THE DRAMA OF
ATHEIST HUMANISM

HENRI DE LUBAC, S.J.

THE DRAMA OF
ATHEIST HUMANISM

IGNATIUS PRESS   SAN FRANCISCO

Title of the French original:
Le Drame de l'humanisme athée
Seventh edition © 1983
Les Éditions du Cerf, Paris
First French edition © 1944, Spes, Paris

First English edition © 1949
Sheed & Ward, London
Reprinted with permission

Parts 1–3 translated by
Edith M. Riley and Anne Englund Nash

Part 4, Chapter 1
translated by Anne Englund Nash

Part 4, Chapter 2
translated by Mark Sebanc

Cover by Roxanne Mei Lum

© 1995 Ignatius Press, San Francisco
Second printing 1998
ISBN 0–89870–443–x
Library of Congress catalogue number 92–75066
Printed in the United States of America ∞

CONTENTS

CONTENTS

FOREWORD

Despite their historical and scholarly appearance, all Henri de Lubac's works clearly refer to the present. As he investigates the sources of modern atheism, particularly in its claim to have definitely moved beyond the idea of God, he is thinking of an ideology prevalent today in East and West that regards the Christian faith as completely outdated: In the West this ideology is even more sharply expressed than in the East (specifically) in the positivism of linguistics scholars who assert not only that every sentence containing the word "God" is a meaningless one that precludes any further conversation but also that that word virtually "destroys meaning". But this extreme statement is firmly grounded in the great sources of that contemporary atheism that purports to have "moved beyond God" and whose basic forms are represented here. They are Feuerbach (before him Hegel and, after him and influenced by him, Marx); then Nietzsche, who is discussed in the book in three places—as the polar opposite of Kierkegaard and later of Dostoevsky, and finally with reference to his "mysticism" of the Eternal Return, and lastly, Auguste Comte. The detailed and meticulous treatment of Comte might surprise readers who do not immediately realize that this "high priest" of his own brand of "positive religion" is, of the three great figures of the last century, the most commanding—though largely unnoticed —presence in all forms of present-day positivism and anthropological antimetaphysics. Thus it might be prudent to read this book with modern eyes while recognizing that its scholarly presentations discuss, in part, seemingly familiar material. Only then will the reader comprehend why the author pursues all available sources with such care and sobriety, while simultaneously hiding his personal feelings.

The book is a new and enlarged edition that was augmented by an appendix discussing Nietzsche's mysticism that was included in the latest revised and enlarged French edition at the occasion of the author's elevation to the cardinalate (*Le Drame de l'humanisme athée* [Paris: Cerf, 1983], 7th edition, revised and enlarged). The essay is also important for our modern understanding of Nietzsche since, with his characteristic lucidity, Henri de Lubac attempts to solve the psychological riddle of Nietzsche's efforts to overcome or sustain the contradiction between the "Overman" and "Eternal Return".

The third part of the work is dedicated to the "prophet" Dostoevsky because his work reflects a poetic treatment of the Christian response to the claims and presumptions of positivist atheistic humanism. De Lubac preserves (like Guardini) a keen critical awareness of the ambiguous solutions offered by the great Russian, but he manages to go beyond them and arrive at clear positions that have remained as guidelines for the conversations of Christians with their atheistic brothers. This fact will probably prove to be a greater testimony to life than the theoretical discussion of the issue of whether or not a real human being is capable of assuming a position beyond God.

— HANS URS VON BALTHASAR

PREFACE

If the different chapters of this book have not been organized into a systematic whole, their object, as intended by the author, is nonetheless the same. Beneath the numerous surface-currents that carry contemporary thought in every direction, it seems possible to detect a deep undercurrent, by no means new— or rather a sort of immense *drift*; through the action of a large proportion of its foremost thinkers, the peoples of the West are denying their Christian past and turning away from God. This is not the everyday type of atheism that crops up in all ages and is of no particular significance; nor is it the purely critical atheism so fashionable in the last two hundred years: for, though the effects of this are still conspicuously in evidence today, it does not represent a living force, since it is manifestly incapable of replacing what it destroys—its only function being to hollow out a channel for that other atheism which is my real subject. Contemporary atheism is increasingly positive, organic, constructive. Combining a mystical immanentism with a clear perception of the human trend, it has three principal aspects, which can be symbolized by three names: Auguste Comte, Ludwig Feuerbach (who must share the honor with his disciple, Karl Marx) and Friedrich Nietzsche. Through a number of intermediaries, and with a number of accretions, admixtures and, in many cases, distortions, the doctrines of these three nineteenth-century thinkers are, even today, the inspiration of three philosophies of life (social and political as well as individual) that all exercise a powerful attraction. Thus the immediate interest they present is only too manifest; and, whatever the vicissitudes of the causes and parties whose clashes occupy the front of the stage, there is a danger that these philosophies, perhaps in new forms, will long continue to be a matter of direct concern.

The negation that underlies positivist humanism, Marxist

humanism and Nietzschean humanism is not so much *a*theism, in the strict sense of the word, as *anti*theism, or, more precisely, anti-Christianism. Great as the contrast is between them, their common foundation in the rejection of God is matched by a certain similarity in results, the chief of which is the annihilation of the human person. This dual character I have tried to place in the strongest light, thinking that this simple exposition would undoubtedly be, if not the most effective "refutation", at least the most appropriate one with which to begin. The reader will find in these pages hardly any theoretical discussion and little of what commonly goes by the name of "theology". What the book offers is merely a historical survey in which special emphasis has been laid upon the essential feature—often passed over too lightly.

First and foremost, then, it is suggested that Christians should take cognizance of the spiritual situation of the world in which they are involved. It is recognized that positivism is an immense edifice of scientific philosophy and practical politics; that Marxism, which has received its Summa if not its Bible in *Das Kapital*, is a vast and powerful system of political and social economy; and that Nietzsche's ideas offer an extraordinary profusion of pedagogic resources (in the profoundest sense of the term). There are many elements to be found in all three on which a Christian, as such, is not required to take a stand; there are many others, often mutually contradictory, that he would have the right to claim as his own, after rescuing them from the synthesis that has warped them. They contain many audacities that do not frighten him. And, even at their most blasphemous, they advance criticisms whose justice he is bound to admit.

These three systems, of course, are not three cast-iron constructions. In the real life of the human mind many dissociations take place, so that not all those who call themselves positivists, Marxists or Nietzscheans are necessarily atheists. Some, for instance, leaving the metaphysical problem open, join the Marxists only for the sake of their social program or, without even examining the details of that program, because of their own aspirations for society; they are, in some cases, more Christian than those who oppose them; and often they have a clearer insight into history. Certain maxims of Comtist origin have served for the expression of what is soundest in conservative circles. Many ideas of a more or less Marxist, Nietzschean or positivist stamp may even find a place in some blueprint for a new synthesis, and neither its orthodoxy nor its value will be called in question on that account. In the Church the work of assimilation never ceases, and it is never too soon to undertake it! Nevertheless, all systems, as shaped and held together by their underlying inspiration, have their own internal logic; and not to see this quite clearly from the outset is to run the risk of going dangerously astray. In the threefold case engaging our attention, this inspiration and this logic are very forcibly thrusting mankind away from God and at the same time urging it along the lines of a double bondage, social and spiritual.

Feuerbach and Marx, like Comte and Nietzsche, were convinced that faith in God was disappearing forever. That sun was sinking on our horizon never to rise again. Their atheism both believed and rejoiced in its own finality, having, it thought, this advantage over former atheisms, that it discarded everything, even to the problem that had brought God to birth in man's consciousness. They were antitheists like Proudhon, but in a still more radical way; and they did not come to his conclusion that the existence of God, like that of man "is proved by the eternal antagonism between them". They did not share his sense of the militant return of mystery, and of a mystery that is not only the mystery of man, after each attempt to overcome it. Beneath the variety of its manifestations, their "humanism" seems equally lightless. Yet the sun did not cease to rise! Marx was not yet dead, and Nietzsche had not yet written his most searing books, when another man, another disturbing but more truly prophetic genius, announced the victory of God in the human soul, and his eternal resurrection.

Dostoevsky was only a novelist. He originated no system, he supplied no solution for the terrible problems with which our age is confronted in its efforts to organize social life. That may well be considered an inferior position. Let us at least be able to recognize the significance of such a fact. It is not true, as is sometimes said, that man cannot organize the world without God. What is true is that, without God, he can ultimately only organize it against man. Exclusive humanism is inhuman humanism. Moreover, it is not the purpose of faith in God, that faith which instills Christianity in us in an ever-present and ever-demanding transcendence, to install us comfortably in our earthly life that we may go to sleep in it—however feverish our sleep might be. On the contrary, faith disturbs us and continually upsets the too beautiful balance of our mental conceptions and our social structures. Bursting into a world that perpetually tends to close in upon itself, God brings it the possibility of a harmony that is certainly superior but is to be attained only at the cost of a series of cleavages and struggles coextensive with time itself. "I came, not to bring peace, but a sword." Christ is, first and foremost, the great disturber. That certainly does not mean that the Church lacks a social doctrine, derived from the Gospel. Still less does it tend to deter Christians, who, like their brothers, are men and members of the city, from seeking to solve the city's problems in accordance with the principles of their faith; on the contrary, it is one more necessity impelling them to do so. But they know at the same time that, the destiny of man being eternal, he is not meant to find ultimate repose here below. The earth, which without God could cease being a chaos only to become a prison, is in reality the magnificent and painful field where our eternal being is worked out. Thus faith in God, which nothing can tear from the heart of man, is the sole flame in which our hope, human and divine, is kept alive.

CHRISTMAS 1943

N.B.—The first and third parts of this work develop a series of studies that appeared in *Cité nouvelle* from 1941 to 1943. I wish to thank here the Rev. Frs. Desbuquois and Bernard for the very kind reception they always gave to these studies.

This work had to make its appearance during the Occupation. In writing it, I had to take into account the necessities imposed by censorship; and it was printed before the liberation of Paris. This explains, on the one hand, some of the emphases and, on the other hand and in particular, some of the omissions, some of the silences. As such, it constitutes a witness. I commit it to the indulgence of the reader without making any changes.

Note for the third edition.—This new edition reproduces almost exactly the two preceding ones. I have made a certain number of slight additions, either in the text or in the footnotes, but without taking away the work's fragmentary character, which was imposed on it by the circumstances of its composition.

JULY 20, 1945

Note for the fourth edition.—If the author had wished to remedy the insufficiency of these pages, to take into account subsequent events, to profit, finally, from the numerous works to which this immense and fundamental subject has given rise in the meantime, a total revision would have been necessary. Since he could not consider such a revision, he is allowing the work to be republished in its original state, except for a very few alterations. For additional material, he refers the reader to a little volume published by Éditions du Témoignage chrétien (1950): *Affrontements mystiques* (Mystical confrontations), especially to chapters one: "The Search for a New Man" and two: "Nietzsche as Mystic". These two chapters form Part Four of this edition.

PART ONE

ATHEIST HUMANISM

CHAPTER I

FEUERBACH AND NIETZSCHE

1. A Tragic Misunderstanding

A wonderful piece of sculpture adorning the cathedral of Chartres represents Adam, head and shoulders barely roughed out, emerging from the earth from which he was made and being molded by the hands of God. The face of the first man reproduces the features of his modeler. This parable in stone translates for the eyes the mysterious words of Genesis: "God made man in his own image and likeness."

From its earliest beginnings Christian tradition has not ceased to annotate this verse, recognizing in it our first title of nobility and the foundation of our greatness. Reason, liberty, immortality and dominion over nature are so many prerogatives of divine origin that God has imparted to his creatures. Establishing man from the outset in God's likeness, each of these prerogatives is meant to grow and unfold until the divine resemblance is brought to perfection. Thus they are the key to the highest of destinies.

"Man, know thyself!" Taking up, after Epictetus, the Socratic *gnôthi seauton*, the Church transformed and deepened it,[1] so that what had been chiefly a piece of moral advice became an exhortation to form a metaphysical judgment. Know yourself, said the Church, that is to say, know your nobility and

---

[1] See, for example, Clement of Alexandria, *Stromates*, 17, c. 3; Basil, *Homilies*. Cf. Dt 15:9. Cf. André Jean Festugière, *L'Idéal religieux des Grecs et l'Évangile* (Paris: J. Gabalda, 1932), pp. 23–24; Étienne Gilson, *La Théologie mystique de saint Bernard* (Paris: Vrin, 1934), pp. 91–93 and 181–82; *L'Esprit de la philosophie médiévale* (Paris: Vrin, 1932), vol. 2, pp. 6–8.

your dignity, understand the greatness of your being and your vocation, of that vocation which constitutes your being. Learn how to see in yourself the spirit, which is a reflection of God, made for God. "O man, scorn not that which is admirable in you! You are a poor thing in your own eyes, but I would teach you that in reality you are a great thing! . . . Realize what you are! Consider your royal dignity! The heavens have not been made in God's image as you have, nor the moon, nor the sun, nor anything to be seen in creation. . . . Behold, of all that exists there is nothing that can contain your greatness."[2] Philosophers have told man that he is a "microcosm", a little world made of the same elements, given the same structure, subject to the same rhythms as the great universe; they have reminded him that he is made in its image and is subject to its laws; they have made him into part of the mechanism or, at most, into an epitome of the cosmic machine. Nor were they completely mistaken. Of man's body and of all that, in man, can be called "nature", it is true. But if man digs deeper and if his reflection is illuminated by what is said in Sacred Scripture, he will be amazed at the depths opening up within him.[3] Unaccountable space extends before his gaze. In a sort of infinitude he overflows this great world on all sides, and in reality it is that world, "macrocosm", which is contained in this apparent "microcosm" . . . *in parvo magnus*. That looks like a paradox borrowed from one of our great modern idealists. Far from it. First formulated by Origen, then by Saint Gregory

---

[2] Gregory of Nyssa, *In cantica*, homily 2; *De mortuis*; Pseudo-Nyssa, *First Homily on the Creation of Man*; Basil, *In psalmum 48, 8*, etc. "The masters", Meister Eckhart also says, "teach that the least noble part of the soul is more noble than what is loftiest in the sky": "Le Livre de la consolation divine", in the French trans.: *Traités et sermons* (1942), p. 76.

[3] Gregory of Nyssa, *On the Creation of Man*, c. 16. John Damascene, *De duabus voluntatibus*. Maximus the Confessor, *Mystagogia*, *Ambiguorum liber*, etc. Cf. Isaac de Stella, sermon 2: "Redi ad cor. Foris pecus es, ad imaginem mundi; unde et minor mundus dicitur homo. Intus homo, ad imaginem Dei: unde potest deificari" (PL 194, 1695).

Nazianzen, it was later repeated by many others.[4] Saint Thomas Aquinas was to give much the same translation of it when he said that the soul is in the world *continens magis quam contenta*— containing it rather than contained by it—and it found fresh utterance through the lips of Bossuet.[5]

Man, to be sure, is made of dust and clay; or, as we should say nowadays, he is of animal origin—which comes to the same thing. The Church is not unmindful of this, finding a warrant for it in the same passage of Genesis. Man, to be sure, is also a sinner. The Church does not cease to remind him of that fact. The self-esteem that she endeavors to instill into him is not the outcome of a superficial and ingenuous view of the matter. Like Christ, she knows "what there is in man". But she also knows that the lowliness of his origin in the flesh cannot detract from the sublimity of his vocation, and that, despite all the blemishes that sin may bring, that vocation is an abiding source of inalienable greatness. The Church thinks that this greatness must reveal itself even in the conditions of present-day life, as a fount of liberty and a principle of progress, the necessary retaliation upon the forces of evil. And she recognizes in the mystery of God-made-man the guarantee of our vocation and the final consecration of our greatness. Thus in her liturgy she can celebrate each day "the dignity of the human substance"[6] even before rising to the contemplation of our rebirth.

These elementary truths of our faith seem commonplace to-

---

[4] Origen, *Fifth Homily on Leviticus*; cf. *First Homily on Genesis*, n. 12. Gregory of Nazianzen, *38th Discourse*, c. 11. Andrew of Crete, *First Sermon on the Assumption of Mary*. Jacob of Edessa, *Hexaemeron*. Meister Eckhart, "Sermon sur Luc 1, 26", in the French trans. by Paul Petit: *Sermons-traités* (1942), pp. 14–15.

[5] Jacques Bossuet, *Sermon sur l'Annunciation*.

[6] Roman Catholic Mass, Offertory: "Deus, qui humanæ substantiæ dignitatem mirabiliter condidisti. . . ." Bruno of Segni: "Magnus honor, magna nobilitas, ad Dei imaginem et similitudinem esse hominem factum!" *Tractatus de interiori domo*: "Intellige dignitatem tuam, nobilis creatura!" (PL 184, 547). Cf. Arnold of Bonneval (PL 189, 1534), etc.

day—though we neglect their implications all too often. It
is difficult for us to imagine the disturbance they created in
the soul of man in the ancient world. At the first tidings of
them humanity was lifted on a wave of hope. It was stirred by
vague premonitions that, at the recoil, sharpened its awareness
of its state of misery. It became conscious of deliverance. To
begin with, needless to say, it was not an external deliverance
—not that social liberation which was to come, for instance,
with the abolition of slavery. That liberation, which presupposed a large number of technical and economic conditions,
was brought about slowly but surely under the influence of
the Christian idea of man.[7] "God", says Origen, in his commentary on Saint John, "made all men in his own image, he
molded them one by one."[8] But from the outset that idea had
produced a more profound effect. Through it, man was freed,
in his own eyes, from the ontological slavery with which Fate
burdened him. The stars, in their unalterable courses, did not,
after all, implacably control our destinies. Man, every man, no
matter who, had a direct link with the Creator, the Ruler of the
stars themselves. And lo, the countless Powers—gods, spirits,

---

[7] We can subscribe to the following reflections of Commander Lefebvre
des Noettes, *L'Attelage; le cheval de selle à travers les âges* (Paris: Picard, 1931), p.
178: "Moral factors are not alone in governing human destinies; there are, in
addition to them, pressing material conditions and, in our opinion, it would
be impossible to understand the social movement of the Middle Ages, one of
the most profound humanity has known, if one were to ignore the brilliant invention that, under the first Capetians, revolutionized methods of transporta-
tion, endowed industry with new and almost unlimited possibilities and made
man a powerful force." But, in his conclusion, the author exceeds the limits of
his own thought by writing that the study of this invention makes us penetrate
"into the profound area of causes". Robert Aron and Arnaud Dandieu put it
better in *La Révolution nécessaire* (Paris: Grasset, 1933), p. 78: "Thanks to those
technical inventions that have remained anonymous, the tendencies proper to
the new society can be freely developed." Cf. Hegel, *Philosophie de l'histoire*
(French trans. by Gibelin of *Vorlesungen über die Philosophie der Geschichte*), vol.
2, p. 116.

[8] Origen, *Commentary on Saint John*, vol. 13, no. 28 (PG 14, 468).

demons—who pinioned human life in the net of their tyrannical wills, weighing upon the soul with all their terrors, now
crumbled into dust, and the sacred principle that had gone astray
in them was rediscovered unified, purified and sublimated in
God the deliverer! It was no longer a small and select company
that, thanks to some secret means of escape, could break the
charmed circle: it was mankind as a whole that found its night
suddenly illumined and took cognizance of its royal liberty. No
more circle! No more blind destiny! No more *Moira*! No more
Fate! Transcendent God, God the "friend of men", revealed in
Jesus, opened for all a way that nothing would ever bar again.[9]
Hence that intense feeling of gladness and of radiant newness
to be found everywhere in early Christian writings. It is much
to be regretted that this literature for so many reasons, not all
of which are insuperable, should be so remote from us today.
What wealth and force our faith is forfeiting by its ignorance
of, for instance, the hymns of triumph and the stirring appeals
that echo in the *Protrepticus* of Clement of Alexandria![10]

But if we look down the course of the ages to the dawn of
modern times we make a strange discovery. That same Christian idea of man that had been welcomed as a deliverance was
now beginning to be felt as a yoke. And that same God in
whom man had learned to see the seal of his own greatness
began to seem to him like an antagonist, the enemy of his dignity. Through what misunderstandings and distortions, what
mutilations and infidelities, what blinding pride and impatience
this came about would take too long to consider. The historical
causes are numerous and complex. But the fact remains, simple
and solid. No less than the Early Fathers, the great medieval
scholars had exalted man by setting forth what the Church had

---

[9] Cf. Festugière, pp. 101–15 and 161–69. Louis Bouyer, *Le Mystère pascal*,
pp. 111 and 115. The Apostles of Christ were "the apostles of freedom": Saint
Irenaeus, *Adversus hæreses*, I, 3, c. 13, and I, 4, c. 56.

[10] Mondésert translation, in the *Sources chrétiennes* series (1943). See particularly the first and last chapter.

always taught of his relation to God: "In this is man's greatness, in this is man's worth, in this he excels every creature."[11] But the time came when man was no longer moved by it. On the contrary, he began to think that henceforward he would forfeit his self-esteem and be unable to develop in freedom unless he broke first with the Church and then with the Transcendent Being upon whom, according to Christian tradition, he was dependent. At first assuming the aspect of a reversion to paganism, this urge to cut loose increased in scope and momentum in the eighteenth and nineteenth centuries until, after many phases and many vicissitudes, it came to a head in the most daring and destructive form of modern atheism: absolute humanism, which claims to be the only genuine kind and inevitably regards a Christian humanism as absurd.

This atheist humanism is not to be confused with a hedonist and coarsely materialist atheism—a commonplace phenomenon to be found in many periods of history. It is also quite contrary in principle—if not in its results—to an atheism of despair. But it would be dangerous to call it a critical atheism and let it go at that. It does not profess to be the simple answer to a speculative problem and certainly not a purely negative solution: as if the understanding, having, on the attainment of maturity, set itself to "reconsider" the problem of God, had at last been obliged to see that its efforts could lead to nothing or even that they were leading to an end that was the opposite of what they had long believed. The phenomenon that has dominated the history of the mind during the last few centuries seems both more profound and more arbitrary. It is not the intelligence alone that is involved. The problem posed was a human problem—it was *the* human problem—and the solution that is being given to it is one that claims to be positive. Man is getting rid of God in order to regain possession of the human greatness that, it seems to him, is being unwar-

---

[11] Saint Thomas, *De malo*, q. 5, a. 1; *Contre gentiles*, I, 3, c. 147. François Tolet, *In primam partem S. Thomas*. All the Scotists, etc.

rantably withheld by another. In God he is overthrowing an obstacle in order to gain his freedom.

Modern humanism, then, is built upon resentment and begins with a choice. It is, in Proudhon's word, an "antitheism". In Proudhon, this antitheism operated first of all in the social field, where it was chiefly a struggle against a false idea of Providence.[12] It was a refusal to be resigned to the "economic contradictions", productive of poverty, for which a more or less conscious conspiracy on the part of economists and property-owners claimed the sanction of heaven and which they sometimes even went so far as to extol as "harmonies". Thus Proudhon laid the blame not so much upon God himself as upon a certain form of recourse to his authority. Subsequently extending his conception to the metaphysical field, he still thought that God was "inexhaustible": the struggle in which man necessarily wrestled with God was an "eternal struggle"; "the hypothesis of a God" was reborn every time "from its resolution in human reality"; always, after the denials and exclusions, there was a resurgence of something beyond man—Proudhon for the most part called it Justice—which imposed itself upon man and prevented him from ever taking himself for God.

Thus Proudhon, even when undergoing the influence and appropriating the language of those whom he calls "the humanists" or "the new atheists", expressly refuses to follow them.[13] Antitheism, as conceived by them, is something more radical. They go farther in opposition and denial because they set out from a more complete refusal. The story is a dramatic one. At its maximum point of concentration, it is the great crisis of modern times, that same crisis in which we are involved today and which takes its outward course in disorder, begets tyrannies and collective crimes, and finds its expression in blood, fire and ruin.

---

[12] He says: "The myth of providence".

[13] *Philosophie de la misère*, vol. 1, pp. 253, 388–89, 397–98, etc.

2. Feuerbach and the Religious Illusion

Let us now take a look at the two men who may be regarded as the protagonists of the drama, whether we consider their actual achievement or take them as symbols. They were two German thinkers of the last century, Ludwig Feuerbach and Friedrich Nietzsche.

The greatness of the second is no longer contested. After having been neglected by professional philosophers, and sometimes brushed aside by them with irritation, he finished by compelling universal recognition. The time has gone by when he could be described as "little more than a nerve-ridden and overexcitable Goethe".[14] The first of these two men, on the other hand, if considered solely in himself, would hardly deserve more than an honorable place, which has never been denied him, in a good history of philosophy. But his importance is chiefly due to the fact that he was the stepping-stone between the great current of speculation known as German idealism and the great current of revolutionary thought and action which were to be its principal, if not its most legitimate, heir. Feuerbach pulled down the Hegelian structure, and he did not found the communist movement. Between Hegel and Marx, he is a rather shadowy figure—even if, as Engels wrote in his study of him, he was, of all the immediate descendants of Hegel, "the only one who amounted to anything as a philosopher".[15] For all that, he is the link connecting Marx with Hegel and the "transformer" thanks to whom Hegel finds his continuation in Marx, though with a change of direction.[16]

In the years that followed Hegel's death in 1831, the focus of

---

[14] Émile Faguet, *En lisant Nietzsche*, p. 33.

[15] Friedrich Engels, *Ludwig Feuerbach et la fin de la philosophie classique allemande* (French trans. by Ollivier of *Ludwig Feuerbach und der Ausgang der klassischen deutschen Philosophie*), chap. 4. Cf. Nikolai Berdyaev, *Les Sources et le sens du communisme russe*, p. 215: "Feuerbach had undoubtedly been the greatest genius of the atheist philosophers of the nineteenth century."

[16] Marx himself wrote in his regard, in his "Lettre au Sozial-Demokrat" of

philosophical debates was the problem of God, and it was on this subject, and not primarily on political or social matters, that the split occurred between the right and left wings of Hegelianism.[17] Feuerbach soon assumed the leadership of the left. His purpose ran parallel to that of his friend Friedrich David Strauss, historian of the origins of Christianity. As Strauss tried to account historically for the Christian illusion, Feuerbach tried to account psychologically for the religious illusion in general, or, as he himself put it, to find in anthropology the secret of theology. The substance of what Strauss said, in his *Life of Jesus* (1835), was that the Gospels are myths expressing the aspirations of the Jewish people. In *Religion* Feuerbach was to make the parallel assertion that God is only a myth in which the aspirations of the human consciousness are expressed. "Those who have no desires have no gods either. . . . Gods are men's wishes in corporeal form."[18]

January 24, 1865: "Compared to Hegel, Feuerbach is very poor. Yet, after Hegel, he was epoch-making, for he stressed points that were unpleasant for the Christian conscience and important for the progress of philosophical criticism but left by Hegel in a mystical twilight": *Misère de la philosophie* (French trans. [1896]), p. 246.

[17] Cf. Auguste Cornu, *Karl Marx, l'homme et l'oeuvre*, p. 79. Strauss, who was one of the principal members of this left, was still a "liberal conservative" in politics (Victor Cherbuliez, *Études sur l'Allemagne* [Paris: Hachette, 1873], p. 124). When Arnold Ruge founded the *Annales de Halle* in 1838 in order to oppose the *Annales de Berlin*, which was the organ of the old Hegelians, he still hoped that the Prussian government would support his religious radicalism; cf. Cornu, *Moses Hess et la gauche hégélienne*, pp. 24–25. Strauss always had an aristocratic disdain for the people; what he dreaded above all was the "rise of the masses": Albert Lévy, *David-Frédéric Strauss* (Paris: Alcan, 1910), pp. 38 and 154.

[18] *La Religion; mort-immortalité-religion* (French trans. by Joseph Roy [Paris: Librairie Internationale, 1864]), pp. 115 and 117. Strauss also thought, and this is one more similarity, that everything that the Church says of Christ was to be understood of humanity; that the first Christian community unconsciously had in mind the idea of humanity when it drew the portrait of Jesus; that all that faith had in a way incarnated in an individual, science was to restore to the Whole, to the Species. Cf. Lévy, pp. 46, 60, 267. He would also say: "The

To explain the mechanism of this "theogony", Feuerbach had recourse to the Hegelian concept of "alienation". But, whereas Hegel applied it to absolute Spirit, Feuerbach, reversing the relation of the idea to the real, applied it in *Das Wesen des Christentums* (*The Essence of Christianity*) to man in his flesh and blood.[19] Alienation, according to him, is for man the fact of finding himself "dispossessed of something essentially belonging to him for the benefit of an illusive reality".[20] Wisdom, will, justice and love, says Feuerbach, are so many infinite attributes that constitute man's own being and that nevertheless affect him "as if it were another being".[21] Thus he spontaneously projects them beyond himself and objectifies them in a fantastic form, the pure product of his imagination, to which he gives the name of God.[22] In this way he defrauds his own self. "It is one and the same act that strips the world of its content and transfers that content to God. The poor man possesses a rich God", or, to be more accurate, he impoverishes himself by enriching his God, in filling whom he empties himself.[23]

---

religion of Christ must open out into the religion of Humanity", *Nouvelle vie de Jésus* (French trans.), vol. 2, p. 420.

[19] *Essence du christianisme* (French trans. [1864] by Joseph Roy of *Das Wesen des Christentums*), pp. VII–X. Cf. *Principes de la philosophie de l'avenir* (French trans. [1849] of *Grundsätze der Philosophie der Zukunft*), pp. 32 and 55: "The new philosophy makes man—including nature, the foundation of man—its sole, universal and supreme object. Anthropology, including physiology, thus becomes the universal science. . . ." "Truth, reality, world of the senses are identical things; the sensual being is the only true one, only real one; the world of the senses alone is truth and reality."

[20] Jean Daniélou, "Le Foi en l'homme chez Marx", in *Chronique sociale de France* (1938), pp. 163 ff.

[21] *Essence du christianisme*, p. 34.

[22] Ibid., pp. 23 and 24: "Reason, love, will, there we have the perfections, the highest powers, the absolute being of man in man and the goal of his existence. . . ."

[23] Ibid., pp. 50–51: "If what is positive, essential in the determination of the nature of God is borrowed from the nature of man, man would be stripped of all that one would give to God. In order for God to be enriched, man would

He "affirms in God what he denies in himself".[24] "Religion is thus transformed into a vampire that feeds upon the substance of mankind, its flesh and its blood."[25]

Such action on the part of man was, moreover, inevitable and therefore justified in occurring when it did. In the Hegelian rhythm it represents the second movement of the dialectic, the phase of denial or antithesis that necessarily precedes the synthesis in which man is to regain possession of his essence, now enriched. Feuerbach knew that this stage could not be skipped. Thus he does not execrate religion in the past but recognizes in it "an essential aspect of the human spirit".[26] Without religion, without the worship of an external God, man would never have had more than a dim and muffled consciousness like that of an animal, for, "strictly speaking, consciousness exists only in beings which can make their essence and their species the object of their thought".[27] It was first necessary to realize one's duality, as it were—which amounts to losing oneself in order to find oneself. But one day the alienation must come to an end. After the movement of religious systole, by which man rejected himself, he must now, by a movement of diastole, "take back into his heart that nature which he had rejected".[28] The hour has at last struck when he must exorcise the phantom. Reflection carries on the work begun by a spontaneous impulse. The kingdom of man has come.

For Feuerbach, then, God is only the sum of the attributes

---

have to be impoverished." And p. 103: "The emptier life is, the fuller, more concrete is divinity. . . ."

[24] Ibid., p. 52.

[25] Jean-Édouard Spenlé, *La Pensée allemande de Luther à Nietzsche* (Paris: Colin, 1934), p. 122. For the reconciliation of the two slightly different explanations given by Feuerbach, in *Das Wesen des Christentums* and in *Religion*, of the process of dividing or alienation that ends in establishing God, see Albert Lévy, *La Philosophie de Feuerbach* (Paris, 1904), p. 294.

[26] *La Religion*, p. 77.

[27] *Essence du christianisme*, pp. 21–22.

[28] Ibid., p. 56.

that make up the greatness of man. The Christian God carries
this to perfection (and that is why man has never been more
alienated than in Christianity,[29] the worst of religions because
the highest). He is "the mirror of man", he is "the great book
in which man expressed his loftiest thoughts, his purest feelings".[30] In a maxim closely reminiscent of Auguste Comte's
law of the three states, Feuerbach wrote in *Religion*: "God was
my first thought, reason my second, and man my third and
last."[31] Elsewhere he says, "It is the essence of man that is the
supreme being. . . . If the divinity of nature is the basis of all
religions, including Christianity, the divinity of man is its final aim. . . . The turning point of history will be the moment
when man becomes aware that the only God of man is man
himself. *Homo homini Deus!*"[32]

Be it noted, however, that this "humanist" Feuerbach does
not say, as Max Stirner was soon to say, *Ego mihi deus*.[33] He
believes that the human essence, with its prerogatives, which
call for worship, is not inherent in the individual considered
in isolation but only in the community, in the generic being
(*Gattungswesen*); indeed, by substituting for that generic being
the illusion of an external God, it is the mistaken religion that
is responsible for disintegrating mankind into a dust of individuals, thus leaving each of them to himself and turning him into
a being naturally isolated and thrown back upon himself; for

---

[29] *La Religion*, pp. 45–46.

[30] *Essence du christianisme*, pp. 92 and 93.

[31] "Pensées diverses", in *La Religion*, p. 348. This maxim will be quoted by
Georgii Plekhanov in *Les Questions fondamentales du marxisme* (French trans.),
2d ed. (Paris: Ed. Sociales internationales, 1927), p. 15.

[32] *Essence du christianisme*, p. 27: "The absolute being, the God of man, is the
very being of man." *La Religion*, p. 112.

[33] In *L'Unique et sa propriété* (French trans. [1845] of *Einzige und sein Eigen-
tum*), Max Stirner criticizes Feuerbach's doctrine sharply, and he has no difficulty in showing in fact that it in no way frees man in the individualist and an-
archist sense of which he dreams. Cf. Victor Basch, *L'Individualisme anarchiste
Max Stirner* (Paris: Alcan, 1904), pp. 65–66.

"man spontaneously conceives his own essence as individual in himself and generic in God; as limited in himself and infinite in God." But when, abandoning that chimerical view, man comes actually to participate in the common essence, to that extent he really assumes divinity. Thus the principle that sums up real religion is a principle of practical action: it is a law of love, which takes the individual out of himself and obliges him to find himself in fellowship with those of his own species. It is the principle of an altruist morality. For, in the last analysis, "the distinction between human and divine is neither more nor less than the distinction between the individual and mankind."[34] Thus Feuerbach clears himself of the charge of preaching egoism.

He is equally on the defensive against the charge of preaching atheism. Insofar as the term is a negative one, he rejects the title of atheist. In his view this name should rather be applied to the idolater, who mistakenly regards himself as a true believer. Such a man, without faith in the divinity of qualities, feels the need to attach them to an imaginary subject, which he takes as the object of his worship:

> The true atheist is not the man who denies God, the subject; it is the man for whom the attributes of divinity, such as love, wisdom and justice, are nothing. And denial of the subject is by no means necessarily denial of the attributes. The attributes have an independent significance of their own; by their value they force men to recognize them; they impose themselves upon him; they immediately convince his understanding that they are true in themselves; they are their own warrant, their own guarantee. . . . A quality is not divine because God possesses it; God

---

[34] *Essence du christianisme*, p. 38. *Principes*, pp. 61 and 62: "The isolated man, who lives for himself alone, does not have within himself the human essence, either as a moral being or as a thinking being. The latter is contained only within society. . . . Man for himself is man, in the usual sense; man with man, the unity of you and me, is God." Earlier, p. 42, Feuerbach had this fine formula: "In the single gaze of man shines the light of conscience and reason in man."

must possess it because without it he would be an imperfect
being. . . . When God, as subject, is the thing determined, and
the attribute is the determinant, it is not to the subject but to
the attribute that the rank of supreme being, of divinity, really
belongs.[35]

The inference is that, in order not to sacrifice love to "God",
we must sacrifice "God" to love.[36] In so doing, moreover,
we shall be accomplishing the secret purpose of religion. For,
rightly understood, religion "ceremoniously unveils the hidden treasures of man's nature; it is the avowal of his inmost
thoughts, it is the public revelation of the secrets, the mysteries of his love."[37]

Thus, far from being unfaithful to the spirit of Christianity,
which is the perfect religion, we shall at last explain its mystery.[38]

Feuerbach had at first intended to give a different title to
Das Wesen des Christentums, the first of the works in which he
expressed his essential idea. It was to be called Gnôthi seauton
—a truly symbolic point. His atheistic humanism thus took as
its banner the old precept that the Fathers of the Church had
taken over long before. To reveal to mankind its own essence
in order to give it faith in itself—that was his sole aim. But
in order to attain it he thought it necessary to overthrow the
God of the Christian conscience. Toward the end of his life he

---

[35] Ibid., pp. 46–47.

[36] Ibid., p. 82; cf. p. 81: "Insofar as love is not raised to the rank of substance, of being itself, there remains behind a subject who, without love, is yet
something else, a monster without sympathy. . . ."

[37] Ibid., p. 36. Cf. Joseph Roy, introduction to La Religion, pp. VII–VIII and
XXIV.

[38] Essence du christianisme, pp. X–XII: "I let religion express and disclose itself; I listen, I am its interpreter, and never its prompter. . . . It is not I, it is
religion that adores man, although it, or rather theology, would not want to
admit it. . . ." On the other hand, Feuerbach pays little attention to what he
calls "the dissolute, spineless, comfortable, well-read, flirtatious and epicurean
Christianity of the modern world."

wrote: "The only thing I am anxious to leave in the memory of man after my death is my fundamental thought. I will let everything else go. . . . All that I want is to have introduced one single idea into the speech of conscious humanity."[39] It must be recognized that he succeeded only too well.

He had an immediate following. Engels mentions the extraordinary "impression of deliverance" felt by many young men of his generation in November 1841 on reading *Das Wesen des Christentums*. Hegel's disciples were at that time laboriously threshing about in the toils of contradiction. "At one blow it was demolished. This was a potent stimulus." "There was widespread enthusiasm", Engels adds. "We all straightway became Feuerbachians."[40] He is scarcely exaggerating. The impression made on people was of something definitive; of a perfectly clear revelation, as if the scales had at last fallen from all eyes; of a full stop put to discussions that had been going on for a thousand years and had suddenly become pointless; of an end to the illusion of religious faith and the adventures of idealist speculation. The solution to the human problem had been found; there was nothing left to look for.

What had happened in Germany very soon happened in Russia also. We learn from Dostoevsky's *Journal of an Author* that Bielinsky, until then the uncontested master of the younger

---

[39] Lévy, *La Philosophie de Feuerbach*, p. XXI. Cf. *Sämmtliche Werke*, vol. 8, p. 29: "The goal of my work is to make men no longer theologians but anthropologists, to lead them from the love of God to the love of men, from hopes for the beyond to the study of things here below; to make them, no longer the base religious or political servants of a monarchy and an aristocracy of heaven and earth, but free and independent citizens of this universe."

[40] Engels, chap. 3 (in the French trans. by Ollivier, p. 47). "Even the defects of the book", Engels also says, "contributed to its success at that time. The literary and even, in places, bombastic style in which it was written assured it a large public, since, despite everything, it was invigorating after the long years of abstract and abstruse Hegelianism." Cf. Célestin C. A. Bouglé, *Chez les prophètes socialistes* (Paris: Alcan, 1918), p. 164. It was Strauss' *Das Leben Jesu* that had shaken the Christian faith of Engels, who had at first been a devout believer.

generation, revered Feuerbach and Strauss.[41] Later, Herzen was
to recount how Feuerbach, read at Novgorod, was responsible for his innermost transformation, so that he turned "from
mysticism to the most ruthless realism".[42] From 1843 we find
Bakunin, then a refugee in Switzerland, explaining that communism is only Feuerbach's humanism carried into the social
field;[43] he extolled Feuerbach for having made the great pro-
nouncement on religion that Hegel had failed to arrive at and
for having thereby put an end to "the mirage of God", thus giving back to the earth what heaven had stolen from it.[44] Bakunin
adopted Feuerbach's doctrine in its entirety, and forty years
later he was still trying to popularize it. Comparing Feuerbach
with Auguste Comte, he marveled at the agreement between
these "two great minds", though "they had never heard of each
other"; and in his tract on *Dieu et l'état* he wrote:

> The heaven of religion is nothing but a mirage in which man,
> uplifted by ignorance and faith, rediscovers his own image, but
> magnified and transposed—in other words, deified. . . . Chris-
> tianity is the religion of religions because, in its fullness, it lays
> bare and reveals the nature, the peculiar essence, of every religious
> system; that is to say, the impoverishment, the enslavement and
> the annihilation of mankind for the benefit of the deity. . . . God
> appears, man is extinguished, and the greater the godhead, the
> more wretched man becomes. That is the history of all religions;
> that is the effect of all divine inspiration and divine lawgiving.
> In history the name of God is the terrible club with which men
> of manifold inspiration, the great geniuses, have struck down the
> liberty, dignity, reason and prosperity of men. . . .[45]

---

[41] Fyodor Dostoevsky, *Journal d'un écrivain* (French trans. by Chuzeville),
vol. 1, p. 201.

[42] Cf. Milyukov, "Alexandre et Nathalie Herzen", in *Le Mouvement intel-
lectuel russe* (French trans. [1918]), p. 248.

[43] Cf. Cornu, *Moses Hess*, pp. 69–70.

[44] Mikhail Aleksandrovich Bakunin, *Dieu et l'État* (Geneva, 1882), p. 82; cf.
pp. 19–20.

[45] Ibid., pp. 35, 58, 73, etc.

From the outset, too, Karl Grün had become a missionary of the same doctrine in Paris, where he lived as a refugee. As Ruge had sought to convince Louis Blanc, so he tried to convince Pierre Leroux. It was no good;[46] but, in the fever of his zeal, he fancied that, to make up for it, he had achieved a more important conversion, namely, that of Proudhon—which was true only to a very limited extent.[47] In 1844, Marx was commenting on *Die Religion der Zukunft* at a club in Lausanne. In England Engels was an active propagandist; he championed the cause of his master in atheism with Carlyle, while George Eliot translated *Das Wesen des Christentums*. Among those of a later generation, Nikolai Chernyshevski, the chief forerunner of Russian communism, went through the same school and recognized in Feuerbach the first of his "great Western masters".[48] But the disciple who eclipsed all others was Karl Marx.

---

[46] Karl Grün, *Die soziale Bewegung in Frankreich und Belgien* (Darmstadt: Leske, 1845): "We have a good opportunity to make him be within an inch of humanity, to show him how its heart beats, loves, hopes, how infinite and eternal it is; it is no use. He persists in his incredulity like Saint Thomas and remains with his eyes firmly fixed on that shadow that humanity, for six thousand years, has projected to the top of the heavens." Quoted and translated by Saint-René Taillandier, "L'Athéisme allemand et le socialisme français", in *Revue des deux-mondes*, October 15, 1848, p. 288.

[47] "I spoke to him of German philosophy and of the dissolution of it achieved by Feuerbach. . . . I sought to show him by what series of ideas Feuerbach was succeeding in annihilating religion, how the science of the absolute had through him become an anthropology. I saw how he was able to profit from translations and analyses by those striking words he expressed to me about Feuerbach: But, it is the completion of Strauss' work! . . . I hope to have thereby prepared the way for an immense result; there will now be but one single social science on both sides of the Rhine." In Charles Augustin Sainte-Beuve, *Proudhon* (Paris: C. Lévy), pp. 211–13. In reality, almost immediately after their conversation, Proudhon set about refuting Feuerbach, whose importance he did not deny but whose philosophy had hardly more effect upon him than Strauss' exegesis. From its first page, *La Philosophie de la misère* adopts a standpoint very definitely opposed to Feuerbach's humanism.

[48] Georgii Plekhanov, *Le Matérialisme militant* (French trans.), p. 144. Berdyaev, pp. 66–69: "Chernyshevski", says Berdyaev, "is the brain not only of the contemporary intelligentsia but also of the following generations."

In *Die heilige Familie* (*The Holy Family*), written in collaboration with his friend Engels and published in 1845, Marx warmly praises his master for having dispelled "the old quibbles" and set up man in their place.[49] Feuerbach, to be sure, never went deeply into economic problems. While clearly indicating the social import of his doctrine,[50] he left it to others to make it explicit. To the young men who brought him their reforming impatience and wanted him to join them in the fight, he replied in the introduction to his collected works in 1846:

> The only ills I cure are those that come from the head or from the heart; it is from the stomach that men suffer chiefly, I know, and anything that does not help to eradicate that fundamental ill is mere useless rubbish. Must my complete works be considered as among such rubbish, then? I'm afraid so. But are there not many ailments, even of the stomach, which come from the head? I have set out, once for all, to attack the maladies of humanity's head and heart. But what you have set out to do you should carry out conscientiously, keeping faith with yourself.[51]

Thus Feuerbach certainly cannot be regarded as the founder of Marxism in all but name. But its "spiritual father" he certainly is.

It is true that Marx very soon broke with his friends, the "young Hegelians", who contented themselves with daring speculations and political radicalism; it is true that he broke with his own past and bade the philosophy of his youth and all speculation a farewell that was at the same time a declaration of war and that he even, to some extent, renounced his first works, including, maybe, the articles Feuerbach had inspired.[52]

---

[49] Karl Marx, *Die heilige Familie*, vol. 2.

[50] "Temporary Theses for the Reform of Philosophy", in *Anekdota*, March 1842.

[51] Introduction to his *Sämmtliche Werke* (1846); quoted by Lévy, *La Philosophie de Feuerbach*, p. 49.

[52] Bernhard Groethuysen, "Les Jeunes hégéliens et les origines du socialisme contemporain en Allemagne", in *Revue philosophique*, vol. 1 (1923), pp.

But for all that he did not go back upon the conclusions he owed to *Das Wesen des Christentums*. They always remained for him something definitive. Not that he did not criticize Feuerbach's doctrine: but when he did so it was not to call it in question in the slightest degree; it was only to pronounce it incomplete and still too abstract and vague. He reproached it with making religious alienation in some sort a metaphysical act, instead of explaining it more positively as a sociological fact. He endeavored to go beyond what Engels irreverently called Feuerbach's "banalities" by substituting, as Otto Ruhle said,[53] the "materialism of social situations" for the "materialism of the objective data of nature". To quote Engels' book on Feuerbach once more, Marx wanted to replace "the cult of abstract man", which was the center of Feuerbach's new religion, "by the science of real men and their historical development".[54] Thus he stripped from the human essence the mystic halo with which Feuerbach had kept it surrounded.[55] Soon everything else seemed to pale, in his thought, before the technique of economics and the tactics of class warfare. No other philosophical or religious influence, however, made any profound change in the thesis of humanist metaphysics that he had taken over from his master.[56] If he hardly ever referred to it again after reaching his maturity, this was because

---

379–402. In the single issue of *Annales franco-allemandes* that appeared in February 1844, Marx had published two articles inspired by Feuerbach: "Introduction à la Philosophie du droit de Hegel" and "La Question juive".

[53] Otto Ruhle, *Karl Marx* (Hellerau bei Dresden: Avalun-verlag, 1928), p. 113. Marcel Moré, "Les Années d'apprentissage de Karl Marx", in *Esprit*, September 1, 1935, p. 761: "While Feuerbach had been content to show the mode of alienation of the human essence in religion, Marx now sought the reasons for this alienation in the social reality."

[54] Engels, chap. 3.

[55] Cf. Nikolai Berdyaev, *Problème du communisme*, p. 37: "Marx no longer has the Feuerbachian faith in man as divinity"; and *Le Marxisme et la religion*, p. 5: "Marx had little interest in general philosophical questions, he turned his attention only to the social reality."

[56] Jules Monnerot, "Marx et le romantisme": Feuerbach was the final philo-

it seemed to him a thing settled once for all, a starting point at which there was no further need to linger. Thus it remains true that "Marx traces his spiritual descent from the humanist religion of Feuerbach."[57] He cannot be accounted for in any other way. And that spiritual fact is fraught with the gravest consequences; it is among those that dominate the history of our times.

Nor did Marx content himself with admiring what he called the "inspired demonstration" by which the mystification of men's minds was at last brought to an end or with extolling Feuerbach as a second Luther in the history of human emancipation. He stated that Feuerbach went "as far as a theorist can go without ceasing to be a theorist and philosopher"[58] and that after him "the criticism of religion is substantially complete";[59] in 1844 he took Feuerbach's work under his protection, in *Die heilige Familie*, where he instituted a complete defense of it against Bruno Bauer,[60] improving upon the dithyrambic eulogy he had already bestowed upon it two years ear-

---

sophical influence exercised on Marx. French socialists, the English political economy would bring him scientific materials, not ideological or spiritual elements", in *Le Romantisme allemand* (*Cahiers du Sud*), p. 159.

[57] Paul Vignaux, "Retour à Marx", in *Politique*, vol. 9, no. 2 (1935), p. 904. Henri Holstein, "Marx et la critique de la religion", in the *Dossiers de l'Action populaire*, June 10, 1937. Berdyaev, *Sources et sens*, pp. 215–16.

[58] *L'Idéologie allemande* (French trans. by Molitor of *Die deutsche Ideologie*, written by Marx [1845–1846] in collaboration with Engels and Hess), p. 192.

[59] Karl Marx, *Contribution à la critique de la philosophie de Hegel* (French trans. by Costes of *Beitrag zu der Kritik von Hegels Philosophie*), p. 83.

[60] "Feuerbach was the first to complete Hegel and to criticize him in an Hegelian manner by reducing the absolute of the metaphysical Spirit to the reality of man rooted in nature. . . . He established masterfully the governing principles of a criticism of Hegelian speculation and of all metaphysics. . . . Is it a question of removing the veil from the mystery of the 'system'? It is Feuerbach who does it. Is it a question of putting an end to this war of the gods; to this verbal dialectic that is of interest only to philosophers? It is again he who does it. Who, therefore, has put man in the place of the old imagery, in the place of the infinite conscience, for example, if not he?" Quoted by Alexandre Marc in "Marx et Hegel", *Archives de philosophie*, vol. 15, no. 2 (1939), p. 152.

lier, in his short anonymous article on "Luther as Umpire between Strauss and Feuerbach". He not only copied his master's religious criticism in his own social criticism, analyzing
the "secular form" of alienation[61] to arrive at the conclusion
that humanity must abolish the State as it had abolished religion; he adapted the Feuerbachian conception of religion to
social life.

For him, too, as he states in his *Kritik* of Hegel's philosophy,
"man makes religion, it is not religion that makes man; religion
is in reality man's own consciousness and feeling that has not
yet found itself or has lost itself again." Such is "the foundation
of religious criticism". Only:

> Man is not an abstract being outside the real world. Man is
> the world of men, the State, society. This State and this society
> produce religion, a mistaken attitude to the world, because they
> themselves constitute a false world. Religion is the general theory
> of this world, its encyclopaedic compendium, its popular logic,
> its spiritual point of honor, its inspiration, its moral sanction,
> its solemn completion, its general consoling and justifying rea-
> son. . . . It is the imaginative realization of the human essence,
> because that essence has no true reality. The misery of religion
> is, on the one hand, the expression of real misery and, on the
> other, a protest against real misery. Religion is the sigh of the
> creature overwhelmed by unhappiness, the soul of a world that
> has no heart, as it is the mind of an era that has no mind. It is
> the opium of the people.[62]

Thus, at the rebound, the fight that must be put up against
religion will be a "fight against this world", against "this perverted world whose spiritual aroma is religion". "Atheism is
humanism mediatized to itself through the suppression of reli-

---

[61] For example, *Le Capital* (French trans. of *Das Kapital*), vol. 1, p. 608:
"Just as in religion man is governed by the products of his own brain, thus in
the capitalist production he is dominated by the products of his own hands."

[62] *Contribution à la critique de la Philosophie du droit de Hegel* (from the *Œuvres
philosophiques*, trans. by Molitor, vol. 1: pp. 83–84).

gion"[63]—a thoroughly Feuerbachian way of putting it. But, in order that man may one day be freed from the mystical illusion and all the evils it brings with it, Marx thinks it is necessary to transform society, since it is bad social organization that is the true cause of human belief and consequently of human alienation. Or, rather, its two forms, social alienation and spiritual alienation, help to produce each other, and it is impossible to overcome one without attacking the other. And this results in a combined struggle, the two parts of which serve each other as means to an end. "The only point on which I do not agree with Feuerbach", Marx wrote to Ruge on March 13, 1843, "is that, to my mind, he attaches too much importance to nature and not enough to politics."[64] And again in *Die deutsche Ideologie* he says that Feuerbach

> does not see that the perceptible world surrounding him is not a direct datum, from all eternity and always the same, but is the product of industry and of the state of society, and is so in the sense that, in every period of history, it is the result and product of the activity of a whole succession of generations, each of which lifted itself on the shoulders of the one before, whose social order it changed in accordance with changing needs. . . . He never arrives at active man, really existing, but always stops short at an abstract idea. . . . He offers no criticism of the conditions of actual existence. . . .[65]

Thus, in preaching practical means of emancipating man, Marx may be said to have shown himself "more Feuerbachian than Feuerbach himself".[66] In that way he ensured his own success in revolutionary circles[67] and, right to the end, he re-

---

[63] Quoted by Gaston Fessard, *Le Dialogue catholique-communiste est-il possible?*, p. 233.

[64] Cf. Cornu, *Karl Marx*, p. 248.

[65] Molitor trans., pp. 161 and 164.

[66] Blaise Romeyer, "L'Athéisme marxiste", in *Archives de philosophie*, vol. 15, no. 2 (1939), p. 201. Cf. Jules Monnerot, p. 163.

[67] Bakunin, for example, interpreted Feuerbach via Marx and found in this

mained faithful to his inspiration, thanks to the addition that he thus made to it in point of method. Marx's doctrine, never plain naturalism, always paid as much attention to man's spiritual life as to his material existence. His communism offered itself as the only concrete realization of humanism; it quite deliberately claimed to be a total solution for the whole human problem; moving to the plane of reality, it did not propose to figure there only as a social phenomenon but as a spiritual phenomenon also.[68] This is what gives it greatness, but this is also the radical flaw in it; it is this that bathes even its sound elements in a baneful atmosphere, and it is this that chiefly arouses Christian opposition. "The religion of the workers has no God," Marx wrote,[69] "because it seeks to restore the divinity of man."

The combination of French socialism, English economics and German metaphysics might have produced something quite different from Marxism if Marx had not found a master in Feuerbach. It was through Feuerbach that his feet were firmly planted on one of the slopes of the Hegelian system. It has been said that, before being the right-wing Hegelian who sees in dogmas the symbols of his philosophy, Hegel had been for a short time the left-wing Hegelian who wants to destroy dogmas in order to make way for truth.[70] In one of his earliest writings, noting man's need, first of all, to think his way "out

interpretation a fresh theme for his militant atheism. *Dieu et l'État*, pp. 78–79: "Once the supernatural world, the divine world, had been well established in the imagination of the peoples, the development of different religious systems followed its natural and logical course, conforming, moreover, to the contemporaneous development of economic and political relations, of which, in the world of religious fantasy, it has always been the faithful echo and the divine sanction."

[68] Berdyaev, *Sources et sens*, p. 208. Cf. p. 214: "Communism wants to be universal, it wants to command all existence and not only some of its moments."

[69] Letter to Hartmann.

[70] Jean Wahl, *Le Malheur de la conscience dans la philosophie de Hegel* (Paris: Rieder, 1929), p. 73, cf. pp. 52 and 61.

of his own consciousness", he made this short but lucid observation that seems to forecast the double program of Feuerbach and Marx: "It was one of the merits of our age that, at least in theory, it claimed as man's property the treasures that had been squandered on the heavens; but what age will have the strength to take practical advantage of that right and secure that property?"

The second part of the prophecy presupposed the realization of the first. Feuerbach was indispensable to Marx. Arnold Ruge's *mot*,[71] repeated by Karl Grün and by Marx himself,[72] offers the historian a suggestive symbol: on the threshold of the Marxist paradise there is the "purgatory" of Feuerbach.[73]

3. Nietzsche and the "Death of God"

Nietzsche published his first work in the year of Feuerbach's death. He showed no esteem for that philosopher.[74] Neverthe-

---

[71] Feuer-bach = stream of fire, burning brook. Letter to Feuerbach, October 14, 1840.

[72] "Luther arbitre entre Strauss et Feuerbach", in *Anekdota*, vol. 2, no. 7 (1843), p. 206: "No other path to freedom and truth exists for you [theologians and philosophers] than through Feuer-bach. Feuer-bach is the purgatory of our time" (quoted by Alexandre Marc, 269). Cf. Heinrich Heine, *De l'Allemagne*, vol. 2 (edition of 1884), p. 285: "The most consistent of these *enfants terribles* of philosophy, our modern Porphyrius, who actually bears the name of River of Fire (Feuerbach), proclaims, together with his friends, the most radical atheism as the last word of our metaphysics."

[73] Lenin, too, proclaimed this Feuerbachian relation, for example, in *Matérialisme et empiriocriticisme* (French trans.), p. 288: "Stemming from Feuerbach, Marx and Engels. . . ." Cf. pp. 60, 125, 170, 198, 287, etc. This is a point very well observed by Marcel Moré, pp. 25–26: "Marxism, coming from the religious criticism of Feuerbach, can only be, by its very origin, antireligious. It is therefore with this point of transmission that all intelligent criticism of Marxist atheism should be concerned."

[74] "There we have one of those stupid blunders à la Feuerbach", he wrote one day to Deussen (Daniel Halévy, *La Vie de Frédéric Nietzsche* [Paris: Calmann-Lévy, 1922], p. 30).

less, he had received from Feuerbach more than he admitted—
more, I dare say, than he thought—through his two masters,
Schopenhauer and Wagner.[75] Written between 1844 and 1850,
Schopenhauer's *Parerga* bear incontestable witness to the deep
impression that *Das Wesen des Christentums* had made upon their
author.[76] As for Wagner, before being "initiated into the profound and tragic meaning of the world and the vanity of its
appearances" by reading *Die Welt als Wille und Vorstellung* (*The
World as Will and Idea*), he too had been fascinated by Feuerbach. At the time when he was at work on his *Memoirs*—those
memoirs of which Nietzsche himself corrected the proofs—
Wagner still considered Feuerbach the "only real philosopher of
modern times" and "the representative of the radical and categorical liberation of the individual".[77] Before he broke away,
he had not only found in Feuerbach's doctrine the idea for a
play called *Jesus of Nazareth* (which he never finished), and dedicated to the philosopher his work on *Religion und Kunst* (Religion and Art), but it was from Feuerbach that he had received
the inspiration for his Siegfried, described by Mr. René Berthelot as "a wonderful incarnation of the hero as conceived by
Nietzsche".[78] Thus it is not surprising to find that, even in the

---

[75] We should also note the relationship of trust and cordiality he maintained
with the aging Bruno Bauer, whose thought recalls *Das Wesen des Christentums*
and foreshadows *Der Antichrist*.

[76] *Fragment sur la philosophie de la religion*: "The word 'God' is antipathetic
to me, for in every case it shifts to the outside what lies within. . . . 'God' is
essentially an object and not the subject. Thus as soon as God is posed, I am
nothing" (quoted by Dietrich, *Sur la religion*, p. 128).

[77] Richard Wagner, *Ma vie* (French trans. of *Mein Leben*), vol. 2, pp. 335–
38; vol. 3, pp. 99–101 and 254. It was between 1848 and 1853 that Wagner
read Feuerbach; he had been urged to do so by Metzdorff, "Catholic preacher
and political agitator"; correspondence was established between them, and the
artist at that time tried to lure the philosopher to Zurich. It was in October
1854 that Wagner read Schopenhauer for the first time.

[78] "Friedrich Nietzsche", in *Evolutionnisme et platonisme*, p. 101: Siegfried
was "imagined by Wagner around 1850, under the influence of Bakunin and
Feuerbach"; he achieved "the ideal of Feuerbach, for whom man must live

last phase before madness overtook him, Nietzsche's notes for the great synthesis on *Der Wille zur Macht* (*The Will to Power*) —a project he was continually postponing—included an explanation of belief in God that comes close to Feuerbach's, but with an added element of passion.[79]

Religion is conceived as the result of a kind of psychological duplication. God, according to Nietzsche, is nothing more than the mirror of man, who, in certain intense, exceptional states, becomes aware of the power that is in him or of the love that exalts him. But, as these sensations take him more or less by surprise and he does not seem to be accountable for them, man, not daring to ascribe such power or love to himself, makes them the attributes of a superhuman being who is a stranger to him. He accordingly divides the two aspects of his own nature between two spheres, the ordinary weak and pitiable aspect appertaining to the sphere he calls "man", while the rare, strong and surprising aspect belongs to the sphere he calls "God". Thus by his own action he is defrauded of what is best in him. "Religion is a matter of adulteration of the personality." It is a process by which man is debased. The whole essence of the human problem will therefore consist in remounting that fatal slope so as "gradually to regain possession of those lofty and proud states of the soul" of which we have wrongfully despoiled ourselves.[80]

In Christianity this process of self-despoilment and self-

---

without fear of the death of human life in all its fullness". *Jesus von Nazareth*, a play begun in 1848, was also inspired by Feuerbach. Wagner acknowledged this influence on several occasions.

[79] We should also note that Karl Friedrich Koeppen, the historian of Buddhism whom Nietzsche followed so closely, was "an old Feuerbachian thinker" and that his work on the religion of Buddha (1857) is "imbued with an irreligious Hegelianism": Charles Andler, *Nietzsche, sa vie et sa pensée* (Paris: Bossard, 1920–31), vol. 4, p. 245.

[80] *Volonté de puissance* (French trans. by Bianquis [1885] of *Der Wille zur Macht*), vol. 1, pp. 153–56. Feuerbachian, too, is the idea of making religion an illusion of desire even before making it an illusion of knowledge.

debasement is carried to extremes. There is nothing good, great and true that is not solely bestowed by grace. "It is a deplorable story: man seeks a principle in the name of which he can despise man: he invents another world in order to be able to slander and besmirch this one; in actual fact he never grasps anything but nothingness and makes of that nothingness a 'God', a 'Truth', called upon to judge and condemn this present existence. . . ."[81]

Moreover, Nietzsche's aversion to Christianity and to all faith in God did not date only from the end of his career. It showed itself very early, and from the beginning it was a spontaneous, quite instinctive feeling, as he himself explained in his *Ecce Homo*: "Atheism", he said at that time, "is not, for me, the consequence of something else; still less is it a thing that has befallen me; in my case it is something that goes without saying, a matter of instinct."[82] For some time he dreamed of an organization of the forces of atheism.[83] Thus, in this new protagonist of the great drama, even more plainly than in Feuerbach and his disciples, atheism is, at the very root of it, an antitheism.

Nietzsche takes it as an accepted fact that God cannot "live" anywhere but in the human mind. But he is an undesirable guest there: he is, according to *Zarathustra*, "a thought that bends everything that is straight".[84] The way to get rid of him is not so

---

[81] Ibid., and p. 103. Cf. p. 145: "Men have thus been given a bad reputation and a bad conscience by imagining a holy God placed above them and by imprinting thereby the seal of evil on all their acts, whatever they might be, especially as the human sensibility became more delicate and more noble."

[82] *Ecce Homo* (French trans. by Albert [Paris, 1909]), p. 42. Cf. Lou Andreas-Salomé, *Nietzsche* (French trans. of *Friedrich Nietzsche in seinen Werken*), p. 49.

[83] *Aurore* (French trans. by Albert of *Morgenröthe*), no. 96 (p. 105): "There are now perhaps ten to twenty million men among the different peoples of Europe who 'no longer believe in God'. Is it too much to ask that they get in touch with each other on their own accord?"

[84] *Ainsi parlait Zarathoustra* (French trans. by Albert of *Also sprach Zarathustra*), p. 117.

much to refute the proofs of his existence as to show how such an idea came to be formed and how it succeeded in establishing itself in the human mind and in "gaining weight" there. This "historical refutation" is "the only one that will carry finality". It will make any counterproof unavailing, whereas without it a doubt will always subsist; for, in spite of themselves, men will always keep on wondering whether there is not perhaps some better proof than the one that has just been refuted. That being so, belief will not have been destroyed at the root, and it will not fail to put forth new shoots at the first opportunity.[85] Is not Kant a case in point? Although his first *Kritik* seemed to have broken "the bars of the cage" in which faith in God keeps us shut up, Kant of his own accord, through the postulates on which he based his ethics, went into captivity again.[86] He had, however, given evidence of a force and skill hitherto unknown! For the rest, his criticism was bound to be incomplete because it remained wholly speculative and did not proceed from a decision. Kant was only an intellectual, a "journeyman of philosophy":[87] it is man who has to free himself, by an act of will. He must dare. Faith in God, especially as inculcated by Christianity, has served to tame man (*zähmen*): what is necessary is to raise (*züchten*) him (in the sense of improving the breed) by rooting out that faith, so as to enable

---

[85] *Aurore*, no. 95, p. 103. Note the connection with Bakunin, p. 17: "As long as we are not able to account for the way in which the idea of a supernatural or divine world was produced and had inevitably to be produced in the historical development of the human consciousness, no matter how scientifically convinced we are of the absurdity of this idea, we will never succeed in destroying it in the opinion of the majority, because we will never be able to attack it in the very depths of the human being where it originated. . . . As long as the roots of all the absurdities that torment the world are not destroyed, belief in God will remain intact and will never fail to produce new shoots."

[86] *Le Gai savoir* (French trans. by Vialatte of *Die fröhliche Wissenschaft*), no. 335, p. 165.

[87] *Par delà le bien et le mal* (French trans. by Albert of *Jenseit von Gut und Böse*), no. 211, p. 201.

him in the end to raise himself. Come then: let "the death of God" be boldly proclaimed.

This expression "the death of God" had its place in the most traditional theology as signifying what happened on Calvary. Nietzsche had doubtless, on various occasions, heard Luther's chorale "God himself is dead"; he may even have joined in the singing of it. Nor was he unaware of the use that Hegel had made of it. "That hard saying is at the same time just the opposite", Hegel had said; and he had taken it and turned it into one of the essential categories of his own thought, applying it both to the Christ who dies and comes to life again and to human reason, which must pass through the moment of negation in order to join the universal spirit: "the Good Friday of speculation", the death of the "abstract God", necessary for the life of the concrete God. In this connection Hegel had quoted Pascal, who had said "in a quite empirical way" but in a sense not so far removed from Nietzsche's, though with a completely different intention: "Nature bears traces of a lost God everywhere, both in man and outside him."[88] The same expression also occurred in the mystics, such as Jakob Boehme and Angelus Silesius: through love, the latter sang, "God is led into dying", "God dies in order to live in thee."[89] But this is obviously not the sense in which Nietzsche understands it. Wagner came closer to him when recounting, in his *Nibelungen* trilogy, the death of a race of gods. Schopenhauer, in a letter Nietzsche may have read, made use of terms rather similar to

---

[88] To be found in Hegel's early works and in *La Phénoménologie de l'esprit* (French trans. by Jean Hyppolite [Paris: Aubier, 1941] of *Die Phänomenologie des Geistes*), vol. 2, pp. 270 and 286). For the early works, cf. Wahl, passim; J. R. Badelle, "Foi religieuse et connaissance philosophique", in *Revue philosophique*, September 1942–1943, p. 73.

[89] *Cherubinic Wanderer*, l. 2, 2; l. 1, 33, etc. (Henri Plard, *La Mystique d'Angelus Silesius* [Paris: Aubier, 1943], p. 57). Meister Eckhart had also spoken, in his mystical language, of "divine death" and even of "killing God": *Sermons-Traités* (trans. by P. Petit), pp. 308–10; *Traités et sermons* (Aubier trans.), pp. 137 and 221.

those that he himself was later to adopt. This letter, written to Frauenstaedt on August 21, 1852, says:

> The "Thing in itself", for you, is the absolute, the ontological proof, in disguise, with the God of the Jews astride it. And as for you, you go in front of it like King David before the Ark of the Lord, dancing and singing, puffed up with vanity. And yet, despite the aforesaid definition, which should have made it unshakable (the "original, eternal being, which had no beginning and cannot perish"), it has been well and truly cast forth by Kant. It has been handed down to me as a corpse, and when the smell of it comes back to me, as it did in your letter, I am filled with impatience.[90]

No doubt Nietzsche likewise recalled the cry of horror that symbolizes the end of the ancient paganism: "The great Pan is dead! The great Pan is dead!" In any case he must have read the passage in which Heinrich Heine[91]—one of his favorite writers—set forth the "catastrophe" in which the development of German thought had culminated.

> Our hearts [said Heine, with his usual irony] are thrilled with compassion, for it is old Jehovah himself who is making ready to die. We have known him so well, from his cradle in Egypt, where he was brought up among the divine crocodiles and calves, the onions and ibises and sacred cats. . . . We saw him bid farewell to those companions of his childhood, the obelisks and sphinxes of the Nile, to become a little god-king in Palestine to a poor nation of shepherds. . . . Later we saw him in contact with the Assyro-Babylonian civilization; at that stage he gave up his far too human passions and refrained from spitting wrath and vengeance; at any rate, he no longer thundered for the least trifle. . . . We saw him

---

[90] Adolphe Bossert, *Schopenhauer, l'homme et le philosophie* (Paris: Hachette, 1904), p. 288.

[91] We know that, from a literary point of view, Nietzsche professed great admiration for Heine. "It is Heinrich Heine", he wrote, "who has given me the loftiest image of the lyrical poet. . . . And what mastery of the German language he had! Heine and I, we are very nearly the first artists of the German language: a day will come when all the world will say so" (*Ecce Homo*).

move to Rome, the capital, where he abjured everything in the way of national prejudice and proclaimed the celestial equality of all peoples; with these fine phrases he set up in opposition to old Jupiter and, thanks to intriguing, he got into power and, from the heights of the Capital, ruled the city and the world, *urbem et orbem*. . . . We have seen him purify himself, spiritualize himself still more, become paternal, compassionate, the benefactor of the human race, a philanthropist. . . . But nothing could save him!

Don't you hear the bell? Down on your knees! The sacrament is being carried to a dying God.[92]

Whatever its antecedents may have been, the meaning Nietzsche attaches to this phrase, "the death of God", is new. On his lips it is not a mere statement of fact. Nor is it a lament or a piece of sarcasm. It expresses a choice. "Now," says Nietzsche, "it is our preference that decides against Christianity— not arguments."[93] It is an act. An act as definite and brutal as

---

[92] Heinrich Heine "De l'Allemagne depuis Luther", in *Revue des deux-mondes*, vol. 4 (1834), p. 408. This light, quizzical tone is the very opposite of Nietzsche's habitual manner, though the two pieces of storytelling are so much alike that the hypothesis of direct imitation can hardly be ruled out. Cf. "Hors de service" in *Zarathoustra*, p. 367:

"When he was young, this God from the East, he was hard and vindictive and fashioned a hell, for the diversion of his favorites.

"But as time went on, he became old and soft and flabby and compassionate, more like a grandfather than a father, but still more like a shaky old grandmother.

"There he sat, shriveled up, in the chimney-corner, fretting over the weakness of his legs, world-weary and weary-willed, until one day he was suffocated by his own excess of pity."

Or "L'Insensé", in *Le Gai savoir*, p. 105: "It is still reported how this madman entered the same day into various churches and intoned there his *Requiem aeternam Deo*. . . ."

Or *L'Antéchrist*: "In the past, God had only his people. . . . Since then he has gone off to the stranger, just like his people, he began to travel, until he was at home everywhere, the great cosmopolitan . . ." (*Le Crépuscule des idoles*, p. 262).

[93] *Le Gai savoir*. Bauemler is thus mistaken when he writes: "In order to understand precisely Nietzsche's attitude with regard to Christianity, it is nec-

that of a murderer. For him "the death of God is not merely a terrible fact, it is something willed by him."[94] If God is dead, he expressly adds, "it is we who have killed him". "We are the assassins of God."[95]

A great many men, the vast majority, are unaware of it; and, if someone comes to tell them the news, they take him for a madman. They fall into two huge categories: believers and common atheists. The first, failing to understand what it is all about, are not even disturbed. Their faith makes them blind and deaf, so to speak. They go on with their dream in the midst of a world that is waking. The second, who have never believed in anything, laugh heartily at the news. They have never suspected the existence of anything living beyond the life of sense perception. Nietzsche wants to shake these scoffers out of their complacency; he wants to make them perceive the void that has been hollowed out within them, and he accosts them in violent terms. Toward believers, on the other hand, if he feels that they are sincere and simple, his manner is circumspect, as if he feared to cause them suffering by making himself too

---

essary never to lose sight of the fact that the decisive phrase: 'God is dead' has the sense of a historical observation", *Nietzsche, le philosophe et le politique* (1931), p. 98. Nietzsche did much more than observe.

[94] Jean Wahl, "Le Nietzsche de Jaspers", in *Recherches philosophiques*, vol. 6, p. 356; and "Nietzsche et la mort de Dieu, note à propos du Nietzsche de Jaspers", in *Acèphale*, January 1937, p. 22: "This death is not only a fact, it is an action of a will."

[95] *Le Gai savoir*, no. 125, "L'Insensé" (pp. 104–5). The expression "to kill God" is also found in Max Stirner, *L'Unique et sa propriété*: "Can the man-God truly die if only the God in him dies? To be truly free of him, it is necessary to kill not only God but man!" (quoted by Victor Basch, p. 66). Among those who would subsequently use the expression, we cite Miguel de Unamuno, *Le Sentiment tragique de la vie* (French trans. [Paris: Gallimard, 1937] of *Del sentimiento trágico de la vida en los hombres y en los pueblos*), p. 124: Many ask, like Pilate: What is truth? "without having the heart to wait for the reply, just to wash one's hands of having helped to kill God in their own conscience or in that of others." Wanting to go farther, Montherlant would write: "To stab Jesus Christ."

well understood.[96] His attitude is even respectful, seeming to say: "Take care lest, in revealing my secret to you, I deprive you of your treasure. . . ."[97] But at first he even gave *himself* the impression of being mad. The bewildered or contemptuous surprise he encountered might well have made him doubt his message. And so might the enormity of that message. . . . "I have come too soon", he said to himself; "my time is not yet." It is because "the most important things that happen are also the slowest in making themselves felt." And here was a "terrible innovation", indeed the most terrible and the newest of all.[98] "It takes time for the lightning and the thunder, it takes time for the light of the stars, it takes time for actions, even when they are over, to be seen and heard." It would take hundreds, perhaps thousands of years yet, before the shadow of the dead God would disappear entirely from the walls of the cave in which the great mass of human beings vegetated.[99]

The death of God! "This immense happening is still on the

---

[96] "Every deep thinker is more afraid of being understood than of being misunderstood. In the latter event, his vanity suffers perhaps; in the former, what suffers is his heart, his sympathy, which keeps on saying: 'Alas! Why do you want the road to be as hard for you as it is for me?' "

[97] The first man Zarathustra meets descending from his solitude is an old man who spends his time, in the forest, singing the praises of his God. "What present do you bring us?", asks the holy man of the prophet. Zarathustra replies to him: "What would I have to give you? But let me leave quickly so that I do not take anything from you!" Alone again, he says to himself: "Could this be possible? the old holy one in his forest has not yet heard that God is dead!" *Zarathoustra*, pp. 10–11 (cf. pp. 364–65).

[98] *Œuvres posthumes*, texts translated into French by H. J. Bolle, no. 188, p. 88 (years 1882–1888).

[99] *Le Gai savoir*, no. 108, "Luttes nouvelles": "With Buddha dead, his shadow in a cave will still be shown for centuries; an enormous and terrifying shadow. God is dead; but men are such that there will still be caves perhaps for millennia in which his shadow will be shown. . . . And we . . . it is still necessary for us to conquer his shadow" (p. 95). Compare Heinrich Heine, "De l'Allemagne depuis Luther", p. 644: "Deism has vanished. . . . It will perhaps still take millennia for this new funeral to spread universally. . . . But we others have been in mourning for a long time. *De profundis.*"

way", he wrote in *Menschliches, Allzumenschliches* (*Human, All-too-human*), "it is progressing, and it has not yet reached men's ears." "The sun has already set, but it still illumines and kindles the firmament of our life."[100] Already, however, a few, more clearsighted than the rest, emerging from the great mass, are beginning to feel frightened. They are in the grip of a strange impression. Everything seems to have "lost its weight".[101] Or rather, on the earthly horizon, the sun seems to have disappeared forever. "Day by day, our old world appears more vesperal, more suspicious, more alien, more obsolete." Without having as yet formed a clear idea of what has happened, these few feel that henceforth the ground is mined beneath their feet, and they dimly perceive the catastrophe that is bound to destroy everything by which they live. With a confused understanding of the crime that has been committed and of the fact that they themselves have had a hand in it, they begin to lament:

How did we come to do that? How did we manage to empty the sea? Who gave us a sponge to wipe out the whole horizon? What were we about when we undid the chain that linked this earth to the sun? Are we not continually falling? Forward, backward, sideways, in every direction? Is there still an above, a below? Are we not wandering as through an endless nothingness? Do we not feel the breath of the void on our faces? Isn't it growing colder? Is not night always coming on, one night after another, more and more?[102]

---

[100] *Humain, trop humain* (French trans. of *Menschliches, Allzumenschliches*), vol. I, p. 232.

[101] *Œuvres posthumes*, p. 89.

[102] *Le Gai savoir*, n. 125, "L'Insensé", and no. 343, "Notre sérénité" (pp. 104–5 and 173). Similar images and a rather close symbolism in Gérard de Nerval, *Aurelia* (Éd. de la Pléiade, 1927), pp. 111–14. The poet goes out into the night from a service at Notre-Dame de Loretto: "The stars were shining in the firmament. Suddenly it seemed to me that they had just been extinguished all at once like the candles I had seen in church. . . . I thought I saw

At last a very few, rare spirits who carry in them the destiny of mankind resist the dizziness that assails them. They feel it at first, like the others, for they are human, and more than all the rest they are aware of the enormity of what has happened and the losses involved. But very soon they master this sensation. Their energy is equal to their perspicacity. Alone in their power to see things as they are, they bring a perfectly clear mind to bear upon the outrage they have perpetrated and thus transform the crime into an exploit.[103]

It is from them that we receive Nietzsche's message, which does not entirely reside in the confident pride of his Zarathustra: "But, friends, let me open my whole heart to you: If there were

---

a black sun in the desert sky and a blood-red globe above the Tuileries. I said to myself: 'The eternal night is beginning, and it is going to be terrible. What is going to happen when men perceive that there is no longer a sun?' . . . Through clouds quickly driven away by the wind, I saw several moons that passed by with great speed. I thought that the earth had left its orbit and that it was wandering in the firmament like a vessel without a mast. . . . Exhausted, I returned home and threw myself on my bed. Upon waking, I was astonished to see the light again. A kind of mysterious choir reached my ear; children's voices repeated in chorus: 'Christ! Christ! Christ!' I thought a great number of children had been gathered in the nearby church (Notre-Dame-des-Victoires) to invoke Christ. 'But Christ is no more', I said to myself, 'they do not know it yet!'. . . I finally rose and went under the galleries of the Palais-Royal. I said to myself that probably the sun had still conserved enough light to light the earth for three days, but that it was using its own substance. . . . [Entering the home of a friend], I said to him that all was finished and that we must prepare to die. He called his wife, who said to me: 'What is the matter with you?' 'I don't know', I said to her, 'I'm lost.' "

[103] Cf. *Par delà le bien et le mal*, 109, p. 125: "The criminal is not often at the same level as his deed; he belittles and slanders it." Already in *Aurore*: "I have killed the law, and I have for the law the horror that the living have for a corpse; unless I am above the law, I am the greatest of all transgressors." Cf. the letter dated March 1884 to Overbeck (*Lettres choisies*, ed. Walz, p. 417): "Great heavens! Who has any idea of the burden that weighs upon me and of the strength it takes to endure myself! I don't know why it should fall upon me of all people—but it may be that I am *the first* to light upon an idea that will divide the history of mankind in two. . . . It takes some courage for me to face that thought."

gods in existence, how could I endure not to be a god?"[104] Nor is it merely an instance of the attitude habitual to Nietzsche, which consisted in saying No to everything that was dear and estimable to him, in order that he might free himself from everything.[105] Charles Du Bos, in an entry in his *Journal*, has hit upon one of its distinguishing traits. He observes that Nietzsche is, above all, up in arms against the great convenience that belief in God too often affords:

> "God", Nietzsche might have said, "is that to which we look to make good our shortcomings and to supply an explanation where we feel the need of one." That is why in *Zarathustra* and elsewhere he so often repeats: "They cannot all know that God is dead. . . ." It is here above all that the idea of God finds champions, because of the too great advantages that it offers. Nietzsche is one who continually says to us (and on a much more profound plane than that on which we ask ourselves "How far can man go?"): "O man, to what point can you stand firm against this, and against that, and, last of all, against the fact that there is nothing left for you but absolute denudation? And more than that . . . can you taste and feel in denudation itself the utmost fullness?"[106]

Zarathustra, indeed, says to his disciple: "The laggard demon in you, the one that likes to fold his arms and take his ease—it is this laggard demon that says to you: 'There is a God!' "[107]

---

[104] *Zarathoustra*, p. 116.

[105] That, as we know, is one of the basic aspects of the Nietzschean metamorphoses: that of the camel as lion. *Zarathustra*, pp. 31–34. Cf. Yves de Montcheuil, "Nietzsche et la critique de l'idéal chrétien", in *Cité nouvelle*, June 25, 1941.

[106] *Extraits d'un journal*, pp. 177–79. Solely from the intellectual point of view, is it not true that God is in fact too often the "verbal symbol" under which we arrange "all the difficulties we have in explaining and generalizing particular facts"? Cf. Eugène de Roberty, *L'Inconnaissable* (1889), p. 129.

[107] *Zarathoustra*, p. 253. See already the letter to his sister, written from Bonn on June 11, 1865 (he was twenty years old): Walz, pp. 87–88. Geneviève Bianquis has well observed in Nietzsche "that fatal taste for the truths that

What is needed is courage to reject his promptings and "stand firm" in spite of all. But the very fact of "standing firm" means growing in stature. Nietzsche did not stop short at a new kind of stoicism. If he deliberately set out to be "godless"[108]—the word, which later scored such a success in Soviet Russia, came from him—it was neither to clench his teeth in unspoken distress nor to give himself up to selfish enjoyment. If his first feeling was one of instinctive revolt, atheism in the end seemed to him "the result of an arduous and hazardous conquest".[109] "If we do not make the death of God a splendid renunciation on our part and a continual victory over ourselves," he said in *Also sprach Zarathustra* (*Thus Spoke Zarathustra*), "we shall have to pay dearly for that loss."[110] Jaspers notes that there is in Nietzsche "a universal negativity, an immeasurable lack of satisfaction with every aspect of being: and this dissatisfaction and denial are so passionate and full of the will to sacrifice that they seem to come from the same depths as the great religions and the faith of the prophets."[111] Thus they are transformed into a positive urge, spurring us on to greatness. To quote Zarathustra once more: "What would there be left to create, if there were any gods?"[112] Bereft of the God in whom it used to repose, to whom it used to appeal, mankind must henceforth go forward and upward. It is forced into creating. To quote from *Der Wille zur Macht*: "Since there ceased to be a God,

---

hurt, that defiance with respect to all that favors laziness or weakness of character": *Nietzsche* (Paris: Rieder, 1933), p. 62.

[108] *Zarathoustra*, p. 141: "Starved, violent, solitary, godless: so the will of the lion chooses to be." *Généalogie* (French trans. of *Zur Genealogie der Moral*), 2, 25: "Zarathustra, the atheist".

[109] Alphonse de Waelhens, *La Philosophie de Martin Heidegger* (Louvain: Éd. de l'Institut superieur de philosophie, 1942), p. 354.

[110] *Zarathoustra* (French trans. by Betz), appendix, no. 61, p. 310 [1881–1882]).

[111] Karl Jaspers, *Nietzsche* (Berlin: De Gruyter, 1936), French trans. by Jean Wahl.

[112] *Zarathoustra* (Albert trans.), p. 118; cf. p. 26: "The destroyer, the criminal: but that is the creator."

loneliness has become intolerable; the man who overtops the
rest *must* set to work."[113] He must produce out of himself—
out of nothingness—something with which to transcend humanity; let him trample his own head under foot and shoot
forth beyond his shadow. . . .[114] The endurance test to which
he has condemned himself will reveal to him his own divinity
by bringing it into being. God is dead, long live the Overman!
Remorse and despair will be overcome simultaneously, by the
same effort:

> How shall we console ourselves, murderers that we are, among
> the murderers? What was most holy and powerful in the world
> up to now has bled beneath our knife. . . . Who will cleanse us
> of this blood? What expiations, what sacred charade shall we be
> forced to invent? The greatness of this deed is too great for us.
> Shall we not have to become gods ourselves simply in order to
> seem worthy of it? There was never a more stupendous action,
> and those who are born after us, whatever they may be, will,
> because of it, belong to a history nobler than any history ever
> was ere this. . . .[115]

At this prospect the "free minds" exult. Such a revelation
is in very truth "joyful wisdom". Before their delighted eyes
the horrible twilight gives place to dawn. They have the triumphant feeling of being the "freed men" of *Der Wille zur
Macht*, "to whom nothing now is forbidden".[116] "The greatest danger" that threatened them has been removed from their

---

[113] *Volonté*, vol. 2, p. 133.

[114] Cf. Gustave Thibon, "Nietzsche et saint Jean de la Croix", in *Études
carmélitaines*, October 1934, p. 62.

[115] "L'Insensé", *Le Gai savoir* (pp. 104–5). Wahl, "Nietzsche et la mort de
Dieu": "In order for man to be truly great, a genuine creator, God must be
dead, God must be killed, he must be absent. By depriving him of God, I
bring man the immense gift of perfect solitude as well as the possibility for
greatness and for creation." Cf. Jean-Paul Sartre: "Human life begins on the
other side of despair" (*Les Mouches* [Oreste]).

[116] "Midi et éternité" (1888), in *Volonté*, p. 381.

path.[117] This corpse of God in decomposition is not, for them,
a sign of death: it is the sign of a gigantic change. God will
find himself again in man, beyond good and evil.[118] Such is
the power of a heroic decision! By it the meaning of facts is
reversed. Now at last "twenty centuries of flouting nature, of
doing violence to humanity" are at an end forever. The sublime adventure can begin:

> Hearing that the old god is dead, we feel ourselves illumined as
> by a new dawn. Our hearts overflow with gratitude, surprise,
> foreknowledge and suspense. . . . Now at last the horizon, even
> if it is not clear, is free once more; now at last our ships can
> weigh anchor and sail to meet any danger; now once more the
> pioneer of knowledge has license to attempt whatever he will:

---

[117] *Zarathoustra* (Albert trans.), part 4, p. 406:

"Now this God is dead! You higher men, this God was your greatest danger.

"It is only since he lay in the grave that you have risen again. Only now the
great noontide comes; only now the higher man becomes lord!

"Do you understand this saying, O my brothers? You are frightened: Do
your hearts fail you? Does the abyss yawn at your feet? Does the hound of
hell bay at you?

"What of it? Forward! Higher men! Now at last the mountain of man's future is about to give birth. God is dead; now it is our will that the Superman
shall live."

Cf. "Le Chemin de la sagesse" (1884): "Neither God nor man above me
from now on!" (In *Volonté*, vol. 2, p. 133.)

[118] Fragment from 1882–1884 (*Volonté*, p. 329): "You say that it is a spontaneous decomposition of God, but this is only a shedding of skins: he is
stripped of his moral epidermis. And soon you will find him again—beyond
good and evil." Fragment from 1885–1886 (vol. 2, p. 150): "The refutation
of God: basically only the *moral* God is refuted."

A Nietzschean socialist wrote in his notebook around 1908: "The Gods are
dead, long live the Superman! Nietzsche predicts an early return to the ideal,
but to an entirely different and new ideal. To understand this ideal there will
be a category of free minds, fortified by war, solitude and danger. They will
know the wind, the glaciers, the Alpine snows; they will be able to plumb the
deepest gulfs without wavering. Endowed with a kind of sublime perversity,
they will deliver us from loving our neighbors and from the desire of nothingness, that the earth may recover its purpose and men their hopes."

the whole expanse of the seas, *our* sea, is accessible to us once more. Never before, perhaps, was there such an open sea.[119]

"I am alone and I would have it so", said Zarathustra. "Alone with a clear sky and an open sea."[120]

4. The Dissolution of Man

Such an outburst of lyricism, coupled with such magnificent promises, was contagious. Already at work in the preceding generation, the urge to do without God now became a greater ferment than ever in souls which were not all lacking in nobility[121] and which would have been the first to reject an atheism of the ordinary complacent type. It was this urge that inspired the ideas of men like Dietrich Heinrich Kerler, for instance, who declared, "Even if it could be proved by mathematics that God exists, I do not want him to exist, because he would set limits to my greatness."[122] Nor was it enough for a man like Martin Heidegger to deny God: in order to rule out more completely any risk of a swing toward belief again, he had to go beyond a mere denial and refuse to allow the question of God even to be raised.[123] And, in a study that caused a great stir in

---

[119] "Notre sérénité", in *Le Gai savoir*, p. 174.

[120] *Zarathoustra* (Albert trans.), p. 226.

[121] Cf. Charles Du Bos, *Approximations*, 5th series (Paris: R. A. Correa, 1932), foreword, p. 14: "Nietzsche, the loftiest and most noble adversary with whom they [the Christian writers] have to dialogue."

[122] Letter to Max Scheler.

[123] Cf. De Waelhens, pp. 355–56: "He sees that the violence of negation in Nietzsche is turned into an affirmation, and he wants to be the one whose No will not give evidence of a Yes. The institution of an idea radically freed from the idea of God could not be conceived by the *negation* of this idea. It has to be formulated without the least reference to the latter. A philosophy—such as Nietzsche's teaching—would have shaken off the yoke of the divine if, and only if, it succeeded in completing the circle of philosophical problems outside *any* use of the theist hypothesis. There we have, at least with respect to

Germany not long ago, Max Scheler went so far as to speak of "postulatory atheism" as the essential characteristic of modern man.

There were many, indeed, who still more or less vaguely thought, with Feuerbach, that "the question of the existence or nonexistence of God is the question of the nonexistence or existence of man";[124] there was Nicolai Hartmann, for instance, holding the view that, if there was a God, this would be the end of man "as an ethical essence, as a person".[125] Many, like Nietzsche in *Die fröhliche Wissenschaft* (*The Gay Science*), said to themselves that "perhaps man would rise higher and higher from the moment when he ceased to flow into God":[126] there was Emil Bergmann, who proclaimed, in the language of the stud-farm, that "it is possible to breed not only animals but the man-God". Both types traced their descent from Prometheus, whom they acclaimed as "the first of the martyrs".[127] They recognized themselves in that man who heroically stood up to

---

the essentials—and in our opinion—the profound and ultimate intent of Heideggerean existentialism. Its success would tend to prove—as Heidegger implies somewhere—that there is no philosophical problem of God or, to keep to the author's terms, no philosophical decision touching a possible existence in view of God [*Sein zu Gott*]."

[124] Quoted by Lévy, p. 48.

[125] *Ethik* (Berlin: De Gruyter, 1926), p. 179. Nicolai Hartmann is here strictly Feuerbachian: "Ethics accomplishes and must accomplish what in the eyes of the faithful is a blasphemy: it gives man the attributes of the Divinity. It renders him what he himself, unaware of his own essence, had taken from himself and given to God, or, to express it otherwise, it makes the Divinity descend from its cosmic throne to dwell in the will of man. The metaphysical heritage of God falls to man" (p. 180). Texts quoted by Gaston Rabeau, "L'État religieux de l'Allemagne protestante", in *Mélanges de science religieuse*, 1945, p. 126.

[126] *Le Gai savoir*, p. 285; *Excelsior*, p. 142.

[127] Karl Marx, *Différence de la philosophie de la nature chez Démocrite et chez Epicure* (in *Œuvres philosophiques*, trans. by Molitor [Paris: Costes, 1937–1948], vol. 1, pp. XIV–XV). Nietzsche, *Naissance de la tragédie* (French trans. by Bianquis [Paris: Gallimard, 1941] of *Die Geburt der Tragödie aus dem Geiste der Musik*), pp. 53–54.

the gods. They too wanted to "kill God" so that man could at last live a fully human, or rather "superhuman", life, and atheism seemed to them that indispensable foundation of the high ideal that they proposed for such a man: either an ideal of rationality and love or an ideal of strength and heroic life. They might subsequently differ on every point and fight each other without mercy; but to begin with they were of one mind in their determined rejection of God.

To achieve their aim, both camps made abundant use of the resources that generations of historians and thinkers had piled up: resources of dialectic, of genetic analysis, of psychology, of the history of ideas, of the study of religion. A vast accumulation of work, most of it distorted by a mass of prejudices, supplied them with a whole arsenal. But, unlike many of those who had thus prepared the ground for them, they hardly troubled to apply the patient methods of the intellectual. They preferred a more active approach. Had not Feuerbach taught that the Hegelian synthesis marked "the end of classical philosophy"?[128] True, Feuerbach himself, although "the real conqueror of the old philosophy", "never stopped philosophizing". As Dühring observed later,[129] Feuerbach found it "a slow and painful business to expel from his naturally generous blood the academic poison with which Hegel had infected him". Without going so far as to adopt, like Hegel, the maxim: "It is only at eventide that Minerva's bird comes forth", he put off his young disciples (who, as we have seen, pressed him to join them in more direct action) with the answer: "We have not got far enough yet to put theory into practice."[130]

But soon, even "more realistic" than his master in his con-

---

[128] Cf. the title of the celebrated work by Engels. Already Heinrich Heine: "Our philosophical revolution is over; Hegel has closed that great circle": *Revue des deux-mondes*, vol. 4 (1834), p. 674.

[129] Eugen Karl Dühring, *Cursus der Philosophie als streng wissenschaftlicher Weltanschauung und Lebengestaltung* (Leipzig: K. Koschny, 1875), p. 486.

[130] Letters to Ruge, March 13 and June 20, 1843, in Auguste Cornu, *Le Jeunesse de Karl Marx*, pp. 248 and 265.

ception of man,[131] Marx was to proclaim in the sixth of his Theses on Feuerbach the interdependence between man's spiritual alienation and his temporal and social alienation—that is to say, what he had lost to God through religion and what he had lost to other men through their exploitation of him. Refusing to "crouch" any longer "in the speculative concept",[132] he declared that "the driving force of history is not criticism but revolution"[133] and finally, in the last of the Theses, uttered his famous watchword: "So far the philosophers have done nothing but explain the world; now we have got to transform it."[134] Engels, too, referred to "the defunct philosophy";[135] and since then all true Marxists, accepting, like Marx and Feuerbach, Hegel's own idea about his work[136] and acting accordingly, have contemptuously left systems to "the professors",[137]

---

[131] Karl Marx, *Thesen über Feuerbach*, thesis 6, etc.

[132] Karl Marx, letter to Friedrich Engels (against Lassalle).

[133] Study of 1845–1846 (at the time unpublished) on *Die deutsche Ideologie*. A little earlier he had written that the solution of the theological problem was itself a task of practical activity (1844 manuscript on *Economie politique et philosophie*).

[134] *Thesen über Feuerbach*, thesis 11. Léon Brunschvicg does not give full justice to Marx' originality and power when he comments: "Marx proposes a return to the practical concept, which has, since Descartes, been that of all properly rational doctrine and whose invention, with his naïve arrogance, he attributes to himself": *Le Progrès de la conscience dans la philosophie occidentale* (Paris: Alcan, 1927), vol. 2, p. 428. What is more true is that Marx' attitude was prepared by that of Ruge, von Ciesztowski and Hess in the course of the years 1839–1841.

[135] *Anti-Dühring*, p. 19.

[136] Hegel had ended his *Geschichte der Philosophie* with the following reflection: "This is the point now reached by the intellect of mankind: the latest philosophy is the outcome of all those that went before it; nothing is lost, all the principles are preserved. This concrete idea is the result of the efforts of the human mind through nearly 1,500 years (Thales was born in 640 B.C.) of its most serious effort to objectify and recognize itself. *Tantæ molis erat seipsam cognoscere mentem!*"

[137] Cf. Lenin's scoffing remarks aimed at "professors of philosophy". . . . In their introduction to Hegel's *Morceaux choisis*, Henri Lefebvre and Norbert

in order to prepare direct action.[138] As for Nietzsche, given
to "philosophizing with a hammer", did not he, too, smash
all speculation so that life might triumph? Did not he, too,
scorn all "professorial philosophy"? According to him, there
was no need to be held up by what the "ruminants of the higher
education", the common "journeymen of philosophy", or, as
Wagner put it, the "hired porters of philosophy", called "the
search for truth".[139]

There was to be no more contemplation of the real in order to discover its essence, no more submission to any object
whatsoever. Let us, said Nietzsche, reject "this last bondage";
"we have abolished the world of truth"; "nothing is true."[140]
Is the very idea of truth anything more than a shadow of the
dead God? "Perhaps", indeed, "falsehood is a divine thing? . . .

Gutermann will also say, in accordance with Marxist orthodoxy: "He was the
last of the geniuses who wished to content themselves with 'thinking' their
time and with establishing contact with things through pure theory. Since
Hegel and after him—as if he had exhausted pure philosophy—something
else is necessary for thought to find contact with things. Action, practice, life
are necessary." And again: "He has been overtaken, but because speculative
philosophy has been overtaken by action. . . . Hegel is for us 'the Philosopher', with all that this word now entails of strangeness and deficiency; with
a good percentage of irony mixed in with the admiration. He is 'the Philosopher' because he was the last of them" (pp. 9-10). Cf. the naïve remark of Mr.
Matter, De l'état moral, politique et littéraire de l'Allemagne (1847), vol. 1, p. 239:
observing that socialist and communist ideas are spreading beyond the Rhine,
he reassures himself by saying: "but these doctrines are not professed in the
pulpit. . . ."

[138] For Marxism, as we know, religious criticism and revolutionary action
must go hand in hand; spiritual revolution and social revolution are linked.
Communism alone would achieve atheism, but the atheist propaganda must
nonetheless accompany and sustain from the beginning the effort to achieve
communism. Atheist ideology is essential to the Party, even if in individual
cases it admits believers into its midst.

[139] As early as 1875, Nietzsche wanted to consider philosophical effort only
as a series of attempts "to arrive at a form of life that we have not yet attained".
"Le Conflit de la science et de la sagesse" (in La Naissance de la philosophie, p.
212). Cf. the letter to Erwin Rohde, November 9, 1868 (in Walz, p. 138).

[140] Volonté, vol. 2, p. 45.

Perhaps there is value, significance and purpose in the lie, the
artificial introduction of a meaning?" At all events, the cult of
lucidity should replace the search for truth. Let us get to the
bottom of what our denial entails: let us be consistent in our
choice. If God is really dead: how could that "reason", that
"truth" and that "morality" that owed their existence to him
be anything but idols? Here, then, is their "twilight". . . . "Aggressive rejection of a law of being, of an extrahuman order,
of a coherent universe", of an "ontological harmony prior to
the 'I will' " of man; hatred of the intelligible, of final causes,
of an absolute practical order: the decision to kill God entails
all that.[141] Value in itself no more exists than objective essence
exists. It must not exist. Just as it is absurd to submit to a law, so
"pure knowledge", "immaculate knowledge", is a false ideal,
or rather it is a hypocritical ideal fashioned by impotence.[142]
One must live. But "to live is to invent."[143] One must appraise.
But "to appraise is to create."[144] Invention and creation: these
are the two words that henceforth define the task of the genuine philosopher, who is to be "the bad conscience of his age".
He will make hay of accepted values, overthrowing them and
scrapping them so that something new can be got out of them,
remolded to suit his fancy. And this task, which will have to
be done over and over again, is not confined to the realm of

---

[141] Cf. Thibon, pp. 61–63.

[142] *Zarathoustra* (Albert trans.), pp. 169–73, to the partisans of contemplation: "O sensitive and lascivious hypocrites! You lack innocence in desire:
that is why you slander desire! In truth, you do not love the earth like creators,
generators, joyful to create!" Stirner had already said in a similar vein: "The
ancient Apollonian inscription 'Know thyself' is no longer engraved over the
threshold of our epoch, but this new inscription: Make the most of yourself,
Verwerte Dich!" On the immediate meaning of this passage from *Zarathoustra*,
which deals with art and not science, see Charles Andler, "La Morale de Nietzsche dans le 'Zarathoustra' ", in *Revue d'histoire de la philosophie*, 1930, pp.
139–40. Cf. *Volonté*: "The whole system of knowledge has domination as its
goal."

[143] *Aurore*, p. 140.

[144] *Zarathoustra* (Albert trans.), p. 77.

thought; the philosopher is "a terrible explosive from which nothing is safe"; he is "the man of violence, Caesarean creator of civilization"; "it is his mission to command and lay down the law; his research is creation, his creation is legislation, his will to truth is will to power."[145]

Thus, like the Marxist, though after another fashion and for other ends, the Nietzschean is a revolutionary.[146]

That being so, it was not surprising that the drama that had taken shape in human minds quickly reached the point at which it burst forth in fire and slaughter. Nietzsche, indeed, had predicted it. More than a too reasonable farsightedness could have done, the lightning flashes of a mind stalked by madness made him a prophet. "I herald the coming of a tragic era", he said, at a time when his days of sanity were numbered.[147] "We must be prepared for a long succession of demolitions, devastations and upheavals"; "there will be wars such as the world has never yet seen"; "Europe will soon be enveloped in darkness"; we shall watch "the rising of a black tide".[148] "Thanks to me," he wrote, "a catastrophe is at hand. A catastrophe whose name I know, whose name I shall not tell. . . . Then all the earth will writhe in convulsions."[149]

---

[145] *Ecce Homo*, p. 101. *Par-delà le bien et le mal*, pp. 189 and 201–2. "The radical renewal of values will thus not be reduced to setting up a table of oppositions on the Pythagorean model, in order then to make *positive* and *negative* signs intervene in it. It signifies that the values do not at all have an internal stability, that they are destined to be endlessly renewed, by the very vitality of the being that perpetual renewal is": Brunschvicg, vol. 2, pp. 415–16.

[146] Cf. the comparison of the Nietzschean superman and the Aristotelian wise man in Lucien Laberthonnière, *Esquisse d'une philosophie personnaliste*, pp. 88–91.

[147] *Ecce Homo*, p. 94.

[148] "Notre sérénité", in *Le Gai savoir*, p. 174.

[149] *Der Wille zur Macht*: "What I am recounting is the history of the two centuries that are going to come, the advent of nihilism. It is possible to recount this history already today, for it is Necessity that one sees at work here in person. The future speaks to us already through innumerable signs; all that our eyes see foretells the inevitable decline; our ears have become sensitive

In a word, he adds, "it will be the coming of nihilism."[150]

But all this is only the effect, the manifestation of a deeper and a purely inward crisis. For "thought comes before action as lightning before thunder".[151] Events take place in the reality of the mind before they make their appearance in the external reality of history, and what is happening today "should not surprise those who have watched the movements of the spirit". There was something shaken and overthrown in the soul of man before his historical values were shaken and overthrown. The "death of God" was bound to have fatal repercussions. Thus we are confronted with what Nicholas Berdyaev, likewise endowed with a "prophetic" gift, but one coupled with accurate diagnosis, has rightly called "the self-destruction of humanism". We are proving by experience that "where there is no God, there is no man either."[152]

---

enough to perceive this music of the future. Our whole European civilization is in a state of anguished anticipation; it is making its way, decade by decade, toward catastrophe with a restless, irresistible movement, increasingly hastened by a river that runs to its end, that no longer reflects, that would be afraid to reflect" (quoted by Spenlé, p. 167).

[150] Letters to Overbeck, April 16, 1887, and to Brandes, November 20, 1888.

[151] Henrich Heine, p. 677. "Great events, Nietzsche himself says, are great thoughts." Cf. Charles Péguy, *Compte rendu de congrès*, p. 9: "The events of the interior life, which are the first events." And Le Mennais, preface to *Troisièmes mélanges* (1835), p. 11: "All that is accomplished in the social world has previously been accomplished in the world of the intelligence."

[152] *Un nouveau moyen âge*, p. 21, etc. Already Léon Bloy, *Le Fils de Louis XVI* (1900): "It is very permissible to wonder if, truly, the Image is not as absent as the Prototype, and if there could be men in a society without God?" Cf. Synchronë, "Mort et résurrection", in *Le Mot d'ordre*, May 5, 1943, p. 2: "The main event of our times is that we have lost man. God knows, however, if we are anxious to keep him, that old man who was not so handsome but whom we had wanted to make wholly polite and authentic by shielding him from a secular subjection that was not proceeding, it was judged, without including much filth with much ignorance (filthy ignorance, in the end), in order to strip him of his halo and dusting him of a radiance foreign to his nature. Man thus freed, man liberated from the dogmatic chains that restricted his progress

What has actually become of the lofty ambitions of this humanism, not only in fact but in the very way of thought of its initiates? What has become of man as conceived by this atheist humanism? A being that can still hardly be called a "being"—a thing that has no content, a cell completely merged in a mass that is in process of becoming: "social-and-historical man", of whom all that remains is pure abstraction, apart from the social relations and the position in time by which he is defined. There is no stability or depth left in him, and it is no good looking for any inviolable retreat there or claiming to discover any value exacting universal respect. There is nothing to prevent his being used as material or as a tool either for the preparation of some future society or for ensuring, here and now, the dominance of one privileged group. There is not even anything to prevent his being cast aside as useless. Moreover, the types of man conceivable vary even to the point of contradiction, according as, for instance, a biological or an economic system of explanation comes to the fore, or according as the history of mankind is, or is not, credited with a meaning and a purpose. But beneath these diversities there is always the same fundamental creature, or rather the same absence of any creature. For this man has literally been dissolved. Whether in the name of myth or in the name of dialectic, losing truth, he has lost himself. In reality there is no longer any man because there is no longer anything that is greater than man.

It cannot be said that this is only a temporary setback. Nor should the blame be laid on certain clumsy distortions that are only too real and palpable. The descendants of Marx did not all inherit his genius. The heirs of Nietzsche are even more mixed, and there is no doubt that today the prophet in *Zara-*

---

on the route of happiness, man whose Father was suppressed in order to make him a joyful orphan, this man does not know how to profit from his happiness. Despite the oracles that had assisted at his rebirth, despite the godfathers who had answered for his future and said the *non credo* for him, which is *de rigueur* at the baptismal ceremony, it will be agreed that the launching of the free man has not succeeded. . . ."

thustra would be the first to find abundant reasons for cursing a great many of those who invoke his name.[153] But these distortions are often not so much betrayals as the effects of an inevitable corruption.[154] Atheist humanism was bound to end in bankruptcy. Man is himself only because his face is illumined by a divine ray. "The godhead is reflected in the slime of the earth like the image in a mirror."[155] If the fire disappears, the reflected gleam immediately dies out. "If, in everything that takes place in our sublunary world, the relation to eternity is destroyed, it needs no more than that to destroy, at the same time, all depth and all real content in this world."[156] For man, God is not only a norm that is imposed upon him and, by guiding him, lifts him up again: God is the Absolute upon which he rests, the Magnet that draws him, the Beyond that calls him, the Eternal that provides him with the only atmosphere in which he can breathe and, in some sort, that third dimension in which man finds his depth. If man takes himself as god, he can, for a time, cherish the illusion that he has raised and freed himself. But it is a fleeting exaltation! In reality, he has merely abased God, and it is not long before he finds that in doing

---

[153] In *Der Mythus des zwanzigsten Jahrhunderts*, Alfred Rosenberg, in opposition to other interpreters, claims Nietzsche as an inspirer of National Socialism. Bäumler and others as well.

[154] Cf. Jean Wahl, "Le Nietzsche de Jaspers", p. 362: "An explanation is necessary of the possible misuse that has been made of Nietzsche in Germany. For it is a point of the thought of Nietzsche himself that explains how he could—rightly or wrongly—appear to be the one who prepared the way for false ideologies. One can see this particularly in reading Spengler. The criticism of the misuse made of Nietzsche must be accompanied by a criticism of Nietzsche himself, as the profoundly historical origin of the influence he exerted."

[155] Franco (d. 1130), *De gratia Dei*, 1, 2 (166, 725). Cf. Gregory of Nyssa: "Imitation of the Being superior to all thought, resemblance of incorruptible Beauty, stamped with true Light" (PG 44, 805). On man, the reflection of God: Maurice Nédoncelle, *La Réciprocité des consciences* (Paris: Aubier, 1942), pp. 74–75.

[156] Dietrich von Hildebrand, "Le Mythe des races", in *Archives de philosophie du droit et de sociologie juridique*, 1937, p. 143.

so he has abased himself.[157] Soon the old forces of Fate, exorcised by Christianity, begin to weigh him down again. What though a few still dream of boundless paradise? Others, more clearsighted, will lose no time in reminding them that this Fate cannot be conquered; that it is at the beginning as at the end of all things; and that the only resource left for man is to endeavor to transform it into an "uplifting idea" by persuading himself that he forms part of it;[158] to endeavor to love it: *ego Fatum, -amor Fati*.[159] Let them drink deep of a life whose sap seems to them all-powerful, the pledge of more and more exalted victories: soon one of them, having seen that, at bottom, "noth-

---

[157] Cf. Gustave Thibon, *L'Échelle de Jacob* (Lyons: Lardanchet, 1946), p. 178: "The gesture that divinizes is the first phase of the gesture that destroys; when a finite being feels "that it is becoming god", he is like Vespasian, on the eve of decomposing. . . ." Paul Evdokimoff, *Dostoïevski et le problème du mal*, pp. 132–33: "*Heteronomy* oppresses freedom, *autonomy* leads man to the divinization of the arbitrary, from which he will sink down into demonism. It is only in the free and creative acceptance of *theonomy* that man finds true freedom, for in God, all 'hetero' disappears, in him man recognizes his homeland, in him he finds himself once again. 'All is in Thee, Lord, I am myself in Thee, receive me' (*L'Adolescent*)."

[158] Nietzsche, *Volonté*, nos. 636, 637, 639 (vol. 2, p. 389).

[159] Nietzsche, *Le Gai savoir*, p. 137; *Ecce Homo*, p. 71; *Maximes et chants de Zarathoustra*, p. 231. In Nietzsche, the Schopenhauerian pessimism was never really overcome. Thierry Maulnier has observed this failure very well: "The cult of life prevails over the demand for freedom and leads to the submission to determinism just as it led to the preference for pain. From then on, man, whose dignity is undoubtedly the rejection of universal innocence, became a moment of universal innocence; he is only one face among other faces of a force that makes sap rise in plants, crystallizes minerals and makes the stars obey . . .", *Nietzsche* (Paris: Gallimard, 1925).

See also Richard Wagner, *L'État et la religion*, with respect to *Der Ring des Nibelungen*: "With this work, I had admitted to myself, without really giving myself a precise explanation of it, the true foundation of human things. For a tragic necessity runs through the whole of it. The Will, which at first thought to transform the world in the direction of its desires, finds in the end no other satisfactory solution than to break its own will to live and to prepare for its decline with dignity" (quoted by Spenlé, p. 147; cf. ibid., pp. 170–71, on Nietzsche).

ingness characterizes the human being", will show them that their essence, in itself, spells defeat and that they are nothing but "beings made for death".[160]

"Oh, heaven above me!" cried Zarathustra, speaking for man in the days of his illusion. "Pure and lofty heaven! This is what your purity means to me now: that there is no everlasting spider and spider's web of reason; that you are a dancing-place for divine hazards; that you are a divine table for the dice of divine gamesters!"[161] Or, in another of his dreams: "Oh, Earth ahead of us! Earth of deliverance and fellowship! Earth promised to our Promethean exertions! This is what your beauty means to us now: that there is no heaven above you to keep us under the yoke, no everlasting precept to clip our wings! But that a day will dawn over you, a day of reconciliation, marking the end of history, in which man and Nature will celebrate their espousals!"[162] He does not see that, in reality, the One whom he

---

[160] Cf. Heidegger, in Karl Rahner, "Le Concept de philosophie existentiale chez Martin Heidegger", in *Recherches de science religieuse*, 1940, pp. 168–69. "Nothingness, Heidegger also says (*Sein und Zeit*, p. 300), which basically characterizes the human being." And, although the being of each is essentially a "being with", an existence in common, "on the common basis of that existence . . . , the abrupt unveiling of my being-in-order-to-die will suddenly cut me out of an absolute 'solitude-in-common', while raising others at the same time to that solitude": Jean-Paul Sartre, commenting on and completing Heidegger, in *L'Être et le néant* (Paris: Gallimard, 1943), p. 303.

[161] Nietzsche, *Zarathoustra* (Albert trans.), p. 234; cf. pp. 315 and 450: "Spider, why do you weave your web around me?" Cf. Betz trans., appendix, no. 47: "In that I consider the world like a divine game beyond good and evil, I have the philosophy of Vedanta and Heraclitus as precursors" (p. 308).

[162] See, for example, the famous piece from Marx, commented on by Gaston Fessard, appendix. Cf. Friedrich Engels, *Socialisme utopique et socialisme scientifique* (French trans. by P. Lafargue of *Entwicklung des Sozialismus von der Utopie zur Wissenschaft*), p. 23: "All the conditions of existence, which up to now have dominated men, will then be submitted to their control. . . . Humanity will finally leave the rule of fatality and enter into that of freedom. . . . Men will become the real and conscious masters of nature." A great dream, whose degree of utopia it would not be our place to say, if it were not condemned by his basic atheism.

thus blasphemes and exorcises constitutes his whole strength
and his whole greatness. At the goal of his dreams of complete
emancipation, he does not perceive the impending menace of
slavery.[163] A tragic misconception, and one that, it may be, has
not finished bringing forth its fruits of death.

Other forms of atheistic humanism than those briefly described
have existed and still exist. But, in the contest now in progress
in the depths of men's souls, they can (apart from positivism)[164]
be dismissed as negligible. Not that they have failed to produce
effects that are still far-reaching and likely to make themselves
felt for a long time to come. But in the world of today they
no longer represent a creative force. Critical atheism, liberal
atheism, atheism resulting from laicism, all these are marks of
an age that is dying. Like deism before them, they often preserved a number of values that were Christian in origin; but,
having cut off these values from their source, they were powerless to maintain them in their full strength or even in their
authentic integrity. Spirit, reason, liberty, truth, brotherhood,
justice: these great things, without which there is no true humanity, which ancient paganism had half perceived and Christianity had instituted, quickly become unreal when no longer
seen as a radiation from God, when faith in the living God
no longer provides their vital substance. Then they become
empty forms. Soon they are no more than a lifeless ideal, ready
to fall a prey to lurking lies and offering an even apter application for Péguy's terrible dictum: "Kantism has clean hands,

---

[163] "Starting from unlimited freedom, I ended in unlimited despotism", says
the revolutionary theoretician Shigalev, in *The Possessed* by Dostoevsky. How
many facts prove the deductions of this maniac correct!

[164] Which is sometimes looked on as a direct precursor, almost a forerunner. Cf. Charles Maurras, *L'Avenir de l'intelligence* (Paris: Flammarion, 1927),
p. 108; or the reflections on "theistic hypocrisy" in *Trois idées politiques* (Paris:
Champion, 1912), p. 60.

only it has no hands."[165] Without God, even truth is an idol, even justice is an idol. Idols too pure and pale in face of the flesh-and-blood idols that are regaining their pedestals; ideals too abstract in the face of the great collective myths that are reawakening the strongest instincts—"de-germed wheat", as they have been called.[166] Thus the laicism of this present-day society has, though often despite itself, prepared the way for the great revolutionary systems now loosed with the enveloping sweep of an avalanche.

These great systems are not, first and foremost, social and political facts but systems of living. The principle that inspired them was not devoid of nobility. Some of their intuitions have been sound. Their ambitions are not purely utopian. The criticisms that served as their starting point were often shrewd, with a shrewdness cruel in its accuracy; and certain of their manifestations have an imposing grandeur that, for many fascinated eyes, masks the horrors that were their purchase price. I have not made it my business to discuss them or even to subject them to a primary analysis, but merely to bring out in full relief the passionate denial that underlies them and vitiates them beyond all hope. True, the problems—not only social but also and predominantly spiritual—with which they grapple are only too real, and their inability to find a human solution should not be made a pretext for ruling out the examination of these problems. For the world they spew forth has often no right to call itself Christian in any but a purely sociological sense, and the God they reject is all too often a mere caricature of the God we worship.[167] It is equally certain that many of those who feel the attraction of these revolutionary systems do not

---

[165] Charles Péguy, *Note conjointe* (Paris: Gallimard, 1935). "He who takes away the Word destroys speech" is a profound saying of Claudel's, *Correspondance de Paul Claudel et de Jacques Rivière* (Paris: Plan-Nourrit, 1926), p. 25.

[166] Jacques Maritain, *Humanisme intégral* (Paris: Aubier, 1936), p. 14.

[167] Jacques Maritain has rightly observed, with respect to atheist communism: "At the root of it, and chiefly through the fault of a Christian world unfaithful to its principles, there is a deep resentment against the Christian world

grasp their full import; they choose to see no more in these systems than programs for temporal organization, and they leave the religious problem on one side or, in some cases, solve it for themselves in quite a different way. How few people see what is at the bottom of the movements by which they are carried away! Nor may we lightly decline to take on a task of dissociation. The denial we have witnessed is, for all its negativeness, a fundamental fact—too fundamental for accidents of history or of thought to get rid of it for a very long time yet. Overcome in one form, it can reappear in another and renew its strength thanks to unforeseen conjunctions. We have not seen the end of it. And as long as this threat persists, it is man himself who is threatened.

Nicholas Berdyaev has spoken of an "end of the Renaissance" and of a return to a kind of Middle Ages for our era. "A new Middle Ages?" Such a hypothesis cannot be ruled out, but the phrase may have two meanings. For two elements were mingled in the Middle Ages of history: barbarism and the Church, which endeavored to educate the barbarians by converting them to belief in God. Shall we revert to barbarism, a barbarism no doubt very different from the old one, but surely much more horrible, a centralized, technically efficient and inhuman barbarism? Or shall we, in conditions themselves very different, with deeper knowledge and lifted by a freer, more magnificent impetus, succeed in rediscovering the God which the same Church still sets before us, the living God who made us in his own image? That, above all the problems that press for our attention, is the great question today.

—and not only against the Christian world but (and that is the tragedy of it) against Christianity itself, which transcends the Christian world and should not be confused with it. . . . Resentment against those who have not been able to give effect to the truth of which they were the bearers; resentment that is rebounding against that truth itself": ibid., pp. 49 and 52.

NIETZSCHE AND KIERKEGAARD

1. The Birth of Tragedy

When war broke out between France and Germany in the summer of 1870, young Friedrich Nietzsche, who, in consequence of his recent appointment to a professorship at the university of Basel, had become a Swiss citizen, at first considered that this conflict did not concern him. But, changing his mind before very long, he joined an ambulance unit, since he had no legal right to serve in the armed forces. Along the roads of Alsace and Lorraine he carried with him the first drafts of the great work that he was then meditating on Greek civilization. Something of this work was already known, in embryo, from the two lectures he had given at Basel, in January and February, on "Greek Musical Drama" and "Socrates and Tragedy". The work matured "to the sound of the guns at the battle of Woerth" and "under the walls of Metz during chilly September nights".[1] Home from the war, and hardly waiting to have done with the illness that he had brought back with him, Nietzsche continued to work at this book throughout the winter of 1870–1871. The title he intended for it at that time was "Greek Serenity". But only a fragment was ever written, and for this completed part, after a number of tentative choices,[2] he finally adopted the title

---

[1] "Essai d'autocritique", in *Naissance de la tragédie* (French trans. by Geneviève Bianquis [Paris: Gallimard, 1941] of *Die Geburt der Tragödie aus dem Geiste der Musik*), p. 127. *Ecce Homo* (French trans. by Albert), p. 142. See the letter to the Baron von Gersdorff, October 20, 1870 (*Lettres choisies*, trans. by Vialatte, pp. 37–38).

[2] At first he wanted to entitle it *Tragedy and Free Spirits*, then *The Beginning and End of Tragedy*; then *The Dionysiac Conception of the World*. Other titles

Die Geburt der Tragödie aus dem Geiste der Musik (*The Birth of Tragedy from the Spirit of Music*).[3] He had difficulty in finding a publisher. Brought out in 1871 by Fritzsch, who specialized in the publication of music, the work was not a success. It seemed more calculated to damage the young philologist's career than to advance it. Only a few close friends of the author appreciated it. Among those to whom he sent it, and whom he had had in mind in writing it, there were a number who did not realize its full significance.

Die Geburt der Tragödie is a work of genius. "An enigmatic, shocking, wonderful book", said Andler.[4] And Ernst Bertram called it "perhaps the most profound, purest and most moving of Nietzsche's books, though not the most important or the finest". A youthful work, but like *Le Cid* or like *Die Einheit in der Kirche* by his compatriot Möhler. "One of the strangest love stories of all time," was another of Bertram's comments, "a truly magnificent explosion, due to the kindling of Nietzsche's spirit by an unparalleled enthusiasm."[5]

The principal theme of the book is well known. The Nietzschean opposition of Apollinism and Dionysism, which at first seemed only a fantastic antithesis and one that need not be taken seriously,[6] has become a commonplace in the study of Greek history as well as in aesthetics. Apollo, the god of

tempted him too: *The Musical Origins of Tragedy*, or *The Music of Tragedy.* . . . Later, he gave it the subtitle: *Hellenism and Pessimism.*

[3] Or: *De l'enfantement de la tragédie par le génie de la musique* (Of the childbirth of tragedy through the guarding spirit of music), according to the translation that Edouard Schuré gave it in *Revue des deux-mondes*, August 15, 1895, p. 780.

[4] Charles Andler, *La Jeunesse de Nietzsche*, vol. 2, 2d ed., of *Nietzsche, sa vie et sa pensée* (Paris: Bossard, 1920–1931), p. 216.

[5] Ernst Bertram, *Nietzsche, essai de mythologie* (French trans. of *Nietzsche: Versuch einer Mythologie*), pp. 366 and 367. We will not say, however, with Émile Faguet, *En lisant Nietzsche*, p. 16: "In truth Nietzsche is totally complete in *Les Origines de la tragédie grecque.*"

[6] This is the judgment of Ernest Seillière, *Appollon ou Dionysos?* (Paris: Plon-Nourrit, 1905), pp. 13 and 51. Cf. pp. 11–12: "A strange theory that in turn opposes and combines the Apollonian dream and the Dionysian rap-

dreams and also of plastic form, symbolizes the luminous aspect of being, the organization of chaos, the radiant achievement of individuality. He is the god of appearance. Dionysus, god of music and of the ecstasy of wine, is the hidden life; he is universal energy, the force that creates and destroys worlds. He is the god of the depths of being. Greek tragedy, that marvelous apex of art, is the offspring of their union.[7] In it, epic and lyricism blend and surpass themselves. Apollo was needed to give it that serenity that makes it a work of art; but it is Dionysus who provides the inspiration, who brings the tragic element and who, in the last analysis, always remains the one and only character in it. Apollo heals Dionysus of his delirium, but without Dionysus he would himself be colorless and tame. People are apt to form a false idea of Greek serenity, like a man "who, looking at very clear water lit by sunshine, imagines that the bottom of the lake is quite near and that he could touch it with his fingers"; in reality there is no glittering surface without formidable depth.[8] The serene hierarchy of the Olympian gods sprang from the frightening family of the Titanic gods, and luminous Apollinism, in its turn, emerges from the subterranean kingdom of dark Dionysus.[9]

---

ture! . . . To keep our attention fixed for long on this monument of sterile ingenuity and arbitrary symbolism would not at all be worth the effort."

[7] Cf. *Naissance de la tragédie*, p. 17: "We would have made decisive progress in aesthetics if we had understood, not as a view based on reason but with the immediate certitude of intuition, that the evolution of art is linked to the dualism of *Apollinism* and *Dionysism*, just as generation is linked to the duality of the sexes, to their continual battle, broken by temporary agreements."

[8] "Projet de préface à Richard Wagner", February 22, 1871 (ibid., p. 196). Cf. "Dionysos philosophos", in *Volonté de puissance* (French trans. by Geneviève Bianquis of *Der Wille zur Macht*), vol. 2, p. 372: "I have endeavored to guess why Greek Apollinism had to arise from a Dionysian subsoil."

[9] *Naissance de la tragédie*, pp. 26 and 25: "It seems at present that the enchanted mountain of Olympus is opening to us and showing us its foundations. The Greek knew and experienced the terrors and horrors of existence: he could not have lived if he had not interposed between the world and himself that dazzling dream creation: Mount Olympus. . . ." Cf. letter to

Beneath the theme with its manifold orchestrations, in vigorous reaction against the radiant Greece of Winckelmann and Goethe, there is another, more basic theme: that of the relation that art and culture as a whole (that is to say, everything that counts in humanity) bears to suffering. This is the theme that Nietzsche himself underlines right at the end of his book, when, imagining an admirer of the Greeks transported in a dream into the midst of their harmonious creations, and celebrating the greatness of Dionysus, who is the fountainhead of all that magnificent plenitude, he pictures an old Athenian lifting "the sublime gaze of Aeschylus" upon the enthusiast and answering him thus: "Add this to thy words, remarkable stranger: how much this people must have had to suffer before attaining to so much beauty!"[10] But what makes this double theme so comprehensive is that it is not concerned merely with an interpretation of Greek art, nor even, in a more general way, with a philosophy of art. Apollo and Dionysus are divinities too great for such a specialized function. The kingdom beneath their sway is vaster and more profound. Their dual myth embraces a whole conception of the world and of man and a whole ideal of life.[11] And that conception is an aesthetic conception, and the ideal a tragic ideal.

Is such an ideal contrary to Christianity? Nietzsche came

Erwin Rohde: "This serene and harmonious beauty has not fallen from the sky: tremendous convulsions, gigantic battles were necessary in order to make it emerge gradually from the shadows of a savage and inhuman prehistory. Homer was the victor who appeared at the end of this long period of despair."

[10] P. 124. See his "Essai d'autocritique" (French trans. of "Selbstkritik"): "The fundamental problem is the relation of the Greeks to suffering" (*Naissance de la tragédie*, p. 131). Later, in the second part of *Zarathustra*, Nietzsche said: "To create is the great release from suffering and the alleviation of life. But much suffering and many metamorphoses are needed to bring the creator to birth" (from *Ainsi parle Zarathoustra*, the French trans. by Albert of *Also sprach Zarathustra*, p. 117).

[11] "Projet de préface à Richard Wagner": "In the end I was obliged to locate this problem at the very center of the universe" (*Naissance de la tragédie*, p. 195).

back to this book several times to explain its meaning. In a self-criticism written in 1886, he said that he had been guided, from that time, by a strong instinct to set up against the Christian view of life a contrasting, deliberately anti-Christian view: "As a philologist, a man concerned with words, I baptized it, not without temerity—for who knows the true name of Antichrist? —with the name of a Greek God: I called it *Dionysism.*"[12] The following year, in a letter to his mother, he declared: "If people had understood one word of the first thing I wrote, they would have been scared and would have crossed themselves forthwith." A little later again, in 1888, in *Ecce Homo*, he noted "the deep and hostile silence with regard to Christianity" underlying the *Geburt der Tragödie.*[13] This interpretation seems a little forced. If it is true that his first work could, after the event, seem big with all the ideas that explode in Nietzsche's last works, it is not less true that those ideas were still only in the embryonic stage: germs that were sometimes closely sheathed and were warred upon by other germs. Thus, of Dionysism and Apollinism, those two complementary forces from whose balance beauty is born, it is at first impossible to guess, despite Nietzsche's marked predilection for Dionysus, which will triumph over the other, or whether one of the two must necessarily triumph.[14] Moreover, in the 1870 lecture on "Greek Musical Drama" (to which the *Geburt der Tragödie* brought no essential change of thought), Nietzsche admired "that mysterious and infinite symbolism that is peculiar to the Christian church" and that lifts the ritual of the Mass, in a sense, above ancient drama.[15] In the *Geburt* itself, he speaks of "those profound and terrible natures, produced by the first four centuries

---

[12] Cf. 5 (ibid., p. 124).

[13] Ibid., p. 143. "Essai d'autocritique", ibid., pp. 132–33. Letter of October 30, 1887.

[14] The book ends with a vague tribute: "Come with me and offer a sacrifice in this temple of our two deities" (p. 124). Cf. Charles Andler, *Le Pessimisme esthétique de Nietzsche*, vol. 3 of *Nietzsche*, pp. 47–48.

[15] *Naissance de la tragédie*, p. 161.

of Christianity", which rejected an effeminate Greece;[16] and the Christian movement, coming from the East, sometimes seemed to him a fresh wave of Dionysism. Soon, in *Schopenhauer als Erzieher* (*Schopenhauer as Educator*), Nietzsche was to exalt the saint even more than the artist—the saint in whom nature rises to the height that releases it from itself and attains perfect humanization.[17] That, of course, is not a sufficient reason for asserting that Nietzsche's first Dionysism might have quite naturally taken a Christian turn (as it has been possible to assume, with some probability, in the case of Hölderlin).[18] When Nietzsche wrote his first work, Christianity had long been not only abandoned but condemned by him, and it has been said, without undue exaggeration, that "the whole of *Der Antichrist* already existed in embryo in the letter he wrote to his sister" in 1865 "to let her know that he had given up his theological studies."[19] At any rate, at the time of the *Geburt der Tragödie*, he did not yet see in Dionysus, as he did later,[20] the symbol of a pagan type of religion to be set up against Christ. His way of looking at things was not primarily anti-Christian at that time. It was anti-Socratic.

Nietzsche has been credited by Ernst Bertram with "loving hatreds".[21] Whether loving or not, his hatred for Socrates bursts forth from the outset. It is this which, in the last analysis, gives the book its significance. Nietzsche himself, in a letter to his friend Erwin Rohde, called the book his *Anti-Socrates*. Noting that Euripides had hounded Dionysus off the tragic stage, he

---

[16] Ibid., p. 61.

[17] "Schopenhauer éducateur", in *Considérations inactuelles* (French trans. by Albert of *Unzeitgemässe Betrachtungen*), pp. 65–68.

[18] Cf. Albert Béguin, *L'Ame romantique et le rêve*, 5th ed. (Paris: Corti), p. 164. See in fact the beautiful poem of 1803, "Der Einzige", with the later corrections: *Poèmes* (French trans. by Geneviève Bianquis), pp. 401–7.

[19] Théodore de Wysewa, in *Revue des deux-mondes*, February 1, 1896, p. 695.

[20] *Volonté*, vol. 2, p. 345: "Les Deux types: Dionysos le Crucifié" (fragment from 1888). *Ecce Homo*, end.

[21] Bertram, p. 112.

added: "Euripides himself was, in a sense, nothing but a mask: the deity which spoke through his mouth was neither Dionysus nor Apollo but an entirely new demon called Socrates. Such is the new antinomy: Dionysism or Socratism."[22] Antagonism between the two deities had been a productive opposition; it led to their completely successful fusion. But antagonism between the god and the demon was an irreducible antinomy. It was a war without mercy; one or the other must be expelled. Greek civilization went under because Socrates vanquished Dionysus.

What had Nietzsche against Socrates? To begin with, it was not (as he said later, especially from 1885 onward) his moralism. If at that time Nietzsche spoke of his work, in the *Selbstkritik*, as profoundly "hostile to morality",[23] he was under the influence of that retrospective illusion to which reference has already been made. The grudge Nietzsche bore Socrates was rather on account of rationalism. An aesthetic conception of the world is, it is true, antimoralist; but a conception both aesthetic and tragic is, more fundamentally, antirationalist. In Greece, the sixth century B.C. was that marvelous era when human culture reached its acme: a unique time, the "noontide of history", whose decline set in with and through Socrates. It was in him that the dialectical instinct of knowledge triumphed over dark forces; or to put it another way: in him "theory" dispelled "magic":

> Wherever it bends its enquiring glance, Socratism is confronted with a lack of conscious clarity and with the power of illusion, and from this lack it infers the profound absurdity of everything that exists. It was with this datum as his starting point that Socrates thought himself under obligation to correct the real; he

---

[22] *Naissance de la tragédie*, p. 65; cf. pp. 68–69.

[23] "Essai d'autocritique", ibid., pp. 133–34: "Life, being essentially immoral, will always and inevitably appear in the wrong before the tribunal of morality. . . . And would not morality itself be the 'will to deny life', a secret instinct of destruction, a principle of decadence, of decay, of slander, the beginning of the end? And consequently the danger of dangers? It is therefore against morality that my instinct in this shocking book is turned."

came forward, all by himself, with an air of disdain and superiority, as the forerunner of a wholly different civilization, art and
morality, whereas the world in which he lived was such that we
should be only too happy to clutch with devotion the very hem
of its garment. . . ."[24]

There is no more disastrous illusion than this victory over
illusion, celebrated as a step forward. The Socratic man is no
more clearsighted than the man he plumes himself on having
surpassed: actually he is less so. He is classifiable as "deficient
to the point of monstrosity". "He is monstrously deficient in
a sense of mysticism"—so much so that Socrates might serve
as the type of nonmystical man, in whom "the logical bent
is developed to excess by superfetation, as instinctive wisdom
is in the mystic."[25] The Socratic spirit is essentially a "myth-
destroying spirit". But man starved of myths is a man without
roots. He is a man who is "perpetually hungry", an "abstract"
man, devitalized by the ebbing of the sap in him.

Nietzsche notes this in the *Geburt der Tragödie*, and he was
soon to stress it in *Unzeitgemässe Betrachtungen* (*Thoughts out of
Season*):[26] there is a close connection between the rationalism
of modern times, inherited from Socrates, and the historicism
that is increasingly characteristic of it. When the feeling for
myths is lost, they become narrowed down to something that
has had its day and is henceforth subjected to the requirements

---

[24] Ibid., p. 70: "What demonic force is this that is permitted to spread magic
potion in the dust." See also the study on "Socrate et la tragédie": Socratism
is older than Socrates; . . . dialectic is the distinctive element in it" (*Naissance
de la tragédie*, p. 164). And this note from the summer of 1872: "In Socrates,
everything is false" (p. 131).

[25] P. 71. Cf. p. 88: "If the ancient tragedy was led astray by the dialectical instinct of knowledge, we could conclude from this fact that there is
an eternal conflict between the *theoretical conception* and the *tragic conception* of
the world. . . ." See also *Human trop humain* (French trans. by Desrousseaux
of *Menschliches, Allzumenschliches*), vol. 2, pp. 45–46. Cf. Pierre Lasserre, *La
Morale de Nietzsche* (new ed.), p. 103.

[26] Particularly in the second: "De l'utilité et des inconvénients des études
historiques".

of historical criticism. Then they cease to live and to proliferate; their leaves wither, they die.[27] It is because it has lost the substratum of myth, which gave it stability and nutriment, that our civilization is now condemned "to exhaust all possibilities and to sustain its wretched existence at the cost of other civilizations. . . . What accounts for the prodigious appetite of modern civilized man for historical knowledge, his way of gathering round him innumerable civilizations, his need to know everything? What can it be but that we have lost the breast that fed us, we have lost Myth?"[28] Thus rationalist fever is inevitably followed by "historical consumption". We become "walking encyclopaedias", and this "historical sense", of which we are so proud, is "the precursor of senility".[29] In one or other of its two forms, it will have to be recognized one day that "an excessive need for knowledge is as barbarous as hatred of knowledge",[30] and that, in the end, to use a dictum that suggested itself to Nietzsche only at a late stage, but which well expresses his earliest sentiments, "Wisdom is always a crow feeding upon corpses."[31] But the struggle between Dionysus and Socrates is not finished. Tragic thought, which seemed to be dead, will come into its own again.[32] The conquered god is preparing his

---

[27] *Naissance de la tragédie*, pp. 57–58; cf. p. 115.

[28] Ibid., pp. 115–16.

[29] *Considérations inactuelles*, pp. 121 and 162. *Le Gai savoir* (French trans. by Vialatte of *Die fröhliche Wissenschaft*) p. 167.

[30] *La Naissance de la philosophie à l'époque de la tragédie grecque* (French trans. by Geneviève Bianquis of *Die Philosophie im tragischen Zeitalter der Griechen*), p. 34.

[31] In 1888.

[32] Cf. "Richard Wagner à Bayreuth" in *Considérations inactuelles*, vol. 2, p. 161. It is a well-known fact that Nietzsche counted on Germany for this awakening, while counting on Dionysism to enable Germany to get rid of her alien elements and be herself again with her "native gods": *Naissance de la tragédie*, pp. 118–19: "And if the German, feeling helpless, looks round for a guide to bring him back to his long-lost home, to which he hardly knows the approaches and paths, let him but listen to the sweet and seductive call of the Dionysian bird perched above his head, who will show him the way."

revenge, and Nietzsche is the prophet who heralds his return by opening up the way for him:

> What a sudden transformation in the dreary wilderness of our jaded civilization, the moment the Dionysian spell has touched it! A hurricane snatches up everything that is out of date, worm-eaten, broken or stunted, envelops it in a whirlwind of red dust and carries it off like a vulture into the air. In bewilderment we look about for those vanished things; for what now meets our eyes seems to have thrust its way upward from an abyss to the golden light—everything is so lusty and green, luxuriant and vigorous, quick with a boundless nostalgia. Tragedy is enthroned in sublime ecstasy in the midst of this profusion of life, of pain and of pleasure; it lends its ear to a far-off, poignant song that speaks of the Mother of Being, whose names are Illusion, Will, Suffering. Yes, my friends, join with me in belief in the Dionysian life and the rebirth of tragedy. *The age of Socratic man is over.* Crown yourself with ivy, take the thyrsus in your hands and do not be surprised to see the tiger and the panther crouch, fawning, at your knees. Dare to be tragic men, for then you will be saved! You will follow in the train of Dionysus from India to Greece. Prepare yourselves for a hard fight and have faith in the miracles of our God![33]

2. Myth and Mystery

As I have said, the book is a work of genius. A tumultuous and brilliant book, an intoxicating book. Since Wilamowitz's attack —to which, it is true, Rohde put in a rejoinder—philologists and strictly orthodox historians have not wearied of denouncing its shortcomings, its bias, its mistakes—especially the use of late Orphic texts—and that belief in the connection between Euripides and Socrates which is essential to the scheme of the book. From other points of view Nietzsche himself criticized the work. In his *Selbstkritik* he notes that it contains "the worst

---

[33] Ibid., pp. 104–5.

defects of youth: excessive length and revolutionary efferves-
cence"; he finds it "ill-written, heavy, labored, inflamed with
a veritable frenzy of imagery in which confusion reigns"; he
declares that he is distressed "at having clouded Dionysian prescience with Schopenhauerian and Kantian formulas".[34] What
he reproached himself with above all, now that the rupture
with Wagner had long been complete, was with "having marred
this sublime Greek problem by mixing it up with ultra-modern
things", with having pinned his hope for a rebirth of tragedy
"on something that no longer warranted any hope but was all
too clearly indicative of a decline".[35] "Flame and smoke of
a youthful sacrifice, and more smoke than flame."[36] There is
no doubt that Wagner's ascendancy over this young mind was
too strong at that time to allow him the least objectivity. And
other influences were not always completely mastered. Nietzsche was not yet fully himself.[37] The whole work exhales
a romanticism[38] of which it took the author years of critical
reflection to rid himself—not that he ever succeeded in doing so completely.[39] But these considerations, plain enough at

---

[34] An example of a Schopenhauerian formula, p. 35: "To the degree that the
subject is an artist, he is already freed from his individual will, he has become
a kind of medium through which the sole truly existing subject celebrates his
redemption in the appearance."

[35] "Essai d'autocritique", *Naissance de la tragédie*, pp. 129 and 134.

[36] Fragment from 1885–1886, in *Volonté*, vol. 2, p. 370.

[37] This book "that most resembles those that everyone writes", Leo Shestov
will say, *La Philosophie de la tragédie: Dostoievsky et Nietzsche* (French trans.), p.
146.

[38] A description of the nocturne mystique of romanticism, which is one
of the factors of Nietzschean Dionysism, will be found in *Le Nocturne*, by
Vladimir Jankelevitch (Lyons, 1942).

[39] We can subscribe to the judgment of Thierry Maulnier: "He will rediscover romanticism from the day he claims to rediscover life. . . . He will
reestablish, in his final philosophy, the need for climax and dangerous tension,
self-satisfaction in suffering, the will for final innocence and the attempt at a
fusion with nature, indisputable symptoms of aggravated romantic delirium":
Nietzsche (Paris: Gallimard, 1925), p. 279. René Berthelot had already con-

a distance of seventy years, are after all of minor importance. They will not do duty for an appraisal of the substance of the work. Nietzsche proudly intimates what that is: "How miserably timid", he says in the *Selbstkritik*, "to have spoken like a scholar on matters of which I should have spoken from personal experience!" "This writing is pregnant with a tremendous hope. . . . Everything in it is prophecy. . . . Truth was speaking in me from the depths of a dizzy gulf." And again: "The speaker knows what he is talking about; he is an initiate and a disciple of his god."[40]

A work of such power and vehemence presents a complex of confused values, in which the true and the false are inextricably mingled. Or rather, these values are found there still in such a state of development that they must often be called ambivalent and that a process of discernment is indispensable in their regard. "Our genius is for discernment," wrote the Rev. Daniélou in a remarkable study on "Culture française et mystère [French culture and mystery]",[41] which deals with a subject closely related to our own. If this discernment must be exercised on works as reliably Catholic as those of Guardini,

---

cluded his article in the *Grande Encyclopédie* on "Friedrich Nietzsche" by relating him again to romanticism: *Evolutionnisme et platonisme* (Paris: Alcan, 1908), pp. 129–30.

[40] "Essai d'autocritique", p. 130. Ibid.: "What was speaking here was a strange voice, the disciple of a god as yet unknown, who was hiding temporarily under the cowl of the wise man. . . . There was a spirit there for strange and as yet nameless needs. . . . It was something like a mystical soul, prey to the delirium of maenads. . . . It should have sung, this new soul, not talked! I was reading the *Geburt*, it is of such inexpressible depth, it is tender, what a shame I have not yet dared to say in poetry what I had to say!" Against, on December 22, 1888, to Pierre Gast: "The day before yesterday, I was happy. . . ." As early as February 4, 1872, relating to Gersdorff the work's lack of success: "But I am counting on seeing it advance discreetly through the centuries; I am absolutely convinced of it, for it declares for the first time some eternal ideas; they will continue to echo" (*Lettres choisies*, ed. by Walz, p. 199). *Ecce Homo*, pp. 92–94.

[41] *Esprit*, May 1941, p. 478. The analyses contained in this study will spare us several analogous explanations, and we will simply refer the reader to them.

Rademaker and Doms, how much more on the work of Nietzsche!

There is probably no thinking person today who does not feel the shallowness and impoverishment of a certain kind of intellectualism and the barrenness of a certain abuse of the historic discipline. We all know what there is to be said, with Péguy, on "the dust and must" of rational or "positive" criticism. During the last fifty years we have had, thank God, Bergson himself and many others. Jules Lachelier himself was already writing before the end of the last century: "Up to now we have believed in the light, and we are rather bad at finding it, perhaps because we have, in the end, sought it only in knowledge and interest."[42] In the Church herself, reaching out beyond logical forms and methods of exposition that owed much to a Cartesian tradition of scholarship, we have linked up again with a more substantial tradition. There has been a more and more decided return to the golden age of medieval thought, that of Saint Thomas and Saint Bonaventure; and this movement of return, increasingly apparent, is gradually restoring the climate of "mystery" that was eminently the climate of patristic thought. We are relearning, if not the use, at least the understanding of symbols. In every province we are feeling the need to go back to the deep springs, to investigate them with other instruments than clear ideas alone, to reestablish a life-giving and fruitful contact with the fostering soil. We recognize, too, that "wine has to ferment before it becomes clear"[43] and that "rationality at any price" is "a dangerous force that undermines life".[44] We know that mere abstract principles are no substitute for a *mystique*; that the most penetrating criticism cannot produce one atom of being; that an endless exploration of history and

---

[42] Letter to Friedrich Rauh, December 2, 1892. He added: "Will salvation in the twentieth century come to us from obscurity?" (Quoted by Léon Brunschvicg, *Congrès philosophique de Lyon*, 1939.)

[43] Kierkegaard, quoted by Torsten Böhlin, *Sören Kierkegaard* (French trans. by Tisseau), p. 17.

[44] Nietzsche, *Ecce Homo* (*Naissance de la tragédie*, p. 143).

of human diversities is by no means enough for that "progress of mankind" that is the aim of all culture. We will no longer tolerate a divorce between knowledge and life. . . .

It would be easy to continue in this strain. Does it mean that we ought to abandon ourselves, as we have been urged to do for some time past, to a sort of blind "dynamism", to yield without reflection to every vital urge, to renounce the use of our critical faculties? We are certainly cured of our infatuation for a world wholly explainable and indeterminately perfectible by pure reason.[45] We have learned how brittle is that "palace of glass" that symbolizes a life "rationalized through and through":[46] even if it could really be built, we should find it nothing but a prison. More than ever, even outside the dogmas of our faith, we recognize, with Pascal, a "lack of clarity". Are we therefore to set about creating a mythology in willful darkness, any mythology, no matter what? Such a consent to illusion, with all it implies of contempt for truth, can never be ours. Vertigo must not be confused with ecstasy. We will never cease to believe—as Pascal (again) and Saint John of the Cross believed—that "the whole dignity of man lies in the power of thought." We intend that life shall be coupled with understanding, and enthusiasm with lucidity. Our God "is a God hidden indeed", but in himself he is light. "God is light, and in him there is no darkness."[47] That saying of Saint John the Apostle remains a normative principle for us. All Christian philosophy is a "metaphysics of light". So we refuse to make "an idol of darkness",[48] and we are prepared to defend our-

---

[45] Cf. Pierre Teilhard de Chardin, "La Mystique de la science", in *Études*, vol. 238, p. 735.

[46] Cf. Paul Evdokimoff, *Dostoïevsky et le problème du mal*, p. 139.

[47] 1 Jn 1. This is what is proclaimed by the very ones, among the Christian mystics, who put the greatest emphasis on "darkness". Cf. Gregory of Nyssa, *Life of Moses* (French trans. by Jean Daniélou, pp. 40–41, in the series *Sources chrétiennes*). Saint Bernard, *On consideration*, book 5, no. 10: "God is full of light and absolutely pure of any night."

[48] Pascal, *Pensées* (Chevalier ed., 584, p. 400).

selves against enthusiasms uncontrolled by any reasoning. We think that "it is a great misfortune to be drawn to God not by a desire for light but by an inclination for darkness",[49]—and there is Plato's reminder (directly aimed at the worshippers of Dionysus) that "many bear the thyrsus, but there are few true Bacchantes."

The zone of clarity of consciousness (too narrow and too superficial, indeed, for us to rest content in it) lies between two infinities. The great thing is to go forward beyond it and not to fall back on the hither side. The Bergsonian criticism of the "understanding" (in any case, not properly understood) has been accused of taking us back to instinct: that, at any rate, is a risk one does not wish to run. "We no longer make man descend from 'the spirit' ", Nietzsche was to write in *Der Antichrist*. "We have put him back among the animals."[50] That is, indeed, where Dionysian fervor is in danger of leading us. Socrates, on the other hand, represents consciousness prevailing over instinct; he represents reason that forms judgments and teaches man to kow himself. This is why we will never condemn Socrates as a supporter of decadence. Against forces in which the best of man is threatened with

---

[49] Georges Bernanos, *Nous autres Français* (Paris: Gallimard, 1939). Cf. Charles Péguy, *Note sur M. Bergson et la philosophie bergsonienne* (Paris: Gallimard, 1935): "As if the verses by Racine that are the fullest of light were not also the most mysterious. What is profound and mysterious is not of necessity somber and tormented. Nothing is as pure as the fold of the mantle of ancient prayer." Dostoevsky was supporting his inner life on moments "of entire serenity" that God sent him and in which he composed a profession of faith "in which everything", he said, "is clear and holy" (letter written on leaving the prison of Omsk).

[50] *L'Antéchrist*, no. 14 (*Le Crépuscule des idoles*, French trans. by Albert, p. 257). Nietzsche had for a moment thought of *Socrates and Instinct* as a title for his first work (letter to Rhodz, April 30, 1870). Cf. Ernst Jünger (quoted by Jacques Maritain, *Sort de l'homme* [Neuchâtel, Éd. de la Baconnière, 1943], p. 74): "The best response to betrayal of life by the spirit is the betrayal of the spirit by the spirit. And one of the greatest and most cruel delights of our time is to participate in this work of destruction."

foundering, we would much rather choose him for an ally.
And not only Socrates with his dialectic, but Descartes, too,
with his clear and distinct ideas—and even Voltaire's irony, on
occasion.[51]

We shall not make them our masters; being too well aware of
their limitations. But their services will be valuable in helping
us to keep our heads. "Myth," says Nietzsche in *Die Geburt
der Tragödie*, "that epitome of the universe, cannot dispense
with miracles." Very well. But one can never feel at ease with
a mind that rejects miracles and at the same time welcomes
myths; a mind that, while denying the only true God, feels the
need to create gods for itself. And when, in order to justify
his dual standpoint, he continues: "For want of myths, every
civilization loses the healthy fruitfulness of its native energy;
only a horizon circumscribed on all sides by myths can ensure
the unity of the living civilization it encloses",[52] we fully appreciate the weight of the argument, but it seems to us that
those who believe in myths and feel the benefit of them have
never dreamed of making excuses for them; and, now that reason has done its work, we are too much attached to reason to
entertain such reasons. In the old days there were those who
quite simply offered man a serviceable lie (before the phrase
"vital lie" came in). It is their voice that echoes in the words
of the believer Joseph de Maistre: "Whether religious ideas are
denied or venerated is immaterial; true or false, they form the
sole basis of all durable institutions."[53] The new temptation
is more subtle and doubtless more pernicious too. For what it
promises is not just order but rapture, and in what it insinu-

---

[51] Cf. Louis Lavelle, *La Philosophie française entre les deux guerres* (Paris: Aubier,
1942), p. 17. Thierry Maulnier, "Vers an ordre français", in *Revue universelle*
of December 25, 1941, pp. 782–83. "They wish to break with Cartesian spirituality", Mr. Jankelevitch wrote, "and in truth they refute only Condillac's
analysis": *Le Nocturne*, p. 5.

[52] *Naissance de la tragédie*, p. 115.

[53] Joseph de Maistre, *Considérations sur la France*, cf. 5, in *Œuvres* (Lyons:
Vitte, 1884–1928), vol. 1, p. 56.

ates there is no longer any question of lies: the very idea of truth disappears, replaced as it is by this idea of myth.[54] Nietzsche is bent on vanquishing knowledge by "forces that generate myths"; according to him it is "a moral prejudice to believe that truth is worth more than outward appearance". After the days of the *Geburt*, he was not long in freeing himself from this philosophy of illusion, borrowed from Schopenhauer; but it was not in order to reestablish truth in its former rights— quite the contrary, since he specified "the will for nontruth" as first among the "new forces and new territories"[55] he had acquired, and, in order not to sink into passivity, his "nihilism" always had need of myths. . . . There is a double danger there, against which we need to mobilize all the resources of the critical mind, just as against certain similar dangers of neglect all the resources of energy are called to the rescue.[56]

Such are the findings of the first process of discernment, wholly intellectual still and, for that reason, largely critical and negative. Necessary though such a process is, it is not enough.

---

[54] See the fragment of September 22, 1870, on "La Tragédie et les esprits libres", *Naissance de la tragédie*, pp. 186 and 187. Cf. "Midi et eternité", in *Volonté*, vol. 2, p. 226: "The author (of *Die Geburt*) knows from experience that art has more value than truth."

[55] Fragment from 1872, and *Par delà le bien et le mal* (French trans. by Albert of *Jenseit von Gut und Böse*), p. 69. Fragment from 1884–1888, in *Œuvres posthumes* (French trans. by H. J. Bolle), p. 225.

[56] Cf. Jean Lacroix, *Semaine sociale de Clermont-Ferrand*, 1937, p. 117: "The triumph of abstract rationalism has made the atmosphere unbreathable: this is the accusation made by the young. And the danger is that all means risk seeming good to those who want to escape this invasive rationalism, even an integral resignation of thought. . . . Under cover of the pursuit of entities, which is in danger of being adopted today, is the reign of violence. . . ." Compare a contemporaneous text by Jacques Maritain, *Bulletin de l'Union pour la vérité*, April-May 1937, pp. 308–9: "If one wants to prevent the powerful irrationalist reaction aroused by Cartesian rationalism from sweeping away everything, civilization and reason itself, it is necessary to proceed to a self-criticism of reason and to recognize that the essential fault of Cartesian reason has been to deny and reject the world of the irrational below it, and particularly the world of the suprarational above."

Nietzsche, a few months after having finished the *Geburt*, noted that "it is impossible to found a civilization on knowledge."[57] And (as Mr. Albert Béguin shrewdly observes)[58] immediately after a period in which man has intensively and exclusively cultivated his own conscious powers and sought to rule the world solely by the laws of reason, there is bound to be a reemergence, in full force, of those myths "which tend to lift the creature out of his solitude and reintegrate him in the general scheme of things". In any case the profoundly disturbing question arises which Nietzsche was not the only one to raise, and which Michelet, for instance—inspired by Vico—had already posed: As soon as man ceases to be in contact with great mystical or religious forces, does he not inevitably come under the yoke of a harsher and blinder force, which leads him to perdition? It is what Vico called the age of "deliberate barbarism", and that is the age in which we live. Will it be possible, we ask ourselves, to rediscover some myth for our salvation, or shall we be engulfed by a catastrophe?[59] The question is primordial. It confronts us with the urgency of Hamlet's dilemma: to be or not to be. If Socrates, then—this Socrates of Nietzsche's who is himself a myth, for that matter—is modern man, then we too repudiate Socrates. If Socratism is the "modern world"—our rationalized world that has been robbed of its vitality because a shortsighted and arrogant reason has made it wholly profane —or even if it is the world of pure knowledge, we condemn Socratism and consign it to extinction. But that does not imply our adherence to the Nietzschean program of "surpassing knowledge by mythological invention",[60] still less our submis-

---

[57] Fragment from 1872, in *Volonté*, vol. 2, p. 272.

[58] Béguin, p. 396.

[59] Daniel Halévy has brought out this point very well in his *Jules Michelet* (Paris: Hachette, 1928); see particularly pages 37–38, 102, 184–85. Michelet has also said: "Life is a mystery that perishes when it ends in revealing itself": "Discours d'ouverture à la Faculté des Lettres", January 9, 1834; in *Introduction à l'histoire universelle*, new ed. (Paris: Hachette, 1879), p. 114.

[60] Fragment from 1872, *Volonté*, vol. 2, p. 271.

sion to Dionysus: for that disturbing deity is not necessarily the only one that can restore our saving contact with sacred forces.

It is at this point that a second discernment becomes necessary, a spiritual discernment. As we have already seen, Nietzsche spoke of myth and of mystery without making any distinction between them, whereas a selective use could be made of these words to signify two opposite types of sacredness. The zone of superficial clarity in man to which reference has already been made is also a zone of nonreligious clarity, and the two infinities between which it lies have each their own sacredness. But what a gulf separates them! There is the sacredness of myth which, like vapor rising from the earth, emanates from infrahuman regions; and there is the sacredness of mystery, which is like peace descending from the heavens. The one links us with Nature and attunes us to her rhythm but also enslaves us to her fatal powers; the other is the gift of the spirit that makes us free. One finds its embodiment in symbols that man molds as he pleases, and into which he projects his terrors and his desires; the symbols of the other are received from on high by man who, in contemplating them, discovers the secret of his own nobility. In concrete terms, there is the pagan myth and the Christian mystery.

Myth and mystery may both be said to engender a *mystique*, and each provides a way of escape from "the prison of things that are clear". But these two *mystiques* are as opposite in character as in origin: one is the Dionysian state, with its "heady, feverish, ambiguous" irrationality;[61] the other is the chaste and sober rapture of the Spirit. If both shatter individuality, "the

---

[61] Geneviève Bianquis, preface to *Naissance de la tragédie*, p. 7. Nietzsche, "Dionysos philosophos", in *Volonté*, vol. 2, p. 370: "Dionysus, that great equivocal god and tempter, to whom I had recently offered my premises. . . . There, it is a question of new, strange, equivocal, indeed, sinister, things. . . ." Cf. Édouard Schuré, "L'Individualisme et l'anarchie en littérature", p. 780: "If there is a weak point in his essay, which is otherwise so remarkable, it is in not having thrown light on Greek tragedy through the mysteries of Eleusis, it is in

wretched screen of glass",[62] their ways of doing so are very different; for the first only succeeds in merging the human being in the life of the cosmos—or in that of a society itself wholly of this earth—while the second exalts the most personal element[63] in each individual in order to create a fellowship among all men.[64] Not that the second rejects the first out of hand. Mystery does not refuse to make use of myth, any more than reason does in the human order; on the contrary, mystery takes over a part of it, filters it, purifies it—exorcises it, as it were. There is an authentic sacredness in the cosmos, for it is full of "vestiges" of divinity. There *is* a "*mystique* of the earth". But it needs to be christianized. When it aspires to reign alone, it is no longer even terrestrial; the mark of the Spirit of Evil is upon it.

Socrates, or modern man. In this sense, we shall side against him. Against him, but not, consequently, with Nietzsche. Much rather with Péguy. Péguy will save us from Nietzsche. It would be tempting to compare them or at any rate to show them

---

confusing the Dionysus divided up by earthly life with the Liberator of celestial life and in diving into the elements for the mystical union of the regenerated and revived soul with the divine Spirit."

[62] Nietzsche, *Naissance de la tragédie*, p. 107. Cf. "Dionysos philosophos": "The word Dionysian expresses the need for unity, all that surpasses the personality, etc., the great pantheistic participation in all joy and in all pain . . ." (p. 372).

[63] Cf. Michelet, p. 136: "The last people in the world in whom the personality would consent to be absorbed into pantheism is the French."

[64] Cf. these words from one of Gabriel Marcel's characters: "Perhaps it is mystery alone that reunites. Without mystery, life would be contemptible." And Jean Daniélou, pp. 472–73: "Thus the idea of mystery is found at the juncture of two great orientations today: the search for values and the search for communion. We can define it in a general way as something beyond individual interests that is the object of faith and principle of communion. As beyond particular interests, mystery charges the realities that it invests with a higher content, which imposes respect for it: it gives them a new dimension, it connects them with something that goes beyond them and thus it makes them sacred; it allows one to go beyond the boundaries of individual life and to participate in a common reality."

competing for the same goal. Did not Péguy curse the modern world, this laicizing, rationalizing world that ends up in sterile criticism, this world that "disparages" everything? And did he not set up against it a sacred world,[65] pagan as well as Christian? Undoubtedly. But in order to understand him it is necessary to know what kind of paganism he had in mind and to take into account the circumstances. Péguy, be it noted, had in mind the "ancient" world, that is to say, the pagan world before Christ, in its highest moral and religious endeavor. He had in mind that part of the soul of the ancients that was worth more than their gods, than their myths. He was thinking of Sophocles and his Antigone, he was thinking of the Severus of *Polyeucte*, he was thinking of Plato. And since the days when he composed, and lived, his dialogue of the soul of the ancients and the Christian soul, the problem has shifted its ground. Strong to destroy, the laicism he denounced had no strength to construct. It hollowed out the channel for a new paganism whose waves are now breaking over us and which is quite different from the paganism that Péguy honored: not a symbol of Christian light to come, but anti-Christian paganism, which begins by proclaiming the "death of God", with Nietzsche as its prophet.

Nietzsche and Péguy are two prophets who dominate our age. They are at one in embracing the task of criticism. Both execrate the "modern world". In part, their diagnoses coincide.[66] Yet their messages remain contradictory. Both link up with a past that reaches far back down the ages, but they do not choose the same vein. Both announce a new age, but they do not forge it of the same metal. While Nietzsche is the prophet

---

[65] Péguy's work is not only full of the sacred, but it contains, and very explicitly, a reflection on the sacred. See particularly *Les Suppliants parallèles, Victor-Marie comte Hugo* and *Clio*.

[66] Péguy's satire on the "intellectual party", too, is not unrelated to Nietzsche's satire on the "Philistines of culture". Compare also Péguy (*Œuvres*, vol. 11, p. 249) and Nietzsche, in the second study of *Unzeitgemässe Betrachtungen*, on the true historian, who should be not "disinterested" but "passionate".

of scission, Péguy is the prophet of fidelity.[67] And while Nietzsche, in order to chain us to the reeling chariot of his Dionysus, is led on to curse the Cross of Christ, Péguy shows in Jesus
the one in whom the whole of ancient tragedy is concentrated
and transfigured:

> He was to inherit tragic terror;
> He was to inherit tragic pity,
> In him they were turned to ardent charity.[68]

At a time when Christians in France were suffering doubly
in the humiliation of their country and in the threat to their
faith, he found matter for hope in that. It was France that produced this extraordinary prophet, our contemporary; it was
France that nourished him entirely. There was never a man
more rooted in the soil of France and at the same time in the
soil of Christendom. He makes no vain promises like the false
prophets. He does not incite us to rash courses. His program
is simple and modest as well as bold. He teaches to "rediscover France", to use Stanislas Fumet's apt expression, and to
rediscover Christianity at the same time. Not to "invent new
myths"—a puerile and pretentious thing—but to rekindle in
ourselves the sense of mystery. May that be primarily the endeavor of those among us who are believers; may they show
themselves more at pains to live by the mystery than eager to
defend its formulas[69] or impose the hard outer crust of it; and

---

[67] Cf. "Un Nouveau théologien", in Œuvres, vol. 13, pp. 100–108. "It is
a question of whether our modern fidelities, I mean our Christian fidelities,
washed by the tides of the modern world, beset and belabored by all the winds,
belabored by so many trials but emerging intact from these two centuries of
intellectual ordeal, are not thereby invested with a singular beauty, a beauty
not hitherto theirs, and a singular grandeur in the eyes of God. . . . Our fidelities are citadels. Those crusades that carried people away and hurled con-
tinents one upon the other . . . have flowed back upon us, returning into our
very houses. . . . The least among us is literally a crusader. . . . We are all islets
buffeted by incessant storms and our houses are all sea-girt fortresses."

[68] Suite d'Eve.

[69] Cf. Nietzsche, Naissance de la tragédie, pp. 57–58.

the world, impelled by its instinct to live, will follow in their footsteps.[70]

3. *"Deeper Immersion in Existence"*

From Nietzsche the iconoclast to Kierkegaard the believer, the author of "edifying discourses", there is quite a change of climate. Yet they have much in common,[71] and it was perhaps because he had a presentiment of this that Nietzsche wrote to Georg Brandes on February 19, 1888: "I propose to deal with the psychological problem of Kierkegaard." "Both", it has been said, "were passionate and subjective thinkers; both were individualists, pushing their individualism to the point of justifying dissimulation; both were enemies of system and abstraction; both were philosophers of 'becoming' and of time. . . ."[72] Kierkegaard's language is "masked",[73] and Nietzsche, thinking of his own case, wrote in *Jenseit von Gut und Böse*: "Covering every profound mind there is a mask that grows and develops continually, thanks to the invariably false, that is to say, *shallow*, construction put upon every one of its owner's words, his movements, the least sign of life that he gives."[74] Both were

---

[70] Cf. André Rousseaux, discussing *Combats préliminaires* by André Petitjean, in *Le Figaro littéraire* of December 6, 1941.

[71] There is first of all the external similarity that Jaspers stresses: Both "lived the problem of existence in an entirely original way" and "the present position of philosophy is characterized by the fact that these thinkers, so long without influence, are now gaining more and more ground. They dominate all the other thinkers of our day": Torsten Böhlin, *Sören Kierkegaard* (French trans. by Tisseau), p. 234.

[72] Jean Wahl, *Études kierkegaardiennes* (Paris: Aubier, 1938), p. 429. Henri Lichtenberger had already sketched these points of similarity: "The development of the personality, of the 'unique' and incomparable I, is also the essential doctrine of the Dane Sören Kierkegaard . . .": *Le Philosophie de Nietzsche*, (Paris: Alcan), pp. 174–75.

[73] Jean Lacroix, *Le Sens du dialogue* (Neuchâtel: Éd. de la Baconnière, 1944).

[74] *Par delà le bien et le mal*, p. 40. Among numerous other similar texts, see

exceptional men, men who really lived their thoughts, but lived them remote from life.[75] Both of them, passionate readers of Schopenhauer,[76] attached a fundamental importance to suffering[77] and showed themselves no mercy. Both criticized the established Christianity of their age. Both were chiefly preoccupied, not with objective doctrine, but with the inward "form" or "style of life". And both, tragic and lonely heroes,[78] taught that resistance, even self-resistance and harshness toward oneself, was the only road to freedom. "What man", wrote Nietzsche, "ever explored the path of truth in such conditions as I have done, resisting and gainsaying everything that gratifies my spontaneous feelings?" And Kierkegaard: "The really serious part does not begin until man, equipped with the necessary experience, finds himself forced by a higher power to undertake something that goes against the grain." Both of them, fighting for a cause, modeled themselves upon the ancient Greeks and opposed the philosophy of their own day, which increasingly

---

the letter to his sister of May 20, 1885: "The feeling that there is in me something distant and foreign, that my words have other shades than the same words in the mouths of others. . . ." "Everything I have written up till now belongs in the foreground, and as for myself, everything begins only after the lines of suspension. . . ." His books are "above all hiding places in which I can take cover at times" (*Lettres choisies*, p. 429). He wants to expand on his thought "of mantles of light", which conceal it.

[75] Jean Wahl, "Le Nietzsche de Jaspers", in *Recherches philosophiques*, vol. 6, pp. 358 and 359.

[76] For Kierkegaard, see Böhlin, p. 198. Cf. Karl Koch, *Sören Kierkegaard* (French trans.), p. 206.

[77] Cf. Kierkegaard, *Post-scriptum aux miettes philosophiques* (French trans. by Paul Petit [Paris: Gallimard, 1941] of *Afsluttende uvidenskabelig efterskrift*), p. 301: "When Scripture says that God dwells in a broken heart, it does not refer to a momentary, fortuitous and transitory relation but, on the contrary, to the essential significance of suffering for the relationship with God." And p. 293.

[78] Kierkegaard, *Journal* (French trans. of *Efterladte papirer*), 1847: "Every time the history of the world is taking a real step forward and getting over an awkward bit of the road, a team of extra horses comes forward: the celibates, the solitaries, who live only for an idea" (Wahl, *Études*, p. 25).

tended to become professorial philosophy.[79] Their very opposition was another point of resemblance, and, as Nietzsche's atheism should not be mistaken for an incredulity incapable of faith, neither should Kierkegaard's faith be mistaken for a credulity incapable of doubt.[80]

An essential trait links them: the struggle against Hegelianism both as a rational system and as a "historicist" way of thought.[81] For Nietzsche and Kierkegaard were both men of the alternative—"either or"—demanding clarity of thought and rejecting a method of "conglomeration" that leaves nothing in its original purity[82] and that seemed to them to become, in practice, a method of accommodation, a philosophy of courting success. . . . On these last points there are surprising coincidences between the two controversialists. Which of them do you think penned this criticism of the theologian who judges Christianity from the standpoint of its "idea"?

Having distinguished between "the idea of Christianity" and its manifold and common "appearances", one comes to believe that this "idea" takes a mischievous pleasure in manifesting itself in

---

[79] Compare, for example, Nietzsche, "Schopenhauer éducateur", p. 25, and Kierkegaard, *Post-scriptum*, p. 223, etc. Nietzsche "writes with blood", and Kierkegaard says scornfully of Hegel: "Hegel was a professor of the grand style: he explained everything"; he observes that, in the whole of Martensen's *Dogmatique*, there is neither a true Yes nor a true No (Wahl, *Études*, p. 120 and p. 124, note).

[80] Cf. Rachel Bespaloff, "Les 'Études kierkegaardiennes' de Jean Wahl", in *Revue philosophique*, vol. 1 (1939), p. 317.

[81] Cf. Wahl, *Études*, p. 123: "Like Nietzsche, Kierkegaard denounces the historical passion. History cannot attain the essential. . . . By adding historicism to the philosophy of identity, Hegelianism united two of the idols of modern philosophy."

[82] Ibid., p. 131: "The absolute for Hegel was what unites absolutely: for Kierkegaard it is, at any rate primarily, what separates absolutely. . . . Kierkegaard's thought is the sword that separates; the inward is not outward; reason is not history; the subjective is not the objective; culture is not religion. . . ." And p. 130: "Against synthesis he will set up dilemma, '*Elten Elter*'. . . , against mediation paradox, against immanence transcendence. . . ."

purer and purer forms and finally chooses its most translucid
form in the brain of the present *theologus liberalis vulgaris*. But,
when he hears these purer Christianities passing judgment on the
earlier Christianities, which were impure, the impartial listener
often has the impression that Christianity does not enter into it
at all. . . .

This passage is taken from the second of Nietzsche's *Unzeitgemässe Betrachtungen*.[83] And now here is Kierkegaard in the
Postscript: after having set forth the religion of the "speculative
man", that is, the man who claims to understand Christianity
and to explain the "idea" of it in order to judge its concrete
manifestations, he concludes: "Whether the speculative man
is right is another matter. All that concerns us here is the question of whether his explanation of Christianity has any bearing
upon the Christianity he explains." "Modern speculation", he
adds, "performs the feat of understanding the whole of Christianity, but in a speculative way: which is precisely where the
misunderstanding comes in, for Christianity is the antithesis
of speculation."[84]

From the second of the *Unzeitgemässe Betrachtungen* comes
this satire on the fruits of Hegelian historicism:

Hegel implanted in the generations imbued with his doctrine
that admiration for the "power of history" which, in practice,
is continually transformed into an unconcealed admiration for
success and which leads to the idolatrous worship of facts. For
this idolatry that very mythological expression "to take facts into
account" has now been adopted. Thus those who have learned
to bend their backs and bow their heads before the "power of
history" will have a mechanical gesture of approval for every
kind of power, be it a government, or public opinion, or a majority. They will jerk their limbs according to whatever rhythm
"authority" adopts for pulling the strings. If every success has

---

[83] "De l'utilité et des inconvénients des études historiques", pp. 198–99.

[84] *Post-scriptum*, pp. 147 and 181–82. Cf. pp. 142–43 and the similar criticism of the Hegelian "up to a certain point", pp. 151–52.

in it a necessity of reason, if every event is the victory of logic or the "idea", well then! let us fall on our knees with all celerity and thus progress from step to step of "success"! What? There are to be no more sovereign myths? What? Religions are dying out? Just look at the religion of the power of history; look at the priests of the mythology of "ideas", with their bruised knees. Are not all the virtues lining up for this new faith? For is it not disinterestedness when historical man lets himself be transformed into the mirror of history? Is it not magnanimity to renounce all power in heaven and upon earth in order to worship Power in itself with all one's power? Is it not justice to hold the balance of forces in one's hand, watching which side it tips?[85]

That passage (whose aptness surely needs no stressing) would have appealed to Kierkegaard, who took up the cudgels with such warmth against the moralists, with their "world-history-minded" view of duty.

Modern speculation [says the *Postscript*] rests on an assumption that is not false but comic, a kind of preoccupation with world history having made it forget what it means to be human. . . . We are told that those who give their minds to universal history gladly leave popular ethics to seminarists and village schoolmasters; that they have no objection to the lower classes' endeavoring to live according to such ethics while the world-history interest concentrates on something higher, on much greater duties. . . . As for these "much greater duties", let us speak of them in all simplicity, like two neighbors chatting at dusk. . . .[86]

---

[85] Pp. 217–18. It would, moreover, be unjust to see in this philosophy of the *fait accompli*, as Kierkegaard seems to do at times, a pure and simple fruit of Hegelianism.

[86] Pp. 80 and 95. Cf. pp. 88–89: "The continual reading of world history makes one unsuited for action. True ethical enthusiasm consists in that which one wishes with all one's will but, at the same time, elevated by divine gaiety, one never thinks of the eventual results of one's action. . . ." It is clear, moreover, that this criticism, like Nietzsche's charge against the idolaters of success, does not reach Hegel himself but only certain more or less self-seeking interpretations of his philosophy. Just as he did not want to justify, purely and simply, the *fait accompli*—although "the most patent result of his philosophy is,

Here again, is not Nietzsche entirely of the same mind?

> When, in connection with the term "morality", one thinks of a
> higher usefulness, of ecumenical aims, it must be admitted that
> there is more morality in trade than in the Kantian precept: "Do
> as you would be done by", or than in the Christian life conceived
> in accordance with the saying: "Love your neighbor out of love
> for God."[87]

But Kierkegaard is far more vigorous than Nietzsche in his
criticism of Hegelianism (that is to say, of the official and popularized system rather than of the actual ideas of the philosopher
in his first phase of invention). This is because Kierkegaard,
far from repudiating all dialectic, is himself a doughty dialecti-
cian.[88] His dialectic is qualitative, it concerns diversity of planes
and of "spheres of existence",[89] it pursues the confusions of
the Hegelian synthesis as formidably as the equally appalling
confusions of unsystematized thinking. For him the "religious"
does not reside in some sort of "immediacy", but it is placed
in its specific sphere, equally distinct from the "aesthetic" and
the "ethical". If, in a sense, it can be called irrational, at least
there is no danger of its being confused with any form of the
infrarational. Kierkegaard restores faith to its towering height,
and he brings man back into genuine contact with God. An-

---

according to Émile Bréhier (*Histoire de la philosophie* [Paris: Presses Universitaires de France, 1930–1938], vol. 2, p. 783), "to confer the divine seal on
all the realities of nature and history"—Hegel clearly distinguished objective
morality (*Sittlichkeit*) and subjective morality (*Moralität*), to which alone he accorded an absolute value. Yet he seems not to have succeeded in synthesizing
them in a satisfactory manner. Cf. Hegel *Philosophie de l'histoire* (French trans.
by Gibelin of *Vorlesung über die Philosophie der Geschichte*), vol. 1, p. 12, etc.

[87] *Sur le christianisme* (French trans. by H. J. Bolle of *Über das Christentum*),
in *Œuvres posthumes*, p. 79.

[88] Wahl, *Études*, p. 104: "This master of anti-Hegelianism is still rather
Hegelian, so that one could connect him with the doctrine he is combat-
ting and follow in his expression the very explanation he opposes. Had not
Socrates been infinitely ambiguous like this?" Cf. p. 75, note 1.

[89] *Post-scriptum*, p. 339. Cf. Wahl, *Études*, pp. 57 and 113.

other feature of his superiority, as artist no less than as thinker, may be added: his Socratism. If Nietzsche is the anti-Socrates, Kierkegaard is certainly the most Socratic of the moderns. His use of pseudonyms is a form of the Socratic method of drawing out ideas. Irony and humor are two essential categories of his thought; they also permeate his style. By this means he escapes the heaviness in jesting from which Nietzsche was not immune,[90] even when in *Zarathustra* he proclaimed "the spirit of heaviness" his "archenemy".[91] Kierkegaard steers clear of the too ceremonious splendor for which the exalter of Zarathustra always retained a liking;[92] of the thick vapors exhaled by his Dionysism; of the sectarian fanaticism that disfigures all the "philosophizing with a hammer". The occasional "extravagance" that the poet of *Morgenrothe* would like to see in his disciples, the "little tail of farce" that, with Dionysus, he would have "attached, even to what is holiest",[93] the watchword: "Be something of a buffoon, something of a god",[94]—all these things add up to a clumsy substitute for the Socratic atticism of Kierkegaard. Socrates is not blasphemed with impunity.

Is the *Concluding Unscientific Postscript to the Philosophical Fragments of Johannes Climacus* (published by Søren Kierkegaard with the

---

[90] See, for example, in his correspondence, the letters to Malwida von Meysenbug (August 11, 1875) or to Bernhardt Foerster (April 16, 1885).

[91] *Zarathoustra*, pp. 270–76: "De l'esprit de lourdeur". P. 278: "My old demon and my born-enemy, the spirit of heaviness"; p. 438: "The spirit of heaviness, my old mortal enemy"; p. 418: "Zarathustra the dancer. Zarathustra the light one, the one who flutters his wings, ready for flight, signaling to all the birds, ready and agile, divinely light."

[92] Cf. Charles Andler, *La Dernière philosophie de Nietzsche*, vol. 6 of *Nietzsche*, p. 52.

[93] Cf. Seillière, pp. 299–303.

[94] "Dionysos philosophos", in *Volonté*, vol. 2, p. 381. Jaspers noted this lack of humor in Nietzsche (cf. Wahl, "Le Nietzsche de Jaspers", p. 346).

firm of Reitzel in Copenhagen in 1846) Kierkegaard's master-piece? It is not so easy to judge. Kierkegaard himself, it seems, had a predilection for *Fear and Trembling*. After all, the *Postscript* really is a postscript, incomparably longer, to be sure, than the *Fragments* it follows—like Péguy's *Note conjointe*—but presupposing their existence. In any case, the work itself presents difficulties for the twentieth-century reader in a different country on account of the large number of allusions it contains. Despite all the skill of an exceptionally competent translator, this dazzling prose is often dull for us. To follow the author with ease in all his sallies, to enjoy all his malice, would require knowledge of current events in Denmark and of the Danish literature of the day—not omitting the theatre—which one may be excused for not possessing. In addition, Kierkegaard, in this work, is sometimes unduly prolix and repetitious, given to digressions and parentheses. . . . These factors make for obscurity, but they are not an insuperable obstacle. If the subtle power of the construction can be savored only by specialists, numerous pages are impressive in their classical beauty. It does not take one long to perceive that the *Postscript* is a great work, perhaps Kierkegaard's masterpiece and in any case one of the masterpieces of the philosophical and religious literature of all time.

In France we have already had for some time Jean Wahl's *Études kierkegaardiennes*, a true Summa, a monument of intelligent insight.[95] This essential work allows us to situate and understand the other works. Kierkegaard's thought, one of the most foreign summits of human thought in the nineteenth century, is henceforth accessible to us. Jean Wahl and Paul Petit [who translated Kierkegaard's works into French] deserve the gratitude not only of ardent followers of Kierkegaard but of all who value man and who believe in the life of the spirit.

The *Philosophical Fragments* presented, by way of hypothesis, the fact of the Incarnation, that supreme paradox of the in-

---

[95] (Paris: Aubier, 1938).

cursion of God into history, or of the eternal into time. They formed a kind of philosophy of dogma. The *Postscript* completes them with a philosophy of faith. It sets out to show in what conditions the individual receives the mystery (Kierkegaard calls it the paradox) into himself without stripping it of its essentially mysterious quality. Thus, after the objective standpoint of the *Fragments*, it is the subjective point of view that now prevails. It should not be inferred that Kierkegaard has returned, by a devious route, to subjectivism: this would be an enormous misinterpretation.[96] As he is the philosopher of transcendence, Kierkegaard is the theologian of objectivity. But he is at the same time the theologian of *inwardness*, that is to say, of personal appropriation. The problem he handles in the *Postscript* is consequently a subjective problem: it is a question of determining the relation of the subject to the truth of Christianity —more concretely, the relation of the individual to Christian reality: most simply of all, it is a question of how to become a Christian. It may be said that the essential question discussed all through these 430 closely printed pages is the question of the nature of faith.

To believe is neither to know nor to understand, still less, of course, is it simply to profess a doctrine. Mystery is not a rational system; faith is not a "starting point for thought"; belief is not speculative; the real individual is face to face with a real God: that is the quite simple truth that Kierkegaard is never weary of repeating, turning it this way and that (so to speak), against Hegelian intellectualism. "What I am writing here should be considered, not in the sense of speculation, but

---

[96] This misinterpretation is not fanciful. It is found in Høffding, according to whom the principle of subjectivity invoked by Kierkegaard would place the latter on the same line of thought as Feuerbach in *Das Wesen des Christentums*. Cf. Böhlin, p. 166. See also R. Vancourt, "Deux conceptions de la philosophie", in *Mélanges de sciences religieuses*, 1944, pp. 229–30; the author, without declaring it, nevertheless does not dismiss the hypothesis according to which, for Kierkegaard, "we would always adhere only to truths we have created ourselves."

in a simple sense, as an elementary teaching, as an ABC."[97]
Thus Socrates pretended to know nothing, the better to lead
his interlocutors to the essential point, which their pretensions
to learning inclined them to forget. Does not the vanity of our
age come from the fact that, with all its knowledge, lost in
the objectivism of its theories, it forgets those two little things
that are so simple: "the meaning of existence and the meaning
of inwardness"?[98] Johannes Climacus proposes to recall them
to the attention of the age in order to recall the age itself to
Christianity. Not that he sets up to be a Christian, any more
than he sets up to be a philosopher. He is nothing but a man
"wholly engrossed in the thought that it must be very difficult
to become one"; but at least, he adds, he is *not* a man who,
"having been a Christian, has ceased to be one by going beyond Christianity".[99]

Now that precisely is the misfortune of our philosophers.
They are not ignorant of Christianity, and it is not of their
own wish that they reject it. But according to them—even
if they do not put it so crudely—"faith is a refuge for weak
heads"; they reduce it to the status of an initial impetus, a starting point for thought. They "go beyond" the Christianity of
the Apostles! "Not only", they say, "do we believe in Christianity, but we can explain it"—without perceiving that for
that very reason it eludes them. They think that their speculation will transform into "real truth" what was hitherto only
"relative truth", hidden from itself in the mind of a simple
believer; and they manfully set forth to solve the paradox to
which that believer clings—not realizing that wisdom lies in
seeing it more clearly as a paradox. In their naïve and complacent pedantry, they think they possess and can "offer for sale
the secrets of the Godhead" as well as the secrets of humanity.
Thus they end by transforming "the fact that God has existed"

[97] *Post-scriptum*, p. 363.

[98] Ibid., p. 160; see also pp. 202–6.

[99] Ibid., p. 419; cf. p. 420.

into a beautiful system: they "haul" this fact "to the plane of intellectuality", so as to have no relation to it in future but an intellectual one and to save themselves from the passionate entanglement of faith.[100]

This "thinker's" attitude is perhaps "distinguished". It is in any case convenient, since it automatically confers immunity from any martyrdom. What it can have in common with the Christian attitude remains to be seen. "The speculative man is perhaps farther from Christianity than anyone, and it is conceivably much better to be shocked by Christianity—thus, after all, still bearing some relation to it—rather than to be a speculative man who 'understands' it."[101] The attitude of the man who is aware of his own real existence will be very different;[102] and very different that of the believer who grasps that "faith is a sphere in itself" and welcomes the paradox in it for its own sake. Faith does not seek to transcend itself but to grow deeper, that is to say, to find itself more completely, to realize itself more thoroughly *as faith*. It does not attempt to "enter into God's counsels", it does not perpetually cry that "from the eternal, divine, theocentric standpoint, there is no paradox." Far from confusing "spiritual penetration" with "speculation", it resists the latter as "the gravest temptation of all". It knows that Christianity does not merely happen to be a secret; it is essentially a secret—and a secret that "has no desire to be understood".[103] Faith struggles—and triumphantly—"with the understanding against it, like those Romans of old, blinded by the light of the sun".[104] In proportion as its inwardness grows, probability diminishes rather than increases. In any case faith

---

[100] Ibid., pp. 150–53, 160, 218–19.

[101] Ibid., pp. 143 and 153; cf. pp. 181–82 and 147.

[102] Ibid., p. 204: "A man is forbidden to forget that he exists." And p. 170: "One can really, with a pure intention, wish for humanity that this excess of knowledge might be withdrawn anew from it, so that one might learn again to know what it is to live like a man."

[103] Ibid., pp. 141–42 and 52.

[104] Ibid., pp. 148–49; cf. p. 151.

has no liking for this probability. "One is apt to imagine that the improbable, the paradox, is something with which faith is loath to have dealings; that it temporarily puts up with this state of affairs, hoping to improve it gradually." No, the improbable is not the enemy but the food of faith. Faith spends its time in discovering it and firmly maintaining it—in order to be able to believe:

> To be sitting quietly in a boat in calm weather is not an image of faith. But when the boat has sprung a leak, to keep it afloat by enthusiastically manning the pumps, yet with no thought of returning to port—that is an image of faith. . . . While the understanding, like a desperate passenger, stretches out its arms to terra firma but in vain, faith works with all its might in the deep waters: joyfully and triumphantly it saves the soul.[105]

There is an epic grandeur in this hand-to-hand fight between a faith determined to keep itself pure and a plausible speculation that would dissolve it. A powerful virtue goes out from this challenge to all thought that proposes to "overcome religion by philosophy".[106] As, in another part of his work, he reclaims the specific character of Christian faith from the hands of romantic sentimentalism, Kierkegaard, in the *Postscript*, reclaims it from Hegelian intellectualism and, in so doing, from the eternal temptation of philosophy. Here, so to speak, he saves the Christian from the temptation of logic, as elsewhere he saved him from the aesthetic illusion. As he reestablished the frontiers between the spiritual life and the emotions or pleasures of the aesthete, so he reestablishes them between faith and speculation.[107] And as, in the campaign he conducted, toward the

[105] Ibid., p. 149, note; pp. 153–54.

[106] Alain, *Histoire de mes pensées* (Paris: Gallimard, 1936), p. 250. Hegel's philosophy "dissolves religion in itself and substitutes itself for it", says Benedetto Croce with justification, *Ce qui est vivant et ce qui est mort de la philosophie de Hegel* (French trans. by Henri Buriot [Paris: Giard and Brière, 1910] of *Cio che e vivo*), p. 58.

[107] *Point de vue explicatif de mon oeuvre* (French trans. by Tisseau, 1940), p. 36;

end of his life, against the established Church of his country, he wanted to save that "shocking" element which is essential to Christianity, so in his struggle against Hegelianism he wanted to save the element of "paradox", which is no less essential. He was in the right against Hegel; he had been in the right against romanticism and was to be in the right against the admirers of Bishop Mynster. But is he always quite clear as to what the philosopher is getting at? Does he do justice to his efforts, to the very ambition of reason? Does he recognize how much a "converted" Hegelianism could contribute—like all great human thought—to an authentic "understanding through faith"? Has he even a dim idea of what such an understanding could be? After having extricated Christianity in its purity, does he not tend to relegate it to an inhuman solitude? . . . These are altogether different questions.[108]

One cannot help wondering, too, whether it is only rationalism that comes in for a drubbing. Does not reason itself emerge with a few bruises? Fewer, perhaps, than one is tempted to believe if one reads Kierkegaard without first examining the exact nature of his set of problems. In spite of appearances to the contrary in some of his writings, it is the narrow limits of the terrain that would seem to call for criticism rather than the actual import of the theses involved. Kierkegaard, says Mr. Bachelard, marches the destiny of mankind "into a defile".[109] He marches the whole process of thought there along with it.

---

on the *Post-scriptum*: "After having cited as his authority the whole pseudonymous aesthetic production considered as a description of a way by which one must pass to become Christian, that is, the way by which one returns from aesthetics in order to become Christian, this work describes the second way, that is, that by which one returns from the system of speculation, etc., in order to become Christian."

[108] Cf. Henri Rondet, S.J., "Hégélianisme et christianisme", in *Recherches de science religieuse*, June and October 1936. For a theological restatement of the doctrine of Kierkegaard: M. J. Congar, "Actualité de Kierkegaard", in *Vie intellectuelle*, vol. 32, pp. 9–36.

[109] Preface to the French translation (*Je et Tu*) of Martin Buber's *Ich und Du*.

In order to give a fair hearing to this new and powerful echo of the *credo quia absurdum*, we must take up the concrete, existential position into which Kierkegaard is doing his best to lead us.

That in itself, moreover, is big with consequences. I certainly should not go so far as to say, with a recent historian, that "the God of Kierkegaard is only a myth", that he is merely "nothingness in disguise", on the grounds that the path that leads Kierkegaard to God does not seem to conform to any given dialectical schema. To judge faith solely according to the value of its rational "preambles" would, I think, be to place it on a naturalistic basis. It should not be forgotten that the "despair" analyzed by our author implies consciousness of eternity, or at any rate is to be accounted for by eternity.[110] I do not admit that the distinction which he draws between aesthetic existence and religious existence "is only an optical illusion". I find no equivalence between his faith and the nihilism of men like Nietzsche or Heidegger.[111] If the filiation of Heidegger to Nietzsche is a matter of history, that of Nietzsche to Kierkegaard is not; and the kinship that can be discovered between these two men of genius should not blind us to their fundamental antithesis. Heidegger no doubt owes much to Kierkegaard, but the debt is not such that Kierkegaard can be held responsible

---

[110] *Traité du désespoir* (French trans. by Ferlov-Gateau [Neuchâtel: Éd. de la Baconnière, 1944] of *Sygdommen til doden*), pp. 68, 70, 75, 139, 147: "Despair is a category of the mind, and in man its application is to his eternity. . . . It is hopelessness of even being able to die. . . . The eternity of man can be demonstrated by the impotence of despair to destroy the ego, by that dreadful contradiction of despair. . . . To despair as regards the eternal is impossible without an idea of the ego, without the idea that there is or has been eternity in it. . . ."

[111] Cf. Alphonse de Waelhens, *La Philosophie de Martin Heidegger* (Louvain: Éditions de l'Institut superieur de philosophie, 1942), pp. 338–39 and 356. "Kierkegaard", the author concludes, "is still only the representative of a nihilism that deceives itself; Nietzsche, that of a nihilism that knows itself but tries to overcome itself; would Heidegger not be the herald of a greater nihilism that professes itself?"

for Heidegger's nihilism. I shall not look to Kierkegaard for an ontology he never proposed to construct; but it seems futile to attempt to show that, without wishing it and without realizing it, he chose nothingness because he could not choose anything else. To refuse a man the right to inform us of what he thinks and to arrogate to oneself the right to understand him, not as he understands himself but "as he *ought* to be understood", is a very subjective principle of exegesis. The principle is not, perhaps, completely false, but it is at least dangerous. It is particularly arbitrary when the thing to be judged is not just a system of concepts but a faith—and a faith that is amply, richly expressed: Whatever the preliminaries may be, should not such a faith be judged first of all in itself?[112]

However that may be, it must be recognized that Kierkegaard is a stimulating writer rather than a safe one. His ideas are not so much a food as a tonic and, taken in too large a dose, they might become a toxin. Anyone who, thinking to follow in his footsteps, entrenched himself forthwith in Kierkegaard's positions, would run the risk of cutting himself off from all rational life and perhaps from all culture—an inhuman attitude that was certainly not Kierkegaard's and that would be of no benefit to Christianity in the end. In any case, Kierkegaard cannot be considered a teacher, and he would have been the first to deny himself that title. "A strange man", "a morbid and complicated mind",[113] he himself referred in his *Journals* to "the queer intimacy of the machinery" that produced his writings, and all of them show the effects of an origin so closely personal. His

---

[112] Besides, it is rather difficult to see why "the subject who has been raised to the dignity of subject through the intensity of his inner reflection, is immured in nothingness, wants this and is only through that will. . . ." That such is Heidegger's thesis, we are ready to believe the author; but why adopt it in some way and apply it to Kierkegaard? In addition, what necessary relation is there between such a metaphysical affirmation and the remark by Mynster saying that the writings of Kierkegaard are "a profane play on sacred themes"?

[113] These are M. H. Hatzfeld's expressions, *Correspondance de la Fédération française des associations chrétiennes d'étudiants* (June 1942).

"twisted" thought, deep and incisive though it is, lacks breadth and balance. Beyond those illusory unities that it unmasks and explodes, it has not found that other unity that is like the seal of God upon its work.[114] His soul knew moments of peace and joy, whose witness remains,[115] but it was not settled in serenity. The faith of this true believer[116] retains a strongly Lutheran flavor, though it escapes the distortions that Lutheranism had engendered in most of his contemporaries. The mere fact that he constantly uses the words "paradox" and "improbable" where we should say "mystery" and "marvelous" may serve to illustrate these observations. Is he not in danger of causing those who become his undiscriminating disciples to confuse what, in things of the spirit, is improbable to carnal man with what is simply unreasonable in things that are within the province of reason? And when he complains in *Training in Christianity* that, among those who have become scholars in regard to history or religious doctrine, "the paradox has become slack",[117] the justification for such a complaint is only too apparent; but does it not seem, at the same time, as if he wished to keep

---

[114] Note, however, the penetrating remark by Jean Wahl, *Études*, p. 156: "There are souls made for unity, unity in love that can become unity in reason. There are souls who, made, too, for unity perhaps, are not made to receive it, and who because they are closed to this gift receive perhaps still greater ones."

[115] *Journal*, May 19, 1838, at ten-thirty in the morning: "There is an indescribable joy that embraces us in a way that is as inexplicable as the cry of the Apostle ringing out without knowing why: 'Rejoice, I say it again, rejoice.' It is not a joy of this or that, but the full cry of the soul. . . . A heavenly refrain, which suddenly interrupts, so to speak, the rest of our song; joy that caresses and refreshes like a breeze; a gust of wind that breathes from the oaks of Mamre all the way to the eternal dwelling-places" (quoted by Böhlen, p. 31).

[116] Cf. *Crainte et tremblement* (French trans. by Tisseau [Paris: Aubier, 1935] of *Frygt og bæven*), p. 41: "Love finds its priests among the poets, and one hears at times a voice who knows how to sing it; but faith does not have any cantor who speaks in praise of this passion."

[117] *L'École du christianisme* (French trans. by Tisseau of *Indøvelse i Christendom*), p. 41.

Christians in a state of paradoxical tension that finds no more recommendation in the Gospel than in psychology?

In spite of this unilateral character of a body of thought strongly marked with the heritage of the Reformation, Mr. Paul Petit observes that, in the last years of his short life, Kierkegaard seems to have increasingly followed a course that was clearly taking him toward positions not far removed from Catholicism. He is ready to admit, in the train of critics like Brandes and Høffding, that if Kierkegaard had been born later he would have been a Catholic.[118] I shall not attempt an opinion on that point (and I confess that I see no very clear indications). It is sufficient that this free-lance, outlawed by his Church, was the witness chosen by God to compel a world that increasingly disowned it to contemplate the greatness of faith; that, in a century carried away by immanentism, he was the herald of transcendence. It is sufficient that this despiser of all apologetics was, in his own way, himself a powerful apologist. His whole work finds a fitting commentary in this maxim from the *Postscript*: "Preparation for becoming attentive to Christianity does not consist in reading books or in making surveys of world history, but in *deeper immersion in existence*."[119]

---

[118] Cf. his introduction to *Miettes philosophiques* (the French translation in the Caillou blanc series [1947] of *Philosophiske smuler*). That, with slight shades of difference, is the contention of the Rev. Fr. Przywara also. In his book *Das Geheimnis Kierkegaards*, he "proposes to show that in Kierkegaard an anonymous Catholicism is to be found"; by his call for objective authority and by his views on the ordination of priests as an intermediate objective authority, Kierkegaard is asserted to have crossed the border-line of Lutheranism and pointed the way to "Holy Mother Church" (Böhlin, p. 239).

[119] *Post-scriptum*, p. 378; cf. p. 98.

CHAPTER III

THE SPIRITUAL BATTLE

Every age has its heresies. Every age also sees a renewal of the general rule that faith must be attacked. For a long time now —ever since its foundation—Christianity has never ceased to be assailed; but not always from the same quarter, nor by the same type of adversary, nor with the same weapons. Sometimes it is the historical substructure of our beliefs that seems shaken: biblical criticism and exegesis or the history of Christian origins or of the Church's dogmas and institutions provides the battleground. Sometimes this is shifted to the metaphysical field. The very existence of a reality higher than the things of this world is then denied or declared unknowable; thought falls back upon immanent positions. Or else, taking the opposite course, it seeks to invade the whole field of being and to leave nothing outside the clutches of a reason that insists on understanding everything; and that means (without prejudice to more specific objections against such and such a dogma) the disappearance of the very idea of a mystery to believe in. Often the politicians take over from the historians and metaphysicians or work side by side with them: the political attacks are directed against the Church, against what is termed her thirst for earthly domination; many politicians, not content with opposing any meddling by the Church with the State, are also out to destroy all Christian influence on the course of human affairs; and the most ambitious go so far as to reject, in the State's favor, that distinction between temporal and spiritual that the world owes to the Gospel. Lastly, there are the objections of a social character, objections so strong and so insistent that they have more than once seemed preponderant. Has it not been, latterly, the chief concern of a number of apostles to prove, by an exposition of Catholic social doctrine and by an endeavor to achieve material results in the social field, that religion is not the "opium of the people", that the Church is not indifferent to man's lot on earth and that, as mother of all, she is not by any means in league with the rich and the mighty?

None of these types of objections is obsolete today. In none of these different sectors can we afford to relax our vigilance. Yet the principal attack comes from elsewhere. What is in the foreground—in reality, if not always in appearance—is no longer an historical, metaphysical, political or social problem. It is a *spiritual* problem. It is the human problem as a whole. Today it is not one of the bases or one of the consequences of Christianity that is exposed to attack: the stroke is aimed directly at its heart. The Christian conception of life, Christian spirituality, the inward attitude which, more than any particular act or outward gesture, bespeaks the Christian—that is what is at stake. How timid those men now seem who, for instance, fought against the Church but wanted to keep the Gospel! Or those who, while claiming to be released from all authority and all faith, still invoked principles derived from a Christian source! They had persuaded themselves that "it was possible to preserve the benefits of Christianity while ceasing to be Christians".[1] "Free thinkers", but not very bold and not very "free" as yet! Those who have come after them deride their illogicality as much as their impotence and lump them together with believers in a common reprobation. Those of the new generation do not intend to be satisfied with "the shadow of a shadow". They have no desire to live upon the perfume of an empty vase. They are pouring quite a different fluid into it. It is the *whole* of Christianity that they are setting aside—and replacing. They no longer say, as Renouvier and many others said not so long ago: "Everything is being called in question again, but none of the great principles of the Gospel tradition have been effaced

---

[1] Henri Lacordaire, *Considérations sur le système philosophique de M. de la Mennais* (1834), p. 21.

from men's minds."[2] Jesus had brought about a "reversal of values": it is a reversal of values that *they* are undertaking in their turn. To the Christian ideal they oppose a pagan ideal. Against the God worshipped by Christians they proudly set up their new deities. In doing so they are conscious of attacking essentials and sweeping everything away at one stroke; for they profess, with Schopenhauer, that "it is the spirit and the moral tendency that constitute the essence of a religion, and not the myths in which it is clothed."[3]

1. The Battlefield

Such was Nietzsche's conviction and such was his intent. The God whose death Nietzsche proclaimed and desired is not only the God of metaphysics but, very definitely, the Christian God. Hostile to Christianity from the time when, at about the age of twenty, he lost his faith, Nietzsche opposed it with an absolute No. His denial, radical from the outset, became more

---

[2] Charles Renouvier, *Manuel de philosophie moderne* (Paris: Paulin, 1842), p. 8: "Something [he added] will henceforth be gained, it is the sacred right of man, freedom of the spirit, the definitive fall of the principle of slavery and castes in all its forms." In a similar sense, Béranger wrote to Lamennais, on May 28, 1834: "I believe like you in the gradual but complete transformation of today's society. Evangelical morality has created a world that has not yet had the form its principle claims" (Georges Goyau, *Le Portefeuille de Lamennais, 1818–1836* [Paris: La Renaissance du livre, 1930], p. 140). And Lamennais himself, in *Le Livre du peuple* (Paris: Pagnerre, 1838), p. 104, "Examine everywhere the reason that no prejudice alters, the conscience that no interest, no passion corrupts; they will reply to you that man is sacred to man; that to attack him in his person, his freedom, his property, is to overturn the basis of order, to violate moral laws, the conservator of the human race; to commit one of those acts, in all centuries with all peoples, has received the terrible name of CRIME." Numerous quotations like this could be cited. But do they not have the effect of pieces drawn from an archeological museum?

[3] Schopenhauer, *Le Monde comme volonté et comme représentation* (French trans. by Burdeau of *Welt als Wille und Vorstellung*), supplement to book 4, chap. 48: vol. 3, p. 434.

and more violent and frantic. His last writings are full of outbursts of hatred and invective. But he never took the trouble
to outline any sort of refutation.[4] For him, as for men like
Comte and Feuerbach, Christianity was dead and done with.
Christian history could not be anything but a legend and its
dogmatics a mythology. Thus there was no point in dwelling
on them. "That mythology", he wrote in *Der Wille zur Macht*,
"which Kant himself did not completely abandon, which Plato
prepared for Europe, to its misfortune . . . that mythology has
had its day."[5] In any event, that was not what interested him.
"All those absurd remains of Christian fable," he said later,
in the same work, "that cobwebbery of concepts, that theology, matter very little to us; though they were a thousand
times more absurd, we should not lift a finger to overthrow
them."[6] The essential question lies elsewhere. It is not a question of truth—is there such a thing as truth?—but a question of
value.

> Up to the present the assault against Christianity has not only
> been fainthearted, it has been wide of the mark. So long as Chris-
> tian *ethics* are not felt to be a *capital crime against life*, their defenders
> will have the game in their hands. The problem of the "truth"
> of Christianity—the existence of its God or the historicity of its
> legend, to say nothing of its astronomy and its natural science
> —is in itself a very subsidiary problem so long as the value of
> Christian ethics goes unquestioned.[7]

"Have Christian ethics any value, or are they a profanation
and a shame, despite all the sanctity of their means of seduc-

---

[4] "I am not speaking", he said, "of *lived* things, and I am not presenting any
cerebral process": *Ainsi parlait Zarathoustra* (French trans. by Betz of *Also sprach
Zarathustra*), appendix, no. 5, p. 301.

[5] Nietzsche, written in 1885; *Volonté de puissance* (French trans. by Geneviève Bianquis of *Der Wille zur Macht*), vol. 1, p. 70.

[6] Written in 1887–1888; ibid., vol. 1, p. 185. Cf. already his letter to his
mother and sister, November 1865: *Lettres choisies* (Walz ed.), pp. 101–2.

[7] Written in 1888; ibid., vol. 1, p. 140.

tion?" That was for Nietzsche the real problem, the only one. How he solved it is well known. "War against the Christian ideal," he cried, "against the doctrine that makes beatitude and salvation the aim of life, against the supremacy of the poor in spirit, the pure in heart, the suffering, the failures. . . . When and where was there ever a man worthy of the name who resembled that Christian ideal?"[8] He did not fight against faith in God. "What do God and faith in God matter in our day? God is no more than a faded word today—not even a concept."[9] But what he fought in Christianity, and what he declared "must be fought without ceasing", was "its ideal of man": "that ideal whose morbid beauty and feminine seduction, its insinuating and calumnious eloquence, flatter all that is vain and craven in weary souls—and even the strongest have hours of weariness." What he fought was "trustfulness, ingenuousness, simplicity, patience, love for one's neighbor, resignation, submission to God, a sort of disarming and repudiation of one's own ego", all those virtues that Christianity sets before man in order to tempt him. The establishment of such an ideal, ministering to the small and the weak, had threatened the vigorous exceptions with death; it had imperilled the great human achievements,

> as if that inconsiderable runt of a soul, that virtuous middle-sized animal, that docile sheep of a man, not only ranked higher than the race of men more malignant, rapacious, daring and prodigal, and thus a hundred times more exposed to danger, but as if he

---

[8] Written in 1887; ibid., vol. 1, p. 184. Cf. *L'Antéchrist* (French trans. by Albert of *Der Antichrist*): "This eternal denunciation of Christianity, I will write it on all the walls so long as I find walls to blacken. I have at my disposition letters that give sight to the blind. I call Christianity the great scourge among all, for which no means is poisonous, secret, underhanded, small enough. Christianity, I call it the most shameful, ineradicable stain of humanity" (quoted by Daniel Halévy, *Nietzsche* [Paris: Grasset, 1944], p. 536).

[9] *Volonté*, ibid. He also said, as early as 1873, in the same spirit: "Christianity will soon be ripe for historical criticism, which is to say, for the dissecting table": ibid., vol. 2, p. 59.

were even the ideal, the aim, the norm for man in general, the supreme good.[10]

Nietzsche realized that along this path he was a pioneer. "I am inaugurating", he said, "a new kind of free thought." "Nobody yet has regarded Christian morality as something beneath him. . . . Hitherto Christian morality has been the Circe of all thinkers. They have entered her service. Did anyone, before me, go down into the chasms that vent the poisonous breath of such an ideal, the ideal of those who slander the world? Did anyone even dare to suspect that there were chasms there?" For this, so he said in *Ecce Homo*, he had needed "a quite unparalleled prominence, farsightedness and psychological penetration".[11] Nietzsche flattered himself. As a matter of fact, Christian ethics had never been wholly free from adversaries of that kind. Without going back to the earliest centuries, one may recall, for instance, the pagan surge of the Renaissance, with a Machiavelli setting up against "our religion", for which "the highest happiness lies in humility, abasement and contempt for things human", the old religion that "found the supreme good in greatness of soul, strength of body and all the qualities that make man formidable". In the eighteenth century, in the group of publicists revolving round Diderot and Baron d'Holbach, there were several who professed an equally decided anti-Christianism: Grimm, for instance, called Christian dogma a "base and ignoble mythology", reproached it with

---

[10] Written in 1887–1888; ibid., vol. 1, pp. 185–86. *Ecce Homo* (French trans. by Albert), p. 45: "Humanity has let itself be seduced by a negative corruptive instinct . . . by the instinct of decadence."

[11] *Ecce Homo*, pp. 170–71. Cf. *L'Antéchrist* in *Le Crépuscule des idoles* (Albert trans.) p. 293: "Christian values and noble values: we other, free spirits, we have been the first to reestablish this contrast, the greatest there is!" Compare in fact Nietzsche's position with that, for example, of Strauss, writing in the *New Life of Jesus*, with respect to the characteristics of the person and teaching of Jesus: "They have remained a part of human nature, and it is through them that all that we call humanity today was able to germinate and develop."

exercising "the most sinister influences" and teaching "abject-ness, ignominy, slavery", vilified "the spirit of Christian char-ity" and declared that "the spirit of the Gospel has never been able to go hand in hand with the principles of good govern-ment."[12] But these "philosophers" were of too poor a quality to have any lasting lure for the élite. As for Machiavelli (whom Nietzsche had read with close attention just before the com-position of his last works), it is only in a few passages that his most profound thoughts are allowed to come to the surface; he did not as a rule claim to be a master of moral philosophy but only of politics. Renan, too, had shrewdly observed, in the letter written to Strauss in 1870: "What gains one admission to Valhalla is what shuts one out of the kingdom of God", but his ideas were too flabby for him to push his point very far. . . . It must be agreed, then, that never, before Nietzsche, had so mighty an adversary arisen, one who had so clear, broad and explicit a conception of his destiny and who pursued it in all domains with such systematic and deliberate zeal. Nietzsche was thoroughly imbued with a sense of his prophetic mission. He laid down laws for future ages. "Another ideal", he said in *Ecce Homo*, "runs ahead of us, prodigious, alluring and rich in dangers . . . the idea of a mind that ingenuously, that is to say unintentionally, makes game of all that up to now has been held sacred, good, inviolable, divine." He considered himself called upon to inaugurate a new era, "to be the first to put the great question mark in its place, to change the destiny of the soul, to move the hands of the clock, to raise the curtain upon the tragedy".[13] With him, eternal paganism proudly lifts its head again but brings with it new equipment. It prepares to remold individual life and intimate feelings just as much as public life and the exercise of power. It takes charge of man's destiny, with a view to new conquests.

---

[12] Friedrich Melchior Grimm, *Correspondance littéraire, philosophique et critique*, vol. 5, April 1763, pp. 261, 264, 265.

[13] *Ecce Homo*, pp. 125–26.

I do not propose to embark upon yet another exposition of Nietzschean anti-Christianism;[14] the call to a powerful, heroic, creative life; the morality of strength and hardness; the accusation of "resentment" brought against the founders of Christian ethics and their precursors, the great prophets of Israel; the confronting of the "baseness of the Christian slave" with the "nobility" of the Greek hero; the exaltation of Dionysus, the god of orgiastic and perpetually renascent life, in contrast to his scorn of the Crucified who, on the tree of the Cross, "the most poisonous of all trees", is "a malediction upon Life".[15] Suffice it to note the very serious nature of the attack. It is not, like others, directed against a few specialists in history or metaphysics; its action is not at first confined to intellectual circles; without needing men of science as its interpreters, it comes to shake souls. It is aimed at the spiritual élite and, when it has attained its aim, it succeeds in perverting that élite while sparing them the sensation of having fallen. Like everything that is of the spirit, it is at the same time ubiquitous in its infiltration and very difficult to nail down, so that it has time to spread great havoc before the first warning is sounded. Under cover of impeccable enunciations of faith, sometimes even screened by an apparent increase of orthodoxy, souls may already be gangrened. Though intellectual laziness is a potent safeguard against many objections, and the interests of social security may become a very strong argument for religion, neither intellectual laziness nor the interests of social security are a safeguard against the inroads of the pagan spirit. To the connivances which that spirit has always found in our nature, it

---

[14] Refer especially to the study by the Rev. Fr. Yves de Montcheuil, "Nietzsche et la critique de l'idéal chrétien", in *Cité nouvelle*, June 25, 1941. As early as 1901, Alfred Fouillée was defining Nietzscheanism as a "neopagan religion": "La Religion de Nietzsche", *Revue des deux-mondes*, February 1, 1901, p. 587.

[15] Nietzsche, written in 1888; *Volonté*, vol. 2, p. 345. Cf. *Ecce Homo*, p. 177: "Have they understood me?—Dionysus before the Crucified."

has been Nietzsche's forte to add others, by appealing to man's instinctive will to be great.[16]

The facts testify that he has succeeded all too well. His influence today is worldwide. Neopaganism is the great spiritual phenomenon of our age. In spite of the horror and the vulgarity of the forms that it assumes in its dissemination, it continues to suck in noble souls, sometimes even Christian souls, whose blindness is frightening. For forty or fifty years now numbers of young men have been taking it into their heads that a "profound contempt for man" is the fitting apanage of "great souls";[17] many have taken to dreaming "heroic ecstasies" and thinking longingly of "the pride of the heroes of old"; many have made much the same reflections as Rainer Maria Rilke recorded after enthusiastically reading the new prophet:

> He whom men worship as the Messiah turns the whole world into an infirmary. He calls the weak, the unfortunate, the disabled his children and his loved ones. What about the strong? How are we ourselves to climb if we lend our strength to the unfortunate and the oppressed, to idle rogues with no wits and no energy? Let them fall, let them die, alone and wretched. Be hard, be terrible, be pitiless! You must thrust yourselves forward, forward! A few men, but great ones, will build a world with their strong, muscular, masterful arms on the corpses of the weak, the sick and the infirm![18]

Others, after having repeated the cry: "The gods are dead, long live the Overman!" celebrate the new Nietzschean ideal

---

[16] Cf. *Zarathoustra*, Betz. trans., appendix, no. 11, p. 302: "All my books up to today have been nets I have thrown: I was hoping to catch some men of profound, rich and exuberant souls."

[17] Cf. Gustave Thibon, *Destin de l'homme* (Paris: Desclée de Brouwer, 1942), p. 78.

[18] Rainer Maria Rilke, *Les Apôtres*, new ed. (1896). Quoted by Christiane Osann, *Rainer Maria Rilke, destinée d'un poète* (French trans. by Gnia Tchernosvitow [Neuchâtel: Delachaux & Niestlé, 1942]), p. 47. This early text does not represent Rilke's thinking in later years, however.

in terms that none can afford to ignore as a clue to some of the dominant facts of contemporary history:

> Nietzsche predicts an early return to the ideal, but to an entirely different and new ideal. To understand this ideal there will be a category of free minds, fortified by war, solitude and danger. They will know the wind, the glaciers, the Alpine snows; they will be able to plumb the deepest gulfs without wavering. Endowed with a kind of sublime perversity, they will deliver us from loving our neighbors and from the desire of nothingness, that the earth may recover its purpose and men their hopes.

In France itself, since the beginning of this century, the gospel of Zarathustra has found less wholesale but not less powerful echoes. The Nietzschean current mingled its waters with one of the branches of the great stream of positivism. Thus men like Hugues Rebell began to harry "that Christian spirit with which [he said] everything is infected today, including those who profess to be its enemies".[19] Men like Pierre Lasserre, author of an admiring work on *Le Morale de Nietzsche*, reproached Christianity with having turned suffering into a mystery and thus "made ugly the eyes of sufferers":

> Cruelty hunted down by the arrows of Apollo, Christian eyes fill with wrath, hatred and despair. . . . Suspicion and rancor have their abode in them. . . . If sometimes they seem to have at last found repose, if they meet yours with a calm, serene, ethereal look, beware! It is then that they express mischief of the most purposeful and arrogant kind. They want to persuade you that they have foiled the enemy for all time and that they are already fixed upon the first gleams of the Beyond. . . . The hatred I read in Christian eyes of this kind is something definite; it is the quintessence of Christian hatred of the earth. It is when they are gentlest that Christian eyes are shiftiest. . . . At bottom, is it not the last trick of incurables to set about loving their infirmity and exalting it?[20]

---

[19] Hugues Rebell, *Union des trois aristocraties*, p. 21.
[20] Pierre Lasserre, in *L'Action française*, vol. 5, p. 277.

A labored exercise in rhetoric, a clumsy imitation of the master by a disciple without genius? Granted. The effect of such writings was not negligible, however. But today we are up against something very different! Christianity is besieged on all sides, and the hearts of many of the baptized have already begun to yield. Stories of apostasy are going round. Drunkenness can make even the wisest stagger. . . .

2. The Spirit of Christianity

Nietzsche's feelings with regard to Jesus always remained mixed, and so did his judgments on Christianity. There are times when he sees in it not so much a *false* ideal as one that is *worn out*. "It is our stricter and more finely tempered piety", he says, "that stops us from still being Christians today."[21] Thus his animosity is against the Christians of our day, against *us*. The lash of his scorn is for our mediocrities and our hypocrisies. It searches out our weaknesses, adorned with fine names. In reminding us of the robust and joyous austerity of "primitive Christianity" he calls shame on our "present-day Christianity", as "mawkish and nebulous". Can it be contended that he is quite wrong? Should "everything that now goes by the name of Christian" be defended against him? When he says of us, for instance: "If they want me to believe in their Savior, they'll have to sing me better hymns! His followers will have to look more like men who have been saved!"[22]—are we entitled to be indignant? To how many of us does Christianity really seem "something big, something growing, to which we can give ourselves up completely with joy and enthusiasm"?[23] Do the unbelievers who jostle us at every turn observe on our brows the radiance of that gladness which, twenty centuries ago, captivated the

---

[21] Nietzsche, *Zarathoustra*, Betz trans., appendix, no. 165, p. 326.

[22] Ibid., p. 99.

[23] Msgr. Bruno de Solages, *Pour rebâtir une chrétienté*, p. 245.

fine flower of the pagan world? Are our hearts the hearts of men risen with Christ? Do we, in our time, bear witness to the Beatitudes? In a word, while we are fully alive to the blasphemy in Nietzsche's terrible phrase and in its whole context, are we not also forced to see in ourselves something of what drove him to such blasphemy?

That is the tragedy of the present situation. However things may have been in the past (we are told), the Christianity of today, *your* Christianity, is the enemy of Life, because it is itself no longer alive. "I can see", Jacques Rivière wrote, as far back as 1907, in a letter to Paul Claudel, "that Christianity is dying. . . . People don't know why our towns are still surmounted by those spires, which are no longer the prayers of any of us; they don't know what is the point of those great buildings, which are now hemmed in by railway stations and hospitals and from which the people themselves have expelled the monks; they don't know why the graveyards display pretentious stucco crosses of execrable design."[24] And Claudel's answer to that cry of anguish was undoubtedly a good one: "Truth is not concerned with how many people it convinces." But if those who have remained faithful to truth have apparently no "virtue", that is to say, no inward strength, does not that seem to justify the surrender of the others? The grounds for thinking so are, indeed, often strong enough to command our assent. It is a matter of almost daily experience that some of the harshest reproaches leveled against us come both from our worst enemies and from men of good will. The tone, the intention and the underlying inspiration are different, but (surprising yet significant convergence!) the judgments are, in the last analysis, the same. Among the best of those whom we thus disappoint, some

---

[24] Jacques Rivière, letter to Paul Claudel, March 17, 1907. *Correspondance de Jacques Rivière et de Paul Claudel*, p. 15. Cf. to Alain-Fournier, Easter 1907: "This morning's Mass, dreadfully bungled, without grandeur, without desire, disgusted me. Everything was ugly, and I felt so keenly that no one was understanding anything any more." Jacques Rivière and Alain-Fournier, *Correspondance*, vol. 3, p. 93.

of the most clearsighted and the most spiritual find themselves caught between two conflicting sentiments: they are strongly attracted by the Gospel, whose teaching seems to them full of strength and freshness still; they are drawn toward the Church, which, giving them a sense of superhuman reality, impresses them as the only institution capable of providing both the remedy for our ills and a solution of the problem of our destiny. But on the threshold they pause, repelled by the spectacle that we present—we, the Christians of today, "the Church which we form". They are moved to think and "to say that what still remains of the Gospel ideal in the world survives outside our camps".[25] Not that they necessarily condemn us; it is rather that they cannot take us seriously. Does history condemn Romulus Augustulus for not having given fresh impetus to the work of Caesar or Augustus? It merely notes that in that last heir to the Empire the sap had dried up. . . . In the eyes of a number of our contemporaries it is the same with us and the Church we represent. Their sentiments are comprised of an admiration mixed with scorn.

Hence the temptation that lies in wait for some Christians today. While too many continue to grow more inert, daily adding to their blasphemy of the Savior to whom they still pay lip service, though understanding him less and less; while pious circles, "edifying" circles, so often reveal such a mediocre level of culture and spiritual life; there are in the Church men who see, who hear, who reflect. There are Christians who refuse to protect their faith with a rampart of illusions. "Yes," they say, "it is only too true. Taken as a whole, our Christianity has become insipid. Despite so many grand endeavors to restore life and freshness to it, it is humdrum, listless, sclerotic. It is lapsing into formalism and routine. As we practice it, and as, in the first place, we think of it, it is a feeble, unavailing religion; a religion of ceremonies and observances, of ornaments and trivial solaces, with no depth of seriousness, no real hold

---

[25] Msgr. de Solages, p. 238.

upon human activities—sometimes with no sincerity, either. A religion outside life, or one through which we ourselves lose touch with life. That is what we have made of the Gospel, of that immense hope that had dawned upon the world! Is there any trace left of the breath of that spirit which was to recreate all things and revolutionize the face of the earth? Do not many of us today make profession of Catholicism from the same considerations of comfortableness and social conformism that, twenty centuries ago, would have prompted rejection of the Glad Tidings as a disturbing innovation? And what is to be said of that alternation, or rather that mixture, of politics and 'piety', in which religion is hard put to find a place? Though of a different nature, the evil is just as serious among the most 'practicing' Catholics as among the worldly. The most virtuous themselves are not always the least affected. Are not impatience of all criticism, incapacity for any reform, fear of intelligence —are not these manifest signs? Clerical Christianity, formalist Christianity, quenched and hardened Christianity. . . . The great current of Life, whose flow is never checked, seems to have deposited it some time ago, high and dry upon the bank. . . ."

It is at this stage of their reflections, when courageous lucidity begins to give place to satirical distortion, that temptation creeps in. Temptation to look covertly (the prophets' reproach of old) toward the new paganism, in order to lay hold upon some of that strength and life with which it seems haloed. Insensibly the reproaches leveled against *our* Christianity are transformed into a criticism of Christianity itself. After having denounced the negative fashion in which we often practice the Christian virtues, the next step is an arraignment of the "negative virtues" that make up the Christian. The satirizing of the false Christian who, being "neither of nature nor of grace", is a diminished being, finishes by joining forces with the Nietzschean satire of the genuine Christian in the grips of "hemiplegia". In the name of moral health, heroism or virility, it is the Cross itself that, in the end, comes in for attack, it is "the figure of the Crucified" that is rejected. There is a strange concordance between the utterances that fall from the lips of certain young Christians, when moved to painful confidences or sudden outbursts, and the gallery of caricatures in, for instance, Raymond de Becker's *Livre des vivants et des morts*.[26] In the end, this may be apostasy once more. Such cases are not unknown. They exhibit, in an advanced state, a tendency that, in a mild form, is already widespread.

There is no point in shutting one's eyes to the causes of this deep-seated trouble. Stubbornness in one's own shortcomings is no more excusable than refusal to see the good in one's adversary. An attitude of that sort bears only a false resemblance to intrepidity of faith. The faithful soul is always an open soul. On the other hand, it would be no less fatal to lose any of our confidence in the resources of our Christian heritage and to go in search of a remedy from outside. If we wish to regain a strong Christianity (that "galvanic Christianity", as it has been aptly called), our first care should be to save it from deviating —as it now threatens to do—toward a "power" Christianity. Otherwise the expected cure will be merely an aggravation of the disease. If the pursuit of a "power" Christianity were not a betrayal, it would at the very least be a reaction of weakness.[27]

---

[26] Raymond de Becker, *Livre des vivants et des morts*; see, for example, pp. 52–54 and 154. If we descend yet another degree, here is what we can read in a very recent work: "An idea is true when it is forcefully affirmed. . . . A system is true in the mouth of a genius and false, a few centuries later, in the mouth of the common people. Uttered by the mouth of Christ, Christianity is true, without any doubt. But who would dare maintain that it is true, uttered twenty centuries later by the mouth of one of his so-called disciples? The man closest to Christ in the future will be the one who throws Christianity to the ground. . . . How could the Church survive, since the Spirit is leaving her? This retraction, this disgust of the noble, it is the arrow of death in her side."

[27] One could read recently, in an excellent religious journal, this review of a men's retreat that had just taken place: "Retreat devoted to the search for a forceful mysticism, drawn from our Christian and French heritage." The subject was undoubtedly too naïve not to be inoffensive. But it expresses a ten-

For, is it not obvious that, wishing despite everything to remain Christian, we should never be able to set up more than a pale imitation of the ideal of Force that goes on its way triumphant? We should then be doubly conquered in advance. Instead of giving Christianity a new value, as was intended, we should have weakened it by adulteration. What needs to be done is something quite different. Christianity must be given back its strength in *us*, which means, first and foremost, that we must rediscover it as it is in itself, in its purity and its authenticity. In the last analysis, what is needed is not a Christianity that is more virile, or more efficacious, or more heroic, or stronger; it is that we should live our Christianity with more virility, more efficacy, more strength, and, if necessary, more heroism —but we must live it as it is. There is nothing that should be changed in it, nothing that should be corrected, nothing that should be added (which does not mean, however, that there is not a continual need to keep its channels from silting up); it is not a case of adapting it to the fashion of the day. It must come into its own again in our souls. We must give our souls back to it.

The question, be it repeated, is a spiritual one, and the solution is always the same: insofar as we have allowed it to be lost, we must rediscover the *spirit* of Christianity. In order to do so we must be plunged once more in its wellsprings, and above all in the Gospel. The Gospel that the Church unvaryingly offers us is enough for us.[28] Only, always new, it always needs to be rediscovered. The best among those who criticize us are sometimes better able to appreciate it than we are. They do not blame it for its supposed weaknesses: they blame *us* for not making the most of its strength. Can we grasp the lesson?

---

dency, a distortion observable today on all sides, distortions that are not always equally inoffensive.

[28] We well know that the Gospel is not a political treatise, and a moral code, properly speaking, is not to be sought there. But from it alone we will receive our final inspiration in everything, to it alone, without any kind of alteration, we will surrender our souls.

Lord, if the world is seduced by so much enchantment, if there is such an aggressive return of paganism today, it is because we have let the salt of your doctrine lose its savor. Lord, today as yesterday and as at all times, there is no salvation except in you —and who are we that we should dare to discuss or revise thy teachings? Lord, keep us from such delusions and restore to us, if need be, not only a submissive faith but an ardent respect for your Gospel!

Christianity, if we would go straight to the heart of it, is the religion of love. "God is love," says the Apostle John, "and he who abides in love abides in God and God in him."[29] Every advance in awareness of our faith should increase our comprehension of this. There must, of course, be no misconception of the conditions of that love and of its natural foundations, especially of that justice without which it is only a false love— that justice which today is no less scoffed at than love itself. We must beware of clumsy or subtle counterfeits, of which there are so many today, as well as of over-simple recipes. But, when all is said and done, everything is for love. It is the absolute to which everything orders itself, in relation to which everything should be judged. But, now by violent assaults, now in a thousand more subtle ways, attempts are being made to rob it of that primacy. The prestige of strength insinuates itself even into Christian hearts, driving out or at any rate lessening their esteem for love. Against these assaults, may the Holy Spirit impart to us the gift of strength! But against more insidious attacks, may that Spirit impart to us the gift of wisdom, that we may understand in what the strength of Christianity consists.[30] It is not something to be set up beside or in opposition to love, as an adversary: it is to be fostered in the service of love.

---

[29] 1 Jn 4:16.

[30] Cf. the prayer *super populum* of Thursday in the first week of Lent: "Da, quæsumus, Domine, populis christianis . . . *quæ profitentur agnoscere*. . . ." On true Christian heroism, see the accurate reflections of Charles Du Bos, *Approximations*, sixth series (Paris: Correa, 1934), pp. 352–54.

In the present state of the world, a virile, strong Christianity must become a heroic Christianity. But this adjective is a description, it must not be a definition, in which case it would be a falsification. Above all, this heroism will certainly not consist in constantly talking of heroism and raving about the virtue of strength—which would perhaps prove that one is under the influence of someone stronger and that one has begun to give up. It will consist, *above all*, in resisting with courage, in face of the world and perhaps against one's own self, the lures and seductions of a false ideal and in proudly maintaining, in their paradoxical intransigence, the Christian values that are threatened and derided. Maintaining them with humble pride. For, if Christianity can and should assume the virtues of ancient paganism, the Christian who would remain faithful is bound to reject with a categorical No a neopaganism that has set itself up against Christ. Gentleness and goodness, considerateness toward the lowly, pity for those who suffer, rejection of perverse methods, protection of the oppressed, unostentatious self-sacrifice, resistance to lies, the courage to call evil by its proper name, love of justice, the spirit of peace and concord, open-heartedness, mindfulness of heaven; those are the things that Christian heroism will rescue. All this so-called "slave morality" will be shown to be a morality of free men and the sole source of man's freedom.

Christians have not been promised that they will always be in the majority. (Rather the reverse.) Nor that they will always seem the strongest and that men will never be conquered by another ideal than theirs. But, whatever happens, Christianity will never have any real efficacy, it will never have any real existence or make any real conquests, except by the strength of its own spirit, *by the strength of charity*.

PART TWO

AUGUSTE COMTE
AND CHRISTIANITY

LIST OF COMTE'S WORKS REFERRED TO IN THIS PART, WITH THE ABBREVIATIONS USED

Appel aux conservateurs
   (Paris: Dalmont, 1855) . . . .   *Appel*
Catéchisme positiviste (Paris, 1842) . . . . . .   *Catéch.*
Circulaires annuelles . . . .   *Circ.*
Correspondance inédite (Paris: 1903–1904) . . .   *Inéd.*
Cours de philosophie positive
   (2d ed., Paris: Baillière, 1864) . . . . . .   *Cours*
Discours sur l'esprit positif
   (Paris: Dalmont, 1844) . . . .   *Disc.*
Lettres à Henri Dix Hutton . . . .   *Hutton*
Lettres d'Auguste Comte à divers . . . .   *Div.*
Lettres d'Auguste Comte à M. Valat
   (Paris: Dunot, 1870) . . . .   *Val.*
Lettres d'Auguste Comte à Stuart Mill
   (Paris: E. Leroux, 1877) . . . .   *Mill*
Lettres inédites à C. de Blignières
   (Paris: Vrin, 1932) . . . .   *Blign.*
Nouvelles lettres inédites . . . .   *Nouv.*
Opuscules de philosophie sociale, 1819–1828
   (Paris: Leroux, 1883) . . . .   *Opusc.*
Synthèse subjective (Paris: Dalmont, 1856) . . .   *Synthèse*
Système de politique positive
   (Paris: Vrin, 1929) . . . .   *Polit.*
Testament d'Auguste Comte (Paris, 1896) . . . .   *Test.*

In 1842 AUGUSTE COMTE completed the publication of his vast *Cours de philosophie positive*. It was the very year in which Ludwig Feuerbach published *Das Wesen des Christentums*. This coincidence of dates emphasizes the convergence of the two designs. Shortly afterward Emile Saisset wrote: "Herr Feuerbach in Berlin, like Monsieur Comte in Paris, offers Christian Europe a new god to worship—the human race."[1] We have seen the success that Karl Marx was to secure for his master's humanism by founding the communist movement upon it. Positivism was destined to score as great a success, though by different means. Neither the *Cours* nor Comte's later writings won their author the enthusiastic adherence of the intellectual youth of the day. At the time of his death, the church he had founded and of which he had been the first high priest numbered but a small handful of believers, already threatened with schism. Yet at the end of the nineteenth century it could be said that "the positive spirit", which he had done more than anyone else to isolate and define, was "so closely interfused with the general thought" of the age that it had become almost unnoticeable, "like the air one breathes".[2] A number of coteries, varying in character but all equally active, professed a Comtian orthodoxy that in some cases was as strict as Marxist orthodoxy. If complete positivism remained more or less esoteric, this did not detract from its potency; and even today there are many whom it still inspires with intense faith and fervor.

---

[1] Émile Saisset, "Les Écoles philosophiques en France", in *Revue des deux-mondes*, August 1, 1850, p. 681. The same comparison in Dühring (Grüber, *Le Positivisme depuis Comte jusqu'à nos jours* [French trans. by Mazoyer, 1893], pp. 371–72) and in Edward Caird, *La Philosophie sociale et religieuse d'Auguste Comte* (French trans. of *The Social Philosophy and Religion of Comte* [Glasgow: J. Maclehose & Sons, 1885; reprint: New York: Kraus, 1968]), p. 96. Cf. Friedrich Albert Lange, *Histoire du matérialisme* (French trans. of *Geschichte des Materialismus*), vol. 2, p. 89: "This theory [of Feuerbach] presents a remarkable analogy with that which the noble Comte sought to establish around the same time in Paris."

[2] Lucien Lévy-Brühl, "Le Centenaire d'Auguste Comte", in *Revue des deux-mondes*, January 15, 1898, p. 398.

Positivism comes forward as one of the three or four systems that offer mankind a blueprint of a way of life claiming to answer all its needs. Like the others, but more than the others, positivism does not propose to be "critical" and destructive but "organic": that is, indeed, the principal meaning it attaches to the word "positive".[3] Like the others, it aspires to replace Christianity in Europe, in order to set the whole world upon a new course. Like the others, it proposes to strengthen its foundations by first of all revolutionizing thought: to find, as Comte says, a "mental coherence" that will ensure a final "social cohesion". The spiritual reorganization of the West, "the only possible basis of temporal regeneration", is the first of its objectives.[4] To anyone observing the great spiritual currents of our age from a certain altitude, positivism will seem less the antagonist than the ally of the Marxist and Nietzschean currents. By other methods, in another spirit and in competition with them, it strives for the same essential object. Like them, it is one of the ways in which modern man seeks to escape from any kind of transcendency and to shake off the thing it regards as an unbearable yoke—namely, faith in God. "To discover a man with no trace of God in him" is how Mr. Henri Gouhier defines Auguste Comte's self-appointed task.[5] Just what this

---

[3] *Disc.*, p. 51. *Polit.* vol. 1, p. 57.

[4] *Synthèse*, p. 2. *Polit.*, vol. 1, p. 2 ("Discours sur l'ensemble du positivisme"): "A real systematization of all human thoughts constitutes, therefore, our first social need." *Appel*, p. XIX: "The spiritual reorganization of Occidentalism." *Circ.*, p. 22. *Disc.*, p. 65: "The final reorganization, which must at first be at work in ideas in order to pass then to customs and, in the final place, to institutions." *Val.*, December 25, 1824: "I regard all the discussions on institutions to be pure rubbish until the spiritual reorganization of society is effectuated, or at least greatly advanced." *Plan des travaux scientifiques nécessaires pour réorganiser la société, May 1822*: "Spiritual anarchy has preceded and engendered temporal anarchy . . ." (p. 88). To Barbot de Chement, September 13, 1846: It is necessary first "to regenerate opinions, then customs or feelings, finally institutions or acts": *Nouv.*, p. 52.

[5] Henri Gouhier, *Le Jeunesse d'Auguste Comte et la formation du positivisme* (Paris: Vrin, 1933–41), vol. 1, p. 23.

Comtian atheism stands for, what attitude it engenders toward the Catholic religion and by what transpositions it gives the positive doctrine a religious character, the present study proposes to show. While necessarily leaving certain phases of Comtism out of account, this limited aim should enable prominence to be given to some of its most important aspects, of particular interest at the present time.

CHAPTER I

THE MEANING OF COMTIAN ATHEISM

1. The Law of the Three States

Every undergraduate in France knows "the law of the three states". Comte was twenty-four years old when, in April 1822, he formulated it for the first time, in a paper he later referred to as his *opuscule fondamental*, and which, under the name of *Prospectus des travaux scientifiques nécessaires pour réorganiser la société*, was incorporated in a book published by his master, Saint-Simon.[1] Before very long—in November 1825—he took it up again, to give it more precision, in the *Considérations philosophiques sur les sciences et les savants*.[2] "From the very nature of the human mind," he said, "every branch of our knowledge has necessarily to pass through three successive theoretical states: the theological or fictitious state, the metaphysical or abstract state, and the scientific or positive state." Thus man "began by conceiving phenomena of all kinds as due to the direct and continuous influence of supernatural agents; later he came to regard them as having been produced by various abstract forces inherent in bodies but distinct and heterogeneous; in the end he confined himself to considering them as subject to a certain number of

---

[1] The volume was entitled: *Suite des travaux ayant pour objet de fonder le système industriel. Du contrat social.* Comte republished his paper in 1824, under the new title *Système de politique positive* in the *Catéchisme des Industriels, par Saint-Simon.* He was to reproduce it, along with other early papers, in the General Appendix to volume 4 of his *Système de politique positive* under the title *Plan des travaux scientifiques nécessaires pour réorganiser la société, May 1822.*

Several anticipatory expressions of the law are already found in the paper of April 1820, *Sommaire appréciation du passé moderne.*

[2] In the form of three articles published in *Le Producteur*, issues 7, 8 and 10.

invariable natural laws that are nothing but the general expression of the relations observed in their development." Such are the three great stages of human evolution that history reveals to us in connection with every science and that the examination of human nature leads us to postulate a priori as "inevitable" and "indispensable", both from the intellectual and from the moral and social points of view.

Within the initial stage, Comte distinguishes three influences that seem to him, in the first place, to sum up the whole history of religions: fetishism, polytheism and theism. In the metaphysical state he sees little more than an intermediate phase with no really original character, the mind linking facts together in accordance with ideas that are no longer wholly supernatural but not yet entirely natural; so that "metaphysical conceptions are related both to theology and to 'physics' (or natural science) or rather are merely theological conceptions modified by physics." He then shows the various kinds of phenomena leaving "the domain of theology and metaphysics", in order of increasing complexity, "and entering the physical domain": it is now the turn of the very last, the "moral phenomena" that are to form "social physics" (later Comte also used the term "sociology") "as positive as any other science based on observation", as scientific as celestial, terrestrial, vegetable or animal ologies. Thus the scientists will soon have gained "all the territory successively lost by the clergy", and they will then constitute "a new spiritual power".[3]

Resumed and developed in later works, especially in the *Cours de philosophie positive*,[4] this law of the "three general states of the human mind and of society" forms the framework into which Auguste Comte fits the whole of his doctrine. Not that

---

[3] Papers (*opuscules*) written in 1822 and 1825; in *Opusc.*, pp. 100–106, 172, 181–228. The following paper (1826), the so-called "decisive opuscule" (*Circ.*, p. 413) was in fact given the name "Considérations sur le pouvoir spirituel".

[4] *Cours*, lessons 1, 48, 51, 52, 58, 60 (vols. 1, 4, 5, 6), etc. *Disc.*, *Catéch.*, pp. 154–60. *Polit.*, pp. 3, 28ff., etc. *Cours*, vol. 4, p. VI, note.

he failed to make substantial amendments in it, bit by bit. He showed a growing tendency to consider the second state as one that was purely critical and to interpret it in a pejorative way, while increasingly exalting fetishism. Partly forsaking his original standpoint, which had been almost exclusively rational, he came to study human evolution more and more from the standpoint of sentiment, and this applies particularly to his value judgments; after having tried to "systematize speculative existence" and the "active existence" that corresponds to it, he undertook to systematize the affective life, then recognized as "the really preponderant element in all human existence", the one which "gives the others a continuous impulse and direction".[5]

Linking up religion above all with sentiment, he thus came to distinguish more and more clearly between "religion" and "theology"; without denying the law that relegates theology to a dead past, he rediscovered religion in his own way, so that, according to him, "the history of mankind can be represented, in a sense, as development from the primitive religion (fetishism) to the definitive religion (positivism)."[6] He even

---

[5] Cf. Léon de Montesquiou, *Le Système politique d'Auguste Comte* (Paris: Nouvelle Libraire Nationale), pp. 308-10: "It was in 1851 that Comte published his first volume of *Politique positive*, thus it was over a quarter of a century ago that he affirmed for the first time his law of three states. During this whole long period of time, his mind has been penetrated by this law, has been oriented according to it. He has built a monument on it, his whole course of *Philosophy*. Assuming that this law of evolution required some modifications in order to conform exactly to the fundamental concepts of the *Politique positive*, one can imagine that it had become impossible for Comte to effectuate them. His whole intellectual past weighed too heavily on his thought. So it must rather have impelled him to seek an explanation that permitted him to maintain his law while affirming the preponderance of feeling. . . ."

[6] Lucien Lévy-Brühl, *La Philosophie d'Auguste Comte* (Paris: Alcan, 1900), pp. 42-43. If it is thus a little excessive to say, with Mr. Lévy-Brühl (ibid.), that "it is not the object of the law of the three states to express the religious evolution of humanity"—since Comte himself was to write, a little before his death, that: "the principal application of this law must naturally concern reli-

came to assert the necessity for a kind of fourth state, in which the mind frees itself from science "as it freed itself from ontology and theology"; so that the scientific state, at any rate such as it is still conceived by too many scientists, should constitute "only a final transition into the truly positive state": so long as "scientific prestige survives the theological and metaphysical yoke," he said, "we are still unfit to direct the final reorganization."[7] But all this did not prevent the law of the three states from remaining for Comte, as long as he lived, "the fundamental law of intellectual evolution".[8] Right at the end of his life, he noted with satisfaction that his "thirty years of work" had "already secured the admission of this law by all thinkers really abreast of the times".[9] He made a point of claiming paternity, proudly calling it *his* law, *his* great law, and relating how he had suddenly *discovered* it after a night of intense thought and how he had henceforth found in it his "cerebral unity" and the fullness of "philosophic harmony".[10]

It has been said that this was an illusion on his part. Earlier writings have been cited. Saint-Simon, referring to the statements of Dr. Burdin, had distinguished in every science two successive states, conjectural and positive, and had predicted that ethics, politics and philosophy would become positive sci-

---

gion"—this is primarily a question of terminology. Comte immediately distinguished between religion as sentiment, which is unchangeable, and religion as conception, which is profoundly modifiable: *Div.*, vol. 1, p. 367. "If, as sentiment, religion is unchangeable and must simply develop itself continually, it is, insofar as conception, subject, in its nature, to the universal progress that regenerates the whole according to the parts." It therefore remains true that the law "concerns only the progress of human intellect. It sets forth the successive philosophies that this intelligence has been obliged by turn to adopt in the interpretation of natural phenomena. It is, in a word, the general law of the evolution of thought" (Lévy-Brühl, *Philosophie*, p. 43).

[7] *Div.*, vol. 2, p. 326 (to Ellis).

[8] *Polit.*, vol. 3, p. 28.

[9] *Div.*, vol. 2, p. 325.

[10] *Polit.*, vol. 3, p. 40; vol. 1, p. 33: "this great law, which already is no longer contested". *Cours*, vol. 5, p. 1; vol. 6, p. VIII.

ences; at a later date, in his *Système industriel*, he had even spoken of an "intermediate state" between "purely theological ideas" and "positive ideas".[11] Turgot, in the preface to his *Discours sur les progrès de l'esprit humain*, had clearly described the three phases through which the human mind passes in order to formulate the natural sciences.[12] Does this mean that, "combining Turgot's law with, and applying it to, the conceptions of Burdin" and of Saint-Simon, Comte had really contributed nothing new and that, "if the word Comtism, sometimes used as a synonym for positivism, came to oust the latter, there would be justification for saying that Turgot and Burdin are the Columbuses of a system of which Auguste Comte is the Amerigo Vespucci"?[13] That would be going too far. For the observations on which Saint-Simon enlarged were hardly more than ingenious ideas[14] thrown off in passing; as for Turgot, if he gave the law of the three states its first formulation, this was only for one category of phenomena, with no thought of extending it "to conceptions of a moral and social order" and, above all, with no thought of ever fettering the whole of our intellectual activity with the shackles of the positive state. That is what several disciples of Auguste Comte—Dr. Audiffrent, Dr. Robinet and E. Sémerie—rightly pointed out in opposition to Renouvier and Pillon.[15] They adduced this simple and incontestable proof: Turgot believed in God. What constitutes Comte's orig-

---

[11] Cf. *La Critique philosophique*, April 8 and 15, 1875, pp. 160 and 153. Burdin, too, formulates the trinary series: idolatry, polytheism, deism.

[12] Anne Robert Jacques Turgot, *Œuvres* (Paris: Belin, 1808–1811), vol. 2, pp. 294–98.

[13] *La Critique philosophique*, April 8, 1875, p. 160.

[14] This is not to deny the profound influence exercised by Saint-Simon on Comte, who owed him undoubtedly much more than he admitted, and perhaps a little more than Henri Gouhier says.

[15] Georges Audiffrent, *Du cerveau et de l'innervation d'après Auguste Comte* (Paris: Dunod, 1869), p. 63. Jean François Robinet, "Lettre à M. le Directeur de la Critique philosophique", in *La Critique philosophique*, July 15, 1875, pp. 373–74. Eugène Sémerie, *La Loi des trois états, réponse à M. Renouvier* (1875).

inality in this connection is precisely that he makes the three
states a universal rule, thus providing positivism with its basis
both as method and as doctrine: it is the constitution of a vast
synthesis that crystallizes into one single formula a philosophy
embracing "nature, history and the mind."[16]

But is this a matter for congratulation? If criticism has sometimes shown itself rather small-minded in contesting the originality of Comte's achievement, it is fully within its rights in
questioning its value. Comte's mind, no sooner formed than
fixed, left out of his survey many series of facts, already known
at that time, which would have forced him to abate the rigor
of his law: he himself recognizes it in his own fashion, with
an easy artlessness[17]—and if he rejects "too detailed investigations", if he criticizes the "puerile and unseasonable display of
a barren and undigested erudition which in these days tends to
hamper the study of our social evolution",[18] it is for a reason.

Again, where Comte saw three successive states, it is actually
a case of "three coexistent modes of thought", corresponding
to three different aspects of things; thus progress consists in
an increasingly clear distinction between these three aspects,
at first perceived in a kind of chaotic unity. If, then, it is true
to say that "physics" (in the sense of the whole of science)
began by being theological, it would be just as true to say that
theology began by being physical, and the law of evolution

---

[16] Gouhier, vol. 3, p. 400. With his intuition of 1822, Mr. Gouhier also
says, p. 395, "Comte sees a reunion, despite the distances, between the intuition of Condorcet and the program of the École Polytechnique, the industrial
conception of history and the opposition of the law to the cause, generalized
relativity and the regeneration of the West." Cf. Jean Lacroix, *Vocation personnelle et tradition nationale* (Paris: Bloud & Gay, 1942), p. 59: "When all is said
and done, the law of the three states is less a historical law than a theory of
knowledge."

[17] *Cours*, vol. 4, p. 245: "No law of social succession, even when indicated
with all the authority possible by the historical method, should be finally admitted except after having been rationally connected, directly or indirectly,
with the positive theory of human nature."

[18] *Cours*, vol. 6, p. 638, etc. Cf. below, chap. 3, pp. 232–33.

does not tend to expel theology any more than science, but to "purify" both by differentiating them.[19]

Finally, the generalization of the law of the three states—that generalization which gives Comte his principal claim to originality and which, in the eyes of his disciples, is his glory—seems to me, rather, to mark the essential defect in his thought. Not that he should be blamed for having extended the positivist method to human facts in order to constitute a social science. But his offense lies in trying to reduce the whole knowledge of man to such a science; in other words, having wished to reduce man to no more than the subject matter of sociology.[20] Emile Durkheim found that admirable: he celebrated the victory that Saint-Simon and Comte had won in breaking down the "obstinate resistances" of the human mind to submission to science

---

[19] Robert Flint, *Le Philosophie de l'histoire en France et en Allemagne* (French trans. by Carran [1878] of *The Philosophy of History in France and Germany* [Edinburgh, London: Blackwood, 1874]). The "theological state" would thus be the state of primitive confusion in which a science and a religion are found in infancy. These views have been taken up and renewed by Jacques Maritain, distinguishing the "nocturnal" state and the "solar" state of science and religion: "Signe et symbole", in *Revue thomiste*, 1938. Note the law that the young Ernest Renan opposed, in 1845, to that of Comte: "In his infancy, man and humanity does not conceive of the law of nature. . . . He sees everywhere a supernatural action, God everywhere. In his second state, he observes the law through observation and induction, then he drives God out of the world, for he believes he no longer has need of him; from there, we have atheist philosophy. . . . In his third state, he preserves the result acquired in the second, which is true; only he connects the laws themselves to God, the universal cause and true effector. From there, we have true, complete science. . . . Instinct sees God everywhere and sees him nowhere; observation sees the law everywhere (hence its mocking, proud tone) and God nowhere. True philosophy sees God everywhere, acting freely through invariable laws because they are perfect": *Cahiers de jeunesse* (Paris: Calmann-Lévy, 1906), pp. 37–40. An outline of the theory that would soon be set forth in *L'Avenir de la science.*

[20] In other words, Comte is not wrong to say that positive philosophy must embrace all orders of phenomena (*Cours*, vol. 1, pp. 10–12)—social phenomena as well as the others—but to claim that the knowledge man has of himself must be reduced to a science of these social phenomena.

on the same terms as other objects, in resolutely freeing themselves from the prejudice that leads us "to place ourselves on a different footing from things" and "to claim a special place in the universe". In doing so, he said, they achieved not only "one of the most important conquests made by science" but "one of those that have done most toward giving the mind a new orientation. Is not to think scientifically to think objectively, that is to say, to strip our ideas of what is exclusively human in them, in order to make them as adequate as possible in the expression of things? Is it not, in short, to make the human understanding bow before things?"[21] Here we have the first part of that famous and ambiguous principle "submission to the object", with its practical corollary of "realism", which has, of course, been so misused by other disciples of Comte. Can the mind be reduced to its object? Is not the mere fact that the mind *thinks* the object—and does so as objectively as it can—sufficient indication that something in it overflows, and always will overflow, any "object" whatsoever? Auguste Comte not merely fails to solve the problem that the mind has become to itself by the mere fact that it knows objectively and that it constitutes positive science, even if this positive science is that of the human mind: he is not even aware of the problem.[22]

The law of the three states, as he systematized and turned it to account, nevertheless presupposed great power of cerebral organization, and he had a right to show pride in it. In any case, his pride was also modesty. For, in presenting his "new philosophy of history", he did not claim to be giving the world an original system. He only wanted to be the interpreter of the age into which he had been born. His whole ambition was limited to describing in broad outline "the evolution of man"

---

[21] *Le Socialisme*, pp. 149 and 161.

[22] A similar criticism in a different form by Charles Renouvier: "La Loi des trois états", in *La Critique philosophique*, March 11, 1875 (particularly pp. 82–83).

and to defining clearly the state that had been brought about by that evolution,[23] in order to pave the way for the future.

2. The Monotheistic Transition

So the positive age had arrived: it was a fact that had to be duly noted. Whatever still remained from earlier ages was only a survival. "The deplorable state of arrested development in which social science still languished" was itself destined to come to an end, at any rate in a few choice brains. That science was not doomed to remain indefinitely, "as a disastrous exception", in the theologico-metaphysical state in which even eminent minds were still keeping it. The day was approaching when, in everything, "theology would necessarily die out as physics advanced."[24] It was toward the end of the Middle Ages that the decisive crisis in the history of mankind had arisen in the West. Since then "the positive spirit, making more progress in two centuries than it had been able to do in the whole length of its previous career, had left no possibility for any other mental unity than that resulting from its own universal ascendancy."[25] Thus any serious attempt at the "social reorganization" that would clear the way out of the horrible anarchy ensuing from the revolution of 1789 must be made "without theological intervention".

Comte has a ceaseless flow of sarcasm to lavish upon "the reactionary doctrine that, in truly ridiculous fashion, ventures to recommend today, as the only possible solution for the present intellectual anarchy, so fantastic an expedient as the social reestablishment of those same futile principles whose inevitable decrepitude was the original cause of that anarchy."[26]

---

[23] *Cours*, vol. 5, p. 157.
[24] *Cours*, vol. 4, p. 108.
[25] *Disc.*, p. 58.
[26] *Cours*, vol. 4, p. 42, note, and p. 62.

Today, he repeatedly declares, Catholicism is rotten to the core, all theologism is "outmoded",[27] and everything that comes from it is now in a state of hopeless decrepitude: things have reached such a pass that even the most illustrious exponents of this way of thinking have long ceased to understand it, and those who would fain resuscitate it with the aid of a "reactionary policy" are, despite their "ineffectual moral pretensions", doomed to "hypocrisy".[28] Those who, in this age, think that certain signs of a "recrudescence of theology" are to be noted need not be anxious: there is "nothing of real religious conviction in it, but only a further manifestation of vulgar and ridiculous Machiavellianism, based on the vague social necessity claimed for such a mental regime"—and "the more that systematic hypocrisy spreads, the less consistency it retains."[29]

There was no doubt about it, then; the "great organic func-

---

[27] *Inéd.*, vol. 3, p. 96 (to Mr. de Tholouze, 25 Charlemagne 62). To Miss Henriette Martineau, April 6, 1854: "Without maintaining any more the existence, long since fictitious, of Christianity and Islamism, hopelessly outmoded" (in Émile Littré, *Auguste Comte et la philosophie positive* [Paris: Hachette, 1863], p. 643). *Cours*, vol. 4, p. 53. *Polit.*, vol. 2, p. 129; vol. 3, pp. 511 and 518, etc.

[28] *Cours*, vol. 4, pp. 17, 19, 89. *Polit.*, vol. 4, p. 541 ("degrading hypocrisy"). *Div.*, vol. 1, p. 79 ("theological hypocrisy"). *Circ.*, p. 9: "system of hypocrisy"; p. 54: "theological hypocrisy, as degrading when one exercises it as oppressive when one suffers it"; p. 95: "in a century in which the need to construct imposes on all the sceptics the most degrading hypocrisy"; etc.

[29] *Div.*, vol. 1:2, pp. 386. *Cours*, vol. 4, p. 76: "With respect to reactionary politics, the special kind of corruption that belongs to it consists in the systematic hypocrisy of which it has had so great a need since that decomposition of the Catholic-feudal regime became deep enough so as no longer to include, in most educated minds, anything but weak and incomplete convictions. From the beginning of the revolutionary period, in the sixteenth century, this system of increasingly elaborate hypocrisy could be seen to develop, principally in the religious order, which easily consented, in a more or less explicit way, to the real emancipation of all minds of a certain capacity, on the sole, at least tacit, condition of helping to prolong the submission of the masses: this was eminently the policy of the Jesuits. . . ." And, in a note: "This theological Machiavellianism was to be radically ruined when the spread of the philosophical

tion previously performed by theology had now devolved upon positive science. If the latter had sometimes had a disintegrating effect, it was because it had not then been systematized. This had been done now. . . ." Having founded "sociology", having placed it at the apex of his classification of the sciences, Comte had completed the edifice.[30] Without being rash, he could forecast the decisive events that would follow. The day of fulfillment was at hand. "When the generation of transmission had come to an end", a ceremony would "finally inaugurate the new religious regime", and he hoped to live long enough to preside over it.[31] He became still more explicit. "I am convinced", he wrote to Mr. de Tholouze, "that before the year 1860 I shall be preaching positivism at Notre Dame as the only real and complete religion."[32] That letter is dated 23rd Archimedes 63, that is to say, for us laymen, April 22, 1851! Such are the calculations of the positive mind.

Since the principal tendency of this positive mind was to "substitute the relative for the absolute in all cases",[33] it was possible for Comte to understand and justify the preceding states. He knew that "everything that develops spontaneously is necessarily legitimate for a certain time",[34] that each stage of human progress has played an indispensable part and could not have been skipped. Far from copying "the ingratitude of Catholicism to its Graeco-Roman forebears", he regarded

---

movement finally obliged it, as we see today, to extend such a privilege gradually to all active minds. This has resulted, in fact, in that kind of reciprocally universal mystification in which, even in the less educated classes, each recognizes religion as indispensable for others but superfluous for himself. At bottom, this is the strange, definitive effect of three centuries of a laborious resistance to the fundamental movement of the human reason!"

[30] *Circ.*, p. 55.

[31] *Div.*, vol. 1:2, pp. 27 and 102.

[32] *Inéd.*, vol. 3, p. 101.

[33] *Disc.*, p. 53.

[34] *Opusc.*, p. 240; fifth opuscule, March 1826: "Considérations sur le pouvoir spirituel".

"Saint Augustine's reproaches against the whole system of polytheism and Voltaire's recriminations against Catholicism" as equally "frivolous".[35] "The encyclopaedists of the last century, kept by metaphysics to the purely individual point of view and thus incapable of any feeling for history, had seriously attributed theological beliefs to unbelieving legislators, who were supposed to have forged them in order to secure dominance." That superficial explanation was rejected by Comte as by all thinkers of his day. Able to "bring everything into harmony without making any concessions", positivism showed that the old religions "were spontaneous institutions by which mankind, during its infancy, created imaginary guides, because the dominating species could not find any in the real order".[36] A still deeper need called them forth. If "man everywhere began with the crassest fetishism", if he later invented all his gods, it was because "without theological principles our intelligence could never have emerged from its initial torpor"; it would have gone round and round forever "in a radically vicious circle". Thus the first of the three states was, "to begin with, indispensable from every point of view", although "purely temporary and preparatory".[37]

In theory Comte had the same ideas about the following state, which, when its turn came, played an equally indispensable part in the transition to positivity. But in practice he always preferred the first of the two. For the part played by the second was an unattractive one, its age was the awkward age of mankind. Whereas the theological spirit is, in its way, organic, the metaphysical spirit proves incapable of "ever organizing anything of its own", from the mental, let alone from the social, standpoint; it is not "spontaneously capable of anything but a merely *critical* or disintegrating activity" (the equivalence

---

[35] *Polit.*, vol. 4, p. 15; vol. 2, p. 362. *Catéch.*, p. 344. *Cours*, vol. 5, p. 28, note.

[36] *Div.*, vol. 1:2, p. 333.

[37] *Cours*, vol. 5, p. 17; vol. 4, p. 351. *Disc.*, pp. 6 and 10. *Polit.*, vol. 2, p. 80.

of these two epithets in Comte's language may be noted in passing). "Radically inconsistent, this ambiguous spirit retains all the fundamental principles of the theological system, while increasingly depriving them of that vigor and stability that are indispensable to their effectual authority." It has no real unity. It is only a "variable mixture of two kinds of ideas that are radically antagonistic, the second being, in fact, a mere denial of the first, with no new dogma of its own".[38] Thus it is all askew. "Metaphysics is, at bottom, only a kind of theology that has been gradually devitalized by the solvent action of simplifications." If, in spite of everything, it helps the flowering of civilization, it does so only in a negative and transitory fashion, encouraging the decomposition of the preceding regime, when the latter "has inevitably arrived at such a point of over-prolongation that it tends to perpetuate indefinitely the state of childhood that it had at first directed so successfully"; and the progress then achieved is due, in reality, to the secret action of nascent positivity.[39] Thus, whereas this first regime had "long been a progressive one for the whole evolution of man", giving proof of a wonderful creative fertility, metaphysics, on the contrary, develops more as a parasite than anything else and may very soon become "the most dangerous obstacle to the final establishment of a true philosophy".[40] "Always inspired by pride", it can never "lead to anything but doubt".[41] In the *Prospectus* of 1822, Comte had already pointed out "a shade of bastard theology" in metaphysics; later, without going so far as to deny the necessity for it, he spoke of it chiefly as an evil —is not evil itself sometimes forced to contribute to good?—

---

[38] *Cours*, vol. 4, p. 7.

[39] *Polit.*, vol. 3, p. 39. Certain phenomena are rather simple, in fact, in order to escape "spontaneously" from the beginning "the reign of causes" (vol. 3, p. 127). It is this "minimum of positivity, acting from the beginning, that slowly eats away all theological explanations": Lacroix, p. 67.

[40] *Disc.*, pp. 14–17; 64: "Critical passions" are always detestable, while the opposite passions are so only when they become "reactionary".

[41] *Polit.*, vol. 2, p. 130.

he wished its reign to be regarded as "a kind of chronic transitional malady",[42] and, in his writings, the Western transition which it constituted became, for the most part, an "immense malady", the "Western malady".[43]

In the succession of different phases, monotheism is itself intermediate, between the theological state and the metaphysical state. On the one hand, it contributes no new principle, "never being anything more than a reduced and concentrated polytheism"; thus, in a simpler form, it preserves all the fantastic elements of theology: "monotheistic concentration"[44] has changed neither the nature of divinity nor the mechanism of the conceptions that brought it to birth in the human consciousness; the one god is still made of the same stuff as the gods of polytheism; he is required to supply an answer to the same problems: the dogma of Providence is still nothing but "the earlier dogma of fate, gradually transformed". On the other hand, it is only under "the growing influence of the metaphysical spirit"[45] that this transformation is possible, thanks to a critical activity that tends to push abstraction to greater and greater lengths. That is why monotheism is late in making its appearance. It "always presupposes a long succession of philosophical meditations—and that is something that can only happen in a theoretical corporation."[46] The example of peoples like the Jews or the Moslems should not lead us astray: for these people are, in a sense, exceptions, having "prematurely arrived at an abortive monotheism before having duly completed the various social preparations indispensable to the efficacy of such

---

[42] *Cours*, vol. 5, p. 147.

[43] *Polit.*, vol. 3, p. XXIX, "a kind of chronic alienation". *Circ.*, pp. 16, 57, 93, etc.

[44] *Polit.*, vol. 3, p. 241. *Appel*, pp. 21 and 60. Cf. Jules Soury, *Essais de critique religieuse* (1878), p. 262: "Monotheism is only a more refined form of polytheism, an abstraction of abstractions, a quintessence of subtle essences, a voids of voids."

[45] *Cours*, vol. 5, pp. 148–49.

[46] *Polit.*, vol. 3, p. 241.

a transformation". For the rest, the "Hebraic initiative" in itself, if closely examined, will be found to conform to the laws of general evolution. "The exceptional monotheism that distinguishes the Jewish theocracy" seems after all to represent a normal instance of "concentrated polytheism",[47] if it be borne in mind that it is most probably a case of "monotheistic colonization" due to the priestly caste of Egypt, whose mental development was much more advanced than that of the "inferior population" in the midst of which "so premature an institution"[48] had come into being. So "strange an anomaly" is thus anomalous only in appearance, and it may be maintained that monotheism is an outstanding example of a tardy state of transition.[49]

This state of transition, which in itself is of no interest, is a phenomenon "essentially peculiar to Western peoples."[50] If it can be dispensed with elsewhere, so much the better. Such was the case with Chinese civilization, which was able to system-

---

[47] *Cours*, vol. 5, p. 96. *Polit.*, vol. 2, p. 116; vol. 3, pp. 407 and 425.

[48] *Cours*, vol. 5, pp. 154–55. In a note, Comte adds details that throw new light on his method. "It is quite conceivable", he says, "that the Egyptian and later the Chaldean priests were led or even forced to attempt such a monotheistic colonization in a twofold hope: namely, that this would bring sacerdotal civilization to a higher stage of development there by the more complete subalternization of the warriors, and that it would secure a safe refuge for those of their caste who might find themselves threatened by the frequent insurrections in the mother country." Then he adds: "Although the nature of my specific work does not permit me to deal adequately with such a particular explanation of Judaism, I have no doubt that this new outlook on history, acquired as the result of a direct and profound study of the subject as a whole, in accordance with my basic theory of human evolution may some time or other be sufficiently confirmed by its detailed application to the general analysis of this strange anomaly, if such an appraisal is one day actually carried out by a philosopher suitably stationed beforehand at this new rational standpoint." O "positive" history!

[49] Cf. *Cours*, vol. 5, p. 24: "The modern social state has, so to speak, constituted until now only an immense transition, under the indispensable directorship of monotheism."

[50] *Appel*.

atize the original fetishism by adopting only an outward polytheism and "never extending a welcome to monotheism".[51]
Such will be preeminently the case with the numerous populations that are still in one or other of the first two phases
of theologism. "A protective rampart" must be established on
their behalf, with the abolition of "disturbing missions in which
monotheism, having run its course in its own home, claims
universal superiority" over their religious practices. Soon other
missionaries will be sent out by the High Priest of Humanity,
to enable fetishists and polytheists to pass directly and "peace-
ably" into the positive state. They will thus be saved for ever
from the monotheistic transition—the Western malady.[52]

In the *Cours de philosophie positive* Comte was already an apologist of polytheism. This religious system, "so little understood
today", was distinguished in the first place by "outstanding
intellectual qualities"; the practice of taking the auspices led
to the study of anatomy, the astrologers gradually became as-
tronomers, and in this way scientific progress was the fruit of
superstition. In addition, polytheism "spontaneously gave the
aesthetic faculties a minor but direct share in fundamental theological operations", so that art acquired an importance and a
dignity that it never subsequently regained. In these ancient religions, so "highly national in character", primitive attachment
to the soil became exalted into "the most profound and vigor-

---

[51] *Synthèse*, pp. 20–23.

[52] *Appel*, p. 69. *Catéch.*, p. 326. *Polit.*, vol. 2, pp. 99–101. *Div.*, vol. 1, pp.
195–96: "When the positivists would espouse polytheists and even fetishists
in order to hasten human fusion." Vol. 1, pp. 107–8: "Fetishistic China has
been waiting for many centuries . . . for the universal religion that was to arise
in the West. The priesthood of Humanity is to find there special affinities in
worship, dogma and regime that are more pronounced than anywhere else, in
the adoration of ancestors, the apotheosis of the real world and the preponderance of the social end. It belongs to Positivism to be received by the Chinese
according to the same motives that made them rightly reject Christian or even
Muslim contacts." So Comte wished that some of his disciples would devote
themselves to "a serious study of the Chinese language".

ous patriotism". In a word, "by its greater homogeneity and the closer connection between its various essential elements", polytheism "automatically tended to develop men who were much more consistent and complete than any who had a chance to exist subsequently, when the state of mankind had become less uniformly and purely theological without being as yet quite frankly positive".[53]

In the following works, *Catéchisme positiviste*, *Système de politique positive* and *Synthèse subjective*, it was chiefly fetishism that was rehabilitated, and that increasingly. Without expressly going back upon his distinction of the three states, Comte nevertheless made of fetishism an age apart, a sort of vast "preamble" to human history, a first idyllic age, distinct from the theological age properly so called. Fetishism was still immune from the "divagations peculiar to theology". Even more than polytheism, it paved the way for science and encouraged the fine arts. How, indeed, can one fail to see that a system "that directly places all beings, even the most inert, on the same footing as ourselves is admirably in keeping with man's creative urge in poetry, music and even the plastic arts"? This "aesthetic aptitude" was coupled with a wonderful "gift for philosophy": all human thought was then unified in that great idea ("subsequently overshadowed by the whims of the gods") of "the necessary subordination of man to the world"; and that great idea expressed itself in the religious sphere in "universal worship". Is it not to fetishism, moreover, that we owe "the family and even the first rough plan of the city"?

Such a eulogy is not really surprising: if, as Comte makes out, fetishism really consists in the predominance of sentiment over the other human faculties, it is quite understand-

---

[53] *Cours*, vol. 5, pp. 70–72, 76–77, 115, 119. In *Polit.*, vol. 2, p. 85 (cf. pp. 90–98). Comte adds that polytheism has prepared the way intellectually for positivism "by rejecting the material life". There is also an apology for polytheism in Renouvier and in P. J. Proudhon, *De la Justice*, new ed. (Brussels: A. Lacroix, 1868–1870), vol. 1, p. 445.

able that it should have been regarded more and more favorably by a philosopher who increasingly exalted sentiment. So Comte celebrates "the underlying kinship between positivism and fetishism". Do not these "two extreme cases of synthesis" offer "an equivalent subjectivity—the necessary condition for the linking-up of the whole world"? Does not "the touching logic of the humblest negro" (so much "wiser than our academic aridity") anticipate the new logic to which the "subjective synthesis" invites us? Does the perfect fatalism of the first man need anything more than "positive systematization, in order to serve as basis for our normal meditations"? Thus the law of the three states, which, in diagrammatic form, at first represented progress along a straight line, is about to undergo yet another modification, without departing from the same formula. Evolution ends by assuming in Comte's eyes the aspect of a circle. He returns to the old idea, the old dream: *prima novissima*. A "direct *rapprochement* of our two extreme regimes", it seems to him, "is obligatory for the true philosophy of history, in which unity of conception would otherwise be impossible". Thus "the final order of the positive religion" must consist in "systematizing the instinctive usage of our earliest infancy". "Fetishity" is spontaneous positivity, just as positivity will be deliberate fetishity. The first must be incorporated in the second, and that fusion must be so complete that it will extend "even to the field of mathematics". . . . The first mental regime, which is the only "fictitious" regime that is "really inevitable", is also the only one that ought to be carried over *in toto*—with one exception, to be mentioned later—into the final regime. On the face of it, it might even be imagined that mankind could pass "without any intermediate state", and by a mere process of adding depth through reflection, "from its primitive existence to its final state, avoiding all the intellectual and moral dangers peculiar to the theological transition followed by metaphysical anarchy". Such a hope would doubtless be chimerical, in actual fact "original evolution . . . had always to be brought about empirically." Nevertheless it remains true that "our maturity is led to perpetuate and develop the fundamental dispositions of our childhood, while overcoming the obstacles due to the absolute character of primitive conceptions."[54]

Such is the magnanimity of the positive spirit toward its earlier states. But monotheism cannot benefit by it, being much too dependent on those metaphysical fluids of which it is positivism's task to rid us.[55] In monotheism, imagination, which characterized the age of the creation of the gods, is corroded by criticisms; it is not strengthened by reason. From the standpoint of moral education, in which it "disdained the two earlier modes and proclaimed its own superiority", it was "in all respects the most ill-equipped of the three for the achievement of its object". It was with monotheism that "the direct and growing decadence of the religious spirit really set in",[56] as is shown by its doctrine of miracles[57]; it is monotheism that pushes "theological arbitrariness" to its extreme limit. It is in monotheism, above all, that "the artificial nature of the temporary religion"[58] is most glaringly apparent. At the same time it is through monotheism that "the first germs of metaphysical anarchy"[59] develop. Causing violent disturbances in society and

---

[54] *Polit.*, vol. 3, pp. 37, 92–123, 154–61, 181–85; vol. 4, p. 213; vol. 2, pp. 135–36: "Positivism will always pride itself on borrowing from this spontaneous system the subjective method, the sole possible source of mental unity"; if there was great mental affinity between the two, "the moral affinity is still more complete and more direct". *Catéch.*, p. 327. *Synthèse*, pp. 6–12.

[55] *Synthèse*, p. 9.

[56] *Polit.*, vol. 3, p. 193. *Cours*, vol. 5, p. 65.

[57] *Cours*, vol. 4, p. 354: "Since the decrease in religious spirit, one has consequently had to create naturally the notion of miracle, properly speaking, in order to characterize exceptional events, those attributed to a special divine intervention. In the beginning, and while theological philosophy was fully dominant, there were no miracles, since everything seemed equally marvelous. Minerva intervened to pick up the whip of a warrior in simple military games as well as to protect against a whole army. . . ."

[58] *Synthèse*, p. 18. *Polit.*, vol. 4, etc.

[59] *Polit.*, vol. 3, p. XLIV ("Lettre au tzar").

in the mind, it encourages the most dangerous fanaticism.[60] It opens the door for "ontology", which can only disorganize everything without constructing anything, since it preserves the "vicious unity" of theology while "eliminating its necessary corrective".[61] So long as it remained polytheistic, theologism at least remained compatible with two essential attributes: "rational prevision" and "the sympathetic instincts"; but, in its monotheistic form, it is strikingly opposed to both: so much so that the positive state can be considered as the reestablishment of "the normal state, interrupted during the Western transition, or rather in the last phase of it",[62] which was the monotheistic transition or, shall we say, parenthesis.

3. Beyond Atheism

That parenthesis is now closed. "The positive mind has now reached its systematic maturity", and it is to this mind that "the privilege of logical coherence has irrevocably passed." In what does it essentially consist? For a clear understanding of this, it is necessary that, after having set forth the differences between the theological state and the metaphysical state (with which monotheism was very closely bound up), we should now stress the characteristic they have in common. In both of these first two states, the infant or adolescent human mind asks why: it is always in search of something absolute—whether a personal being or an abstract principle—which is the cause of everything that happens in our world. "In their first flight, necessarily theological, all our speculations show . . . a characteristic predilection for the most unsolvable questions", and, if

---

[60] *Catéch.*, p. 345.

[61] *Polit.*, vol. 2, p. 115.

[62] Ibid., vol. 4, pp. 22–23 and 213. It was with respect to heaven and to our relation to the stars, which "a disposition as ungrateful as blind, coming from fictitious and passing beliefs, can alone" represent to us "as purely passive", that Comte wrote these last words.

the metaphysical state brings a change in the kind of answers, it brings no change in the kind of questions put. In the positive state, on the other hand, "our understanding, gradually emancipated", does not perplex itself with all kinds of curious and vain "whys"; it no longer wonders what are the causes of phenomena but strives to ascertain the laws according to which they happen. As Mr. Léon Brunschvicg would say, it has gone on a "slimming cure". Having reached "its final state of rational positivity . . . , the human mind abandons its quest of the absolute."[63] If it is true that the mind chiefly progresses, not by altering or perfecting the solutions first proposed, but by revolutionizing the presentation of the problem,[64] then certainly no other revolution is comparable.

Some have drawn from this the inference that Comte was an agnostic. "Methodical neglect of causes" (an ambiguous phrase) has been noted as characteristic of positivism. According to other interpretations, Comtian thought immured itself in the relative as a last resource after having found itself powerless to decide the question of the absolute.[65] Separating "positive knowledge" from "belief",[66] it took the terrestrial horizon as its boundary, without prejudice to what might lie beyond it. Abandoning too high a level of speculation, it retired to lowlier positions of more immediate interest. For rea-

---

[63] *Disc.*, p. 122, 33, 6, 17. Already the atheist Baron Paul Henri d'Holbach, *Système de la nature* (Paris, 1820), vol. 1, chap. 1 (vol. 1, p. 2): "Let him submit in silence to laws from which nothing can remove him, let him consent to ignore the causes surrounded for him by an impenetrable veil."

[64] Cf. Renan, *Cahiers de jeunesse*, pp. 94–95.

[65] Charles Maurras, *L'Action française et la religion catholique*, p. 206. "The positivist negations come from a disappointed love", Albert Rivaud also said recently, "L'Enseignment de la philosophie", in *Revue des deux-mondes*, November 1, 1943.

[66] Fortunat Strowski, *Histoire des lettres*, vol. 2, p. 537 (in Gabriel Hanotaux, *Histoire de la nation française* [Paris: Société de l'histoire nationale, Plon-Nourrit, 1920-1929]); Comte would relegate in belief "all religious postulates; he would thus avoid any conflict between science and religion, but he would thereby destroy the unity of the human mind. . . ."

sons similar to Kant's, though in the train of a historical rather than a metaphysical dialectic, Comte is said to have declared the problem of God unsolvable.[67] Presumably he was not very long in making up his mind to that, and then devoted all his vital energies to the "positive" organization of this world—quite unlike Kant, who sought to regain by faith what he had perforce allowed to elude reason. But agnosticism is not atheism. "The agnostic considers it equally impossible to prove the existence or to prove the nonexistence of God; he believes that any solution of the problem of the origins and ends of man and of the world is beyond him." Strictly speaking, he is not an atheist, since he does not formally deny God. For him God is only the unknowable. It is the same for the positivist with regard to the causes of phenomena and their final cause. "He knows nothing about such things; all he knows is that he never *will* know. . . . He is neither deist nor atheist: he is ignorant"; and he proclaims his ignorance.[68] More than this—some would add—there are advantages in such a position; it

---

[67] So, too, Raymond de Boyer de Sainte-Suzanne, *Essai sur la pensée religieuse d'Auguste Comte* (Paris: Nourry, 1923), p. 51: "Man has long wanted to know the universe in its origins and its ends. It is impossible for him today to hope to shed light on these questions. It is very clear, in fact, that we cannot hope for a positive certitude in what concerns God. Comte professes on this point a radical agnosticism. That is an 'inaccessible mystery' (*Polit.*, vol. 1, p. 50), which must be left aside, since neither the present state of our knowledge nor probably the nature of our intelligence permits us to study it fruitfully. We can deny nothing and affirm nothing in this order of ideas. Henceforth, we do not have to be preoccupied with these questions.

[68] Émile Faguet, "Auguste Comte", in *Politiques et moralists du xixe siècle* (Paris: Boivin, 1890–1893), p. 294; and p. 343, still commenting on Comte: "Science excludes metaphysics, it goes beyond it and must go beyond it. This is not to say that it denies it; it merely resists the right to enter it. But minds intoxicated by scientific certitude, by the fact that science could prove God, conclude that it proved he did not exist. It would be as ridiculous for science to claim to prove the nonexistence of God as it would be to claim his existence; but from the abstention of science in this regard, idle minds have concluded his negation." A commentary of pure fantasy; as is that of Fortunat Strowski, in Hanotaux, vol. 13, p. 537 (see footnote 66 above).

may be "rich in happy consequences", for an expert apologist, starting out from the premises that positivism provides, will be able to show that this philosophy of the relative "necessarily implies an affirmation of the absolute".

That was the "use" which Brunetière, about forty years ago, attempted to make of positivism "on the road to belief".[69] It is certainly not illegitimate to carry on another man's thought and bring to light its necessary implications, even in the author's despite. That has been done, for example, for Marx—against Marx—by the study of his writings on the end of history and the reconciliation of man with all things. But, in such a case, it is at least necessary that the ideas that are thus being turned against themselves should first be clearly grasped. Now Brunetière, when he wished to set forth "the Comtian theory of the Unknowable", had to admit that Comte himself "had nowhere formulated it with sufficient clarity"; so he based his summary on Herbert Spencer, to whom, he said, must be accorded "the honor of having first enunciated it". As a matter of fact, Spencer never intended to play the part of a mere exegete of Comtism, and his own theory is quite a different one.

It is a fact that Comte did not like to be called an atheist. He wrote to John Stuart Mill on July 14, 1845: "That description does not fit people like us in any but the strictly etymological sense . . . for, apart from nonbelief in God, we have really nothing in common with those who are called atheists, and we in no way share their idle metaphysical musings about the origin of the world and of man, and still less their narrow and dangerous attempts to systematize ethics." Atheism is no more than a "mere temporary negativism", and "true system-

---

[69] Ferdinand Brunetière, *Sur les chemins de la croyance, première étape , l'utilisation du positivisme*, 9th ed. (Paris: Perrin, 1912), pp. 46 and 51. Father Xavier Moisant also "used" Comte's texts a little quickly when he said "He does not profess to be an atheist, he makes statements that are more or less contrary to the scientific and historical spirit, conformed to proclaiming the existence of God than to deny it": "A l'École d'Auguste Comte", in *Études*, vol. 91, p. 628.

atic positivism" is separated from it by such "radical differences" that there is only a "purely negative coincidence" between the two.[70]

But, as these lines would suffice to show, if Comte does not profess the ordinary atheism of those who argue in the abstract to prove that there is no God, it is not his intention to remain in an agnostic position, on the hither side of their denial; he proposes to go beyond it. He proposes to leave atheism behind. His historical dialectic strikes "the last blow at theologism". More inexorable than any other, for "theology and metaphysics cannot be finally extinguished without such a concatenation of historical facts",[71] his dialectic eliminates God by explaining what illusion accounts for that belief and what role that belief has temporarily played. It explains the "birth and death of the gods"[72]—without forgetting the birth and death of the latest of them. More simply still, it brings upon the scene a state of mind—a final state—in which there is no room for that belief. "I dare say nobody has ever logically demonstrated the nonexistence of Apollo, Minerva, and so on," he says, "nor that of the fairies of the East or the various creations of poetry; but that has in no way prevented the human mind from inevitably forsaking ancient dogmas when they became out of keeping with its situation as a whole."[73] If it comes to that, positivists do not affirm or deny the existence of God either: but that is because it is one of those "undiscussable hypotheses" that "do not lend themselves to denial any more than to affirmation", being not merely "unapproachable" but "devoid of meaning".

---

[70] Mill, pp. 352–53 (July 14, 1845).

[71] Polit., vol. 2, p. 357. Inéd., vol. 1, p. 8 (to Friedrich Buchholz, November 18, 1825).

[72] André Poëy, M. Littré et Auguste Comte, Bibliothèque positiviste, p. 54, note.

[73] Disc., p. 52. On 17 Archimedes 68, Comte wrote to A. Ellis that one has never ceased to believe in Apollo, in Jupiter, etc., "quite as respectable, however, for the corresponding case as your God." Div., vol. 1:2, p. 322.

Can one decide, the old Buddhists would say, whether the hairs of a tortoise are long or short? Similarly, "the profound inanity", not only of any solution but of any problem infected with the theological spirit, is "quite obvious".[74]

Thus, in the cautious attitude of the positivist who refrains from denial, there is nothing more than a purely "apparent" concession (it is still Comte speaking), which "is essentially cancelled" by the explanation he gives of it:

> True positivists everywhere . . . will content themselves with ruling out [belief in any deity whatsoever], not for the time and place to which it might be suited, but for the present-day West, which, according to the fundamental law of human evolution, has now, in the minds of its true guides, gone beyond the theological state, henceforth irreconcilable with the final structure of the universal religion.[75]

Our mental activity has found "a better food".

Thus a comparison with Kant is inappropriate here. If, on this cardinal point, analogies with positivism are to be sought, it is again Feuerbach's thought that comes to mind,[76] and that of Nietzsche and Heidegger.

---

[74] *Cours*, vol. 4, p. 12; vol. 1, pp. 14–15: We must consider "the search for what is called causes, whether first or final, as absolutely inaccessible and senseless for us"; vol. 6, pp. 701–2: "to the degree that our mental activity finds better nourishment, these inaccessible questions are gradually abandoned and finally judged senseless for us."

[75] *Div.*, vol. 1:2, pp. 2, 321. Guillaume de Greef, *Problèmes de philosophie positive* (1900), was therefore in the right line of Comtism when he reproached Spencer for still being haunted by the problem of God in his theory of the Unknowable. In his preface to the republication of the *Cours* (1864, vol. 1, pp. XLI–XLV), Littré distinguished between the "Spencerian unknowable" and the "positivist unknowable". See also François Pillon, "Quelques mots sur l'agnosticisme", in *La Critique philosophique*, vol. 1 (1881), pp. 347–59. Cf. Jules Soury, p. XV: "God has become more and more useless. Even at the time of Descartes, he scarcely intervened any more except to give a gentle push. At the time of Laplace, he was only a hypothesis for which there was no need. What do you want, today, for us to do with your God, O believers?"

[76] For Marx, too, atheism that remains on the level of rational discussion "is

We have it on Comte's own authority that he wished to go beyond atheism, considering it a position that was over-timid and not proof against certain counteroffensives. He thought, for instance, that the eighteenth-century atheists had rendered great services, but that it was not enough to repeat their arguments or stop short at their denial. One of the passages in which he goes into this, anticipating the misapprehension that we are now concerned with dissipating, is so clear and definite and at the same time so important that it calls for extensive quotation. It is taken from the *Discours sur l'ensemble du positivisme*, which was a work of Comte's full maturity, written at the point of transition between his two "careers" (when he had already laid the foundations of his religion) and published by him in 1851, at the beginning of his *Système de politique positive*. It will be seen how he dissociates his cause from that of atheism:

> Since complete emancipation from theology is today an indispensable preparation for the fully positive state, superficial observers, misled by this preliminary position, often genuinely confuse the final regime with a purely negative situation which, even in the last century, displayed a truly progressive character but which, in societies where it is becoming improperly permanent, is now degenerating into an essential obstacle to any real social or even mental organization. Although I have long denied any solidarity, whether dogmatic or historical, between true positivism and what is called atheism, I must, at this juncture, add a brief but pointed explanation in regard to this mistaken notion.
>
> Even in its intellectual aspect, *atheism represents no more than an inadequate emancipation*, since it tends to prolong the metaphysical state indefinitely by continually seeking new solutions of theoretical problems, instead of ruling out all accessible researches as inherently fruitless. The true positive spirit consists above all in perpetually substituting the study of the invariable laws of phenomena for the study of their causes properly so called, whether

---

only an abstraction", and in the communist perspective "atheism, like negation of God, no longer makes sense": *Economie politique et philosophique*. Cf. *Revue marxiste*, February 1, 1929, p. 125.

first or final, or, to put it briefly, it seeks to ascertain *how* rather than *why*. It is therefore incompatible with the vainglorious musings of a vague atheism about the formation of the universe, the origin of animals, and so forth. So long as we persist in solving the questions prior to our childhood, we are in a very bad position for rejecting the naïve method which our imagination brings to bear on them and which is, indeed, the only one suited to their nature. Thus confirmed atheists can be regarded as the most inconsistent of theologians, since they occupy themselves with the same questions but reject the only suitable approach to them.[77]

Furthermore, classical atheism has the defect of being a purely negative system. That being so, it is at a disadvantage in relation to "backward beliefs", since it is impossible for it to satisfy all the moral and social needs that those beliefs used to meet. It is therefore in danger of prolonging their reign instead of abolishing it. After all, it is another species of the same genus as deism, and the two of them have many traits in common—many flaws. Of the representatives of both it can equally be said that "when something constructive is needed one is soon conscious of the profound inanity of all those schools that confine themselves to incessant protests against theological institutions, while nevertheless accepting their fundamental principles."

Comte also saw in this same classical atheism a manifestation of that "speculative arrogance" that he abhorred and at that time was attacking more and more relentlessly; he saw in it the extreme limit of that metaphysical spirit he had already denounced in theism and which was opposing positivist "regeneration" in the name of an "alleged reign of the spirit". But all these reproaches are merged in the fundamental grievance: atheism does not go far enough, it does not pluck out the root of the evil. Preserving, along with the terms of the problem of God, the believer's habits of thought and methods of reasoning, it exposes itself to reactionary attacks. It maintains the rut in

---

[77] *Polit.*, vol. 1, pp. 66–68.

which the mind is in danger of sticking fast once more. Experience shows, moreover, that it is exceptional for it to remain in a pure state. "In most cases, what is described as atheism is a state of pantheism that is, at bottom, only an academic relapse into a vague and abstract fetishism from which all the phases of theology may reemerge in new forms." It is impossible to overemphasize the fact that atheists and pantheists, parodying positivity, are at bottom the last representatives of the theological mind. "Having, without any social excuse, become the most inconsistent spokesmen of the regime that is preoccupied with causes, they continue the quest of the absolute, while banning the only solution it permits."[78]

"The great revolution of the West", of which Auguste Comte is the prophet and artificer, does not fall into that trap. It goes beyond atheism, the better to liquidate theism. It nonsuits both "reactionary beliefs and anarchic dogmas". By driving out all "metaphysical abstractions" as well as all "theological figments",[79] it proclaims and at the same time ensures "the hopeless outmodedness of the reign of God".[80] That reign was only a regency corresponding to "the long minority of mankind". Now that mankind has grown up, the only absolute principle that is real shines forth in all its brilliance: "everything is relative"; and this principle rules out forever all spurious problems, while making it clear how they managed to present themselves in former times. For the atheist there might be new shocks in store: however absolute his denial, uneasiness might still creep in under cover of the question that his mind had rashly admitted at the outset: positivism alone does its work

---

[78] *Polit.*, vol. 1, pp. 73 and 88; vol. 3, p. 91.

[79] *Appel*, pp. 3 and 4.

[80] *Polit.*, vol. 4, p. 531. This is one of the words Comte was fond of repeating. Cf. above, 2, note 4. *Appel*, p. XIII: "Outdated theologism"; p. 2: "the entire depletion of theologism and the organic impotence of ontologism"; p. 62: "Irrevocably decayed system", etc. Cf. *Polit.*, vol. 2, p. 57: "Taken together, the positive studies radically exclude" the hypothesis of a providence higher than humanity, "our common mother".

thoroughly. Thanks to it, "God has gone, unquestionably and forever."[81]

4. God Excluded and Replaced

That is not simply a conclusion that was bound to result from the inevitable development of the mind in the course of history. We have sufficient evidence that Auguste Comte did not forgo value judgments. If he was not an atheist in the most current acceptation of the word, he was a confirmed antitheist —like Feuerbach, like Nietzsche—and it was on good grounds

---

[81] The expression is that of Henri Gouhier, vol. 1, p. 23; it sums up Comtian thought rather successfully. Stuart Mill had already seen quite well that if Comte "indeed disclaimed, with some acrimony, dogmatic atheism", it was with a still more radical intention. He concluded: "Those who accept his theory of the progressive stages of opinion are not obliged to follow him. The positive mode of thinking is not necessarily a denial of the supernatural; it merely throws back that question to the origin of all things. . . . It is one of M. Comte's mistakes that he never allows of open questions": *Auguste Comte et le positivisme* (French trans. by G. Clemenceau [Paris: Baillière, 1868] of *Auguste Comte and Positivism* [London: Trubner, 1865]), pp. 14 and 15.

The commentary by Mr. Lévy-Brühl is equally enlightening. He ends with an inverse but equivalent metaphor: "In fact, we no longer imagine any supernatural intervention in the simplest and most general phenomena of nature, such as the movement of the stars or the fall of bodies. When all the orders of phenomena are habitually conceived like those, when the idea of their laws has become familiar everywhere, one will not demonstrate, in addition, that there is no place for belief in a Providence. One will simply have ceased to believe in it. To be an atheist is still one way of being a theologian. It is thus not very accurate to say that Comte did not want to leave open questions. On the contrary, all theological and metaphysical questions, according to him, will eternally remain open. Only no one will broach them any more": "Le Centenaire d'Auguste Comte", in *Revue des deux-mondes*, January 15, 1898, p. 404.

Because Comte speaks of the "insoluble mystery of the essential production of phenomena" (*Polit.*, vol. 1, p. 46), Paul Labérenne, spokesman for Marxist orthodoxy, can write: "Such an attitude always leaves a door through which to enter reactionary philosophy": *A la lumière du marxisme*, vol. 2:1, p. 82. Such was not, in any case, Comte's intention.

that Robert Flint gave the name of *Anti-theistic Theories* to the book containing the doctrines of unbelief professed in England that owed their origin, at least in part, to the founder of positivism.[82] Positivism was not born solely of a renunciation of the "lower forms of explanation". The law of the three states may well be simply the appearance in an intellectual disguise of a deeper spiritual choice—the decision to do without God.

Needless to say, no suspicion is being cast upon Comte's sincerity, which is unqualified and obvious; and it is that solid and self-confident honesty that accounts for the extraordinary influence exercised by a system of thought whose genius for simplification so often turns to distortion and whose "positive" claims are so often at fault. "A man of real superiority", Comte wrote, "has never managed to produce a great effect upon his fellow men without having first profoundly convinced himself."[83] These words apply to nobody more than to himself. Everything, then, took place on the hither side of the zone of consciousness. There is no trickery in this most consistent of systems.

Moreover, Auguste Comte's mind was far less the servant of a personal choice than the instrument of the will of a particular age. Yet it is nonetheless true that the whole thing was, so to speak, a foregone conclusion. When, at the age of thirteen, he cut loose from "all supernatural beliefs, without excepting the most fundamental and the most universal", the Montpellier schoolboy was not impelled by the logic of the "sociological laws" which, as he tells us, he discovered ten or eleven years later. "The farther I got in working out the dogmas of positivism," he says elsewhere, "the more incapable I became of returning to supernatural beliefs."[84] We can well believe it.

---

[82] Robert Flint, *Anti-Theistic Theories*, 2d ed. (Edinburgh and London: Blackwood, 1880). Cf. Grüber, p. 307.

[83] *Cours*, vol. 5, p. 41.

[84] *Test.*, p. 9. *Div.*, vol. 1:2, p. 379 (to Louis Comte, 26 Moses 69).

But it seems no less obvious that, in the reverse direction, the farther he went in building up the Comtian "Trilogy", the more a secret instinct, which antedated it, took charge of the whole construction of the huge edifice.

There were times when that instinct came out into the open. Consider, for instance, Comte in the presence of the revolutionary cults that seem to have struck his young imagination so forcibly. Why does he condemn the cult of the Supreme Being? Why does he despise "Theophilanthropy"? Why, on the other hand, does he see in the cult of Reason a sort of anticipation of positivism that failed to establish itself? Yet the last of the three has just as metaphysical an aspect as the first, and the second might justifiably be regarded as a rough draft for the cult of Humanity. But that is not the criterion: "There is a cleavage between the sects that retain the monotheistic idol and those that discard it."[85]

"Inconsistent synthesis", "empty unity", the work of "pure babblers" and the fruit of their "mental debility", Comte does not stop at these scornful remarks when dealing with monotheism. It is not merely that he has a grudge against the "monotheistic sophisms" that, "by a vain quest for objective universality", have "so greatly hindered the working-out of final unity". It is not merely that the idea of God seems to him vague and incoherent.[86] He finds belief in God disastrous. He considers that it leads man to pay homage to a being who, if he existed,

---

[85] Gouhier, vol. 1, p. 12. Likewise, if for some time Comte marvelled at "the admirable philosophical impulse" of the Parisian proletariat, it was because he believed he could observe that their "crude but energetic instinct had definitively overcome" the "temporary halt" of deism that was still delaying the "literate world": *Mill*, pp. 229–31 (May 1, 1844).

[86] *Polit.*, vol. 3, pp. 247, 331, 492, 332: "Then, as today, ontology becomes the principal food only of dissolute or ill-prepared minds, which, better fit for exposition than for conception, aspire to universal systematization by contenting themselves with an illusory but facile synthesis." Vol. 2, p. 100: "Our intelligence would be better guided by a wisely compressed polytheism than by any monotheism"; p. 101.

would be degrading himself by "puerile vanity".[87] Much more than polytheism, it exalts that passion for the absolute which is the antipode of the positive spirit and thus exposes the mind to an unhealthy climate. Everywhere it fosters incomprehension and fanaticism. Monotheistic ways are blind, they are at the root of all kinds of injustice.[88] They encourage reaction no less than anarchy.[89] These grievances recur in connection with Christianity. They help us to understand that "strict need to have done with God" of which one of Comte's most eminent disciples[90] spoke not long ago in connection with Charles Jundzill. In the few scraps of prose and verse that this young Polish convert to the positivist doctrine left behind him and that were handed down to us by the master, there is nothing that literally warrants so strong an expression. Nevertheless, it very aptly expresses the spirit that is at the root of positivism and that animates the principal representatives of that system, as it animated the founder. Comte had welcomed Jundzill like a son; and, after the young man's premature death in 1855, he honored him with a long notice in the preface to the *Synthèse subjective*. But before receiving Jundzill into his "positivist society", Comte had waited for his "emancipation from theology" to be quite complete and, as a worthy crown for his

---

[87] *Polit.*, vol. 1, p. 353.

[88] *Disc.*, pp. 43 and 73.

[89] *Div.*, vol. 1, p. 75: "Sincere and judicious conservatives . . . have noted that the device of anarchists is *God* and the people, just as that of reactionaries was already *God* and the king."

[90] Charles Maurras, "Auguste Comte", in *L'Avenir de l'intelligence*, p. 112: He "was of purely Roman birth and formation; before his nineteenth year, he had noted very clearly his inaptitude for faith and particularly for faith in God, principle and end of the Catholic organization. Was it philosophy, was it science that had reduced him to this impossibility of believing? Whatever the influence undergone by the young man, such was the fact. He no longer believed and that was the source of his concern. It would be to use very imprecise language to say that he missed God. Not only did his mind not miss God, but his mind felt, if one can put it this way, a rigorous need to miss God: no theological interpretation of the world and man was tolerable to him."

novitiate, he had set him to make a study of Diderot.[91] On various occasions Comte vaunted "the great Diderot" and his "robust wisdom"; he wished him to be celebrated, in the positivist cult, as a forerunner.[92] As to Marx and later to Lenin, the propeadeutical role of the atheism of the Encylopaedists seemed to Comte a salutary one.

But once God has been shut out, his place must be taken by something else, if you do not want him to come back. A prolonged "interregnum" would be disastrous. For "only what is replaced is destroyed." Comte borrowed that aphorism from a speech by the Prince-President, and he continually applied it to his subject.[93] "In obedience, then, to that maxim, as well expressed as it is well considered, Catholicism must be replaced by a real religion, on pain of seeing its 'vile decrepitude' prolonged indefinitely."[94] As we have seen, it was precisely one of the weaknesses of atheism, in its purely critical attitude, that it left unsatisfied the needs that God had answered. But positivism, the most organic of all doctrines, "for the first time supplies complete satisfaction to all the tendencies of the many-sided nature of man".[95] Above all, it supplies an object for that urge to worship which is at the heart of our nature. It concentrates "our feelings, our thoughts and our actions around Humanity", "the one truly great Being, of which we are wittingly the necessary members".[96] Thus, by its efforts, Humanity is

---

[91] *Synthèse*, pp. XXII–XXIV (Letters of Charles Jundzill). *Blign.*, p. 102.

[92] *Polit.*, vol. 3, p. 584. *Synthèse*, p. 22. *Inéd.*, vol. 2, p. 165: "the great school of Diderot". Compare Strauss, who, while also rejecting the narrow idea that the eighteenth century developed of religion and its origin, republished Reimarus, popularized Voltaire, translated the "Dîner du comte de Boulainvilliers" and the "Testament du curé Meslier".

[93] *Catéch.*, p. 6. *Div.*, vol. 1, p. 160. *Inéd.*, vol. 2, p. 331: "Only true positivists are preserved today (from the Catholic yoke), because they have replaced it with what the others think they have destroyed"; etc.

[94] *Inéd.*, vol. 3, p. 117 (To M. de Tholouse, 15 Gutenberg 64).

[95] Cf. Caird, p. 96.

[96] *Polit.*, vol. 3, p. 618; vol. 1, p. 330, etc.

finally substituted for God, and, if its cult cannot be really systematized until God has been eliminated, his elimination will at last become a complete certainty thanks to that systematization.[97] One day, in Notre Dame de Paris, turned into "the great Temple of the West", "the statue of Humanity will have as its pedestal the altar of God"[98]—of the vanquished God who has become "its footstool". . . . Positivism is essentially a "religion of Humanity".[99] That is the deity, the true Great Being that acts as Providence, the "new Supreme Being"[100] that is to make man forget the absolute God—the God of Abraham, the God of the metaphysicians—not only "left behind" but driven out.

In one of his lectures in 1851, Comte squarely contrasted the "slaves of God" with "the servants of Humanity". "In the name of the past and of the future" it behooved the latter, alone capable of "organizing the true Providence", to get rid of the former everywhere "as disturbing and backward elements".[101] Two years later he reverted to the same proposition in the *Catéchisme positiviste*, thus showing once more that it was not only the necessities of mental evolution that gave birth to the last of religions. Some of his English disciples were shocked. The master had to explain himself. On 6th Bichat 65 (December 8, 1853) he wrote to Henry Dix Hutton:

> In contrast to the title "servants of Humanity", the designation "slaves of God" was then intended to indicate a decisive antagonism between true positivists and any kind of theologists, from

---

[97] *Catéch.*, p. 380. *Test.*, p. 9. *Polit.*, vol. 3, p. 618; vol. 4, p. 531. On this substitution of Humanity for God, the missionary positivists "must never make the least concession": *Inéd.*, vol. 1, pp. 275–76. Cf. pp. 209 and 211.

[98] *Div.*, vol. 1:2, p. 27.

[99] *Appel*, p. XIII, etc.

[100] *Polit.*, vol. 1, p. 329; vol. 2, p. 63, etc.

[101] *Div.*, vol. 1, p. 75 (11 Shakespeare 63). Comte proved happy with "this decisive proclamation, which it would be good", he added, "to propagate with all expediency".

the fundamental nature of their respective doctrines. The relative Being, to whom the first group dedicate themselves, has only a limited power, though one that is always superior to our strength, individual or collective; its impulses are always regulated by laws that are completely open to appraisal. The second group, on the other hand, worship an absolute Being, whose power is boundless, so that its wishes necessarily remain arbitrary. Thus, if they were really consistent, they would have to regard themselves as genuine slaves, subject to the whims of an inscrutable power. Positivism alone can make us systematically free, that is to say, subject to known and immutable laws that enfranchise us from all personal domination. Such is the decisive contrast implied by the expressions I used for the two groups. . . .[102]

Clearly the explanation was not a withdrawal, and in the following year, completing his *Système de politique positive*, Comte once more inexorably and indiscriminately excluded from leading positions in his city "Catholics, Protestants and deists"— in short, "all the various slaves of God"[103]—"as being both backward and disturbing elements". The very idea of religion, which implies the idea of a tie, was enough to make him ban that faith in an absolute Being which plucks man away from his natural ties: "While the Protestants and the deists have always

---

[102] *Hutton*, pp. 8–9. Comte added, it is true, that his expressions "apply, besides, only to the claim to govern *earthly* affairs, henceforth incompatible with all theological preoccupation. My sincere theologians, who today restrict their belief to directing the search for their *heavenly* salvation, are in no way touched by these terms. . . ." But this concession, apart from the fact that it could in no way satisfy a believer (for it is an obvious expulsion), must be understood as one of those "wise cautions" that he recommended with regard to certain "theologians" and that he distinguished with great care from a "degrading hypocrisy". Cf. *Circ.*, p. 41, etc. Other positivists would make similar remarks; for example, Jean Coutrot, "Lettre d'invitation à une recherche collective visant à étendre aux problèmes de l'homme—individuel et social—la connaissance solide que nous avons déjà de l'univers des choses", in *Entretien sur les sciences de l'homme, un essai collectif de coordination, document no. 1*, (1937), p. 28. See also Comte, *Polit.*, vol. 4, p. 534.

[103] *Polit.*, vol. 4, p. 533.

attacked religion in the name of God, we must discard God, once and for all, in the name of religion"[104]—in the name of that religion which finds the fullness of its concept in the cult of Humanity.

True, the Humanity that Comte offers for our worship is not quite the same as Feuerbach's. This Great Being, this "huge organism",[105] is certainly formed of the beings which are ourselves, it certainly comprises individuals of all generations; but it does not retain them all within its midst. It is only "the continuous whole of convergent beings".[106] Criminals are excluded, even those among them who are called great men—the Neros, the Robespierres, the Bonapartes, "all those who break the human harmony";[107] "parasites" likewise, mere "dung-producers", "who transmit to their successors no equivalent for what they received from their predecessors". Only those are incorporated who have made themselves fit for "assimilation", that is, "all the men who have cooperated in the great human task, those who live on in us, of whom we are the continuation, those whose genuine debtors we are".[108] A conception that is perhaps less aristocratic than it subsequently became in the hands of this or that later disciple, but quite different, less vague, less "humanitarian" and also more deliberately religious than Feuerbach's conception. Furthermore, the Homeland and

---

[104] *Inéd.*, vol. 2, p. 107; and p. 89: "In a free conversation before dining, in the midst of the forest of Saint-Germain, I was able finally to observe that the systematic use of the indispensable word 'religion', with its derivatives, no longer offended Mr. Littré, who was even very touched by the hope of finally dismissing *God* as irreligious" (A. Laffitte, 17 Shakespeare and 11 Descartes 61). For the Comtian concept of religion, see *Polit.*, vol. 2, chap. 1.

[105] *Cours*, vol. 6, pp. 810–11: "immense and eternal social unity".

[106] *Polit.*, vol. 4, p. 30.

[107] *Inéd.*, vol. 3, p. 114.

[108] *Polit.*, vol. 1, p. 411; vol. 2, p. 62. *Catéch.*, pp. 66–70. Cf. Henri Gouhier, *Le Vie d'Auguste Comte* (Paris: Gallimard, 1931), p. 260; Maurras, *L'Avenir de l'intelligence*, p. 130. The expression "dung-producers" figured in the *Caté-chisme*; Comte promised to replace it with a word "in better taste" following an observation offered by "one of our lady positivists": *Div.*, vol. 1:2, p. 300.

"Occidentalism" have in it an intermediate place that has no parallel in the system of the German philosopher.[109] But for both of them Humanity plays the same part in relation to the former "God". "In it," says Auguste Comte, "we live and move and have our being." It is "the center of our affections". Those whose heart it has captured return no more to their former slavery (Feuerbach, in his Hegelian language, called it the former alienation). They are won over forever to "the true religion".

In 1847 Comte had given a series of lectures that formed the basis of his *Discours sur l'ensemble du positivisme*. Alluding to these lectures a few years later, one of his hearers, Dr. Robinet, expressed himself as follows: "In those hallowed hours that heralded such great destinies, we felt the breath of Humanity, we caught a glimpse of its reality, its greatness, we bowed before it, and the holy enthusiasm of demonstrated faith was kindled forever in our hearts."[110] In the following generation, E. Sémerie, another fervent positivist whom the master had adopted to take the place of "poor Jundzill", addressed the Catholics in these terms:

> We have faith that inspires great things and the courage that spurs us on to achieve them. Against the fragrance of your incense and the harmony of your canticles we set up the splendid festivals of Humanity in the holy city of the Revolution: against the cult of God we set the cult of woman and of the great men who have made us what we are: against the narrow mysticism of the Catholic, the noble activity of the citizen and the enthusiasm of the Republicans of '92. We shall convince the men, we shall persuade the women, and the day is not far off when we shall enter your forsaken temples as masters, bearing above our heads the banner of triumphant Humanity.[111]

---

[109] *Appel*, p. 25. *Polit.*, vol. 2, p. 83: "Homeland prepares the way for Humanity, and national egoism disposes one for universal love."

[110] Jean François Robinet, *Notice sur l'oeuvre et sur la vie d'Auguste Comte*, (Paris: Richilieu, 1864), p. 273.

[111] Eugène Sémerie, *Positivistes et catholiques* (1870), p. 135: quoted by Grüber,

Closer to our times, coming from a completely different social and spiritual direction, "a young patrician, Léon de Montesquiou, transfigured by having read Auguste Comte"[112] and having become a member of his "testamentary execution", explained as a true believer the "positivist consecrations of human life".[113] It is well known how profound his influence was on a small group of active minds. One of those who shared in this influence, Antoine Baumann, declared that, like him, he had "finally found repose of mind and heart" the day he assimilated "the work of the great thinker".[114] Still nearer to our times, the whole work of Alfred Loisy is, in the last analysis, an attempt to verify by history the truth proclaimed by Feuerbach and by Comte that mankind, through all the manifold forms of creed and cult that it has invented, has always worshipped itself. The works of his modernist period, dominated by an "intellectualist" and critical viewpoint, left a void in Loisy's soul, and, in his need to rediscover a faith, he turned, if not to the teacher of positivism, at least toward a doctrine similar to his.[115] Not content with finding, as an historian, that reli-

---

pp. 150–51. It was to Sémerie that Comte had confided the work on Diderot with which Jundzill had first been charged: to Audiffrent, 15 Caesar 69 (*Div.*, vol. 1, pp. 391–92).

[112] Charles Maurras, *Le Contre-révolution spontanée* (Lyons: Lardanchet, 1943), p. 122.

[113] This work was a continuation of *Système politique d'Auguste Comte* by the same author (Paris: Nouvelle librairie nationale). On February 23, 1907, sending a copy of Auguste Comte's *Testament* to a friend: "This is not an ordinary book I am sending you here. It is something that grips me to the soul, or rather, it is something to which I owe a little of my soul. . . . You will judge the man in the closeness with which I have lived for four years. I owe him much (of my soul)." He had on his table the two portraits of Comte and of Clotilde de Vaux. (Mme. de Coudekerque-Lambrecht, *Léon de Montesquiou* [Paris: Nouvelle Librairie Nationale, 1925], pp. 173 and 178).

[114] Antoine Baumann, *La Vie sociale de notre temps, opinions et rêveries d'un positiviste* (1900), pp. 1–2. Likewise, *La Religion positive* (Paris: Perrin, 1903).

[115] "I have never had the least intention of standing in for Auguste Comte, and I am not inspired by him", declared Alfred Loisy in 1922 (cf. *Mémoires*

gion is "primarily a social phenomenon", he professed, as a believer, that "the holy is the same thing as the social", and, without embracing the letter of the cult that Auguste Comte "had
proposed to establish", he occupied himself in constructing or
musing upon that "religion of Humanity" which, he said, "has
been in preparation from the very beginning".[116]

Still more significant, because apparently more paradoxical,
was the attitude adopted by one of our most militant philosophers, Alain. With him, it is not only historical criticism, it
is rational criticism itself that surrenders. The author of the
Citoyen contre les pouvoirs, for whom the mind was "that which
scoffs" and "to think is to say no"; for whom doubt and refusal
to surrender were the crown of the wise man; who wished "to
overcome religion by philosophy"; who, in addition, readily
admired the Bible and declared that the *Imitation* "is not from
its books".[117] Alain made Comte his master and almost his

[Paris: E. Nourry, 1930–1931], vol. 3, p. 419). This is thus a reference to a
general influence, not of a filiation, properly speaking. Let us add, without
wishing to encroach upon the mystery of souls, that Mr. Loisy seems to have
preserved to the end more of a religious spirit—and perhaps more Christian
faith—than his critical works allow to appear. This seems to be evident in
some of his reactions in the face of works of a rationalistic or scientistic inspiration. His mysticism has in any case a different accent from that of Comte.

[116] *La Religion*, 2d. ed. (1924). *Religion et humanité* (1926). Cf. pp. 7–12, 20–
27, 234, 246; p. 50: "It is in religions that the spiritual notion of humanity
gradually becomes distinct, an essentially religious notion and one which, in
managing to define itself, will by that very fact define the religion that is heir
to all the religions that prepared the way for it": *La Crise morale du temps présent*
(Paris: Nourry, 1937).

[117] Alain, *Les Dieux* (Paris: Gallimard, 1934), p. 305; *Propos sur le christianisme*, pp. 24 and 170; *Histoire de mes pensées* (Paris: Gallimard, 1936), p. 250,
etc. Alain is also the one whose individualist temperament was stressed to the
extreme and whose spirit has been defined as "an idealism of the will"; the
one who wishes the minister to be incessantly controlled by the deputy, the
deputy by the elector; the one who laughs at the type of "polytechnician",
who demands that one never believe any knowledge but that one reinvent his
thought each time. In brief, in all things, it seems, the perfect antagonist for
Comte.

God. He took the ten volumes of the *Cours* and of the *Politique* for his breviary, admiring the strictness of the history of humanity he found there.[118] Most probably tired of always destroying, he too aspired to found something. Thanks to Auguste Comte, he thought, he could fill the void that criticism had left in him, without being constrained to restore any part of a transcendency that he had demolished. The "physiology of religions" with which Comte supplied him enabled him, in his turn, to dream of a new Catholicism, based on science and stripped of all "fantastic beliefs". Comte's speculations helped him "to keep the gods on earth" and to establish himself once for all in "immanence". Such is the "great secret" that accounts for a subjection that is so odd at first sight.[119]

In the case of Georges Deherme it is no longer submission but sheer bewitchment. Comte is "a genius, a hero, a saint"; he is "the greatest of men", he is "the purest and most exact representative of the apostolic soul of universal France"; "his thought contains everything", he offers "the redeeming doctrine that saves", and the religion that he has founded will leave its mark upon the twentieth century, for "all his thoughts are for mankind."[120]

One further example, a contemporary one, will serve to show that the positivist faith has not yet grown cold and that, unchecked by differences of period and mentality, it lives on

---

[118] *Histoire de mes pensées*, pp. 139–45. *Abrégés pour les aveugles* (Paris: Hartmann, 1943), pp. 99–175; etc. When Comte was in question, even the best attested facts of his life or the most patent traits of his character, Alain lost all critical spirit; for example, the attack of insanity was only "a state of fatigue, which made people believe it was some mental illness" (*Abrégés*, p. 99; cf. *Idées* [Paris: Hartmann, 1932], p. 292); etc.

[119] *Propos sur le christianisme*, p. 129. *Histoire de mes pensées*, pp. 243 and 281; cf. p. 144: "This torrent of totally new and unknown ideas cast me completely into the future, and everywhere on the earth. . . ." Together with Hegel, Comte tore him from his "metaphysical purgatory" (p. 145).

[120] *Aux jeunes gens: un maître, Auguste Comte; une direction: le Positivisme* (1921); *Le Positivisme dans l'action* (1923), etc.

unchanged. "Objectively," wrote M. Jean Coutrot on the very eve of the present war,

> the only being that surpasses the individual is his species, carrying in it . . . that extraordinary additive faculty that enables man to outclass the animals. This suggests an inspiring extension of the humanist attitude. We seek to divert religious feeling toward the species, as the Marxists tried to divert it toward class warfare, the dictatorship of the proletariat or the organization of industrial production.[121]

Thus, for the disciple as for the master, today as yesterday, positivism is much more than a mere doctrine on a par with other doctrines. It is "the true religion", as it is "the true philosophy". To make itself safe from any aggressive recurrence of theologism, the positive spirit has found its redoubt. It has placed itself "forever under the just rule of the heart".[122] Exactly what ceremonies were organized in Comte's day around the armchair of Clotilde de Vaux is a matter of minor importance; outside the circle of the rigidly orthodox who bow the knee with the proper ritual, positivism has its faithful followers and its worship, because it has its idol. God's place has been well and truly taken.

---

[121] Loc. cit., p. 136. Several signs, however, would lead one to think that the author of these lines had finally considered going beyond positivism to be possible.

[122] *Polit.*, vol. 1, pp. 8 and 37.

CHAPTER II

CHRISTIANITY AND CATHOLICISM

In his philosophy of history, Auguste Comte finds himself constantly up against the great fact of Christianity. It is clear that he does not attribute any truth value to it as doctrine. But how does he regard the spirit of Christianity? Something of his attitude may already be guessed from the views set forth up to the present. His judgment is not a simple one, however. It is colored and even turned almost inside out according as Christianity appears to him in its pure state, in all the virulence of its monotheistic principle, or more or less modified, corrected, neutralized by another inspiration. In a word, between Christianity and Catholicism he thinks it possible to establish a contrast that will enable him, while condemning the former, to exalt the latter (or his own idea of it) and even go to the length of seeking a temporary alliance with its leaders.

1. Antisocial Christianity

During the first three centuries of its history, the noblest minds of the Roman world felt a strong repulsion for the new religion that aspired to conquer them. As a particularly powerful vehicle of "monotheistic belief" and of all the evils it brings with it, Christianity, indeed, deserved their reprobation.

> Unable at that time to judge the system otherwise than by its doctrine, they did not hesitate to reject, as hostile to the human race, a provisional religion that situated perfection in the solitude of heaven. The modern instinct still more strongly disapproves of a system of ethics that proclaims that benevolent tendencies are foreign to our nature; which, far from recognizing the dignity

of labor, attributes its origin to a divine curse; and which makes
woman the source of all evil.

It cannot reconcile itself to that perpetual preoccupation with
death that Christianity inculcates in its disciples and that leads
them to abandon the tasks of this life. If, in quite recent times,
such a religion could nevertheless deserve "accommodating
treatment at the hands of cautious conservatives", this was so
"only insofar as it was impossible to replace that religion by a
better conception of the world and of man—to which a gradual
advance of the positive spirit was alone conducive"; and because the policy in question did, after all, exercise some slight
check upon the effects of Christianity. But in itself, at bottom,
that religion is immoral and, if we go straight to essentials, we
shall maintain that its "immoral character" is "inherent in its
antisocial nature".[1]

Christianity is antisocial in two ways: in its conception of
man and in its conception of salvation; or, to put it differently,
in its doctrine and in its ethics, in its ontology and in its practical standpoint. The one is "anarchic", the other "selfish".
There is, moreover, a close connection between the two; the
anarchism of Christian doctrine inevitably entails the egoism
of Christian practice, so that there is no need to deal with them
separately.

In Comte it would be vain to look for anything even remotely resembling those recent doctrines that, while disapprov-
ing of individualism, seek to establish a salutary tension between
the "personal" and the "communal" elements, or even see in
the second one of the characteristics inherent in the first. The
word "community" does not figure in Comte's vocabulary. As
for "personal", he takes it as the synonym of "individual" used
in a depreciatory sense. He says, for instance, that the whole
aim of positivism is to overcome the "personal instincts" and
to substitute "the social viewpoint for the personal viewpoint"

---

[1] *Catéch.*, pp. 12–13. *Div.*, vol. 1, p. 259. *Polit.*, vol. 3, p. 412.

that had unfortunately hitherto prevailed.[2] "Not less saintly, in our way, than the early Christians, we must concentrate our solicitude and our ambition upon real life, at first objective, then subjective, whereas they scorned it in their preoccupation with a chimerical existence: they were essentially personal and we shall be preeminently social."[3] The great mistake made by theologism was, indeed, that, in "giving rise to purely inward observations", it had "sanctified personality with an existence that, by linking each man directly with an infinite power, profoundly isolated him from Humanity".[4] "This quality of constant personality" has its source and its immediate strength in "theological thought", but it is only in monotheism that it bursts forth in full force. There (it may be said) lies the radical evil: this linking-up of each man to God, which has the effect of "exaggerating the human type", making every man an absolute like God himself, and leading him to subordinate the world to himself.[5] This accounts for the "shamelessness" of "monotheistic aspirations" and the "anarchic utopias"[6] from which we are suffering today. For theology has infected metaphysics. In other words, on the plane of concrete facts, it is the personalism of the Christian religion that has given birth to the personalism of modern philosophy—that philosophy whose "dominating thought is constantly that of the ego", all other existences

---

[2] *Synthèse*, pp. 25–26. *Inédit.*, vol. 2, p. 320.

[3] *Inédit.*, vol. 3, p. 290.

[4] *Catéch.*, pp. 166–67. Similarly, according to Barthémely Enfantin, *La Vie éternelle* (Paris: Ancienne Librairie Germer Ballière), the faith that binds the believer to his God unbinds him from his neighbor (Sébastien Charléty, *Histoire du saint-simonisme, 1825–1864* [Paris: Hartmann, 1931], p. 322).

[5] *Polit.*, vol. 4, p. 526; vol. 3, pp. 444 and 166. Cf. Alain, *Histoire de mes pensées* (Paris: Gallimard, 1934), pp. 141–42: "As for monotheism . . . , it is already the metaphysical spirit, the spirit that reasons without matter, the spirit that imposes on society and nature its own, completely empty laws." Comte is opposing here very directly the Augustinian principle often formulated in the Christian tradition, for example by Saint Albert the Great, *Summa theologica*, second part, 2, 6, 2: "Inter mentem hominis et Deum nihil est medium".

[6] *Polit.*, vol. 3, p. 336. *Div.*, vol. 1, p. 200.

being hazily shrouded in a negative conception, their vague sum total constituting the nonego, while "the notion of we" secures "no direct and distinct place in it".[7]

To be explicit: the fault lies in the Christian religion far more than in the theological spirit in general. Neither fetishism nor even polytheism gave such prominence to the human person. Polytheism had at any rate some inkling of the natural existence of the benevolent tendencies that keep the individual immersed in the great social body. But monotheistic faith, whose triumph Christianity is for a time ensuring, sees in all "altruistic inclination" only the principle of a "reprehensible diversion, forbidden to the truly devout in the name of their best interests, which are always necessarily personal". Thus it is chiefly in the eyes of this faith that social life may be truly said to have no existence. It does not exist because it has no purpose of its own: human society is, for the believer, "merely an agglomeration of individuals whose coming together is almost as fortuitous as it is transitory and who, each exclusively occupied with his own salvation, regard cooperation in the salvation of others merely as a good means of working out their own".[8] This "Christian egoism" is still more understandable if one recalls the fact that it is an echo of "absolute egoism of the supreme type". It is modeled on "divine egoism".[9] It was this, for instance, that inspired Saint Peter with "the characteristic maxim: 'Let us look upon ourselves on earth as strangers or pilgrims.' "[10] It fosters "a continual habit of personal calculation", which in the long run goes so far as to change the tendencies of human nature, so that "even in quite other respects" it acquires, "by gradual affinity, an excess of circumspection, of caution and, ultimately, of egoism, which its basic organization did not demand and which might therefore abate some day, under a bet-

---

[7] *Disc.*, p. 85.

[8] *Polit.*, vol. 3, pp. XXXV ("Lettre au tzar"), 446. *Disc.*, p. 87.

[9] *Polit.*, vol. 2, p. 110; vol. 3, p. 447. *Div.*, 13, vol. 2, p. 43.

[10] *Catéch.*, p. 71.

ter mental regime".[11] In short, by "a continual and excessive
appeal to the spirit of pure egoism"—always this word, which
recurs time after time in the indictment running through all
Comte's works—Christian ethics "bring the noblest part of
our moral organism to atrophy for want of proper exercise".

It is no good protesting that, on the contrary, Christianity
is the religion of brotherly charity and consequently of mutual
help in social matters, its second commandment being that we
should love our neighbor as ourselves. For the same quality of
personal calculation underlies this "great precept": "not only
is egoism thereby sanctioned rather than repressed, it is directly
provoked by the reason given for this rule: *for the sake of the
love of God*, without any human sympathy: apart from the fact
that such love ordinarily amounted to fear."[12] There we have a
fine example of that "Christian boasting", that "Gospel boasting", which makes a display of admirable sentiments but has
really nothing in it. Just such another is that sublime precept
of forgiveness for injuries: "when the Christians arrogated this
prerogative to themselves", it had long been "widely practiced,
especially by Alexander and by Caesar": while the Christians
themselves, claiming, by an exaggeration as reprehensible as
it is impossible, to push forgiving to the point of forgetting,
immediately give the lie to their pretensions by "proscribing
forever the whole Jewish nation in order to avenge one single
victim. . . ."[13]

Lastly, Christian doctrine is even more unfavorable to "sociability than to intelligence. . . . The omnipotence" of the God
whom it places at the apex of all things "sanctifies egoism"
even "more than stupidity, first of all in the type of the deity
and then among his worshippers". Thus it has been incapable
of rising, of its own accord, to social conceptions and giving
civic cares their proper place. "Its own spirit was necessarily

---

[11] *Disc.*, pp. 86–87.
[12] *Catéch.*, p. 281.
[13] *Div.*, vol. 1, p. 169. *Polit.*, vol. 3, p. 413. *Inéd.*, vol. 2, p. 371.

personal, either as regards the aim set for each existence as a whole or as regards the feeling represented as dominant." Thus the typical Christian life was not put fully into practice anywhere "except among the hermits of the Thebaid". It is an anarchical type of existence, rejecting all social influences, repulsing all human interest and acting as a solvent of public life.[14] The man who believes he is in direct touch with an Absolute Being can only be a ferment of social disintegration. He is lifted up by an "abstract urge" that continually runs counter to "the collective order", and he disregards all solidarities. He cannot recognize them in time any more than in space: consider Christian injustice to the Graeco-Roman past, an injustice that extends also to its Jewish antecedents. Christianity has none of the sense of continuity that is part of the sense of relativity and one of the essential characteristics of the social sense. Arrogant in its own idea of itself, it develops arrogance in its initiates, fostering in them that rebellion of the mind against the heart, that is to say, of the personal instincts against the collective instincts, which is at the root of the deep-seated anarchy of the modern world. Social anarchy and intellectual anarchy,[15]

---

[14] *Polit.*, vol. 3, pp. 445, 451, 454; vol. 4, pp. 8, 93. Cf. Edward Caird, *La Philosophie sociale et religieuse d'Auguste Comte* (French trans of: *The Social Philosophy and Religion of Comte* [Glasgow: J. Maclehose & Sons, 1885; reprint: New York: Kraus, 1968]), p. 163. Compare the Baron d'Holbach, *Système social* (Paris: Niogret, 1822), chap. 3, on "The God of the Christians": "The misanthrope God, in his gloomy and unsociable lessons, seems to have entirely ignored the fact that he was speaking to men living in society. What, in fact, does his morality say to us, this morality so vaunted by those who have never seriously examined it? It counsels us to flee the world . . ."; or *Le Christianisme dévoilé* (Paris: Libraires Associés, 1767), chap. 14. Compare Rousseau as well: if he, too, believes that Christianity in the pure state would be unfavorable to "particular societies" because it "weakens the strength of political scope", he at least maintains that it is "very advantageous to the general society"; he does not make the Gospel the "citizen's religion", but he sees in it "the religion of man": *Contrat social*, I, 4, c. 8; *Première lettre de la montagne*, etc.

[15] One could also say: "literary anarchy"; this is how Comte designates the romanticism of his time, *Cours*, vol. 4, p. 18, note.

Christianity is responsible for both: if it were to prevail forever, "a mystic excitement would sweep man and Humanity
into endless fluctuations or infinite divagations. . . ."[16]

2. Jesus and Saint Paul

Auguste Comte's ideas on the subject of Christianity are so
shocking both to the historical sense and to Christian feeling that, although they are expressed, as we have seen, in the
plainest terms, a number of sound minds seem to have made
themselves blind in order not to see them. Thus Emile Faguet
made Comte say: "As they were in the beginning, Christian
ethics are our ethics, they are excellent; but in their debased
state they are immoral"—contending that the whole trouble
came from the "modern distortion" they had undergone, gradually forsaking "love one another" for "save your soul", leaving the human for the ascetic, passing from the Gospel to the
Imitation.[17] A more inaccurate and unfortunate choice of terms
it would be difficult to find: Auguste Comte is known to have
professed the most lively admiration for the *Imitation*, while he
always made a point of disparaging the Gospel, with a kind of
rancorous pertinacity. He speaks with contempt of "the mental
and moral void" that characterizes the Gospels,[18] and he never
cites any one of their precepts without immediately criticizing

---

[16] *Catéch.*, p. 360; *Synthèse*, p. 26. *Polit.*, vol. 1, p. 19. *Test.*, p. 114. Cf. *Polit.*,
vol. 3, p. 453: "Monotheistic doctrine was always very hostile to continuity as
well as to solidarity, because of its necessary disapproval of all our polytheistic
or fetishistic predecessors. The adoption of Hebraic antecedents was tending
to make up for this anarchic rupture of human filiation, if the ingratitude of
the Christians toward the Jews had not neutralized this artificial bond." *Circ.*,
p. 28: "The instinct of continuity, the principal attribute of our sociability,
was at first profoundly altered by Catholicism, whose brutal advent rejected
all our Graeco-Roman antecedents."

[17] Émile Faguet, *Politiques et moralists du xixe siècle* (Paris: Boivin, 1890–
1903), pp. 326–27.

[18] *Polit.*, vol. 3, p. 409. One disciple, Georges Deherme, will write: "Chris-

it, although he does not disdain now and then to transpose one of them into his own system.[19]

This systematic hostility is directed in the first place against the very person of Jesus. The space given in Comte's religion to the cult of great men is well known. The "Positivist Calendar" honors them one after the other, with a broadminded eclecticism, in its months and in its days. These benefactors of humanity are not exclusively men of science or of thought, great captains or great statesmen: there are founders of religions among them. But in this list, which includes Confucius, Moses and Muhammad, the name of Jesus would be sought in vain. In a first version of the Calendar, in 1848, Comte had thought of making Jesus "Saint John the Baptist's deputy", "but I soon recognized", he said later, "that he did not deserve even that humble rank." To a disciple who expressed surprise, he replied that he had made up his mind "quite irrevocably" on that point and that he would uphold the "total exclusion"[20] of Jesus. "The founder of the religion of Humanity" declared that he "would always regard the just glorification of all his forerunners as a sacred obligation", and he would not consider that he discharged this duty if he omitted to celebrate even the nameless company of the founders of fetishism.[21] But he systematically ignored the greatest of his precursors. When he has to refer to Jesus, he habitually resorts to circumlocution. He refuses to recognize a forerunner in Jesus, however indirectly. "That person"

---

tianity . . . exalts the individual, that is to say, the instinct, and diverts him from social reason. . . . All the ferment of rebellion, of logomachy, and of sentimental profligacy are in the Gospel" (*Aux jeunes gens: Un maître, Auguste Comte; une direction: le Positivisme* [1921], p. 95).

[19] *Polit.*, vol. 2, p. 71: "Each generation must give freely to the following generation what it itself received freely from the preceding."

[20] *Div.*, vol. 1, pp. 512–13 (to Hutton, 20 Descartes 65). It had been discussed at the Positivist Society; Littré had wanted the name of Jesus to be placed on the calendar; *Notes sur Auguste Comte par un de ses disciples* (1909), p. 164.

[21] *Polit.*, vol. 3, p. 204.

was only a "religious adventurer" and had contributed nothing to mankind. He was "essentially a charlatan".[22] He should be regarded as no more than a "false founder", a "supposititious founder" "whose long apotheosis will henceforth be greeted with irrevocable silence".[23]

Christ's contribution would have been purely destructive if it had not been almost immediately amended by Saint Paul, who comes in for a fervent cult on Comte's part. He is "the great", "the wonderful"', "the incomparable Saint Paul". True, he shares that last title with a number of other great men.[24] With Caesar and Charlemagne, he is one of the three principal founders of the West, whose memory is to be solemnly celebrated every year. "Despite his theological apotheosis", his value has not yet been appreciated.[25] The first benefit he

---

[22] Comte's imperviousness to the spirit of the Gospel reminds one of the remarks Claudel attributes to his Judas: "My whole misfortune is that at no moment could I lose my faculties of control and criticism. I am like that. The people of Carioth are like that. A kind of great good sense. When I heard that it was necessary to turn the other cheek and to pay as much for one hour of work as for ten, and hate one's father and mother, and leave the dead to bury the dead, and to curse the fig tree because it did not produce apricots in the month of March, and not to lift an eyelash on a pretty woman, and this continual defiance of common sense, nature and equity, obviously I took eloquence and exaggeration into consideration, but I don't like that, I am offended. There is in me an appetite for logic, or, if you prefer, a kind of middle feeling, that is not satisfied. An instinct for measure. We are all like that in the city of Carioth. In three years I have not heard the shadow of a reasonable discussion . . ." "Mort de Judas", in *Figures et paraboles* (Paris: Gallimard, 1936).

[23] *Catéch.*, pp. 11, 353, 358. *Div.*, vol. 1, p. 513. *Polit.*, vol. 3, p. 356; p. 413: "Those who, for several centuries, admired familiarly the real devotion of Curtius and Decius must have scorned the childish fiction in which personal abnegation consisted in suffering death with the certitude of being resurrected three days later." Is this not the place to recall as well Rousseau's indignant words about "those base and stupid interpretations given to Jesus Christ" by men who think themselves superior?

[24] Aristotle, Muhammad, Charlemagne, Hildebrand, Saint Bernard, Bichat. *Polit.*, vol. 2, pp. 121, 321; vol. 3, pp. 428, 470, 478, 484, 485.

[25] *Div.*, vol. 1:2, p. 262, etc. *Polit.*, vol. 3, pp. 102–3. "More than three cen-

conferred consisted in "his general doctrine of the permanent struggle between nature and grace". By setting up this doctrine, he "actually outlined, in his own way, the whole of the moral problem. . . . For that valuable fiction temporarily offset the radical incompatibility of monotheism with the natural existence of benevolent inclinations that impel all creatures to unite with one another instead of devoting themselves in solitude to their creator." But in a more direct way he was able to "anticipate, in feeling, the conception of Humanity, in that moving but contradictory image: 'We are everyone members one of another'."[26] Above all, is it not to him that we owe that most wonderful of all doctrines, soon to be universally recognized by a Humanity that has entered upon its normal state, that it is in complete submission that true freedom is found?[27] Such are the overwhelming services rendered by this great man. In correcting the Gospel teaching on these three essential points and in thus rejecting anarchism and "Christian egoism", to replace them by an exactly opposite spirit, Paul was, at least by anticipation, the "true founder of Catholicism".[28]

History was for a long time mistaken on this point. But "no sound mind will be surprised that such a correction has been so slow in coming, since it had hitherto had no rules and no organs

---

turies after Saint Paul", wrote Comte, *Disc.*, p. 76, where anyone else would have said: "after Christ". Cf. Charles de Rouvre, *L'Amoureuse histoire d'Auguste Comte et de Clotilde de Vaux* (Paris: Calmann-Lévy, 1917), p. 407: "Just as, according to him, it was Fourier and not Sturm who was the author of Sturm's Theorem, so it was Saint Paul, and not Christ, who founded the doctrine of Christ."

[26] *Catéch.*, pp. 227 and 27.

[27] *Div.*, vol. 1:2, p. 169. *Inéd.*, vol. 2, p. 188; etc. Note that Comte, a founder himself, likes to compare his epistolary role with that of the Apostle: to P. Laffitte, 20 Gutenberg, 63 (*Div.*, vol. 2, p. 127).

[28] *Polit.*, vol. 2, p. 115: Paul is "the true creator" of "Catholic dogma", etc. Having recalled that Comte swears only by Saint Paul, Charles de Rouvre adds, p. 408: "If we remember that the Church of Saint Paul was the one where Comte mystically wed Clotilde, we see that his philosophy took counsel from his love." That is very possible.

with which to counter a belief that had always been admired or cursed but never judged."[29] It took the coming of positivism, with the sovereign equity and lucidity conferred upon it by the constant relativity of its standpoint, to reestablish the truth "by historically representing this great man as the true founder of what is improperly called Christianity". Truth to tell, Paul is himself responsible for that wrong designation. By a sublime abnegation, he wished to be considered only as the apostle. But this was not purely a desire for self-effacement on his part. For a proper understanding of his attitude, it is indispensable to recall the conditions that governed the "establishment of Western monotheism". It could not be founded except by a "divine revealer", without whom its principal historical role, "the separation of the two powers", would have been a failure. But such a need seems

> to require, in the founder, a mixture of hypocrisy and fascination, forever incompatible with a true superiority of heart and mind. There was no way out of this difficulty but the spontaneous readiness of the true originator to subordinate himself to one of the adventurers who must, at that time, have been often attempting to inaugurate monotheism, by aspiring, like their Greek forerunners, to personal deification. Saint Paul was soon led to adopt this relation toward that one, among the many prophets, who was best able to play such a part. Born a Jew, but brought up under Greek influence and having already become truly Roman, he at first despised such a type of person. In meditating on the construction of monotheism, however, he was not long in coming to appreciate the advantage this nascent success would afford it. Thus preserved from all personal degradation, Saint Paul could freely develop his fundamental mission, the scope of which made him so alive to the importance of such a solution that he became imbued with a deep veneration for a type of person henceforth idealized.[30]

---

[29] *Polit.*, vol. 3, p. 409. Cf. Antoine Baumann, p. 236.

[30] *Polit.*, vol. 3, pp. 410–11. One of Comte's closest disciples, Doctor Audiffrent, was to write a book on *Saint Paul et son oeuvre*.

Evidently Comte was not altogether devoid of a novelist's imagination. Saint Paul coming to worship Jesus sincerely, because the latter saved him from the necessity (always hateful to an upright man) of letting himself be worshipped, is a pretty idea to have hit upon. The great apostle was within an ace of infecting his admirer with his own enthusiasm. . . . The latter, however, regained possession of himself; it was sufficient for him to recognize "the true, though involuntary, usefulness" of the part played by Jesus, which was limited to "dispensing Saint Paul from the necessity of self-deification, without, however, ceasing to fulfill the condition essential to Western monotheism". Actually it is on the Greeks that Saint Paul depends much more than on Jesus. He has "an intimate acquaintance with the true thinkers of Greece"; there is between Aristotle and him a "spontaneous affinity",[31] while all the essentials of his doctrine are opposed to the spirit of the Gospel.

Thus, if it is fitting to glorify him as a founder, it is not by any means because he founded monotheism. It is because he ensured its success at a time when it had become expedient but at the same time laid the foundations of the true faith that was to triumph over it one day. "A fantastic and ridiculous belief", monotheism was kept in reserve by "an exceptional people" for the office it had to fill. Thus there was no reason for it to be hatched out, four centuries before Saint Paul, under the influence of the "divagations" of men like Socrates and Plato. These "would-be philosophers" do not come in for much better treatment at Comte's hands than Jesus himself. He denounces both the error in their minds and the flaw in their hearts and deplores the "disastrous influence" they exercised right up to our own times.[32] Saint Paul's influence was quite different. Through him the "monotheistic transition", that extreme phase of the provisional synthesis, took on an entirely

---

[31] *Polit.*, vol. 3, pp. 428–29.

[32] Ibid., vol. 3, pp. 341–43 and 331; p. 427: "Starting with Socrates and Plato, speechifiers prevailed over thinkers." *Test.*, p. 115.

different character. It was able to play its part, "which was really necessary only in a social way". So far as that was possible, Paul knew how to restrain "the divagations peculiar to the theological mind".[33] He is truly the head of that priestly line that succeeded in constructing the incomparable masterpiece known as Catholicism. If Comte believed in miracles, it would be necessary to say here: behold the miracle, the greatest of all. At any rate it may be said that here is the most paradoxical fact that history has to offer. Under the apparent continuity of one and the same tradition, Christianity was to transform itself into its opposite. The worst was to become the best. It is true that there were certain favorable circumstances, especially the influence of that Roman order with which the genius of Paul was so strongly stamped. Be that as it may, "Tacitus and Trajan could not foresee that, for several centuries, priestly wisdom . . . would so far restrain the natural flaws" of the religion which rightly made them uneasy that "admirable social effects could be derived from it for the time being."[34] That is nevertheless what happened. The persecutions failed, but, through other channels, the priesthood, heir of Saint Paul, succeeded.

3. The Work of the Catholic Priesthood

Auguste Comte's admiration for Catholicism is well known. He himself says in his *Testament*: "Since the year 1825 our writings have shown an increasing respect for Catholicism, the immediate and necessary precursor of the religion that has, above all, to consolidate and develop the structure that first took shape in the twelfth century."[35] And in his *Politique positive* he says, with a certain pride: "Already more complete justice has been done to Catholicism by positivism than by any of its own de-

---

[33] *Polit.*, vol. 2, pp. 100 and 107.

[34] *Catéch.*, p. 13.

[35] *Test.*, p. 9.

fenders, not even excepting the eminent de Maistre."[36] What he sees in it above all is what he calls its "social genius";[37] it is a great human achievement, the most powerful and the latest in date before the beginning of the crisis of the West, which preceded the advent of positivism. It is a vast system that, strictly speaking, did not come into being until the eleventh century and which, by the thirteenth, had already passed into the phase of decadence. More precisely, it is the spiritual aspect of the system which, in its temporal aspect, is called the "feudal system".[38] The complete system, or "catholic-feudal synthesis", was chiefly the work of two men, Charlemagne in the temporal sphere and Hildebrand in the spiritual. But its foundations were older. Caesar and Saint Paul had laid them. In the days of its splendor it had no equal for vigor and steadfastness. No later system has been capable of taking its place.[39]

The chief cause of such a perfect success is to be sought in "that great and beautiful conception" that distinguishes temporal from spiritual power. Bazard had already said, in 1829, in the *Exposition de la doctrine saint-simonienne*:

> Far from continuing to accuse the Church of having constantly sought to extend her power, of having ceaselessly worked to exempt that power from the law of the State, we ought rather to bless the efforts she made to this end and recognize that the

---

[36] *Polit.*, vol. 1, p. 87.

[37] *Div.*, vol. 1:2, p. 129: "The exposition of Catholic doctrine constitutes a very weak paper by the great Bossuet, who fails to make one feel the social genius of Catholicism."

[38] Note here, in both the concepts and the terminology, the dependence on Saint-Simon.

[39] To d'Eichtal, December 10, 1824 (Émile Littré, *Notes sur Auguste Comte par un de ses disciples* [1909], p. 152). *Cours*, vol. 4, pp. 36, 46, etc. *Polit.*, vol. 1, p. 102; vol. 3, p. 556: "the title of Catholicism [will be reserved] for the normal state of the Middle Ages". *Opusc.*, pp. 84, 86, 244. Since then, "the various European powers have reentered, with respect to each other, the savage state; kings have had engraved on their cannons the inscription '*Ultima ratio regum*', which since then has been precisely true" ("Considérations sur le pouvoir spirituel").

> division of power that resulted from the struggle she put up was
> the most important conquest that mankind has been able to make
> in the course of the epoch that has just come to an end.[40]

Now such a distinction itself presupposed the preliminary constitution of a priesthood distinct from the other authorities.
Therein lay the grave inferiority of fetishism, otherwise so
complete as a religious system: it was a regime that did not "allow any sort of priesthood to arise until very late in the day".
Polytheism had been able "to separate, and ultimately to segre-
gate, from the main body of society a highly speculative class,
equally released from military and industrial preoccupations
and capable, by its natural ascendancy, of gradually conferring
upon human society a lasting stability and a regular organization".[41] The ancient world, however, was not destined to attain full knowledge of the valuable distinction "between purely
moral power, whose essential function it is to govern thought
and inclinations, and political power properly so called, which
is directly concerned with actions and results". In this respect,
at any rate, monotheism marks a step forward, and that is why,
historically, much might be forgiven it. There is a tendency
in it "to separate spiritual from temporal power, at least when
it springs up spontaneously in the midst of a suitably prepared
population where, without such preparation, it cannot fulfill its
principal social purpose".[42] Even so, this happens solely with a
view to the work to be accomplished, and its true significance
will not be apparent until later. Suffice it to say that it would
be a mistake to understand this distinction or this "separation"
of the two powers in the light of any patterns offered for our
consideration by modern forms of society that have been the
outcome of 1789, or according to the schemata of theology.

---

[40] Bazard, *Exposition de la doctrine saint-simonienne* (Cinquième séance, Du
pouvoir spirituel et du pouvoir temporel), in *Œuvres de Saint-Simon et d'Enfantin* (Paris: Dentu and Leroux, 1865–1878), vol. 42 (1877), p. 263.

[41] *Catéch.*, p. 338.

[42] *Cours*, vol. 5, pp. 89, 104, 107. *Polit.*, vol. 2, p. 105; etc.

The Catholic priesthood, after having patiently built itself up, imposed its spiritual power upon Europe for the purpose of directing it.[43]

But the sole reason why it was actually able to direct Europe successfully was because it had at the same time transformed the religion it had the mission of transmitting. The medieval order, which is its handiwork, was, according to Comte, something quite different from a Christian order. It was a "Catholic" order, and Catholicism can rightly be called "the polytheism of the Middle Ages".[44] In a general way monotheism gives "a very dangerous impetus" to the religious spirit, "as is clearly illustrated by the example of the Jews, habitually swamped with prophets and visionaries". Christianity could not fail to increase the evil. But, thanks to the slow work of its priesthood,

> Catholicism, at the time of its greatness, directly and successfully endeavored to lessen, as far as possible, the political dangers of the religious spirit by more and more restricting claims to supernatural inspiration—claims that no spiritual rule based on theological doctrines can wholly abstain from sanctioning in principle but which the Catholic organization has notably reduced and checked by wise and effective usages.[45]

---

[43] Cf. Charles Maurras, L'Action française et la religion catholique, p. 135. Comte also expresses the same idea in a slightly different form when he says, Cours, vol. 5, p. 185, that "the eminently social genius of Catholicism has particularly consisted . . . in making morality gradually penetrate, as far as possible, into politics, to which, until then, morality had always been, on the contrary, . . . essentially subordinate."

Rousseau had better understood (although only to criticize it immediately) the principle of the distinction of the two authorities, the "theological system" and the "political system", the first being relative to the "spiritual kingdom" established on earth by Jesus.

[44] Polit., vol. 2, p. 134. It will be observed that Catholicism evokes Comte's admiration only insofar as he distinguishes it from, and contrasts it with, Christianity. When he happens to speak of it in a more general sense, it is in order to criticize it.

[45] Cours, vol. 5, pp. 186–87. Saint-Simon's judgments here were almost the reverse. "The Christian religion", he wrote, "made civilization take a great

The priesthood discountenanced miracles; above all, it discountenanced revelations; in a word, it "centralized all the oracles in the visible head of the Church, who thus became the permanent mouthpiece of the divine precepts, and eventually the universal judge of the Western peoples".[46] By this means the bonds of society were strengthened. "Catholic organization", "the Catholic constitution", "Catholic systematization", "Catholic discipline" are words our author is fond of using. In his system of thought they denote the victory won over evangelical anarchy.

This victory was so complete, the Christian elements were for some time so well held in check, that they could no longer serve as common denominator or connecting link between Catholicism and the other branches put forth by the Christian trunk. That is why, "beneath an empty conformity of dogmas", "Byzantine monotheism . . . is, at bottom, almost as different from it as Muhammedanism."[47] That is also why "Islamism comes nearer to Catholicism than Protestantism does."[48] We should be wrong, moreover, in judging medieval beliefs by those of our own day: "As a result of modern anarchy, the disposition now prevailing with regard to monotheism has an absolute character that it lacked in the Middle Ages, when, preoccupied with its final transition, the West only appreciated in Catholicism its aptitude to direct it without asking of it an outcome that was still undetermined."[49] If one feels surprise and contests this interpretation of the Catholic faith, Auguste

---

step forward by reuniting all men by a belief in a single God and by the dogma of universal brotherhood. By this means, it was possible to organize a more vast society . . ."; but the Catholic clergy, unfaithful to its origins, developed "mystical conceptions" without relation to "the principles of the sublime morality of Christ" (*Œuvres*, vol. 3, pp. 33–34; vol. 7, p. 123; cf. Émile Durkheim, *Le Socialisme*, p. 273).

[46] *Polit.*, vol. 3, p. 434.

[47] *Cours*, vol. 5, p. 182.

[48] *Appel*, p. 76.

[49] *Polit.*, vol. 3, p. 433.

Comte replies by quoting the doctrine of the Incarnation, the cult of the saints and above all the cult of the Virgin: Are not these so many breaches made in the monotheistic absolute, in uncompromising faith in God? Are they not so many stones ready for the building of the new religion? In a higher degree than the most human creations of ancient polytheism, "the incarnation of the prime mover" manifests "our growing tendency toward a real homogeneity between worshippers and worshipped"; "receiving its first contribution from the institution of the Trinity, which perpetuated a fugitive conformity, and a further contribution from the mystery in which everyone repeatedly took the body of the Deity into his own body", this parallel "enabled the God of the Middle Ages to offer Western hearts an image foreshadowing Humanity". Thus,

> in borrowing from polytheism the hypothesis of incarnation, Catholicism not only enhanced its dignity as dogma but, above all, improved its social character. This divine mediator, moreover, proclaimed, even if obscurely, the growing tendency of mankind to look for its supreme Providence in its own midst. . . . Catholicism brought out this tendency more strongly. . . . Such a progression was to end in the complete elimination of the fictitious being, when the real being should have acquired sufficient greatness and stability to replace its necessary forerunner completely.[50]

The cult of the saints, too, was to contribute greatly toward removing the danger of God. When it had attained a sufficient development, that is to say, from about the tenth century, it

---

[50] *Polit.*, vol. 2, p. 108; vol. 3, p. 455. Contrast Comte's assertions with Kierkegaard's declaration in *Traité du désespoir* (French trans. by Ferlov-Gateau of *Sygdommen til doden* [*Sickness unto Death*]), p. 230, which is perfectly in accordance with Catholic orthodoxy: "No other human doctrine has ever drawn God and man together in actual fact as Christianity has; no other has ever been capable of it. God in person has alone the ability to do it: Is any invention of man anything more than a dream, a precarious illusion? But no doctrine has ever taken more care to guard against the most dreadful of blasphemies—that which, since God made himself man, consists in profaning his deed by acting as if God and man were but one."

"improved the dogmatic constitution of Catholicism by an admixture of polytheism of the type, and to the extent, demanded by the popular purpose of the monotheistic faith". The irrational criticisms voiced by Protestants and deists are an indication that it was possible to retain it, with the necessary modifications, in the positive religion.[51] But it was above all the cult of the Virgin that wrought a deep and auspicious change in Western monotheism. For here it is a case of real "worship". In the century of the Crusades, "with the double flowering of feminine influence and chivalrous manners", the Virgin acquired over Western hearts a growing ascendancy that Saint Bernard, for instance, sanctioned while trying to systematize it. From then onward, "the fundamental flaw resulting from the omnipotence of the supreme mover" was in process of correction. The cult of God became "almost extinct". If the cult of the saints reintroduced polytheism, it may be said that the cult of the Virgin went one better: it reintroduced fetishism. Nothing was more suited than "this holy idealization of the feminine type" to pave the way for "the final conception" of which it was "the mystical forerunner". "Better than the divine mediator", "this truly human mediatrix foreshadowed our cult in its normal state." The only really poetic fruit of Catholicism, the "sweet creation of the Virgin" wonderfully predisposed souls for "positive worship". It was she, and not the Eucharist, which should serve as a transition to this final cult "under the gradual impulsion of the positivists, assisted by the women and the regenerate Jesuits". It was the image of the Virgin Mother that should accustom people to the emblem of "our goddess", Humanity.[52]

---

[51] *Polit.*, vol. 3, p. 475.

[52] *Catéch.*, p. 363. *Appel*, p. 77. *Polit.*, vol. 2, p. 122; vol. 3, pp. 485–86, 548. *Div.*, vol. 1:2, pp. 28, 41, 160, 179, 233, 344. One must admire, says Alain, p. 142: "Comte's remarks on the popular cult of the Virgin, in which he perceives that fetishism, which is closer to the truth than its ambitious successors, here energetically resists monotheistic simplification, which corresponds to the abstract, cruel age of our race."

"A vast and wonderful organization", medieval religion, with all its cultural flowering and all its array of social and political institutions as well, is thus the result of "the outstanding wisdom of the Catholic priesthood".[53] It is not in any way a divine religion, of course; but neither is it the outcome of an inspiration that considered itself divine; it is an

> outstanding political masterpiece of human wisdom, worked out gradually during the course of centuries, in forms that varied considerably but were all parts of a whole, from the time of the great Saint Paul, who first conceived the general spirit of it, to that of the energetic Hildebrand, who finally coordinated the complete social constitution.[54]

All this progress was due "rather to its situation than to its doctrine", which, indeed, being full of "the moral dangers peculiar to monotheism", did not cease to disturb "the social functions of the priesthood".[55] But the practical instinct of the priests made them doggedly amend the logical effects of the theological principle in accordance with social needs, while "their subordinate material position . . . compelled them to use spiritual means of persuasion in preference to the ruder weapons of material force." Thus they became "the true heirs of social polytheism" and of the incomparable prestige that the name of Rome[56] possessed in former times.

Even when its true character has been recognized, it has not been sufficiently noticed that Auguste Comte's eulogy of the Catholic priesthood is an exact echo of the one he had already bestowed upon the priesthood of pagan antiquity. Supernatural beliefs, he said, threatened to disturb human reason; it was partially preserved by priestly wisdom. Freed from material cares in order the better to meditate upon public welfare, the priests of polytheism embodied "the normal type of the contemplative

---

[53] *Catéch.*, p. 361.

[54] *Cours*, vol. 5, p. 205.

[55] *Polit.*, vol. 2, p. 112.

[56] Ibid., vol. 3, pp. 449, 464; vol. 4, p. 526. Cf. Caird, p. 361.

life"; and the precepts they laid down were always directed toward a social end. However much the theological system based
these precepts on purely individual motives, the sacerdotal instinct knew how to turn them to the advantage of society.[57]
Thus, whether in paganism or in Christianity, the historical
role of the priesthood is the same: to use the religion officially
under its protection in such a way as to counter the antisocial
effects of that religion, even at the cost of betraying its spirit.
But in the case of Christianity this last necessity is more urgent
because Christianity is more profoundly antisocial.

Thus that disciple of Comte's was being faithful to his master as well as being sincere who said one day to a Catholic:
"I have always considered that Catholicism saved the human
race."[58] But it is now sufficiently clear what a great gulf there
is, in every respect, between this idea of salvation and the one
that Catholics themselves receive from their faith. It is therefore difficult to agree with Mr. Georges Dumas that Auguste
Comte had "the Catholic Spirit" and that this Catholic spirit
makes of him, "despite all differences, the heir of the great
doctors of the Church".[59] It is even permissible to express surprise that a serious historian should have emitted so strange
a judgment. As we know, Comte himself spoke of a "systematic predilection" for what he called Catholicism. But he took
adequate care to narrow down its meaning; it was "the general

---

[57] *Polit.*, vol. 3, pp. 161, 214, 231–32.

[58] Charles Maurras to the Count de Lantivy, February 15, 1902. Cf. Maurras, *La Politique religieuse*, 2d. ed. (Paris: Nouvelle Libraire Nationale, 1912),
p. 23: "If I said from what, M. de Lantivy would be shocked. Now, I find it
pointless to shock any of us when we have been brought together."

[59] Georges Dumas, *Psychologie des deux Messies positivistes, Saint-Simon et Auguste Comte* (Paris: Alcan, 1898), p. 232. A similar error of judgment in Faguet,
p. 286: "A man born a Catholic and who, basically, has always remained so."
There is more truth in this opinion by Mr. Maurras, *L'Action française*, p. 200:
"With the founder of positivism, the resemblances and affinities with Catholicism are so numerous and so strong that they could rightly alarm religious
authorities and make them fear confusion on the part of thoughtless or non-
chalant listeners."

perfecting that the social organism received in the Middle Ages under the political ascendancy of Catholic philosophy".[60] And that, he adds, was possible only so long as the principal flaws of the deplorable Catholic "doctrine" could be neutralized by exceptional wisdom.[61]

The miracle, however, was not complete. It could not be. "The admirable attempt at human systematization . . . set the goal and indicated the conditions", but it miscarried all the same. "The Catholic principle never adapted itself to the social direction that the wonderful perseverance of the priesthood attempted to impress upon it." Thus medieval Catholicism suffered from an inward contradiction that, despite its magnificent success, was to render it unstable and short-lived. "Its full splendor" was "to all intents and purposes" limited "to the twelfth century".[62] This was because its nature was eminently transitory.[63] On the intellectual plane the scholastic doctrine, by a true compromise, was already restricting "the ascendancy of theology in monotheism" and was tending more and more to abstraction, condemning providential power to a "sublime inertia" and bestowing all the real activity upon a "great metaphysical entity". The "most cultivated minds" and

---

[60] *Cours*, vol. 5, p. 231. Around the same time, Lamennais wrote: "this social system, which is all Catholicism . . .": "De l'avenir de la société", in *L'Avenir* of June 29, 1831.

[61] *Catéch.*, p. 361. *Polit.*, vol. 2, p. 344: The priesthood is "obliged to overcome, through its own wisdom . . . the radical vices of a doctrine profoundly dissimilar to the existence it must regulate."

[62] *Polit.*, vol. 1, p. 351; vol. 3, p. 418 (cf. Ferdinand Brunetière, *Sur les chemins de la croyance, première étape, l'utilisation du positivisme*, 9th ed. [Paris: Perrin, 1912], p. 53); vol. 2, p. 124. On the "fragility" of the Catholic-feudal regime, vol. 2, pp. 124–28: "By setting its hopes always on an eternal ascendancy, monotheism, Eastern as well as Western, involuntarily reveals its natural fragility; while fetishism and polytheism were too deep-rooted ever to experience the need to reassure themselves thus."

[63] *Appel*, p. 21: "The contradictory attitude of Catholicism". *Catéch.*, p. 353: "The profoundly contradictory nature of such a construction". *Cours*, vol. 5, p. 273.

the "most energetic characters" had always regretted the old polytheism, and, "in the doctrine of the two principles", its spirit had uttered a protest that could never be overcome. From the beginning of the fourteenth century, the whole system tottered, and it was then that "the vast Occidental revolution that positivism has just concluded"[64] had its inception. Be it noted:

> The Catholic-feudal synthesis did not succumb, like all the preceding syntheses, under the continued impulsion of the one that was to succeed it: it disintegrated through its own brand of incoherence, the natural antagonism of its chief elements. Having cursed all its ancestors, Occidental monotheism wanted to be blessed by whatever descendants it had. . . . [But] the more it tried to coordinate everything, the more clearly it displayed the impotence of theologism with regard to a systematization that was reserved for the only doctrine capable, in virtue of its reality, of embracing the whole of an indivisible problem. . . .[65]

Thus its disintegration was spontaneous, and it has now long been in decay. The "mental dissolution of Catholicism" was inevitable, and its social decadence merely followed its intellectual decadence.[66] The opinions it provoked (now completely

---

[64] *Disc.*, pp. 46–47. *Polit.*, vol. 2, p. 114: "This strange combination of an absolute will with immutable laws was consecrated in the great scholastic transaction that ended the Middle Ages"; vol. 2, pp. 100, 124. *Catéch.*, p. 364.

[65] *Appel*, p. 60. Formerly, in the *Sommaire appréciation de l'ensemble du passé moderne* (April 1820), Comte had insisted on the fact that the Catholic synthesis was threatened because, from the beginning, the positive principle had been introduced into it by Arab science; so "all this splendor rested on a minefield": *Opusc.*, pp. 12–13.

[66] *Appel*, p. 62; p. 61: Catholicism is nothing any more but a cult, its system of government and its dogma have decomposed, "its so-vaunted morality no longer inspires anything but some vague declamations, which can, according to the impulse, become alternately oppressive with regard to the poor and subversive against the rich, while preaching servility like sedition." *Cours*, vol. 5, pp. 186, 255.

retrospective) are inevitably divided. While doing justice to "the merits and advantages of Catholicism", the historian must regret "the inevitable breach" it made in "human continuity", a breach whose disadvantages it could never really palliate.[67] He is forced to note that "Catholicism proved competent only in regard to personal life, whence its influence barely extended to domestic relations, without in any way being able to embrace social life", so that its efficacy "has been greatly exaggerated"; that it was, moreover, "so shocking in itself, for both mind and heart", that "our pious and chivalrous ancestors" would, like ourselves, have been very well aware of its natural flaws, but for the social efficacy that the priesthood stamped upon it and which alone caused its rule to be endured; that in spite of everything it preserved "the fantastic spirit and egotistical character proper to even the purest theologism"; that its philosophic influence would have become disastrous "without the whole set of polytheistic antecedents" from which it never succeeded in purging the understanding.[68] Lastly, let it not be forgotten that in Catholicism "most of the thanks addressed to the fictitious being represented as many acts of ingratitude toward Humanity, the only real author of the benefits in question."[69] In short, "the positive religion", for which this "provisional regime" had in some respects paved the way, is now nevertheless obliged "directly to repair all the ravages ensuing from the Catholic synthesis".[70]

---

[67] *Polit.*, vol. 1, p. 351; vol. 4, p. 533: "The ascendance of Catholicism broke the continuity." *Catéch.*, p. 369. Catholicism "breaks the chain of time by cursing its true ancestors". Cf. Brunetière, p. 53.

[68] *Polit.*, vol. 2, pp. 111, 123; vol. 3, pp. 436, 496, 507. Cf. to Barbot de Cheffent, November 8, 1846: the "dying theologism", by its nature, develops an exorbitant personality". *Nouv.*, p. 74.

[69] *Polit.*, vol. 2, p. 58.

[70] *Appel*, p. 21; p. 24: "The dogma of Humanity gradually arose under fictitious guardianship, which is irrevocably outdated."

4. A Holy Alliance

While this synthesis was thus in the process of disintegration, the Christian principle, released, once more developed its seeds of anarchism. "The Western priesthood irrevocably became retrograde" and, during this time, "its belief, left to itself, tended to develop freely the immoral character inherent in its antisocial nature."[71] The immense egoism that this belief sanctified in God and encouraged in man was thus set free from the bonds in which the Church had sought to confine it. This first becomes apparent in the sixteenth century, among the "would-be reformers". They caused a "retrogression toward God of the worship that, since the time of the Crusades, the peoples of the West had increasingly transferred to the sweet figure who was the spontaneous forerunner of Humanity".[72] Hence the "aridity" of Protestantism; hence its danger, too. Shattering that "initiative of the heart", it provoked "the revolt of the mind". While Catholicism tended to "give the forms of worship their natural ascendancy", Protestantism "gives a false preponderance to dogma".[73] With it, absolute influences and individualist tendencies are once more unleashed. It sets up personal investigation against the opinion of society.[74] Wherever it establishes itself, "the anarchic principle, although kept in check by the transitional system, creeps in on every hand, in line with the individual examination of biblical beliefs."[75] Comte does not like the Bible. He never understood its greatness or

---

[71] *Catéch.*, p. 30.

[72] *Synthèse*, dedication (to Daniel Encontre). *Div.*, vol. 1:2, p. 233: "It deferred to God the preoccupation that was beginning to be directed toward the sweet forerunner of Humanity." Cf. Caird, p. 166.

[73] *Circ.*, p. 70.

[74] *Div.*, vol. 1:2, p. 321. *Polit.*, vol. 3, p. 550.

[75] *Hutton*, p. 34. Yet, right at the end, in memory of his mentor of Montpellier, Daniel Encontre, who was a Protestant, Comte would at times bring a more benign judgment to bear on Protestantism. He would point out "the tendency of positivism to treat as auxiliaries all provisional religions, even the

appreciated its poetry. Thus he reproaches Protestantism with a "constant tendency . . . to put forward as guide for modern peoples the most backward and dangerous part of the Scriptures, namely, the part concerning Jewish antiquity".[76] Protestants, he thinks, show their bad taste and even "their religious ineptitude" by scorning that "incomparable summary of Western monotheism", the *Imitation* (in which it is so easy to replace "God" by "Humanity")[77] and by preferring to it "the universal and daily reading of the sacred books of Judaism".[78] Such reading is full of dangers, and it may truly be described as constituting "a relapse into anarchy".[79]

In the advance toward absolute liberalism, that is to say, anarchy, Protestantism was only a "halt", after the first phase of spontaneous disintegration.[80] "The Protestant insurrection"[81]

---

less consistent ones". "Since", he would add, "the universal religion is irrevocably constituted, its installation demands, during the whole course of organic transition, the character that I recently formulated by means of this systematic verse: Conciliatory in fact, inflexible in principle": *Synthèse*, p. XIII. Whence the idea, scarcely compatible with the one we have just seen, of a vast "religious alliance that would bond together, under positivism, first the Catholics, then the Muslims, finally the Protestants hoping for the reconstruction of spiritual power, and even the deists and pantheists, if the principle of the separation of the two powers has prevailed over their revolutionary tendencies." *Div.*, vol. 1, p. 238 (1 Homer 67). And, vol. 1:2, p. 208 (1 Saint Paul 69): "Although in this holy alliance Catholicism merits the principal attention of positivist presidency, one must not at all neglect Protestantism, even the closest neighbor of the purely revolutionary state."

[76] *Cours*, vol. 4, p. 121, note.

[77] Not always absolutely; but the rare contrary cases are an invaluable occasion to feel all the better the superiority of the new religion over the old. *Div.*, vol. 1, p. 439: "This substitution, nearly always possible, makes evident the moral superiority of positivism over Catholicism. Even when it becomes impossible, one easily recognizes that that adheres to the egotistical and chimerical nature of Christian beliefs" (to M. Laurent, weaver at Tarare, 21 Gutenberg 63).

[78] *Appel*, p. 73.

[79] *Hutton*, p. 118.

[80] *Cours*, vol. 4, p. 31. *Polit.*, vol. 3, p. 533.

[81] Cf. Maurras, *L'Action française*, p. 236; ibid.: "Judaic anarchy".

was itself soon followed by a purely metaphysical deism, which was a still more effective solvent. And Comte goes on to analyze, not without perspicacity, the developments leading, "in the intellectual order", to "a more and more attenuated or simplified Christianity, finally reduced to that vague and impotent theism that, by a monstrous juxtaposition of terms, the metaphysicians called *natural religion*, as if all religion were not necessarily supernatural".[82] It should not be forgotten that the *Cours de philosophie positive* appeared at a time when eclecticism, in official thought, had reached its apogee, and that it is this, above all, that Auguste Comte had in mind when attacking a certain form of belief in God as well as when arraigning psychology. Here he is on common ground with Proudhon, who was, however, much better able to understand at least certain aspects of faith and who had been brought up on the Bible. It is distressing to read the charges, often only too just on both sides, which the critics and partisans of deism bandied in that nineteenth century. The youth of today, Mazzini wrote to Edgar Quinet, "denies God . . . , belief in an intelligent providential law, and all that is good, great, beautiful and holy in the world; it denies a whole heroic tradition of great religious thinkers, from Prometheus to Christ, from Socrates to Kepler, in order to kneel before Comte, Büchner. . . ."[83] A noble lament! But is not this a case of deploring the effect after having provided the cause? Was the faith criticized by Comte really consistent? And, despite all his incomprehensions, Comte had logic on his side when, as a young man still, he wrote to his friend Valat, who had just been converted: "I own that I was glad to hear that in returning to the theological state, your mind and your heart did not stop short in the ineffectual phase of metaphysical

---

[82] *Cours*, vol. 4, p. 41. This last thought would be much more just if Comte did not understand "supernatural" in a sense that is very far from the Catholic sense.

[83] Quoted by Mme. Edgar Quinet, *Mémoires d'exil* (Paris: Le Chevalier, 1870), vol. 2, p. 434.

deism that is at present preventing any fundamental regeneration. . . . I much prefer to see you frankly Catholic."

In accordance with that preference, Comte wishes the positivists to become "the systematic defenders of Catholic customs against the impact of Protestantism"; he is glad to note that "Catholic resistance protects the Occidentals of the south against Protestant or deist metaphysics"[84]—which means, in the first place, against faith in God. He thinks that there would be "great advantages in narrowing down social discussions today to a straight contest between the Catholic spirit and the positive spirit, the only ones that can now fight it out to any purpose since, on different bases, both are conducive to the establishment of a real organization"; to this end, "Protestant metaphysics would be eliminated by common consent." This is an idea that is dear to him, he reverts to it in his correspondence, he pleads "for the concentration of philosophical and social discussions between positivists and Catholics"—Protestants, deists, sceptics and, in a word, all metaphysicians, being, *by common agreement*, treated as hopeless bunglers.[85] This word "agreement" runs through his head. It takes on a more and more definite meaning. At first it was merely a question of an understanding between two adversaries to get rid of the lukewarm and leave only their extreme positions confronting one another; it was the idea of "an issue directly joined be-

---

[84] *Catéch.*, p. 23. Cf. Léon de Montesquiou, *Le Système politique d'Auguste Comte* (Paris: Nouvelle Libraire Nationale), p. 117. To Benedetto Profumo, 25 Caesar, 63: "The great French initiative must increasingly rely principally on populations preserved from Protestantism and deism" (*Nouv.*, p. 225).

[85] *Cours*, vol. 5, pp. 173–74, note. *Hutton*, p. 92 (10 Dante 68). *Div.*, vol. I, p. 242: "The agreement of positivism and Catholicism to dismiss Protestantism from any discussion as incapable of any result" (19 Homer 67). Cf. Maurras, *La Politique religieuse*, p. 4: "It was necessary that we even merge in agreement about the nature and the existence of a God. But all, Catholics as well as atheists and positivists as well as pantheists and pagans, find that we reject the philosophical deism, such as it appeared with a Kant, a Rousseau, a Cousin or a Jules Simon. Deism, Protestantism and with every greater reason Judaism are naturally eliminated from our thought."

tween the two organic systems, all intervention in the form of criticism being ruled out", the idea of "a serious and dignified rivalry" in a clearly defined field,[86] once all "the metaphysical schools" had irrevocably disappeared. Soon the idea took a different turn and incorporated the notion of "due accommodation" that positivism ought to admit or even prescribe toward former beliefs: rather than a stark opposition, it was to be a sort of temporary apportionment of spheres of influence, all those who still believed in God being urged to return to Catholicism, while the elect souls would join the positivist faith; the latter, thanks to their system of accommodation, would obtain the consent of the former to their program of social reorganization; they would be "at the head of the party of order" and "would lead the movement"[87] to its normal consummation in the noble league that the positivists were to organize for all the theologists properly impressed with the need to reconstruct spiritual discipline.[88]

Thereupon a plan began to take shape, to materialize. Auguste Comte remembered that long ago, in 1826, after the publication of the "decisive opuscule" in which he had publicly vowed his life "to the establishment in the West of the true spiritual power", he had had three interviews with Abbé de Lamennais, who was at that time "the real leader of the Catholic party". "Without any idle hope of converting one another",

---

[86] *Polit.*, vol. 3, p. 73. *Div.*, vol. 1:2, p. 33; p. 467: "The noble and patent concurrence of positivism toward Catholicism for the true reconstruction of the intellectual and moral order". *Mill*, November 20, 1841 (pp. 7–8).

[87] *Hutton*, p. 21 (7 Moses 66). *Div.*, vol. 1:2, p. 217 (22 Descartes 66), p. 337 (7 Gutenberg 68). *Circ.*, p. 41 (1854): "The system of hypocrisy must therefore be transformed into a system of management, in preferring the reactionary state to the negative state, in a generation in which the directors alone can attain the normal state."

[88] *Appel*, pp. 74–75. *Div.*, vol. 1:2, p. 332: "The holy League, which must rally the Catholics to the positivists against the Protestants" (to John Metcalf, 3 Aristotle 68). *Inédit.*, vol. 2, p. 346: "All equivocal souls [must be obliged] to choose between the only two beliefs that can truly pose the question of order" (to Hadery, 15 Charlemagne 68).

they had both been "spontaneously led to draw the groundplan of the great religious league" that had now to be built up in earnest. Thirty-one years had passed. Comte had become the High Priest of Humanity. He had "publicly taken possession of the pontificate that had devolved upon him in the normal course". He was exercising his powers with conscientious and unfaltering resolution. He was "the common father", and he meant to assume all the responsibilities of his title.[89] Had not the time come for "this holy plan" to be taken up again? His two addresses, to Czar Nicholas I, for the Orthodox Church, and to Reschi Pasha, for Islamism, had remained unanswered; scant hearing had been given to his *Appel aux conservateurs*. A stronger move must be made with regard to the Catholic Church. Despite many "individual disappointments" he was convinced that the realization of his plan might be "decisive": the alliance he offered could not fail to be accepted "by the best remnants of the ancient priesthood". Already (as he was soon to write) "two eminent disciples in New York" were "preparing *his* personal contacts with the American Catholics who, in that country, under no domination even as regards ideas, were more accessible to *his* influence". After "the masculine impacts" it would be necessary to ensure the active aid of "feminine sympathies", indispensable if the holy league was to be constituted at last.[90] But a more important and urgent step was necessary, the success of which would decide everything.

At the heart of Catholicism there was a privileged body in whom its spirit was incarnate and its power maintained: the Jesuits. The Order founded in the sixteenth century by Ignatius and Xavier had taken as its mission, says Comte, "the regeneration of the papacy, whose spiritual office had really fallen vacant since its temporal transformation"; the reform miscarried, even sooner and more completely than the attempt

---

[89] *Blign.*, p. 135 (10 Charlemagne 69). *Inédit.*, vol. 2, pp. 393 and 394; etc.
[90] *Div.*, vol. 1, p. 2 (to Sabatier, 8 Archimedes 69).

made in the thirteenth century "by a more highly developed
but equally inevitable influence". Far from rehabilitating a debased spiritual power, the Jesuits' endeavor itself speedily de-
generated into "hypocritical tactics" and, "in order to check
the mental anarchy" that was still making headway, they soon
confined themselves to systematizing the retrograde tendency
of Catholicism and passed by way of intrigue into corruption.[91]
Nevertheless their head was a real Pope (alongside the official
Pope, who, for three centuries now, had been "irrevocably reduced to the status of a mere Italian prince"). So he was the
man to approach. There was still a hope that, during the coming
period of transition, the Jesuits—abandoning their "corruptive
intrigues" and returning to "their original vocation in the reconstruction of spiritual power"—would "give the Catholic
dogma short shrift in order to concentrate upon ritual, so as
to prepare a backward but estimable public for the worship of
Humanity". "Regenerated as Ignatians", they would become
"useful auxiliaries"; they could help the positivists "to reor-
ganize the West"—provided, of course, "that they recognized
the natural superiority" of the positive "religion".

Positivism's Supreme Pontiff determined not to miss this
opportunity. One of his disciples, John Metcalf, was given the
mission of establishing "special contact" with the Jesuits in the
United States: without allowing them "any concessions calculated to encourage or revive their habitual leanings toward domination", he proposed that they should serve "as auxiliaries" in
the work of reconstructing spiritual power, vainly attempted
in the past by their founders. Others, Sémerie and Dr. Audiffrent, were to do the same in Paris.[92] But the great coup was

---

[91] *Polit.*, vol. 3, pp. 553–55. *Div.*, vol. 1, p. 452 (to M. Laurent, weaver at la
Croix-Rousse, 2 Frederick 63).

[92] *Div.*, vol. 1:2, p. 332 (to Sabatier, 8 Shakespeare 68), p. 334 (to John
Metcalf, 3 Aristotle); vol. 1, p. 401 (to Audiffrent, 8 Saint Paul 69). In calling
them Ignatians, Comte wanted to free the Jesuits of a name "that is in itself
corrupt".

to be attempted in Rome. In 1862 Auguste Comte intended to publish an *Appel aux ignaciens* in which he would call upon "their General to proclaim himself the spiritual head of the Catholics, declaring the Pope prince-bishop of Rome. In order to implement this proclamation, the General of the Ignatians would be publicly invited by the founder of positivism to take up his residence in Paris." But now he could not help being frightened by that bold proposition. So, in his offer of alliance, Alfred Sabatier, the disciple chosen for the embassy, was to confine himself at first to a definite program: the abolition of the budget of church expenses.[93] This would be the "necessary preamble". Such a program could not fail to attract the Jesuits, since it would promptly lead to "the result which for three hundred years they had vainly been striving to attain: the supplanting of the local clergy, whose resistance was really the source of their downfall in the eighteenth century among all Catholic peoples. . . ."[94]

The course that events took is well known[95]—the letter sent by Sabatier on behalf of the Pope of positivism to the General of the Jesuits and at first left unanswered; the confusion of Auguste Comte with Charles Comte, the economist; the belated interview with the Assistant for France; the visitor tactfully shown out. The positivist Catechism, sent with the founder's compliments, was even left with its pages uncut. . . . Obviously these men of Jesus had no idea of how much had been offered to them! Alfred Sabatier, somewhat put out, made a report to his master. The Pontiff was disappointed but not

---

[93] Ibid., vol. 1:2, pp. 360 and 361 (to Sabatier, 8 Shakespeare 68, September 17, 1856); pp. 196, 354. *Circ.*, p. 59: "So, from all sides, the germs of the great alliance have already arisen so that the principal needs of the nineteenth century must soon develop among religious souls, against irreligious instincts."

[94] *Inédit.*, vol. 2, pp. 318–19 (to Hadery, 12 Bichat 67): "All the discipline that the bishops exercise rests, basically, on the official budget, the suppression of which would deliver the priests to the only body endowed with a true consistency in today's Catholicism." And p. 312 (to the same, 19 Frederick).

[95] Cf. Georges Dumas, in *Revue de Paris*, October 1, 1898.

shaken. If the Ignatian negotiations had had no immediate effect, they had surely, he thought, "sown seeds that the pressure
of events might soon develop".[96] On 9th Aristotle 69, replying
to Sabatier, he drew the following lessons from the incident:

> In the memorable interview you have described to me, you have
> nobly manifested the natural superiority of Positivism over all
> theologism, not only as regards elevation of thought but also as
> regards the moderation and magnanimity of its sentiments, and
> even the courtesy of its procedure. It is no more your fault than
> mine if those whom I already regarded as true Ignatians are still
> merely Jesuits, failing to recognize the position in the West and
> sacrificing the end to the means, until new upheavals come to
> enlighten their empiricism as to the dangers they are running,
> when they might instead be helping us to prevent or mitigate
> them. No better proof could have been given of the involuntary
> abdication of true spiritual power, and no more complete accep-
> tance of the social supremacy of Positivism, than that afforded
> by your artless interlocutor, who was probably so backward that
> he did not even feel how superior Ignatius Loyola is in every
> way to their Jesus Christ. But, despite their limited scope and
> their inadequate emancipation, these empiricists, whom I persist
> in believing sincere, will be involuntarily influenced by your ad-
> mirable preliminary letter. . . .[97]

It would be easy to take this for a made-up tale and laugh
at it. The thing certainly has its laughable side. The embassies
despatched across the globe from the sanctuary in the Rue
Monsieur-le-Prince; the new "holy alliance", proposed by an
old atheist philosopher who modestly regards Aristotle and

---

[96] *Inédit.*, vol. 2, p. 380 (to Hadery, 26 Caesar 69). Cf. *Div.*, vol. 2, p. 375.

[97] *Div.*, vol. 1:2; cf. p. 378, 27 Aristotle: "You see that positivism is
henceforth devoid of any real concurrence in the intellectual and moral
organization of the West." And to M. Edger, 1 Saint Paul 69 (p. 209): "Catholicism, too blinded by official protection, could not, I fear, appreciate sufficiently such a bond as under the hard pressure of recent events; while Protestantism, deprived of legal authority, is more susceptible to anticipating that
painful necessity."

Saint Paul as his two forerunners; the conviction that believers will readily agree to admit the superiority of positivism to their own faith; the surprise that a Jesuit should be submissive to Jesus Christ and place him even above Ignatius Loyola . . . clearly the founder of positivism—the name primarily signifies realism!—is a long way from reality. It all sounds like a madman's dream: but it would be wrong not to see the serious side of it too. The episode is highly symbolic. Auguste Comte is here the instrument of a temptation that, always latent, becomes particularly strong when Catholicism *seems* to have its back against the wall. What he proposes to the Church, with the utmost naïveté, is a betrayal. In exchange for temporal salvation (of a pretty precarious sort) she is to deny herself in denying her Master and Bridegroom. His avowed plan was to "use obsolete beliefs in order to make them work suitably toward the final transition".[98] It must be said, and he himself would say, of this alliance what he had said some years earlier of the dictatorship of Louis Napoleon: "Even if it would seem officially to benefit theologians", "certainly [they] will always end by gaining nothing from it".[99] But apart from any expectation of self-interest, apart from any calculation, who does not see that a man of the Church, aware of his mission—that supernatural mission which Auguste Comte so incredibly misunderstood —could respond in no other way than did the Jesuit whom Alfred Sabatier visited? This temptation has been repeated in various forms, at times more serious and more specious in appearance,[100] and it will arise again; but the Church, assisted by the Spirit of Christ, will not succumb to it.

---

[98] *Inédit.*, vol. 2, p. 381 (to Madery, 26 Caesar 69). Thus "doctrines empirically dedicated to heaven" would serve "on earth".

[99] *Blign.*, p. 53 (4 Moses 64 = January 1852).

[100] Other appeals have not been lacking. Cf. the letter from a group of positivists to the Archbishop of Paris, July 7, 1925: "We thus express the hope that Your Eminence, as well as the Church to which he is attached, might indeed recognize in the Religion of Humanity, not a rival and still less an enemy of his high moral mission, but, on the contrary, a friendly and allied Religion,

What fruits did Auguste Comte expect of such an alliance? What future was at stake? To find the answer to those questions, it is necessary to consider, at least in broad outline, the *positivist transpositions*.

---

a useful collaborator in the work of regeneration of a gravely ill Society . . ." (quoted by Georges Bouyx, *L'Église de l'Ordre*, vol. 1, p. 139). The positive faith, declared the same group, is "the affectionate daughter, the grateful and respectful heir of the religious, philosophical and scientific teachings of that great and venerable Past, and in particular of the admirable religious culture of Catholicism." Georges Deherme, *Auguste Comte et son oeuvre, le Positivisme* (Paris: Giard and Brière, 1909), pp. 114‒15: the Catholic Church must understand "that such an alliance is indispensable to her". Léon de Montesquiou, *Le Réalisme de Bonald*, pp. 11‒12: "By bringing out the agreement of thought that exists on a host of important questions between a Comte and a Bonald, I hope to have facilitated that alliance which Comte had hoped for and sought between all the defenders of the social order.

CHAPTER III

POSITIVIST TRANSPOSITIONS

1. The True Catholicism

The alliance that Auguste Comte, toward the end of his life, attempted to conclude with the Catholic Church was intended to be purely temporary. He thought it expedient because he no longer hoped that the triumph of his own Church, at any rate among the masses, was as near as he had at first predicted.[1] Nevertheless, "since the termination of (its) religious construction", that is to say since about 1843, the true universal Church was no longer merely a desire, a dream, an idea: it had begun to live. Having completed "the generation of gestation and birth", positivism began "the generation of establishment". The various local "churches" were firmly attached to the center. A new "spiritual power" was in existence and at work: "the positivist papacy" was a reality.[2] And Comte was quite sure that, in face of it, the other one, the old theologist papacy, could not but fade away more or less rapidly. . . .

During the first part of his career, the founder's role had

---

[1] In 1856, at the time he was publishing the *Synthèse subjective*, he wrote: "I suppose that I am writing in the year 1927, which, in my eyes, should constitute the seventy-third of the normal state. So the Western reorganization is sufficiently accomplished to have regenerated souls everywhere."

[2] *Div.*, vol. 1:2, p. 238 (1 Homer 67). *Blign.*, pp. 126–28 (10 Charlemagne 63). One of the links was constituted by the *Circulaires annuelles*, which Comte had been sending since 1850 to "each cooperator of the free subsidy constituted exceptionally for him". One can follow, throughout his correspondence, the jealous solicitude with which Comte surrounded his "precious Lyonnaise church" and the trouble it caused him: *Div.*, vol. 1, pp. 76, 105, 130–32, 140–43, etc. *Inéd.*, vol. 2, pp. 148–59, 263–72.

been chiefly that of a philosopher. Then the new Aristotle had changed into a new Saint Paul, in order to complete the edifice. "I have systematically devoted my life", he says in the *Système de politique positive*, "to making real science ultimately provide the necessary basis for the sound philosophy according to which I should then build up the true religion."[3] He says elsewhere that he was "the man whom the Great Being entrusted with the establishment of the true religion".[4] It had "at first taken shape as a mere philosophy, intended solely to establish a real and lasting harmony between all our sound logical and scientific conceptions"; but now the religion of Humanity stood revealed and, once it had given full assurance of "the normal satisfaction that the modern revolution claimed", it secured the "free submission of the mind to the just rule of the heart".[5] Some of those, however, who seemed to have adopted the conclusions of the *Cours* refused to commit themselves beyond that point. Only those who recognized both parts of the master's mission and followed him to the end were his disciples. "Positivists calling themselves intellectuals" were no more than "abortive positivists". "Complete positivists", "consistent positivists" were "religious positivists". They did not linger indefinitely in "the philosophical preamble" but accepted all their leader's work: they did not merely bring their convictions into conformity with it but regenerated "their feelings" and reformed "their habits" to correspond.[6] They grouped them-

---

[3] *Polit.*, vol. 2, p. XX. *Circ.*, p. 3.

[4] *Polit.*, vol. 4, p. 551.

[5] Ibid., vol. 2, p. 68.

[6] Ibid., vol. 4, pp. 535, 537, 548. *Hutton*, p. 58 (21 Moses 67): "One of the aborted positivists with whom M. Littré surrounds himself". *Div.*, vol. 1, pp. 348–49. *Inéd.*, vol. 1, pp. 84, 261. *Circ.*, pp. 20, 26, 27–28. Comte foresaw (*Div.*, vol. 1, p. 123; 8 Gutenberg 64) in the rather near future "the battle between the true positivists and the false . . . , between the religious and the irreligious, the latter fortified by whoever is afraid of any religion whatever, particularly positive religion." "The war", he added, in alluding to his two "spouses", "will be pursued under two feminine banners, one green, the

selves around Comte's "sacerdotal fatherhood".[7] Without any mental reservations, they sang with Charles Jundzill:

> Mankind becomes the focus
> Of all speculations:
> Centered in that locus
> Are all our heart's affections.
> It is the fair ideal and hope
> Toward which the infant race did grope
> While still confined in error's maze.
> Now all men worship at its fane,
> And all men hail its coming reign
> To end the tempest of our days.[8]

If the positivist religion thus seemed a final one, it was because it was the religion of Humanity in yet another sense: in the sense in which Catholicism had claimed to be that, through the etymology of the name it had assumed. This name was, in reality, "suited to positivism alone", so that "the Western revolution" could be "reduced to the replacement of the Catholicism of Rome by the Catholicism of Paris, when the human metropolis had become exclusively a spiritual one".[9] More than the first, indeed, the second possessed "that great attribute of universality that essentially characterizes spiritual organization".[10] That is what gave it confidence in the missionary task it assumed: it was this conviction that sustained its members in the pains they took to edify the "infidels" every-

---

other red, between the angel who never ceases to be thirty years old and the demon who has just reached his fifty-first year."

[7] *Div.*, vol. 2, p. 107.

[8] Charles Jundzill, "to Auguste Comte" (22 Descartes 64).

[9] *Polit.*, vol. 4, p. 463. Yet, in order to avoid confusion, they would not misuse the word "catholicism", even though it was very just etymologically, to describe the "new Church". *Div.*, vol. 1:2, pp. 193–94.

[10] *Cours*, vol. 5, p. 159, note. *Polit.*, vol. 4, p. 533: "Exclusively capable of a true universality".

where.[11] It was the final outcome of all the generations. It took over "all the meritorious programs" that Humanity had ever contemplated, in order to "carry them out, in a purer form".[12] Contrary to the view held by superficial observers, man in the course of history had become "more and more religious": that was the "epitome of human development", and even "the one and only law".[13] After the period of remote preparation, the West, for twenty centuries, had been groping its way toward "the universal religion, but without having the power either to abandon it or to establish it":[14] now it had at last found it.

Auguste Comte did not, of course, stop at a few vague indications on this subject. To the religious spirit of his doctrine he meant to give a body. The positivist religion is really a positive religion. "A dignified pomp is as suited to positivism as it is to Catholicism."[15] Dogmas and practices, ceremonies and intimate feelings were all thought out and ordered, down to the last particular, by the founder. This new Saint Paul was also a new Moses.

There is no need to go into the details of the legislation

---

[11] *Blign.*, p. 118. See above, chapter 1, section 2. Comte was actively interested, in his last years, in the "propagation of the true religion"; *Circ.*, pp. 82–84, etc.; he praised highly the "continued zeal of an eminent apostle" of "our nascent American Church". In 1884 and 1887, in his thirty-sixth and thirty-ninth circulars, Pierre Laffitte was to organize, according to his views, a whole "system of missions" with the intention of spreading "the good news": Grüber: *Le Positivisme depuis Comte jusqu'à nos jours* (French trans. by Mazoyer, 1893), p. 135.

[12] *Hutton*, p. 38: "Relative religion, the normal result of all the others". *Div.*, vol. 1:2, p. 261.

[13] *Polit.*, vol. 2, p. 19; vol. 3, p. 10. *Div.*, vol. 1, pp. 270, 276; vol. 1:2, p. 312. Comte added, according to his own experience, that this law sums up evolution, "individual as well as collective".

[14] *Synthèse*, dedication, and p. XVIII: "To terminate the Western revolution by gradually making the universal religion prevail", etc. *Polit.*, vol. 3, p. 621: "When the battles and the factions were exhausted, Humanity, prepared under their preponderance, necessarily arose by founding, upon peace and unity, the irrevocable advent of the universal religion."

[15] *Hutton*, pp. 42–43.

he laid down. Chiefly interesting is the recurrence of Comte's "Catholic allusions";[16] and the constant process of transposition by which the new Catholicism is modeled on the old. The Church had her sacraments—sacred rites with which she encircled the life of her children in order to sanctify it, leading them from the cradle to the grave: positivism has its rites, too, "consecrations" or "social sacraments" by which it similarly sanctifies "all the actual phases of private life", at the same time "systematically linking them to public life".[17] Hence their superiority over those of the old cult. There are nine of these sacraments, including one that is received *after* death—the additional sacrament of "incorporation", which may rather be compared with canonization.[18] This last rite symbolically expresses the positivist faith in immortality: all those who in the course of their objective existence have shown themselves worthy of it subsequently enter upon a subjective life in accordance with their deserts, the wonderful privilege of this life "consisting above all in the fact that it purifies the objective life, selecting from it only impressions worthy to survive"—a purification so perfect that the individual, ceasing to exist as a distinct being,

---

[16] Pierre Ducassé, *Méthode et intuition chez Auguste Comte* (Paris: Alcan, 1939), p. 563. Yet Comte is not referring to the center of Catholic worship; nothing in his inventions recalls the Sacrifice of the Mass.

[17] *Catéch.*, pp. 115–21. *Div.*, vol. 1, pp. 17–20; vol. 1, p. 451: The sacraments embrace "the whole economy of real existence, according to the solemn bond between each normal phase of private evolution and the collective organism". *Inéd.*, vol. 2, pp. 51–53; vol. 3, pp. 94, 197–200, 267–68. *Nouv.*, pp. 92–94.

[18] *Catéch.*, p. 122: "Seven years after death, when all disturbing passions have sufficiently died down but before the best special documents are already lost, a solemn judgment, the principle of which has been borrowed by sociocracy from theocracy, will irrevocably fix the lot of each. The priest, having announced incorporation, will preside over the ceremonial transfer of the sanctified remains, which, lodged until then in the civic cemetery, will now take their eternal place in the sacred grove that surrounds the temple of Humanity. Each tomb there is adorned with a simple inscription, a bust or a statue, according to the degree of glorification attained."

then becomes "a veritable organ of the Great Being"; he no longer forms part of it merely in hope but is henceforth incorporated in it, he becomes inseparable from it. Every individual aberration having been eliminated, "the continual influence of the social sense on the personality" is established forever. How superior such an immortality is, both in dignity and in sweetness, to that lonely immortality conjured up by "the objective Utopia of the theologians"![19]

The chief among these incorporated beings are the great men who are benefactors of Humanity. The cult of these great ones, which is above all a public cult, is copied from the cult of the saints, and it composes a liturgical year. The domestic cult is organized for the most part around marriage. As for the "private" or "secret" cult, which also has to have its rules, it knows the intercession of "angels"—those mothers, sisters, wives, daughters, beloved women, dead or still alive, whose affections or virtues have made them worthy objects of "private worship".[20] Thus this cult envelops life in "holy feminine in-

---

[19] *Blign.*, p. 15. *Polit.*, vol. 2, pp. 61–62; 68–71; 362–63: "The religion of Humanity definitively transforms the fanciful and crude notion of objective immortality, all of whose provisional efficacy is exhausted, in the definitive dogma, as noble as it is real, of the subjective immortality proper to all dignified human nature. As antisocial as the primitive hypothesis was in itself, when priestly wisdom could not sufficiently correct the vices of it, so the final conception is fit to consolidate and develop our true sociability, still more relative to time than to space." Vol. 3, p. XXXIII ("Lettre au tsar"). *Div.*, vol. 1, p. 10: "After this final transformation, the better part of ourselves always subsists, that part which binds us to others, the personality alone has disappeared"; pp. 33, 328, etc.

Cf. Antoine Baumann, *La Religion positive* (Paris: Perrin, 1903; 2d ed., 1924), pp. 247–48: "O dead . . . , they lie who say you disappeared into the void. . . . You are the dust of whom the best part of Humanity is formed."

There is also a "positivist hell", destined for "the unworthy spouse": *Div.*, vol. 2, p. 389.

[20] *Div.*, vol. 1, pp. 441, 450. *Polit.*, vol. 2, p. 64; vol. 4, pp. 118–19; Mother, spouse and daughter are the three "personal patrons" of man, "guardian angels" or "domestic goddesses". *Circ.*, pp. 95–96. *Inéd.*, vol. 1, p. 213: In ma-

fluences".[21] Rising above the saints and the angels, to complete the "sociolatrous system", "positive prayers" are addressed to the supreme deity. Humanity, as we know, is enthroned in the place of the traditional God; or, rather, surely it was Humanity that the true worshippers of the old God adored without knowing it—especially those devotees of the Virgin Mother who had a foretaste of its sweetness. Now their worship is fully conscious. They have learned that this is the "true Providence".[22] They know that the well-being of Humanity is the only real kingdom of God.[23]

But Humanity is not an abstract monad. It evolved on the Earth, which is itself contained in space "beyond what were once gods and, later, their unique condenser".[24] And there a triad is constituted, a "religious triumvirate", which is the pos-

---

turity, "we have submitted to the holy influence, in all its fullness, of the woman, who, having first given shape to us like a mother, and incidentally as a sister, is then to act on us like a spouse, and even secondarily like a daughter, so that our whole moral nature is sufficiently cultivated." Vol. 2, p. 66: "My great religious theory on the public and private worship of Woman as the indispensable preamble to and continuous stimulant of the worship of Humanity." *Blign.*, p. 32: "All that I have left to desire for your inner flight is a sufficient organization and a suitable practice of the secret cult that you must render to your angelic sister. . . ." *Hutton*, p. 35: "Adoration is particularly destined to develop our sympathetic instincts. . . . By improving us, it perfects the beings it concerns, which provides a new motive for extending it to the living."

[21] *Blign.*, p. 27: "The holy feminine influence that subjectively dominates my second life and which has so shared in the moral effort of the final religion". On 10 Charlemagne 69, Comte would reproach Blignières for "your radical dryness toward this sister whose personal adoration I could not formerly in any way make you institute as the necessary foundation of true positive worship. Yet it is impossible to write or speak suitably about the whole of positivism without having sufficiently submitted to the feminine influence." *Inéd.*, vol. 3, pp. 196, 202; etc.

[22] *Polit.*, vol. 3, p. 621. *Circ.*, p. 11: "The religion that is coming to reduce our race to its own providence."

[23] Cf. Baumann, p. 275.

[24] *Inéd.*, vol. 3, p. 305.

itive equivalent of the fantastic Christian Trinity and forms the only true and unchangeable Trinity:[25]

> An unchangeable Trinity guides our conceptions and our adorations, always related in the first place to the Great Being, then to the Great Fetish, finally to the Great Environment. . . . In it, first and foremost, veneration is paid to the human type in its perfection, in which the understanding helps pure feeling to govern activity. Next, our homage glorifies in it the active and benevolent habitation, whose assistance, willing though blind, is always indispensable to the supreme existence. . . . To this second cult succeeds that of the theatre, passive as well as blind, but still benevolent; to it we refer all material attributes, since its sympathetic flexibility helps our hearts and minds to an abstract appraisal of them.[26]

"Few minds", says Mr. Charles Maurras in this connection, "would follow an operation like Comte's without sacred awe. . . ." Indeed, we are naturally inclined to think that the time of great religious foundations has passed; "such prodigies are easier to imagine in the perspective of History than close at hand in a contemporary brain." Mr. Maurras himself, overcom-

---

[25] We will also suppress here some of the foliation of the new mythical tree in order to keep to its threefold trunk. Cf. *Div.*, vol. 1, p. 349; "You will see . . . Space, Earth and Humanity constitute the religious triumvirate, in which the Great Milieu is tied to the Great Fetish by heaven and the twofold earthly envelope, like the Great Fetish to the Great Being, by vegetality followed by animality. Such are the seven degrees of the sacred ladder that incorporates us, sympathetically and synthetically, the whole relative economy, simultaneously the domain of our feelings, our theories, our private or public activity." And vol. 2, pp. 363, 372–73.

[26] *Synthèse*, p. 24; cf. pp. 18–23, 48, 53. *Inéd.*, vol. 2, p. 375. The subjective synthesis achieved "the irrevocable institution of the religious triumvirate between Space, the Earth and Humanity, which closely links abstract reason with concrete reason. I regret that so complete a positivist as yourself should still be a stranger to this decisive progress, inaugurating the poetic age of our doctrine, after my first Treatise had established its philosophic superiority, and my principal work had thence deduced its religious supremacy" (to Hadery, 11 Caesar 69).

ing this prejudice, admires Comte's way of reducing things to systems, and to systems that effectually govern conduct, "the most spontaneous impulses of the life of the heart".[27] In face of passages like the one just quoted, and despite all that we know of the psychological condition of the old man who wrote them, it would be a mistake to take refuge in irony. This is the place in which to meditate upon Comte's teachings on the vanity of the critical spirit and to recall, as well, that all those who set out to *build* have at first seemed strange and laughable; that many were so, indeed; but that, even among them, some were the carriers of a great idea and sowed for the future.

Auguste Comte was one of these. In forms that couple the mazes of a dream with a coherence carried "to the verge of the ridiculous",[28] his last works sometimes conceal a wisdom that is too habitually abandoned by the partisans of "reason". Having, in his youth, broken with his master, Saint-Simon, partly because, as he says himself, he began to "see signs in him" of a tendency toward "the reconstruction of a religious theory"; having indignantly refused to "dabble in the manufacture of any new religion, and especially of a wretched travesty of Catholicism",[29] Comte ultimately followed the same line and, with greater thoroughness, carried out the same experiment.[30] Af-

---

[27] Charles Maurras, *L'Avenir de l'intelligence* (Paris: Fontemoing, 1905), p. 157.

[28] Cf. Maurice Muller, characterizing Comte: "The contrary of an artist, but a genius of coherence, all the way to the frontiers of the absurd": "De Descartes à Marcel Proust", in *Être et Penser*, vol. 2, p. 73.

[29] *Div.*, vol. 2, pp. 178–79 (to Armand Marrast, January 7, 1832). And to d'Eichtal, December 6, 1828, on the Saint-Simonians: "It will not be long before they die out in ridicule and disrepute. Imagine that their heads have gradually been raised to the point where it is a question of nothing less than a true new religion, a kind of incarnation of the divinity in Saint-Simon. Finally, there is nothing left but to say the new Mass, and that will not be long, the way things are going": Émile Littré, *Auguste Comte et la philosophie positive* (Paris: Hachette, 1863), p. 167.

[30] Cf. the final words of Saint-Simon, according to the *Globe* of December

ter having first conceived these works "in radical and absolute opposition to any kind of religious tendency",[31] he later
departed farther and farther from a too intellectual scientism,
but without wishing to give up what he always believed to be
the final conquest of the positive spirit; and he systematized
as well as he could some of the great fundamental, natural and
sound instincts of human nature. He tended to strengthen—by
powerfully appealing to them—the feelings corresponding to
the great natural institutions by which humanity, daily resisting
the forces of disintegration, perpetuates itself and survives as a
whole. He felt something of the "great human fellowship"[32] to
which he summoned his disciples. Beneath the eddies of transitory theories, beyond the ascending line of Progress, he contemplated Order, and to that great word, which he held sacred,
he was able to give a meaning that is not, perhaps, complete but
is much deeper than the sense in which so many doctrinarians
invoke it.

There is also much to admire in the "tender respect for
the human soul, the desire to let nothing be lost (not even
fetishism) from among mankind's arduous conquests, the deep
feeling of the unity of the human family", in which Charles
Gillouin wondered whether he should recognize "philosophic

30, 1831: "The last part of my works, the new Christianity, will not be immediately understood. People believed that the whole religious system had to
disappear because they had succeeded in proving the decrepitude of the Catholic system. They were mistaken, religion cannot disappear from the world. It
is only being transformed." Comte himself would come to this.

[31] *Inéd.*, vol. 1, p. 69 (to Michel Chevalier, January 5, 1832). Cf. the letter from d'Eichtal to Lamoricière, January 15, 1830: "Comte is a man whom
the exclusive culture of scientific ideas has reduced to a true degradation;
he is a moral eunuch. All feeling, all poetry, which is to say, all manifestation of feeling, is something he has completely disregarded, or rather that is
completely unknown to him . . .": Charles de Rouvre, *L'Amoureuse histoire
d'Auguste Comte et de Clotilde de Vaux* (Paris: Calmann-Lévy, 1917), p. 138,
note.

[32] *Nouv.*, p. 51.

principles or Christian virtues".[33] But the question remains whether Comte does not actually go too far in reverting to those "most spontaneous impulses" to which Mr. Maurras refers; whether he does not thus prune our reason of an essential part; whether the religion to which he summons us does not simply tend to revive the state of mind characteristic of what he called fetishism; whether the unity to which he aspires is not absorption pure and simple. . . . Here again, despite an apparent continuity with the spirit of Catholicism, are we not confronted with an attempt to break away from the requirements of monotheism? Is it not a rejection of the Glad Tidings? Comte does not conceal it: the whole aim of his later work is to show "systematic effect being given to the disposition to absorb fetishism once for all"; for "our maturity" should set its seal upon "the tendencies of our childhood".[34] But such a program, carried to extremes, will induce us to change many "habits" that monotheism had led us to contract; it is incompatible with them. A Christian cannot forget that.

It is unnecessary to dwell upon the psychological impossibilities of such a religious attitude. Comte was able to put his religion into practice only because, in his last years, he had partly lost his sense of reality. The marriage of fetishism and positivism is the union of fire and water. Comte said that by

---

[33] *Journal d'un chrétien philosophe*, pp. 245–46 (September 8, 1921). Pierre Ducassé quotes this testimony, *Essai sur les origines intuitives du positivisme* (Paris: Alcan, 1939), p. 263. But it is right to note that Gillouin reached such an interpretation only by means of an interpretation that seems to us something less than objective. According to him, Comte himself had supposedly considered his system to be unfinished; toward the end of his life, "he was on his way toward the Christian faith", his thought had remained open. On December 19, noting that Comte was unaware of all the "new birth", Gillouin again wrote: "Positivism must thus be 'accomplished' to the point where it becomes praise of God and service of Jesus Christ and where, having rid us of individual pride, it does not connect us to the law of the world or of appearance, but leads us, through humility, to adoration" (p. 282).

[34] *Hutton*, p. 35.

this means he proposed to "satisfy the theoretical and practical need" that he summed up in this formula:

What is missing from laws must be supplied by volitions.

For, he added, "regenerate man feels a need to show his constant gratitude to the unchangeable order on which his whole existence rests."[35] This urge has found expression in a number of forms which, if taken literally, would carry us back to the heyday of the "primitive mentality" and which, if regarded only as symbols, poetic fictions, would discourage all sincere religion. Religious feeling, it is quite true, demands that "volitions" should fill the gap left by "laws"; but are they not known to be mutually exclusive? "If science", says Comte, "becomes the basis of dogma, poetry remains the soul of worship";[36] but what principle will unite the two? And what, for example, will my worship of the Great Environment amount to, and my gratitude for its universal benevolence, if, even "in a religious sense", it is no more to me than the habitation to which I attribute "supreme inevitability"?[37] After that, it is all very well for Comte to denounce "the fictitious nature of the temporary religion"![38] In his "reconstruction of religion", as Edward Caird rightly observes, "there seems to be something artificial and factitious, something 'subjective' in the worst sense of the

---

[35] *Synthèse*, pp. 25 and 14. Cf. Baumann, p. 256: "My thought goes, then, to those primitive men who adored with naïve tenderness the tree that gave them its fruit, the star that warmed them with its rays, the animal that provided them with its milk, its fleece and its flesh. I admire the obscure wisdom that is hidden in these childish acts. And if, in contrast to the fetishist, I cannot attribute thought and will to beings that I know are devoid of them, I still have, nevertheless, good reason to envelop them, too, with my grateful sympathy."

[36] *Polit.*, vol. 2, p. 76.

[37] *Div.*, vol. 1:2, pp. 372–73; the Great Milieu "will always be conceived . . . as a totally artificial institution". *Synthèse*, p. 15: "To venerate the Fatality on which the whole of our existence rests."

[38] *Polit.*, vol. 4, p. 87.

word. It is a religion made, so to speak, on purpose"; it takes shape only by pushing "the poetic license of worship . . . to the point of self-deception".[39]

Should one refrain from censuring an only too obvious want of logic because of the high spiritual value of the system? Should one adopt the opposite attitude to John Stuart Mill's, for instance, and admire Comte as a man of religion while condemning him as a philosopher? Comte stoutly believed that he had gone beyond Catholicism. "The new spirituality", he says, "enjoys moral advantages that Catholic spirituality did not offer."[40] He thought he had discovered pure love.

> The theologians . . . meditated solely with a view to contemplating beings that continually eluded them. . . . Positivism, in its secret outpourings, closes its eyes, the better to perceive the inward image, while the theologian opens his in order to descry a chimerical object outside. . . . There is no longer any interested motive to sully the purity of our effusions.[41]

---

[39] Edward Caird, *La Philosophie sociale et religieuse d'Auguste Comte* (French trans. of: *The Social Philosophy and Religion of Comte* [Glasgow: J. Maclehose & Sons, 1885; reprint: New York: Kraus, 1968], pp. 130 and 132–33. Cf. pp. 129–30 (Eng. ed.: pp. 161–62): Comte feels that "the idea of an indifferent outward necessity must be a hindrance to the perfect combination of submission and love. Hence he calls in the aid of poetry to revive the spirit of Fetishism, and to reanimate the dead world by the image of benevolent divine agencies. . . . Comte therefore ends in what some one has called the system of 'spiritual book-keeping by double entry', in which the imagination is allowed to revive, for practical purposes, the fictions which science has destroyed. In this way, poetry . . . has to make us forget in our worship the dualism of Nature and Humanity, and to reconcile us to Fate by giving it the semblance of a Providence. It is obvious that poetry is thus made into a kind of deliberate superstition. . . ."

[40] *Polit.*, vol. 1, p. 101. The same persuasion with respect to grace. *Inéd.*, p. 69: "Positivism takes definitive hold of the old domain of grace. . . . Grace . . . depended only on divine caprices; it would have been a sacrilege to seek laws in it. We, on the contrary, regard these sublime cerebral functions as still more capable than all others of being worthily regulated. . . ."

[41] *Catéch.*, pp. 84–85, 96. Yet, on "the sublime contradiction" of such disinterestedness, see the letters to Tholouze, 28 Aristotle 67 (*Div.*, vol. 3, p. 139).

(Shades of Fénelon!) In point of fact, if there is much impressionable "devotion" in Comte, many "pious outpourings" and a whole art of evoking "cherished images",[42] there is very little spirituality in evidence; nothing that, even remotely, resembles a mystic transport; and it would be dangerous to subject the vaunted purity of these "effusions" to an over-strict analysis, for fear of finding, perhaps, that they are mostly sublimated sensuality. After all, applying his precept of "living in broad daylight", he lets us observe in him the transition—and a late one—from "carnal emotions" to "sweet sensations", and the transformation of "brutish instincts into the necessary stimuli to the most elevated affections". Objectively, this religious system is an illusionism; subjectively, is his religious life anything but an illusion put into practice? Clotilde was for her worshipper the symbol of Humanity; but was not Humanity, insofar as it provoked all these effusions, chiefly an irradiation of Clotilde? . . .[43] Comte was one of those men who, as the saying goes, "grow devout as they grow grey". A vulgar expression, but is not the reality vulgar too?[44]

I would repeat, the feelings he wishes to arouse and develop are healthy feelings. It is a good thing to exhort men to cultivate

---

[42] *Polit.*, vol. 2, p. 77. *Inéd.*, vol. 2, pp. 33–34; etc. Cf. Charles de Rouvre, pp. 462–63.

[43] See particularly "Ma quatrième Sainte-Clotilde", June 25, 1848, in *Test.*, pp. 128–29; cf. p. 135: "Far from making me cool toward Humanity, you make it all the more dear to me, since I see its image in you"; p. 129: "Your worship has permitted me to taste well the satisfaction of pure sacrifices and the direct charm of universal sympathies. . . ." *Polit.*, vol. 3, p. XXVII: "These high holy walls, forever imprinted with the adored image, helped me to develop daily the intimate worship of the best personification of the Great Being."

[44] Before he became, sincerely but belatedly, a professor of chastity, we know what the life of Auguste Comte was, and he himself has not left us ignorant about any of his regrettable pressures with regard to Clotilde de Vaux. The latter, writes the Rev. Fr. Antonin Sertillanges, *Le Christianisme et les philosophies* (Paris: Aubier, 1939–1941), vol. 2, p. 244, "brought him . . . the ardent idealism for which he was waiting." That is to idealize quite a lot.

"sympathetic inclinations" and "kindly affections"; it is not a bad thing to feel oneself "imbued with a delightful emotion of social sympathy" and to go in search of the times and places that revive that emotion;[45] nor is positivism wrong in consecrating and wishing to intensify those "natural inclinations" thanks to which "one will never prevent a son from adoring his mother, or a lover his lady."[46] Only when these sublimities are offered to us as crowning and eclipsing Catholic teaching, we shrug our shoulders. Apart from all question of doctrine, one cannot take seriously the musings of a man who never understood a word of the Gospel and who sank deeper, every day, into a monstrous egocentricity; the crude and lachrymose "consolations" to which Comte innocently abandoned himself in his sanctuary cannot be taken for genuine spirituality.

2. The Priesthood of the Scientists

So far only the most general of the transpositions from Catholicism has been considered. There are two others that complete it and essentially contribute to the distinctive appearance of the new religion. This is made up of three great sections, to which the three parts of its Catechism correspond: a form of worship, a dogma and a regime: in other words, it has its poetry, its philosophy and its politics.[47] The actual doctrinal elements

---

[45] *Blign.* pp. 63, 64. Cf. Léon de Montesquiou, *Le Système politique d'Auguste Comte* (Paris: Nouvelle Libraire Nationale), p. 24.

[46] *Hutton*, p. 35. "No one", writes Mr. Henri Gouhier writes of Comte, "will deny . . . his sense of the inner life": "Réflexions sur l'expérience positiviste", in *La Philosophie et son histoire* (Paris: Vrin, 1944), p. 114. Probably not—always provided that the words "inner life" are given a very broad interpretation.

[47] *Catéch.*, p. 62. *Inéd.*, vol. 2, p. 42: "Theocracy as regime and theolatry as cult responded to theology as dogma. Similarly, sociocracy as regime and sociolatry as cult must correspond to sociology as final dogma." And vol. 3, pp. 78–79.

we have so far considered should be classed under cult, on account of the symbols in which they are clothed. At bottom, in all ages of mankind, "our faith has always had the same essential object: to form a conception of the universal order that governs human existence, for the purpose of determining our general relation to it."[48] In our ideas of this universal order, we have now at last rid it of those "artificial causes" that preceding ages assigned to it; we know that in all fields, from mathematics to ethics, it consists in laws that are purely immanent. For the first time, thanks to a knowledge of these "real laws" and their hierarchy, the human mind is finding its true balance. On concluding his *Cours de philosophie positive*, at the end of the sixtieth and last lesson, Auguste Comte proclaimed: "The chief characteristic of the positive state will certainly consist in its natural aptitude to establish and maintain a complete mental coherence."[49]

But that would still be nothing if such coherence were to remain purely mental and, still worse, the property of a small enlightened minority. It must be a principle of action that, spreading to one and all, will become a principle of union. And such is indeed its privilege. The positive spirit is "the sole effectual principle of that great intellectual fellowship that is becoming the necessary basis of all real human association". There is, in fact, no "true commonalty of opinion, except on subjects already resolved into positive theories". As yet, alas! these subjects are not "the most important—far from it"; thus the object has not yet been attained, and that is why Auguste Comte first of all patiently embarks upon an intellectual career. It is nonetheless obvious that

> the positive philosophy is alone capable of gradually carrying out the noble plan of universal union that Catholicism had prematurely drafted in the Middle Ages but which, as experience has recently shown, was at bottom necessarily incompatible with the

---

[48] *Catéch.*, p. 53.
[49] *Cours*, vol. 6, p. 518.

theological nature of its philosophy, since that philosophy had not the logical coherence necessary to ensure such social efficacy.[50]

Positivism was, therefore, to be the new "moral power" with the mission of performing "the great social functions that Catholicism no longer exercises"[51] and which, truth to tell, it had never fully exercised. But what does that amount to in concrete terms? If Catholicism had formerly accomplished its task, even though in a very limited and entirely temporary fashion, it was thanks to the institution of its priesthood, and, indeed, history shows that "no society can maintain and develop itself without a priesthood of some kind."[52] Thus the new power must not remain diffused, without any accredited representatives. It must be exercised by a new priesthood. Ever since 1824 Comte had seen this quite clearly: social physics were to create "a new spiritual power capable of replacing the clergy and reorganizing Europe by means of education".[53] It was to be, as he said later, "the positive priesthood", the "priesthood of Humanity".[54] Anyone who does not neglect the end for the means must recognize that the advent of a new spiritual power, that is to say, of an organized priesthood, is the only solution directly suited to the Western revolution."[55] A "regenerative priesthood", the *Testament* calls it.[56]

But in whose hands should it be placed? The positive spirit suggests the answer—and again Comte had indicated it from the outset: in the hands of the scientists.[57] The *Synthèse* sub-

---

[50] *Disc.*, p. 34.

[51] Ibid., p. 83.

[52] *Catéch.*, p. 253.

[53] *Val.*, p. 120 (May 21, 1824).

[54] *Synthèse*, preface. *Blign.*, p. 68.

[55] *Hutton*, p. 72.

[56] *Test.*, p. 22.

[57] Already Henri Saint-Simon, *Œuvres* (Paris: Capelle, 1841), vol. 4, pp. 153–55 (Émile Durkheim, *Le Socialisme* pp. 168–69).

jective, which dates from November 1856, remains faithful to the ideas of the "opuscule" of November 1825 when it calls for "masters of synthesis directing students of synthesis in the positive schools attached, as a regular thing, to the temples of Humanity".[58] Similarly, when the high priest of Humanity demands a long scientific training for those whom he intends to make his collaborators, he is carrying out the great design he had already conceived as a young man. Only, as is normal, everything is organized gradually: the conditions of approach are laid down; the functions of officiants, teachers and administrators are distinguished; a "sacerdotal subsidy" is created, or at any rate contemplated, "which will become the central budget of the positive clergy *pari passu* with the conversion of the governors and the governed to the true faith". For, in order to devote themselves entirely to their ministry, the priests must be released from all the cares of the bread-winner; "the positivist subsidy" will secure "the full and free development of the priesthood of Humanity".[59]

But what type of scientist would be worthy to belong to such a priesthood? Auguste Comte never cared for "empty learning", the "cloudy erudition" that contents itself with mechanically accumulating facts and which is "equally fitted to serve the most contradictory opinions". "The true positive spirit", as he conceives it, "is, at bottom, just as far removed from empiricism as from mysticism."[60] With empiricism, Comte classes specialization. He blames "the exaggerated intellectual narrowness" that comes from "an empirical specialization". Most of the scientists of the day seem to him to be warped by that "spirit

---

[58] *Synthèse*, preface.

[59] *Test.*, p. 21. *Blign.*, pp. 68–69; 79, 98, 121. *Div.*, vol. 1, p. 319: "The positivist subsidy, on which the flight of the priestly nucleus depends." *Circ.*, passim.

[60] *Cours*, vol. 5, p. 50. *Disc.*, pp. 21–22. So "true science, very far from being formed of simple observations, always tends to dispense, as far as possible, with direct observation, substituting for it that rational foresight that constitutes, in all regards, the principal character of the positive spirit."

of particularism and division",[61] by that "blind and dispersive specialization" that makes them incapable of ever becoming true positivists. Their whole mind is occupied with "a few limited questions that are seldom important". The academies and scientific societies serve only to strengthen these "analytical prejudices".[62] That is not "true science", which is always "necessarily relative to humanity"; that is not the real scientific spirit, which is always a "spirit of integration".[63] The aim in view should be "systematic generality".[64] Analysis should be subordinated to synthesis, as progress is to order, and egoism to altruism. All particular knowledge should be brought into line with total knowledge. "At bottom", the whole thing should be "one single science, namely, human or, rather, social science, of which our existence is both the origin and the aim, and with which the rational study of the external world naturally merges as a necessary element and at the same time a fundamental preamble."[65]

Thus the scientist according to Comte is to be a man with an "encyclopaedic mind". No task is more important than that of ensuring a solid "encyclopaedic training" for those who are to enter the priesthood. Or, rather, they must receive "a genuinely encyclopaedic initiation", to which a series of graduated tests will bear witness.[66] These tests are to be severe, for the priesthood must not be invaded by "literary men" and "stump

---

[61] *Cours*, pp. 6, 8. "They accumulate experiences", said Bazard likewise, in 1829, "they dissect the entire nature. . . . They add more or less curious facts to facts observed previously. . . . But what are the wise men who classify and coordinate these riches accumulated in disorder?"

[62] *Disc.*, pp. 92–94. *Mill*, p. 404 (January 23, 1846): "Our whole provisional regime of dispersive specialty must disappear." Letter of Charles Jundzill to Auguste Comte, February 1, 1848: "The deplorable spirit of dispersive specialization".

[63] *Cours*, vol. 5, p. 69. Cf. Montesquiou, pp. 236–37.

[64] *Polit.*, vol. 4, p. 535.

[65] *Disc.*, p. 38. *Synthèse*, p. 1.

[66] *Blign.*, pp. 61, 102, 110. *Div.*, vol. 1:2, pp. 93, 117, 159, 163. *Synthèse*, preface; etc. *Test.*, pp. 21–22: "I have recently determined, for priests and vi-

orators", for this would soon open the way for hypocrites.[67] Zealous positivists who, through mental inadequacy, are unable to fulfill these conditions can, "while confining themselves to apostleship", still "make a very valuable contribution toward the advent of the universal religion".[68] But only the priests, fully initiated, will ensure the stability of an encyclopaedic regime that is the essence of the positive regime.[69] They will be the living refutation of the reproach of aridity blindly leveled against the scientific spirit. That aridity is "characteristic of science only in its academic degeneration, when dispersive particularity hampers aesthetic culture and the moral urge"; genuine science, on the other hand, establishes a double synthesis, first between the various branches of intellectual research and then between poetry and philosophy (there being a necessary connection between them that only absurd modern prejudices fail to recognize); it sets a seal upon the mutual harmony between "fiction" and "demonstration", which are both indispensable for the "continued development of personal and social unity"; essentially relative, it knows that it is so and does not wish it to be otherwise; instead of vaingloriously pursuing an impossible objectivity, it takes advantage of the "privileges of relativity" to sanction ideal conceptions that answer the needs of the heart.[70] To use three words dear to Comte;

---

cars, the encyclopaedic conditions that will guarantee to the public, as well as to the Great Priest, the theoretical aptitude of the philosophers, when their moral qualities will be sufficiently ascertained. These tests, which follow each other at intervals of one to three months, consist in seven printed theses, at the pleasure of the candidate, on the seven fundamental sciences; seven days after his reception, each thesis is publicly completed by an oral examination. . . ."

[67] *Div.*, vol. 1, p. 131.

[68] Ibid., pp. 179, 182; vol. 1:2, p. 298.

[69] *Blign.*, p. 112.

[70] *Synthèse*, pp. XI and 10–12; cf. p. 9: "Poetry needs to assimilate the world to man as much as all the notions emanating from philosophy allow." There, in other words, we have "that union of positivity and fetishism that combine to institute the subjective synthesis so as to consolidate the synergy by developing sympathy."

being a "synthesis", it constitutes a "synergy" in the service of "sympathy".[71]

These considerations dictate the task that "the priesthood of humanity" finds "exclusively reserved for it". Left to their natural impulses, the great forces of feeling and action "could not accomplish their sacred and difficult mission". It is for the priesthood to systematize them by concentrating their intellectual influence. Accordingly, "its indispensable office, without which the universal movement would miscarry", falls into two parts, "two successive constructions, one philosophic and the other poetic, the second presupposing the first",[72] but the first being at the service of the second. Imbued with such a spirit, the positive clergy will really be the "regenerative body" capable of "reconstructing occidentalism". For that purpose it will have the right of "at last establishing a real and complete discipline".[73] In all things it will decide what should be thought: man's understanding will be subjected to it. In the positive regime, in fact, there can be no more question of free thought or of freedom of conscience. There is no freedom of conscience in positive sciences; and all human knowledge will henceforth be positive.[74] Revolutionary dogma may have been useful in its time, to help to undermine the old beliefs; but a short-lived interregnum must not be "given the status of a normal and permanent order". It is clear that the principle that underlies critical doctrine cannot possibly be "an organic principle"; on the contrary, it "even has a direct tendency, now, to become more and more of a systematic obstacle to all real social reorganization". It perpetuates anarchic empiricism; it spreads the

---

[71] Baumann, p. 263, summed up in this way Comte's requirements with respect to the positivist priest: "The Master wanted him to join the power of love that the woman possesses and the energy of the proletariat to a high intelligence and an encyclopaedic knowledge. This is not asking too much, given what we expect from him."

[72] *Div.*, vol. 1:2, p. 58 (to Thalès Bernard, 28 Aristotle 62).

[73] *Circ.*, pp. 30, 76.

[74] *Opusc.*, p. 68 (third opuscule).

metaphysical scourge of which it is the new priesthood's mission to rid us.[75] What Catholic priests have wrongly demanded of their flock, positive priests have the right to demand from the whole of mankind. In the society of the future, men will be "emancipated" but at the same time "subjugated". The positivist doctrine is a faith, its initiates are believers, they are "true believers".[76]

Admittedly, "lost faith is not easy to build up again"—that faith which is the indispensable cement of all society and whose chronic dissolution is our Western malady. Today dissolution has reached such an advanced stage that, "through habitual exacerbation of pride and vanity, everyone is in a state bordering on madness." The evil is all the more serious since people have no desire to be cured of it; they regard it as a good thing, and the mere announcement of the "spiritual reconstruction" brought about by the positive spirit is shocking to many of them. Yet submission to the new faith is the only thing that can rescue us from anarchy; it alone can cure modern man from "the boredom, doubt and irresolution" that prey upon him; and, far from setting itself limits by becoming positive, faith will spread. "All the precepts of Catholicism regarding the submission of reason to faith are so many programs to be carried out." We must not lessen them but go beyond them.[77]

In Catholicism these precepts were oppressive because they were related to chimerical beliefs. They became so more especially "when the degenerate priesthood, taking the means for the end, endeavored to prolong, by violence, the outmoded rule of the least enduring form of theologism". The Inquisi-

---

[75] *Cours*, vol. 4, pp. 25–30: "Without the conquest and use of this unlimited freedom of thought, no true reorganization could be prepared"; on the other hand, "is it not obvious that such a tendency is, by its very nature, radically anarchic in that, if it were able to persist indefinitely, it would prevent any true spiritual organization?" *Polit.*, vol. 3, p. 619.

[76] *Blign.*, pp. 8, 118, 120.

[77] *Hutton*, pp. 76–77 (1 Homer 68). It is necessary to satisfy the "present need for a worthy fanaticism", to Leblais, 15 Moses: *Div.*, vol. 1, p. 132.

tion was a desperate effort to restrain an inevitable urge for independence. There is nothing of that kind to be feared in positivism. It is "the normal regime", it is "the final religion" that will know no decline, and the faith that it demands is a positive faith, that is to say, a "real faith", the object of which is always "demonstrated or demonstrable".[78] Known by some, believed by others, that object is the same for all. Thus there is no cleavage between those who know and those who believe; no danger of Machiavellianism and hypocrisy.[79] And why not rely on those who know? Why persist in seeking the synthesis when it has been found? That would be going against the new religious unity and making oneself "an unhappy as well as a disturbing element".[80] To ask for proof of what has been accepted by the human race in the person of its qualified scientists would be a sign "of mistrust if not hostility toward the priestly order". Furthermore, there is nothing now to fear from complete subordination of the reason to faith: it is tantamount to that of the mind to the heart; that is to say, it subordinates personal to social instincts, or, more briefly, man to Humanity.[81] Can Humanity be a tyrant?

---

[78] *Mill*, pp. 289–90 (December 25, 1844). *Synthèse*, p. 31. *Blign.*, pp. 7–8. *Polit.*, vol. 4, p. 533: The universal religion is "more positive than any science".

[79] Cf. Henri Gouhier, *La Jeunesse d'Auguste Comte et la formation du positivisme* (Paris: Vrin, 1933–1941), vol. 1, p. 25, note 33: "It was freely said, at the end of the eighteenth century, that religion was necessary for the people. This is not the idea expressed here. Comte's idea is just the opposite: he reestablishes the spiritual unity of the classes, beyond the diversity of cultures, through communion in the same knowledge. The content of popular thought is that of scientific thought; the seafaring man and the astronomer know the same laws of heaven; but the seaman believes what the learned man says, while the learned man knows the reasons for what he says. Positive science will be the object of faith for those who would have neither the time nor the means to acquire it."

[80] *Blign.*, p. 19. *Hutton*, p. 77.

[81] *Synthèse*, p. 31.

3. Spiritual Despotism

Auguste Comte did not always give exactly the same interpretation to this need for belief and to "the real distinction between demonstrated and demonstrable faith".[82] "The way things happened", Mr. Jean Lacroix writes on this subject,

> would seem to suggest that, after having at first had confidence in the universalization value of his doctrine, considered as true, he had later doubted the swiftness of its triumph. *Competent men* are so far ahead of the masses that all sorts of political and social catastrophes have time to happen before the latter have reached the positive stage. Besides, the community as a whole must always lag behind the élite.[83]

But even this does not affect Comte's underlying thought, which once more displays a surprising continuity. The things that change are emphasis and perspective; a certain hardening takes place. The confidence at first shown by the young reformer in a spontaneous consensus of opinion, which would make it unnecessary to require any submissiveness of mind,[84] did not apply to the masses;[85] and, if comparative liberalism conceded a few divergencies on "secondary questions", this

---

[82] *Blign.*, p. 131.

[83] Jean Lacroix, *Vocation personnelle et tradition nationale* (Paris: Bloud & Gay, 1942), p. 93. Comte, *Opusc.*, p. 98.

[84] *Inéd.*, vol. 1, p. 7 (to Buchholz, November 18, 1825): "What an admirable property of the positive philosophy to be able thus, despite all the differences in organization, age, education, climate and language, in government and social customs, and finally without any relation whatever, to determine spontaneously a communion of ideas that could be produced and maintained in other periods only through the combined, ceaseless action of artificial and violent means, by demanding even as a first condition a certain general and permanent compression of intellectual activity!"

[85] *Val.*, p. 121: "This is a doctrine to be preached and spread everywhere, just as the Gospel was in its time; except that it is addressed solely today to enlightened men, the masses are to participate in it only later." This letter is from 1822; but as early as 1820, in the "Sommaire appréciation de l'ensemble du passé moderne" (*Opusc.*, pp. 10–11), Comte wrote: "Spiritual authority,

only concerned the "revolutionary transition", during which progress had to be made by methods of persuasion, until the final achievement of "mental regularity" should enable pressure to be brought to bear upon those who favored personal opinions.[86] In any case, the *Cours de philosophie positive* already contained a clear statement of doctrine; it took it as self-evident that "the social order will always be incompatible with permanent freedom to reopen, at will, an indefinite discussion of the very foundations of society", so that "systematic tolerance cannot exist and has never really existed except in connection with opinions regarded as indifferent or doubtful."[87] The *Politique positive* had only to draw the necessary conclusions, by making a sharper distinction between the two categories: scientists and believers.

> Faith, that is to say, the disposition to believe spontaneously, without previous demonstration, the dogmas proclaimed by a competent authority, is a fundamental virtue, the immutable and indispensable basis of social order. . . . For in the positive state, characterized by a more complete and ever-increasing separation of functions, everyone, no matter what his capacity, is only in a position to conceive an infinitely small part of the doctrine that he needs for his behavior.[88]

In short, the positive faith "is not open to abuses" because it is "always demonstrable", but people cannot "demand that

---

being conjectural by nature, had necessarily to require the highest degree of trust and submission of spirit. That was an indispensable condition for its existence and its action. On the other hand, the positive scientific capacity, conceived as directing the spiritual affairs of society, requires neither blind belief nor even trust, at least on the part of all those who are capable of understanding the proofs; as for the others, experience has sufficiently shown that their trust in the proofs unanimously settled on by the positive scholars can never be prejudicial to them in that this kind of trust, in a word, is not susceptible to abuse."

[86] *Mill*, p. 399 (January 27, 1846).

[87] *Cours*, vol. 4, p. 58.

[88] *Polit.*, vol. 4, pp. 205–6.

it should be demonstrated here and now". Thus no "conversion" is really complete unless the convert adopts, with the intention of putting them into practice, "notions taken quite on trust", the proof being left to the scientists as "spiritual fathers".[89] That is why, among the virtues he recommended to his disciples, Comte gave the first place to love of discipline and a tendency to veneration. Those were the conditions of true submissiveness of mind. He had great hopes for Henry Dix Hutton because, if that young man was not yet "really disciplined", he was at any rate "disciplinable";[90] on the other hand, he came to despair of Célestin de Blignières, because the "positivist half-convictions" of that erstwhile ardent disciple "would only serve to arouse in him an indisciplinable theoretical vanity" and because he showed "no signs of any aptitude for veneration"; he was still among those who, while believing themselves to be positivists, more or less reserved the right to set up "their own brand of universal synthesis". Yet Comte had, at first, thought he recognized in this disciple a "distinct propensity for veneration"—that veneration which alone induces the "prompt and complete" absorption of "ideas that useless discussion would make obscure and doubtful. . . ."[91] It is, at any rate, "on the decisive reconstruction of this great sentiment, which is more essential and has been more perverted than any other", that positivism must base "its best title to spiritual rule".[92]

---

[89] *Div.*, vol. 1, p. 289 (12 Descartes 67). *Val.*, January 18, 1826.

[90] *Hutton*, p. 69.

[91] *Blign.*, pp. 14, 132. *Hutton*, p. 59. *Inéd.*, vol. 1, p. 84: The irreligious positivists "all carry, like M. Littré, the stamp of moral reprobation on their own brain, through the absence of the great feeling of veneration, the sole possible source of Western regeneration."

[92] Montesquiou, p. 121. An analysis of the Comtian feeling of veneration can be found in Baumann, p. 257: "In truth, our nature will always be too imperfect to allow us to do away entirely with the duty of what, in our eyes, necessarily appears a little severe. So the religion of Humanity preserves submission as an indispensable virtue. But it is particularly a restrictive virtue,

Thus the authority of the new priesthood is not to be an empty word. Should it not be spontaneously recognized by the veneration of the faithful, it will know how to enforce itself. It will also know how to come down from conviction to action, and Comte does not hesitate to speak of "subjecting all conduct to examination by an inexorable priesthood".[93] More than that, heresy is an indication of secret perversity, which must be run to earth without pity. As the heir of Catholicism, "positivism will systematize and expand [its] purely empirical maxim regarding the basis of the connection between errors of mind and defects of heart." That maxim, says Comte in a threatening tone, "will not be left inactive; I shall apply it increasingly to unmasking my false adherents."[94] The purge was beginning! Inveighing against "the revolutionary malady" which consisted in "a constant overexacerbation of pride and vanity" and in "a highly contagious tendency to personal infallibility", he reached a point where he would admit, in the last analysis, only one authority, only one infallibility: his own. In other people he increasingly preferred the faith of the heart to "scientific faith", and that is one of the reasons why he in-

---

which prevents us from acting badly, rather than one that incites us to act well. Love can be mixed with it, however, and ennoble it. This is what veneration does, that is, love being aware that it is addressed to something much greater and much stronger than it. The saint will love Humanity like Saint Thérèse loved Jesus: it will be enough for others never to forget the state of close dependence in which they find themselves with respect to it."

[93] *Blign.*, p. 58.

[94] *Hutton*, p. 91 (10 Dante 68). *Inéd.*, vol. 2, pp. 254-55 (to Hadery, 6 Gutenberg 65): "M. Etex is profoundly affected, to the point of incurability, with the Western illness to which I have given a place in the positive table of cerebral pathology under the title of chronic pride-vanity with an attack of sharpness. But however expressive this name might be, drawn with the most intense characters, it does not indicate at all the source of such a perturbation, which is essentially mental. Nevertheless, although this revolt of the individual against the race always begins through the intelligence, it is not long in corrupting the feelings, whose trouble strengthens and develops spiritual disorder. Reactionaries, without knowing it, are nearly as affected by it as revolutionaries, since they also lack any reflective submission."

creasingly dissuaded would-be readers from studying his *Cours*. In the society governed by positivism, the priests themselves must display as much veneration as the faithful. That would be the surest mark of their "sacerdotal vocation"; "indispensable to all believers whatsoever, this attitude is particularly seemly for the priests of Humanity, to ensure their proper devotion to the world pontiff, whose worthy appendages they must become."[95] To the founder of the final religion, to the first High Priest, "the supreme spokesman of Humanity",[96] to him who has the power to bind and to loose, all will owe absolute obedience in deed, thought and heart.[97]

These personal eccentricities and extravagances may be left out of account. If the Comtian structure of "spiritual power" is to be judged with fairness, it must first be recognized that we are confronted with a few simple and powerful ideas that it seems impossible to reject completely. In the ideal he sets forth of a synthesis of knowledge, Comte certainly shows himself more of a "teacher" than a "seeker". That ideal—which Plato had had before him—nonetheless corresponds to a need that is making itself more and more felt as discoveries and specializations increase. Consequently this is one of the points that Comte's disciples are most inclined to stress today. Mr. Aldous Huxley recently complained that "our universities have no chair of synthesis"; "intensive specialization", he added,

> tends to reduce every branch of science to a state in which they are very nearly meaningless. . . . [That] comes to be considered,

---

[95] *Circ.*, p. 22. *Div.*, vol. 1, p. 290: "I will never bestow the priesthood on anyone who does not fulfill such a condition."

[96] *Circ.*, pp. 24; 75: "As founder, it was necessary for me to have worthily submissive auxiliaries."

[97] Comte wrote to Armand Marrast, on January 7, 1832, in criticizing Saint-Simon: "To exercise, through vague and emphatic declarations, a sovereign influence over a few devout men or women who have generally sacrificed their intellectual and moral individuality has never seemed to me to be capable of inspiring any attraction except to mediocre minds combined with weak characters. If I had the taste to reign, I would want less docile subjects."

in certain circles, as a kind of diploma of true science. Those who try to establish relations between the small particular results of specialization and human life as a whole . . . are accused of being the wrong kind of scientists, charlatans, publicity-hunters. . . .

Mr. Huxley continues in a vein of diatribe that is not unreminiscent of Comte's personal differences with the scientists of the *École Polytechnique*.[98] By way of remedy for the state of affairs thus described, Mr. Jean Coutrot not long ago laid the foundations of what he called "an integral and up-to-date humanism, that is to say, an intellectual attitude that seeks to embrace simultaneously all the problems that condition human activity and human equilibrium". Noting the extreme rareness of "strictly encyclopaedic minds" such as Comte desired, he proposed to fill the gap by teams organized for collective work. "The nineteenth century", he concluded, "was the age of research in depth, each specialist working the placer or claim assigned to him by his profession or his diplomas; the task of the twentieth century will be the *horizontal coordination* of all these vertical workings."[99] But in Comte the spirit of synthesis deviated into a spirit of generalization, as it does in everyone who has not, at the same time, a feeling for research. Specialists find in his work plenty of opportunity to take their revenge by catching him out, not only because our knowledge has advanced since his day, but because he was very far from possessing the scientific learning necessary for his undertaking. For the rest, the system of "cerebral hygiene" that he prided himself on practicing very strictly—it is well known that from 1838 onward he denied himself, with very rare exceptions, all reading in any

---

[98] *La Fin et les moyens* (French trans. by Jules Castier [Paris: Plon, 1939] of *Ends and Means* [London, Chatto and Windus, 1937; New York: Greenwood Press, 1969]), p. 326 (Eng. ed.: p. 320): "The people who make such accusations do so, of course, because they do not wish to take any responsibility for anything, but merely to retire to their cloistered laboratories, and there amuse themselves by performing delightfully interesting researches. . . ."

[99] *Mémoire introductif à la recherche collective*, pp. 18 and 83.

way connected "even indirectly" with the subject of his work
—may be conducive to "purity" and "harmony" in the lines
of a system; but, even allowing for our abstainer's excellent
memory, it seems less compatible with the requirements of an
"encyclopaedic" task.[100]

Another simple and powerful idea is the suggestion that science is not an end in itself, that it is not all-sufficient, that
synthesis in itself is of value only as enabling man to recognize
himself in his actions. But how quickly this idea, too, begins to
deviate! One may agree with Pascal that there is a philosophy
that is not worth an hour's trouble and yet find cause for uneasiness in the frame of mind of the young Comte, declaring
that he has a "supreme aversion" for any scientific work whose
"utility is not clear" to him.[101] One need not be a supporter
of "science for its own sake", any more than of "art for art's
sake", to feel that science, like art, should in the first place
be disinterested. But with Comte it became less and less so.
Seeing it all in relation to man, he showed little strictness as to
the quality, provided that it served his purpose. "Mr. Comte",
said John Stuart Mill, "was not so solicitous about the com-
pleteness of proof as becomes a positive philosopher."[102] He

---

[100] *Cours*, vol. 6, pp. XXV–VI, and note. *Div.*, vol. 1:2, p. 152: "Sixteen
years of scrupulous practice have made this cerebral hygiene more and more
dear to me" (April 6, 1854), pp. 238, 320, etc. *Inéd.*, vol. 3, p. 27: "A cerebral
diet that has, for long years, served to assure better the purity, originality and
consistency of my own conceptions" (October 25, 1846). *Mill*, pp. 2, 48–49,
121.

[101] *Val.*, p. 99 (1819). "I would set very little value on scientific works if
I were not always thinking of their usefulness for the race; I would like just
as well to amuse myself with deciphering some very complicated word puz-
zles." According to Comte, writes Georges Cantecor, *Le Positivisme*, p. 48, "it
is no longer the true that is the criterion of the legitimate elements of science,
it is usefulness and particularly social usefulness. That is indeed undoubtedly
within the logic of the system, but it is not, whatever Comte may say, within
the logic of history. He does not continue in that vein with Galileo and New-
ton, he condemns them."

[102] *Mill*, p. 59. Cf. Caird, p. 133 (Eng. ed.: pp. 166–67): Comte energeti-

had a way of speaking of the "real progress of science" and of "our real intellectual needs" that was one way of discarding many researches as "idle and chimerical".[103] Feeling and saying "how morally dangerous the study of science is when it is not regarded merely as a means but is elevated into an end",[104] he came to rule out everything whose immediate application was not apparent and to show himself impatient of any thought that was at all free.[105]

Further, he is not to be blamed for wishing to "base the whole systematization on the natural preponderance of the heart", or, in other words, for having "strictly subordinated the intelligence to the social sense". Only a mind seriously distorted by intellectualism would dispute the rightness of preferring sympathy even to synthesis. But there is another form of distortion to beware of: with regard to science itself, the preference in question was made to cover an "emancipation" such as opens the way for arbitrary judgments of the most subjective character. In the "final structure", sympathy was to rule synthesis and fashion it to its own liking.[106] Criticism of

---

cally affirms in his last works "that art, rather than science, is the true field for man's intelligence, and that it is a desirable and useful thing to allow our minds to dwell on ideal conceptions, which are beyond the reach of scientific proof, provided these conceptions are favourable to the development of altruistic sentiment."

[103] *Cours*, vol. 2, p. 11; vol. 3, p. 279, etc. Does this go as far as saying, *Polit.*, p. 4, that it would be enough to study the sun and the moon in astronomy, perhaps possibly the planets known by the ancients? See the commentary by Paul Labérenne, in *A la lumière du marxisme*, from the Cercle de la Russie neuve (Paris: Ed. sociales internationales, 1935), vol. 2, p. 93. There are more details on this attitude in Victor Delbos, *La Philosophie française* (Paris: Plon, 1919), pp. 351–53.

[104] *Blign.*, p. 8.

[105] Stuart Mill also noted it with much regret, pp. 177–78. *Test.*, p. 123: "A blind tendency to accumulate indefinitely any speculations whatsoever, nearly always pointless even when they are not fanciful" ("Ma troisième Sainte-Clotilde", June 2, 1847).

[106] *Div.*, vol. 1:2, p. 299: "I can thus verify how much the synthesis depends

the "empty presidence of the mind" tended more and more to become distrust of the understanding, the mere exercise of which was to be regarded as a manifestation of egoism and vanity. There was no admission for anything that did not bow to that "subjective synthesis" which, by "a close coordination between the reality of speculations and their utility", came to constitute the only "true positivity".[107]

This last point brings us to one that towers far above all others—the requirement that minds should submit to the decrees of the positive priesthood. Mr. Lévy-Brühl, commenting on the "famous paper on liberty of conscience", written in 1822 and reproduced in the fourth volume of the Cours, tells us that "There is no question of imposing upon men, by a sort of spiritual despotism, beliefs that they would not be allowed to judge; Comte only wishes to extend to politics, considered as a positive science, what is unanimously admitted in other sciences."[108] But this is decidedly sugaring the pill. Comte *did* institute a "spiritual despotism", in the strict sense of the term. If he was not aware of it in 1822, he certainly saw and intended it later on; and at the time of the Cours he let it be clearly understood that he meant to take advantage of the current principle of "unlimited freedom of thought" to set forth the doctrine thanks to which he would later on subject all minds to "a continual strict discipline", as soon as "the new social order" had at last been established.[109] Admittedly, it is good to

on sympathy." Letter to Papot: "The normal order in which sympathy leads to synthesis, and finally to synergy". *Circ.*, p. 59: "Truly religious souls, disposed to synthesis by sympathy". *Polit.*, vol. 1, p. 679: "The preponderance of the heart over the mind must first be established in my own nature. . . ."

[107] *Div.*, vol. 1, pp. 368–69.

[108] Lucien Lévy-Brühl, *La Philosophie d'Auguste Comte* (Paris: Alcan, 1900), p. 345. The same watering down in Alain, *Éléments d'une doctrine radicale* (Paris: Gallimard, 1925), p. 69: "True spiritual authority, according to our philosopher, is solely spiritual, it acts by enlightening opinion, that is to say, through word and writing only." Likewise, F. Pécaut, in the introduction to his edition of the *Catéchisme*, p. XXX.

[109] *Cours*, vol. 4, pp. 26–28.

be reminded of that elementary but so often disregarded truth that "obedience is the foundation of self-improvement"; and what well-disposed mind would not be grateful to the author of the beautiful maxim: "Without veneration, it is impossible to learn or even enjoy anything, and, above all, it is impossible to arrive at any settled state of mind or heart"?[110] Great and powerful, too, was the idea of a "mental fellowship" to be established among all men, as a noble possession for which men at that time seemed to have lost even the inclination; there, indeed, was the proper remedy for the sickness of the social body, and it was thinking realistically to think that a faith was needed.

But Comte ended by trapping himself within the terms of an insoluble problem. For he had made that faith doubly impossible in advance—in its content and even in its form. By a paradox to which he was doomed by the narrowness of the positivist doctrine, he was obliged to demand what no religion has ever wanted from any of its initiates; and, in founding his priesthood, he established the harshest and at the same time the most unjustifiable of intellectual tyrannies. As one of his most orthodox disciples expressly states, the "theoretic or philosophical class", which consists of the priests of positivism, is specially charged to think for us.[111] Henceforth man was to bow no more before God; nothing higher than his own understanding was to solicit the free adherence of his faith; but he was to submit the depths of his being, the part by which he was most himself, to other men, and in matters that depend solely upon man. Fortunately, said John Stuart Mill, with a touch of humor, "mankind have not yet been under the rule of one who assumes that he knows all there is to be known and that, when he has put himself at the head of humanity, the book of human knowledge may be closed."[112] Of a man, one might

---

[110] *Blign.*, p. 131. *Hutton* (1855).

[111] Ibid., p. 262.

[112] *Mill*, p. 182.

add, who, concentrating the whole of "spiritual power"[113] in his own person, has decreed once for all, and for everyone, that there are no mysteries and that it is one's duty to believe.

4. Sociocracy

That is only the first and most fundamental of the obligations that positivism imposes upon us. The whole thing is not carried out on a purely spiritual plane. It should not be forgotten that this man who knows and who does our thinking for us is essentially a sociologist meditating social reconstruction. Philosophic positivism is marked by the advent of sociology: religious positivism was therefore to take the form of a "sociolatry" and a "sociocracy". In it "social physics" was to culminate in a social mysticism, and the religion of Humanity, which would otherwise have remained an abstract or purely inward religion, was to become incarnate in the reign of Society. In the last analysis, Christianity in general had been a looking-forward to the kingdom of heaven; positivism in general is, in the last analysis, an organization of the kingdom of the earth. Thus there is no point in trying to distinguish between a religious part and a political part: politics, in the broad sense of the word, form the whole of that religion, constituting "the final object of the dogma and of the cult, thus preserved from any ascetic or quietist deviation, following the impulse of real love".[114] If

---

[113] *Polit.*, vol. 3, p. XXXIX: "Spiritual authority, although more difficult than any other . . . is also the most susceptible of condensation. It necessarily begins through a single head, in which, however, all its essential institutions reside, worship and even rule as well as dogma. That law, verifiable in the great Saint Paul, the sole real founder of Catholicism, is even more appropriate for positivism, more complete and better coordinated. . . ."

[114] *Polit.*, vol. 2, pp. 77, 20, 110: "The asceticism and quietism inherent in Catholic beliefs". P. 343: "The positive religion . . . decides irrevocably for the preponderance of the State", "the religious society is particularly destined to consolidate and develop the civil society", and "the superior extension of

the advent of sociology had meant the elevation of politics to the rank of an exact science,[115] the advent of sociocracy was to be the religious consecration of the said politics.

There was to be a distinction, however, between those who inspired and those who directly practiced politics, that is to say, there was to be a spiritual and a temporal authority. "Spiritual power will be in the hands of the scientists, and temporal power will be exercised by those in charge of industrial enterprises."[116] But naturally the latter would only be the instruments of the former: they were to be a kind of "overseers of Western affairs" under the direction of the priesthood.[117] This distribution of functions, first suggested in the *Opuscules*, was taken up unchanged in the *Politique positive* and was firmly maintained in the *Circulaires annuelles*. It is in this sense that the "natural distinction between education and action, or between ethics and politics, must be understood".[118] It is similar to the classic distinction between theoretical and applied science. There is no duality of purpose. "Free from all temporal ambition", the nobly contemplative class was "to inspire a wise policy everywhere",[119] and this was to be effectually carried out by a temporal authority that would confine itself to "presiding over the

---

the Church never authorizes her to regard herself as representing the true Great Priest better than the States can do. . . ."

[115] *Opusc.*, p. 39.

[116] Ibid., p. 93.

[117] *Circ.*, pp. 28–29.

[118] *Polit.*, vol. 1, p. 89. *Div.*, vol. 1, p. 231. *Mill*, pp. 13–14: "I know that by proclaiming the present necessity of a frank systematic separation between the speculative and the active life, between philosophical action and political action, corresponding to the old Catholic division between spiritual power and temporal power, I am directly attacking the most universal and the most profound of the revolutionary prejudices proper to the great modern tradition" (January 17, 1842). Cf. Saint-Simon, according to Durkheim, p. 207.

[119] *Circ.*, p. 51; p. 81: "Posterity will regard the normal state of Humanity as having spiritually begun during the year that has just ended, since the positive religion, fully instituted the preceding year, then applied itself to the political installation of the final transition."

habitual improvement of our material lot, in accordance with the knowledge of the external order taught and developed by the priesthood".[120]

Comte, who admired the theocracy of the Middle Ages (as he pictured it in a very rough and ready view of history), equally admired the Jacobin Club, and it is now to the first and now to the second of these organizations that he compares his priesthood. The positivists, he says, are "the true successors of the Jacobins", for "the Jacobin Club, standing outside the government properly so called, then represented a sort of spiritual authority, in that combination, so remarkable and so little understood, which was characteristic of the revolutionary regime."[121] In the circular that "the Founder of Positivism" addressed, on March 8, 1848, "to all those who wish to join in", the same comparison is made: "I have just founded, with the characteristic motto 'Order and Progress', a Political Society destined to perform, in the second and essentially organic part of the great revolution, a function equivalent to that which the Jacobin Club so usefully performed in the first and necessarily critical part."[122] Just as "the outstanding social genius peculiar to the Middle Ages" came from the circumstance that the temporal leaders at that time followed the promptings of the Catholic priesthood, so "the admirable political instinct of the Convention" was infused into it by the Jacobins. It was a cooperation of the same kind that would enable the positivists to "rule the world".[123] In order to establish, at last, the final regime that would bring men the happiness of perfect order, the High Priest of Humanity must summon to his banner the "nobly ambitious men" of energetic character. He would have nothing to gain in being overscrupulous in the choice of them. There was not much danger of serious excesses, since those

---

[120] *Polit.*, vol. 3, p. XXXVII.

[121] To Hardery, January 20, 1853. *Mill*, p. 23 (March 4, 1842).

[122] Cf. Gouhier, vol. 1, pp. 17–18, note.

[123] *Polit.*, vol. 1, p. 90. *Blign.*, p. 120.

who were out to "make political capital of positivism would soon be swept along beyond their original intentions by the obligation to become religious in order to exercise a real influence upon society".[124] Like Muhammed "to his predestinates" or Cromwell "to his saints", he thus promised them "universal mastery", addressing them in "this bold language":

> Seize hold of the world of society, for it belongs to you, not according to any law but because of a manifest duty, resting on your exclusive capacity to direct it properly, either as speculative counsellors or as active commanders. Let there be no dissembling the fact that today the servants of Humanity are ousting the servants of God, root and branch, from all control of public affairs, as incapable of really concerning themselves with such affairs and understanding them properly. . . . Those who cannot seriously believe either in God or in mankind are morally unworthy, so long as their sceptical sickness lasts. As for those who, on the other hand, claim to combine God and Humanity, their mental inferiority is at once evident, since they propose to reconcile two wholly incompatible regimes, and thereby prove themselves unaware of the true conditions of either. . . .[125]

Thus the alliance sought with the theologists was, as we have seen, certainly no more than temporary. It was an expedient to get rid of the intermediates, so as to enable the two principal antagonists to try their strength in a combat whose outcome could not be in doubt. As soon as the opportunity presented itself of acceding to power, all "accommodations" would disappear. In its latest historical form, which was the Catholic form, the only thing that theologism could do prior to disappearing forever was to help positivism to take the fate of the world into its own hands, before society had been completely disin-

---

[124] *Div.*, vol. 1:2, p. 107.

[125] *Blign.*, pp. 35–36 (27 Dante 63). *Inéd.*, vol. 1, p. 188; vol. 2, p. 324. *Circ.*, p. 80: ". . . soon to achieve, purified and combined, the universal empire that Muhammad promised to true believers and the general kingdom that Cromwell announced to the saints."

tegrated by the forces of revolution. But, in contributing to this work by the alliance it agreed to, it would accomplish its own ruin. The more merit it possessed, indeed, the more implacably the rivalry of positivism must confront it. It was the rivalry of the heir presumptive toward the old sovereign unable to make up his mind to die; undeclared at first, it must break forth in the end. To accomplish its object, positivism would, moreover, employ more brutal methods than its predecessor; its "political advance" would not resemble that of Catholicism. The latter "did not obtain the reins of government until it had conquered society; for positivism, on the other hand, ascendancy in the social field in particular would come only after experience of its political efficacy".[126] "Its chief triumph as theory" would come to it "through a spontaneous appreciation of its superiority" in practice; "its dogma and even its form of worship, despite their preeminence in their own right", would "receive their greatest recommendation, in the eyes of the public of the West, from the excellence of its regime". Thus, "although necessarily destined to a complete universality", the positivist doctrine would be, "for a generation at least, the religion of the leaders, before becoming that of the subjects". It would impose itself before making converts. Only when "the positivist party" had gained the upper hand in the political field would the religion of Humanity be able to acquire its "final influence". Thus the watchword was still "Mental approach first", since without any doctrine it would be useless to attempt a social reconstruction, and since nothing could be done

---

[126] *Blign.*, p. 74. *Inéd.*, vol. 3, p. 219: "The political installation of positivism must be accomplished in a wholly different way than that of Catholicism. The latter, directly unsuited to public life, and arising, moreover, under a still very powerful rule, could be raised to government only by penetrating society. Positivism, on the contrary, is immediately fit to regulate sociability, and reaching the midst of an anarchy in which authority is essentially lacking, will prevail in society only after having seized government, temporal as well as spiritual, by the spontaneous preponderance of its practical commanders and its theoretical counsellors." And vol. 2, pp. 119–21.

unless a "proper nucleus of true sociocrats" was formed; but in the field of action the watchword was "Politics first". From the very outset "the new system must seek to lay hands on power."[127]

With regard to the organization of that power and of the society it was to govern, Auguste Comte did not stop short at a general outline, any more than he had done in the case of the form of worship. This new Saint Paul and new Moses was also a new Ezekiel and a new Saint John. "The positivist New Jerusalem is as definitely determined and measured as the Holy City of the Apocalypse", and everything in it is carefully arranged in advance. But the main interest of such details, Caird adds, "is for the Church and not for the world".[128] We shall be sufficiently edified in learning that all the men in it are allotted to one of two hierarchies, according as they belong to the speculative or the active class; that, in the active class, the first category is that of the bankers; that these men, possessing great wealth, must, provided that they keep up to the pitch of their social vocation, also have the leading part in the government; that they are naturally trained for this role by their habit of seeing things in perspective and by their spirit of calculation;[129] that the middle classes are to disappear, leaving only a patriciate and a proletariat; that for the whole of the West, with its hundred and twenty million inhabitants, the patriciate is to number two thousand bankers, one for each temple of hu-

---

[127] *Polit.*, vol. 3, p. XLIII. *Div.*, vol. 1, pp. 69–71. *Opusc.*, p. 59. The same phase of constitution of the system is brief. Comte writes to Deullin, on 20 Homer 65 (*Inéd.*, vol. 1, p. 246): "The social advent of positivism has more need now of worthy practicians than of eminent theoreticians."

[128] Caird, p. 53.

[129] *Div.* vol. 1, pp. 216–17 (to Deullin, 18 Saint Paul 64): "Bankers are the natural generals of modern industry. Because of this, positivism reserves to them the temporal supremacy of the West, when their moral and mental dispositions will be on the level of their social destination and when the worthy advent of true spiritual authority will have rid the government, properly speaking, of all theoretical office. It is particularly from it (this industry of the elite) that the new knighthood must emanate. . . ."

manity; that States must be split up into small republics of the
size of Holland or Sardinia (for the present territory of France,
for instance, there will be seventeen), each of which will be
independent in temporal matters, authority being exercised in
them by the three principal bankers, and so forth.[130]

Such a regime should produce a powerful "synergy", with a
view of "universal harmony".[131] All the forces of discord would
be excluded from it: thus it was not surprising that, "by a secret presentiment", "all vicious influences" already "feared the
power that, coming at last to judge the dead irrevocably, would
never hesitate to judge the living too".[132] It would be pure of all
liberalism and would make no concessions to public opinion.
In his youth, Comte had written that "public opinion must will
what is to be done, the publicists must propose the means of action, and the rulers must put them into effect." At that time he
thought that "the people, as a body", could arrive at a sufficient
degree of enlightenment to "guide itself", without needing to
be governed "arbitrarily".[133] Soon, however, he came to think
that the "anti-feudal dogma", that is to say, the principle of the
sovereignty of the people, ought to be as transitory as "the an-
titheological dogma", that is to say, the principle of freedom of
conscience. These twin dogmas could not have any but a critical
purpose: "both born to destroy", they were "equally unsuited
as a foundation"; the first "could not form the political basis
of social reorganization" any more than the second could form

---

[130] *Cours*, vol. 6, pp. 570–620. *Polit.*, vol. 2, p. 306; vol. 4, p. 348, etc. The
Marxists point out that, in contrast to Comte, "Marx has always rejected these
naïve descriptions of the future city." Lucy Prenant in *A la lumière du marxism*,
vol. 2, p. 56.

[131] "Synergy" was a word used with increasing frequency by Comte in the
last years. Already *Mill*, March 4, 1842: "The new European synergy of five
Western populations."

[132] *Circ.*, p. 30.

[133] *Opusc.*, p. 4: "Séparation générale entre les opinions et les désirs", July
1819. And p. 46: "Sommaire appréciation de l'ensemble du passé moderne",
April 1820.

its "moral foundation".[134] "Positive philosophy and positive religion" increasingly declared themselves opposed to the "anarchic ambition" and "backward metaphysics" of the revolutionaries. "Since progressive tendencies are increasingly swallowed up by the requirements of order", Comte turned more and more toward the conservatives, to whom he launched a public appeal in August 1855.[135] "The ranks of the conservatives or reactionaries", he wrote to Pierre Laffitte, "must be regarded as the proper environment for positivism. . . . Positivism will become, for them, the only systematic defense of order against communist or socialist subversion."[136] Although "the regenerators of the West" had assumed the task of curing "anarchists and reactionaries" impartially, they could no longer "hesitate to prefer the latter", and, in order to win over to his cause "the leading conservatives of the United States" and to persuade them to a proper acceptance of "the strict moral obligations" that the "new spiritual authority" would impose upon them, Comte could, in all sincerity, stress the "proper respect" that this authority would secure "for their free use of a wealth owned by the community".[137]

Such assurances greatly restrict the bearing of certain statements in which Comte represents positivism as "a philosophy intended, in the first place, to systematize the social advent of the universal proletariat".[138] Unlike Proudhon, who ridiculed

---

[134] Ibid., p. 69: "Plan des travaux . . .", May 1822. *Catéch.*, p. 309: "In itself, any choice of superiors by inferiors is profoundly anarchic."

[135] *Circ.*, p. 27. *Appel. Hutton*, pp. 13–14 (25 Bichat 65): "Until now conservatives have shrunk from positivism, seeing as they regard us, according to our initial contacts, as a new sect of revolutionaries. But this gross mistake cannot fail to be dissipated to the degree that the positive religion is more developed and better known."

[136] *Inéd.* vol. 2, p. 167 (8 Gutenberg 65).

[137] *Circ.*, pp. 17, 40, 53: "In order to hasten the expansion of the regenerative doctrine, it must be transplanted today among the conservatives, who alone represent the dispositions and the habits that its installation demand."

[138] *Circ.*, pp. 5; 8–9: "This termination of Western anarchy demands two

liberal and parliamentary democracy as purely formal and called for the establishment of a real social democracy, Comte rejected democracy of every kind.[139] True, he hoped to recruit initiates for the "sound philosophy" chiefly from the "lower classes", "for the very reason that their fortunate lack of scholastic culture makes them less prone to vague and sophistical ways", and also because of that "wise improvidence that, whenever there is a natural pause in the work required, leaves the mind completely open again". True, he likes to suggest that these classes have a "necessary affinity" for positive philosophy, while theological philosophy is no longer suited to any but the upper classes, whose political pull it tends to perpetuate; just as metaphysical philosophy appeals chiefly to the middle classes, whose active ambition it fosters.[140] Consequently he thinks that "our proletarians are alone capable of becoming the decisive auxiliaries of the new philosophers", every proletarian being a "born philosopher", as every real philosopher is a "systematic proletarian"; and in his *Testament* he goes so far as to provide for a positivist dictatorship, to be temporarily exercised, "for the space of one generation", by three "eminent proletarians" whose names he mentions.[141] But this dictatorship by prole-

---

principal constructions: one is theory, the other is practice, which are naturally connected: the establishment of a new spiritual authority and the normal incorporation of the proletariat in modern society. The Middle Ages have irresistibly bequeathed to us this twofold program that presupposes an intimate combination between true philosophers and worthy proletarians."

[139] Much good will and trust in the elasticity of words are necessary in order to come to say, with F. Pécaut (introduction to the *Catéchisme positiviste* [new ed.: Paris: Garnier Frères, 1842], p. XXXIX) that Comte "brings out and proclaims the moral principle of democracy". . . .

[140] *Disc.*, pp. 100, 102, 109. *Circ.*, p. 83: "The proletarians of both sexes must, with heart and even mind, have a better sense than the learned of the true philosophy of history." *Mill*, pp. 229–30 (May 1, 1844); these praises seem particularly due to the fidelity of the popular audience gathered together by Comte for his weekly public course.

[141] *Polit.*, vol. 1, p. 129; vol. 3, pp. XLI–XLII. *Test.*, p. 21. *Inéd.*, vol. 2, p. 211.

tarians has nothing in common with the Marxist dictatorship of the proletariat! Comte maintains that the social condition of the proletarians is unavoidable. "The vast majority of workers" must always live on "a periodic wage", carrying out, "with a kind of abstract intention, each separate elementary action, without any special interest in their final coordination".[142] Precautions will be taken to combat the tendency of the majority to misuse its "characteristic energy".[143] Positivism actually claims to ensure "more effectually than communism, the happiness and dignity of the workman": "but it is by developing the preponderance of the employers". To the great mass of operatives Comte allows no part in the handling of public affairs. As he demands their faith, so in everything he demands their unquestioning obedience.[144]

To facilitate their task and forestall any risk of insubordination, the rulers would look to the initiative of the true believers, who "would feel bound to supply the priesthood with the private information without which its influence would remain too uncertain". Thus, after the pattern provided by the "Cath-

---

[142] *Disc.*, pp. 101–3. *Inéd.*, vol. 2, p. 206.

[143] They are curious precautions, too: *Polit.*, vol. 1, p. 222: "Proletarian hearts will adopt the habit of purifying themselves, in feminine salons, from the renascent germs of violence or envy, under the influence of an irresistible solicitude whose sanctity they will appreciate." Let us admit, with Paul Labérenne, p. 97, that "the praises that Comte makes workers still have, despite their evident sincerity, something naïve, indeed, even conventional, about them, which is miles from the relentlessly precise and yet so humane analyses of Marx or Engels on the fate of the working classes in certain countries."

[144] *Circ.*, p. 81. Yet the significance of Comte's words that "the proletariat camps in the midst of Western society without being settled there yet" (*Polit.*, vol. 2, p. 411) has been much exaggerated. It is necessary to take these words in their most literal sense: it is purely a question, Comte himself says, of "furniture" and "domicile". He advocates a system to facilitate the "sale of apartments" to proletarians. Thereby, he also says, "our barbarians" will finally be settled, this will be the "mere final complement of sedentary existence" (*Inéd.*, vol. 2, pp. 60–61). It could also well be, we would add, progress in their enslavement.

olic regime" and by 1793, the best possible police force would be available "at practically no expense". This might, of course, lead to certain abuses, but it should nevertheless be "regarded as an institution greatly to the advantage of society, its desuetude having been solely due to an indifference to the general interest that came from a total lack of real convictions".[145] It would be still better, however, if there were no more need to rely upon informers than to rely upon force. The ideal way to secure obedience is to prepare the ground by persuasion. In order not to be always obliged to impose its orders, an authority should be able to "discipline the public will".[146]

Two methods of persuasion were successively contemplated by Comte. In 1822, in that *opuscule* that he described as "fundamental", he favored an appeal to the imagination. "Whatever the particular system," he said, "you will never inspire the bulk of mankind with enthusiasm for it by proving to them that it is the one toward which civilization has been tending from the outset." What was needed was to "paint them a vivid picture of the improvements that the new system would bring into the human lot"; in that picture "imagination must play the leading part"; it must be "given free rein . . . the franker and freer it appears, the more complete and salutary will be the indispensable influence it must exercise".[147] In this way it would be possible to organize "a formidable public opinion".[148] But this method of propaganda[149] was more especially suited to the preliminary phase, when the positive regime was being first established. And perhaps it allowed too much latitude, still, to the critical principle, to the spirit of examination. . . . As we have

---

[145] *Div.*, vol. 1, pp. 367–68 (1 Homer 69).

[146] *Circ.*, pp. 72–73.

[147] "Plan des travaux . . .", *Opusc.*, pp. 135–39.

[148] *Circ.*, p. 9.

[149] The expression is Henri Gouhier's, *La Vie d'Auguste Comte* (Paris: Gallimard, 1931), p. 221; cf. *La Jeunesse*, vol. 3, pp. 320–21. There is already in that a view similar to the modern theory of myth.

seen, after having made himself the apologist of polytheism, in which the imagination is paramount, Comte tended more and more to exalt fetishism, where sentiment rules. Hence the second method, more truly in conformity with the spirit of positivism. Instead of working up the enthusiasm of the people for one after another of the aims that (having first been established scientifically by its sociologists) were successively assigned to it by its temporal leaders, would it not be better to inculcate a general disposition toward respect, veneration and even "fondness", which would consolidate the submission of the people once for all? The strong must devote themselves to the weak and the weak must venerate the strong. Such was the principal aim of the reorganization of the West, and such was the supreme and lasting service that the revival of fetishism was called upon to render to positivism.[150]

Admirable submission of the mind to the heart! It is in this that the principle of the unity of mankind lies.[151] This alone, uprooting "critical prejudices", can make "universal sociocracy" a living reality—that sociocracy for which the people of the West had been laboriously preparing for thirty centuries and whose establishment would leave nothing more to seek.[152] In order to bring out the total subordination of individuals to society, which is the characteristic of this regime, it is less correct to speak of an *adherence* by passionate spirits than of an *adhesion* on the part of "sympathetic and synthetic souls".[153]

---

[150] *Circ.*, p. 102. *Polit.*, vol. 4, pp. 42–45.

[151] *Circ.*, p. 27.

[152] *Cours*, vol. 4, p. 135. *Appel*, pp. 14–15. *Catéch.*, pp. 6, 359 ("the final sociocracy"), p. 368 ("the final state of the West"). *Polit.*, vol. 3, p. XXXI: "So arose an unimpeachable discipline, fit to deliver the West at last from sophists and orators . . .", "to return worthily to domination by the heart".

[153] *Appel*, p. 54. Léon de Montesquiou, *Les Consécrations positivistes*, p. 34: "The sentiment that permits social conservation is attachment"; pp. 62–63: "It is to attachment and to veneration that we owe what there is in us of what I call social reason. It is to attachment and to veneration that we owe our most precious lights for directing our lives."

An adhesion as deep and perfect as that of the believer to his God. No private precinct is reserved for the self.[154] It is inconceivable that the believer should make a stand against his God, set a limit he may not pass and claim rights against his exigencies. So it is with the new faith. Transferring to humanity the prerogatives that Christians acknowledge to be God's, positivism, by that very fact, reverses, in the social field, the attitude of Christianity, whose heir it means to be. Without rights vis-à-vis God, since he receives his whole being from God, the individual thought he had rights vis-à-vis society: however organically incorporated in it, however subject to its authority in all things temporal, however sincerely devoted to its welfare, he was aware of transcending it by his first beginnings and his latter end. He knew that, by what lay deepest in himself, he formed part of a greater and vaster society and that, in the last analysis, everything rested with an authority that was not human.

But, if temporal society is an adequate manifestation of the only true deity, from whom the individual receives all that he is, how can he have any rights as against society? That notion of right is essentially "theological-metaphysical". This means that it is completely out of date. It is "as false as it is immoral". It "must disappear from the political domain as the notion of cause has disappeared from the philosophical domain". The positive faith, everywhere substituting the relative for the absolute, substitutes "laws for causes and duties for rights". It replaces "the futile and heated discussion of rights" by a "fruitful and salutary realization of duties".[155] All claims to rights are anarchic. All idea of rights should be completely wiped out,

---

[154] *Polit.*, vol. 2, p. 182: "The continued development of the true Great Being identifies domestic existence more and more with political existence, according to a growing connectedness between private life and public life."

[155] *Catéch.*, p. 298. *Appel*, p. 71. *Disc.*, p. 145. *Polit.*, vol. 1, pp. 129, 311. Cf. *Nouv.*, p. 30. Lévy-Brühl's effort, pp. 374–75, to demonstrate that Comte reconciled authority and freedom, right and duty, seems to us to have been in vain.

as applicable solely to the preliminary regime and directly incompatible with the final state, which admits only duties corresponding to functions. The individual is a mere abstraction if he is not an organ of the Great Being.[156] There is no salvation for him save in "community spirit and sense of duty".[157]

---

[156] *Inéd.*, vol. 3, p. 114 (to M. de Tholouze, 15 Gutenberg 64): "This whole is alone real, and the individual exists only through an abstraction that is, however, indispensable. If you had made biological meditations, you would feel, according to their eminently synthetic nature, that it is basically the same for the whole animal kingdom, especially the higher animals, where biological unity consists in the species and in no way in the individual, who is only one really inseparable, or henceforth unintelligible, part of it." *Polit.*, vol. 2, p. 13: "This great sociological dogma is basically only the full development of the fundamental notion elaborated by true biology on the necessary subordination of the organism to the milieu."

[157] *Polit.*, vol. 3, p. 499. *Catéch.*, pp. 299–300: "Positivism never admits anything but duties, with all, for all, for its point of view, which is always social, cannot contain any notion of right, constantly founded on individuality. . . . On what human foundation could the idea of right thus rest? . . . Since divine rights no longer exist, this notion must be completely effaced. . . ." *Polit.*, vol. 3, p. XXXVI: "Any worthy citizen then becomes a social functionary."

CONCLUSION

Such is that "religion of Humanity" and that "positive regime" that are offered for our "enthusiasm".[1] With all due apologies to Comte, they contain a whole "social metaphysics" of which (echoing Maine de Biran's criticism of Bonald's system, which it so greatly resembles) we can only say: "Let anyone make what he can of it!"[2] As for the consequences, they are only too clear. The positivist formula spells total tyranny. In practice it leads to the dictatorship of a party or, rather, of a sect. It refuses man any freedom, any rights, because it refuses him any reality. Because of the sincere altruism that inspired him, Auguste Comte was able to harbor illusions regarding the character of the "harmony" he wished to establish. He was steeped in sheer utopianism.[3] Nevertheless, he illustrated that too-often-neglected truth that charity without justice inevitably turns into oppression and ruins the human character it ought to ennoble. This comes out strongly in Proudhon—Proudhon whose name is often associated with Comte's, whereas (not without going

---

[1] *Div.*, vol. 1, p. 297 (to Audiffrent, 25 Descartes 67).

[2] Pierre Maine de Biran, *Défense de la philosophie*, in *Œuvres*, ed. by Ernest Naville, vol. 3, p. 209.

[3] *Inéd.*, vol. 2, pp. 302–3: "Positivism will renew human existence by developing the systematic culture of sympathetic instincts. As long as they remained unknown through official beliefs, their expansion could only be empirical. It will now be able to receive the assistance of theory. The principal superiority of the positive religion consists in establishing itself essentially in the domain of grace, previously rebel to all laws. Henceforth the knowledge and improvement of our nature are to procure for us means of happiness whose past cannot provide any idea of it" (to Hadery, 36 Dante 67). *Polit.*, vol. 4, p. 526: "The final state is fully conceived, in view of the expansion related to sociological foresight and universal love, replacing theologism and war."

to the other extreme) he set out to be the philosopher of Rights and the prophet of Justice. "Love as the principle", says the positivist motto. Alas! One can but add: "and tyranny as the outcome".[4]

It must be admitted, however, that in his denial of all rights Auguste Comte appears logical. It was a necessary consequence of denial of God. Antoine Baumann says with truth:

> If one rules out the hypothesis of a God who is master of the world . . . , I cannot see on what reality you can base the notion of a right enabling the individual, as an isolated monad, to set himself up in front of the other beings around him and to say to them: 'There is something intangible in me that I conjure you to respect because its principle is independent of you"[5]

—words which may well provide food for thought to those who, at the present time, are alive to the horror of the regimes toward which mankind without God is heading. If there is no Absolute, how can there be anything absolute in man? God's cause in the human conscience and man's cause in society are bound up with each other.

Thus, if man, in his moral being, is crushed by society, it is because, in his essence, he is first crushed by the universe. The positivist order is an acceptance of Inevitability. There is nothing in man that escapes its blind force. The "Great Being" itself is completely dominated by the "Great Environment", which will one day swallow it up. Comte may well exhort us to love what we cannot avoid. He may well entreat us to "ennoble our necessary resignation by converting it into deliberate submission", into "affectionate submission".[6] The reality is still there. And this almost brings us to Nietzsche again. . . . The solutions to the problem of man and his destiny are not so numerous!

---

[4] Cf. *Polit.*, vol. 3, p. XXXV: "Altruism, whose authority can never become oppressive".

[5] Baumann, *La Religion positive* (Paris: Perrin, 1903; 2d ed., 1924), p. 222.

[6] *Polit.*, vol. 2, pp. 42 and 674.

So it is to be a double bondage, social and metaphysical—the inevitable outcome of a passionate double denial! Comte will not have it that man has a soul made in God's image. We have seen what message he proposes as a counterblast to the Glad Tidings: it is what one of his disciples calls the "Gospel of systematized common sense".[7] Here, it is true, there is nothing to remind us of Nietzsche. "Auguste Comte", says the same disciple, "did not embark upon a mad attempt to overthrow the table of values." But common sense by no means suffices to bring us the Word of Salvation! In its name the better can be repressed no less than the worse. Moreover, when it comes to "systematizing" itself, it is not immune from madness either.

Can it at least be said that the positivist menace is not very formidable? To my mind it is, on the contrary, one of the most dangerous that beset us. At any moment the failure of other nostrums, with greater outward attractions, may suddenly send its stock up. Many of the present campaigns against individualism already derive their inspiration from the ideas of Comte and his disciples, too often at the cost of the human person. They may loudly proclaim their agreement with traditional philosophy, but what they understand by that term, too, is often nothing but a traditionalist philosophy—completely heterodox in some of its fundamental propositions—which is actually one of the sources of Comtian thought.[8] They lead believers astray by

---

[7] Georges Deherme, *Aux jeunes gens: un maître, Auguste Comte; une direction: le Positivisme* (1921), p. IV; cf. pp. 45, 51–101.

[8] Cf. Charles Maurras, *La Contre-révolution spontanée* (Lyons: Lardanchet, 1943), p. 92: "To the bi-monthly Review was added an Institute whose teaching was founded on the practical agreement of the ideas of Bonald and Comte, of Maistre and Renan, of traditional Catholic dogma and historical experience. . . ." The relationship between positivism and traditionalism was recently shown, in depth, by Jean Lacroix, *Vocation personnelle et tradition nationale* (Paris: Bloud & Gay, 1942); this is why we have refrained from discussing it. For Comte, "Catholic philosophy" was the system of Maistre (*Du Pape*) or of Bonald: *Cours*, vol. 4, p. 146 (46th lesson).

ambiguous pronouncements.[9] They pay homage to Catholicism; but, in varying degrees and often without being clearly aware of it, their purpose is to rid it more effectually of the Christian spirit. They stress the elements of superstition that still subsist in a body so large as the Church and which it is so easy to exacerbate, especially in periods of unrest. It sometimes happens that churchmen, paying too little heed to the Gospel, let themselves be caught by this. Positivism is gaining ground, as its founder repeatedly predicted,[10] far less by any conquest over former "metaphysicians" or "revolutionaries" than by a slow and imperceptible dechristianization of a large number of Catholic souls. The "accommodations" and "alliances" favored by Comte have actually borne fruit. They were followed by a period of spontaneous assimilation, and the faith that used to be a living adherence to the Mystery of Christ then came to be no more than attachment to a social program, itself twisted and diverted from its purpose.[11] Without any apparent crisis, under a surface that sometimes seemed the reverse of apostasy, that faith has slowly been drained of its substance.

Nevertheless, positivism, in its way, bears witness to a vocation that man cannot stifle. Comte's spiritual itinerary is that of

---

[9] Such was the famous formula on authority that comes "from above". Cf. *Cité nouvelle*, June 1944: "La Malfaisance de Rousseau".

[10] *Inéd.*, vol. 2, p. 142: "My daily experience increasingly goes to prove that sincere Catholics . . . will be more accessible to positivism than revolutionaries"; p. 130; vol. 1, p. 273: "We shall see more and more cases (there have already been some) of a direct ascent from Catholicism to positivism, without any intervening negativism", etc. Cf. Deherme, p. 60: "Comte tried to contrive a primrose path between the decaying theologism and the nascent positivism." "We will destroy nothing: we will absorb everything", said his disciple Baumann, after having participated in the celebration of December 8 in Lyons (p. 292).

[11] "We are divided", said a leading positivist to an eminent Catholic, "only when it is a question of God" (Georges Bouyx, *L'Église de l'Ordre*, vol. 1, p. 127). The gravity of the danger that we point out would consist precisely in that, little by little, Catholics would come to think in fact that such a distance was, in practical terms, negligible.

man himself. Lost faith cannot long remain unreplaced. Thus a more and more religious aspect was assumed by the very doctrine that, in the name of science, had liquidated the whole religious past; and the religion of the "Great Being", in which it found its consummation, enabled a few souls to cross the desert of the scientistic era with something to cheat their thirst. But the illusion cannot possibly continue.[12] The virtue of a religion in which there is nothing transcendent, of a mysticism in which there is nothing supernatural, must soon show signs of exhaustion. Auguste Comte, the worshipper of Humanity, profoundly misjudged human nature. He thought to satisfy it by offering it a deity that was perfectly "homogeneous" with itself, a Being "composed of its own worshippers".[13] He was, indeed, surprisingly lacking in that sense of transcendency that was so keen (though wretchedly perverted) in Nietzsche, for instance, and that had its parallel, or at any rate its substitute, in a man like Marx. What was only impotence or blindness, he exalted as the victory of the positive age. His gravest weakness came from the fact that he never allowed any room in his mind for "those great critical questionings that challenge all purely human interpretations, those great questionings from the beyond",[14] which alone reveal man to himself. He thought he had exorcised them forever. Never, perhaps, has their voice been so strong and insistent as it is today.

---

[12] An in-depth criticism of Comte's religion and of his idea of the Great Being will be found in an article by Jean Delvolvé, "Auguste Comte et la religion", in *Revue d'histoire de la philosophie*, 1937. A criticism that is especially significant since it proceeds from a sympathy that was at first total and since it ends in showing how the imaginary elements of the Comtian religion delineate, at the heart of the practical doctrine, a void that could only be filled by the Divine Being.

[13] *Polit.*, vol. 1, p. 354; vol. 2, p. 59; vol. 3, p. 455.

[14] Eduard Thurneysen, *Dostoïevski ou les confins de l'homme* (French trans. by Maury of *Dostojewski* [Zurich: Gotthelf-Verlag, 1948]), p. 156.

PART THREE

DOSTOEVSKY AS PROPHET

How DIFFICULT IT IS TO MEASURE true greatness from the outset! In the celebrated work in which he brought "the Russian
novel" within the reach of French readers, Vogüé could still
claim that *Crime and Punishment* marked Dostoevsky's apogee.
"With that book," he said, "his talent had soared to its greatest
height. The mighty beat of his wings still continued, but he cir-
cled in the mist, in a darkling sky, like a huge bat at twilight." In
this way Vogüé excused his neglect of *The Brothers Karamazov*,
an "interminable narrative" in which he saw not much more
than "clouds of smoke" and "unpardonable digressions".[1] "It
is the weakest, heaviest and longest of Dostoevsky's novels",
he wrote, about the same time, advising against a translation of
it; "not many Russians can get through it; French taste would
certainly find it unpalatable."[2] For long enough after Vogüé,
translators would not let us approach such major works of the
great writer until they had shorn them of their "intolerable pro-
lixities", which actually means of some of the most important
passages. The genre of the "adaptation" enjoyed, so to speak, a
forced currency.[3] There was so much Russian queerness about

---

[1] Eugène-Marie Vogüé: *Le Roman russe* (Paris: Plon-Nourrit, 1886), chapter 5, pp. 246, 255, 256.

[2] Letter to the publisher Plon, October 30, 1884. Compare Henri Troyat,
Dostoïevski (1940), p. 95: "The miraculous symphony of the *Brothers Karamazov*". The German Scholz was the first among the European critics (1889)
to express the opinion that Dostoevsky had not begun to decline with *Crime
and Punishment*. Cf. Maxime Herman, *Dostoïevski et Przybyszewski* (Lille: Sau-
tai, 1938), p. 20.

Let us not speak of Jules Lemaître, who, in an article famous in its time
(published in *Revue des deux-mondes*, October 15, 1895), summed up Dostoevsky's contribution in the character of Sonia, in order to conclude that we
[French] had one better than that in Fantine of *Les Misérables*.

[3] Read, for example, the astonishing preface that M. E. Halpérine-Kaminski
placed in the volume he entitled *L'Esprit souterrain*; or, indeed, that foreword
by the same translator to the narrative that he entitles *Précoces* and which he
published following the *Journal de Raskolnikov* (1930), p. 110: "Even today,
when Dostoevsky's work enjoys a universal value, his major novel could not
usefully be disseminated except in the adapted form we have given it from

Dostoevsky![4] How could people help being completely baf-
fled? Excision was a convenient way of guarding against the
too harsh and upsetting revelations brought by his work.

Little by little, however, these revelations obtruded themselves. The riddle began to be unraveled. Beyond that vague
"religion of suffering" with humanitarian echoes, which had
at first been taken as the essence of these powerful and gloomy
productions; beyond the analogies, which critics had not been
slow to stress, with the vein of realism and naturalism in the
Western novel of the period,[5] we were brought to discern the
fathomless depths of a psychology that anticipated the most
surprising discoveries of contemporary psychiatry. We were
rightly asked to admire how "things had revealed themselves
much more quickly to the great artist than to the scientist."[6]

---

the beginning." *Précoces* is, in fact, composed of the passages from the *Brothers
Karamazov* concerning the children with whom Alyosha enters into relation.
These passages, thus treated "out of context", are nevertheless essential both
for the work's aesthetics and for its profound meaning; Dostoevsky wrote, on
March 16, 1878: "I have imagined and will soon begin a large novel, in which
there will be many children, among other characters."

[4] With respect to *The Possessed*, assuredly one of the strangest of his novels, which Dostoevsky conceived and wrote at Dresden, the Russian public
thought that it was indeed a work that had ripened abroad, that one could easily see that the author had lost contact with the Russian land. . . . Henri Troyat
is right to say that it is "absurd to claim, as some do, that Dostoevsky's heroes
are essentially Russian". Cf. Eduard Thurneysen, *Dostoïevski ou les confins de
l'homme* (French trans. by P. Maury [for Éd. Je Sers] of *Dostojewski* [Zurich:
Gotthelf-Verlag, 1948), p. 94: "We well know the scornful manner that some
have of getting rid of him by saying that it is a question 'of Russian men and
souls'."

[5] Charles Andler also wrote in 1930: "All things considered, the work
of the Russian novelist, like that of Zola or Flaubert, has swept along into
the muddy stream that carries naturalistic art, which is to say, the art of the
most decadent pessimism, into the abyss": "Nietzsche et Dostoïevski", in
Mélanges d'histoire littéraire, générale et comparée, offerts à Fernand Baldensperger
(Paris: Champion, 1930), vol. 1, p. 14.

[6] Nikolai Berdyaev, *L'Esprit de Dostoïevski* (French trans. by Lucienne Julien
Cain [Paris: Éd. Saint Michel]), p. 125. Cf. Serge Persky, *La Vie et l'oeuvre de*

What light was thrown on our common nature by those cases of dualism that continually recur in Dostoevsky, as if to compel us to see, under what seems exceptional and abnormal, the only too real law of our own hearts! What a commentary on the terrible text, "Man of himself has nothing but falsehood"![7]

But all this leads to the suspicion that, even when Dostoevsky stands revealed as a genius, he has not yet been understood. While taking such successful soundings in subliminal regions, it is really an entirely different domain that he is exploring—the domain of the spirit. Looking into and through a "formidable unconscious", he catches a glimpse of a "mysterious beyond".[8] He compels us to follow him in uncovering

---

Dostoïevsky (Paris: Payot, 1918), p. 25: "He had no notion of psychiatry, and if it can be said that he was the best depicter of neuroses, this was due to his divinatory genius and not at all to his education." The same author, p. 162, gives the example of Nelly, in *The Insulted and Injured*: "We observe in her what is called the 'epileptic character'. Dostoevsky describes the singularities of it with such accuracy that it was believed that he had copied them from a modern treatise of psychiatry. But it must be added that when he wrote his novels, the 'epileptic character' was not yet as well known as it is at present: the writer was thus in advance of science."

[7] The Second Council of Orange (529), canon 22. Augustine, *In Joannem*, 5, 1. "Everything in the world is a lie", Dostoevsky had Svidrigailov say, *Les Carnets de Crime et Châtiment* (French trans. by Boris de Schloezer), p. 187. Cf. to Strakhov: "What most people call fantastic and exceptional is the most profound reality for me": Troyat, p. 351. And, in *L'Homme souterrain* (French trans. by M. E. Halpérine-Kaminski), p. 139: "It is an illness to have too acute an awareness of one's thoughts and actions, a true illness." Mr. Troyat has analyzed very well, it seems to us, the process by which the novelist illuminates the depths of ourselves by giving life to characters who, at first, seem so distant: pp. 348–49 and 380–81.

[8] These two expressions are from Maxime Herman, p. 23. Nowhere is this symbolic duality better verified than in the major work *Notes from the Underground*. In it, Dostoevsky declares some of the most exalted truths of any of his writings through the spokesman of a miserable and abject failure who explores the lower depths of his nature with cynicism. Dostoevsky's underground represents both "the hidden world of the subconscious" (Paul Evdokimoff, *Dostoïevski et le problème du mal*, originally published as the author's the-

the spiritual depths of being. "They call me a psychologist,"
he said (that word already coming into his own self-criticism),
"but it is not true: I am a realist in the highest sense of the
term; that is to say, I show the depths of the human soul."[9] In
other words, he is, in his own way, a metaphysician. There is
no danger of taking anything away from him by recognizing
what he tells us about himself: "It is not the novel that I set
most store by, but the idea."[10] Not that there is anything there
that prejudices the novel as such, provided that we also recognize that, for Dostoevsky, the real plot of the book is none
other than that spiritual adventure to which he summons us—
that same adventure which metaphysical research, when it is
in earnest, simply transposes into abstract terms. Had we been
looking merely for some casual story, enhanced, if you like, by
psychology, we should have been on the wrong track.

On this point André Gide has gone to the heart of the matter: "In all our Western literature, the novel, with very few exceptions, deals only with the relations between man and man,
relations of the passions or the intellect, family, social or class
relations—but never, practically never, does it trouble itself
about the relations of the individual with himself or with God
—which, in this writer, come before all the others."[11] This
accounts for the initial impression of "prolixity" or "digression" made upon readers as yet unaccustomed to the Dostoevskian atmosphere. It accounts for that impression but at the
same time brands it as erroneous. Anything could be called a
"digression" rather than those inward altercations, those confidences and those interminable dialogues which, cropping up

---

sis [Université d'Aix-en-Provence, 1942], p. 138) and the sacred cave in which
the prophetic voice is raised.

[9] Quoted by Evdokimoff, p. 43.

[10] Letter quoted above to Strakhov.

[11] André Gide, Dostoïevski, vol. 11 of Œuvres complètes (Paris: NRF, 1932–
1939), p. 149. We would dispute the final interpretation that Gide proposes of
Dostoevsky, but let us first recognize that he undoubtedly helped more than
anyone else to make him known and understood in France.

unexpectedly, seem to interrupt the story in the most arbitrary and tiresome fashion, for the sake of leading the characters into strange reflections upon the immortality of the soul and the existence of God. In the meantime, has not the drama that had begun to grip us by the throat been forgotten? On the contrary, this is its center and vital point, as it is the kernel of the writer's thought. Though Dostoevsky's heroes say to themselves that "there is nothing more foolish than this eternal conversation",[12] they continually go back to it. That is because they live the problem that he himself lived and which, as he wants to show us, is our problem too. "What torments these beings is not illness or fear of tomorrow: it is God. Their author obligingly relieves them of petty everyday worries in order to leave them, naked, face to face with Mystery. Their active life corresponds to our underlying life."[13]

More than that. As the years go by, Dostoevsky grows in stature. The novelist no longer seems merely a psychologist and a metaphysician: he has the look of a prophet. Not because he foretold this or that event that has since come to pass: he tried that several times in the writings which make up the *Journal of an Author*, but, for the most part, he had no luck (similarly, when he begins to dogmatize on his own account, he very often disappoints us).[14] Inspiration rarely came to him save through the creations of his art. A lot of goodwill is needed to see in *The Possessed*, as some have done, a kind of prophetic description of the Bolshevik revolution. But, in a deeper way,

---

[12] *The Brothers Karamazov*, vol. 1. But they also say (here Ivan Karamazov is talking to his brother Alyosha): "What do young Russians do—some of them at any rate? They go into a stinking tavern, like this one, and sit down in a corner. These young fellows don't know one another and it will be forty years before they meet again. What do they discuss in those brief moments? *Only essential questions* . . ." (pp. 246–47 of French trans. by Mongault: *Les Frères Karamazov*).

[13] Henri Troyat, p. 567: cf. pp. 234–35. See also what Dostoevsky himself said with respect to *Anna Karenina*: *Journal d'un écrivain*, vol. 3, pp. 80–82.

[14] Gide, p. 212.

Dostoevsky drew in advance upon new forms of thought and of inward life which, through him, imposed themselves upon man and became part of his heritage. It is not a question of doctrine, strictly speaking: "One man can believe in God and the other not believe in him; one can be a Russian patriot and the other a patriot of the West; and yet both can belong to one and the same psychical formation and be woven of the same stuff. But, since Dostoevsky, it is the very stuff of the soul that has been changed in those who adopt his spirit."[15] Few are the men of genius of whom so much can be said; very few those to whom it applies with such force. Yes, Dostoevsky was a prophet: because he not only revealed to man the depths that are in him but opened up fresh ones for him, giving him, as it were, a new dimension; because, in this way, he foreshadowed a new state of humanity (that is to say, he heralded it by giving a preview of it);[16] because in him the crisis of our modern world was concentrated into a spearhead and reduced to its quintessence; and because there is the vital adumbration of a solution there, a light-fringed cloud for our present journey through the wilderness.

[15] Berdyaev, p. 256. The idea would not occur to us to dress Dostoevsky up as a scholar and enroll in his school in order to receive "theses".

[16] Cf. Evdokimoff, p. 378: "If, as Bêm has written, Dostoevsky's novels are dreams, they are prophetic dreams." For a study of Dostoevsky as metaphysician and prophet, the works of Berdyaev and Evdokimoff are essential. Very important, too, is the study by Romano Guardini, a French translation of which (as yet unpublished) we owe to MM. Engelmann and Givord. Let us also point out the profound exegesis made from the Barthian point of view by Eduard Thurneysen, in a brief writing translated into French from German by P. Maury (published by Je Sers): *Dostoïevski, ou les confins de l'homme.*

CHAPTER I

COMPARISON WITH NIETZSCHE

1. Hostile Brothers

We are immediately reminded of another prophet, of *the* other prophet of our times: Nietzsche. The comparison is inevitable. Everything suggests it, especially the grim contest that is now in progress in the human mind under their combined and contrasted constellations. What is at stake in the drama we are watching, and in which we are all actors, is the victory of Nietzsche or of Dostoevsky, and the outcome of the struggle will decide which of them was, in the fullest sense of the word, a prophet.

Their conjunction dates from 1887. Dostoevsky had been dead for six years. Nietzsche, doomed to lead a wandering life, was then at Nice. He wrote to Franz Overbeck on February 23:

> In a bookshop I came upon *L'Esprit souterrain* [*Notes from Underground*] by Dostoevsky. . . . It was pure chance—just like my discovery of Schopenhauer when I was twenty-one and Stendhal when I was thirty-five. Immediately I heard the call of the blood (how else can I describe it?) and my heart rejoiced.[1]

Nietzsche was lucky in his find. The hero of *Notes from Underground*—that man "disowned by the common mentality"[2] and disowning it with a gust of laughter—was just the one to give Nietzsche that sense of "affinity" to which he refers

---

[1] *Lettres choisies*, ed. by Walz, p. 455. Cf. Charles Andler, p. 14.

[2] Leo Shestov, *Les Révélations de la mort* (French trans. by Boris de Schloezer, 5th ed. [Paris: Plon, 1923]), p. 101. "I am alone, and they are everyone", says the underground man.

(Nietzsche who had celebrated "the joyful wisdom" and who, in a recent allusion to the writing of *Morgenröthe* (*The Dawn*), had actually used the words "the subterranean man at work"[3] to describe himself as he was at that time). His discovery had come late in the day, however. He had now only two years of unclouded mental activity before him. Moreover, with no knowledge of Russian, he had access to his great senior only through a few French translations and had no opportunity of reading either *The Possessed* or *The Brothers Karamazov*. *The Idiot* probably suggested some of the traits that appeared in his portrait of Jesus and the group of early Christians. It is possible, too, that the character of Raskolnikov (if he had the opportunity of studying it)[4] helped to confirm him in his aggressive immoralism.[5]

Yet, although Dostoevsky is in more than one respect the forerunner of Nietzsche, and although Nietzsche said: "He is the only person who has taught me anything about psychology", it cannot really be said that the one profoundly influenced the other. Nietzsche's enthusiasm soon waned. Without disowning his first feeling, he had time for second thoughts. In a note in *Der Wille zur Macht* dated 1888, he still spoke of the "release" that came from reading Dostoevsky.[6] But on November 20 of the same year, when Georg Brandes was warning him

---

[3] Written in 1886, *Aurore* (French trans. by Albert of *Morgenrothe*), preface, p. 5, no. 1: "In this book, an 'underground' man will be found, a man who thinks, digs and gnaws."

[4] He had the chance of seeing a French adaptation of *Crime and Punishment* performed in Turin, but he did not read the novel itself.

[5] Let us note, too, Daniel Halévy's remark, *Nietzsche* (Paris: Grasset, 1944), p. 458: "Nietzsche, prompted by Dostoevsky, was soon going to write the history of 'that cold, poisonous, eternal malice', of that *resentment*, whose expressive name had just been provided him by the French translator of Dostoevsky and that he would soon carry, as such, and implant in the German vocabulary, in the language of social psychology, thus procuring for it an unexpected fortune."

[6] *Volonté de puissance* (French trans. by Bianquis [1885] of *Der Wille zur Macht*), vol. 2, p. 343. The Russian author would free it from the rational-

against Dostoevsky as "wholly Christian in sentiment" and an adherent of "slave morality", he replied: "I have vowed a queer kind of gratitude to him, although he goes against my deepest instincts."[7] "It is much the same as with Pascal", he added. And in *Ecce Homo*, enumerating the writers who had been his spiritual sustenance, he did not mention Dostoevsky. The initial attraction was coupled with an equally violent repulsion.

From the very outset it is impossible not to be struck by the similarity of the judgments they pronounce on their age. There is the same criticism of Western rationalism and humanism; the same condemnation of the ideology of progress; the same impatience with the reign of scientism and the foolishly idyllic prospects it opened up for so many; the same disdain of a wholly superficial civilization, from which they both remove the gloss; the same foreboding of the catastrophe that should soon engulf it. Nietzsche rebels against idealism and morality: Dostoevsky attacks what he calls "Genevese ideas"[8]—which come to much the same thing. Both predict the vengeance of the "irrational elements" that the modern world tramples underfoot but does not succeed in rooting out. They call down that vengeance, even at the cost of the most dreadful cataclysms. A will to destruction is apparent in both, and the iconoclastic hammer of the German thinker plays much the same part as the apocalyptic visions of the Russian dreamer.[9] Nietzsche's mockery at the very idea of truth and his revolt against the "established order" of knowledge come close to Dostoevsky's protest against "two and two make four" and his denial of the "wall of evidence". Both represent humanity's attempt to es-

---

ist psychology inherited from the Greeks: "Ah, those Greeks!", he said in his letter to Overbeck, "what things they have on their conscience! Their principal trade is that of falsifying. All European psychology is sick from Greek 'superficiality'. . . . And without this, what little Judaism remains to us!"

[7] *Lettres choisies*, pp. 455 and 512. For several other details, see Andler, pp. 1–14.

[8] *L'Adolescent* (French trans. by Pierre Pascal), p. 201.

[9] Cf. Berdyaev, pp. 257–58 and 266–69.

cape from the prison in which a narrow-visioned civilization has confined it. They will not agree to avoid contradiction by mutilating man: smashing down the artificial but comfortable universe in which man has let himself be parked, they give him back the sense of his tragic destiny.

As we know, Nietzsche loved life. As we know, he despised happiness and sought after heroism. And we know, too, the essential part he attributed to suffering and sickness in forming heroes: "Only this noble anguish will suffice to set the spirit free"; "The great innovators were all without exception ailing and epileptic."[10] Dostoevsky, before him, had put these words into the mouth of Versilov, in *A Raw Youth*: "My dear fellow, I am not out to seduce you with any sort of good middle-class virtue in exchange for your ideals. I'm not making out that happiness is better than heroism. On the contrary, heroism is superior to any happiness whatsoever."[11] He, too, thought that the healthy man is doomed to live too commonplace a life in this normal workaday world and that the only way of escape is by a derangement of the organism.[12] In analyzing his books, it would be possible to trace a mysticism of life, or, more precisely, a telluric mysticism not unlike the cult of Dionysus.

---

[10] *Volonté*, vol. 2, p. 345 (1888). Cf. André Gide, *Journal* (1918, *Feuillets* [Paris: Gallimard, Éd. de la Pléiade], pp. 665–66). And, speaking of "that long and slow suffering, which takes its time, which burns us as if with green wood": "I doubt", he says, "that such suffering makes one better, but I know that it makes one more profound." Or again, to Malwida de M., January 14, 1880: "I have learned much from these years of suffering for the purification and polishing of the soul."

[11] *L'Adolescent*, p. 202. Cf. *Journal d'un écrivain*, vol. 3, p. 37. The same antithesis between happiness and freedom. Cf. Nikolai Berdyaev, *Destination de l'homme*, pp. 136–37: "Neither his freedom nor his dignity authorizes man to see in happiness and satisfaction the end and unique good of life. To tell the truth, there even exists an unsurmountable antagonism between freedom and happiness. It was around this that Dostoevsky created the Legend of the Grand Inquisitor."

[12] Cf. Svidrigailov to Raskolnikov, in *Crime and Punishment*, commentary in Evdokimoff, p. 76.

The whole Karamazov family, upon whom he so strongly set his stamp, is possessed by a "thirst for living", by a "raging appetite for life" that no despair can quell, and the gentle, the pure, the wise Alyosha himself says to his brother Ivan:

> "You were quite right in saying one would fain love with one's heart and one's bowels. I am thrilled with your ardor for life. To my mind, we ought to love life more than anything."
>
> "Love life rather than the meaning of life?"
>
> "Yes. Love it before finding reasons why; without logic, as you said; that's the only way to get at its meaning." [13]

The parallel has been pushed too far. Some have tried to make out that these two prophets were bearers of one and the same message. It has been said that the affinity to be found in their critical work cannot be explained solely by certain common characteristics; that they have the same positive orientation; that Raskolnikov cursing "this devil's good" reveals an audacity in every way similar to that of the despiser of morality; that the *will to power*, before Nietzsche glorified it, already represented Dostoevsky's secret aim—and that, in spite of himself, he must have been aware of it from the time of his penal servitude. The only appreciable difference, it is maintained, is that for him it had been the revelation of a "hideous truth, which he did not dare to proclaim through the utterances of his heroes save with shame and terror", hiding behind them even from himself; whereas for Nietzsche, who came later, it

---

[13] *Les Frères Karamazov*, vol. 1, pp. 243–44. "Only live, live, live!", cry the heroes of *Crime and Punishment*. "How? It doesn't matter, just live!" Cf. the extraordinary letter from Dostoevsky to his brother Mikhail, dated from the Peter and Paul fortress, December 22, 1849: "This head that created, that lived from the higher life of art, that knew the higher needs of the spirit and became used to it, this head is already detached from my shoulders; memories remain, images created by me and not yet incarnated. It is true that they make me suffer; but my heart has remained in me—and the same flesh and blood—which can also love, suffer, desire, remember; and that is life all the same. One sees the sun!": *Les Inédits de Dostoïevski* (French trans. with notes by J. W. Bienstock), pp. 3–4.

was a "declaration of rights". The first had spoken of a transformation of his convictions, while the second speaks of a transmutation of values: but it was the same process for both: from the time that he at last became his true self and dared to admit it to himself, at the end of a humanitarian and liberal period, Dostoevsky was a Nietzschean ahead of Nietzsche.

So argued Leo Shestov in a profound but highly subjective book;[14] and the idea still crops up here and there. It is not wholly untrue. Several of the characters created by the great novelist are, in some ways, precursors of the Nietzschean ideal, and these creations are "flesh of Dostoevsky's flesh". The "subterranean man", Raskolnikov, Stavrogin, Ivan Karamazov and the Grand Inquisitor himself all strive to reach a region situated "beyond good and evil", and each of them is but one of the masks of their author. Ivan Karamazov tells Alyosha in so many words that he has never been able to understand how it is possible to love one's neighbor;[15] Stavrogin, too, confesses that he has never been able to love anyone;[16] Versilov repeats to his son that "man was created physically incapable of loving his neighbor" and that "to love men as they are is impossible", giving him this watchword: "Be able to despise them even when they are good."[17] They are all of them giving expression to something deeply felt by the man who put the words in their mouths: *Journal of an Author* contains a similar confession, made with the utmost directness.[18]

But one cannot leave it at that. If he teaches contempt for others, Versilov immediately adds that he is speaking like this

---

[14] Leo Shestov, *La Philosophie de la tragédie, Dostoïevski et Nietzsche* (French trans. by Boris de Schloezer, vol. 3 of *Œuvres* [Paris: J. Schiffrin, 1926]). Shestov gave a distinctly different interpretation of Dostoevsky in *Les Révélations de la mort*.

[15] *Les Frères Karamazov*, vol. 1, p. 250.

[16] "La Confession de Stavroguine", in *Les Possédés* (French trans. by Chuzeville), vol. 3, p. 410.

[17] *L'Adolescent*, p. 203.

[18] *Journal d'un écrivain*, vol. 2, p. 314.

because he knows himself thoroughly and that "anyone who is not too stupid cannot live without despising himself, it being of little importance whether he is honest or dishonest!" This places the cynicism of these remarks in a different light.[19] Ivan and Stavrogin are doubtless only too right; yes, "a man must be hidden if we are to be able to love him; as soon as he shows his face, love disappears":[20] who, having thought it over, will deny that? But what right have we to transform this harsh and painful fact of observation into a declaration of principle? And why refuse to grant credence to the opposite side—to what are called the "monotonous and importunate lispings" of a child? Alyosha, to be sure, does not tell us what Dostoevsky was; yet his witness, like that of the Elder Zossima, nonetheless sheds light on what Dostoevsky thought. It would be a complete misconception to see in it only the echo of a conformism to which the novelist offered incense in public, either because of a lingering scruple or because he did not want to show his own self too openly. Alyosha's importance will be examined later. As for Dostoevsky in person, listen to his complete profession of faith: "I declare that love for mankind is something completely inconceivable, incomprehensible and even impossible without faith in the immortality of the human soul." Will anyone suggest that he regarded this condition as a purely chimerical one, irrevocably ruled out?[21]

Yet Shestov's idea must not be rejected out of hand. The

---

[19] *L'Esprit souterrain*, p. 149: "Can a conscious man judge himself?"

[20] Saint Bernard says the same thing with less asperity: "I know that perfect knowledge of either cannot be obtained in this life; perhaps we ought not even to desire it. If, in the heavenly mansions, knowledge indeed feeds love, down here it may serve it an ill turn; for who can flatter himself that his heart is absolutely clean? Thus there would soon ensue both confusion for the one who is known and an unpleasant surprise for the one who knows. Only where there are no more blemishes will there be happiness in knowing oneself" (*Second Sermon for the Dedication*, French trans. by the monks of Tamié, p. 28).

[21] He also says, in the *Journal d'un écrivain*: "The idea of immortality is life itself, the definitive formula and the initial source of the truth and right of the

two heroics are brothers in a profound sense.[22] Dostoevsky penetrated, in advance, into the lonely world where Nietzsche was soon to venture. He had a prophetic awareness of the crisis (perhaps the most formidable of all) of which Nietzsche was to make himself the herald and the artificer. He lived it. He was present at the "death of God". He saw the murderer springing into the saddle for a stupendous career. He envisioned both atheism and the ideal of the overman in all their force. Then —despite all the complicities he was aware of harboring he very deliberately, though not without repeated struggles, decided against them.

Thus, in a sense, he did more than foreshadow and serve as a rough sketch for his successor. To put the matter succinctly, he forestalled Nietzsche. He overcame the temptation to which Nietzsche was to succumb. That is what gives his work its extraordinary scope. Whoever plunges into it comes out immunized against the Nietzschean poison while aware of the greatness of Nietzsche. Dostoevsky does not compel the reader either to close his eyes or to take fright and shrink away. He does not thrust him back to the hither side of the newly discovered regions; he carries him beyond them. Dostoevsky, too, dispels comforting illusions and cruelly rends the veils that man ceaselessly weaves in order not to see himself as he really is. But God is not, for him, one of those veils. Dostoevsky, too, condemns this world and its falsehoods. But God is not, for him, part of the machinery of this world nor the sun of a dying universe. For, if it is more precisely our own age that

---

conscience"; cf. Berdyaev, *L'Esprit de Dostoïevski*, pp. 121–23. On the primordial interest that Dostoevsky attached to his character of Zossima, see his letters to Strakhov, August and September 1879, in *Les Inédits*, pp. 127 and 130–31.

[22] Yet one will note the justice of Mme. Geneviève Bianquis' reflection, with respect to Nietzsche: "His virile way of considering the mediocrity of the virtuous man, the fruitful virtualities of the criminal, join in a cult of energy that is much more Stendhalian than Russian": *Nietzsche* (Paris: Rieder, 1933), p. 62.

is in question, the parallel we have recognized in the critical attitude of the two thinkers with regard to it should not make us overlook the clash between their sources of inspiration. Nietzsche, in cursing our age, sees in it the heritage of the Gospel, while Dostoevsky, cursing it just as vigorously, sees in it the result of a denial of the Gospel. In the last analysis, disagreeing as to man and as to God, they disagree just as completely on the meaning of the world and on our human history, since between them is planted the sign of contradiction.[23]

Nor should we seek in our novelist proofs that it was not in his genius to fashion and that were unnecessary for his purpose. His flesh-and-blood creations are no more syllogisms than are his antagonist's burning aphorisms and visions. His novels are not theses, and it is questions rather than answers that he offers us. Or rather he is continually forcing us to reopen questions that peremptory answers claimed to have settled once for all. *Pro* and *contra* fight it out in him. He shakes us out of our blissful tranquillity. That is the foremost of the reasons why his testimony is valuable.

2. The Torment of God

"God has tormented me all my life." This confession by the atheist Kirillov, in *The Possessed*,[24] is Dostoevsky's own cry. He

---

[23] Shestov seems to us to have made a more accurate guess when he wrote, p. 6: "I think if they had lived together, they would have had that particular hatred for each other that Kirillov and Shatov experienced for each other (in *The Possessed*), after their trip in America, where they spent four months, lying side by side, dying of hunger, in a shed."

"Thus", notes Daniel Halèvy, p. 457, "the Dostoevskian chaos meets the Nietzschean chaos. Each of the two men loves what the other does not, but each of them detests what the other detests." Endorsing this judgment, we would nevertheless prefer to reverse the order of these two propositions.

[24] *The Possessed*, vol. 1. Cf. *Les Carnets de l'Idiot* (French trans. by Boris de Schloezer), p. 136: "Lebedev suddenly asks: 'Prince, what do you think: Does

dreamed of writing a comprehensive work, split up into five novels, which should recount "the life of a great sinner" and contain "everything for which (he himself had) lived":

> The chief problem, which will be propounded in all the different sections of the work, will be the one that has consciously and unconsciously tortured me all my life: the problem of the existence of God. In the course of his life the hero will be now an atheist, now a believer, now a fanatic, now a heresiarch, and then an atheist once more. . . .[25]

The book, which was originally to have been called *Atheism*,[26] was never written.[27] The idea recurs, however, in the life of the Elder Zossima, as he recalls it in the presence of his disciples, just before his death. Moreover, *The Brothers Karamazov* may be regarded as the beginning of a *Life of Alyosha*,

---

God exist?' 'You ask that so lightly?' 'If you knew how that torments me! But I always put off the solution till later, I have too many things to do, and as a precaution, I pray on occasion. . . .' "

[25] Cf. Troyat, pp. 458–59.

[26] *Dostoïevski*, by his wife, Anna Grigorievna Dostoevskaia (French trans. by André Beucler), p. 198. Conceived as early as 1868, the project had taken shape during the winter of 1869–1870. The first title considered was "Atheism"; it was in 1870 that it became "Life of a Great Sinner". To Mme. Ivanov, March 20, 1869: "I have conceived an idea, in the form of a novel, which will be called *Atheism*, in which I think I will totally experiment." To Maikhov, May 27: "I have a literary idea, a novel, a parable of atheism, to which all my former literary career is only an insignificant introduction, and I am going henceforth to dedicate my whole life to it"; and again: "Afterward, never mind if I die, I will have said everything."

With regard to the title "Life of a Great Sinner", Mr. Evdokimoff has pointed out that "in Russian, the coupling of these words in itself brings out the mystical character of the plan. The word *Jitie* (life) is the Slavonic form of the word *jisn* (life), used only in hagiographic language, for the life of a saint. This word denotes the essential and complete orientation of a life toward God, life actually *in* God. Sin is life outside God. In coupling these two notions, Dostoevsky wished to underline the paradoxical character of human destiny" (p. 33).

[27] A reconstruction of his outline has been attempted by Komarovich, following Dostoevsky's notes; French trans. in *Les Inédits*, pp. 295–308.

who, after his blameless adolescence, would have figured as the great sinner in whom faith was to triumph in the end. But the canvas was too large, the idea too ambitious! Even if he had lived longer and if he had been able to make that lengthy sojourn in a monastery that he considered an indispensable preliminary, Dostoevsky would probably never have managed to give us more than a sketch or a few fragments of this work. His art, faithful to human realities, could only have depicted a mangled destiny. In any case, he has distributed among the various characters of *The Brothers Karamazov* all the aspects that, in the projected work, were to have been arranged in a time sequence. And other novels, *The Idiot*, *The Possessed* and *A Raw Youth*, also throw light on some of these aspects. So that the main episodes of that tortured existence have really been presented to us; the main forms of atheism are there for us to see.

The first form is evoked symbolically, with extraordinary power, in *The Idiot*. Dostoevsky is transposing a personal impression of which his wife, Anna Grigorievna, has left us a record. She and her husband, on their way to Geneva in 1867, broke their journey in Basel in order to see a picture they had been told about. "It was a painting by Holbein, in which Christ, who has just suffered an inhuman martyrdom, is represented as having been taken down from the Cross and abandoned to decomposition." Unable to endure so painful a spectacle for long, Anna Grigorievna went on into another room.

> But my husband [she says] seemed shattered. . . . When I returned, twenty minutes later, he was still there, in the same place, rooted to the spot. His stricken face wore that expression of dread that I had very often noticed at the beginning of epileptic fits. I took him gently by the arm and made him sit down on a seat, expecting every minute the onset of the fit, which fortunately did not come. He gradually calmed down, but on leaving the gallery he was very anxious to look at the picture once more.[28]

---

[28] Anna Grigorievna, pp. 173–74.

What had he been contemplating? What had he seen be-neath the bloodless lineaments of that body removed from the Cross? *The Idiot* gives us the answer. There is a copy of Hol-bein's picture in Rogozhin's house, and it catches the eye of Prince Myshkin, who is visiting his friend. "That picture!" exclaims the prince in the course of their conversation. "Do you know that to look at it might make a believer lose his faith?"[29] Later Dostoevsky explained himself at greater length and, after a long description of which Charles Ledré has said: "It is hard as a Grünewald",[30] he would reveal the thoughts that had seized him at the time:

"... The strangest thing about it was the singular and engrossing question that the sight of that corpse suggested. ... Confronted with such a spectacle, how can the faithful have believed that the martyr would come to life again? One cannot help saying to oneself: If death is such a terrible thing, if the laws of nature are so strong, how can one triumph over them? How is one to conquer them if they did not even yield before him who had subjugated nature, who had said: 'Talitha cumi', and the damsel arose; 'Lazarus, come forth!' and the dead man had come out of the sepulchre? When you look at this picture, you imagine nature as a huge beast, dumb and implacable. Or, rather, how-ever unexpected the comparison may seem, it would be nearer, much nearer, to the truth to compare it to an enormous machine of modern construction that, deaf and insensible, had stupidly caught, crushed and swallowed a great Being, a Being beyond all price, one that was worth the whole of nature and all the laws that govern it, worth the whole earth, which had perhaps been created solely for the advent of that Being!

"What this picture seemed to me to express was the notion of an obscure force, insolent and stupidly eternal, to which ev-erything is subjected. ... The men who surrounded the dead body must have suffered anguish and a dreadful dismay on that

---

[29] *L'Idiot* (French trans. by Mousset), vol. 1, p. 391.

[30] Charles Ledré, "La Lutte du bien et du mal chez Tolstoï et Dostoïevski", in *La Vie intellectuelle*, vol. 41 (1936), p. 143.

evening which, at one blow, shattered all their hopes and very nearly shattered their faith. They must have gone from one another, a prey to a terrible dread, although each of them carried away in his inmost self a prodigious and ineradicable thought. And if, on the eve of the Passion, the Master himself had been able to behold his own image, would even he have been able to walk to his crucifixion as he did. . . ?"

These thoughts continued to haunt the mind of Myshkin, driving him almost to delirium. Starting as scattered thoughts, they presently became fixed in a concrete form, a hallucination:

> Can the imagination give a definite shape to what, in reality, has none? There were moments when I seemed to see that boundless force, that heavy, dark and silent being, materialize into something strange and indestructible. I remember having had the impression that somebody who was holding a candle took me by the hand and showed me a huge, repulsive tarantula, assuring me that this was the same dark, deaf and all-powerful being, and laughing at my indignation. . . .[31]

Let us recall the date of Dostoevsky's visit to the gallery in Basel: 1867. In that second part of the nineteenth century, everything conspired to intensify the rivalry in which universal Necessity has always competed with the living God. German metaphysics and French positivism led to the construction of that prison whose bars were one day to be shaken by Bergson, from which Claudel, like Saint Peter of old, was to be miraculously freed.[32] Many at that time were blind enough to mingle with their stifling scientism the illusions of a philosophy

---

[31] *L'Idiot*, vol. 2, pp. 727–29.

[32] Paul Claudel, letter to Jacques Rivière, March 12, 1908: "I am finally leaving this hideous world of Taine, of Renan and of the other Molochs of the nineteenth century, this prison, this frightful mechanics governed entirely by perfectly inflexible and, most horrible of all, knowable and teachable laws." In a page where he also evokes the early period of his liberation, Claudel cites precisely Dostoevsky among his "masters". Jacques Rivière and Paul Claudel, *Correspondance*, p. 142.

of progress.[33] Others thought that man was at last reaching his maturity in the collapse of his illusions. It was the time when Taine, the over docile mouthpiece of the prevailing ideas, pictured nature as a great lady whose indifference was about to destroy him like an ant with the uncaring sweep of her gown. At the moment when he set eyes upon Holbein's painting, the whole burden of the century suddenly weighed upon the soul of Fyodor Mikhailovich and, if he found such arresting terms in which to express the objection then prevalent and triumphant, it was because he himself was encompassed by it. It had shaken him to the heart.[34]

"I feel myself", he wrote to Pobedonostzev, "that atheism seems to be the stronger".[35] Perhaps he felt it even more in connection with the objection regarding evil. This crops up continually in his work. Take, for instance, Hippolyt's confession in *The Idiot*: "Can't I be devoured without having to bless the devourer?" . . . But it is chiefly Ivan Karamazov whom he uses to present this view, and it has been more than once remarked that he seems to side with him, Ivan's blasphemies being so very spirited! The "sacrilege" is, at first, so much more arresting than the "refutation".[36] He wrote Ivan's pages in the space of a few days, in a state of exaltation, while it cost him

---

[33] Cf. Maurice Barrès, *Les Déracinés* (Paris: Plon-Nourrit, n.d.): "The new [religion] is in agreement with scientific method and promises us through it, in the name of necessary and indefinite progress, that future of peace and love of which all the prophets have the hallucinated spirit."

[34] The same idea, perhaps still more gripping, and mixed with the dream of the "God-man", in *Les Possédés*, vol. 2, pp. 305–7. Cf. Ivan's comment, in the *Carnets des Frères Karamazov*: "The elect, the strong and the powerful, after they have supported his Cross, will find nothing of what was promised, just as he himself found nothing after his Cross. . . . Here below, there is nothing, religion is an absurdity and a stupid attempt. . . . We know, of course, that he found nothing." Here we have the parallel of the anguish of Pascal, musing about the "eternal silence of those infinite spaces" that the new science had just revealed to him. . . .

[35] Evdokimoff, p. 228.

[36] Cf. Letter to Strakhov, May 19, 1879: (*Les Inédits*, p. 123).

a laborious and protracted effort to put the other side of the case.[37] He is quite in agreement with the second Karamazov in rejecting the world as it is at present—without hoping for the advent of a really better state. With Ivan, again, he rebels "against all optimistic theology, shorn of its tragic element, with evil appearing only as a necessary note in the universal harmony, while the ways of Providence fit in only too well with philosophic reason".[38] Rather than a theodicy, he would compose a "satanodicy"! And when Ivan musters the whole force of his argument in the thought of the little girl, ill-treated and weeping with grief and shame, Dostoevsky is thinking in the depths of his heart that, on the plane of reason, there is no answer. Christ did not come to explain suffering or solve the problem of evil: he took evil upon his own shoulders to deliver us from it.

There is something else, too, in Ivan. Something else, above all, in people like Raskolnikov, Kirillov and Stavrogin: diabolical pride that will not brook the existence of a God; a yearning for irresponsibility in human conduct; the idea, too, that man would be able to do more as soon as the specter of the deity

---

[37] Boris de Schloezer, "Les Brouillons des Frères Karamazov" (*Mesures*, October 15, 1953). To Strakhov, May 19, 1875: "This part of my novel is the culminating point, its title is "Pro and Contra", the substance of it is sacrilege and the refutation of sacrilege. Sacrilege is finished and sent off; the refutation will be for the month of June. I have taken this sacrilege as I feel it and as I understand it, which is to say, precisely as it is presented today, all over Russia, in nearly all the upper classes, particularly in the young . . . the refutation of all this will appear in the last words of the dying old man": *Les Inédits*, p. 123.

[38] Evdokimoff, pp. 232 and 233; cf. p. 36. With Nicholas Berdyaev, *Les Sources et le sens du communisme russe*, pp. 53–56, one will note that this problem of suffering, which is universally human, is also "fundamentally Russian". "Through the impossibility of admitting suffering, the Russians became atheists. . . . Russian atheists judge that God does not exist precisely because, if he did exist, he could only be cruel." And Berdyaev quotes a page from Bielinski that is so characteristic that it seems very likely to have inspired Dostoevsky in the comments he gives to Ivan Karamazov. See also M. Zdziechovski, in "L'Ame russe", in *Nouvelle Journée*, cahier 8, pp. 74 and 85.

had been removed from his horizon. Here we come upon Nietzsche again. André Gide has already made the comparison. After having recalled the questions over which "the constant anguish of humanity has lingered so long": What is man? Where does he come from? What is truth?—he writes:

> But since Nietzsche, and with Nietzsche, a new question has arisen . . . and not so much one that is grafted on those other questions as one that brushes them aside and takes their place. . . . "What", it asks, "is mankind capable of? What is a man capable of?" That question is coupled with the terrible perception that man could have been something different, could have been more, could yet be more; that he is ignobly relaxing at the end of the first stage. . . . "What is a man capable of?" That question is peculiarly the atheist's question and Dostoevsky understood it through and through. . . .[39]

To that question there are ultimately two opposite answers: "Where Nietzsche hails an apogee, Dostoevsky only foresees bankruptcy."[40] These two men "came to a fork in the road that proceeds from man" and, while one yielded to the lure of the path ostensibly leading to man who has become a god —to the "overman"—the other took the way that leads to God who has been made man. Nevertheless Dostoevsky, too, had begun by thoroughly exploring the path of human self-assertion.[41] The Nietzschean temptation had laid hold of him. He had made a rough sketch of an apologia for Satan.[42] He

[39] Gide, *Dostoïevski*, pp. 267–68.

[40] Ibid., p. 289; cf. p. 269: "Every time, in the books of Dostoevsky, that we see one of his heroes ask himself this question, we can be sure that shortly after we will be present at his bankruptcy."

[41] Berdyaev, *L'Esprit de Dostoïevski*, pp. 67 and 68.

[42] This apology, moreover, goes beyond the Nietzschean aspect of Dostoevsky: it can be considered, on the one hand, to be an apology of the mysterious ways of Providence; more profoundly, it is perhaps tied to an ill-considered tradition on the integration of "evil" (which from then on is no longer such) in the very Being of the Divinity. Cf. Evdokimoff and Berdyaev,

had inquired whether evil were not the artificer of good, its indispensable harbinger, and whether that were not its justification. He had wondered whether these notions of good and evil were not prejudices of the weak. He had pictured a being that could rise above them and had clothed him with strength and beauty: his enigmatic Stavrogin does not show any of the defects that doom Raskolnikov to failure; he is not, like Kirillov, a maniac inevitably destined to kill himself; and those who come into contact with him cannot escape his fascination.[43] From this passage through immoralism, Dostoevsky's ethics acquired a note of great freedom that makes it impossible to confuse them with any vestige of prejudice. Like the most aloof immoralist, he enjoys an independent development far away from our world of conventions. Thus, if he judges the immoralist, it is not without having understood him. For, just as he felt the overwhelming impact of universal suffering, he was alive to the glamor of evil. His gaze did not only plumb the horror of man in the denial of God: it measured his greatness too.

It is Bishop Tykhone who is entrusted with this message. Moved by it is hard to say what impulse—perhaps on the advice of Shatov[44]—Stavrogin has decided to confess his crimes. In the monastery to which he repairs he is received by an old

---

ibid., p. 62: "For Dostoevsky, the terms 'divine' and 'diabolical' do not cover, the wholly external notions of 'good' and 'bad'. If Dostoevsky had developed his teaching on God and the Absolute completely, he would have been forced to recognize an antinomy in the very nature of God, to discover in God an obscure abyss, thus bearing a close resemblance to Jacob Boehme's theory on the *Urgrund*. . . ."

[43] Cf. *Les Possédés*, vol. 1, pp. 230, 240, 248–49 (Derély trans.). "Remember that you have stood for something in my life", Kirillov says to him. And Shatov: "What you call our conversation was no such thing. A master pronouncing grave words was face to face with a disciple raised from the dead; I was that disciple, you were the master"; "Shall I not kiss your footprints when you have gone? I cannot pluck you out of my heart, Nicholas Stavrogin!"

[44] *Les Possédés*, vol. 1, p. 249: "Listen, go see Tykhone."

man who is ending his days in retreat there. Stavrogin makes it clear that he is not prompted by any feeling of repentance, that he is an atheist:

"Perfect atheism is worth more than worldly indifference", Tykhone replied, with cheerful good humor.

"Oh! So that's what you think. . . ."

"Perfect atheism stands high up the ladder, on the rung below that which leads to perfect faith (the whole question is whether it will take that step or not), while indifference has no trace of faith, except, perhaps, craven fear; and then only at times, if the man is impressionable. . . ."[45]

But is the believer himself sure of his faith? Is he not human, like everyone else, and, when he takes a shrewd look at himself, can he fail to see that "strength of the earth", a "violent and brutal force" that impels him to oppose God? Father Païssy rightly tells Alyosha that it is peculiar to the Karamazovs; but what are the Karamazovs, that "sulphurous family",[46] if not men of Adam's breed? Alyosha himself has days when it works in him. He could not help confiding this to Lisa, who was talking about his brother. The accursed power is in him as in them:

"I do not know whether the spirit of God controls this power. I only know that I am myself a Karamazov. . . . I am a monk, a monk. . . . You said just now that I was a monk."

"Yes, I did say that."

"Well, perhaps I don't believe in God."

"You don't believe? What are you saying?" Lisa murmured, with constraint. But Alyosha made no reply. In those sudden words there was something mysterious, something too subjective, perhaps, which he himself could not account for and which worried him.[47]

---

[45] "La Confession de Stavroguine", in Les Possédés, vol. 2, p. 371.

[46] Ledré, p. 138.

[47] Les Frères Karamazov, vol. 1, pp. 233–34.

That again is Dostoevsky! And how many other confessions there are, which it would take too long to analyze! In him, wrote Mr. Paul Evdokimoff,

> the cry that there is nothing mingles with a serene and joyful affirmation of life. In his experience the dark deity of Kirillov, with his attribute of "arbitrariness", lives side by side with the luminous God of Mitya Karamazov and his "privilege of giving joy". He leads us in pursuit of his argument, but sometimes his guiding hand forsakes us, the light goes out, the ground gives way, and it is the same Dostoevsky who looks out through the eyes of the gentle Alyosha and through the clearsighted sarcasm of Ivan.[48]

One might add that Ivan himself has glimmerings of faith and that Alyosha, as we have just seen, is surprised, at times, by feelings of disbelief. . . . Anyone whose chief desire is for reassurance will not take Dostoevsky as his confidant. Without going so far as one of his Soviet publishers, who says that he has "left magnificent models of antireligious propaganda",[49] we may admit that his work bears scant resemblance to a treatise of apologetics on standard lines. But that is just what gives it its value. Through the characters in his novels, who all have something of himself in them, he delivers himself from his temptations and by this we know that, though he has not been insensible to the power of denial, that power has not conquered him.

Freud and his followers argue that, if Dostoevsky did not succeed in shaking off a faith when its difficulties were quite plain to him, "it is because the universal feeling of filial guilt —the feeling on which religious sentiment is based—had in his case attained a supraindividual strength and could not be quelled even by his great intellect."[50] One is more inclined to

---

[48] Evdokimoff, p. 22.

[49] Gorbatchev, Preface to the first volume of Dostoevsky's *Letters* (Leningrad: State Publications, 1928). Quoted by Evdokimoff, p. 227, note.

[50] Freud, "Dostoïevski et le parricide", a study oddly placed in the introduc-

see him as Shestov did, standing anxiously before the balance in which man's destiny is weighed: "One of these scales is filled by Nature, huge, infinitely weighty with its principles and its laws, dumb, blind and deaf. Into the other, with a trembling hand, he throws his imponderables, which have no protection, no defense . . . ; and with beating heart he waits to see which of the two will tilt the scale. . . ."[51] All the probabilities seem against God, but experience must decide. And lo! like Galileo after he had examined all the apparently convincing reasons for the doctrine of immovability, Dostoevsky exclaims: *Eppur si muove!*[52] The new judges of the scientific inquisition can do nothing about it: God lives! As Berdyaev sums the matter up: "Dostoevsky knew everything that Nietzsche was to know" —and that is what went into the first scale—"but something else as well."[53]

Lastly, there is his own testimony. Shortly before his death, he noted in his diary, in connection with criticisms of his last novel, *The Brothers Karamazov*:

> The dolts have ridiculed my obscurantism and the reactionary character of my faith. These fools could not even conceive so strong a denial of God as the one to which I gave expression. . . . The whole book is an answer to *that*.
>
> You might search Europe in vain for so powerful an expression of atheism. Thus it is not like a child that I believe in Christ and confess him. My hosanna has come forth from the crucible of doubt.[54]

---

tion to the reminiscences of Anna Grigorievna about her husband, translated into French by Beucler, p. 27: "We know", adds Freud, "that we risk incurring reproach by renouncing the impartiality necessary for psychoanalysis and by submitting Dostoevsky to a sectarian judgment, or at least to a judgment resulting from a certain conception of the world."

[51] Shestov, *Les Révélations*, p. 91.

[52] Cf. Miguel de Unamuno, *Le Sentiment tragique de la vie* (French trans. [Paris: Gallimard, 1937] of *Del sentimiento trágico de la vida en los hombres y en los pueblos*), p. 184.

[53] Berdyaev, *L'Esprit de Dostoïevski*, p. 66.

[54] In Evdokimoff, p. 227; cf. Berdyaev, *L'Esprit de Dostoïevski*, p. 30.

3. In the Presence of Jesus

These last words are a warning: Dostoevsky does not separate faith in God from faith in Christ. Not for a moment would it occur to him that the God who triumphs in his soul could be other than the God of Jesus. There again, is not the same thing true of Nietzsche? The God whose death the prophet of *Die fröhliche Wissenschaft* goes about announcing is also the God of the Bible, the God whose portrayal was completed for us by the Gospel and whose faith the Church has handed down as our heritage. And in neither case was it a matter of mere habit, as if it had not occurred to them to dissociate two elements that an ancient tradition had presented to them in conjunction. No. If the God which the one worshipped and the other rejected was still the God of Jesus, each of them had very definite reasons for this: the first being that both of them were equally fascinated and equally impressed by the personality of Jesus, although their reactions were completely different.

André Gide was not mistaken in regarding this point as "of extreme interest". "In the presence of the Gospel," he writes,

> Nietzsche's immediate and profound reaction was—it must be admitted—jealousy. It does not seem to me that Nietzsche's work can be really understood without allowing for that feeling. Nietzsche was jealous of Christ, jealous to the point of madness. In writing his *Zarathustra* Nietzsche was continually tormented with the desire to contradict the Gospel. Often he adopted the actual form of the Beatitudes in order to reverse them. He wrote *Anti-Christ* and, in his last work, *Ecce Homo*, set himself up as the victorious rival of him whose teaching he proposed to supplant.[55]

That is shrewdly observed, and a host of details could be cited that go to prove it. In *Ecce Homo* Nietzsche claimed to

---

[55] Gide, *Dostoïevski*, p. 185. Cf. *Journal* (1937, *Feuillets*; p. 1282): "Rather than rally around the One whose teaching surpassed his own, Nietzsche thought to grow by confronting him."

have been inspired like Jesus, and, after having described the
experience, he added: "I have no doubt that it is necessary
to go back thousands of years to find someone who has the
right to say: That was my experience too."[56] Like Jesus, he
was destined to come into conflict with the Pharisees, "the
good and the just", he says in *Zarathustra*, who were incapable
of understanding him, for "their mind is the captive of their
good consciences" and "the stupidity of the good is an unfath-
omable wisdom."[57] One feels that it was a kind of happiness
for him to be able to write: "These last few years everyone
has been scandalized in me." In *Zarathustra* there is not only
an echo of the Sermon on the Mount and an imitation of the
parables, there is also a copy—or rather a parody—of the Last
Supper, ending with the same words: "This do in remembrance
of me."[58] The prophet has his disciples; he also has his solitude
on the Mount of Olives.[59] Nietzsche was haunted by the idea
of the crucifixion and it was this that made him attempt the
insane synthesis between Dionysus and Jesus.[60] At moments
the idea that he was another Christ, coming after the first one
(though to oust and replace him), gave Nietzsche a feeling of

---

[56] *Ecce Homo*: "Comment naquit Zarathoustra", French trans. by Albert
(Paris, 1909). There is also perhaps an emulation with respect to Saint Paul; cf.
M. A. Cochet, "Nietzsche d'après son interprète français", in *Revue philosophique* (1932), vol. 2, pp. 242–43. He presents his poem as "a fifth Gospel": to
the publisher Schmeltzner, February 14, 1883.

[57] *Ainsi parlait Zarathoustra*, part 3 (French trans. by Albert of *Also sprach
Zarathustra*, p. 301). Cf. Betz trans., appendix, n. 134 (p. 321): "Jesus of
Nazareth loved the wicked, not the good. The sight of their moral indigna-
tion led him to swear himself. Everywhere someone was making a judgment,
he sided against those who were judging: he wanted to be the destroyer of
Morality." To Peter Gast, September 11, 1879, in *Lettres choisies*, ed. Walz, p.
302.

[58] *Zarathoustra*, part 4, pp. 401–4.

[59] Ibid., part 3, pp. 241–46.

[60] It is known that he signed several of his letters sent at the beginning of his
madness "the Crucified". An allusion to the quartering of Dionysus.

brotherhood toward the one who still inspired him and whom, *nolens volens*, he took as his model; or else he enveloped Jesus in mystery, so as to be able to stop short of condemning him in condemning his message. More often, however, he was carried away by the feeling of rivalry and poured out his hatred. "What", he asked, for instance, "has so far been the greatest sin on earth? Is it not the utterance of him who said: Woe unto you who laugh in this world?"[61] Or he delighted in twisting, with sarcastic intent, the maxims of the Gospel. "Let him who would be first take care that he is not last!"[62] He had a grudge against "this presumptuous being who is to blame for the fact that the little men have long been riding the high horse",[63] and he offered his own teaching as the formal antithesis of the teaching of Jesus:

---

[61] *Zarathoustra*, part 4, p. 416.

[62] Ibid., p. 414.

[63] Ibid., p. 374. These words, it is true, are placed in the mouth of the "ugliest of men", not of Zarathustra himself. But there is no doubt that they here translate well the thought of the author. Nietzsche indeed writes of Jesus that he was "the loftiest of human souls" (*Humain, trop humain* [French trans. of *Menschliches, Allzumenschliches*], vol. 1, p. 475), but we could not say with Charles Andler ("La Morale de Nietzsche dans le 'Zarathoustra' ", in *Revue d'histoire de la philosophie*, 1930, pp. 134– 35) that he "never spoke of him except with an infinite respect and a brotherly love". We fear, too, that Daniel Halèvy is laboring somewhat under an illusion and has bent the German prophet in the direction of his own sentiments by writing this fine page (p. 518): "A singular thing: in this wholesale massacre in which nothing escapes the blows (Plato treated by Cagliostro, as Wagner will also be immediately), in which Christianity is going to be denounced as the shame of all shames, Jesus alone is respected. Nietzsche is not one of those who seek to reduce persons in the history of humanity. On the contrary, he goes straight to them, nearly always in order to seize them, at the chink in their armor, and to drive home the point. But when Nietzsche approaches Jesus, his appearance changes. Jesus wears armor without any chinks. He is not touched by the human battle. He crosses it, enigmatic, like a living parable. History remains overturned by him, and the historian understands nothing of it. Whatever might be the explanations he tries on the overall event, that initial given always subsists, resisting any interpretation: Jesus, the immeasurable. . . ."

It is true that if you do not become as little children again you will
not be able to enter into *that* kingdom of heaven (and Zarathustra
pointed to the sky). But we have no wish to enter the kingdom
of heaven: we have become men—that is why we want the kingdom of the earth.[64]

Finally, in a strange transport of melancholy, he coupled his
passionate denial with involuntary admiration, regretting the
premature death of his predecessor. If he had lived longer, Jesus
would not have failed to go back upon his first ideas. Would
he not then have become Nietzsche's real predecessor?

Truly he died too soon, that Hebrew. . . .

All that he knew as yet was the tears and sadness of the Hebrew,
along with hatred of the good and the just, that Hebrew Jesus:
and lo! the wilderness of death laid hold upon him unawares.

Why did he not stay in the wilderness, far from the good and
the just? Perhaps he would have learned to live and to love the
earth, and life too!

Believe me, my brothers, he died too soon. He would have
recanted his own doctrine had he lived to be my age. He was
noble enough to recant!

But he was not yet mature enough. His young man's love lacks
maturity; that is why he hates men and the earth. . . .[65]

Poor Nietzsche, reproaching Christianity with being founded
on resentment!

---

[64] *Zarathoustra*, 4th part, p. 446.

[65] Ibid., part 1, p. 99. The following judgment of Pierre Burgelin, "Actualité
de Nietzsche", in *Foi et Vie*, 1938, p. 162, thus seems too absolute: "He always
made a distinction between Christ and Christians. For the one, he had nothing but respect; for the others, only scorn." See also this passage in *Volonté*,
vol. 1, p. 174 (1887): "In the New Testament, and very particularly in the
Gospels, it is not a 'divine' voice I hear but much rather an indirect form of
the most impenetrable, slanderous and destructive fury—one of the most dishonest forms of hatred. . . . Nothing is more vulgar than this battle against the
Pharisees with the aid of an absurd and impracticable moral evidence; people
had always taken pleasure in such tours de force. The reproach of 'hypocrisy'
in such a mouth! There is nothing more vulgar than this way of treating the
adversary. . . ."

Up to the time of his penal servitude, Dostoevsky does not seem to have been much concerned with seeking God; at any rate he was not "consciously" concerned: he had as yet had no personal encounter with Christ. The "Hundred and Four Stories from the Old and New Testaments" had made a fine book for his childhood, but his childhood was long past when he was arrested by the imperial police. Shut up first of all in the Fortress of Saint Peter and Saint Paul, he wrote to his brother asking for some books and, in particular, for the Bible, in French and Slavonic, if possible.[66] Soon, after having faced the specter of capital punishment, he was deported to Siberia. The convicts were cut off from the world of the living, they were even denied books. But an exception was made in favor of the Gospel, which pious women handed out to them on the road to exile. In the evening, on his return from back-breaking toil, Dostoevsky would take up the little book that was his only treasure, which he kept under his pillow.[67] He read and reread it, meditated upon it, steeped himself in the Gospel. When he came under a less rigorous regime, he immediately asked for the works of the Fathers of the Church, to help him in his commentary.[68] From then onward the Gospel was his inseparable companion. His wretched, tormented life had no power to make him forget it. In his last years he planned to write a book about Jesus Christ.[69] On his deathbed, following an old habit, he asked his wife to open the Gospel at random and read him a passage, sure of finding a light, a sign in it.[70]

In the convict prison, Dostoevsky encountered Christ. That

---

[66] Letter of August 27, 1849 (*Correspondance et voyage à l'étranger*, trans. by Bienstock, p. 99.

[67] *Journal d'un écrivain*, vol. 1, p. 202.

[68] Letters to his brother, February 22 and March 27 (cf. *Nouvelle revue française*, February 1, 1922).

[69] Notebook, December 24, 1877. Cf. Anna Grigorievna, p. 350. For some time now, he had already been attracted more usually by religious subjects and was praying more; ibid., pp. 212 and 351.

[70] Ibid. Evdokimoff, pp. 27–28.

is the cardinal fact without which his work cannot be explained. He was to be a sinner. He was to go through agonies of doubt. He knew that in advance—he did not hope to find the peace vouchsafed to simple believers. He explains this to Mme. von Wisine in an impressive letter, the first one written after his release.

> And yet God sometimes sends me moments of complete seren-
> ity. It is in such moments that I have composed in my mind a
> profession of faith, in which everything is clear and holy. This
> profession of faith is very simple. This is what it is: to believe
> that there is nothing finer, deeper, more lovable, more reason-
> able, braver and more perfect than Christ; and, not only there is
> nothing, but, I tell myself with a jealous love, there cannot be
> anything. More than that: if anyone had told me that Christ is
> outside truth, and if it had really been established that truth is
> outside Christ, I should have preferred to stay with Christ rather
> than with truth.[71]

It would be out of place to clog with commentary such a profession of faith, the intensity of which is accentuated by its paradoxical form. But anyone in danger of being shocked by it might remind himself of Dostoevsky's instinctive disdain for the absolute, unassailable proofs of a "reason" impervious to the things of the spirit; he might also recall the many "impossible suppositions" that mystics of all ages are wont to invent for the better utterance of their love. Dostoevsky was not destined to forget his paradox. When he came to objectify in the character of Kirillov some of the denials that burst from him,

---

[71] Troyat, pp. 235–36. Mr. Troyat, whose commentary is often so dependable, sees here a "solution of distrust toward the official doctrine of the Church". Yet, even if it is true that, for example, the Legend of the Grand Inquisitor presupposes a criticism of official Orthodoxy as well as of the papacy, we do not see in Dostoevsky that will for "risk" and "solitude" that Mr. Troyat attributes to him. Dostoevsky is not Kierkegaard. Mr. Thurneysen (p. 109) seems to have been more just in his view, noting that Dostoevsky did not want "to try to set himself up in the void by detaching himself from the Church".

he made that fanatical atheist raise a hymn to Christ;[72] and when he devised the inscrutable character of Stavrogin, who inspires others to make a gift which he will not allow himself to make, Dostoevsky put into his mouth the very words of his own profession of faith.[73]

How ill he could brook the claim made by so many of his contemporaries to do without Christ! He wrote one day to Strakhov, with regard to Bielinsky: "This man has insulted Christ in my presence. . . . But, in insulting him, he has never asked himself: 'Who are we to put in his place? Ourselves?' No, he has never given a thought to that."[74] What makes these denying minds, which are everlastingly arguing and which look down upon believers—what makes these creatures "withered by the drought of liberalism"[75] so pleased with themselves? They make use of noble words and talk of civilization and progress, but their vainglorious denial condemns them:

> And those fellows still boast of their atheism! But, good heavens! theism has given us the Savior, that is to say, that human form which is so noble that it commands veneration and must

---

[72] *Les Possédés* vol. 2, p. 306: "Listen", says Kirillov to Peter Stepanovich, "that man was the highest of all on earth, he was its reason for existing. The whole planet, with all that is on it, is sheer madness without that man. There has never been anyone like *him* before or since, and never will be, not even by a miracle. The miracle consists precisely in that fact, that there never was and never will be such a man as he." Similarly Shatov, obliged to admit that his faith in God is perhaps not sure, nevertheless says: "I believe in the body of Christ" (vol. 1, p. 259). Cf. Evdokimoff, p. 109.

[73] Shatov to Stavrogin, *Les Possédés*, vol. 1, p. 255: "Was it not you who told me once that if it were proved to you by a + b that the truth were outside of Christ, you would still rather remain with Christ than go with the truth? Was it not you who told me that? Did you say it?"

[74] Letter of 1871, quoted by Troyat, p. 138. Cf. *Journal d'un écrivain*, vol. 1, p. 200: "I cannot look at him without surprise, Bielinski suddenly said, interrupting the course of his explanation and pointing at me to his friend. Every time I make some reference to Christ, his face changes as if he wanted to cry."

[75] Dostoevsky, letter to his wife, August 2 and 11, 1876. *Lettres de Dostoïevski à sa femme* (French trans. by W. Bienstock), vol. 2, pp. 139 and 153.

be regarded as the eternal ideal. And what have these Turgenevs, Herzens, Outins and Chernychevskis brought us? Instead of divine beauty, which they scoff at, they offer us the spectacle of a loathsome vanity, an empty pride. . . . [76]

I quite agree that here speaks a man who is giving vent to his natural ill-nature; political rivalry, literary spite and personal jealousy make their contributions to his judgment. But, when he is alone with himself, noting down his most serious reflections, Dostoevsky also says: "We continually go astray if we have not Christ and his faith to guide us"; "Repudiate Christ, and the human mind can arrive at the most astounding conclusions."[77] Reflecting upon the West, which a strong party in his own country would have liked Russia to take as its model, he says: "The West has lost Christ, and that is why it is dying; that is the only reason."[78] This idea underlies *The Possessed*. He expresses it quite clearly in the notes that served as a preparation for the book. His faith is revealed there without any compromise:

> True, it is possible to argue, and even to assert, that Christianity will not fall to the ground if Christ is regarded as no more than a man, as a philosopher who goes about doing good, and that, moreover, Christianity is neither a necessity for mankind nor a source of living life . . . but that it is science that will be able to vitalize life and set up a perfect ideal. The world is full of these discussions. But we know, as you do, that all that is utterly absurd; we know that Christ, considered as merely man, is not

[76] Letter to Maïkov, August 28, 1867.

[77] Notebooks, 1879. *Journal d'un écrivain*, 1873 (vol. 1, p. 348). *Les Frères Karamazov*, vol. 1, p. 334 (teachings of the staretz Zossima): "On earth, we are walking about blindly, and, but for the precious image of Christ before us, we would have perished and lost our way altogether, like the human race before the flood." Cf. *Correspondance et voyage à l'étranger*, appendix, p. 571.

[78] Notebooks, 1871. He adds that it is Catholicism that is to blame for this loss. His views on the Catholic Church are, as we know, harsh and unjust as a rule. They are much the same as those that were generally held in Orthodox circles.

the Savior and the source of life; we know that no science will
serve to realize the human ideal and that, for mankind, peace,
the source of life and salvation and the indispensable condition
for the existence of the whole world, is contained in the saying:
"The Word was made flesh", and in faith in that saying.[79]

What sort of a "Life of Jesus Christ" had he in mind to write?
Assuredly not a nondescript popularization of the Gospel nar-
ratives. Not such a life as Dickens wrote, or Papini or Mauriac.
His Christ would have been, first and foremost, the messenger
and author of spiritual freedom. If Dostoevsky has not left the
slightest sketch of this book, Mr. Paul Evdokimoff considers
that we have at least the prologue to it in the "Legend of the
Grand Inquisitor".[80] Only two features of that most celebrated
composition will be dealt with here. The author of the legend
is Ivan Karamazov, the representative of all Western denials,
who recounts it to Alyosha during their long conversation at
an inn. Thus the avowed intention is not in doubt. The Grand
Inquisitor opens the case against Jesus, whose delusions and
evil-doing he denounces. Gradually he lays bare the whole of
his thought: the one who inspires him is the Denier, "the profound Spirit", the only one who holds the secrets of human
happiness. Ivan is with him, that is certain.[81] The purpose of
the scene that this atheist imagines is to present his denial in all
its force and to bring it to its climax. Alyosha quite understands
this. What, then, is the impression it produces? Alyosha shows
us what it is, and it may be confidently asserted that it is the

---

[79] *Carnets des Possédés*; quoted by Evdokimoff, p. 401.

[80] Ibid., p. 25.

[81] Romano Guardini, *Der Mensch und der Glaube* (French trans. by Engel-
mann-Givord [1933] of the German ed. [Leipzig: Hegner, 1932]), insists on
that: "Ivan's admitted intention is to justify himself and his conception of
the world." Perhaps he even exaggerates a little when he continues: "This
false Christ makes the transformation of the real world by a true Christianity
impossible, and thus hands it over as a prey to usurpation, to Ivan's usurpation. . . . The Christ of the Legend thus represents the justification of Ivan in
his own eyes."

impression produced on all Dostoevsky's readers. "He had lis-
tened in silence, with the greatest emotion. Several times over
he had made as if to interrupt his brother but had restrained
himself. 'But . . . it's absurd!' he exclaimed at last, flushing.
'Brother, your poem is a hymn to the glory of Jesus and not
a reproach as you intended!' "[82] Is this the deliberate effect of
consummate art? May it not, rather, be the spontaneous result
of a love which, even when it has to let the adversary speak,
cannot wholly restrain itself? In any case, Dostoevsky here reveals the depths of his heart. And Ivan himself, as one can see
at the end, is in his turn impressed by the majesty and the truth
of Christ. To be sure, he does not surrender (incidentally that
would have upset the balance of the novel). The demoniac old
man "persists in his idea", but the kiss he has received from
the pale lips of his Prisoner burns his heart forever.[83]

How did Jesus set about producing such an effect? Did he
confute the Grand Inquisitor? Did he, at any rate, take up one
or other of the themes of his Sermon on the Mount or one of
his parables? Did he confront the exaltation of Satan with an
apologia for God? The Inquisitor put no obstacles in his way.
He found the silence of the accused oppressive. "He would
have liked him to say something, even if his words were harsh
and terrible." But Dostoevsky did not want to use any other
methods than the one that Jesus himself had used in the presence of other accusers: *Jesus autem tacebat*. Nicholas Berdyaev
stresses the power of this:

> The artistic method that Dostoevsky adopts in his narrative is ad-
> mirable: his Christ is silent all the time and remains in the shadow.
> The effective religious idea is not expressed in any words. The
> truth about freedom is inexpressible. But the truth about con-
> straint is easily expressed. In the end it is through the contra-

---

[82] *Les Frères Karamazov*, vol. 1, pp. 277–78.

[83] Cf. Evdokimoff, p. 265: "Ivan himself is conquered aesthetically by the
immediate beauty of Christ's apparition, and he grasps the essence of it."

dictions of the Grand Inquisitor's ideas that the truth regarding freedom emerges: it shines forth in dazzling brightness from all his utterances against it. This relegation of Christ and his truth to the background is, artistically, most effective. The Grand Inquisitor produces arguments, he is convincing: he is endowed with a potent logic and a strong will bent on carrying out a definite plan. But Christ's silence, his gentle refusal to speak, carry more persuasion and a more decisive influence than all the Grand Inquisitor's force of argument.[84]

Thus behind the aesthetic device there is a conviction. So long as we talk and argue and busy ourselves on the plane of this world, "evil seems the stronger". More than that: whether evil distresses us or whether we exalt it (and the character of Ivan Karamazov is a peculiarly powerful combination of these two attitudes), it alone seems real. The thing is to enter upon another plane, to find that fourth dimension that represents the kingdom of the Spirit. Then Freedom is queen, then God triumphs and man with him.

This will become clear as we proceed. But one observation may be made here and now. The great humanists—Shakespeare and Goethe, for instance—are generally pagans, and there is an established prejudice that anyone who goes deep in his exploration of man must needs be a pagan. If by any chance he happens to be a Christian, this can only be a kind of veneer; or else he became Christian as the result of an acute attack of

---

[84] Berdyaev, *L'Esprit de Dostoïevski*, p. 224. A similar quality of silence in Sonia before Raskolnikov. *Crime et châtiment*, vol. 2, p. 559: "At the beginning of his captivity, he was expecting her to torment him with her religion, for her never to cease talking to him of the Gospel and knocking him out with that book. But to his great astonishment, not a single time did she turn the conversation to that subject, not a single time did she propose the Gospel to him. It was he himself who had asked it of her shortly after his illness, and without a word she had brought him the book. . . ." And already this dialogue, vol. 1, pp. 331–32: "What would become of me without God? —But what does God do for you, then? —Be quiet! Don't question me! He does everything, she murmured rapidly, her gaze brought back to earth."

pessimism, which made him renounce man and all his riches. But what kind of Christianity is that?

Dostoevsky's type of genius is at once profoundly human (let us avoid the word "humanist", which is ambiguous) and profoundly Christian; he is human *because* he is Christian. Whatever may be thought of his "orthodoxy", which is doubly in question, the thing can hardly be denied. His Christianity is genuine; it is, at bottom, the Christianity of the Gospel, and it is this Christianity which, reaching beyond his great gifts as a psychologist, lends so much depth to his vision of man. "He saw the light of Christ."

CHAPTER II

THE BANKRUPTCY OF ATHEISM

Dostoevsky's books abound in atheists. There are all kinds, from the everyday atheist, like old Fyodor Pavlovich, to the mystical atheist, like Kirillov. Fyodor Pavlovich, the father of the three Karamazovs, is quite ready to believe Ivan's assurance that there is neither God nor immortality. Truth to tell, the question hardly troubles him. But, if there is really no God, there is all the more reason for getting rid of those confounded monks whose fields, adjoining his own, would be just the thing for him. Only—he had not thought of that at first—how is public order to be maintained, thanks to which he can sip his brandy in peace? Between "progress", which should be helped on, and civilization, which should be maintained, the old man is puzzled. He may be left to ponder his difficulty with the aid of another dram.[1] There is no need to dwell on this aspect of his vile character.

Nor is it proposed to pass in review the whole of the rich gallery in which he is but a minor figure.[2] Since Dostoevsky the psychologist is not the object of the present study, there is the more reason for limiting that review to the analysis of the most striking cases, in order to throw into relief the principal types of atheism whose bankruptcy he successively demon-

---

[1] *Les Frères Karamazov*, (French trans. by Montgault) vol. 1, pp. 145-47. Dostoevsky does not bring his satire to bear any less on the political conformism of the partisans of God. *Les Possédés* (French trans. by Derély), vol. 2, p. 104 (von Lembke to his wife): "I will not permit the negation of God, he cried, I will close your antinational as well as antireligious salon; to believe in God is an obligation for a governor and, consequently, for his wife as well."

[2] For this, refer to two articles, of a very detailed psychology, that Fr. Stanislas de Lestapis devoted, in *Études* of 1937, vol. 233, to the "Problème de l'athéisme vu par Dostoïevski".

strates. The ideal of the "man-God", the ideal of the "Tower of Babel" and the ideal of the "palace of glass"—these three images are ready to hand, respectively denoting the spiritual ideal of the individual who is a law unto himself, the social ideal of the revolutionary who proposes to ensure, without God, the happiness of mankind, and the rational ideal of the philosopher who rejects every kind of mystery. In the concrete reality of the Dostoevskian universe, these three types —types of inverted faith rather than of pure disbelief[3]—are intermingled in a variety of permutations and combinations. A brief examination of them will afford an illustration of those divinatory intuitions that made Dostoevsky a prophet and, one might add, a judge of our age.

1. The Man-God

First of all there is Raskolnikov, the weakest of our "man-Gods". Raskolnikov, or the unsuccessful Nietzschean.[4] The wretched student, shut up in his little room in St. Petersburg, had conceived an idea, a "cardinal idea". He had embodied it in a newspaper article that he was to summarize later for the examining magistrate, Porfiry Petrovich. According to him, men are divided into two categories: the lower, comprising or-

---

[3] Cf. *L'Idiot* (French trans. by Mousset), vol. 2, p. 971: "Our compatriots do not become simply atheists, they have faith in atheism, as if it were a new religion. . . . We have such a thirst to believe!"

[4] Charles Andler rightly judged that the anarchistic immorality of characters such as Prince Walkusky in *The Insulted and Injured* is far from Nietzsche: "When the cynicism of these privileged ones grows bold in professions of faith, they are all the more Stirnerian." So, let us leave them outside our perspective. Yet, he added, with a Raskolnikov, "We come close to the more dangerous zone of Nietzschean immorality": "Nietzsche et Dostoïevski", in *Mélanges d'histoire littéraire, générale et comparée, offerts à Fernand Baldensperger* (Paris: Campion, 1930), vol. 1, p. 6. He remarks that Raskolnikov seems to alternate between faith and negation according as he is more or less under the obsession of his idea.

dinary men whose only function is the procreation of beings like themselves; and the other, comprising men who have the gift of saying something new in their environment. The first have only one duty: to obey—and that, in any case, is where their inclination lies; the second are bound to transgress the law, for a power within them demands the destruction of the present in the name of something better. They may be disgraced by their contemporaries, but they are masters of the future.[5]

Such is the theory. We know how Raskolnikov applied it, persuading himself that he was one of these superior, predestinate men. But, once the murder had been committed, the poor young man saw what he really was. "It was not a human being that I killed," he says in his ravings, "but a principle, *the* principle; I have managed to murder it, but, as for going beyond it, I have not managed that. . . ." And he scourges himself in a fury of self-revilement. " 'Oh! I am nothing but a kind of vermin', he exclaimed suddenly, with a burst of wild laughter. 'Yes, vermin, that's what I am. . . . Yes, yes, for I am perhaps something even viler and more repulsive than the vermin I have killed; because I knew beforehand that I should say that, once I had done it.' "[6] He could not stand firm, he was not capable of standing firm, he was not, like the others, "a true master, to whom everything is permitted": long afterward, when he had given himself up and was undergoing penal servitude, this single thought tortured him. He did not repent of his crime. Meditating on other murderers, he said to himself: "Those men went forward, and that was their justification; whereas I have not been able to stand firm and consequently I had no right to make the attempt."

"So that was what he confessed as his crime: only the fact of not having been able to stand firm and of having given him-

---

[5] *Crime et châtiment*, vol. 1, pp. 267–68.
[6] Ibid., pp. 281–82.

self up." He had made the attempt, and his attempt had borne
witness against him.[7]

Is that the author's whole moral? Some have thought so. After having recalled that Nietzsche "considered crime as necessary to human greatness", Charles Andler added:

> But, according to Dostoevsky, this boldness must also be success-
> ful. The weakling who kills and robs an old woman as a means
> of extricating himself from poverty has no right to crime, for
> he is not of the stuff that great conquerors are made of. Racked
> with remorse, he will remain submerged among the common
> thieves dedicated to hard labor.[8]

That is how the sinister Svidrigailov, in the same novel, draws
the moral of the story for the sister of the wretched murderer.[9]
But Svidrigailov was not acquainted with the epilogue, that final moment when, under the persevering influence of Sonia,
the heart of the condemned man came to life again in finding
repentance. Even if he had known of it, however, there is every
reason to suppose that he would not have understood it. It is
more surprising that Leo Shestov should have gone astray on
this point. According to him, Dostoevsky blamed his hero only
for his weakness: if he held out to him, right at the end, the

---

[7] Ibid., vol. 2, pp. 552 and 553; cf. p. 426: "Money wasn't the main thing
I needed. It wasn't money I needed, it was something else. . . . I had to know,
and I had to know right away: Was I a louse like all the rest, or was I a man?
Could I clear the obstacle, or could I not? I asked myself. . . . Was I a trem-
bling creature or did I have the right? . . . The time I went to the old woman's,
I was just going to give it a try. . . . I killed myself, not the old woman!"

[8] Andler, p. 8.

[9] *Crime et châtiment*, vol. 2, pp. 499–500: "He had his little theory about
it. . . . He was really taken personally by the fact that there have been people
of genius who never stopped to look at individual cases of injustice but strode
on their way without giving them a thought. Seems he imagined he too was a
man of genius—or at least he was convinced of it for a while. He has suffered
much and still suffers from the notion he was able to construct such a theory
and yet was unable to stride on his way without reflecting. So it must follow
he is not a man of genius. . . ."

prospect of a new life, it was a life in which his mishap would be justified, in which he would see that he had been right in not repenting and that he had been guided by a sure instinct in not feeling guilty.[10] It may be said that, according to this hypothesis, Raskolnikov's failure as a practician in no way invalidates his argument as a writer. On the contrary, his conversion in the end gives him complete reassurance with regard to his theory and, with new-found calm, he will now dream of an existence in which his character, more finely tempered, would be able to sustain crime and in which his will to power would be satisfied. He will dream of a world in which the selfishness of the strong man could be lived out in broad daylight. Such is, more or less, Shestov's interpretation. It is a complete misapprehension of the novelist's intention. Far from there being any necessity to interpret the last episode—contrary to its most normal meaning—by reference to Raskolnikov's former feelings, its light should be thrown upon the past in order to show up the secret symptoms of conversion already to be found there. Dostoevsky shows us Raskolnikov in the penal settlement, shortly before the crowning conversation with Sonia, going over and over his story in his own mind like a nightmare. Not that he refuses repentance. Quite the contrary! He sighs for it, however scalding it must be, as the deer thirsts for running water. But repentance does not visit him.

All the same

> This thought afflicted him: Why did he not kill himself at the time? Why, after watching the river flowing under the bridge,

---

[10] Leo Shestov, *La Philosophie de la tragédie, Dostoïevski et Nietzsche*, in *Œuvres* (French trans. by Boris de Schloezer [Paris: J. Schiffrin, 1926]), vol. 3, pp. 116–18. Having quoted these words: "He did not repent of having committed his crime", Shestov adds that they are "the conclusion of the terrible story of Raskolnikov". What leads Shestov into error is always his persuasion that Dostoevsky's thought is already Nietzschean, even though he does not dare express it without certain artifices and certain retreats, which are only exoteric.

had he preferred to give himself up? Is the desire to live so hard and difficult to crush?

He tormented himself with these questions and could not understand that even at that time, when he was leaning over the river, he had already, perhaps, a presentiment of an underlying error in himself and his convictions. He did not understand that this feeling could be the herald of a future crisis in his life, of his future resurrection and of a new way of looking at life. . . .[11]

Thus the fact that he is an unsuccessful Nietzschean does not alter, in any essential, the statement of the problem that Raskolnikov has to solve. It only adds a new element of tragedy, which Dostoevsky's realism knows to be the rule in a case like that. The weakness that is so long a source of vexation to his hero in no way affects the final solution. "Am I capable of rising above myself or not?" he asks himself one day, in one of his merciless self-examinations. That is another of his Nietzschean expressions! But in the sense in which he uses it, which is Nietzsche's sense, no man is capable of rising above himself. It is not because he is weak, it is because he is a man, that Raskolnikov is finally obliged to recognize the truth about man and that, in order to find the divine life, he has to give up trying to be a god.

Others, stronger than the St. Petersburg student, are equally defeated. But it is not by pity. Stavrogin's pride, the pride of a Lucifer, leads to suicide, and that tragic end reflects the spiritual suicide of the being who has refused himself to Being, and

---

[11] *Crime et châtiment*, vol. 2, p. 554. Charles Ledré has brought out perfectly Dostoevsky's underlying idea in his article "Le Lutte du bien et du mal chez Tolstoï et Dostoïevski", in *La Vie intellectuelle*, vol. 41 (1936), p. 146: "The whole debate, the true debate . . . is going to consist in leading him [Raskolnikov] from the ideological and 'superman' plane to which he has improperly hoisted himself, to which he still believes that any can hoist themselves, to which he understands only that he did not deserve to hoist himself—to the simply human plane, to the moral and universal plane governed by the eternal words: You shall not kill."

who has arrogantly willed his own emptiness.[12] As for Ivan Fyodorovich, he is the victim of a nasty trick! He does not believe in God, but the devil thrusts himself upon him. He has lied to himself and the spirit of falsehood holds him. He is aware that it is a hallucination, a phantom of his sick brain. But this phantom is his *double*, which confronts him with the secret thoughts that have inspired his conduct:

> As God and immortality do not exist, the new man is permitted to become man-God, even if he is the only one in the world to live in that way. With a light heart he can now free himself from the rules of traditional morality, to which man used to be in bondage. For God, no law exists. Wherever God is, he is in his place."[13]

In these two scenes of Ivan's hallucination, Dostoevsky's art reached one of its highest points. Clinical experts will extol their psychological truth. Their spiritual truth is no less wonderful. It is because he is ill that Ivan sees the devil, and that should satisfy the lovers of "positive" explanations. Have we

---

[12] *Les Possédés*, vol. 2, pp. 362–63. Romano Guardini has commented on this "void", this "terrible coldness" of Stavrogin, recognizing in the heroes of *The Possessed* "the incarnation of the darkest books of Kierkegaard: *The Concept of Dread*". "The series of degrees of dread", he says, "the process of progressive obliteration, the nothingness and the demoniac stand in relief here." "Stavrogin", Guardini also says, "does not commit himself, he is not bound. He is, as it were, the destiny of his fellow creatures, but no destiny comes to influence him himself. And certainly he suffers terribly from this state of things, but he in no way seeks to remedy it. Men are degraded at his touch, but a demoniacal force urges him, despite everything, to exercise influence, to drive home an idea, to unleash a movement. And not through some desire for an experience, in order to observe, for example, how such and such a man in general is built; the motive here is not intellectual, and, besides, there is no curiosity, in the proper sense of the word, in Stavrogin. What urges him is a true instinct (*Trieb*): the pleasure of holding a bit of life in his hands, of dominating it, of torturing it, of destroying it. He knows that he is committing an injustice, but nothing can stop him. Only that very instinct is cold, and this is what gives the impression of pure curiosity."

[13] *Les Frères Karamazov*, vol. 2, p. 651.

not been shown that Raskolnikov might, after all, be only a case of disappointed ambition, a man who has fallen short of his dream? We shall also be shown that the whole character of the Idiot can be accounted for by a physical deficiency. For anyone who wants it, there is always a means of escape from the urgency of the spiritual drama. Dostoevsky knows that, and he does not try to impose the miraculous upon us by any short-cuts. But are not Ivan Karamazov's illness and the form it takes the inevitable climax of his life of falsehood, thus vividly illustrating the impossibility of escape from the human law? True, it is only a case of dual personality! But that makes the witness who rises up all the more irrefutable, and this incipient madness is indeed the most authentic punishment.[14]

Those who would claim complicity between Dostoevsky and characters like Raskolnikov, Ivan and Stavrogin may do so more plausibly in the case of Kirillov. If there is one of his characters in whom Dostoevsky frees himself from a real temptation, it is certainly this one. Nor is there any other who symbolizes a temptation so like the Nietzschean temptation in what may be called its purest form. Kirillov is a kind of mystic. Kirillov has a feeling of fervent admiration for Christ; and when he lights the little lamp before his image, it is this feeling that inspires his action, although he makes the excuse that he is retrieving an old woman's forgetfulness. He has a self-sacrificing love for his neighbor. He is athirst for abnegation, and, in making up his mind to take his own life, he is conscious

---

[14] "It is not a nervous fever", writes Eduard Thurneysen, *Dostoïevski ou les confins de l'homme* (French trans. by P. Maury [pub. by Je Sers] of *Dostojewski* [Zurich: Gotthelf-Verlag, 1948]), p. 160, "it is his demons that destroy Ivan, and Dostoevsky lets the devil laugh sardonically at the doctors who want to cure him. Only the timid adolescent, the profound Alyosha, understands Ivan's illness: 'The tortures of a proud decision, of a deep conscience! The God in whom Ivan did not believe and his Truth have overcome his heart that had not wanted to surrender.'. . ." Another comparison is inevitable. Cf. Albert Camus, *Le Mythe de Sisyphe* (Paris: Gallimard, 1942), p. 148: "Like Nietzsche, the most famous of the assassins of God, he [Ivan] ends in madness."

of offering it on the altar of duty. In short, "in him extreme atheism joins hands with sainthood."[15] Now Kirillov is a man with an obsession; the word is hardly strong enough—he is a madman. Dostoevsky could not have given clearer evidence of the fact that, in the last analysis, he not only rejects Kirillov's idea but condemns this type of atheism as a metaphysical deviation even more than as a transgression. The moral plane has been left behind.

The idea from which Kirillov sets out is a simple one:

> "Life presents itself to man today in the aspect of suffering and terror, and that is what leads him astray. Man is not yet what he will one day become. There will be a new kind of man, happy and proud. He who does not care whether he lives or not will be the new man! The one who overcomes suffering and terror will himself be a god. And the God above will no longer exist."[16]

For that God has, in fact, never existed except in man's mind, where the form he takes is precisely that fear of death which keeps man in bondage and from which he ought to free himself. Then the second phase of human history will open—its divine phase. The first began with the gorilla, the second will begin with the annihilation of God. But there must be someone who dares to make a start; there must be someone who will kill himself in order to kill the fear of death, that is to say, in order to kill God:

> "It is open to anyone now to act in such a way that there will be no God and no anything. But nobody has done it yet."
>
> "There are millions of suicides."
>
> "But never for that reason; always in fear, and not in order to kill fear. Anyone who kills himself solely in order to kill fear will straightway become a god."

---

[15] Jacques Madaule, *Le Christianisme de Dostoïevski* (Paris: Bloud & Gay, 1939), p. 175. "One might wonder", Madaule adds, "to what degree, sometimes, Dostoevsky was not ready to decide in Kirillov's favor." Cf. Henri Troyat, *Dostoïevski* (1940), pp. 491–92.

[16] *Les Possédés*, vol. 1, p. 119.

"Perhaps he won't have time", I observed.

"That does not matter", he replied gently, with quiet pride, almost with contempt.[17]

Kirillov is both the theorist and the practician of atheist humanism. According to him "there is nothing higher than the idea of the existence of God." Until he appeared, men had not ceased to invent God "in order to be able to live without killing themselves". He was going to cut short that unbroken tradition. He was going to put an end to that bondage. He was going to proclaim the god-man, and not the man-God. The latter had already appeared; he was "the most sublime being in the whole world", but his sacrifice had not brought deliverance, for he had not been able to dispel the mirage of faith. He had died for a lie. Nevertheless, he had said: "There is nothing covered that shall not be revealed." Kirillov makes use of his words. He proposes to take up his work. A second Christ, he will complete the other's sacrifice. He will kill himself.

> "I shall manifest my will; I am required to believe firmly that I do not believe. I shall begin, I shall make an end, and I shall open the door. And I shall be a savior. This is the only thing that will save all men and transform them physically, from the next generation onward; for in their present physical state it seems to me that it is impossible for man to do without the old God. . . ."[18]

---

[17] Ibid., p. 120.

[18] Ibid., vol. 2, pp. 305–7; p. 297: "I want to reach the culminating point of independence and kill myself"; cf. vol. 1, p. 243. Paul Evdokimoff, *Dostoïevski et le problème du mal* (originally published as the author's thesis by the Université d'Aix-en-Provence, 1942), p. 150, sets forth and gives an in-depth judgment of the spiritual ambition that guides Kirillov: "The first freedom precedes the determination and, in this sense, it is without foundation, *ungrund*, it is freedom from but not yet freedom in and through. It easily degenerates into revolt, into anarchy of the spirit, into arbitrary appraisal of values. Kirillov divinizes it by raising the arbitrary to the level of a divine attribute; in the first freedom he finds the object of the second freedom, in such a way that freedom in the good appears to be freedom in itself, the good and I are identical with each other and give access to the man-God of Kirillov."

Thus his obsession reels off its logic in his mind, and we feel that he will go through with it to the end. In his somber zeal he acts like a man under a spell or a prey to delirium. Such is the man in whom Dostoevsky has embodied his highest idea of the overman. Kirillov is, moreover, sociable and good. He is a likeable person.[19] If he could read what is at the bottom of his own heart, the chances are he would find something quite different from what he thinks are his convictions. Stavrogin and Verkhovensky laugh at him. "I'm prepared to bet that when I come back I shall find you already believing in God", Stavrogin says, on taking his leave; and Verkhovensky, more brutally, asserts: "You are even fuller of belief than a pope!" Verkhovensky is perhaps right. It may be noted too (and this is a point of the utmost importance) that Kirillov is by no means a fool and that, on subjects outside his mania, he can reason with the best. Just as Raskolnikov made up his mind to murder, Kirillov makes up his mind to kill himself. But he is in a very different position from Raskolnikov, who was not big enough for his own idea. Kirillov's idea does not become a mania because it has taken root in a weak brain; it is *he* who becomes a maniac because of the madness of the idea that has taken root in him. Kirillov is a victim. "His idea does not liberate him, it devours him."[20] His divinity preys upon him.

Dostoevsky took up, on his own account, the phrase that he had placed on Kirillov's lips and had later put into the mouth of Ivan's double. In it he summed up the characteristics of the age he felt was coming and its claims. "The two most opposite ideas in the world are coming into collision", he says in the *Journal of an Author*, "the man-God has met the god-man."[21] It is the Nietzschean experience over again.[22] It is the mul-

---

[19] On the plane of current life, he is modest. Are not these qualities of the engineer Kirillov also those that we remark in Professor Nietzsche, in the hotels where he stays?

[20] Evdokimoff, p. 73.

[21] *Journal d'un écrivain*, quoted by Evdokimoff, p. 292.

[22] Kirillov constitutes, according to the remark of Romano Guardini, "a

tiform experience of our day. We can see what he thought
of it.

2. The Tower of Babel

The experience symbolized by the Tower of Babel will be generally regarded as of more topical interest. Dostoevsky adapts
the old biblical symbol to represent the socialist venture, which
he understands in a special sense. For him "socialism is not only
the labor question, or that of the fourth estate: it is above all the
question of atheism, of its contemporary incarnation; it is the
question of the Tower of Babel, which is being built without
God, not to reach heaven from earth but to bring heaven down
to earth."[23] There is no denying that the history of the strongest
current of socialist thought gives some grounds for that definition, which might have seemed arbitrary at first sight.[24] The
point is that this Tower is something that man is powerless to
build. If it is not God who helps him, then it must be devils.
It will be the work of those who are really "possessed"; and, if
they do not succeed by themselves, then others, more realistic,

---

better formal commentary, a better representational elucidation of philosophy
of Zarathustra's message of salvation. . . . Here and there, it is self-liberation
from dread and resentment by a will uniquely applied to the finite and to what
is this side of it; it is the battle against an inner will of torment, the awareness
of man's potentiality and of the capacity of renewal that sleeps in him; it is the
definition of that being as something physically and ontologically transformed
in which man takes responsibility for God's prerogatives; it is the idea that the
passage must be effected by horror and destruction and lead to an existence
in which freedom and joy are today something terrible for our souls. . . ; and
all that proceeding from the inner persuasion (in a mystical and extraordinary
sense, but altogether absolutely real and within the world) that the end-time
has come. And in both cases, it is not a question of states of soul or of feelings
that one could call occasional or uncontrolled, but in fact from a perfectly
clear position that is translated into an attitude devoid of equivocation and can
be expressed in a very definite conceptual construction."

[23] Les Frères Karamazov, vol. 1, p. 32.

[24] See above, chapter 1.

will send in secret to the leader of the hosts of evil, to Satan. "The Tower of Babel will certainly remain unfinished like the first one", the Grand Inquisitor says to himself. "After having toiled a thousand years at it, men will come and seek us out, and it will be for us to finish it!"[25] Dostoevsky thus offers us two formulas for an atheist socialism, both diabolical: one is the subject of his novel *The Possessed*; the other is set forth by the Grand Inquisitor, created by Ivan in *The Brothers Karamazov*.

The Possessed was at first intended only as a polemic. Dostoevsky was at Dresden when his brother-in-law, arriving from Russia, told him of the recent murder of the student Ivanov, suspected of treachery, by the band of Nechayevians to which he had belonged.[26] This news overwhelmed Dostoevsky. "His hatred of the new ideas was increasing daily. He resolved to strike a resounding blow. Making use of data published in the press", he set to work at once.[27] The novel bears unmistakable marks of such an origin. The murder of Shatov is modeled on that of Ivanov; Peter Verkhovensky, head of the terrorist band, is a caricature of Nechayev; Stavrogin, too, displays a number of features borrowed from Nechayev but even more from Spiechnev, the conspirator who long before had lured young Fyodor Mikhailovich into dangerous paths.[28] But soon the subject gripped the writer and carried him far beyond his original conception. The work was transformed into something of epic proportions. It was no longer a political pamphlet or a social satire. It was a descent into the darkest depths of the human soul and at the same time the great prophetic *geste* in which Eu-

---

[25] *Les Frères Karamazov*, vol. 1, p. 267.

[26] *Dostoïevski*, by his wife Anna Grigorievna Dostoevskaia (French trans. by André Beucler), pp. 199–200.

[27] Troyat, pp. 459–60.

[28] Berdyaev, *Les Sources et le sens du communisme russe*, pp. 44 and 83. Hanns-Erich Kaminski, *Michel Bakounine: La Vie d'un révolutionnaire*, pp. 250–68. There are still other "keys": it is thus that Dostoevsky profited from the occasion to ridicule Turgenev, whom he detested, by modeling the character of the wordly poet Karmazinov after him.

rope was to read its destiny.[29] As a piece of story-telling it may provoke criticism; the plot is put together clumsily, confusedly; the drama sometimes becomes melodrama; affected by a certain bias, the character of Verkhovensky seems the creation of an oversimplified psychology; and the romantic atmosphere with which the book is still suffused does not reflect the social reality of the great upheaval that was in store for Russia. And "how can we recognize socialism", asks Guardini, "in that unclean and decadent thing, *The Possessed*? How can Western reason and technical progress be recognized in that fiendish materialism that parades itself everywhere?" But on the spiritual plane Dostoevsky turns the tables, with what force of suggestion and penetrating diagnosis! And let there be no mistake about it: his ferocity toward the revolutionaries whose portraits he etches is matched by an equal lack of pity for the world they are undermining; "he would be the last person", says Berdyaev, "to defend the old bourgeois world; in spirit he is a revolutionary; but he wants a revolution with God and with Christ".[30] Something in his soul conspires even with the demolishers whom he execrates, and the apocalyptic vision that rises before his eyes does not derive its whole substance from horrors actually experienced; it is partly inspired by his own "apocalyptic bent".[31]

The revolutionary socialists are the heirs of the liberals who, in the Western school, embraced atheism.[32] "To annihilate God" is the first point in their program and the first watchword spread abroad by their tracts.[33] They draw the inferences

---

[29] Cf. André Gide, *Dostoïevski*, in *Œuvres complètes*, vol. 11 (Paris: NRF, 1932–1939), p. 277: "*The Possessed*, that extraordinary book which I, personally, consider to be the great novelist's most powerful, most admirable."

[30] Berdyaev, p. 116.

[31] Cf. Berdyaev, *L'Esprit de Dostoïevski* (French trans. by Lucienne Julien Cain [Paris: Éd. Saint Michel]), pp. 268–69.

[32] *The Possessed*, one must not forget, was first of all a lampoon against the liberals.

[33] *Les Possédés*, vol. 1, p. 275.

of that atheism. No longer contenting themselves with a vague belief in progress, they undertake to build up humanity without God. They are logical; "if Alyosha had not believed in God, he would have become a socialist."[34] But where will that logic lead them?

The first phase of this work is destructive: destruction of the old society (that is what the story of the "possessed" brings before our eyes) and especially destruction of everything that owes its origin to faith in God. Not only is heaven emptied but man is secularized; henceforth nothing about him must recall a transcendent origin and a sacred destiny. Dreams must be banned. Then it will be possible to begin building the new edifice, on the basis of science. It will be possible to organize the happiness of mankind. Stepan Trophimovich has celebrated it in advance in a pageant, of which he expects great things (it is still a question of the famous Tower):

> "In the last scene the Tower of Babel suddenly appears; the 'athletes', singing the anthem of the new hope, are putting the finishing touches to it; and, when it is completed to the very top, the owner (let us call him the Master of Olympus) decamps (this bit should be made grotesque), and mankind, not knowing where it stands, takes his place and immediately inaugurates a new era, at the same time forming a new conception of the universe."[35]

But, having freed himself from God, will man be so very free after all? Those who want to make him happy are not long in realizing that it will have to be done in spite of himself. Among the conspirators whom Verkhovensky has gathered round him, only one has given serious thought to the problem; only one has devised a complete plan of what is to follow the revolution. That is Shigalev, the theorist of the band. His system is a simple one; he sums it up as follows: "Having set out from unlimited freedom, I have ended up with unlimited despotism." Here

---

[34] *Les Frères Karamazov*, vol. 1, pp. 31–32.
[35] *Les Possédés*, vol. 1, p. 14.

we have yet another fanatic, yet another maniac: but this time a maniac who is a realist. He has come to the conclusion that "all the framers of social systems, from the remotest times up to the present year 187–, have been dreamers, tellers of fairy tales, simpletons who contradicted themselves and knew nothing of natural science and that strange animal called man." So let mankind be divided into two sections: one-tenth will exercise absolute authority over the other nine-tenths. That is the *sine qua non* for the establishment of paradise. Shigalev accepts the suggestion that it would be more logical to exterminate the other nine-tenths; then there would be nothing left but "a handful of educated men who, organizing themselves according to scientific principles, would live happy ever after". There is only one thing against this idea: it is too difficult to put it into practice. So Shigalev goes back to his paradise: "there cannot be any other kind on earth." If you want to organize the happiness of mankind, "there is no substitute for the system set forth in my book and there is no other way out; you won't find any alternative."[36] He is right. There is no escape from his conclusion. Nobody can refute Shigalevism.[37]

By this Dostoevsky means to suggest that "social systems that have no Christian basis (the only one capable of transforming man) inevitably become systems of violence and slavery."[38] Facts have perhaps shown that this was no arbitrary conviction! But he also thought that the experiment could not be pushed to extremes. Underlying the venture there was still too much of utopia! Suppose the old society were indeed abolished and the new began to take shape: "The result would be such darkness, such chaos, something so clumsy, blind and inhuman that the

---

[36] Ibid., vol. 2, pp. 91–93.

[37] Dostoevsky perhaps remembered that Bielinski himself called his love for humanity a "love according to Marat". He also said: "If I were tsar, I would be a tyrant!" Cf. Berdyaev, *Problème du communisme*, p. 60.

[38] Evdokimoff, p. 355. Cf. the criticisms addressed by Proudhon to the Jacobin and communist systems.

whole structure would collapse under the curses of mankind before the building had even been completed."[39]

It is here that the Grand Inquisitor comes upon the scene. This man—who, while despising his flock, inspires them with a perfervid faith and has the power to make men deny Jesus after having acclaimed him an hour before—is of quite a different mental stock from the revolutionaries. His brain has never harbored the smallest atom of utopianism. He does not begin by dreaming of "liberation". Aiming, in his turn, at the happiness of mankind, he knows from the outset on what conditions it can be had; he propounds a clear antithesis: freedom or happiness. The reproach he brings against Christ is precisely this: that he placed confidence in man. Why did he load him with this intolerable burden of freedom? His trenchant assertions are unforgettable:

> "You gave men still more freedom instead of taking it from them: Had you forgotten that, rather than freedom to choose between good and evil, man wants peace—though it be the peace of death? . . . You formed too lofty an idea of man; he is a slave, although he was created rebellious! . . . Anxiety, doubt and unhappiness are the lot of the men freed by your sufferings. . . ."

If Christ has failed, if he is so generally denied and cursed, he has no one but himself to blame: "You wanted to be loved with a free love; so you have prepared your own downfall. . . ." And this verdict is paired with the proud declaration: "We have corrected your work. . . . Men are delighted to be led once more like a flock of sheep. . . . We have declared ourselves masters of the earth. . . ."[40]

The Grand Inquisitor's system is Shigalevism in its true and perfect form. It does not stop at outward constraint but enslaves souls as well. Thanks to it, men find "a depository for their consciences". They are henceforth spared "the grave anxiety

---

[39] *Journal d'un écrivain*, 1873 (vol. 1, p. 348).
[40] *Les Frères Karamazov*, vol. 1, p. 464.

of choice"; they have no longer to think or desire; even in the presence of death, they will have no revelation of their destiny: provision has been made for their spiritual euthanasia.[41] In order to be happy, they are completely deprived of their mental faculties. Now the Tower can be built: the foundations are solid. The Inquisitor has dug down to the roots of being, and every disturbing seed has been extirpated. What though the Shigalevs and the Verkhovenskys were "possessed" by frantic devils? He still considers them merely as children. For his part, without losing any of his sovereign calm, it is with Satan himself that he has formed an alliance, with Satan "the terrible and intelligent Spirit, the Spirit of negation and nothingness, the profound, eternal, absolute Spirit". He is the prophet of nothingness, and that is what gives him his formidable strength. He alone can succeed, for he alone is bold enough to confront God as his living antithesis: what is God, indeed, but the creator of freedoms? Thus he alone has the right to say to Christ, when Christ wishes to come and meddle with the affairs of the world again: "Why do you come and disturb us?" He alone can proclaim himself Antichrist.[42]

There is no doubt that here one of Dostoevsky's aims, indeed his chief aim, is to criticize eudaemonism. He wants to show what is doomed to disappearance by the dream of a human race "stripped of all that is tragic in it".[43] Here is a new

---

[41] Ibid.: "They will pass away peacefully in your name, and in the beyond they will find only death."

[42] Paul Evdokimoff, p. 20, noted that the Legend of the Grand Inquisitor and Soloviev's Legend of the Antichrist (in *Trois entretiens*) were born in the same spiritual climate. Cf. Nietzsche, on "The future caste of sovereigns": "These masters of the earth must replace God and be assured of the deep and unreserved trust of those over whom they reign. First of all: their new sanctity, the reward for their renunciation of happiness and comfort. They grant to the most humble a hope of happiness, but not to themselves. They rescue the lost man, through their doctrine of 'rapid death'; they offer religions and systems adapted to the hierarchy" (*Ainsi parlait Zarathoustra* [French trans. by Betz of *Also sprach Zarathustra*], appendix, no. 196; p. 331).

[43] Evdokimoff, p. 285. The Inquisitor and his associates, says Guardini,

point of contact with Nietzsche's mind, although what he and Dostoevsky affirm are contraries, since Nietzsche would fain kill God in order to prevail over eudaemonism, while Dostoevsky's dominating idea is that to kill God in man is to kill man himself. But things are not so simple as all that. For if all that is tragic in it is removed from the "human flock", the same does not apply to its leaders:

> All the millions of beings will thus be happy, apart from about one hundred thousand: apart from ourselves, the guardians of the secret. For we shall be unhappy. The happy will number millions and millions and there will be ten thousand martyrs having exclusive and accursed knowledge of good and evil. . . .[44]

What destiny, indeed, could be more tragic than that of these artificers of falsehood and slavery, who with complete clear-sightedness behold the void into which they are leading man and toward which they are themselves heading? The Grand Inquisitor, with the "party" he allows to share his secret and his work, combines the type of the socialist and the type of the overman, as outlined in the other novels; doubly an atheist —that is to say, always against God—he is, in consequence, doubly against man: in others and in himself. This figure, if it is the most striking, is also assuredly the most prophetic of all those begotten by the genius of Dostoevsky. The setting in which the writer placed him is of little moment. As we know, Dostoevsky really believed, as he wrote in the *Journal of an Author*, that "Roman Catholicism" had "sold Christ in exchange for the kingdom of the earth".[45] This belief, in any case su-

---

"have recognized that men must be treated as a mass and that the happiness they could attain was something very average".

[44] *Les Frères Karamazov*, vol. 1, p. 275. In *Les Possédés* (vol. 2, p. 82), Peter Stepanovich likewise says to Stavrogin: "In Shigalevism there will be no desires. Desire and suffering are for us; the slaves will have Shigalevism."

[45] *Journal d'un écrivain*, vol. 2, p. 177. Cf. Shatov to Stavrogin, *Les Possédés*, vol. 1, p. 242: "According to you, Rome preached a Christ who had given in to the third temptation of the devil."

perficial, supplied him with a symbol but nothing more. He was equally convinced that socialism, in spite of "the air it assumes of being the most vehement protest against the Catholic idea", was really "the most precise continuation of it in the same straight line, its most complete outcome".[46] But this socialism of the Grand Inquisitor's bears little resemblance either to the one that history was already showing Dostoevsky in its first representatives or to the one he had depicted in *The Possessed*, with Russian terrorists as its starting point. It is something other than their logical consequence, although it partly coincides with it. That socialism does not choose to inherit the revolutionary doctrines of the nineteenth century. In taking over from them, it denies them. It rejects their illusions. Its positivist complexion is striking. The Grand Inquisitor and his associates have a family likeness to those "servants of Humanity" that Auguste Comte dreamed of; "men of noble ambition" who "take possession of the world of human society, not in virtue of any right, but because of an obvious duty"—for the purpose of organizing "final order".[47] The power they establish also comes into being, in the first place, as the work of a will to power. Those who will put it into effect are a race of Masters.

In order to establish the new order, they first give their minds to securing control: "We have declared ourselves masters of the earth"; they have to complete their conquest: "We shall achieve our purpose, we shall be Caesar, our kingdom will be deified"; only then will they turn their attention to humanity, which they despise and deceive: "We shall then think about universal happiness." Do they not announce "the age of con-

---

[46] *Journal d'un écrivain*, vol. 3, p. 12. Dostoevsky speaks more precisely of "French socialism", because it was in France that socialism was born, just as it was France that in particular represented, in former times, the Catholic idea. His gifts were not those of the historian, nor of the impartial observer.

[47] Auguste Comte, 27 Dante 63 (August 11, 1851); *Lettre à C. de Blignières* (Paris: Vrin, 1932), pp. 35–36.

tempt"?[48] But prophecy is not prescience. It is spiritual anticipation. For the rest, when creating the universe of the Karamazovs, even more than when engaged upon *The Possessed*, Dostoevsky emancipated himself from immediate data. This prophet must be read in the spirit of all prophecy and, without foregoing the right to find in him signs that will help us to interpret our own age, we should remember that he gives us a type of truth whose significance is not exhaustible by any of its manifestations in history.

According to the Grand Inquisitor, mankind is tormented by a need for universal union, and, if all welcome him with gratitude, it is because they find in him not only a master, not only a depository of their consciences, but "a being who supplies them with the means of uniting into one great anthill". Dostoevsky knows that this is a real need in the human heart. But he also knows that the "anthill", "the great uniform anthill", in no way satisfies that need. There is no union worthy of that name except between persons, and where there is no freedom there are no persons, just as, without God, there is no freedom. The animals forming a "flock" are not united. The law of a world

---

[48] Cf. Bernanos: "Dictators no longer rap the knuckles of their people, they tell them: We only want what is really useful to you, we only want your soul. Give us your consent, just as you consent to the other necessities of life; don't discuss our authority. Let us judge good and evil for you. Give us your soul once and for all, and you will very quickly perceive that it has cost you only a sacrifice of self-love, that it was a responsibility over and above your strength, a ruinous luxury. Renounce your soul, and, once you are thus dispensed from governing yourself, we will administer you like capital, we will make of you such effective material that nothing can resist it. Men without conscience, groups in colonies comparable to those of termites, will easily overcome others. The human Beast, industrious and shrewd, carefully selected, according to the best methods, will gobble up the poor dreamer who was once called the moral man, stupid enough to pay with proofs without number for the vain glory of distinguishing himself from animals by qualities other than superior trickery and cruelty. All the riches of the earth belong in advance to those who will be the first to commit themselves to the new way, who will be the first to renounce their souls. . . ."

that rejects God is a ruthless law of partitioning and isolation, which is more marked in proportion as social links form a closer mesh. "In this age, the whole thing has been split up; everyone keeps away from his fellows and keeps them away from him; instead of giving expression to their personality they fall into a complete solitude"; then "men's efforts lead to nothing but total suicide."[49] "This terrible isolation will certainly come to an end one day", but that day will be the one on which the sign of the Son of Man appears in the heavens.

Thus, against earthly messianism, Dostoevsky sets up the Christian Apocalypse and, against dreams of a paradise somewhere in the human future, the hope of the kingdom of God. We know what sort of an interpretation such ideas may receive, on the political and social plane, from a too facile conservatism. We know that Dostoevsky, as a publicist, was the first to lean in that direction. But that is not what interests us here. A truth should not be set aside for fear of the wrong use that may be made of it, or out of mistrust regarding the psychological conditions that may have favored its emergence. Nor is this a question of adherence, but of understanding; Dostoevsky cannot be comprehended save in depth.

Under yet another aspect he denounces the socialist utopia. Even supposing this Tower of Babel should ever be erected and should eventually offer a habitable dwelling place, in the name of what am I to be constrained, today, to bury myself in its foundations? One generation is as good as another, and the future city cannot mean as much to me as an everlasting kingdom. "I don't want my body, with its sufferings and its shortcomings, to serve simply as manure for the future harmony", says Ivan: and he is right in rebelling if that harmony is only a future one.[50] The same protest bursts forth vehemently from Dolgorouki, the hero of *A Raw Youth*:

[49] *Les Frères Karamazov*, vol. I, p. 317.
[50] Ibid., vol. I, p. 258.

"I may be ready to serve mankind, and I shall serve it perhaps ten times more than all the preachers. Only, nobody shall demand this service of me. . . . I want to remain absolutely free, even if I do not lift a finger. . . . And why should I love my neighbor or posterity, which I shall never see, which will know nothing about me, and which in its turn will disappear without leaving any traces or memories (time makes no difference to this), when the earth in its turn changes into a block of ice and flies through space, without any atmosphere, along with an infinite number of other blocks of the same kind—which is surely the most ridiculous thing that could be imagined?"[51]

In that same novel, *A Raw Youth*, there is also a dream in which Dostoevsky once more expresses his feeling about a human society without God. Unlike so many harsh, bitter and biting passages in his work, this one is very gentle in its melancholy. There is no sarcasm, no invective, but a sad and sensitive tenderness, which recalls the lamentations of Jesus over Jerusalem, in contrast to the violence of the apocalyptic writings. Versilov is speaking to his son, that young Dolgorouki, whose cry of revolt has just been quoted. He tells him how men have driven God out, in a horrible struggle. Now

"calm reigns once more and men are left *alone*, as they wished to be; the great idea that once prevailed has gone from them, the great source of energy that fed and warmed them hitherto has withdrawn like the majestic sun in Claude Lorrain's picture —but now it is mankind's last day. And all at once men realize that they have been left completely alone; suddenly they feel the great forlornness of orphans."

Versilov was never able to imagine thankless and torpid men. Having become orphans, what will they do but press close to one another and clasp hands, understanding that each of them has now only his fellows? With God, immortality has departed from them. Will not "all that great surplus of love", which used

---

[51] *L'Adolescent* (French trans. by Pierre Pascal), p. 55.

to go toward the beyond, henceforth find its object on earth? Will they not work for one another and console one another by each giving all he has to all the rest? Versilov continues his reverie:

> "Each child would feel that everyone on earth is a father and a mother to him. 'Though tomorrow be my last day', each would say, with his eyes on the setting sun, 'what does it matter? They will remain, and after them their children'; and that thought, that they will remain, continuing to love one another and to tremble for one another, would take the place of the idea of reunion beyond the grave! Oh! how they would hasten to love, in order to stifle the great grief in their hearts! They would be proud and bold on their own account, but fearful for the others; each would tremble for the life and happiness of the rest. When meeting, they would look at each other with a profound gaze, full of understanding, and in their eyes there would be love and grief."[52]

Alas! Versilov, or rather Dostoevsky, breaks off his musing. He suddenly realizes that it is only a fancy, "and a most improbable one". Elsewhere he has seen what happened to the orphaned. This is a dream too, a dream of Raskolnikov's in the hospital of the convict prison—and here the style is his usual one. In a night of delirium, Raskolnikov-Dostoevsky has seen an unparalleled plague sweep over Europe:

> "Some parasites of a new species, microscopic beings, had made their appearance, taking up their abode in human bodies. But these animalcules were spirits endowed with understanding and will. The persons affected by them instantly became raving mad. But never, never, were men more convinced that they were in possession of the truth. Never had they a greater belief in the infallibility of their judgment, their scientific conclusions and their moral and religious principles. Whole villages, towns and countries were infected and lost their reason. They all lived in

---

[52] Ibid., pp. 438–39.

dread, and they no longer understood one another. Each thought
that he alone possessed the truth and could discern good and evil.
They did not know whom to condemn and whom to acquit.
People killed one another under the influence of senseless anger.
Great fires sprang up and then came famine. . . . Pestilence raged
over wider and wider areas. In all the world only a few managed
to survive: they were the pure, the elect, predestined to renew
the earth; but nobody anywhere paid heed to these men; none
heard their voices. . . ."[53]

Some such vision must have come to trouble Versilov and
make him break off. But that enigmatic man, now violent, now
gentle, now ardent, now detached, now sceptical, now a believer—a man who "carried in his heart the age of gold and
knew the future of atheism",[54] found grounds for hope again
in a last vision that he confided to his son. No, orphaned men
have not taken their misfortune nobly, and there is decidedly
no remedy for it. . . . And yet—

"I have always completed my picture with a vision, such as
Heine's, of 'Christ on the Baltic'. I have never been able to do
without him. I could not help seeing him among the orphaned
men. He came to them, stretched out his arms to them and said:
'How could you have forgotten me?' Then a sort of veil would
fall from all eyes and they would take up the inspiring anthem
of the new and last resurrection. . . ."

Like Nietzsche, and at about the same time (*A Raw Youth*
dates from 1875 and *Die fröhliche Wissenschaft* from 1882), Dostoevsky saw the divine sun setting on the horizon of our old
Europe. He did not hail the coming night as a triumph. But
he did not despair either. He believed that Europe would turn
to Christ.

---

[53] *Crime et châtiment*, vol. 2, pp. 556–57.
[54] *L'Adolescent*, p. 448.

3. The Palace of Glass

Atheism, however, defended itself stoutly. It had built itself a palace of glass, in which all was light, and outside of which, it decided, there was nothing at all. This palace was the universe of reason, as science and modern philosophy had now completed it.

Dostoevsky was not the more or less uncultivated man it has sometimes been suggested. He did not confuse Kant and Claude Bernard![55] In Siberia, as soon as he came out of the convict prison, he began to study philosophy with his friend Vrangel; he wrote and asked his brother for the *Critique of Pure Reason*; he planned to translate Hegel.[56] These plans remained velleities, but hardly those of an ignoramus. Later his library contained numerous works of philosophy, and he took an interest in Soloviev's lectures.[57] Without being in any way a specialist, he was well able to pick out the fundamental principles of the thought of the age. The reason why this has been doubted is because his criticism of current thought is not, itself, of a scientific or philosophical character. So scientists and philosophers are tempted to shrug their shoulders—which would be a great mistake on their part.

Actually, Dostoevsky attacks neither science nor philosophy: he merely ridicules the man who has become their slave. His respect for them might rather be considered excessive. He trustingly accepts the rational universe as the scientists and philosophers of his age present it. It is not his business to discuss it.

---

[55] As Leo Shestov seems to say, *Les Révélations de la mort* (French trans. by Boris de Schloezer, 5th ed. [Paris: Plon, 1923]), p. 110.

[56] Cf. Evdokimoff, p. 380, note.

[57] Anna Grigorievna, p. 358. The young philosopher and the novelist had been friends since 1873. Cf. to Strakhov, May 28–June 9, 1870: "I am weak in philosophy, but not in the love I have for it; I am strong in the love I have for it"; *Les Inédits de Dostoïevski* (French trans. and note by J. W. Bienstock), p. 106.

He is a novelist, not a theorist. He does not propose to start an argument. He assumes that, in their own province, the people whose job it is know what they are talking about. He bows to their competence. So it is no use expecting a "refutation" of Kantianism or positivism from his pen! But one thing he notes: that all systems of that kind leave one datum out of account; their authors, in their learned calculations, have forgotten one factor. This factor, this datum, is man himself, in that fundamental part of him that will always elude the classifications of science as it always eludes the grasp of reason. And the effect of this simple observation is to shiver and splinter the categories and the law of the three states and universal determinism. . . . The rational universe is not simply the universe. Nobody had bothered to explain how it happens that, in practice, this beautiful palace of glass produces the effect of a dark jail: yet it is a fact that calls for explanation. Nobody had considered whether the experience within whose limits thought was being confined was actually the only kind of experience. . . . It is in this Achilles heel that Dostoevsky wounds the enemy. In a word, he raises the problem of the irrational. And, if it is true that that problem now seems exactly like the great problem of our own times, this again gives the measure of Dostoevsky's importance in the history of thought.

The problem is first raised in the drollest way in a little tale that preceded the great works to which we have confined our attention so far—a tale that paves the way for them and, in a sense, explains them beforehand. *Notes from the Underground*[58] —the story that excited Nietzsche so much—is only a short novel written in a vein of bitter pessimism; but it begins with a lengthy monologue in which the hero introduces himself to the

---

[58] The title is difficult to translate in French. It is sometimes called *Mémoires écrits d'un souterrain*, or *d'un sous-sol* (Notes written from underground), but that suggests a material symbolism that is not in the work. Halpérine-Kaminski says: *L'Esprit souterrain* (The underground spirit); others: *La Voix souterraine* (The underground voice).

reader. This man is "subterranean" in the sense that he looks for his ideas in a region situated far below the level at which the creations of logic and limpid reason display themselves. He is an invalid, obviously neurasthenic, who laughs at "people endowed with a good nervous system, who do not understand the finer pleasures". Things are very simple for such people; they are not tempted to rebel but wisely stop short whenever they come up against the wall:

> "What wall? Why, that goes without saying: the laws of nature; the exclusiveness of natural science; mathematics. When they prove to us that men are descended from monkeys, we have to submit to the evidence, 'there's no wriggling out of it.' Supposing they prove that a bit of your skin is more precious than hundreds of thousands of your fellows and that, in the end, all virtues, all duties and other dreams or prejudices must fade out in face of it: well, what's to be done? You must submit because twice two . . . that's mathematics! Just you try to find an objection."[59]

And, in point of fact, there is no objection. "Twice two are four": you've got to make obeisance. Nature does not ask for our opinion; it hasn't got to pay any attention to our prejudices; we've got to take it as we find it. Its laws are our laws. If you run into a wall, can you turn it into a door? Wise men in good health do not try to go on: they see the wall and turn back. The Subterranean Man is also well aware that he will not be able to knock the wall down; but that is no reason for seeming submissive and content:

> "Heavens above! What does Nature matter to me? What does arithmetic matter if, for one reason or another, I don't want twice two to make four? Naturally I cannot smash this wall with my forehead if I haven't strength enough; but I shall not be reconciled to it on the plea that this is a stone wall and my strength is insufficient. As if there were something reassuring about this

---

[59] *L'Esprit souterrain* (French trans. by Halpérine-Kaminski), p. 146.

wall! As if it were conducive to the slightest feeling of tranquillity just because it is built on twice two are four!"[60]

This arrogant protest is a mixture of two different elements. Dostoevsky rebels against two kinds of evidence. The first consists of the truth that science is said to impose: "physical" or "moral" truths, which, for practical purposes, may all be summed up in the truth that man "is only an organ-stop under the fingers of Nature". There is no such thing as chance and no such thing as freedom! Thus, if you are out to ensure the happiness of mankind, "there is nothing for it but to have a thorough knowledge of the laws of nature: all human actions will then be worked out with the help of a certain moral table of logarithms to the 108,000th and written down in an almanac. Better still: convenient editions will be brought out, like present-day dictionaries, in which everything will be calculated and defined. . . . All the answers will be ready in advance for all the questions. Then the foundations of the Temple of Happiness will be laid, then . . . , in a word, the golden age will then have arrived." Across a warp of universal determinism, utilitarian ethics have woven their ingenious woof, and the doctrinarians of *homo oeconomicus* have lent their aid. The result is not, perhaps, very exhilarating (the Subterranean Man allows himself this incidental comment), but what can one do about it? Science will not allow any other ideal. But how did science come by the idea that this whole structure suggests: that man has never acted from any other motive than self-interest? "Only a child could have originated such a maxim!" As if man were always wise! "Unfortunately man is foolish", and that is what upsets all calculations. He will act against his own interests rather than give up his freedom. His own wishes, his whims, his maddest fancies—these are the most interesting interests, and they refuse to fit in with the forecasts of the scien-

---

[60] Quoted by Henri Troyat, p. 345.

tists. "What man needs is independence, no matter what the cost." An illusion, perhaps? There is no independence? It may be conceded that the reasoning by which this is established is sound. "But it only satisfies the understanding." The will rejects it.[61]

Here the second kind of evidence comes into play. Against it argument is in vain. It is evidence in its pure state, so to speak; formal evidence, the evidence of "twice two are four." But the Subterranean Man will not give in. "I agree that twice-two-are-four is a very fine thing; but, after all, twice-two-are-five is rather nice too."[62] What prompts this humorous objection? The thing that Dostoevsky is rejecting here is not the evidence itself; it is the rationalist claim that it should apply to spheres that are outside its competence; it is the determination to keep man prisoner in "that charmed circle where laws and principles hold sway";[63] it is what Berdyaev was to call the "socialization of the mind". Dostoevsky wants to escape from the atmosphere of "a life rationalized through and through"; he demands a wider universe than "the contracted world of the products of pure thought"; he recalls the rights of man's spiritual self, which is not an objective datum for reason to get its teeth into. Rational evidence is the evidence of life at the surface, of that life in which man really does seem to be a fraction of the universal "twice two are four"—but the Subterranean Man is free of another kingdom![64]

It cannot be denied that he is setting our feet on a dangerous slope. The irrational whose claims he urges has no connection with the rational, and, in itself, it is altogether indeterminate.

---

[61] *L'Esprit souterrain*, pp. 152 and 155–58. Cf. Auguste Comte, "Considérations sur le pouvoir spirituel", in *Opuscules de philosophie sociale, 1819–1828* (Paris: Leroux, 1883), p. 281, denouncing "the frivolity of those metaphysical theories that represent man as an essentially calculating priest".

[62] *L'Esprit souterrain*, p. 160.

[63] Leo Shestov, *Les Révélations de la mort*, pp. 46–47.

[64] Cf. Evdokimoff, pp. 131 and 139.

As we shall see presently, however, it will not wholly remain so; but for a vantage point from which to survey its domain, we must turn elsewhere than to the Subterranean Man, that spleeny hypochondriac. As for this break with the rational, there would be grounds for anxiety only if it occurred in a professional philosopher, whose whole function lies in meditation. To those who have lost it by a wrong use of reason, let Dostoevsky restore the sense of the mysterious regions that are man's true home: it will then be for our philosophers to pick up the trail again by starting out from reason itself.[65]

A wrong use of reason. . . . But why? If Dostoevsky does not even try to refute the systems that obstruct the way to God, it is because he takes them essentially for spiritual matters, and the psychoanalysis he applies to them shows him that they are based on a rejection of God. The age is not atheist because it could no longer find the means of reaching him: its denial is the result of a choice. Like the overman and like the "socialist", the modern rationalist is less atheist than antitheist. This third character, moreover, is often found in association with the second. The building of the palace of glass and the building of the Tower of Babel often go hand in hand. Dostoevsky gives us an example of this in Alyosha's friend Rakitin, the seminarist who dabbles in science and worldliness, an ambitious and conceited young fellow whose monastic life is obviously to be only a stage on the way to a political career. "Seminarists" of this type are, of course, a common phenomenon in the history

---

[65] Another tendency has also been pointed out, a tendency that is, moreover, but one of the aspects of what we are indicating; the Russian tendency to "treat the absolute as the negation of all that is relative, to deny the intermediary strata of human existence"; "a dangerous inclination", but provoked "by the thirst for the ultimate and the absolute"; "the rational doesn't interest him": Evdokimoff, p. 405. Cf. Serge Persky, *Dostoïevsky*, p. 216: "*Notes from the Underground* expresses in axioms the governing thought of Dostoevsky: the idea of the necessarily irrational soul, for which no knowledge, no education can provide." "Man loves to construct", say the *Notes from the Underground* (pp. 159–60), "that is certain; but why does he also love to destroy?"

of the revolutionary movement in Russia.[66] Dostoevsky makes
Mitya, the eldest of the Karamazov brothers, come forward as
their critic. Mitya has no scientific knowledge, and his mind is
not a subtle one. He is a "philosopher tied to the language".[67]
He has not managed to remember Rakitin's explanations very
clearly; he simplifies them and muddles them up. . . . But the
essential point does not escape him. Religious feeling, reborn in
him under the influence of misfortune, has given him shrewd
insight. Rakitin has been to visit him in the prison where he
is awaiting judgment on the charge of having killed his father.
The seminarist has told him of his plan to write an article proving, in the light of science, that Mitya is in no way to blame, that
his act was inevitable, that he is the victim of environment and
heredity; he has spoken to him of Claude Bernard and treated
him to a long harangue on psychological determinism. Mitya
retails this to Alyosha when he too visits the prison.

> "On the whole, I am sorry to lose God, I must say."
> "What do you mean?"
> "Just fancy. In our heads, that is to say, in our brains, there
> are nerves. . . . These nerves have fibers and when they begin
> to vibrate. . . . You see, I look at something, like this, and they
> vibrate, these fibers . . . , and, as soon as they vibrate, an image
> is formed, not immediately but after a second, and an impulse
> is born . . . no, what am I talking about? not an impulse but an
> object or an action . . . that is how perception happens. Then
> comes thought . . . because I have fibers and not because I have
> a soul and was created in God's image, what nonsense! Mikhail

---

[66] Writing to his wife, on August 2 and 11, 1876, with respect to the Elis-
seiev household whom he met at Ems and who displeased him by its negative
spirit and its assurance in atheism, Dostoevsky says: "It is a seminarian's dissatisfaction. . . . Imagine the character and assurance of those seminarians. . . .
The seminarian minds have hurt us a great deal": *Lettres de Dostoievski à sa
femme*, vol. 2, pp. 139, 140, 153. Petersburg is for him "the city of seminarians
and scribes", *Les Carnets de Crime et châtiment*, p. 194; cf. p. 188: "The semi-
narianism in Russia".

[67] Leon Alexander Zander, *Dostoïevski, le problème du bien* (French trans. by
R. Hofmann [Paris: Correa 1946]), p. 43.

explained that to me only yesterday. That fired me. What a wonderful thing science is, Alyosha! Man is undergoing transformation, I quite see that. . . . And yet, I am sorry to lose God!"

"That's something, anyway", said Alyosha.

"That I regret God? Chemistry, brother, chemistry! A thousand apologies, your Reverence, would you mind stepping aside, chemistry is passing by! Rakitin does not love God; oh, no! he does not love him! That's the weak point with all of them, but they hide it, they lie."[68]

Rakitin does not love God. . . . That is the secret of this orgy of scientism. In the universe he has built for himself, modern man has made himself safe from all the forces that hitherto troubled his existence. He has exorcised mystery. Henceforth everything, for him, is clear and final. He has finished with dreams, he can organize his happiness. Why has he that horrible sensation of darkness in the light? Why is his happiness a burden to him? Man has not been able to exorcise himself. Whatever he may say and do, "his attributes are on the scale of eternity. The human Eros, a ceaseless yearning for the infinite, pines at finding nothing on earth that is not alien to it."[69] A living link attaches us to other worlds: it is from them that God took the seeds to sow down here and "his plants, which are ourselves, live only through their feeling of contact with these mysterious worlds; when that feeling subsides or disappears, the thing that had sprouted in us dies"; soon "we become indifferent to life and even learn to hate it."[70] In short, God is necessary to man.

That is what old Stepan Trophimovich discovers on his deathbed, after a wholly superficial life, the futility of which

---

[68] *Les Frères Karamazov*, vol. 2, pp. 592–93.

[69] Evdokimoff, p. 117.

[70] Teachings of the staretz Zossima, *Les Frères Karamazov*, vol. 1, p. 334. Cf. Clement of Alexandria, *Stromates*. Ivan himself recognized it: without faith in immortality, man will no longer have "the strength to continue to live in the world".

he suddenly perceives. "God is necessary to me because he is the only being whom one can love eternally." No, it is not happiness that man is in search of, or at least it is not the sort of happiness he makes for himself in his time of illusion:

"Far more than he needs happiness, man needs to know and to believe, every minute, that somewhere else is a perfect, quiet happiness for each and all. . . . The whole law of human existence consists in this: that man can at all times bow before something infinitely great. If human beings came to be deprived of this infinitely great something, they would no longer want to live and would die in despair. The incommensurable and the infinite are as necessary to man as the little planet on which he moves. . . . My friends, all of you, all of you—long live the great Thought, the eternal, infinite Thought! The whole of man, whatever he may be, feels a need to bow before it. Even the most stupid man has this need to bow before it. Petruchka! oh, how I wish I could see them all again! . . . They do not know that they, too, have within them this great eternal Thought. . . ."[71]

They do not know it, but they cannot do without it. The atheist pays homage to faith when, contrary to all that he affirms, he yields to this need in us that is deeper than the instinct for happiness—the need to worship. Emancipated, a nihilist, he is at the same time an idolater. Such is Verkhovensky, the unworthy son of poor Stepan Trophimovich, who suddenly announces to Stavrogin, after setting forth his plan of revolution: "You are my idol. . . . You are the sun and I am your earthworm."[72] Makar Ivanovich, the moujik, symbol of a believing people, has seen it happen repeatedly: in the course of his long life he has met many atheists; they are men of all kinds, but they all take away joy and beauty from the world; what they say only amounts to words; at bottom, "each is extolling his own death." But "to live without God is nothing but torture. . . . Man cannot live without kneeling, he could

---

[71] *Les Possédés* vol. 2, pp. 348 and 349.
[72] Ibid., p. 350.

not bear it, nobody would be capable of it; if he rejects God, he kneels before an idol of wood or gold, or an imaginary one." And the moujik concludes, as if he had read Origen: "They are all idolaters and not atheists. That's what they ought to be called."[73]

Provided that they are not already believers, as may well happen. Kirillov, as we have seen, seems to be a case in point. He wonders if he is exceptional, he is uneasy and seems at a loss to say what is worrying him. "I don't know how it is with other people," he says, "and I feel that I cannot do as everyone else does. They think, and then immediately think of something else. But I cannot think of anything else. I spend my whole life thinking of the same thing." He need not be perturbed; his case is not so exceptional. And, in putting his trouble into words, he himself has found the solution: if other people are not as he is, it is because in general, flitting from distraction to distraction, they forget to be themselves; fortunate when they have not organized their distraction so as to forget themselves more surely! Were this not the case, they would all see and all confess, too, that God is tormenting them. . . .[74] When Mitya, under stress of misfortune, has shaken off the violence of his passions, it is like Kirillov that he talks, as soon as he has regained possession of himself: "God torments me, I think of nothing but that." And this thought is much the same as Stepan Trophimovich's, the same as Makar Ivanovich's; it is the thought of man throughout the ages: "What are we to do if God does not exist, if Rakitin is right in claiming that this is an idea invented by mankind? If that were so, man would be king of the earth, of the universe. Well and good! Only . . . whom would man love? To whom would he sing hymns of gratitude?" All the Rakitins in the world, moreover, exert themselves in vain, with all their logic and all their science or half-science, with their jealous care to guard from any in-

---

[73] *L'Adolescent*, pp. 348–50. Cf. Origen, *Contra Celsus*, l. 2, n. 40.

[74] *Les Possédés*, vol. I, p. 121.

opportune irruption the so-called happiness they plan for us.
Life will prevail over their systems, and the unhappiness from
which they will not always be able to save us will make the
spring of joy well up in us once more. Listen to Mitya again,
just before he is condemned to work in the mines:

> "If God is driven away from the earth, we shall meet him under
> the earth! From the bowels of the earth the subterranean men
> will raise a tragic hymn to the God of joy!"[75]

That is the point to which Dostoevsky always returns. After having said: "If God is nothing, everything is permitted",
here we have man finding that "if God is nothing, everything
is a matter of indifference", and in this terrible certainty, this
taste of death, temptation vanishes. Man is a "theotropic" being. Violently attacked on all sides, faith is indestructible in his
heart. The atheists may muster impeccable arguments: the true
believer does not worry if he cannot answer them, for it always
seems to him a case of *ignoratio elenchi*. Take Prince Myshkin,
talking to one of them in the train. He admires the intelligence,
knowledge and perfect manners of his chance companion, who
at great length sets forth his reasons for not believing in God.
"Nevertheless," the prince adds, "one thing struck me: in discussing this subject he always seemed to me to be beside the
point. And that is an impression I have had whenever I have
met unbelievers or read their books: they have always seemed
to me to shirk the problem they are pretending to handle. I
made this remark to S. . . . but I must have expressed myself badly or not clearly enough, for he did not understand
me."[76]

Myshkin makes this subtle and far-reaching observation to
his friend Rogozhin, under the famous Holbein. When about
to bid each other goodbye, on the doorstep, they have begun
a conversation that they cannot make up their minds to break

---

[75] *Les Frères Karamazov*, vol. 2, pp. 597 and 595.
[76] *L'Idiot*, vol. 1, p. 396.

off. The sight of the picture has disturbed them both. Rogozhin seems to think that, among people in an advanced state of culture, atheism is inevitable. He asks his friend what he thinks. Without contradicting him, Myshkin for the moment contents himself with recalling a few recent memories. On returning to the hotel an hour after the chance meeting with the atheist on his travels, he had encountered a peasant woman with a baby in her arms:

> "She was quite a young woman and the child would be about six weeks old. It was smiling at its mother—for the first time in its life, she said. I saw her cross herself all of a sudden with the utmost piety. 'Why do you do that, my dear?' I said to her. At that time I was forever asking questions. 'All the joy that a mother feels when she sees her child smiling for the first time,' she replied, 'God feels every time he sees, from up there in heaven, a sinner praying to him from the bottom of his heart.' Those are practically the very words that simple woman said to me; she expressed this deep, subtle and purely religious thought in which the whole essence of Christianity is summed up, which recognizes in God a heavenly Father rejoicing at the sight of man as a father at the sight of his child. It is the fundamental idea of Christ. A simple woman of the people! True, she was a mother. . . . Listen, Parfen. Just now you asked me a question. This is my answer: the essence of religious feeling eludes all arguments; no misdeeds, no crime, no form of atheism can touch it. In this feeling there is and always will be something that cannot be grasped, something beyond the reach of atheist reasoning."[77]

So Rogozhin was right, since it is the learned who are atheists and women of the people who believe. In this century Europe has become learned. Europe has lost her faith. Versilov, that man of dreams, beholds this twilight with dismay and hears a funeral knell tolled over it. He weeps for the old ideas that are departing. But Western atheism will endure only for a time.

---

[77] Ibid.

For "man cannot live without God"[78] and the poor women of the people will triumph over the learned, because they express, more simply but more completely than the Subterranean Man, the incoercible aspiration of the soul made in God's image.

---

[78] *L'Adolescent*, pp. 434 and 437–38.

CHAPTER III

EXPERIENCE OF ETERNITY

To show that atheism in its various forms is bankrupt, making for disintegration and enslavement and leading to suicide, collective or individual, physical or mental—such a result is still too negative. To maintain that religious feeling is something that persists and will not yield to any dialectic—is not that a gratuitous assertion? There are, undeniably, people who have no conscience, no inkling of that "eternal element in man" (as Max Scheler would say) on which Dostoevsky builds. Of such "earthly minds" Ivan's is the true type. As a matter of fact they are not always insensible to the beauty of faith in God. Ivan admits this to Alyosha. "What is surprising", he says, "is not that God should exist in reality but that this idea of the necessity of God should have come into the mind of a savage and ill-conditioned animal like man; it is such a touching, holy, wise idea and does man so much honor." Yes, but it is nonetheless man, he thinks, who has invented God. As for himself, at any rate when he is not carried away by a fury of rebellion at the sight of evil, when he is merely being faithful to the "essence of his being", he feels no more need to deny God than to avow him. He "discards all the hypotheses". Whether or not the earth was created by God, it conforms to the geometry of Euclid. So does his mind, which was made to understand the earth. "Why try to puzzle out anything that is not of this world? I advise you not to rack your brains on that score, my dear Alyosha. Does God exist or not? Questions of that kind are beyond the reach of a mind that can only conceive three dimensions."

Ivan did not need initiation into modern criticism and positivism to enclose him within the terrestrial horizon. He had not become like that by intellectual training but was so by nature. He had never been able to understand the supposition, to which "even eminent geometricians and philosophers" subscribed, that parallel lines, which according to the laws of Euclid can never meet on earth, might meet somewhere in infinity. "I have an essentially Euclidean mind", he concluded.[1] That type of mind is utterly refractory to minds of the "subterranean" type. It will, seemingly, never admit that "the laws of reason are contingent."[2] For it, the mystery of divine things might as well be nonexistent.

Yet Dostoevsky does not abandon the hope of opening such minds to an idea of this kind. To those who see only words in the profession of faith, he proposes to speak in the name of experience. To earthly experience he will oppose the experience of eternity. He will say (as he was in a position to do) what he has seen. Perhaps it will then begin to dawn on Ivan that his "Euclidean mind" does not stand for health but sickness.[3] Perhaps he will let himself be convinced by Alyosha's radiant certainties, and he will even repeat (attaching greater weight to them) the words he had addressed rather condescendingly to his brother: "My dear little brother, I have no intention of perverting you or of shaking your faith; it is much more a case of *my* wishing to be healed by *you*."[4]

1. Ambiguous Experiences

What is this experience that has the merit of giving one something positive to go on? At first glance it seems decidedly unclear. And to what God are we being led by the faith it sustains?

---

[1] *Les Frères Karamazov* (French trans. by Montgault), vol. 1, pp. 247–49.

[2] Paul Evdokimoff, *Dostoïevski et la problème du mal* (originally published as the author's thesis by the Université d'Aix-en-Provence, 1942), p. 109.

[3] Evdokimoff, p. 131: "Ivan's Euclidian illness". *Les Frères Karamazov*, vol. 1, p. 257: "My poor earthly spirit".

[4] Ibid., p. 250. Cf. p. 246: "I am a little boy like you."

Anyone reading Dostoevsky with attention has plenty of cause for uneasiness.

As is well known, Dostoevsky was an epileptic.[5] When, through the medium of the Subterranean Voice, he mocks at those healthy men with sound nerves for whom a wall is a wall, and who turn away satisfied by that evidence, there can be no doubt that he is alluding to his disease, to himself. It is to this disease that he owes not only impatience of the prison in which others submit so meekly to incarceration but also the miracle that opens its doors. Perhaps during his attacks it was given to him to "hoist himself to the top of the wall and survey the forbidden territory. He falls back dazzled, blinded, with anguish in his heart for the loss of that marvelous vision. But he has seen! . . . He is among the only ones who have seen!"[6] It is impossible to blink at the fact that, underlying his most inward thought and what one may venture to call his mysticism, there was that humble, that humiliating physical reality: the epileptic fit. What that meant must now be examined. To make sure of being on the right track, it may first be good to see how he himself describes it to some of his friends:

> For a few seconds I have a feeling of happiness I never experience in my normal state and of which you can form no idea. There is a sense of complete harmony in myself and in the whole world, and that feeling is so sweet, so strong, that, I assure you, one might well give ten years of one's life, nay, one's whole life, for a few seconds of that bliss. . . . But, the crisis having passed, my sensations become extremely painful. I have great difficulty in controlling my distress, my impressionability. . . . It seems to me as if something enormously heavy were weighing upon

---

[5] There are numerous indications in his correspondence. On the exact nature of this epilepsy, the specialists are not in agreement; cf. Freud, "Dostoïevski et le parricide", at the beginning.

[6] Henri Troyat, *Dostoïevski* (1940), p. 347. It was not unintentional that he placed in the mouth of one of the vilest beings of his creation, Svidrigailov, a theory on illness as a condition for the perception of the other world.

me; I seem to have done something appalling, committed some monstrous crime.

A great sense of holiness, a great crime, transcendent joy, transcendent suffering, all these feelings are suddenly united and crystallized in a point as blinding as lightning, and the horrible groans of the epileptic give the impression that it is not he who is crying out but another being which is inside and which is not a man.[7]

How can one help recognizing that Kirillov's experience and Myshkin's were modeled on this? Even so, there would be no occasion to stress the point were it not that Dostoevsky, in both these cases, follows up his description of the experience with a detailed interpretation.

It will be recalled that Kirillov, having come to the conclusion that he must commit suicide in order to banish fear of death, believes that he will forthwith become a god. And when his companion points out to him that there will probably be no time—his deification having to coincide with his death— he receives this ironical comment with proud and almost contemptuous composure. One feels that he has his answer ready. He has his secret, which, for the moment, he does not choose to divulge. Later on, when pressed by Stavrogin, he explains himself unreservedly. It is regrettable to have to summarize this close-knit, breathless dialogue, which takes on so fantastic a guise but is at the same time so thoroughly natural, full of vivid touches and subtle shades and rich in so many beauties.[8] Stavrogin has come upon the engineer playing with a baby girl. Kirillov confesses that he loves children, that he loves life. In that case how can he contemplate blowing his brains out?

> "Why, what is the connection? Life exists and death does not exist."
>
> "You believe in a future and eternal life?"

---

[7] Quoted by Serge Persky, *Le Vie et l'oeuvre de Dostoïevski* (Paris: Payot, 1918, new ed., 1924), p. 159; cf. Troyat, p. 302.

[8] *Les Possédés* (French trans. by Chuzeville), vol. 1, pp. 241–44.

"No, not in a future eternal life but in an earthly eternal life. There are moments—you have moments—when suddenly time stands still and becomes eternity."

"And you hope to attain a moment like that?"

"Yes."

Did not the Angel of the Apocalypse announce the coming of a day when there would be no more time? That idea is very true. When humanity has attained happiness, time will no longer be necessary. There will be no need to get rid of it like a thing one cannot find room for: "Time is not a thing but a concept. It will vanish from the understanding." Kirillov has a foreknowledge of that day because he has already attained happiness: this shines forth in his radiant expression, and he suddenly asks the astonished Stavrogin:

"Have you seen a leaf, just an ordinary leaf of a tree?"

"Of course."

"Some time ago I saw one that was going yellow but was still green here and there and already a bit rotten at the edges. A gust of wind had carried it off. When I was ten years old, I used to shut my eyes, in winter, and think of a bright green leaf, with delicate veins, in a ray of sunshine. When I opened my eyes again I could not believe what I really saw, the dream had been so lovely. I used to shut them again."

"Is that an allegory?"

"No. Why? It is not an allegory. A leaf, an ordinary leaf. The leaf is beautiful. Everything is beautiful."

"Everything?"

"Everything. Man is unhappy because he does not know that he is happy. That's the only reason. That explains everything. Everything! Anyone who realizes that will be happy immediately. . . ."

The little girl who is present at the conversation is soon to be orphaned: but all is well. And if there are poor wretches who starve to death and others who are disgraced, still all is well, all.

> "Those people are happy who know that all is well. If they knew
> that they were happy, then they would *be* happy. . . . That is the
> idea, the whole idea. Beyond that there is nothing."
>
> "When did you discover that you were happy?"
>
> "Last week, on Tuesday, no, Wednesday. It was Wednesday.
> In the night."
>
> "What happened?"
>
> "I don't remember. I was walking about in my room. . . . It's
> of no consequence. I stopped my watch. It was twenty-three
> minutes to three."
>
> "Was that a sign that time must stand still?"

Kirillov leaves the question unanswered. He goes back to
his idea. It is the same with goodness as with happiness. Men
are not good because they do not know that they are good.
They must be taught this, and then they will all become good
immediately. Thus the man who teaches them will bring the
world to an end. He will be the god-man. He, Kirillov, is destined to play this part: for he knows now that he is happy and
that he is good.

Stavrogin is quizzical. But his "man-of-the-world badinage"
cannot shake this new believer. For his faith is not merely the
fruit of fearless logic. It is based on an immediate, incontestable
experience. Later on he explains how he had arrived at that conviction that he expressed in speaking of the leaf—that "all is
well", that all-embracing Yes given in answer to life and capable of arresting time—and how he has access to it periodically,
in all its plenitude. Then we realize that in him it is once more
Dostoevsky himself who is speaking:

> "It happens that for a few seconds [he tells us]—never more
> than five or six at a time—you suddenly feel, in an absolute way,
> the presence of eternal harmony. It is not anything earthly, and
> I don't say that it is heavenly either, but I say that man in his
> earthly form cannot endure it. He must be transformed physi-
> cally or die. It is a clear and indisputable feeling. All at once you
> seem to feel nature in all its fullness and you say: 'Yes, that is
> true!' When God created the world, he said, at the end of each

day of his creation, 'Yes, that is true, that is good.' That . . .
it is not tenderheartedness, it is only joy. You do not forgive
anything, because there is nothing to forgive. Nor do you love
—this is something better than love. The most terrible thing is
that it is all so clear and you feel such joy. If that goes on for
more than five seconds, your soul cannot stand it; it must needs
disappear. . . ."[9]

Shatov, who is the recipient of these confidences, is not for
one moment taken in by them: epilepsy lies in wait for Kirillov.
These blissful states are the premonitory signs of the dread disease, if they are not already the effect of it. They reappear in
Prince Myshkin, whose attacks Dostoevsky analyzes with the
combined precision of a clinical physician and a patient.

When Myshkin is surprised by an attack during his waking
hours, he first of all goes through a phase of apprehension,
coupled with a feeling of stupidity and oppression. Then suddenly his brain takes fire and his vital forces are keyed up to an
extraordinary degree. There is a tenfold intensification of life
and awareness; his mind is illumined with an intense clarity,
all his anxieties die down at once and give place to a sovereign
calm, while reason rises to such a pitch that it can "even grasp
final causes": it is a foretaste of that "eternal harmony" that
Kirillov spoke of. Yet these radiant moments, however fleeting, are but the prelude to one more ephemeral still: the decisive second that precedes the attack. That second is positively
beyond his strength. . . . When, restored to health, he goes
over in his mind the premonitory symptoms of his attacks, he
often thinks: "These flashes of lucidity, in which a kind of
heightened life wells up from my extreme self-awareness, are
nothing but morbid phenomena, deteriorations of the normal

---

[9] Ibid., vol. 2, pp. 278–79. " 'During these five seconds,' he added, 'I saw a
whole existence, and I would give my entire life for them, for they were worth
it. To endure it for ten seconds, one would have to be transformed physically.
I believe that man must cease to beget children. What good are children, what
good is evolution, if the end is attained?' "

condition; far from having any connection with a higher life, they are among the lowest manifestations of being."

Such is the voice of wisdom, which is just as audible to Myshkin as to anyone else. But he has this advantage over other people, that he knows things from the inside:

> Thus he arrived at a most paradoxical conclusion: "What does it matter that my state is a morbid one? What does it matter that this exaltation is an abnormal phenomenon, if the moment that gave rise to it (when I recall and analyze it on my recovery) seems to have been one of supreme harmony and beauty, and if that moment gives me an unparalleled and unimaginable sense of plenitude, of rightness, of reassurance, and feeling that, lifted on the wings of prayer, my being is merged in the highest synthesis of life?"
>
> These nebulous expressions seemed to him perfectly clear though all too weak. He did not doubt, he did not dream of doubting, that the sensations described above were an actual projection of "beauty and prayer" with a "high synthesis of life". But had not these visions something in common with the deceptive hallucinations induced by hashish, opium or wine, which stupefy the mind and deform the soul? He was capable of sound judgment on that subject once the attack was over. Briefly, those few seconds brought a lightning irradiation of the consciousness and an intense heightening of subjective impressionability. If, at that point which represents the last second of consciousness before the fit, he had had time to say to himself clearly and deliberately: "Yes, for this moment one would give one's whole life", it was because in itself that moment was indeed worth a lifetime.[10]

---

[10] *L'Idiot* (French trans. by Mousset), vol. 1, pp. 404–6. Compare these texts with the following passage, in which Tauler notes a more authentic experience: "The one who truly arrives at this point has the impression of having been there eternally. This impression has lasted perhaps only for an instant, but such glances seem like an eternity; an illumination comes to us and a witness that man, having been created, was from all eternity in God": *Sermons* (French trans.) vol. 1, p. 23 and vol. 3, p. 254.

Myshkin does not, of course, take his experience with the fanatical seriousness of a Kirillov. His eyes do not "sparkle", he has not that fixed gaze and that "hard and inflexible expression" characteristic of his rival at such times. As we have seen, he analyzes his own case with a certain detachment. Moreover, there is no forgetting "the prostration, the mental blindness and idiocy" that are the inevitable sequel to his ecstasy. Thus he would be chary of starting a discussion on the subject. He admits that his judgment must be at fault. Yet "for all that, the reality of his sensation continued to perplex him. The fact remained: for an instant he had found time to tell himself that the happiness it brought him was worth a whole life." And, as in the case of Kirillov, this instant brings him understanding of that saying in the Apocalypse: "Then there shall be time no longer."[11]

The similarity between the experience of Myshkin and that of Kirillov is disturbing: disturbing too is the resemblance between the typical atheist and the typical believer; between the one whose mission it is to kill God and the one who proclaims the invincibility of faith.[12] How can doctrines so opposite flow from the same source? But then (and this is still more disturbing) it is soon apparent that the quiet faith and the fanatical disbelief are themselves strangely alike. The psychic state of a man like Myshkin even seems, perhaps, less charged with that *tremendum* and that *sacrum* which announce the presence of the divine; moreover, it is perhaps more encumbered with an element of sensualism. In any case, both men are, at such a time, raised above any normal feeling of love or gratitude

---

[11] *L'Idiot*, vol. 1, p. 407. " 'Undoubtedly', he had added, smiling, 'it was of a moment like this that the epileptic Muhammad was speaking when he said he had visited all the dwelling places of Allah in less time than it took for his pitcher full of water to be emptied."

[12] Leon Alexander Zander, *Dostoïevski, le problème du bien* (French trans. by R. Hofmann [Paris: Correa, 1946]), p. 167, compares the sayings of Myshkin with those of Kirillov; he sees in both the same experience of life and the same conception of eternity.

and know only a heightened acquiescence; both experience a merging of their being in universal life, beyond which there is nothing more to be sought; both are, as it were, projected *outside time*. And, if they come so near to one another, is it not because they both reflect one and the same model: Fyodor Mikhailovich Dostoevsky?

It may be admitted that Kirillov, given up to the obsession that has already laid hold of him, misinterprets his ecstasy. But what about this Prince Myshkin? Has not this author appointed him herald of religious feeling? There should be no need to look elsewhere, then, if we would know what ideal Dostoevsky offers us, bidding us recognize in it "the Christian state par excellence."[13] "Prince Myshkin," says Mr. Serge Persky, for example, "symbolizes Christian wisdom, unconstrained, in its pure essence."[14] This exegesis forms the basis of André Gide's study, which cites both the passage from *The Idiot* and those from *The Possessed* quoted above. According to Gide, Dostoevsky

> suggests that love's real antithesis is not so much hate as cerebral cogitation. The understanding is, in his view, the thing that individualizes itself and sets itself up against the kingdom of God, against eternal life and against the state of beatitude outside time, which can be attained only by sinking one's individuality in a sense of indiscriminate fellowship.

Thus something must be done to "inhibit thought" and to exalt sensation instead, so as to arrive, in the end, at a kind of quietism, thanks to which the final "all is well" can be pronounced. But:

> Is not this state of joy that we find in Dostoevsky the same that the Gospel offers us; that state into which we gain admittance through what Christ called new birth; that felicity that is attainable only by renouncing the individual in us? For it is attachment

---

[13] André Gide, *Dostoïevksi*, in *Œuvres complètes*, vol. 11 (Paris: NRF, 1932–1939), p. 239.

[14] Persky, p. 200.

to self that holds us back from plunging into eternity, from entering the kingdom of God and from participating in the undifferentiated sense of universal life.

This suggests that we are summoned not so much to an excursion beyond good and evil as to a return to the hither side of them; we must regain our innocence by reverting to the primal state of nondifferentiation and reenter the original paradise that the restless promptings of our understanding so unfortunately impelled us to desert. In short, says Gide, Dostoevsky's thought, in its last phase, is found to consist in an "evangelic belittling of the understanding".[15]

This interpretation has decidedly too much of Gide himself in it. The Gospel may be left out of the matter. But Dostoevsky? The question is not so simple. Vogüé had already remarked that Fyodor Mikhailovich reminded him of Jean-Jacques.[16] Is not it a striking fact that, in order to convey what he considers the head and front of his message, he always chooses children, women of the people, the ignorant and the uncultivated, creatures who are close to nature, whose primitive spontaneity has not been ruined by knowledge? After all, he might have got that just as much from Saint Augustine as from Rousseau. Did not the great Christian teacher, himself a faithful echo of Jesus, say: "The unlearned arise and take heaven by storm"?[17] But there is more than that in the character of the Idiot, excellently analyzed by Mr. Henri Troyat:

> The whole novel boils down to this: the incursion of the principal intelligence into the province of the secondary intelligence. This principal intelligence, which is the subterranean intelligence, the intelligence of feeling, is bound to create disturbances in the environment into which it is transplanted. In this confined atmosphere Myshkin's arrival makes, as it were, a kind of draught. He

---

[15] Gide, pp. 257–58, 287, 289–90.

[16] Eugène-Marie Vogüé, *Le Roman russe* (Paris: Plon-Nourrit, 1886), p. 271.

[17] Cf. Leo Shestov, *Les Révélations de la mort* (French trans. by Boris de Schloezer, 5th ed. [Paris: Plon, 1923]), pp. 40–41.

is greeted at first by a roar of laughter. He is grotesque, he is a case of arrested development, he is an idiot—even his mother used to call him an idiot. But gradually this idiot, this case of arrested development, calls in question the most firmly established principles. This half-wit makes wise men think. This intruder becomes indispensable. This weakling subdues the strong and does so without meaning to. He is convinced that everybody around him is magnanimous and that they all love him. . . . People become good because that is how he wants them to be, that is how he sees them. He is at the center of a magnetic field. . . . Each one sees in him the proof of another existence, of the possibility of a different world. . . .[18]

Only, there is another side to this miracle. After the assets, the liabilities have to be reviewed:

Myshkin, the saint, does not know how to act. He only knows how to live. If he tries to act, he makes mistakes. Besides never managing to help anyone, he upsets things when they are going satisfactorily. By the end of the book, the progress of this "absolutely good man" has left in its wake a murder and three or four family crises. As for the "absolutely good man" himself, he has gone mad. He did not know how to adapt himself to human conditions. He did not know how to become a man. . . .[19]

A "pitiable shadow", a "chill and mournful ghost", is Shestov's hard but not altogether unjustified description of

---

[18] Troyat, pp. 334–35.

[19] Ibid., p. 442. Cf. Evdokimoff, pp. 208–9: "Myshkin is almost possessed by a compassion that alters something in his personality, makes it half-passive and half-chaotic, but does not have love in all its fullness and harmony. His compassion can console in moments of grief, but one cannot live from it; it consoles but neither saves nor transfigures: Nastasya Filippovna flees Myshkin; his 'angelic element' bores her. . . . The virile element of decision and the active element of love are lacking in Myshkin; his compassion is divided, two women are in question, and he is incapable of avoiding catastrophe. The dark possession of sensual pleasure in Rogozhin triumphs over the disincarnated compassion of Myshkin. By sinking into gentle madness, the latter demonstrates the insufficiency of a love that is only compassion."

him.[20] And that rebounds upon his goodness itself, which becomes suspect and calls for enquiry. Has not the unfortunate heredity of this epileptic prince a lot to do with it? Perfect physical health, like perfect intelligence, is rarely altruistic. Between that narrowing of the consciousness, into which not even the perception of evil can now find a way, and Myshkin's nervous defect there is a mysterious connection. The man in whom a selfish will no longer exists is smitten with a kind of hemiplegia.[21] This explanation is, perhaps, a little too Nietzschean, but dare one leave it out of account? Shestov considers that such a poor creature cannot be the bearer of a message from Dostoevsky; that the latter reveals his innermost feeling by his very inability to infuse life into characters of that type: "He did not understand, and he was no good at depicting, any but rebellious and adventurous spirits, those who had a quest. As soon as he tried to describe a man without a grievance . . . he immediately lapsed into a disappointing banality."[22] But if Myshkin is indeed a degenerate, that does not make him a commonplace character,[23] and one would have to be impervious indeed to the art of *The Idiot* not to be intrigued by the enigma

---

[20] Leo Shestov, *La Philosophie de la tragédie, Dostoïevksi et Nietzsche*, in *Œuvres*, vol. 3 (French trans. by Boris de Schloezer [Paris: J. Schiffrin, 1926]), p. 102.

[21] Charles Andler, "Nietzsche et Dostoïevski", in *Mélanges d'histoire littéraire, générale et comparée, offerts à Fernand Baldensperger* (Paris: Champion, 1930), p. 11. Cf. Friedrich Nietzsche, "L''homme bon', or l'hémiplégie de la vertu", in *Volonté de puissance* (French trans. by Bianquis of *Der Wille zur Macht*), vol. 1, pp. 128–29.

[22] Shestov, *La Philosophie*, p. 103.

[23] This was felt particularly by Alain-Fournier, writing to Jacques Rivière on March 3, 1909: "By gaining ground on holy evil, *The Idiot* lost the faculty of judgment. But it has been a long time since we have acceded to this degree of wisdom. I, for my part, am haunted in this book by a more profound emotion, a more subtle notion, and, as it were, a new sense that I will call the "touch of the soul". This sudden apperception of the soul has at times something frightening and repulsive about it; then that infinite delicacy in touching it draws tears of blood. This is why Myshkin must, not explain everything, for he explains nothing, but make 'everything explainable' by his presence alone." Cf.

of that extraordinary figure.[24] On this point Gide seems to
me more clearsighted. Only, when he expects us to see in the
prince, apart from any symbolical interpretation,[25] the genuine
spokesman of Dostoevsky, our uneasiness returns.

Before making up our minds, we may continue to take stock
of the reasons for uneasiness. The experience that seems to un-

---

the letter of May 20 (Jacques Rivière et Alain-Fournier: *Correspondance, 1905–
1914* (Paris: Gallimard, 1916–1928), vol. 4, pp. 85 and 128–29.

[24] Let us recall that Myshkin was one of Dostoevsky's favorite characters.
He wrote to Kovner, on February 14, 1877: "I was happy that you consider
The Idiot the best [of my novels]. . . . All those who have spoken of it as my
best work had something particular in the organization of their understanding
that struck me and pleased me very much": *Correspondance et voyage à l'étranger*
(French trans. by J. W. Bienstock), p. 444. See also his letter to Maïkhov, at
the time when he was beginning to write *The Idiot*, on December 31, 1867:
"An idea has been tormenting me for a long time, but I was afraid to take it
for the subject of a novel because it is a very difficult idea for which I am not
prepared, even though it is very seductive and I love it. This idea is to represent *a completely good man*. For me, nothing could be more difficult, especially
in our era . . .": *Les Inédits de Dostoïevski* (French trans. and notes by J. W.
Bienstock), p. 28. He wrote the whole work under impossible conditions, in
the midst of the most extreme financial difficulties and many violent crises.

[25] This reservation is of fundamental importance. For Myshkin is perhaps
the most mysterious of Dostoevsky's characters, as *The Idiot* is perhaps his
most profound creation. Transposed to the plane of symbolism, in accordance
with the author's intentions, the greatest deficiencies and the most disturbing
traits of this sick man take on a sacred value. There is, I think, ample justification for the claim made by Eduard Thurneysen that in this work everything is
calculated to turn our thoughts toward Jesus Christ, and for the attempt made
by Romano Guardini, in a long chapter which is one of the most successful in
his study, to carry that interpretation to its logical conclusion. Cf. *Carnets de
l'Idiot* (French trans.), p. 167: "The prince—Christ" (words written in large
copperplate characters); or on p. 208: "At the end, the prince: his calm and
solemn state. He has forgiven men." And that strange saying at the beginning
of the novel: "Now I am going to men." Only, one should not omit to add, as
Guardini does, that Myshkin is, for all that, "neither the Man-God nor a second Christ: he is a man who has a name—Lyov Nikolayevitch Myshkin; his
life is made up of purely human elements"; "each event of his life has, in the
first place, its proper meaning" and "there is no direct symbolism anywhere".
Mr. Zander concurs with Guardini's interpretation.

derlie all these things is not the only one that is confused: the same applies to expressions of faith. What is this deity which triumphs over all efforts to deny him? In Myshkin it remains decidedly vague; but is it not practically certain that "the highest synthesis of life", which the prince experiences during his ecstasy, comes into existence at the level of the sense life, like the ecstasy that reveals it? When Mitya in prison hymns the "God of joy" and sends this paean forth from "the bowels of the earth", is it not rather a hymn to life?

> "Life is full, life overflows, even under the ground! You cannot conceive, Alexei, how the thirst for life has got hold of me. . . . With the strength that I feel in me, I think I could overcome any kind of suffering, provided I could say to myself every minute: 'I am!' In the pillory I am still alive, I see the sun, and even if I don't see it I know it is shining. And just to know that is the whole of life. . . ."[26]

Is this anything more than an outburst of that fierce vitality that is the peculiarity of the Karamazovs and that is plainly a terrestrial force? And now, from *The Possessed*, comes the testimony of one of those old women in whom Dostoevsky would have us understand the profound soul of the people. She is living in a convent, where she is doing penance for fortune-telling. One day, on leaving church, she falls in with Maria Timopheievna, Stavrogin's ailing wife, and in a low voice questions her about "the Mother of God" and who she really is.

> " 'The great mother,' I answered, 'the hope of the human race.' 'Yes,' she rejoined, 'the Mother of God is the Great Mother, the damp Earth, and there is great joy for me in that. And every earthly pang, every earthly tear is a joy for us, and when you have watered the earth with your tears, to the depth of one foot, then you will rejoice in everything, and your sorrow will have gone, absolutely gone, according to the prophecy.' Those words engraved themselves in my heart. Since then, when prostrating

---

[26] *Les Frères Karamazov*, vol. 2, p. 596.

myself to say my prayers, I have got into the habit of kissing the ground. I kiss it and weep. I tell you, Shatuchka, there is no harm in those tears; and, even if you have no grief to weep for, you shed tears of joy. Tears flow of their own accord, that is the truth! Sometimes I walk along the edge of the lake; our convent is on one side of it, and on the other there is a mountain that goes to a point. They call it the Peak. I sometimes climb that mountain, turn to the East, throw myself down on the ground and weep and weep. I have no idea how long I stay there weeping, and I can remember nothing and don't know anything whatsoever— nothing at all. . . ."

Obviously the old woman's teaching had not been lost. Its slight tinge of esoterism had only heightened its attractions. In any case, Maria Timopheievna was predisposed to receive it, and even the nuns in the convent were probably not at all shocked by it. Had not Maria herself said one day: "It seems to me that God and nature are the same thing"? Everyone there had exclaimed, "Look at that now!" And the Mother Superior had burst out laughing.[27]

It is to Shatov that Maria Timopheievna recounts this incident. He too has his mysticism. After having joined Peter Verkhovensky's terrible gang, he tries to extricate himself from it. He has realized the madness of the socialist venture, which proposes to build a universe exclusively on reason and science. He knows ("history shows") that not a single nation has been able to develop and organize itself on those principles alone; that science and reason have never at any time performed more than minor functions; that nations take shape and act under the compulsion of quite a different force, whose origin is mysterious. This force is "the inextinguishable desire to achieve a

---

[27] *Les Possédés*, vol. 1, p. 150. There is an echo in this of that religion which, according to Bachofeu, was the primitive religion of man, a cult combined of earth and maternity, linked to a regime of matriarchal communism. On the symbolism of the Earth in Dostoevsky and in the Byzantine liturgy, cf. Zander, pp. 66–68. He observes, however: "I doubt that one could avoid here a slight element of paganism."

purpose, and at the same time the constant denial of that purpose"; it is "a constant and tireless affirmation of life": Is it not of this thing—this "spirit of life"—that the Scriptures speak? Those "rivers of the water of life", so the Apocalypse threatens us, will dry up? For Shatov, too, quotes the Apocalypse. "I will merely say", he concludes, "that this force is the search for God." But let us see what he means by that:

> "The sole aim of every popular movement, in every single nation, at every period of its history, is the search for its God, its own God, the God which is its, and faith in that God as the only true God. God is the synthetic personality of the whole nation from its beginnings to the end of its history. It has never yet happened that two or more nations have had the same God; each nation always has its own God. It is the sign of decadence for nations when they begin to share their gods. When gods are pooled, they die, at the same time as the faith they inspired; and the nations die with them. The stronger a nation is, the more exclusively its god is personal to it. There has never yet been a nation without religion, that is to say, without an idea of good and evil. . . . Reason alone has never been capable of distinguishing between good and evil. . . . As for science, it has only been able to supply crude solutions. That has been the great distinguishing mark of superficial science, the most terrible of the plagues that have afflicted mankind, worse than pestilence, famine, war. . . . Superficial science is a tyrant, the like of which had never been known until our times."[28]

There is no doubt that Shatov has been thoroughly converted! He has been overconverted, and rationalists are not the only ones who will take offense at his strictures against the universalism of reason. We have witnessed since a similar *volte-face*, and we know the appearance and the name of the mysticism that has sprung from it. Is that where Dostoevsky is proposing to lead us? His Shatov does not give himself up to vague dreams. If anyone doubts that the Slav genius has a

---

[28] *Les Possédés*, vol. 1, p. 256.

gift for vigorous, clear-cut theories, thoroughly worked out and reduced to the necessary formulas, he should be referred to Shatov. Zarathustra sounds like one of his pupils—but one who did not come up to the master—when he says: "No nation could live without having first considered its values: but, if it wishes to survive, it must not take things at its neighbor's valuation."[29]

Stavrogin, however, to whom Shatov addresses this statement of his theory, does not let it go uncriticized. Shatov immediately protests: "So I reduce God to no more than an attribute of the people? On the contrary, I raise the people to the level of God! The people are the body of God." But this explanation strengthens rather than modifies the theory. "A nation remains a nation only so long as it has its particular God and fiercely disapproves of all the other gods there are; so long as it believes that with its god it will be able to conquer, subjugate and drive out all the other gods." And, as Raskolnikov not long before had distinguished two types of individuals, Shatov now distinguishes two classes of nations: on the one hand, "the great nations of the world, or at least all those who keep their place in history and were at one time in the forefront of humanity", and, on the other hand, mere "ethnographical material". A great nation is one that believes that it is the sole repository of the truth, that it is the only one called and the only one capable of resuscitating and saving the world by its particular truth; as soon as it ceases to believe that, it is done for.

During the last fifty years we have had more than one description of "mystical imperialism": Is not Shatov its forerunner? Today there is much talk of "realism". Did not Shatov, again, observe that it is "impossible to go against facts"?

A philosophy of history can be built up on that foundation. The Jews were a great nation because all they lived for was to

---

[29] Nietzsche, *Ainsi parlait Zarathoustra* (French trans. by Albert of *Also sprach Zarathustra*), p. 77.

await the coming of "the true God" and give him to the world; the Greeks deified Nature and bequeathed to the world their religion, that is to say, their philosophy and their art; Rome deified the people in the form of the State; France was the incarnation of Roman Catholicism, and she is now propagating an atheist socialism that is its natural sequel! When he comes to Russia, Shatov ingeniously rediscovers the only God, and the universalism of conquest that for him is the mark of great nations is found to coincide with the universalism of truth and of the absolute: "As there is only one truth, there cannot be more than one single nation that possesses the true God, however great and mighty the gods of the other nations may be. The only people 'bearing God' is the Russian people. . . ."[30]

Thus after Kirillov, after Prince Myshkin, and after Maria Timopheievna, Shatov too has his religion. But what sort of a "deity" is this which at one moment seems to be no more than man and at another takes on the aspect of Life, the Earth or even the Nation? In what immanent Power can we recognize God? If that is what Dostoevsky offers us, after having conquered atheism, are we to rejoice in his victory? He has plumbed the depths of our flesh-and-blood nature, and he has wonderfully exalted the sense of "holiness". But is it not a decidedly ambiguous "holiness"?

2. Dualisms and Symbols

One is sometimes inclined to form a curious idea of the relations existing between a novelist and his characters. It is quite true that, much more than the writer of a treatise, the novelist

---

[30] *Les Possédés*, vol. 1, p. 257. *Journal d'un écrivain*, vol. 3, pp. 34–41: "Every great nation thinks that it ranks first and wants to impose its ideas upon the others; but the Russian idea is precisely the universal idea, the idea of the social union of all nations. . . ." See also pp. 46–47 and 110, as well as the *Discours sur Pouchkine* and *L'Adolescent*, pp. 434–37.

puts himself into his books. At any rate that is the privilege—or fate—of a certain type of novelist, of which Dostoevsky is an outstanding example. Our theories, even the most cherished of them, can be so unlike ourselves! Even the man who sets out to define himself often cannot. For life is refractory to formulas, and it is easier to surprise it and encircle it, as it were, by the roundabout means of a dramatic action. The chances are that a man will express himself more truly, though unintentionally, when creating other characters than when looking at himself. His secret would have eluded even conscientious self-analysis, but it slips out in the act of creation. How much more vivid an image a son offers of his father than a portrait of its sitter! The novelist is also likely to be more sincere, and can be more completely so, thanks to the variety of his characters. Each of them is an aspect of himself.

These are truisms. But here the difficulty begins. What is the ego? I have in me my nature, my temperament, my character, containing elements some of which I proscribe, some of which I ratify, and some of which I endure. There are the characteristics I have inherited and those I have made for myself. These are the things I hide from myself and the things for which I yearn without possessing them but which are a molding influence because they attract me. How many simplistic, would-be profound explanations there are about it all! No doubt it is essential that I should not be false to the law of my being—that is the first rule of a concrete morality, and that is why moralism, which takes no account of it, is immoral; but does fidelity to my being mean that I should give way to all my tendencies and exercise no discrimination in my inward chaos? Some people argue as if every choice were a mutilation, as if every refusal were hypocrisy, and as if every thought with which a certain substratum of nature is not consonant were, in the worst sense of the word, idealism. As if it were always a lie to form wishes, or even thoughts, which go against oneself! As if the darkest substratum of our nature were necessarily its most profound element! As if the dualism of the flesh and the spirit were not the first real datum in us! One is apt to forget that the life of the conscience cannot be grasped objectively, and it is assumed that complete sincerity excludes any other effort than the courage to read oneself. Moreover, these simplistic explanations, which take themselves for the last word in psychology and ethics, lead to absurd conclusions: the possibilities that swarm in us, more or less preformed, are varied and contradictory: must we, in order to be sincere, put them all into practice? And will sincerity also demand that we should never think, except in accordance with what we are? Or might it not occasionally consist in recognizing that what we are is not in accordance with what we think?

How those two words "realism" and "sincerity" have been misused! And this misuse is particularly serious when it comes to studying Dostoevsky, for whom freedom is the very thing that is characteristic of man and who, beyond any kind of psychology, seeks the truth of man's being. If we find him now materializing one of his own possibilities, now delivering himself from his temptations, now, perhaps, murmuring a confession and now expounding a favorite theory—are we, in each case, to recognize him to such purpose that we think we have solved the riddle of his thought? Some argue that the bad characters, the deniers, stand out admirably in these books, whereas the good, the virtuous, the believers are commonplace figures; and take this as a sign that Dostoevsky's sympathies are with the first—"He himself was afraid of the monsters he exposed, and he exerted all the strength of his soul to hide himself from them by means of the first 'ideal' that came along." This accounts for the second type of character. This is Shestov's argument.[31]

But, as we noted in the case of Myshkin, the characters of the

---

[31] Leo Shestov, *La Philosophie*, p. 3. The remark from which Shestov proceeds is, moreover, incontestable. When Dostoevsky, in the note he adds to *Notes from the Underground*, says that "the author of the journal, as well as the journal itself, are fictitious" and that his sole aim was to paint "a representation of a generation that is dying out", that should not sidetrack us, rather the intention of this explanation is to reassure the author as well as the reader.

second type are not always so insignificant! If their coloring is
rather pale and their gestures sometimes clumsy, is there not a
simple reason for that? Heaven has always been less easy to paint
than hell; but that does not mean that the painter has a greater
belief in hell than in heaven. . . . So, it is actually among the
believers and mystics that we should, especially now, pick out
Dostoevsky's true spokesmen—not those who merely reflect
his psychological reality, nor those through whom he may be
thought to express some "edifying" ideal or other, but those
who represent the real intention of his thought.[32]

There is doubt that Shatov incarnates a tendency that was
very strong in Dostoevsky. He believed in Russia as a people "bearing God" and almost as God himself. He did not
doubt that Russian thought had the mission of regenerating the
world.[33] His "messianic orthodoxy", tending to merge with the
Pan-Slav idea,[34] became more and more fervent during his latter years, and that is the reason why his voice took such a tone

---

[32] Shestov makes a fine game for himself when he refuses to see in Dostoevsky the patron of a "pious idealism". . . . "I will not cease to repeat", he
also says: "Vladimir Soloviev, who considered Dostoevsky a prophet, did not
have a correct view; it is Mikhailovsky who was right, he who called Dostoevsky a 'cruel talent' and a 'seeker of hidden treasures'. Dostoevsky sought, in
fact, hidden treasures, there can be no doubt about it; and the young generation who raised the standard of pious idealism would do better to turn from
the old magician than elect him their spiritual leader, for one would have to
be very myopic or to possess no experience in life not to see in him an ex-
tremely dangerous man": Sur les confins de la vie (Œuvres), vol. 4, pp. 187–88.
A specious antithesis, which does not correspond to reality.

[33] To Maïkov, January 12, 1868; and March 1: "Things are moving toward
regeneration, for the whole world, through Russian thought (which, as you
rightly remark, is firmly welded to Orthodoxy), and it will come within the
next hundred years. That is my passionate faith": Les Inédits de Dostoïevsky, p.
34.

[34] To Maïkov, May 15, 1869: "The horizon of Russia's future is widening.
The principle has been established of a whole new world in which Christianity will find renewal at the hands of Pan-Slav Orthodoxy, and mankind will
be presented with a new system of thought. That will come to pass when the
West has gone rotten, and the West will go rotten when the Pope, having fi-

in the famous address in commemoration of Pushkin. He endeavored to form a "new and pure" idea of him, quite different from "the grist of the Slav mills of Moscow".[35] Nevertheless, he was no dupe: in Shatov's position there is something that is not clear, and Dostoevsky leads his hero to an embarrassed confession of it. The interview with Stavrogin ends in a defeat. Stavrogin declares that he would like very much to assent to all that he has just been told, but what is to be done if God fails men's faith? Then, passing to the counterattack and looking keenly at Shatov, he says:

> "I should just like to know this: Do you yourself believe in God. Yes or no?"
>
> "I believe in Russia, in its Orthodoxy. . . . I believe in the body of Christ. I believe that it is in Russia that the new advent will take place. . . . I believe", stammered Shatov, as if he were raving.
>
> "But in God, do you believe in God?"
>
> "I . . . I shall believe in God."[36]

Is this Dostoevsky reading scruples and painful hesitation in his own heart? Perhaps. In any case, and this is the whole point at the moment, he does not confuse nationalism, even of a mystical and spiritual type, with faith.[37]

---

nally distorted Christ, has, by that very fact, stirred up atheism in the corrupt humanity of the West": ibid., p. 68. Cf. October 9, 1870, p. 89.

[35] Cf. *Journal d'un écrivain*, vol. 3, p. 396, this disturbing phrase from the *Discours sur Pouchkine*: "Why would it not be we who contain the last word of Christ?"

[36] *Les Possédés*, vol. 1, pp. 258–59. "Not a muscle in Stavrogin's face quivered. Shatov fixed an ardent, provocative gaze on him, as if he had wanted to burn him with this gaze. —But I didn't tell you that I did not believe! he finally exclaimed. . . ."

[37] Elsewhere as well, a first appearance is contrary. Cf. Jacques Madaule, *Le Christianisme de Dostoïevski* (Paris: Bloud & Gay, 1939), pp. 100–101: "Does Versilov believe in God? [The question] is complicated by another: Does he believe in Russia? One can complain, with good logic, that in Dostoevsky problems as heterogeneous as these are constantly mixed in such a way that

Myshkin's case is different. For a proper understanding of it, it is indispensable to touch upon the question of dualism and ambiguity in Dostoevsky.

The idea of a second self haunted him all his life. He makes use of it to suggest the punishment of the criminal, who suffers from split personality. "A double appears and materializes. A double which is himself and not himself. A double which is a hideous caricature of him, the distorting mirror in which his human face becomes blotched and bloated, loses its shape and takes on all the signs of an inward life that is under a curse."[38] Ivan Karamazov's is only the extreme case, however, of something that befalls other characters, even "innocent" ones. Golyadkin is the hero of a story that is actually called *The Double*. Versilov is subject to the same phenomenon, which he dreads: while his heart is full of good thoughts, he is, in spite of himself, impelled toward some action that is the reverse; expressions of tenderness and piety have just fallen from his lips, and he smashes an icon. . . .

> "It looks as if you had your other self beside you [he explains, by way of excuse]. You are sensible and reasonable, but the other one, just beside you, insists on doing something absurd, sometimes something very funny; and all at once you notice that it is you who want to do that funny thing—God knows why. You want to do it in spite of yourself, as it were; you want it while doing your utmost not to."[39]

Myshkin himself, the spontaneous creature who moves Eugene Pavlovich to say in wonder: "There is nobody like you. You aren't telling lies the whole time; perhaps you never tell any at all"—Myshkin suffers from a similar malady: two contra-

---

the solution of one seems to govern that of the other. But it is necessary to take the novelist as he is. . . . We reach humanity only through historical Russia, such as it tried to think and conceive of itself shortly after the abolition of serfdom, between 1860 and 1880."

[38] Cf. Troyat, p. 125.

[39] *L'Adolescent*, p. 472.

dictory thoughts cross each other's path in his mind, "God knows where they come from and how they arise." He thinks that this is not good, it is the thing he most blames himself for, although nothing could be less easy than to fight against it; but sometimes he thinks that everyone is like that.[40] Why be surprised, then, that from a man like Lebedev "lies and truth come out all mixed up together without any premeditation"?[41] This splitting of personality sometimes occurs in dreams, then forming a basis for actions to which nothing in one's thoughts —not even in one's involuntary reveries—corresponds; and yet "everything has long been there in embryo" in the depths of one's heart. . . .[42] Thus in every man there is a mystery. Contraries coexist in him: he is two, and these two are one. Sometimes a man perceives within him a caricature of himself, and he is humbled in his own eyes: sometimes, on the other hand, an insignificant person is given a gleam of something that lifts him into higher regions.

It sometimes happens, too, that in the novelist's mind such duplicative tendencies become objectified and crystallized, as it were, and then we have two or three different but identical characters. Smerdyakov, for instance, is Ivan's other self, "an inferior and repulsive double, who will know how to do what Ivan himself has only the power to wish";[43] for making him read what is in his own heart, that vicious lackey is no less indispensable to Ivan than the devil of his hallucinations. Again, when Raskolnikov, after his crime, is talking to the infamous Svidrigailov, he sees himself reflected in the other as in a mirror. "These tragic couples are each of them composed of two beings who are very much alive and quite real, who think themselves complete and seem so in the eyes of others", yet they "are actually nothing more than the complementary

[40] Myshkin to Neller, in *L'Idiot*, vol. 1, p. 554; cf. vol. 2, p. 658.
[41] Lebedev to Myshkin, ibid., vol. 1, p. 556.
[42] *L'Adolescent*, p. 355.
[43] Madaule, p. 155.

fragments of a third person, a split personality whose halves are looking for each other".[44]

This is the simplest type. But there are others. A central character may, like a bursting star, give birth to several satellites: Verkhovensky, Shatov and Kirillov are all three the offspring of Stavrogin, who, "an extinct force, casts off his own unutilized possibilities", each of which becomes incarnate in another creature.[45] Or a number of characters may form a kind of solar spectrum: the four Karamazovs, for example.

---

[44] Dmitri Merejkowski, *Tolstoï et Dostoïevsky* (French trans.), p. 297: "These counterparts persecute each other: Raskolnikov, Stavrogin, Ivan Karamazov would have been able, or at the very least would have wanted to, say to their odious doubles—Svidrigailov, Peter Verkhovensky, Smerdyakov—what Ivan cries with so impotent and unjust a fury to the devil: 'Not for an instant did I take you for the truth. . . .' ".

[45] Evdokimoff, p. 41; cf. p. 218: "Kirillov and Shatov were born of Stavrogin. Peter Verkhovensky is his 'ape'. Through them, the ideology of nihilism, that of anthropotheism and that of religious Slavism live side by side in him." Cf. *Les Possédés*, vol. 1, p. 241 (Dérélis trans.). This is what Romano Guardini also shows:

"The character of Stavrogin not only comprises the climate in which the world of the novel moves, it also achieves, as it were, a synthesis that is developed in the figures of those who surround him. . . . All the ferments of disintegration that seethe in him, scepticism about existence in society, the instinct of destruction, the sensual pleasure of social experiences, all that explodes in Verkhovensky and in his people. And undoubtedly we have fallen here into a weakness of thought and into a carelessness that seem foreign to Stavrogin; how can we not, however, see in their destructive intrigues an elucidation of what is rising within him? Shatov points out to him, at the moment of the great settling of accounts, that it is he who has given the old socialist his concept of the People-God. Stavrogin, in fact, with all his aspirations for an infinite nature, for the great unity and the magic regeneration of existence, with his desire to go to the roots of the earth and the people, Stavrogin is indeed a romantic. . . . [But] Shatov takes the thing with a ferocious seriousness while his master mocks his own doctrines like all the rest. In Stavrogin, finally, the romantic and Promethean revolt of a Kirillov lives again, along with the torment of religious sensation [*Unmittelbar-Religiosen*] and the refusal to respond to it through Christian ways. . . . But, while the others are thereby set in motion and determined with respect to their destiny, he himself remains chained in a gloomy apathy, the lamentable counterfeit of that healthy simplicity whose

Smerdyakov, Dmitry, Ivan and Alyosha can be called increasingly decanted aspects of one and the same individual who, starting from the animal, finds his fulfillment in the "new man". These four brothers are one and the same being, transformed. "The ladder of vice is the same for all", Alyosha says to Dmitry: "I am on the first rung, you are higher, say on the thirteenth; to my mind it is absolutely all one."[46]

Lastly, there are parallels between characters in different novels. Thus Versilov "reflects, although in a softened form, many of the traits of Stavrogin".[47] The Subterranean Man has numerous descendants, and it is assuredly not just by chance that Dmitry Karamazov, foreseeing that he will be sentenced to work in the mines and speaking in the name of his companions in misery, exclaims: "We, the subterranean men . . .";[48] though the tone and the inspiration are different, his reaction against Rakitin's fine speeches is not unlike the ironic apostrophes that the champions of reason come in for. Prince Myshkin has some of Alyosha's qualities; these two young men, different as they are, are linked by a mysterious affinity of soul. Several of Kirillov's assertions recur on the lips of the Elder Zossima: "Life is paradise, and we are all in paradise; only we will not recognize it; but if we would only recognize it we should all be in paradise tomorrow."[49]

These are not trivial resemblances. There is much more in them than that: they are symbolic parallels. And an analysis of these parallels, to which the inner dualism of individual souls serves as a preparation and adds subtlety, is essential for the understanding of Dostoevsky's work as a whole. Dostoevsky did

---

quietude creates movement and life and whose unity makes a multitude of figures and values spring forth."

[46] Troyat, p. 546.

[47] Evdokimoff, p. 41.

[48] *Les Frères Karamazov*, vol. 2, p. 596.

[49] And again: "Each little leaf tends toward the word and praises God. . . ." Ibid., vol. 1, p. 316, etc. Cf. the words of Jesus in John 13:17: "If you know these things, you will be happy."

not put all his cards on the table at once. But the exquisite art he employs—an art that, considering his life and the conditions in which his great novels were composed, seems little short of miraculous—is not merely a means of pursuing the same theme in different registers, correcting one impression by another, and building up a mental universe by the successive revelation of its various aspects. Such an art was indispensable to him. He was obliged to have recourse to parallels of this kind and to make use of symbols. He could not do otherwise than proceed by way of indirect suggestion. For what he had set out to do was to take us as far as the world of the spirit. But that world, as he knew, is invisible. There is no means of reaching it by any direct contact: "A material demonstration of the other world, what a preposterous idea!"[50] Dostoevsky is not an empiricist of the spiritual; in the last analysis he is not a "psychologist", and he does not wish to be one. "The inaccessible reality that solves everything still remains beyond the horizon, at the same remote distance, whatever efforts man may make to reach it. It is transcendent. . . . The vanishing point is outside the picture and yet strictly inherent in it, outside the field of psychology and in the spirit."[51]

Dostoevsky does not think that one can ever look over the top of the wall, so to speak. He does not believe in the absolute value of any of the "experiences" he describes, which are always to some extent his own experience. He knows only too well the imperfections that are, as a rule, the *sine qua non*, the price that must be paid for them. He sees only too clearly that they do not bring salvation. "Idiocy" and epilepsy, on the one hand, and, on the other, inability to act and ineffectual compassion ending in tragedy—that is what his Myshkin's vi-

---

[50] Dostoevsky, quoted by Evdokimoff, p. 187. He was fiercely opposed to spiritism; he rejected it, as well as any experience with suprapsychic pretensions, just as Christ rejected in the desert the temptation to accomplish miracles; cf. the Legend of the Grand Inquisitor.

[51] Evdokimoff, p. 83. Thurneysen, p. 99.

sions bring in their train. Far from denying them or letting himself be distracted by them, he sorts out his material with a sure hand and proceeds to a merciless diagnosis. With the "Idiot", as with Kirillov and the ecstatic worshippers of the "Great Mother", we are still on the plane of nature, which is that of psychology and is bound to be disappointing. There is no observable, strictly describable, transition from the psychological to the metaphysical, from nature to the spirit. "That is of another order, supernatural. . . ."

If Dostoevsky does not believe in a spiritual experience that comes within the competence of psychology and would, so to speak, snare the spirit in its toils, this is because his ideas are not naturalistic. "The last result of his analysis, of his merciless dissection, is the assertion that a *synthetic* connection relates everything human to a viewpoint situated beyond any sort of reality that can be called psychological."[52] He does not picture the spiritual world as a hidden substratum that, while of course impenetrable by the normal, ordinary man, yields to the explorations of a being with better, or different, gifts. For him this spiritual world, this domain of eternity, is, in a concrete sense, the Gospel, and the only way to enter it is by the means referred to in the Gospel: *metanoia*, or "new birth". The gate of the kingdom is opened, as well as guarded, by the mystery of the cross.[53] Myshkin's experience, if taken in isolation or if it had no other possible meaning than the literal one, would simply bring us back to some lost paradise, to a state of childhood and infrahuman innocence. That is how Gide understands it,

---

[52] Thurneysen, p. 100; and pp. 101–2: "This supernature of which he speaks endlessly is not a given reality, a 'superworld', or any unconscious psychic reality. For that which is the presupposition, the foundation, the essential determination of all cannot be something determined or determinable, any more than the point toward which the perspective tends can be a real point situated inside the picture. . . ."

[53] "Christ has called me to carry the Cross", says Alyosha, *Les Frères Karamazov*, vol. 1. Cf. Evdokimoff, p. 134: "The idea of the Cross, the idea of expiation is the spiritual atmosphere of Dostoevsky's novels."

and it cannot be said that he is mistaken; but he is wrong in stopping short at the letter, at the symbol. Such a step backward is impossible for man. Versilov had dreamed of it, he had seen humanity back in its cradle, and the spectacle was so beautiful that a feeling of happiness never yet experienced thrilled his heart; it was a wonderful dream; but the declares that it was only a "sublime aberration".[54] It is useless to seek "the triumph of innocence in unpurified man".[55] Versilov's dream was repeated by someone else—the one whom Dostoevsky in the *Journal of an Author* called "the Ridiculous Man". In the place to which he suddenly found himself transported, "everything was exactly as it is with us, and yet everything shone with a kind of grave and solemn gladness verging on the sublime"; there all men were innocent and beautiful, their faces were untouched by suffering, they lived "in a kind of continual communication with the Great All". But in entering paradise, this man brought evil with him.[56]

Yes, "of all the dreams that have ever been dreamed, the golden age is the most improbable." Yet "for it men have given their whole life and strength, for it the prophets have died and have been killed, without it the nations do not want to live and cannot even die."[57] The speaker is again Versilov, the faithful spokesman of the whole human race. What accounts for this invincible attraction? And why is it coupled with those "ex-

---

[54] *L'Adolescent*, p. 434. This paradise of Versilov, like that of the "ridiculous man", seems like a kind of intermediary between the Greek ideal world (a little like Taine depicts it) and the paradise of Péguy's *Eve*.

[55] Cf. Stanislas Fumet, *L'Impatience des limites, petit traité du firmament* (Fribourg, Librairie de l'Université, 1942), p. 100.

[56] "Le Songe d'un homme ridicule", in the *Journal d'un écrivain*, vol. 3. Cf. Evdokimoff, pp. 53–65. The man in the dream, it must be recognized, gives in completely to one of Dostoevsky's "temptations", and if his sentiment were not corrected by the admission he is to make of his powerlessness to reenter paradise without corrupting it, he would lay himself open to the Gidean interpretation, which is not, therefore, without some foundation.

[57] *L'Adolescent*, p. 434.

periences" that make men believe they have reached heaven? Whatever one may think of them, they are facts. The naturalistic explanation is an obvious one, and Dostoevsky is the first to give it, or rather (for he does not theorize), he provides all the material for that explanation, without cheating. Myshkin's visions are due to his illness, just as Ivan's hallucinations are. That may be so. But, if a man has in him a presentiment of eternity, will he not take all these things as so many signs?

Hence the ambiguous nature of such states, according to whether we just take them literally or see in them signs, that is to say, real symbols. This notion of ambiguity is one of the most important to bear in mind when interpreting Dostoevsky. It is not far removed from that of dualism—with this difference, however, that in dualism, as the name indicates, there are two clearly marked, contrasting poles, whereas in ambiguity the duality that already exists remains latent and not yet differentiated.

Take, for instance, a character like Versilov. What a host of questions present themselves! From beginning to end he seems an enigma. At first one is inclined to lay the blame on one's own misreading or on the author's lack of skill in narration; but these explanations are quite inadequate. The enigma is *real*. Does Versilov believe or doesn't he? Is he good or bad? When is he showing his true self and when is he acting? What mental reservations do his confidences conceal? . . . What was the author's idea? What did he want us to guess? But the author is like ourselves. He has launched his characters into existence, and now he stands before them as if confronted by a mystery. And, it should be added (this is a circumstance of the utmost importance), it is not merely a question of subjective ignorance on his part or on ours: objectively, as Jacques Madaule has noted, people like Versilov inhabit "that uncertain region between good and evil in which one can never be sure how far apparent good overlaps hidden evil, and vice versa".[58]

---

[58] Madaule, p. 90. As for the figure of Myshkin, it is, says Guardini, "of a

The Subterranean Man is also ambiguous in the highest degree, though in a different fashion—and that is why, however
important his monologue may be as a means of admitting us
into Dostoevsky's mind, it does not seem possible to see in
it, as some have done, the "key" to the whole of the writer's
work. For, on the one hand, if it annoys me, if it is personally
distasteful to me that two and two should make four, I may
be quite sure that the lacuna and the sin and the poverty are
inherent in my nature and not in the innocent nature of *things*;
consequently, the Subterranean Man's impatience of the limits
set by reason may be interpreted first as an unavailing protest
against the universal order. All rebellions, all perversions, all
the *mystiques* of hell are potentially contained in it. . . . But, on
the other hand, "did not the viewpoint of the intuitive man
—assuring us that understanding and life are ignorant of one
another" and "that in other spheres two and two do not make
four"—include "the perception of another truth than the one
which it stated"?[59] Is it arbitrary Titanism or a premonition of
transcendence? Neither. Through the "irrational", of which he
is the herald, the Subterranean Man is a tragic introduction to
the higher world of freedom, in which the contrasting destinies
of such men as Stavrogin and Alyosha will intersect.[60]

Thus the ambiguity of souls is matched by an ambiguity of
mental states. Are the insolences of Stavrogin and his wholly

discouraging ambiguity"; this character remains "terribly undecided, so much
so that the path remains open to the most contradictory appraisals. . . . All
that, moreover, in no way results from the fact that Myshkin spends only a
few months with us. This 'gratuitous' character is essential to his being. To
speak with Kierkegaard, we never meet him except in 'simultaneity'. No character of the novel can adopt a detached attitude to him, nor can the reader,
even if he penetrates to the innermost part of the work. . . ."

[59] Fumet, pp. 15 and 42–43.

[60] "Dostoevsky", says Berdyaev, p. 61, "is interested in the man only in his
stormy instability. . . . The latter is due to the instability of his nature, to the
shock of opposites that confront each other in him. Polarity, antinomy, this
is what characterizes the depth of human nature. Neither unity nor repose in
these depths, nothing but passionate movement."

gratuitous provocations[61] due to some affection of the brain, or ought they to be regarded as deliberate expressions of perversity? And what are we to make of Kirillov's visions? So shrewd an analyst as the Rev. Fr. de Lestapis gives us, almost one on top of the other, two opposite interpretations. Observing that Kirillov's frenzy of atheism is a "total inversion of faith", he is moved to lay the blame on "those extraordinary sensations of euphory" without which our visionary would never have "known" that he was happy or that he was good. On the other hand, bearing in mind the whole context, which is that of a noble life, he does not hesitate to recognize in this man who kills himself for the sake of his principles a tragic witness to moral obligation and, in these morbid manifestations of his sensibility, a genuine prophetic sense of the life everlasting.[62]

Both views seem to me correct, and simultaneously so, this being an extreme and paradoxical case of that "ambiguity" which, present everywhere, gives a disturbing depth to the Dostoevskian universe but also imbues it with such symbolic power.

Nature is the sign of the spirit. Christ is our Sun. Dostoevsky repeats it, with the whole Christian tradition. The abnormal experiences that crop up so often in the texture of his work are gleams that point the way into the Forbidden Kingdom. But of this Kingdom nothing can be described by the psychologist. It is impossible for man to enter it by natural means.

3. The New Birth

The central mystery of the Greek Orthodox Church is the mystery of Easter. "Christ is risen!" He draws after him not only men but the whole cosmos. He floods it with his light, and

---

[61] *Les Possédés*, vol. 1, pp. 50–59.

[62] Stanislas de Lestapis, "Le Problème de l'athéisme vu par Dostoïevsky", in *Études*, vol. 233 (1937), pp. 620 and 619.

the believer, for whom everything is transfigured, finds God everywhere. If, for instance, the Earth is sacred to him, that is by no means a return to paganism: it is consistent Christianity. The whole order of nature is permeated by him who is "the life-giving Spirit".

But to arrive at that point it was necessary to experience Death.

Dostoevsky was a child of Orthodoxy. Theologians of his own country may not have been wholly satisfied as to the correctness of his beliefs.[63] But it would be risking a grave mistake in the interpretation of his work to forget that he breathed the atmosphere of Orthodoxy and profoundly assimilated its spirit. The two scenes we have now to examine are of purely Christian inspiration, and it is only in the light of these scenes that the passages already analyzed find their true exegesis and take on their ultimate significance.

We left Raskolnikov in the convict prison, ruminating over his nightmare, in the desert of a heart without repentance. But, even before he went and knelt down in the market-place to confess his crime, a promise of resurrection had sprung up in his hell. The criminal had been to visit Sonia and had picked up from the chest of drawers in her room a little New Testament: it had been a present from Elisabeth, his second victim. Then he had asked Sonia, who now knew all, to read him a passage, the account of the raising of Lazarus.

The moment of the unparalleled miracle was approaching; a feeling of triumph possessed her. Her voice thrilled with a metallic ring; it was the note of triumph and joy that gave it that firm-

---

[63] Berdyaev has recognized that "Dostoevsky did not reflect true Russian Orthodoxy, the traditional Orthodox monarchism, and that he had worked out something entirely new"; "the entire work of Dostoevsky had an accent that was less realistic than prophetic": *Constantin Léontieff* (French trans. by Hélène Iswolsky [Paris: Desclée de Brouwer, 1936]), p. 226. The ecclesiastical censor forbade the edition of the "Teachings of Father Zossima" excerpted from *The Brothers Karamazov* (ibid., p. 330).

ness and resonance. The lines danced before her tear-dimmed eyes; but she knew the words by heart. Lowering her voice at the last verse: "Could not (he that) opened the eyes of the man born blind . . .", she brought out with passionate fervor the perplexity, the reproaches of those blind and incredulous Jews who now railed against him but very soon, in another minute, were to fall on their knees, as if struck by lightning, and, sobbing, believe. . . . "And he who is just as blind and unbelieving, in a minute he too will hear, he too will believe, yes! yes! now, this minute", she thought, trembling with joyful expectation. . . .[64]

Her moment of expectation was prolonged. But she did not despair. She went with the condemned man along the roads of Siberia. Like one of his brothers before him, back in the forties, he now had under his pillow a little Testament, the one that had belonged to Elisabeth and then to Sonia. One evening he took it and opened it mechanically. For some time now he had been less given to arguing about his case; his pride in his theory was shaken. "Life was taking the place of dialectic, and something quite different was taking shape in the depths of his consciousness." Then the miracle happened:

But this is the beginning of another story, the story of the progressive renewal of a man, of his regeneration, of how he gradually passed from one world to another and came to know a new reality that had hitherto been beyond his ken. . . .[65]

So ends *Crime and Punishment*. "Do not these words sound like a solemn promise?" says Shestov. "Has not Dostoevsky undertaken the obligation to show us this new reality and the new possibilities that are opening up for Raskolnikov? But the master left that promise unfulfilled." It could not have been for

---

[64] *Crime et châtiment*, vol. 2, pp. 332–35.

[65] Ibid., pp. 559–60. "That could form the theme of another story, but our own story is ended." And, a little above, this no less evocative sentence: "They wanted to speak, but they could not. Tears filled their eyes. Both were pale and thin, but in those haggard, gaunt faces, a dawn of a new future, of a whole resurrection to a new life, was already rising!"

382 DOSTOEVSKY AS PROPHET

want of time, however—he could still find time to write long novels; but "he did not remember" what he had promised.[66]

That is a forced remark.[67] Its only point is to support the contention that his hero's "new life" was of no interest to Dostoevsky; that in giving his tale a moralizing conclusion he had only been conforming to public opinion, as one puts on a uniform to attend an official funeral; but that, having made the gesture, he had no thought of following it up.[68] To my mind there was a different explanation. Had it merely been a question of recounting the gradual regeneration of an ordinary criminal, his reeducation, his social readaptation, so to speak, with its various episodes, there would certainly have been material for a book there, but Dostoevsky would not have found it very interesting (here I agree with Shestov). He would not have written an analogue to Tolstoy's *Resurrection*. A moral of that kind would have bored him. But, actually, something quite different was involved here: the discovery of a "new reality", the entry into a new world. That, indeed, interested him enormously; but that was untellable. It was very truly "another story", and he could not promise, and had not promised, to write it, for he knew very well that it could not be written. His whole psychology would have broken down. The ways in which God reaches man will always remain a mystery.[69]

For Gide the way the novel ends is not an edifying *passe-*

---

[66] Shestov, *La Philosophie*, pp. 101–2.

[67] We do not see very well, moreover, how it accords with what we have discussed above, in Chapter 2.

[68] It is true that, two pages farther on, Shestov writes: "Men have need of idealism, whatever it might be. And Dostoevsky throws them a handful of it; so much and so well that he himself ends up imagining that his teaching has a certain value. But he believes in it only for an instant, in order to mock it himself a moment later" (p. 104).

[69] Cf. *Les Carnets de Crime et châtiment*: "N.B. the last line: The paths are mysterious by which God reaches man" (p. 243). Cf. Kafka to Max Brod, December 1917, with respect to Tolstoy's *Resurrection*: "One cannot write redemption, one can only live it."

partout, of no import. He finds in it (as in the account of the ecstasies of the "Idiot", but with still more reason) the core of Dostoevsky's thought. But we have seen how he interprets that. Here his interpretation rests upon a translation that, it seems to me, is rather taking liberties with the text for the benefit of the doctrine. "In him life had taken the place of argument. *From now on he had only sensations*."[70] There it is, this return to the paradise of childhood! Raskolnikov has at last found salvation.

How often the supraconsciousness is confused with the infraconsciousness! How often an attempt is made to bring the spirit back to the plane of nature! How often the *denuo nasci* of the Gospel is perverted! "Genius", said Baudelaire, "is the rediscovery of childhood." But the special application that Stanislas Fumet finds for this dictum in the case of the artist is equally pertinent in regard to the man who has ears for the call to sainthood: "The spirit of childhood is for him an irresistible temptation. We like to go back to our beginnings. . . . [Only] the free work of the artist who knows enough about things to forget what he has known may, for a moment, seem like the work of a child; but that is merely a superficial resemblance. . . . The one stumbles for want of experience, the other is lame through having gone so far."[71] Why should a truth so obvious on the plane of art, which is only representation, become dim as soon as it passes to the plane of actual being? Gide had offered us a Gidean interpretation of Dostoevsky to match his Gidean interpretation of the Gospel. Nor does he try to hide this.[72] What

---

[70] Gide, *Dostoïevski*, p. 239. Actually this is an inversion that completely alters the meaning of the words I have italicized. Cf. V. Pozner's [French] translation, vol. 2, p. 280 (NRF, 1931): "He was, moreover, incapable of long reflection or concentrated thought that evening. He could only feel. Life had taken the place of reasoning; his spirit likewise had to be regenerated."

[71] Fumet, pp. 59–60. Hegel rightly observes, at the beginning of the *Phenomenology*, that Christ does not ask us to *remain* children (or, let us add, to become so again), but to *become* so.

[72] *Journal*, April 22, 1922: "Everything that I find the means of saying

made it possible for him to give such an interpretation without immediate improbability was the existence of that series of analogies and symbolic parallels that crop up everywhere in the great novelist's work and have the far-reaching significance that has already been noted.

The kingdom to which Raskolnikov gains access is a world of fellowship. In the name Raskolnikov there is *raskol*, which means schism, division. He has been cut off from his brother-men by his crime, and more especially by his pride in his theory, which led to that crime. That is why Sonia requires of him that he should do public penance.[73] Separated from the human race, he cannot be reunited with it unless his heart is converted. Kirillov, too, by his mad plan of self-deification, imprisons himself in a fatal isolation, of which his insane logic, working in a closed system, is the sign.[74] Such is the fate of every sinner, that is to say, of every man. This earthly world, the objective world of human society, is a world of separation and loneliness, whatever forms of "community" life may be practiced there. For it is a world of sin. Dostoevsky does not oppose its would-be improvers, but he warns us that, in themselves, improvements can do nothing to solve the problem of

---

through Dostoevsky and in connection with him is near to my heart, and I attach great importance to it. Anyone who knows how to read it will find in this volume a book of confessions quite as much as a work of criticism; or, rather, he will find in it a profession of faith." And August 4: "It is not fear of being mistaken, it is a need of sympathy that makes me seek, with an ardent uneasiness, the call or the recall of my own thought in another's; . . . to present my own ethic in the shelter of Dostoevsky's": Éditions de la Pléiade (Paris: Gallimard), pp. 733 and 739. On Gide's evangelical misinterpretation: André Rousseaux, *Ames et visages du xxᵉ siècle: 2d series: Le Paradis perdu* (Paris: Grasset, 1936), pp. 250–83.

[73] Evdokimoff, p. 135.

[74] Evdokimoff, p. 128: "It is thus the very element of resemblance with God that is deflected in Kirillov, and the circle is closed in self-resemblance, absolute isolation. Dostoevsky shows us this isolation, on the one hand, in Kirillov's way of living in communion with others and, on the other hand, in the strangeness of his language."

man and of human fellowship. The most perfect of societies might be the most horrible of hells.[75]

True, the "ordinary man", who is in each of us, feels himself surrounded and sustained by the social environment in which he is immersed and whose thousand habits of behavior he adopts. He has an absolute need of it in order to live. Dostoevsky was keenly aware of this and the elements of a kind of unanimism might be found in him, though chiefly from a negative standpoint. But the man who, having retired into himself, rejects the mental conventions by which man lives in society—that man enters a different solitude: "I am but one, and there are all of them!" exclaims the Subterranean Man. That loneliness is not, strictly speaking, the loneliness of sin. It is not always arrogant; it is often imposed upon the man who experiences it, as the soul sometimes finds itself impelled into mystical paths when it would fain keep to the same prayer as everyone else, and it is afraid of losing its footing. It is a Nietzschean solitude that Dostoevsky also experiences and describes. However —and there is no longer anything Nietzschean about this— beyond every society, in contrast to the separation due to evil, deeper than the "subterranean solitude", there is fellowship. But this, which is the characteristic of the spiritual world, is, like it, incommunicable. The inchoative experience that men can have of it is not a matter for psychology. In entering it, Raskolnikov was to receive a new name, which only the angels know.[76]

---

[75] Cf. Berdyaev, *Esprit et réalité* (Paris: Aubier, 1943), pp. 128–29: "One can conquer social injustices, man's exploitation by man. And this is perhaps the result of a transformation of human society. But by that very fact, far from suppressing it, one only makes the inner tragedy of life grow, the anguish be enlarged still more, and spirituality be manifested in a more intense fashion, since they are no longer crushed by external misfortunes and by social disorder. Man will not consent to becoming a definitively objectified being. . . ."

[76] In *Les Frères Karamazov* (vol. 2, p. 595; cf. pp. 510 and 573), Mitya's conversion—"Brother, since my arrest, I have felt being born within me a new being, a new man has been resurrected!"—also includes this element of com-

This mystery of the new man and of the new birth, glimpsed at the end of *Crime and Punishment*, reappears in *The Brothers Karamazov*. That is the true subject of this horrible story, this "extraordinary epic of turpitude, licentiousness and neurosis".[77] Like Raskolnikov, Mitya is a man who has been brought back to life. But here the action of the mystery is no longer purely retrospective, its evocation is not left for the epilogue, as in *Crime and Punishment*: it shines out from the very heart of the book, where Alyosha foreshadows it.

Alyosha's testimony is of cardinal importance. Its scope has not always been clearly recognized. Some, including Shestov, take little interest in this character, calling him commonplace, unreal, tiresome; according to them the author's failure to make him stand out is a sign that Dostoevsky did not put any of his profound ideas into Alyosha. That view clashes with the preface to *The Brothers Karamazov*, which says just the opposite; and is not Shestov himself obliged to recognize that once, at least, "Dostoevsky felt himself really inspired in speaking of Alyosha and bestowed upon him one of those visions to which he attained when his exaltation was at its height"?[78] Others, including Gide, understand Alyosha in the light of Myshkin. But, if there is an undoubted kinship of soul between these two young men,[79] the differences between them are just as great. Alyosha is neither mentally backward nor maladjusted. He is

---

munion. It is expressed by the acceptance of punishment, although Mitya did not kill his father, in a spirit of expiation for all: "For all are guilty for all. . . . Someone must sacrifice himself for all." And the chain that ties together the workers in the prison thus becomes the symbol of solidarity in expiation. A conversion prepared for and prefigured by the dream in which Mitya saw the "little one" who cried in the arms of its mother, the symbol of human misery.

[77] Persky, p. 279.

[78] Shestov, *Les Révélations*, pp. 118–19. When Dostoevsky depicted Alyosha, if he did not lay emphasis on the characteristics, it is undoubtedly because he was afraid "of soiling with his impure hands the beautiful modern icon", Fumet, p. 82.

[79] "Myshkin goes into the world, penetrates the darkest recesses of life; like a ray of light from the Logos, he pierces the mysteries of the human soul.

capable of manly decision. His innocence does not alter the fact that he has the brutal Karamazov nature. He has not the prince's ambiguous character, nor does he live, like him, "in a perpetual present, tinged with the gradations between smiles and indifference".[80] These contrasts of character are matched by contrasts in their spiritual life, and between Myshkin's experience and Alyosha's there is at once the same distance and the same symbolic link as between nature and spirit.[81]

Alyosha was Zossima's favorite disciple. The old *staretz* had just died. Before entering upon his last rest, he repeated to Alyosha the Gospel phrase that was familiarly on his lips: "Unless the grain of wheat falling into the ground die, itself remaineth alone; but if it die it bringeth forth much fruit."[82] "Remember that!" he said to Alyosha. . . . Then there was the watch beside the dead. According to their custom, the monks gathered round the body lying exposed in its coffin, and one of them slowly read aloud from the Gospel. Overcome by a long day of emotion and fatigue, Alyosha fell asleep. In a dozing state he heard Father Païssy read about the marriage in Cana. And, as he dreamed, Zossima appeared to him; he was alive again, came to Alyosha and expounded the Gospel to him. . . .

Alyosha is necessary to all. His presence brings harmony, makes the meaning of things understood . . .": Evdokimoff, p. 93. Miusov's remarks about Alyosha, *Les Frères Karamazov*, vol. 1, p. 35, would apply as well to Myshkin: "Here you have perhaps the only man in the world who, if he were left alone without a penny in a large, unknown city, would never die of exposure or hunger because he would be instantly fed, people would come to his aid; he would immediately get out of trouble, with neither effort nor humiliation, and it would be a pleasure for others to render him service." There is in Myshkin, nevertheless, a mystery that makes this instinctive sympathy toward him easily change into a no less instinctive hostility. . . .

[80] Albert Camus, *Le Mythe de Sisyphe* (Paris: Gallimard, 1942), p. 149.

[81] Cf. the penetrating remarks of Zander, pp. 168 and 170.

[82] *Les Frères Karamazov*, vol. 1, p. 298. Zossima is fond of this sentence. It is what he had formerly said in response to the mysterious visitor who had come to consult him on the subject of an old and forgotten crime: vol. 1, p. 322. It is what Dostoevsky placed as an introductory quotation to the novel.

Alyosha awoke, the old monk was there, stretched out cold and stiff; the youth gazed at him in his coffin. . . .

Suddenly he turned on his heel and left the cell. He went down the steps without pausing. His soul, in a state of exaltation, cried out for freedom, space. Above his head the vault of heaven was a limitless expanse, the quiet stars glittered. From the zenith to the horizon stretched the Milky Way, as yet indistinct. Calm night enveloped the earth. The white towers and gilded domes stood out against the sapphire sky. Around the house the luxuriant autumn flowers were folded in sleep until morning. The earth seemed to mingle its tranquillity with that of the stars. Alyosha stood motionless, gazing upon it. Suddenly, as if struck down, he prostrated himself.

He did not know why he embraced the earth; he did not understand why he had been irresistibly drawn to clasp it all of a sudden; but he did so, sobbing and watering it with his tears, and he fervently vowed that he would love it, love it forever. "Water the earth with tears of joy and love them"; these words rang through his soul. What was he weeping for? Oh! in his ecstasy he was even weeping over the stars that shone in infinite space, and he "was not ashamed of his exaltation". Threads from these innumerable worlds seemed to converge in his soul, which thrilled "in contact with the other worlds". He wanted to forgive everyone for everything and to ask forgiveness, not for himself, but for others and for everything; "the others will ask it for me", these words, too, came back into his memory. He was more and more keenly aware—and almost as if it were something tangible—that a firm and unshakable feeling was penetrating his soul, that an idea was taking possession of his mind forever. He had cast himself down as a weak youth, and he rose up again a stout fighter for the rest of his days—he was conscious of that at this moment of crisis. And never again could Alyosha forget that moment. "My soul was visited in that hour", he said afterward, firmly believing in the truth of his words.[83]

---

[83] Ibid., vol. 1, pp. 374–75. See the commentary by Berdyaev, *L'Esprit de Dostoïevski*, pp. 246–49.

Do we not feel at this point that those beings whose ambiguous ecstasies had left us perplexed are all gathered round Alyosha? Is it not here that the great mystic current that runs through Dostoevsky's work receives its meaning? Yes, they are all there, amazed at the spectacle before them: Myshkin and Kirillov and the little old woman who recommended kissing the ground, and the Ridiculous Man with his nostalgic dream and even Svidrigailov, who spoke of "fragments of other worlds" that you see floating in visions. . . . Between their experiences and that of the young monk, is there not—with nuances from one to another—some relation similar to that which Clement of Alexandria discerned between the *membra disjecta* of the pagan fables and the whole body of the Christian mystery? Leading up to Alyosha's ecstasy, it should be noted, there are the teachings of the *staretz* on that penitence and sacrifice that are necessary in order to enter into Life—teachings upon which a seal is set by the death of the old man (who thereafter shows himself, alive, to his sleeping disciple) and which are symbolized by the reading of the miracle of Cana. Water is the sign of penitence —for Dostoevsky knows that man is sinful. The changing of the water into wine stands for the process by which the human being becomes divine, the transition from natural life to life according to the spirit. The ecstasy that followed, in the garden, was actually that. We do not know in what it consisted, and neither Dostoevsky nor Alyosha himself could have described its substance. Only the gestures that accompanied it, the feelings it excited and the memories it revived were set down. It was that spiritual miracle, that mystery of "new birth", always the same and always new, symbolized now by the miracle of the marriage of Cana and now by the miracle of the raising of Lazarus.[84] "My soul was visited in that hour. . . ."

---

[84] Evdokimoff, p. 104, discerns besides a more precise symbolism. "Alyosha receives a sophic initiation, in communion with the Alma Mater. The union of the star-shaped cupola and the walls of the monastery, the sophic blue of

Then Alyosha can embrace the earth and water it with his tears. Then the earthly mystery borders upon that of the stars, and God envelops his creation as the tranquil night envelops the earth. In Alyosha's heart "the whole universe throbs".[85] His ecstasy is supernatural, but the cosmos is transfigured with him.

That ecstasy, however, is not an ending. It is a dawn, a promise. Quite unlike those recurring states which, when they had passed, let Myshkin sink back into his passivity, this ecstasy marks a crisis in Alyosha's life, and it brings him strength. It is a viaticum for his journey. Symbolized by the marriage in Cana, it symbolizes, in its turn, a destiny that is not yet fulfilled. "By hope you are saved", said Paul to the Christians who had already passed through mystic death and resurrection. So it is with Alyosha. The mysticism of *The Brothers Karamazov* is the mysticism of the Resurrection. It is eschatological. It is that of the Fourth Gospel but also that of the Apocalypse. Dostoevsky does not dream of some sort of eternity grasped in an instant; that would be, literally, Myshkin's formula, and, as we have seen, it is literally Gide's formula. What Dostoevsky yearns for is to abolish time. In that, Kirillov is his mouthpiece —Kirillov, who is constantly poring over the Apocalypse, although he goes astray in his researches. Eternity is there, at hand. Here and there a strange rent in the web of our human experience affords us a glimpse of it. A spiritual experience of another order gives us the hope of it. . . . "Human, all too human" in his life and in his feelings, he is not rooted in certainty, either. His soul is still tormented. But, toward evening, his doubts are calmed. He believes in immortality. He looks forward to the resurrection.

---

the cosmic spaces and the whiteness of innocence achieve, in a vivid form, the symbolism of iconographic colors and the mystic symbolism of the cult of the Virgin Mother of God."

[85] *Carnets des Frères Karamazov*, p. 171.

"Karamazov," exclaimed Kolya, "is it true, as religion says, that we rise from the dead, that we shall see each other again, all of us, Ilyusha too?"

". . . To be sure, we shall rise again, we shall see one another again, and we shall joyfully recount all that has happened to us", replied Alyosha, half-laughing, half-eager.

"Oh, how lovely that will be!" said Kolya.[86]

With this ingenuous dialogue, this childish conversation which is a pendant to Alyosha's ecstasy, Fyodor Mikhailovich Dostoevsky ends *The Brothers Karamazov*, his last work, completed in the year of his death.

---

[86] *Les Frères Karamazov*, vol. 2, p. 773.

CONCLUSION

Thus all this body of work, this dreadful work, ends in a hymn of hope. The whole of it is a hymn of hope. That is its underlying meaning. Dostoevsky is the prophet of the *other life*. The truth he announces is not a "discarnate" truth, to use a word so often misused today. On the contrary, his realism is of the most vigorous type.[1] But it bears no resemblance to a positivist truth. It is a truth that shocks. Yet, if it sets itself against any attempt on the part of man to "establish eternal life in this world", its purpose is not to leave him weighed down by a miserable lot. It is to reclaim him from a path that leads nowhere. He is the prophet of unity, which presupposes a breach to be healed; the prophet of the Resurrection, which presupposes experience of death.

Death, it has been said, is the only metaphysical experience. Does not Dostoevsky owe his privileged position, and the extraordinary clairvoyance that won for him the title of "man of God",[2] to the fact that he was granted—in two different ways that mingled and corroborated each other—a kind of anticipation of this unique experience? The essential feature of an epileptic fit, according to Eduard Thurneysen, is that it is

> only a presage of quite a different moment; the essential point is the similarity of that moment with the last moment in the life of

---

[1] However gloomy it may be in addition, it is not, at any rate, that "cynical and cruel disparagement" characteristic of so many of our so-called "realistic" or "naturalistic" novelists. Cf. Paul Claudel, *Conversations dans le Loir-et-Cher* (Paris: Gallimard, 1935), "Sunday".

[2] Alain-Fournier, letter to Jacques Rivière, January 3, 1913: "Long conversations with Péguy are the great events of the last few days. . . . I maintain—and I know what I am saying—that, since Dostoevsky, there has surely never been a man who was so clearly a 'Man of God' . . .": *Jacques Rivière et Alain-Fournier: Correspondance, 1905–1914* (Paris: Gallimard, 1916–1928).

a condemned man, when the axe of the executioner is about to fall on his neck; the essential point is the great imminence of the absolute moment of death. And once more a personal experience is involved, when Dostoevsky speaks of the singular light that the fatal moment sheds upon the whole of life. He had lived through it when, as a young man, in the Semenovsky Square in Saint Petersburg, he was on the point of being executed by a firing squad. . . .[3]

Not that (I would repeat) he realized the impossible, that he saw over the wall. . . . But from that time onward he saw the world from the standpoint of death, that is to say, from the standpoint of eternity. (Faith in Christ and meditation on the Gospel had done the rest.) He remained in our world as a man come from elsewhere. That is what makes his vision at once so deep and so strange—so disconcerting for that pseudorealism whose principle Alain-Fournier defined as follows: "To become the soul of everyone in order to see what everyone sees; for what everyone sees is the only reality."[4] Dostoevsky sees something different and, above all, he sees differently from "everyone". He had really reached "the frontiers of man". Nobody had less indulgence for that "impatience of limitations" (to quote Stanislas Fumet), the only effect of which is to enslave us more harshly. But no one, perhaps, has given us so much hope that one day we may be freed from them.

---

[3] Eduard Thurneysen, *Dostoïevsky ou les confins de l'homme* (French trans. by P. Maury [pub. by Je Sers] of: *Dostojewski* [Zurich, Gotthelf-Verlag, 1948]), p. 71. Cf. Dmitri Merejkowski, *Tolstoï et Dostoïevski*, p. 99.

[4] Alain-Fournier, letter to Jacques Rivière, April 2, 1907, *Correspondance*.

PART FOUR

MYSTICAL CONFRONTATIONS

"THE SEARCH FOR A NEW MAN" develops a lecture I was asked to give at the *Semaine sociale* in Paris in 1947. The subject proposed for it was at first, in a general way, "the Christian idea of man". But the character of the *Semaine* as well as the circumstances invited, rather than a mere dogmatic presentation, a confrontation with the Marxist idea that was seducing a number of minds at that time as well as a Christian judgment brought to bear on a whole group of tendencies of which Marxism constituted only one aspect. How will the Christian behave in the presence of all those hopes and that whole search that he observes around him concerning a "new man"?[1] What attitude will he adopt in this great movement that seems to carry away everything in the wake of the discoveries and upheavals of every order that have occurred during these last centuries? What solution will he offer for this new state of the problem of the relations between the temporal and the eternal? In a thousand forms, with respect to a thousand subjects, the question is being posed everywhere today, provoking two antagonistic answers. Optimism or pessimism, social action or eschatological expectation, a search for shelter in the spiritual and intensive cultivation of the one thing necessary or the will to "incarnation" and universal animation: two equally attractive poles, between which two families of minds are divided. The discussions go on, and any occasion makes them spring up again. There is no need to be distressed by them. With the exception of some rare extremes, these differences maintain a fruitful tension within Christian thought. In this way, with respect to the most concrete realities and the most current points of conscience, the diversity of the theological schools is continued and reconstituted. In this way, their vital interest is made man-

---

[1] Since the time these pages were written, this expression has been used increasingly in certain countries as a politico-spiritual slogan and a pretext for religious persecution; it has entered into the language of certain Christian circles, with a meaning completely different from that given in Christian revelation. On this vast subject, the entire work of Fr. Gaston Fessard should be reread. (1983.)

ifest in everyday competition. It could be said of most of the studies devoted to the subject, as Leibniz said of the systems of philosophy, that they are always true in what they affirm; merely incomplete and, in consequence, complementary. I, for my part, have tried, not to bring a complete solution to the problem, nor even to consider it from all sides, but to shed light on it through what seems to me to be the most constant and most authorized tradition of the Catholic Church.

The essay on "Nietzsche as Mystic" sums up in outline a course given to the Theology Faculty of Lyons. Nietzscheism is nearly everywhere today, whether in its aggressive and, in appearance, triumphant form or in its corrupt forms. In illusion or in clarity, it gnaws like an acid at the consciousness of our contemporaries. It has thrown out sparks like incomparable fireworks, but already in its creator it called for a bitter perception of nihilism that disintegrates our civilization to the very degree it thinks to free itself from a yoke by rejecting the Gospel of Christ and even faith in God. It can be instructive to observe at close range, in a privileged case, just where this deadly decision leads. For the tragic destiny of Nietzsche could be an indicator of our own, and it is in this that Nietzsche may, even in his blindness, have been truly a prophet. He unveils with naïveté the eternal temptation of man, which is always resentment toward God. All this is, at bottom, much less new than he believed. And the future that all this prepares is also much less brilliant, much less "superhuman". Starting from such foundations, exaltation quickly leads to catastrophe, nor is heroism slow to change into abjection. . . . There is a lesson in this. Pragmatism, which judges things of the spirit according to ends of another sort, beating the true down over the useful, inspires us only with disgust. But the spiritual fruit can be a test of error or of spiritual truth. Its consideration can at the very least lead the way to a more complete reflection.[2]

---

[2] The numerous publications by Nietzsche (new translations, etc.) and

CHAPTER I

THE SEARCH FOR A NEW MAN

I.

It is a question of knowing if there is a Christian humanism. More than one Christian contests it, and for serious reasons: either this expression risks suggesting that Christianity would come merely to crown a humanism already wholly constituted without it, or one is anxious to recall that the essential object of revelation is not man but God and that the Christian must seek God, not himself: "*And eternal life is this, to know you, the one true God.*"[1] Unbelievers also deny the possibility of Christian humanism, and in a much more radical sense. One of them recently wrote, after having contrasted the believer Pascal, opting for God, and the unbeliever Proudhon, opting for man: "The enemy of Pascal and of Proudhon is the conciliator, who seeks to establish a rough-and-ready settlement between God and man; in a word, it is Christian humanism inhabited by

---

about Nietzsche that have been published since 1949 would obviously oblige many developments, discussions, clarifications, and so forth, if I claimed to offer anything but an essay. Let me point out, however, the works by Fr. Paul Valadier, S.J.: *Nietzsche et la critique du christianisme* (Cerf, 1974), *Essai sur la modernité, Nietzsche et Marx* (Cerf-Desclée, 1974), *Nietzsche l'athée de rigueur* (DDB, 1975), *Jésus-Christ ou Dionysos* (Desclée, 1979). It would still be of interest to read, in *La Vie spirituelle* of November 1949, pp. 339–88, the studies by Fr. Régamey, O.P., on "La Déification de l'homme selon l'athéisme mystique" and by Michel Carrouges on "La Crise de l'espérance théologale dans la littérature prométhéenne". (1983.)

[1] Jn 17:3. Cf. V. H. Debidour, *Le Miroir transparent*, p. 27. We would also agree with J. De Saussure, writing in *A l'école de Calvin*, p. 20: "It is being faithful to the Christian experience to begin by talking of God in order then to descend to man."

the spirit of compromise."[2] In reality, however, Christianity has never proposed such an option. We are not free to change it in order to make ourselves look more uncompromising in the way we profess it. The Gospel was "good news" for man, and it still is today. Christianity does not deny man in order to affirm God. Nor does it seek a compromise between them. In fact, its revelation of God was a promotion of man: that is inscribed in history.[3] And under a thousand forms it repeats with Saint Irenaeus, as the expression of his most profound thought: *Gloria Dei, vivens homo*.[4] As André Blanchet wrote recently in a wonderfully symbolical formula: "The Man-God did not choose between his two natures."[5] So let us drop the equivocal, perhaps in fact too weak, expression "Christian humanism", or let us reserve it for designating certain forms, certain more or less debatable successes offered us by history.[6] It is nevertheless necessary to maintain that Christianity professes a lofty idea of man, that it defends his nobility and wants to assure his salvation.

This Christian idea of man, however, has not been delivered, complete, in some formula that can be analyzed for our purposes. While implied in concrete examples in the sources of revelation, in the Church's attitude, in the teachings of her

---

[2] Aimé Patri, "Proudhon et Dieu", in *Critique*, vols. 3–4 (1946), p. 271.

[3] Cf. Gaston Fessard, *Pax nostra*, pp. 39–40.

[4] Saint Irenaeus, *Adversus hæreses*. It is also necessary to understand well that this "life" of man of which Irenaeus often speaks is not some natural and earthly blossoming: it is the very life that he receives from God.

[5] André Blanchet, "La Religion d'André Malraux", in *Études*, July 1949, p. 43. Ibid., pp. 48–49: With good reason, Malraux praises Christian art for having made the first individual faces appear.

[6] Let us nevertheless observe that much ignorance—or impudence—is necessary for one such recent author to dare to maintain that "Christian humanism" is a new invention by believers as the worst sort of apologetic; he does so in order to denounce the "tactics" of the Church, which is supposedly trying today to provide in this way "new clothes for her old mythology". On the various "humanisms" of our time, there is an excellent chronicle by Henri Niel in *Rythmes du monde* (1948), pp. 98–102

doctors and in the spontaneous reactions of her saints, it has never appeared in a discernable, complete form in itself. We can say of it something similar to what, in the great novel by Roger Martin du Gard, Abbé Vicart says to Antoine Thibaut about the Catholic religion. And this comment, which is addressed to an unbeliever, can be made as well by any believer to himself, since he is always so far from having penetrated the depths of his faith or from having drawn the consequences of it: "It is something completely different, my friend, believe me, it is much, much more than you have ever, up till now, been given to glimpse."[7]

Far from claiming to grasp the whole of it, then, without even seeking to gather together the essence of the rich material that would be provided us by searching through nineteen centuries of Christian tradition, we would merely wish to try shedding light on several more current aspects—aspects which the movement of our century proposes more forcefully to our attention or, on the other hand, which we have all but failed to use in opposition to its most insidious temptations. *Opportune, importunate*: Is this not always the twofold way in which the Christian truth is present? Rather than proceeding to the contemplation of a picture, then, we are faced with a confrontation. Prepared, aroused already by a series of technical and social transformations of which previous centuries offer scarcely any examples, by progress and also by catastrophes previously unknown to us,[8] a new man is sought today: What does our faith say to us about him? In what way will it aid in his birth? From what illusions and what dangers will it protect him? What perspectives will it unveil to him? How, in the final

---

[7] *Les Thibault*, part six, "La Mort du père".

[8] Cf. Pope Pius XII, allocution to the Sacred College on December 24, 1944: On the outcome of this war, "it will not be merely geographical structures . . . that will change their appearance, but it will be men themselves, men in the first place, who will be transformed." *Acta Apost. Sedis*, January 28, 1945, p. 7.

analysis, will it save him from defeat, inviting him by means of the best paths to a higher success? The reply to these questions cannot itself be complete. We will try only to sketch it in its broadest generality.[9] In doing so, moreover, we will not make appeal to any original principle, nor will we seek in it any attractive novelty. Christianity cannot be a "fashionable" doctrine: that is the difference between it and doctrines that come and go. Its eternal newness does not strike one at first glance, and in order to recognize it one must use other methods than the reading of a few journal articles or, indeed, a methodically pursued intellectual reflection, or even the patient application of "Christian principles" to the problems of the day.

2.

We have been witnessing for some time, not only extraordinary events that are drastically changing the face of the world, but *one* event in depth, which is changing something in man himself. This is the fact which we can take as our point of departure. In this "universe in a state of psychic evolution" which is ours, as fixed as it may have been in its essential framework since the appearance of the human race, consciousness is raised through moments, as it were, with the perception of new dimensions and values. Now it seems very likely that we have been in one of these moments of awakening and transformation. A new humanism? That is undoubtedly to say too little; a kind of new man is being constituted, transforming at one stroke the idea that man has had more or less up to now of himself, of his history, of his destiny. In idea, therefore, as well as in fact, it is something like an extraordinary "shedding of skins".

---

[9] Some useful considerations on this same subject will be found in *L'Homme nouveau. Études de pastorale*, vol. 1 (Louvain, 1942), by R. Aubert, C. Moeller, A. Minon and A. Dondeyne.

There have, of course, been many changes since the early ages of our humanity up till the present! But, during the whole course of the historical period, these changes appeared to be circumscribed, in many respects, within rather restricted limits. There were, in particular, at least apparently, periods of ebb and flow; there were alternations between civilization and barbarism, between the foundation and the collapse of empires. Civilization left man close to nature, participating in its rhythm, happy to have attained, like nature, certain moments of fullness and fruitfulness, resigned in advance to falls as fatal as the succession of seasons or as the turns of the wheel of fortune. From the time of his awakening, he was already, to be sure, this impatient animal, discontent with his lot, ready for uprisings and revolts. . . . But these were only sporadic and localized phenomena, like a sudden rise of a fever; not the regular steps of a planned march, not the progressive phases of a conscious and methodical action.

Now here in our own age a new ambition is born. An *idée-force* has emerged. Man has, little by little, raised his head against this destiny that was weighing him down. He wants to escape the fatalities that, from time immemorial, he had learned to believe were invincible. How has this been produced? Under the influence of some distant causes, thanks to the concourse of some favorable conditions? We are not going to analyze it. It will be enough for us to discern, at the foundation of this transformation, three facts of consciousness among others, three simple, very general facts, about the very relative newness, whose whole importance stems from their increasingly vast expansion and their increasingly systematic character.

The first of these facts, as well as the most general and the most banal, is *faith in science*. Built up by experimental research and having achieved its precision thanks to mathematics,[10] pos-

---

[10] "Modern science is the daughter of mathematics; it was born the day algebra acquired enough strength and flexibility to embrace reality and to take it into the net of its calculations" (Bergson).

itive science was not born yesterday. After the long eclipse that followed its beginnings in the Greek and Hellenistic age, it was reborn in the Middle Ages, particularly beginning with the fourteenth century, in order to triumph at the time of Galileo, Descartes and Pascal. But still in the seventeenth century, it was often considered only as the means of satisfying a noble curiosity or of procuring some practical advantages. Despite Descartes, faith in science as having to assure the happiness or the greatness of humanity, worship of research as being the highest ideal that can be set, is much more recent. Moreover, in its beginnings, positive science conquered only a limited field: after that of astronomy, that of the physical sciences. Chemistry and biology really began to be added to it only during the eighteenth century. Then it was the turn of the human sciences: political economy, sociology, psychology. A little more than one century ago, in his celebrated *Cours de philosophie positive*, Auguste Comte proclaimed the advent of the "positive age" (succeeding, he said, the theological and metaphysical ages) through the foundation of "social physics", or "sociology".[11] This was the great novelty—then, it is true, much more imagined than effective, but today very real—man himself became, like external nature, the object of positive science, submitted to the same methods of investigation, and, consequently, it should be readily added, for the first time able finally to know himself, since positive science is the only rigorous type of knowledge, expelling all dreams, all imaginary visions of empty religions and philosophies. Despite its claims, the positivism of the last century still represented a capitulation of science before man. Comte had reproached all "theologism" for having "given man the advantage over the world". But, fearing what he called "a blind and dispersive specialization" and subordinating analysis to synthesis as well as progress to order, he had ended by de-

---

[11] Cf. Edmond Walbecq, *Essai critique sur la religion d'Auguste Comte*, 1947 thesis (Theology Faculty, Catholic Institute of Paris); part one: "Les Présupposés de la religion de l'Humanité".

manding that his disciples, the priests of the future, renounce the pursuit of an impossible objectivity, in order to sanction ideal concepts that responded to the needs of the heart. He had gone so far as to bring back the fetishism of the "primitives".[12] Precisely those who had not followed him on this path had not attained perfect positivity. A vague mysticism still protected humanity from the attacks of knowledge; it constituted a kind of "sentimental entity"[13] in which those now living had to be resolved. This subjectivism having finally been reduced, today the whole man, it is said, is integrated into science. . . .

Now—and this is the second fact—this science is not only theoretical science, the more rigorous and more precise modern analogue of what the aesthetical contemplation of the cosmos was for the ancients. It is an "operating science". It is completely *oriented toward the possession of the world*. It is said that the age of purely critical as well as of purely retrospective thoughts, just as of supposedly disinterested systems, is over. The sciences of the past were themselves only a springboard. Man has a practical end, and he looks ahead. It is no longer for him a matter of tasting some speculative intoxication but, according to the end already glimpsed by Bacon and soon clearly assigned by Descartes, of making himself "master and possessor of the forces of nature". Technique thus no longer appeared to be an inferior genre, like a utilization more or less refused by a science fearing to be degraded: it was recognized as its necessary extension.[14] Knowledge of the laws of the universe is, in the hands of man, a tool to be used in acting on it. And the range of the Cartesian dream is revealed to be increasingly

---

[12] Cf. above, Part Two, Chapter 3, section 2: "The Priesthood of the Scientists".

[13] Henri Wallon, lecture at the Palais de Chaillot, June 10, 1945, for the inauguration of the *Encyclopédie de la Renaissance française*.

[14] Let us add, with M. Guilbaud, this further comment: "It is in the conquest itself that knowledge is achieved. The traditional division into pure science and applied science is subsiding from day to day": *Science et technique*, in the review of the twenty-fourth university days, Easter 1947.

vast, at the same time as this dream is made increasingly attain-
able, to the degree that science is developed and monopolizes
the human domain. The great utopians of the beginning of the
nineteenth century revived it. The mission of man, according
to Fourier, is the "management of the Globe". "Everything by
industry, everything for it": such was the watchword given by
Saint-Simon, whose "new Christianity" looked like an "indus-
trialism". And we know that one of Auguste Comte's slogans
was: "To know, so as to provide". The idea of a new value and
a new significance of human work sprang up everywhere and
gradually conquered minds. In this, capitalism and socialism,
those two great antagonistic forces, were in agreement: they
were like the two faces of the same movement that carried
away the entire century. A new type of civilization was conceived and began to be achieved: the industrial type of civilization, a civilization of work. The work of Proudhon and that
of Karl Marx, just like the activity of the old Saint-Simonians,
converged in its formation. Man felt destined to organize the
planet with a view to its maximal output. He undertook to
transform the world through his work.[15]

But, since man, too, had become an object of science like
all the rest, why would what was true for the external world
be any less true for man himself? The dream of technology
and its first major achievements coincided, moreover, with a
sudden awareness of social unity and with a powerful surge of
social aspirations which were also something new in humanity. To the transformation of nature, they thought, must thus
be added *the transformation of society*. Social science gave rise
to "social engineers". And, since it was the whole man who
had become the object for himself, it was the whole man, too,
who was henceforth going to be manipulated and worked like
an object. One after the other, an applied biology, an applied
psychology, an applied sociology were founded. . . . Through
science, man was going to make himself "master and possessor

---

[15] Cf. Jean Lacroix, *Socialisme?*, "Le Forum" series (E.L.F., 1946).

of the human forces". A whole "technology" of man developed. And this is the third fact.

Let me cite merely two examples. On the one hand, eugenics. The practical idea of a methodically organized "human selection" dawned. Thanks to progress in biology, man could now direct his own biological evolution, and he had to do so if he wanted to be on top of the tasks that awaited him. It would not be a question only of negative measures, like preventing certain undesirable procreation through processes such as sterilization; more must be dared: it was necessary to produce in a positive way the appearance of a superior race; and, in order to do so, to specialize breeders, to refine methods of fertilization, and so forth. Or, another example: political propaganda, so necessary for draining all individual energies toward one great goal, would be based on a systematic exploitation of the fundamental principles of experimental psychology, in particular those of Pavlov's theory of "conditioned reflexes".

The understanding of the behavioral mechanisms brings with it the possibility of manipulating them at will. From then on, one can set off definite reactions from people in directions determined in advance. Of course the possibility of influencing men had already existed from the time man existed, spoke and had relations with his peers; but this was a possibility that worked blindly and that required great experience or special aptitudes: this was, in a way, an art. Here we had this art becoming a science, which could calculate, predict and act according to controllable rules. An immense step forward loomed in the sociological domain.[16]

With this third fact, if we take it in all its complexity, one of the great novelties of our epoch takes shape, fraught with promise and danger: humanity discovered itself, *grasped* itself,

[16] Sergei Chakhotin, *Le Viol des foules par la propagande politique*, French trans. (Paris: Gallimard, 1939), p. 32. The author seems to think that, if the end of propaganda is sound, the latter, remaining unchanged in its processes, would no longer constitute a violation: pp. 43, 113 and 121.

as an object, in the twofold sense of this word "grasp", that is, both to understand by means of one's intelligence and to take hold of with one's hands. With a view to maximal output, it took charge of itself. *It was going to forge its own destiny.* Up until then, thrown into an adventure of which it had neither control nor even, to tell the truth, awareness, it had let itself go, the plaything of obscure forces. So it had not made progress. It had turned, in a way, on itself. This is what had now been set in motion. Its evolution would henceforth be induced, directed, unified. To what progress could it not, then, lay claim! It was in all fields that she said, with Julian Huxley: "It substituted the possibility of conscious control of evolution for the previous mechanism of the blind chances of variation. . . ."[17] Having attained, it thought, mastery of biological, psychic and social phenomena, it had no doubt of being able henceforth to act on itself with the same success that it had already known in the applications of the material sciences.[18] And in those who, being aware of this great fact, wanted to work to increase it, a double tendency arose toward elements that had formerly often been contradictory but which were now united to attain their culmination together: a tendency at once organizational and revolutionary. The two words of the positivist slogan are too weak to describe them; they do not say "order and progress", but "revolution and organization", or rather "organizing revolution". For this was the end of the fantasies, the competi-

---

[17] Julian Huxley, *Essays of a Biologist* (New York: Alfred A. Knopf, 1929), p. x, preface (written in 1923).

[18] Ibid., p. viii: "Furthermore, as the grasp of principles in physico-chemical science led speedily to an immense new extension both of knowledge and of control, so it is not to be doubted that like effects will spring from like causes in biology. . . . Applied physics and chemistry bring more grist to the mill; applied biology will also be capable of changing the mill itself. The possibilities of physiological improvement, of the better combination of existing psychical faculties, of the education of old faculties to new heights, and of the discovery of new faculties altogether—all this is no utopian silliness, but is bound to come about if science continues her current progress."

tion, the squandering of liberal anarchy. It was also the end of romantic, sentimental and libertarian revolts. Only a powerful, realistic and, when need be, hard initiative, unifying the efforts of all to the service of a common plan, would permit humanity to break with its routines and its servitudes in order to construct itself. . . .[19]

3.

That this belief in the power of rational organization was, at least in part, a compensatory phenomenon, in a century in which certain irrational forces were unleashed more violently than ever—and in which the problem of the irrational imposed itself increasingly in all orders of thought—is very possible. It was in this way that we once saw theories of the universal power of the popes develop at a time when the rise of nationalities and the rebirth of the ancient public law brought about a decline of the papacy on the political level. That such a belief penetrated large sectors at the very moment when a serious methodological crisis was opening up in the sciences of man is a fact that seems rather clear. That it was expressed, at

---

[19] Underlying these views, we discern in a certain number a new conception of thought itself. The latter would be by essence constructive, not contemplative; creative, not representative. Its essential function would not be to bring out as objectively as possible a fixed, preestablished order of truths and values but to create new values and to accomplish them in deeds. A conception prepared, or rather already formulated, in the last century by Marx and Nietzsche. Agreement on so fundamental an idea by these two antagonistic thinkers is an indication of its powerful influence. We know the thinking of Marx on Hegelianism, the final end of all speculative philosophy, and the famous declaration at the end of the Theses on Feuerbach: "Up to the present, philosophers have interpreted the world. . . ." As for Nietzsche, the "death of God" marked for him the end of any idea of an objective True or Good. Cf. above, Part One, Chapter 1, sections 3 and 4. F. Alquié has recently risen in opposition to these tendencies: cf. "Une Philosophie de l'ambiguïté", in *Fontaine*, vol. 59, p. 48.

times even by authentic scholars, in a variety of ever-recurring scientistic systems, likely to discourage the most sympathetic examination by the simplism and self-complacency that were displayed there, cannot be denied. That, in fact, the first results of the action that this belief determined proved to be less than encouraging; that, for example, new inventions immediately became engines of death; that so far man has still not been able to master mechanization; that he has succeeded most of the time only in increasing his anguish and in multiplying his sorrows—all this is still only too true. But we will not pay too much attention to this. Is it necessary to stare at the sun for long to be convinced of its brightness? The greatest ideas seem miserable when they have passed through petty minds. The most incontestable innovations do not find adequate interpreters at first glance. And after all, it is not happiness that man seeks, it is not pleasure.[20] Besides, a priori there is no objection to trusting in time. A great experience does not bear fruit immediately, it is natural for it to bring about some disruption at first, and a few initial disappointments do not constitute a peremptory argument against it. Does not the fact that all this atrocious misery has not deterred him from it, or, if one prefers, the fact that this formidable jolt has not awakened him from his dream—does not this fact alone already speak in favor of the profound instinct that propels him? The two wars whose bruises we bear have been two heavy blows of the battering ram against an edifice of dreams: they have shaken the edifice, not destroyed it, and the crisis that was opened in many consciences has often only increased its hold. So it is not the banal, although assuredly powerful, objection of the pessimist that deserves to hold us back at first. Based on a somber present and on still more sinister predictions, this objection is in fact, swept away in many by hope, and all the sarcasm that it arouses leaves this hope intact. This is enough to make us take

---

[20] "There is nothing for which man is less made than happiness or of which he tires more quickly" (Paul Claudel, *Le Soulier de satin*).

it seriously and to make the trouble of examining the solidity of the ideas that form it worthwhile.

But, precisely, after having given a sceptical smile, should one not become indignant? Is it not in fact a forbidden dream that is at issue here? A demoniacal ambition? If catastrophe must be predicted for it, is this not because man is in the process of "biting into the forbidden fruit", of usurping a role that cannot be his, of upsetting the order of the cosmos, of encroaching on the rights of God? Several have wondered this. With some, it is scarcely more than a reflex of timidity or nostalgia for the forms of life and culture whose undeniable charm have vanished forever from our eyes: through the effects of a retrospective illusion, the price paid for these forms of life is often forgotten. With others, an exacerbated romanticism develops an opposition in principle to any technical civilization and substitutes for the outdated idol of progress the "new idol of the curse of progress".[21] Some have given proof of so complete an ignorance of the scientific movement that it is not worth the trouble to discuss it with them. Certain others, however, who do discern the fullness of this movement wish to see in it only an arrogant restlessness. These, without cursing science itself or even technology, condemn the dream of construction they inspire. They consider this will to transform the world, society and even man himself to be an even more monstrous collective revival of the crime of Prometheus. They persistently remind man then that he is a creature, that he is a part of a universe with laws that are independent of his mind just as of his will, that his first duty is to submit in all things to the real, to the object, and to respect the order established by Providence. This traditionalist state of mind, which was not born yesterday, is still alive today. From it proceed those pamphlets denouncing in every respect what is being sought in our time and characterizing it as so many signs of degeneration.[22] This is, for

---

[21] Guilbaud, p. 46.

[22] Cf. Marcel de Corte, in *Chemins du monde*, Civilization (1947), pp. 115-

example, what is being expressed in the following remarks: "It is not we who have made reality, it is God who created it, and we ourselves can only enrich our intelligence, which has created nothing in knowing this reality as it is, which is to say, as God created it. Submission to the real is by definition submission of the created intelligence to God, the Creator of this reality."[23] An excellent principle, but here, at least insofar as we can judge, how poorly applied! Does man truly never have anything to do but record? Does the constancy of natural laws prevent any action upon reality? And is the social universe, such as it is constituted today before our eyes, truly the work of the creator God in the same sense as the physical universe? And do we truly have no hold on the latter universe itself?

Already in the last century, all those who either lacked imagination or lacked any trust in human effort, or who also at times lacked generosity, wanted to maintain a historical situation in which they claimed to see an eternal order and appealed to Providence and to its sacred laws. It was in the name of "providential laws", of "providential order", that they rebelled without discernment against all attempts at better social organization. Any intervention of public powers with a view to suppressing the most blatant abuses was declared utopian or sacrilegious. Any aspiration for more justice was frustrated. In the name of these laws, of this order, they canonized economic

---

23: "Humanity experiments with its planetary affinity and changes its direction through a more intense awareness of its promotion to the universal. This is precisely the crucial sign of decline. Any civilization that universalizes itself is marked with the seal of death and finds itself attacked by a sudden euphoric awareness similar to the one that lays hold of the human body as a prey to 'artificial paradises'. . . . Man is no longer linked to the world as to an end that transcends him. . . . Primacy of the spirit over matter according to an emasculated Christianity. Everywhere the 'civilization' of uprooted man proceeds by breaking in to dissociate the world . . .", etc. Perhaps it would be better not to take all this seriously.

[23] XXX. "Connaître le communisme", *Cahiers d'études sociales et doctrinales* (Haumont, 1946), p. 10.

liberalism, one of the sins of our modern world.[24] Is there not today a similar state of mind that engenders this bitter, unilateral criticism of the paths on which our civilization has embarked? We will certainly not deny that there are in fact many pitfalls; the claims of a certain psycho-technology can wreak devastation, and the two examples cited above of eugenics and propaganda are sufficient to give us a hint of the seriousness of the human problems at stake.[25] Neither must we confuse with such a state of mind the reaction of certain spiritual leaders who are distressed about disregard of the one thing necessary, even if this reaction happens to be expressed in excessive or ill-chosen formulas. As someone has written with good reason, "in order to maintain Christianity's line of sight, it is necessary periodically for us to listen to these abrupt prophets, who are sensitive in particular to the force of doctrine, to the narrowness of the path, to the mystery of the truths, to the intransigence of calls and to the character of dramatic imminence which the Word of God, death, sin, judgment take on for each of us, at every moment of time".[26] Shaken by this, Christians are in less danger of letting themselves "conform to the times", as the Apostle says, and of forgetting that the life of anyone who wants to be faithful will, until the end of time, be "contradiction and struggle". And is there not often cause as well to react against "a monstrous economy, in which man, whom the thinkers had already separated from heaven, is equally uprooted from the

---

[24] Cf., among other papal documents, the encyclical *Quadragesimo anno*.

[25] On the problem of eugenics, see P. de Saint-Seine in *Études*, June 1947, with other references; cf. Dr. Hermann Muckermann, "L'Anthropologie appliquée", in *Études*, October 1947. On the difference between apostolate and propaganda, see the lecture by Msgr. de Solages to the Congrès des Œuvres de Bordeaux (Easter 1947), reproduced in *L'Union*, June 1947. On the illusion that "purely and simply transposes the technical notion of the material order to the social order", see J. Vialatoux, "L'illusion matérialiste du libéralisme économique", in *Philosophie économique*, pp. 55–60.

[26] Emmanuel Mounier, "Pour un temps d'apocalypse", in *Esprit*, January 1947, p. 7.

earth"?[27] But given all that, is it advisable always to oppose "the progress of material life and social organization with a kind of bad prophetic humor"?[28] If we return next to the plane of intellectual analysis, we would indeed have to admit that the traditionalist refusal, in the absolute form it sometimes takes, is inspired by a conception of the world and an ideal of wisdom that are much more a heritage of ancient thought in decline than a corollary of the Christian faith. Similarly, the excessive fear of seeing man's organizing effort cut him off from nature, in the midst of which he will have to continue to live, this fear is rather the reflex of an Eastern (and perhaps pagan) prejudice than that of Christian scruples. Man has his limits, inscribed in the first place in his body. Unrecognized, they call themselves rudely to his attention. But, to permit ourselves a paradoxical expression, these limits are not enough to define him.

This is because, in reality, Providence is not Destiny: it is the force that has conquered it. Submission to Providence is not abandonment to Fatality. Man was not placed in the universe as one thing among other things. Nor has he been installed there in order to enjoy it passively, as if everything had been achieved first without him. He was created, Genesis tell us, "in the image of God". This is the first teaching of the Bible about man. In the image of God, is this to say according, first of all, to the image of the Creator? He should then imitate him in his manner of dominating nature. This trait is undoubtedly not the only one, nor the most important; but it is, so to speak, the most immediate, and it is one of those which the tradition of the Antiochian Fathers liked most to develop.

> Man alone is in the image of God. . . . Theodore of Mopsuestia discovered this privilege in the faculty which man has of being, in his turn, in a certain sense, a creator. Incapable of bringing natures themselves into existence, he can, in imitation of his cre-

---

[27] *Dieu vivant*, cahier 7 (1947), p. 10.

[28] Emmanuel Mounier, in *Foi en Jésus-Christ et monde d'aujourd'hui* (1944), p. 84.

ator, organize, combine as he pleases the elements that are placed at his disposition, produce objects great and small (houses, ships, cities), which had not existed previously. . . .[29]

"It was necessary", Claudel comments, "for nature to hear, to its very depths, this order that we are bringing to it in the name of its Creator."[30] Authentically biblical and Christian, the idea could nevertheless not be fully exploited as long as man did not have in hand the tool which science has just given him. But, in principle, he knew it already. In two little words, which became so much more evocative after we learned to know our distant past and the first stages of our history, Saint Thomas Aquinas here opens to us a great perspective: "*Habet homo rationem et manum.*"[31] Reason and hand: if the Creator has endowed us with this twofold, marvelously constructed instrument, was it simply to allow us to resolve in a roundabout way problems that nature solves directly for the animal? To replace, for example, the missing protection of fur with the protection of woven clothing? Is it merely to endow a higher animal with a few facilities, securities, supplementary pleasures, all the while still keeping him enclosed within the same narrow circle? Assuredly not. Through this indefinitely fruitful association of brain and hand, man is called to pursue the work of the One who made him. No, he has not been installed, blissfully or miserably, in a ready-made world: he cooperates in its genesis. When he created man, Scripture says again, God "rested on the seventh day". This is because henceforth he had someone to take charge of the rest.[32]

---

[29] Robert Devreesse, *Essai sur Théodore de Mopsueste* (Citta del Vaticano, 1948), p. 13. We should recall, too, this other verse from Genesis: "Multiply", God says, "fill the earth and subdue it" (Gen 1:28). And, besides, how could man be faithful very long to the first part of the order if he were unfaithful to the second?

[30] Paul Claudel, *Conversations dans le Loir-et-Cher*, p. 259.

[31] Saint Thomas, *Summa theologiæ*, Prima, q. 91, a. 3, ad 2m.

[32] We have in mind here the changes that have happened particularly in

We hear talk of a transgression of the laws of nature, of a perverse will to tear man away from the rhythm of nature, of a veritable "denaturation" that would be the evil par excellence. These criticisms go too far. To be effective as well as just, they should start by recognizing that there is no systematic discredit to be cast on the artificial. The latter is not necessarily "a counterfeit made by the creature of the work of the Creator". In a certain sense, as someone has written, "the nature of man is artifice."[33] And if material progress often ends badly, even if it is carried out in evil, if it is sometimes promoted in a spirit that

---

practical behavior with respect to the universe. There would be reason to make similar observations on the subject of the changes that have occurred in its representation since the successive discoveries of space and time. Both changes are, moreover, closely tied together. —Nothing is served by clinging to all that might remain in our imaginations or in our sentimental reactions of a time when the universe seemed such a perfect sphere, with harmonious dimensions, hierarchical circles in an eternal order, in which each being had his place and his "degree" in a tiered dwelling, his impassable limit; whose "empyrean sky" formed the circumference and of which man occupied the center. Another movement besides the circular entered into this world; it stretched it, moved it off center; it ruined the harmony that had soothed us for so long. A disconcerting movement, whose law still escapes us: a movement that is apt to make us dizzy, but which we can deny no more than we can deny the sun. Of course, that does not, as many have believed, mean a change in the essential laws of the spirit and the radical ruin of the ancient edifices of thought. Nevertheless, it would be a lack of clearsightedness to fail to understand the profound transformations that result from it in the economy of our knowledge; it would be a lack of virility to linger over a nostalgic regret for the images that it has dissipated, as if over a lost paradise; a lack of vitality to experience its repercussions passively, and as if reluctantly, without cooperating in it ourselves; a lack of faith, finally, to dread the new conditions that are thus created for the awareness of our relations with God. Of course, too, it will always remain a natural symbolism, founded on sensible knowledge, and which no science will affect. But on the plane of knowledge, it is not by seeking to make survive in us a past that can no longer be reborn—and which was in no way tied in its origins to Christian revelation—that we will sustain and develop our faith. It is by taking up its new situations and by anticipating its new syntheses. In this natural domain, the words of the Apostle also apply: "*Quæ retro sunt obliviscens. . . .*"

[33] E. Mounier, p. 15: "The faithful admirers of nature have reason to recall

is not the spirit of good will, is it for all that itself an evil? Has not reflection taught us to dissociate many a synthesis, many an alliance that was not based in the right? And will we condemn, for example, the effort to understand the faith because, in fact, this has nearly always led at first to heresy? Similarly, does the bad use of science condemn scientific effort, even in its social extension? Besides, both of these efforts are inevitable. We are pushed into them by a law of nature and by the need to get out of ever-new dead ends far more than we take the free initiative to do so. Man, who "cannot keep from thinking", cannot at will cease to progress in his technology.

Let us go farther. One may discover a certain kind of opposition, in concrete reality, between the scientific mind and the Christian mind, just as one discovers it between reflection and prayer, between a social orientation and the expectation of the kingdom, and so forth. But if one considers even briefly the fact that man, in his present condition of evolving, is inhabited not only by the two irreconcilable forces of good and evil but by a multiplicity of other opposite movements, tendencies that are at once legitimate and incompatible with each other in their original form, one will no longer conclude right off that one must be sacrificed to the other, that one must be condemned in the name of the other. That would perhaps be the way to lose them both. One will no longer despair of finding some dynamic accord between them, of gradually bringing out of them a harmony of tension. Everything in man seems at first to be antagonistic. Universal war is our original condition and the companion of each of our steps. The most authentic forces, the most essential calls are not in spontaneous concurrence. We

---

that the human condition has not been stretched in any sense and that some time is necessary for humanity to assimilate its own transformations. But the systematic discredit that they cast on the artificial stems from a radically falsified vision of the characteristics of man himself. One could say, with only a slight twist of the words, that the nature of man is artifice. —From this point of view, one can say that European man, around the dawn of modern times, finished a kind of uterine life. . . ."

are often torn apart by them. But it is this very fact that makes us move forward.

That which is true of the physical world is also true for the social world. To transform the first by technology would be nothing if this work did not end in a progressive transformation of society itself. Let us even say that in this above all consists man's faculty as worker, which thus seems in a way, still in the image of his creator, *causa sui*.[34] This is not, to be sure, to criticize unjustly those who did not recognize at first glance the greatness and the truth of such an idea, when it began obscurely to take possession of the human race. Their distrust did not always stem from egotistical motives, even unconsciously, and often they would have needed a rare faculty of discernment to free this idea from the very thick coating that enveloped it. Yet, in the way in which it is all too often invoked, "providentialism" is not a Christian truth. It is not to encroach on Providence to work to modify an order of things which itself is explained in large part by history and by human activity. Certainly finding support from the past, recourse to experience, the sense of tradition are always necessary things, especially when the projects of reform are more radical or when the views of the future are bolder and more grandiose. But let them not be distorted into sacred principles of routine! It is as blasphemous, if not more so, to cover with the name of God things that are simply human, perhaps too human, as it is to utter a cry of revolt against the One who is falsely presented as the eternal guarantor.[35]

---

[34] We are not speaking here of the sense in which man can also be called *causa sui* through the use he makes of his freedom, as Fr. André Bremond explains very well, "Réflexions sur l'homme dans la Philosophie bergsonienne", *Archives de philosophie*, vol. 17, no. 1 (1947), pp. 126–34.

[35] It is in this sense that one can denounce with Proudhon a "myth of Providence" and speak with him of a "methodical atheism" in the work of social reform that always needs to be taken up again. Proudhon also said: "It is for man to take the place of God on the chariot of destinies." Without being blind to the impassioned negations of their author, one could also see in these words

A certain criticism of the appeals to Providence is thus imperative for several reasons, in the name of faith in the true God. Several contemporary thinkers, violently opposed, moreover, to Christianity—it is enough to name Marx and Nietzsche—have liked comparing their work to that of Prometheus. They have proudly proclaimed themselves the spiritual heirs of the rebel hero. We will not let ourselves be manipulated by the adversary to the point of blindly taking the opposite position of his in everything, leaving him thus the full benefit of the sound ideas that he mixes in with his rebellion. The fable of Prometheus, let us consider, is not a Bible story. The rebellion against the gods is not, ipso facto, a rebellion against God. Our God is a jealous God: but his jealousy is quite different from that of the gods in fables.[36] He does not envy his creatures their fire or any of the inventions that followed. On the contrary, a dominion is thereby extended, a construction is thereby achieved that is conformable with his will. Time is given to man in order to perfect himself within the temporal order, and man is right to want to escape all kinds of cosmic or social servitudes with a view to a freer, more humane existence. We do not at all have to mix Christianity closely with initiatives that are situated on a purely natural plane; we do not at all

the expression of that right idea, that, from a certain moment of its history, humanity accedes, in some point of itself, to the reflex awareness of its future and of the unity that it must form, and which, from that moment, must be organized in consequence and be promoted itself. It is necessary to subscribe neither to Proudhon's metaphysical conceptions nor to his economic program to be of the same opinion with him on such an observation, which is expressed elsewhere in less paradoxical terms.

[36] This was recognized in the last century by an often less fortunate author, Edgar Quinet, in the preface to his poem "Prométhée, trilogie dramatique": Prometheus revolted against the power of the established gods; he created humanity in opposition to them. . . . The pagan divinities put him in chains without subduing him. On the Caucasus he prophesied their fall; he awaited a new God who, by overturning them, would deliver him." Cf. "De la fable de Prométhée considérée dans ses rapports avec le christianisme", *Revue des deux-mondes*, vol. 13 (1838), p. 339.

have to involve it in some specific form of political regime or social revolution. Every person can differ with others in his opinion about these things, and even those who are called the "social Catholics", who claim to be the most faithful to the social directives of the teaching Church, do not at all, as we know, have any unanimous program. With all the more reason, most do not consider that there now exists, or that there will ever be constituted, a "Catholic socio-economic system" on the basis of Gospel principles, as someone has unfortunately written. They judge with good reason that the Church does not at all have to "take her part in the quarrels and passions of the century"[37] or to tie her cause to essentially contingent institutions. But perhaps we should often recognize more boldly, not only in words but through our very action and through a certain taste for this action, that our faith approves and encourages this effort of liberation and humanization without dictating its paths. Perhaps we could take more to heart the initiatives born in the very midst of our Church so that the spiritual life might never be a private luxury but bread offered at large to all the children of God. We would, moreover, thereby avoid many temptations and many disappointments for the most generous among us. Let us not forget, however, that Christianity was from the outset—and that it was effectively, because it was much more—a "revolt against destiny".[38]

4.

There could thus be—let us dare this paradox—a Christian Prometheus. In what degree and in what circumstances is another matter, which the following proposes to clarify some-

---

[37] Daniel Pèzeril, "Les Tendances catholiques d'aujourd'hui", *Le Semeur*, 1949, p. 591.

[38] "As for us", said Tatian, for example, *Discourse to the Greeks*, chap. 9, "we are above destiny."

what. But we must first ask ourselves the question: Is our modern Prometheus Christian? Unfortunately, on the whole, we know only too well that the answer is No. The preceding reflections, if they are valid against certain ill-considered criticisms, are nevertheless far from justifying it.

A mysterious law, which one is tempted to believe inevitable, is once again verified before our eyes. Does not the search for a perceived good need to have been stimulated, not only by the observation of deficits or of real needs, but also by the hidden or manifest action of some resentment?[39] Does not the discovery of new values entail the depreciation of other, perhaps more fundamental values? Does it not engender, as modest and as precarious as it might be, an intoxication, and does not the passionate attention one brings to it make one forget all the rest, which is to say, often the essential? Is one not then tempted to reject what one should, on the contrary, deepen and purify? Does not the new power that man feels being born within him incite him, by reawakening and reinforcing the attraction of ancient rebellions, to a false effort of creation, less concerned to collaborate in the divine work than to mimic it and reverse it? In this way ambiguous situations are begun and crises are prepared whose outcomes cannot be foretold with any certainty.

This is very much the case for this advent of a new man which we have briefly described. In one whole part of its active element, humanity no longer sees anything today but its effort toward earthly construction. The successes or the promises of technology have gone to its head. A kind of Dionysian intoxication has seized it. On the other hand, and at the same time, in his desire for a liberation whose instrument must be technology, man goes to the point of renouncing everything that

---

[39] This is what in fact Louis Doucy has shown, for example, for the doctrines of natural law and for the various scientific disciplines applied to the study of the family, which end by suppressing their object: *Introduction à une connaissance de la famille*, pp. 22, 72–82, etc.

makes his condition dependent and would like, so to speak,
not to be born, that is, he would like to exist without having
had to be born. His refusal of providentialism hardens or is
distorted into a rejection of divine paternity. Finally, reversing
the movement that was for millennia the spontaneous movement of his intelligence, instead of seeing in visible and tangible
realities so many signs of the invisible kingdom to which he
believed himself destined, he no longer wanted to recognize
in any of these conceptions any spiritual order except ground-
less symbols, definitively outdated today, of the sole reality of
this world which science is at last handing over to him. After
having, he thinks, long projected into a mystical heaven the
social reality he was living or imagining, he affirms that he has
reached adult age by reducing everything to the earthly plane
and by explaining everything by it. So the essential reproach he
addresses to the Christian mystery is similar to the one which
Origen once addressed in the name of this mystery to the Jewish religion: he reproaches the figure for its refusal to disappear
in the face of the truth that fulfills it. All theology is for him
reducible to an anthropology.[40] Scientific intoxication, ontological rebellion, noetic reduction: such are, in sum, the three
temptations by which the progress of our age is accompanied,
temptations to which it has largely succumbed and which have
opened the spiritual crisis in which we are struggling. Such are
the three elements that, combining to have an effect in all of
life, form what could be called the *organizing scientism*. Already
in 1937, the Rev. Fr. Teilhard de Chardin noted it with respect
to Marxism. "What created the temptation of neo-Marxism
for an elite", he wrote, "was far less its humanitarian message
than its vision of a totalitarian civilization, strongly connected
with the cosmic powers of matter. The true name of commu-

---

[40] We are familiar with Feuerbach's doctrine on this subject; cf. Pierre Mes-
nard, in *La Vie intellectuelle*, December 1946. It was more than prepared for by
Hegel. For the analogous doctrine of Proudhon, cf. *Proudhon et le christianisme*,
chap. 5.

nism should be earthism [*terrénism*]."[41] The diagnosis is true for many others. The traits that we have just discerned are found again in thoughts that give credence to obscure forces and are enveloped with myths as well as in those whose attraction is more classically positivist and which want to lead all to rational clarity. Are they not all condensed in Nietzsche's cry, which has been taken up again by so many of our contemporaries: "Nothing but the earth!"[42]

Now, on these three points, the man of today is taking the wrong road. We need not dwell on the fact that the increased awareness of his "demiurgic vocation" in the consciousness acquired of his new power makes him undoubtedly unjust toward the "archaic man". If the latter, instead of working for the historic progress of the species, is content "to endure time as one dimension of his existence", is the meaning that his successor and critic attaches to such behavior quite certain? Is it really necessary to conclude that up to these recent centuries "humanity had dwelled in nature and was still not detached from it"? In reality, rather than animal innocence, was this not on his part the deliberate (though admittedly still instinctive) refusal of history? And was this refusal not explained by a veritable ontological thirst, by the desire not to let himself lose contact with the archetypal beings who gestures he reproduced? Christian revelation, by making such scruples pointless, freed human development. It allows us to "redeem time", and consequently to accept it, to change what seemed to be only a principle of

---

[41] "La Crise présente", in *Études*, October 20, 1937. This judgment is not without some similarity to that which was brought to bear recently (1947) in the preliminary pages of *Dieu vivant*, no. 7, p. 13, despite a regrettable use of the word "science" where one would have expected "scientism": "Science in our time has gone beyond the stage of ideological conflict with Christianity only to be incarnated in political and social forms that confront the Church and want her death."

[42] Cf. *Also sprach Zarathustra*, preamble, 3: "I beseech you, my brothers, to remain faithful to the earth and not to believe those who speak to you of supraterrestrial hopes. Whether they know it or not, these are poisoners."

corruption and erosion as an instrument of progress. Without wanting, therefore, to return to a "traditional horizon" that has been transcended, without regretting a mentality forever outdated, there is reason to seek, as Mircea Eliade invites us,[43] not to misunderstand completely the profound intention. And that is not important merely as an act of historical justice: for the one who avoids a false solution does not come any closer to the truth if, at the same stroke, he closes himself off from understanding the problem himself. . . . Now is that not precisely what we are seeing happen?

The whole of reality, of which man is an integral part, surrenders something of its meaning only to a loving and disinterested gaze. How could it be *understood* by someone who is seeking only to *explain* the phenomena with a view to submitting them to his manufacturing ends? Hypertrophied in one of its functions, human reason is thus, on the other hand, miserably atrophied.[44] The first result of this is that, far from entering into knowledge of himself, man closes off his own understanding. He no longer perceives that part of his being which cannot be an object of science for him, since it will always be the subject of it. He no longer understands what, in man, studies man[45]—nor what, in man, engages man—and the consequences of this are many and serious. Constructing a universe

---

[43] *Le Mythe de l'éternel retour, archétypes et répétition* (Paris: Gallimard, 1949), pp. 128, 135–36 and 238.

[44] The fine report on *Intelligence et mystère*, presented by Gabriel Madinier at the university days in Strasbourg, April 1949, should be read on this subject.

[45] Cf. F. Alquié, "Marxisme ou Cartésianisme", in *Les Temps modernes*, May 1946, p. 1384. And Joseph Rovan, "L'Allemagne de nos mérites", in *Esprit*, October 1945, p. 540: "We cannot, however, accept without anguish the methods by which humanity reduces itself to the role of an object, subject in its own name to the absolute power of the 'economists'. All the problems of our time meet in this central duty: to maintain, across the 'objectivization' of methods, thoughts and political actions, respect for the human subject of history as for the end of which these methods, thoughts and actions should always remain aware. . . ."

within which he is assigned a place as if to one part in a whole, he contradicts himself, because he fails to understand this indestructible fact, that, whether he likes it or not, man "is always situated beyond the constructions by which he is tempted to define himself".[46] Those who say to us: here is man, never show us anything but the traces of man's passage, the familiar places to which man gives meaning and which reflect his image, but in which man no longer is."[47] Under the influence of methodological abstraction, consciousness and freedom evaporate.

Such an abstraction, of course, is legitimate, it is indispensable. But transformed into a system of thought, it takes away more than it brings: it becomes a deadly negation. And it is in this way that the sciences of man, "when they become an object of worship, resemble those ancient gods who scattered death on their way".[48] The "objective" world, in its most restrictive sense, is taken to be the totality of what is real, which constitutes a first impoverishment; and human reality is treated like the most inert of these "objects" to which it is assimilated. In this adolescent crisis, the essential new searches for the interior man are repulsed for a time, confused as they are with subjectivist maladies and the distortions of interiority. At the same time, the intoxication of the future causes the loss of that sense of being to which one philosopher recently tried, with so much reason, to lead us. "Western man", said Gabriel Marcel,[49] behaves officially more and more as if what I have called the higher soul were a survival, the useless relic of a fossil species." And another philosopher, Karl Jaspers, showed with equal forcefulness how the various scientific disciplines applied

---

[46] H. Niel, p. 102.

[47] F. Alquié, pp. 69–70.

[48] C. M. D'Arcy, *La Double nature de l'amour*, "Théologie" series (Paris: Aubier, 1948), chap. 9, p. 223.

[49] "Science et humanisme", in *La Nef*, February 1946, pp. 69–70. See also C. G. Jung, *L'Homme à la découverte de son âme* (1944).

to man could become the means of losing all understanding, if they threw out another source, another method of knowing, which alone can "meet him as a totality".[50] "It is necessary to recapture this total image of man", he added. Let us also add that the most profound and most certain philosophy would be practically powerless to do so. In order to rediscover this total image of man which is lost, and with it this sense of being, this conception of a stable truth and this confidence in eternal values, which snatches us from a stifling objectivism as well as from a pure subjectivity, we must make appeal to our faith in the creation of man in the image of God.

But this is what man, with good reason, has difficulty in wanting. (It is not enough to say that he no longer knows it.) For it seems to him that this reality as image, as reflection, far from giving him an inner fullness, an ontological density, a spiritual freedom, which scientific and social relativism had alienated, constitutes, quite the contrary, the mark of a servitude—of the essential servitude that maintains all the others. It seems to him that everything that he recognizes in God he steals from himself. God, he concludes, must in the end die in order for man to live. Here we touch on the profound evil of our time: on that rebellion against God which was the temptation of all centuries but which in our own takes the most radical and least disguised forms. Because for the first time this collective persuasion has risen, powerful as a tidal wave, that the hour of man has finally sounded, the hour of the finite being who is self-sufficient in his immanence and his finitude and who, in

---

[50] Allocution for the reopening of the Faculty of Medicine at the University of Heidelberg, August 15, 1945 (trans. by Hessel in *Fontaine*, vol. 46, p. 817). See also, on the ambiguity of the idea of the objective world, on the limits of the sciences of man, etc.: M. Dufrenne and P. Ricoeur, *Karl Jaspers et la philosophie de l'existence* (Paris: Éd. du Seuil, 1947), pp. 73, 88–90, etc. Cf. L. Doucy, op. cit., on the positive applied to the study of the family; it is necessary, he concludes, p. 137, "to free the spirit from a scientific point of view that responds to the familial question by suppressing its object".

his immanence and his finitude, takes over all the prerogatives of God. The folly of Kirillov and the folly of Zarathustra, like the folly of Feuerbach. The folly of the "humanist" and the folly of the "overman". . . . And it is this folly which corrupts the grandiose dream of conquest and organization that modern man has formed. Because of it, "the more he undertakes to dispose of nature entirely, the more he separates himself from it and is enclosed in a lunar world of asphalt and concrete".[51] He was made to be king: his rebellion makes him a slave.

Yet, even in the principal protagonists of the rebellion, it is very rare—if it happens at all—for it to be found in a pure state. One has with good reason spoken of it as a "tragic misunderstanding".[52] There would not be, in any case, anything to be said about it intellectually if it were not encouraged and did not seem in a way legitimated by this illusion of knowledge which we called a moment ago the "noetic reduction". Man excels, it is true, in transmuting into all kinds of dreams the actual conditions of his misery, whether physiological or social. There is of course much truth in the psychoanalyses of a Marx or a Freud, to cite only these two great parallel examples. There is also much truth in the Comtian idea of a first "theological" age and in so many of the analogous reflections of our philosophers and historians. One of the signs of the maturity of the mind is, in fact, the renunciation of mythical imaginations and false transcendencies, of all those wild growths that drain off the sap without giving any solid fruit. But let us not forget, either, the wisdom of the first of the great reducers. When the old Xenophanes of Colophon made his apparently sceptical remarks: "If cattle and horses had hands and could paint . . .", his intention was not at all to destroy the idea of divinity: he was working solely to purify it. The purpose of his criticism of

---

[51] Cf. *Contemplation de la croix*, p. 181.

[52] H. Engelmann and R. Givord, French introduction to Romano Guardini, *L'Univers religieux de Dostoïevski*, p. 13 (from Guardini, *Welt und person*).

the gods of Homer, a criticism "of passionate seriousness",[53] was to lead man to the faceless God, man who, giving in to his inclinations, had lost his way among the gods. Let us not forget that once the reality of nature and the reality of man are rediscovered, it is still necessary to explain it. It is still necessary to penetrate it. Let us take care that the reductions carried out do not become mutilations; that the conquests of science, poorly interpreted, do not produce obsessions; and that one illusion is not replaced by another antithetical one. For there is indeed an illusion of the absolute, but there is also an illusion of the relative; an illusion of the eternal, but also an illusion of the historical; an illusion of transcendence, but also an illusion of immanence; a mystical illusion, but also a positive illusion. Which is to say that, on the one hand, in failing to understand the relative and the historical, it is true that we obtain only a pseudo-absolute, only a pseudo-eternal, a freedom as dream; but, on the other hand, and no less certainly, the failure to understand the eternal and the absolute leaves at hand only a pseudo-historical, a pseudo-temporal, a path that does not lead to liberation. In brief, "mystification" does not have a unique meaning.

Besides, there has been no need to await modern criticism in order to denounce the illusion of mysticism. From the very beginning of Christianity, it has been charged with it. It is not and never has been, as some imagine, a "yogi religion". It has been opposed since its birth as much to acosmic claims as to the old pagan superstitions. Man, according to it, is not at all this being that many dreamed of: a bit of divinity fallen into a bad or illusory world and having, in order to find salvation, to escape this world, not having any work to do there, able only to abandon it to its absurd destiny or to wake up to the awareness of its emptiness. The real work of a good God, the world has a real value. It is more than just the milieu in which

---

[53] G. van der Leeuw, *La Religion dans son essence et ses manifestations*, French tr. (1948), p. 172.

man must act and be engaged, more than the instrument that he must employ; it is, so to speak, the fabric of the world to come, the material of our eternity. It must not be annihilated but transfigured. Man thus has less to free himself from time than to free himself through time; he does not at all have to escape the world but to take it upon himself.[54] A certain primacy of contemplation is quite the opposite of authentic Christian spirituality, as authors such as Hausherr and Festugière have well demonstrated. Only, in order to understand time and the world, it is necessary to focus beyond: for it is its relation to eternity that gives the world its consistency and that makes of time a real future. Time is not, therefore, as the ancients imagined, the simple projection of an eternal; humanity in time is not enclosed in a circle. But if time has a positive face that constructs rather than destroys, if humanity is really progressing, it is because eternity is carrying them.

In other words, we will say that man, according to Christianity, has the twofold character of historicity and interiority, without being able to dissociate one from the other; he has the one only because he has the other: without real, directed, fruitful historicity, his interiority would only be phantasmagoria or empty psychologism; without substantial interiority, his historicity would disintegrate into a time that has itself become dust. Man is made in history and by history, and this is why each generation understands itself fully only as one link of a humanity in progress; but the progress of this humanity would not have any meaning at all or, to be more exact, humanity would not progress, and this very name by which we designate

---

[54] Like the word "world", the words "earthly" and "temporal" are ambiguous, designating either the purely sensible and transitory aspect of present realities or the part of themselves that is to be inscribed in the eternal. When Jacques Rivière wrote (*A la trace de Dieu*, p. 84): "The Christian sees naturally from the point of view of eternity . . . , which leads to a first impression that thrusts him in the path of social indifference . . . , there is nothing better for him to do than to escape time", this can refer only to a "first impression"; let us say, rather, to a "false impression".

it would be only a *flatus vocis*, if there were not, present at the heart of our world and drawing it on as its goal, an Eternal One, who imprints in each of us the seal of his Face and thus confers to each of us his irreducible interiority.[55]

The man that our faith reveals to us is therefore not the being in chains, constrained in routines, fears, servitudes, limits of all kinds from which the normal development of his reason and in particular the modern development of science allow him to escape and will allow him to escape in much greater measure still. Nor is he this dream god, this faceless fragment of divinity which is presupposed by an overly natural mysticism and which thought to free himself only in an illusion suited to maintaining his real slavery by distracting him from any action on the world and from any social task. But neither is he this being that can be encircled by the investigations of positive science thanks to its spatial and temporal coordinates, which also thought to free himself only in order to fall back, on this very earth, into a harder slavery: reduced completely to the state of an object manipulated by technology and subjected to the oppression of social totalitarianism. Made of the earth, whose entire history is summed up, prolonged and transformed in him, animated by a divine breath that makes him eternal, with a "germinal eternity",[56] man must accept his twofold origin, which creates his twofold nature, not as the implacable sign of a twofold oppression, but, on the contrary, as the point of departure for a twofold liberation. May he thus transfigure, without ever denying, the two relationships which he maintains from this twofold origin: on the one hand, making of this universe,

---

[55] If our study claimed to be theological, this would be the place for an explanation of the Christian "mystery", which is essentially the mystery of history, taking up its contradictions and directing it to its end. A very provocative description of it will be found in an article by Fr. Ganne, "Plongée dans le mystère", published by *Plan de travail des Équipes enseignantes*, 1948–1949, pp. 48–57.

[56] Cf. the fine study by Jacques Paliard, "Du temps à l'éternité", in *Ma joie terrestre . . . (Études carmélitaines)*, pp. 248–61.

where he appears at first deprived of everything, thanks to the indefinitely multiplied fruits of his reason and his hands, the means of building himself up by developing all the virtualities of his natural being; humbly recognizing, on the other hand, his dependence and raising himself, by welcoming and appealing to a more sublime destiny, to union with his Creator.

5.

The preceding reflections still leave us very far from the complete idea of man which our faith brings out. A few traits will soon be added. But perhaps we have seen enough already to begin our criticism of the idea most frequently opposed to it today: the Marxist idea of man and of his destiny. It is worth the trouble to pause here, for, more than any other contemporary doctrine, Marxism claims to take up this "new man" whose birth we have noted;[57] more than any other, it presents itself as the heir of the whole scientific and social movement of recent centuries; more than any other, too, perhaps, it has

---

[57] Let us quote here the letter from Fr. Engels to Heinz Starkenburg (January 25, 1894), in which a correct view of the great present phenomenon, which began at that time to be apparent, is mixed with a value judgment coupled with a prophecy inspired by the Marxist faith: "Men make their history themselves, but, up until now, not with a collective will, according to an overall plan. Their efforts thwart each other, and this is the reason why . . . necessity completed and expressed by chance reigns. . . . After society takes possession of the means of production, domination by the product over the producer will be excluded. Conscious organization will succeed the anarchy that now reigns in social production. The struggle for individual existence will cease. Only in this way will man be detached, in a certain sense, from the animal world in a definitive way, he will pass from the conditions of animal existence to conditions of human existence. The whole ensemble of conditions of life which, up till now, have dominated men will pass under their command; they will become in this way for the first time real masters of nature, because they will be masters of their own association. The laws of their social activity, which hold outside of them like foreign laws that dominate them, will be

known how to pose the problem of the total man and to seek a total solution for it. It has not, like so many others, evaded the last questions. For this reason—and although, insofar as it very quickly took on the appearance of an economic system and then became a social movement and political party, it usually moves on an entirely different plane from Christianity—a comparison is legitimate. Let us even say that a confrontation is imperative.[58]

Before being a social phenomenon, in fact, Marxism—Berdyaev has long been saying it—is a spiritual phenomenon. This is what its greatness consists in, it is one of the reasons that explain its longevity. It is also, in my opinion, what makes it most susceptible of criticism. Marx did not only seek a social liberation of man, he sought his spiritual liberation. If he wanted the former, it was, in the final analysis, for the purpose of the latter. The first assuredly held for him, as in the entire movement stemming from him, an incomparably greater place; it is nonetheless true that, in his thinking, it constituted only a means. Even when, in relation to it, the criticism of religion and the antireligious battle became in their turn means, weapons in view of the social battle, the final end that was aimed for always remained the return of man to possession of himself through the elimination of any transcendence. For all social, political or other alienations were in Marx' eyes only "profane forms" of the great, radical, essential human alienation: religious alienation. The ultimate goal was for man, finally be-

---

applied and mastered by them in full knowledge of the facts. The association itself which was presented to man as if imposed by nature and by history will become their free and proper work. The foreign and objective forces that, up till now, dominated history will pass into their control. From then on, men will create their own history in full awareness; from then on, the social causes that they will set in motion will be able to attain, in growing proportion, the desired effects. This will be the salvation of the human race from the reign of necessity into that of freedom."

[58] Les Éditions "Univers" (Lille) have published a collective number entitled *La Russie soviétique à la recherche de l'homme nouveau* (1947).

come reasonable, renouncing the "illusory sun" of religion, "to move henceforth around himself, which is to say, around his true sun".[59] The end of any exploitation of man by man and the return of the worker into full possession of the fruit of his work were thus still nothing if they did not lead to the end of this alienation par excellence, which emptied man not only of his resources but of his very being for the profit of some imaginary power which dominated and weakened him from on high in the heavens. Marx did not reproach Feuerbach for having been mistaken about man's essential evil[60] and, consequently, about the essential goal to be attained by the suppression of this evil: he reproached him only for having remained in the abstract, for not having seen the particular causes that made this evil inevitable and, in consequence, for not having attacked these causes. This is why he himself came to give the social question an unparalleled, exclusive importance. For him, it was expressed on the plane of practical action in a question of politics and economy, but it had in itself the value and the scope of a, of the ontological question. It was the being of man that was in question.[61]

Now, let us freely say here about Marxists something similar to what Saint Augustine once said about "Platonists", with all the implicit reservations that he himself included in his remarks: in one sense, they have seen the end very clearly, but they prevent themselves from ever reaching it by failing to rec-

---

[59] Cf. Karl Marx, *Contribution à la philosophie du droit de Hegel* (in *Œuvres philosophiques*, French trans., vol. 1), p. 85.

[60] He thinks that, after Hegel and Feuerbach, "the criticism of religion was in substance complete": *Contribution à la critique de la philosophie du droit de Hegel*, ed. Costes, vol. 1, p. 83. See also *The Holy Family* (*La Saint famille*), vol. 2 (in *Morceaux choisis*, p. 48).

[61] So, in principle, it is important, according to Marxism, to cut the "social roots" of religious alienation rather than the religious roots of social alienation. See, among other texts, V. Lenin, *De l'attitude du parti ouvrier à l'égard de la religion* (May 1909). Which does not at all exclude the "anticlerical" battle or antireligious propaganda.

ognize the path. Their ideal of the "new man",[62] the ideal of a liberated, unified humanity that has recovered full possession of its essence, reconciled with itself as with the universe, living in fullness until the consummation of History, is the very ideal whose promise we maintain in our Sacred Scripture, and which Saint Augustine expressed vigorously in brief when he spoke of the *unus Christus*, of the *Christus integer*.[63] But, on the one hand, by thinking themselves obliged to attain this ideal by avoiding any transcendence and by wanting to achieve it in time, they denied the very conditions for it and changed it into a contradictory ideal; and, on the other hand, by seeking it through history by heterogeneous means, they prevented themselves even from approaching it and preparing for it. This is what we need to see in a little more detail.

Marx wrote in a surprising text,

> Communism, as the real appropriation of the human essence by man and for man, thus as the return of man to himself insofar as social man, which is to say, human man, a complete, conscious return, with the support of all the wealth of earlier development, this communism, being a perfect naturalism, coincides with humanism. It is the true end of the quarrel between man and nature as well as between man and man, the true end of the quarrel between existence and essence, between objectification and self-affirmation, between freedom and necessity, between the individual and the species. It resolves the mystery of history and it knows that it resolves it.[64]

---

[62] This expression has become current with Marxists more than anywhere else. It came to them, through Hegel, from Saint Paul himself.

[63] Saint Augustine, in *Psalmum 88*, sermo 1, n. 5.

[64] Marx, fragment from 1844 (French trans. in the *Revue marxiste*, n. 1, February 1920). Marx also says, ibid.: "So society is the essential and accomplished unity of man and nature, the true resurrection of nature, the accomplished naturalism of man and the accomplished humanism of nature." On these texts, see Gaston Fessard, *La Main tendue, Le Dialogue catholique-communiste est-il possible?* (Grasset, 1937), and *France, prends garde de perdre ta liberté* (Éd. du Témoignage chrétien, 1946), pp. 129–60.

Corresponding to this text by the founder is this text of recent disciples; the same hope and, under similarly laicized words, the same prophetic impulse can be felt to vibrate in it: At the end of cosmic and social development,

> the total man will really be what these words express. . . . The human being plunges to the depths of nature, both external and interior, which he appropriates, which is his property, which he overcomes and raises in himself to the level of the Spirit. The unity of the individual and the social, the possession by man of nature and of his own nature, defines the total Man. . . . He is indeed the one who is "all", who possesses, seizes and creates his good from all of nature. . . . The human totality remained dispersion, contradiction. It will attain its unity, which is to say, the truth of man, its essence achieved.[65]

Who could not recognize, as it were, a family resemblance between such anticipations and what we ourselves say of the coming of the kingdom of heaven or of the completion of the Body of Christ? Then there will be no more battles, no more antagonisms, no more exteriority, no more inner straining, no more exclusivity. . . . Yes, on both sides, it is indeed a question of an end of history, of a "resurrection of nature", of a culmination, of an access to plenitude, of a perfect unity realized at last. It is a question of the consummate Man, at once unique and collective, as in Saint Paul. Only, what the Christian hopes for in another world, at the end of time, the Marxist dreams of for this present world, within our time. What the Christian awaits from a supernatural intervention, the Marxist anticipates as the natural end of a wholly immanent process. A transfiguration of the here and now without the presence of a Beyond! An end of history in the midst of a time that continues to unfold! A fusion with nature in conditions essentially unchanged by perception and intelligence and without essential modifications

---

[65] Lefebvre and Gutermann, *Introduction à Lénine, Cahiers sur la dialectique de Hegel*, pp. 81 and 98–99. This is what Henri Lefebvre also calls "the total act": *Le Matérialisme dialectique* (1947), p. 151.

either in the support of the organism! A perfect peace, a perfect harmony, a total reciprocity of consciousnesses, without the insertion of any new principle in this humanity, which will not have ceased until then to misunderstand and to tear itself to pieces![66] Has Christianity ever asked such an abdication of the mind? On which side are the miracles the most unbelievable? Supposing that our faith had no other basis, at least it could invoke the coherence of the vision it proposes to us; at least it poses the necessary conditions for achieving it; at least it is conscious of its demands. If it obliges us to believe in mystery, at least it spares us chaos. How could the Marxist vision say as much?[67]

---

[66] When an end has been put to social alienation, each, writes Marx, will exchange "love for love, trust for trust". And again: "If you love without evoking love, that is, if your love insofar as love does not produce love in return, if in manifesting your life insofar as you are a loving man you do not make of yourself a loved man, your love is impotent, it is a misfortune" (Landshut and Mayer, p. 51).

[67] This is what makes Fr. Fessard right in writing (*La Main tendue*, p. 123): "If this page by Marx does not open out on a real and true transcendence, it contains, instead of an existential description of the Humanity-God, only a *general idea* of communism, and all his affirmations become purely verbal, ideological, without real content or practical value." For such a definition of communism "can retain some value only if it aims at Humanity passing the limit of itself, integrating and realizing itself as Humanity-God" (p. 218). But, on the other hand, "does one conceive purely earthly and natural humanity, capable" of working such a transformation of itself? And how can we imagine otherwise than as transcendent a society "in which absolutely all opposition between being and thought will be reduced, in which any perceptible multiplicity will be both conserved and sublimated" (pp. 218–21)? This will be, Marx tells us, a "veritable resurrection of nature". As soon as we try to think truly of the reality that such expressions cover, do we not encounter in its perfect state that "society" of which Saint Paul wrote: "There will be no longer Jew or Greek, slave or free man, man or woman, for you are all but one in Christ Jesus"? Thus we understand that Fr. Fessard could, starting from that, propose "an interpretation of communism which, opening it to a true transcendence, would permit the Christian to assimilate its truth just as the communist to free himself from its errors" (p. 211).

The myth that Marx conceived, the transposition both of the "perfect Man" of Saint Paul and of the "absolute knowledge" of Hegel, is admittedly grandiose. It is not what is generally called utopian, in the sense that he makes any appeal to arbitrary imaginations. It does not want to "anticipate dogmatically", but only to "find the new world through criticism of the old world",[68] and consequently it refuses to enter into any detail concerning the organization of the future city. This is why, among other reasons, Marx believed he could reject with disdain the systems of his predecessors, the "utopian" socialists, who did not hesitate to outline in detail the most enchanting pictures.[69] From this point of view, there is no resemblance between him and, for example, someone like Fourier. Insofar as a socialist, Marx was not a utopian. He was the first to break with the old tradition of "utopias" and "*Uchronies*", which still encumbered the social movement at its beginning, and he seemed more than a little proud of it. That is what permitted a number of his disciples—as it did him, too, already in the second, longest part of his existence—to turn all their attention on the analysis of real society, then to revolutionary method and action, denying that Marxism was a doctrine in the theoretical, complete and traditional sense of the word. From which some conclude with sincerity that the believer can adopt it entirely, adopt at least all that, in it, relates to the "temporal", even it means extending it, or correcting it, if need be, on the level of metaphysics. That is nevertheless a great error (similar to the one that thinks Comtian positivism would not be closed to transcendence and to the supernatural); and this error is at

---

[68] Marx, *Lettre à Engels*, 1843.

[69] A similar contrast in Christianity. Cf. Théo Preiss, "Le Mystère du Fils de l'Homme", in *Dieu vivant*, vol. 8, p. 22: "Are not the discretion, the sobriety of Jesus' evocations about the world to come, when we read the Gospels with regard to the Jewish apocalypses, something poignant?" Joseph Bonsirven, *L'Évangile de Paul*, p. 329: Paul is not concerned "with searching for and explaining what the new world will be, which the eschatological speculations (of that time) were pleased to describe. . . ."

the source of another tragic misunderstanding. It produces fatal compromises.[70]

In fact, such as it is both thought and lived in its inner coherence by the powerful and disciplined bloc that wants it to conquer the world, Marxism is neither a purely empirical doctrine nor a mass of theses without inner connection. It is a whole with closely interdependent sides. Its "temporal" program is wholly permeated by its spiritual negations. One can, of course, desire that some dissociations be produced; one can expect them in a more or less near future. One can work toward it oneself, on the various planes of action and thought. Yet one must nonetheless first judge doctrines and situations such as they are, without blinding oneself to their nature and their strength.

Metaphysical or not, whatever name you call it, Marxism is a complete doctrine, which has like all others its implications and its presuppositions. It tends toward, according to Marx' expression, the "positive suppression of religion". Total relativist as he presents himself, he sets an absolute, analogous and antagonistic to the Absolute in which Christians believe. But if this absolute is not a utopia in the old meaning of the word, if one rejects any description in its regard, is that not itself the sign that it is in reality the radical utopia, the utopia of utopias? For such a rejection is not only prudence and practical moderation, wise understanding of what is unforeseeable in the arrangements of history. It is rather a matter of faith. It stems from the fact that this final state in which humanity culminates is posed as essentially indescribable, as eluding by essence the grasp of the imagination, because radically different from all the relative states through which humanity passes in the course of

---

[70] This is why, if it is true that one can, and even must, wish for "the presence, if possible, of true Christians in every part", with a view to preserving the Church "from the danger of weakening" and of sparing "humanity terrible sufferings", that is true only in general. For it is also only too true that this presence can be in certain cases rendered impossible, even and especially perhaps when the way is obviously smooth for it.

its history. The end of history could not be made of the same elements as its course. Perhaps led onto earth and reduced to the proportions of immanence, the Absolute to which we are tending nonetheless remains the Wholly Other. . . .

Now it is this, this reduction to immanence, this temporalization of the kingdom, that seems contradictory to me. "Marx' ideal is very beautiful: but it is manifestly transhistorical."[71] Engels wrote, in order to criticize Hegel's claims: "With Hegel, one arrives at so-called absolute truth, worldly history is ended, and yet it must continue, although nothing remains for it to do."[72] Is this not still true with Marx? Not that he had, like Hegel perhaps had at the time when he "brooded over his own thought",[73] the naïveté to believe that the advent of his doctrine itself marked the end of history, nor that the latter could be brought about by any solution of pure thought, by any intellectual system. But, in order to postpone it until much later, and to impose on it much more real conditions, he nonetheless always placed this end within time. Henceforth, should one not say, as Engels said: History is ended, and yet, since time continues, it must indeed be carried on; yet, it cannot be, since its engine is contradiction and since all contradiction is henceforth absorbed into harmony. . . . "It is not possible", Jean Lacroix said quite correctly,[74] "to conceive as being still temporal a being in whom all negativity has disappeared." Not

---

[71] Jean Lacroix, "Du Marxisme", in *Le Monde*, July 11, 1947. "In brief", concludes Mr. Lacroix, "Marxism consists in a kind of sociological projection of the ideal Christian. . . . [It is] an immanentism that pushes to its extreme consequences the radical negation of any transcendence. But, as Mr. Jean Hyppolite rightly asks, is this resolution of any transcendence possible on the plane of history as well as on that of thought? Does the human condition contain along with its problem the very solution of that problem?"

[72] Engels, *Ludwig Feuerbach et la fin de la philosophie classique allemande* (French trans. of *Ludwig Feuerbach und der Ausgang der klassischen deutschen Philosophie*), p. 41.

[73] Cf. M. Dufrenne, in *Fontaine*, vol. 61 (September 1947), p. 464.

[74] "L'Homme marxiste", in *La Vie intellectuelle*, August-September 1947, p. 58.

all Marxists, moreover, have failed to perceive this. Several of them have not been without hesitation in revealing to us an earthly horizon "beyond all the fatalities of nature and social contradictions".[75] One senses they are divided "between the rationalism of continuous progress and the mysticism of the true end".[76] Many avoid thinking about it. Others make concessions. Another, recently, in a lecture with a strongly apologetic tone, brought various conciliatory touches to the abrupt thesis of his master. In truth, he abandoned the end of history.[77] But in that case, we are then only dealing with a very diminished humanism. And we are dealing then, too, only with an illegitimate, watered-down Marxism which, in order to escape one of its contradictions, renounces its boldness and its greatness; a Marxism that returns to the inconsistent ideas of the last two centuries on indefinite progress; a Marxism that no longer professes to be a doctrine of salvation, which is no longer, henceforth, a total doctrine of man but one which must consent to be judged by a more complete and higher doctrine.[78]

Let us suppose, nevertheless, that in creating the economy of an "end of the world"—bypassing Christ who forms the real unity of his Mystical Body and through whom God will be "all in all"—man can attain this blessed end that Marx has

---

[75] Roger Garaudy, *Le Communisme et la morale* (Paris: Éditions sociales, 1945).

[76] G. Fessard, p. 134.

[77] Pierre Hervé, "L'Homme marxiste", in *Les Grandes options de l'homme contemporain* (1947). Cf. Jean Hyppolite, "La Conception hégélienne de l'État et sa critique par Karl Marx", in *Cahiers internationaux de sociologie*, vol. 2 (1947), pp. 153 and 158: "It is in the essential tragic of history that Hegel perceived the idea: it is, on the contrary, in the suppression of this historic tragic, in the effective reconciliation or the effective synthesis that Marx discovers the real equivalent of the Hegelian Idea. . . . He believes in the real resolution of the contradictions, in an effective synthesis in which idea and reality are but one, here on earth."

[78] This is because, in fact, "it is impossible to speak of progress without referring to a transcendence. For Marx, this transcendence was the total suppression of alienation that was to achieve the end of history." Henri Niel, "Le Matérialisme dialectique", in *Critique*, vol. 29 (October 1948), pp. 895–96.

dreamed for him. It was in yet another way that, like the Platonians of former years, the latter failed to recognize the path that could lead to this end.

We know how Marxism represents itself as the progress of history, how it explains the motivating forces of it and what moral it draws from it. Jean Lacroix has shown this, with all the sympathy necessary to avoid misinterpretations, or overly superficial interpretations, which are worse sometimes than misinterpretations. We can refer to this.[79] It is not within our purview to undertake a methodical criticism of it any more than it is to express once again all the partial truth that enters into the theses of historical materialism, into the denunciation of hypocrisies, of complicities, or at the very least of the facilities of a certain spiritualism, or into the application of the Hegelian dialectic to the real history of human societies. No more than it is to note in detail how frequently the cause of social justice has found truly effective support only with men already won over to the Marxist and militant ideology in Marxist organizations.[80] But finally, let us simply ask, in what eternal book have the Marxists read this meaning of history that they establish with so much assurance? That they have often, moreover, an acute sense of history, that they know how to observe its progress and analyze its causes in order to take advantage of it admirably in their tactics, that is a totally different matter! But where did they get the idea of the end toward which, according to them, history is infallibly moving? How do they know that in this final state man will finally have the means of resolving all the human problems whose solution is now insoluble for him: "the problems of happiness, of knowledge, of love and of death?"[81] Where have they seen that, from contradiction to

---

[79] *L'Homme marxiste*, lecture to the *Semaine sociale* in Paris, 1947.

[80] From which come so many tragic points of conscience, so many risks of perversion for those who are concerned, not only with generous action, but with efficacy in their action. They do not always have enough distance to see where, in reality, they are being led.

[81] Henri Lefebvre, *Le Matérialisme dialectique*, p. 148.

contradiction, everything was tending toward a universal reconciliation? Who could predict to them the definitive triumph of the Yes and the full reciprocity of love? Who guaranteed them that, little by little, the contradictions would wear out? Experience, in truth, shows us nothing of the kind. It can tell us whether or not there will be progress, provided that one has agreed beforehand on a definition and on a criterion; but not whether, of themselves, if only one assists at their birth, Freedom and Harmony will be present at the end.[82] We can glimpse an outcome to every historical situation: but who will show us the Outcome?

There is more. If it is truly a matter, as they claim, of a final end, the clashes of the dialectic are incapable of procuring it. The latter proceeds by successive negations, it draws the opposite from the opposite, but, in very virtue of its principle, the pendulum always reverses itself anew. Any solution is thus provisional, one extreme calls for the other extreme, and there is no reason for this movement in a broken line to stop. In other words, the opposition breeds and perpetuates itself, definitive harmony cannot emerge from the midst of contradiction. No revolution can give birth to universal reconciliation because all revolution is dialectical. The nondialectical will never come from it. Here the "formidable power of the relative", of which Hegel and, after him, Marx spoke, stops.

---

[82] There are some similar reflections in Nicholas Berdyaev, *Au seuil de la nouvelle époque* (1947), pp. 137–38, or in Maurice Merleau-Ponty, "La querelle de l'existentialisme", *Les Temps modernes*, November 1945, pp. 355–56: "A philosophy that renounces the absolute Spirit as prime mover of history . . . , that recognizes in things no other reasons but those that make their meeting and reciprocal action appear, this philosophy could not affirm a priori the possibility of an integral man, postulate a final synthesis in which all contradictions would be lifted or affirm its inevitable achievement. . . . If Hegel could recover blindly from it in the course of things, because a basis of theology remained in him, Marxist praxis does not have the same resource. . . . It could not assign in advance an end of history. . . . The distinctive feature of Marxism is to invite us to make the logic of history prevail over its contingency, without any metaphysical guarantee."

All that claims to be definitive thus appeals to a principle that is not dialectical, a Yes that is not merely the No of a No.[83] Means that are already homogeneous to it are necessary for its preparation. If not, the dialectic is pursued from reversal to reversal, and what one thought ought to be the final stage toward the "leap" into the absolute is only a link in an infernal cycle. Whoever wants the end wants the means, but whoever does not want any end whatever does not want any means whatever either. No subtlety, for example, will ever make good come from evil, or truth from a lie,[84] or freedom from tyranny, or will show love immanent to hatred, or will ever make actual and practical contempt for man serve effectively the ends that faith in man has conceived. So, we are not indignant about certain features of the Marxist ethic; but, since one takes one's position with some insistence on the plane of effectiveness, we will observe their ineffectiveness. There, too, we will not deny that, in the evolution of history, such an ethic can obtain some fine successes, but we will observe that these successes can never become definitive precisely because this ethic cannot be, as they hope, purely provisional; we will deny that these successes are human successes, first of all because they engender a provisional "order" that is not human, and then because, even at this price, they are incapable of ever ending in the liberation of man. A political success is one thing, the solution of the human problem is another. And they are without common measure.

---

[83] Cf. Marx, *Manuscrit économico-politique* of 1844 (*Molitor*, vol. 6, p. 46): "In conceiving the negation of negations, Hegel found the abstract expression of the movement of History."

[84] Cf. Simone de Beauvoir, *Idéalisme moral et réalisme politique*: "If one has recourse to denouncement, to lies, in order to assure the triumph of man, one will find that the man whom one makes triumph will be a being to which one refuses any respect, a man whom it is legitimate to dupe, to slander, to betray; one will have forbidden him any trust or friendship, one will have saved him only by mutilating him" (*Les Temps modernes*, vol. 2 [November 1945], p. 261).

6.

In addition, what would this glimpsed liberation be from? From humanity? But, for thinking that rejects anything beyond time, any participation of time in an eternal, can the idea of Humanity be anything but a myth? For Marx, man has an essentially historical character, that is to say, the real man "is nothing but man given to one moment of history", nothing in him goes beyond or transcends this moment. "All history", he also says, "is only a continuous transformation of human nature",[85] and this assertion must be taken in the strongest sense. "Nothing exists", comments Engels,[86] "except the uninterrupted process of becoming and of the transitory." Nothing, no part, is total. The Marxist dialectic "advances only on the dead".[87] How then would the essence of a being who has no essence at all finally be realized, this being who is only a common name to designate the succession of generations and the multiplicity of individuals? And the human race does not truly exist any more than the essence of man: What is, from now on, human solidarity? What is the human future? Am I still right to say that, if a liberation is to come, it is humanity that will be freed? These are at the very most only individuals—and why should I admit that, by the fact that they will come later, these future individuals will be worth more than the others? Will they not be just like us, "mediocre inhabitants of the corner of the universe that is called the Earth"? To want and to seek their good, I can still do; but why sacrifice the present generations

---

[85] Marx, *Misère de la philosophie* (1896 ed.) p. 204. Cf. Landsberg, "Marx et le problème de l'homme", in *La Vie intellectuelle*, September 10, 1937. Marx said first of all (ibid.) more modestly, and more correctly, that "when people change utterly their conditions of industrial and political existence", they thereby change "their whole manner of being".

[86] Engels, *Anti-Dühring*; Lenin quotes this text in *Marx, Engels, Marxisme*, French tr., p. 19.

[87] Jacques Maritain, *Humanisme intégral*, p. 102.

to them?[88] Or must we believe that they, too, like us, will have to sacrifice themselves for a Humanity that is only pure concept? No disinterestedness holds firm in the face of the absurd, and to demand an object worth sacrificing oneself for is not to transform sacrifice into calculation: such a demand does not spring from sensitivity or from an egotistical nature but from the spirit.

If, too, one can hope that the liberation of these men to come, supposing that it is achievable in this way, may be, when it takes place, something acquired forever! But we well know that this cannot be. We can believe in new heavens and a new earth; but how can we believe in a totally humanized nature, humanized forever, on our planet? Reconciled with itself, Humanity (let us continue to use this word) cannot be reconciled with nature. One more or less distant day, the latter will sweep everything away. Cosmic forces will overcome the fragile human plant. Thus we will have to immolate ourselves, not only or even especially in our possessions and advantages, but even in our consciousness; not to something that goes beyond us but to something that is exterior to us and which is, in addition, as fatally ephemeral as we ourselves are. . . . If the two Marxist words alienation and mystification are appropriate some place, it is indeed here.

These criticisms go beyond the singular case of Marxism.[89]

---

[88] Cf. Simone de Beauvoir, pp. 263–64: "It is easy to scorn the present, if, cutting it off from the future, one reduces it to itself; but then one also cuts off every instant of the future, and, reduced to themselves, they also lose all their value."

[89] I recently read a similar argumentation in Fr. Lucien Laberthonnière, responding to an atheist who said to him that the effort of each human generation was not lost, considering that "humanity has the infinity of time before itself": "Yes, it is lost. . . . Supposing in fact that there is to be an endless succession of individuals, as from the point of view from which you consider them, these individuals are essentially obsolete and made to appear only in order to disappear, the ideal whose realization they are to work for, for which when need be they must sacrifice themselves, will never be achieved for any-

They apply as well to what concerns the ethic of effectiveness to which we alluded above. Illogical, as we have seen, if its end is considered, the latter is, on the other hand, only too conformed to the negations that are at the foundation of so many other doctrines of our time, and it has, in a way, the advantage of logic over several of them. If, in fact, one denies the transcendent, creator God, of whom man is the living reflection, where will one find the principle of human dignity, of this infinite price, of this absolute value of each "soul", correlative to an absolute of truth and justice, which Christianity has revealed to us? That is a point that Auguste Comte and his disciples had seen very well, and they were not afraid to proclaim it.[90] Their love of Humanity, itself full of illusions, was not in any case coupled with any recognition of the "rights of man". In the order that they dreamed of establishing, they could thus indeed seek the greatest happiness of all: this order was nonetheless tyrannical. No satisfaction, no "happiness" can overcome in man the incoercible demand of Truth and Justice which makes

one. It would have no consistency at all. Everywhere and always, there would only be beings—if one can still call them beings—who would have to exist and act for others; and when these others would appear, it would be the same for them. You thus reduce all individuals to being only means. The ideal under these conditions would be only a dream that each would indefinitely come to have, and destiny would also carry away the dream with the dreamers." About which the Reverend Father also shows that there is no truly human life except through a participation in an eternal Life and that disinterestedness does not consist at all in being "metaphysically a fool". *Critique du laïcisme* (Éd. Canet, 1948), pp. 185–87.

[90] Thus Antoine Baumann, *La Vie sociale de notre temps*, p. 222: "If one takes away the hypothesis of a God as master of the world . . . , I just do not understand on what reality you can establish the notion of a law permitting the individual, an isolated monad, to set himself before the other beings who surround him and say to them: There is something intangible in me which I enjoin you to respect, because its principle is independent of you." Cf. above, Part Two. Marx, it will be recalled, as early as 1842, was speaking of the "supposed rights of man" ("La Question juive"; *Œuvres philosophiques*, tr. by Molitor, vol. 1, p. 195), and, although his criticism of revolutionary ideology was not without foundation, that very expression is loaded with threats.

of him a being not only superior to the other beings of nature but of a totally different essence, in the image of his Creator. Now such a lack of comprehension, once again logical, is not at all peculiar to Comtian positivism. Without a doubt, that is the seed of those totalitarian sociologies in which ideologies often so opposed in other respects naturally converge. There we have what is for the man of today both the greatest temptation and the most terrible threat.[91]

Of course the pressure of facts of all kinds, the development of technology, the necessities of the planned economy with the legitimate hopes that result from it, contribute to a part of the danger. But the profound cause is spiritual. The danger would be less serious, one would have less trouble finding formulas capable of saving, for most of man, a "free sector" beside the "directed sector"—to put it better, capable of promoting a higher freedom, a development of personality by the very means of a more rational organization of the resources of the world and of social life[92]—if the ontological foundation subsisted for it in minds and spirits. But, as we have recalled, it is this foundation that, in the spirit of man, has been ruined. And, since it is, on the other hand, a fact of experience that we

---

[91] Let us add this consequence, that if man is nothing but a knot of social relations, one risks seeing in a social adversary a total enemy. And this other consequence as well, that the "category of the private" is lost: the individual no longer has any safe retreat, any personal home, in which he can set up a shelter from the invasions of all kinds that come in public life. Propaganda hems him in from all sides and molds him; the totalitarian tendencies of the state exert an ever-stronger pressure on him. The family, "the social shelter against society" (Nédoncelle, summarizing Newman, in *La Philosophie religieuse de Newman*, p. 37), is increasingly weakened and externalized. More profoundly, on the ontological plane, what one might also call the "category of interiority" is lost. Man, in his own eyes, is increasingly dissolved into the group of which he is a member. The feeling of collective destiny and collective responsibilities weakens, rather than exalts, the sense of incommunicable personality and of his own responsibilities.

[92] Cf. Pierre Teilhard de Chardin, "Le Formation de la Noosphère", *Revue des questions scientifiques*, January 20, 1947.

are much more men of our means, which form us every day, than of our ends, which are distant, how can we be surprised that not only the hope in a henceforth chimerical ideal or the faith in values which the intelligence can no longer justify but even the nostalgia for this ideal and even the taste for these values come to be blurred and then fade away? The liberation of man can remain the goal, but this goal becomes abstract: it refers above all to succeeding with some magnificent construction. Strength and toughness become the essential virtues. Thus little by little a conception becomes accepted in our century which not only runs counter to the liberal or anarchical tendencies that were so strong in the last century, counter to its individualism and to its social sentimentalism, but which has no consideration for anything but the greatest productivity of the human animal in an all-powerful technocracy. And so, in another context and on a larger scale, that situation, justly condemned by Marx, lives on, in which "man is a mere machine for producing".[93] The exaltation of the worker is transformed, without any words being changed, into the organization of a new slavery. A new Egyptian venture is prepared, more colossal and more learned, but nonetheless inhumane. All the most generous forces of social idealism are drained off, into ambiguity, for the profit of a political realism whose means of oppression have tremendously increased today. Real persons are immolated, not even for a chimerical Humanity, but for some "super-society without heart or face".[94]

The total and exclusive humanism that is professed, by being postponed in its achievement, thus comes to disappear in thought itself. They forget what Marx had recalled so energetically in thinking to speak against "the social principles of Christianity", which seemed "servile" to him, to wit, that "dignity, pride, the sense of independence are still more necessary

---

[93] Communist Manifesto.
[94] Pierre Teilhard de Chardin, "La Crise présente", p. 163.

than bread"[95]—not only for the "proletariat" but for all men. They forget "the freedom of each individual conditioning the freedom of all". They end by becoming used to what had first appeared to be a painful but inevitable phase which they had hoped would have to be brief. They justify it, they set it up as an ideal. They flatter themselves for having found, as Auguste Comte said, "new means for better tying private development to universal progress".[96] This was first of all a dream of the future. Impatience often transforms it into an illusion for the present, and the latter, in order to sustain itself, becomes a lie. Failing to be able really to emerge into the kingdom of freedom dreamed of at first, they imagine a miraculous coincidence between individual freedom and social necessity, and they still speak of perfect freedom, calling it "freedom of membership", there where tyranny reigns. . . .

Thus they could believe, at a time when it was still only a question of emancipation in spirit, that to reduce everything to immanence would give everything to man: this was, on the contrary, to rob him of everything. For it was to reduce everything to time—to a time without eternal foundation, all the moments of which, whatever one has, are dissipated or accumulate without penetrating each other. An Absolute from a dream heaven has not been made to descend onto a real earth; it has not been brought back from God to Man: it has been made to fall into the relative—and all of man with it.

One need not be backward or refuse to have anything to do with the current effort of our race or close one's eyes to the very real bases for formal liberalisms, nor need one be lacking in social boldness in order to dread the lifeless horrors that such aberrations, were they to endure, prepare for us. An appetizer was recently offered us, whose cruel memory will remain with us for a long time—and every day we discover that, whether in-

---

[95] *Morceaux choisis* (Paris: Gallimard, 1934), p. 224.
[96] *Cours de philosophie positive*, vol. 6 (1908), p. 532.

fected directly or by the same process stemming from the same cause, the evil is far from being eradicated. It is spreading, it is establishing itself. In addition, more even than so many recent horrors, more than the current miseries and fears, the total disappointment to which we are on the way and which the most clearsighted cannot fail to sense is in danger of provoking a wave of pessimism whose devastating effect would be difficult to calculate. For a long time the ancient Romans knew how to sacrifice themselves for their eternal Rome, *extra anni solisque vias*;[97] for a long time they believed in the *imperium sine fine* which Jupiter had supposedly accorded them. But when they perceived that this was only a myth, their courage immediately gave way. This was not at first a rebellion of the egotistical instinct: the awakening of reflection was enough. Similarly in our age. The nobility of the human being shines forth, more than ever, in the fact that many proved capable of sacrificing their fleshly being for some cause that transcends them. That at least Humanity might grow! That Humanity might remain! That a future might take shape forever! —And if that were also only a myth? If this idea which we all have of resolving a problem in common, of directing us together toward a goal, were only a totally arbitrary idea whose advantage would be in getting rid of us before becoming an *idée fixe*?[98] If, upon reflection, man were forced to appear, in very virtue of his original positions, to be a solitary being, irremediably alone? If nature, to the degree that it is better known, to the degree one thinks to capture and humanize it, proves always henceforth to be like an immense blind, crushing force? If the universe were absurd? "It is an appalling anguish to foresee and to see

---

[97] Virgil, bk. 6, vv. 791–801. Commentary by Jean Hubaux, *Les Grands mythes de Rome* (Paris: Presses universitaires de Paris, 1945), pp. 138–40.

[98] Cf. Nietzsche, *Der Wille zur Macht*, 339. Some individuals could draw an incentive from such a criticism for their own ambitions: the human race will not, in general, have to be satisfied with it, and nihilism cannot sustain a truly constructive action for very long.

collective death. . . . And as humanity does not have indefinite reserves, it is a strange anguish to think of the death of humanity."[99] In the perspectives of a historicism that refuses man, individually or collectively, any participation in any higher or more stable reality, what Mircea Eliade calls so well "the terror of history"[100] could not be averted. One can overcome the denial of an experience, by judging it temporary, but one cannot overcome indefinitely the logic of thought. Nothing, thus, is more dangerous than a poorly founded optimism: only despair can come from it.

> Lie! The human collective is as fragile as I on the scale of Eternity. Seventy years or seven hundred years, it is the same. . . . The human collective will itself disappear as well. Everything is a mirage. . . .[101]

7.

It is then that Christianity, with its conception of man, comes once again to give hope to the world. Without intoxicating him with dreams, without presenting to him suspect novelties, today just as twenty centuries ago, strengthened by its unchanged doctrine, by its ever-new sap, it comes to save all, to accomplish all! What it did for the ancient soul recom-

---

[99] Charles Péguy, "Encore de la Grippe", *Cahiers de la Quinzaine*, March 20, 1900, p. 7. —We know Nietzsche's apology: "In a lost, hidden corner of this glittering confusion of innumerable solar systems that is called the universe, there was once a star on which wise animals invented knowledge. This was the most pretentious and deceitful second of 'universal history': but it was only a second. After a few sighs from nature, the star went to sleep and the wise animals had to die." "Verité et mensonge au sens extra-moral", translated by Bovard-Simond, in *Europe*, September 15, 1934, p. 5.

[100] *Mircea Eliade*, chap. 4.

[101] These were, according to the *Journal de Krylon*, the last words of a fervent young communist on his deathbed in Moscow, December 31, 1940. Cf. *Journal de Genève*, July 12, 1949.

mends it for humanity today, with a power of assimilation intact. It comes to gather all that is sought in this humanity, the best of its effort and the best of its thought, in order to sublimate it again—and at the same time in order to give it foundation. A historical search would show us that in it we have the deepest source, the most certain origin of the current impulse of our race toward a new type of man. But it is much more. It is a force in the present as well as a source in the past. A force too often asleep but intact. This is due, first of all, to its realism.

This is a mark which cannot be overemphasized. Christianity is, of course, not realistic in the way those systems are which, able to see in man only the "real" that they have conceived, begin by changing his nature; which discern in him only a ready-made, wholly determined being; which, failing to recognize his essential characteristics, take no account, other than to diminish it by treating it as an illusion, of all that is plan, freedom, anticipation, thirst for transcendence in him, in brief, of all to which Christianity gives its true name: vocation, call. Christian realism is a realism of fullness. Without hiding man's misery from him, it shows him his nobility as well. There is therefore no point in asking it how to furnish additional arguments to the sceptics and disenchanted. It will never take sides with those who would sum up the whole possible history of our race in a "parable of the blind" à la Bruegel. It will never, in order to avoid mistakes, invite him back into the rut. It is not in the name of Christian wisdom that laziness of mind or consent to social alienations or the renunciation of dreams of greatness and unity can be preached. Does our faith not teach us that our humanity is one, that it has altogether the same destiny, that a Future is being prepared in which all are invited to collaborate, that the salvation of each is a function of the salvation of all, that the universe has a meaning to which man is the key, that we are all in progress toward a City set free from death and destiny, made for a free and brotherly society, and that we must here on earth serve our apprenticeship for our future condition?[102] That all this would have no effect on the temporal plane is not possible, or rather, not admissible. —But our faith reminds us, too, and with equal force, of two other things.

First of all, that the current ills of man cannot be reduced to some poor organization of the city. "The ills of man are infinitely more profound, more mysterious, his situation infinitely more tragic and his alienation more rigorous."[103] If one is a Christian, it is impossible to forget this very simple, very commonplace little thing—this horrible, invasive leprosy —called *sin*. It is impossible not to take it into account if one is seriously seeking the liberation of man. Naturally egotistical, it is still too little to say: man, that very noble being, is, through something in himself, naturally malicious, and the "unhappy conscience" is first of all a bad conscience, even if it does not yet appear to be so to itself. Already one must observe that, because of free will, all progress is ambivalent; that even progress of conscience does not bring about automatically (far from it!) a growth or consolidation in the good, and that "the state of war", having its seed in all our hearts, will be the state of our earthly condition until the end. Crude or sublime, all dreams of Eldorado are harmful. —But it is another aspect of things that we would particularly like to bring out. To believe that we will dry up the poisoned wellsprings of the heart, or that we will purify it perfectly through any transformation whatever in the external economic, social or political relations between men, to believe that "the state of peace" achieved outside would suppress the whole "state of war" within is once more a utopia. It is disconcerting to note the extraordinary lack of spiritual depth indicated by such an assurance. Does a discovery made in one domain make it fatally blind in another domain of real-

---

[102] On these themes in the patristic tradition, see my book *Catholicisme* [English trans.: *Catholicism* (San Francisco: Ignatius Press, 1988)], chap. 8.

[103] Émile Rideau, *Séduction communiste et réflexion chrétienne* (Éd. de la Proue, 1947), p. 232.

ity? What! Does all this evil that is in man and which so often
makes one person, as has been said, a hell for someone else,
does all this have no other causes at all except those of the social
order? But who, then, first set down these causes? Does man
himself count for nothing in the current functioning of society?
If the division between exploiters and exploited is now—let
us suppose—the sole thing responsible, must we not wonder
how this division itself could have been created? The instinct
for domination existed at the beginning of history, before there
were exploiters and exploited. The instinct for domination and
others besides, which have no fewer social repercussions, such
as that instinct for intolerance, which is characteristic of masses
even more than of individuals and which has been so furiously
awakened once again in our century. . . . This is why there is
no "guarantee of progress". To the very degree that man takes
charge of the direction of his own destiny, as we saw above,
"his existence enters into an extreme danger zone".[104] That is
not to discourage us but must make us clearsighted.

With Marx, as with all those who have seen the importance
of the social question, we thus have no trouble understanding,
in order to reject as pointless, any purely intellectual solution
of the human problem. The "unhappiness of conscience" will
not be suppressed, man will not be liberated by some intellectual process! But let us add that the realism of Marx is incomplete: an economic and social process will not suffice either!
A very different force is necessary in order to overcome "the
great machine of pride and pillage, as old as humanity",[105] always clever at transforming its wheels in order to continue to
crush its victims. Not of course that the historically given social structures are not responsible for many of the varieties of
vices and do not carry many of the seeds of dissension. But the

---

[104] Romano Guardini, "A la recherche de la paix", *Études*, May 1948, p. 252.
Yesterday, the end of human effort still seemed to be the domination of nature; "tomorrow, it must be the domination of its own power."

[105] Jacques Maritain, *Raison et raisons*.

threefold concupiscence is rooted more deeply. The unhappiness of the conscience cannot be reduced to a "reflection of the rifts in society", and the slavery of man is a quite different thing again from social slavery. This unhappiness, this slavery are due to a more primordial—and more internal—fact. Marxism proclaims with good reason the necessity to transcend all philosophy. Christianity has also proclaimed it these twenty centuries. For it, nothing happens in ideas: all is real for it. It does not appeal to principles: it brings us the power of Christ. Come to attack evil, Christ did not come to resolve a problem or dissipate a mirage: he came to destroy an adversary.[106] But philosophy is not the only thing that has to be transcended. Besides, we need not fail to recognize the value of either intellectual activity or social activity. For this latter, the belief in sin is itself another stimulus for us, since it deters us from thinking that an equitable and peaceful order can ever be established by a simple interplay of freedoms. The more one believes man to be naturally egotistical and unjust, the more one must seek to protect his peers from him through a closely woven network of institutions. Social organization is not, of course, composed uniquely of this defensive and negative aspect, but it assuredly involves it. In any case, in whatever way we understand it, it is nonetheless from a wholly different source that we expect the deliverance from evil. The latter can come only from the grace of the Redeemer, freely received. For the evil from which we have been delivered in order to be given back to ourselves, once again, is sin, which touches us and holds us at the root of our being. So, too, it is not indispensable to profess the Catholic doctrine of sin or even to be a believer in order to recognize in man a whole somber and malicious side, a demoniac vein, a power of self-destruction, a spiritual poverty that eats away at him in his depths. Is it not necessary to count among the most certain progress that man has made in our age in knowledge of himself this subterranean exploration

---

[106] This is one of the essential aspects of the mystery of redemption.

in which are joined scholars with the most positive methods and the most intuitive geniuses? We cite simply two symbolic names: Freud and Dostoevsky. Not that, on the other hand, the explanations drawn from psychology (often tied to those of physiology) are not as deficient as the explanation by social relations in the immoderation of their totalitarian ambitions, in which all "pure", theoretical or practical reason is engulfed.[107] Too often, in their respective philosophy of man, sociology and psychiatry prove equally "wrought". At least each of them can serve us, in what it offers us of the positive, to reduce what is exclusive in the claims of the other. Let us add merely that, if psychiatry offers us here the confirmation of its analyses by revealing to us certain "simple bodies" of our deep life,[108] it nevertheless does not succeed any more than its imitator in furnishing us the remedy. And if any man who humbly recognizes himself as a sinner gives proof of more perspicacity than our sociologues, any Christian who opens himself to liberating grace achieves an experience that our psychiatrists do not foresee in any of their categories. It will be enough to call to mind the perfectly clear line with which Augustine of Tagaste, who was a great sinner and a great saint, marks the impassable limit between repression and deliverance: "Multum interest utrum animi desperatione obruatur cupiditas an sanitate pellatur."[109]

But there is another wound in man—a wound which, however completely mixed, concretely, with the first, is not, like it, an obstacle to his greatness: it is, on the contrary, the (in-

---

[107] On Freud's doctrine and on the psychoanalytical method, the best statement seems to me to be that of Fr. de Montcheuil, "Freudisme et psychanalyse devant la morale chrétienne", in *Mélanges théologiques*, "Théologie" series, pp. 297–317. More recently, Maurice Nédoncelle, in *Réflexions sur la psychanalyse* (1949).

[108] The image is from Jean Cassou, *Pour la poésie* (1935), p. 56.

[109] Saint Augustine, *Soliloquies*, I, 19: "There is a great difference between the repression of desire by a desperate soul and its expulsion from a healed soul."

tolerable) sign of it.[110] The form in which it appears to the conscience is multiple. It is an ever-reborn uneasiness, an essential dissatisfaction which prevents man not only from being content with some stable form but from being content with a progress carried on in the same line. It is an impulse of thought that makes him break, one after another, all the circles in which the life of the human animal tends to enclose itself and that overcomes all critical systems, all the positivist wisdoms that believed themselves right. Without an object that is always definite, this can be an agony:

> . . . aliis oppressa malis in pectore cura[111]

an agony whose varieties or psychological substitutes would be infinite to describe. It is at times a presentiment, the presentiment of another existence. The one who experiences it at first communicates around him the taste for it, or at the very least the suspicion of it, thanks to the secret complicity which assures him that the same spirit is spreading everywhere, although numbed in many, and that it, too, is subjected to the mysterious laws of germination. It is what one philosopher recently called the "call of transcendence". One can try to give reassuring explanations for this universal phenomenon. One can also criticize man for its naïve manifestations; one can condemn many

---

[110] Cf. Saint Ambrose, in *Psalmum* 43, n. 88: "Etsi avertis, Domine, faciem tuam a nobis tamen signatum est in nobis lumen vultus tui, Domine" (PL 14:1131).

[111] Lucretius, *De Natura rerum*, bk. 5, v. 1207. This verse occurs in the following context (translated from the version presented by Doctor Logre in his work on *L'Anxiété de Lucrèce* [1946], p. 151):

> When, raising our eyes, we contemplate the immensity
> Of celestial space and the firmament studded with stars
> And when we think of the course of the sun and the moon,
> An anguish, stifled until then beneath other miseries,
> Awakens and lifts up its head: Is there not there, before us,
> An infinite and divine power, which makes
> All these white lights go round to different rhythms?

a distortion of it, denounce many a counterfeit. One can apply
oneself to untangling many of the confusions that a rudimen-
tary mentality entertains with regard to it. One can observe,
besides, that it seems curiously whetted by certain unhealthy
states of the physical or social organism. A very poor observer
would be the one, however, who saw in it only a remnant of
childhood or only a superficial illness, a kind of excrescence
that could one day be rooted out, a phantom that could be
dispelled, a strange voice that could be reduced to silence. A
very poor realist, the one who imagined he could get rid of
it through the development of science or through physical or
social health at last fully acquired. He would fail to understand
the very heart of the reason. He would fail to recognize what
is most human in man and what at the same time makes "man
pass man".

Let us suppose nevertheless that one succeeded in doing so.
We do not hesitate to say: less health would then be better,
if such health were to satisfy us to the point of settling us in
a blissful humanism; if such an equilibrium were to be established that man were as if forever sated with it, that he were no
longer a question to himself.[112] What ideal could be as miserable as that of an earthly existence henceforth without struggle,
without contradiction, without suffering, but also without any
momentum, any search for the Absolute! The ideal of a condition so perfect in its circumscribed reality, so totally adapted
to the surroundings, having so well dried up the spring of all
obstacles of conscience and all scruples, achieving so rigorous
an equation between the objective and the subjective that not
even the least weakness would remain through which to com-

---

[112] This would be the "entire homogeneity" dreamed of by Comte (*Cours*,
vol. 6, p. 536). Cf. M. Nédoncelle, in *Réflexions sur la psychanalyse*, pp. 137–
38: "There is no doubt that the life of the spirit, by introducing into our finite
consciences the perspective of the infinite, makes us forever limp, like Jacob.
Without a head and without a heart, humanity would be a happy beast. But
who would truly want this placidity?"

municate any more with the mystery of being, no play in this great machine of the marvelously organized human universe, nothing that would still permit the debates of man without himself and the commitments of a personal choice![113] One could indeed still speak then of humanism, of culture or of spiritual life: but in what an insipid sense! In Christian terms, what a horror! But simply in human terms, what misery! Is it to this dungeon that the immense effort that is carrying us forward today must lead?[114]

But, in reality, we are not driven to such a dilemma. "God has entered into human life and has introduced into it the essential rupture which removes from all things the natural element with which they are arranged in the totality of the world."[115] Such a rupture is definitive. The "roots of religion" are deep, moreover, in ways other than some still imagine, and it is not up to any social revolution to tear them up. Rather one should say that an excessively unjust or miserable social state—while favoring perhaps certain base aberrations—closes man to the life of the spirit. We can therefore, with full heart and without second thoughts, without fear of ever running the risk of going beyond the desirable limit, work for the rehabilitation of our race and its progress on all fronts: the success will never be such that the noble wound will be healed. Even if that "leap into the kingdom of freedom" that Engels prophesied were

---

[113] When we say that society is for the person, we do not mean to say only that a good social organization must furnish each individual with laws, means to educate himself, to enjoy, as they say, the pleasures of the mind, to taste good music, etc. Man the refined animal, cultivating an "inner life" in new varieties of psychologism is no more the ideal than is man the beast of burden or the cog in a machine. If man does not have at all to decide, to act freely, to struggle, to sacrifice his inferior being for the Good and the True, to commit himself personally in relation to the Absolute, he is a debased being.

[114] Louis Massignon is not wrong to speak in this respect of the "hideous mechanism of our collective incarceration, in which our hardened sins [are combined] as implements of scientific progress": *Dieu vivant*, cahier 7, p. 20.

[115] G. van der Leeuw, p. 516.

to be achieved on earth, the wound would remain open. Our consciousness of it would be only livelier and more pure.[116] We must say what we have already said about the wound of sin: what social disorder has not engendered, social order is powerless to cure.

Why, then, do we see in so many of our contemporaries, along with the persuasion that they themselves are cured, this will to cure our race? Why these cries of triumph at the idea that all metaphysical or religious anguish has drained from their heart? We understand the cry of a Lucretius, celebrating his victory over the fear of the somber Acheron. But after the call of the God of love has sounded directly among us, after a cloud of witnesses, from generation to generation, has never ceased to transmit it to us, do we not see that the situation has changed and that another, more positive way is open? We understand and approve of the struggle against a degrading or paralyzing superstition. But how can we not deplore the blindness of the one who does not know how to discern any prophetic significance in human anguish? There are two ways of being cured of it: by seeking to stifle it, to kill it, to have it removed "surgically"—but then one mutilates oneself, without stopping it from being reborn elsewhere; or else, in opening oneself to the One who assuages it, by changing it into hope. By decreeing that it corresponds to nothing, that there is no mystery at all; or else, taking note of the mystery, by seeking the key which is to open it to us. Now, it is precisely this key that Christianity offers us. It is not one of its dogmas that, in one form or another, reveals and explains us to ourselves. The complete meaning of the great adventure in which we are engaged is revealed to us through it. It shows us, and it alone can show us, the magnif-

---

[116] If we were willing to speak the language of Marx for a moment, we would say that, the more man escapes his natural alienations, the more apt he becomes to understand that kind of alienation—it would be better expressed as ecstasy, promise of a higher and more blessed life—which is his fundamental nature and the movement of his very soul.

icent end of the whole human task. Work is not made to last forever: conceived and served in that way, it would still be an absurd, enslaving idol for him. The new *homo faber* who is being fashioned today will have to be coupled with a new *homo sapiens* as quickly as possible. The latter will not only have the constant concern of renewing with nature and life links that are constantly in danger of being strained. Reflecting on his work activity, he will understand that it cannot be an end in itself but that it has meaning, just like the work of the laborer and the sower, only through the harvest that it prepares: a harvest of eternity. In this temporal existence, it must be at the maximum service of a more pure, more immanent activity: an activity of contemplation.[117] He will likewise understand that, if he enters every day a little more fully into possession of the universe, it is in order to have more to offer; that in the act by which it is achieved, he must not stop but must transcend himself; that only in this way does he accomplish the profound wish of his nature, which is neither to offer himself in a never-ending heroic effort nor to withdraw, satisfied at last, into an egotistical enjoyment, even if noble and collective, but, in contemplating, in offering, to adore.[118]

In the third century of our era, wishing to explain the role of Christians in the world, the author of the epistle to Diognetus compared them to the soul that animates the whole body. This was obviously a strange claim. The paradox today is scarcely less, and yet we affirm it with the same confidence: the disciples of Christ do not feel they are survivors of a shipwrecked world but pilots charged with guiding it into port. In this age when, bypassing the alternatives of optimism and despair, a new man is sought, they want to help him find his way and point out to him the conditions of success. Everything confirms them in

---

[117] Cf. J. Lacroix, *Socialisme?*, pp. 57–62: "The role of work, of all work, is to free captive thought. . . ."

[118] Cf. Émile Rideau, *Consécration* (1946), and J. Mouroux, *Sens chrétien de l'homme*, 4th ed. (1949).

the assurance that they alone have the power to do so. They have not been promised that they will always be heard; they must even usually expect the contrary. They know only too well, moreover, the failures of courage and clearsightedness that make them individually inferior to their task. Yet, strengthened by the words of their Master and the action within them of his Spirit, nothing will make them renounce it. Tomorrow just as yesterday, they will prove to be effectively what they are by vocation: the conscience of the human race.[119]

8.

These are, one will say, very general considerations. At least some of them are, however, unfortunately only too practical and too immediate in application. But, above all, this has been a very incomplete picture of man according to Christianity. The inadequacy due not so much to the biases that an unavoidable distribution of subjects makes imperative as to the perspective adopted. How, in fact, can we penetrate to the depths some point of revealed teaching when, instead of studying the point in itself, we ask of it a judgment about facts, ideas, attitudes which, at least at first glance, are of a totally different order? Such confrontations are legitimate, they are even often necessary, if it is true that the great problems of our temporal life can be resolved only in the light of our total destiny and that Chris-

---

[119] These truths were forcefully recalled by the pastoral letter of Cardinal Suhard in 1947, and in a more recent discourse Pope Pius XII bound all the faithful to fight against the wave of pessimism that is threatening to invade the world: a radio discourse in response to the wishes expressed by the dean of the Sacred College on the occasion of his feast (*Documentation catholique*, June 12, 1947). And already in the same sense, on Christianity coming to save human hope and to achieve the "new man" in human society: the letter of Cardinal Pacelli with respect to the *Semaine sociale* at Versailles in 1936. This text along with other similar ones will be found in J. F. Noubel, "L'Église, vivant modèle de sociologie d'après Sa Sainteté Pie XII", *Bulletin de littérature ecclésiastique*, 1949, pp. 3–25.

tianity, on the other hand, is really lived only on condition of being, as they say today, fully incarnated.[120] It is nonetheless true that these confrontations are always in danger (as we have had occasion to imply above) of misleading and blurring somewhat in minds the distinction between the plane of nature and that of the supernatural. Now, in one sense or another, many positions taken today with respect to temporal action, many judgments formulated about the value of history, about that of scientific research or social effort, seem to us ill-founded precisely due to the lack of a relatively clear doctrine on this subject. While some tend to refer to the ends of human activity the whole impulse of faith that the proclamation of the Good News has aroused in our hearts,[121] others, disparaging this activity unduly, would seem ready to admit that the Christian

---

[120] Again it is necessary to understand well this "incarnation" of Christianity, and for that purpose, not to misjudge the meaning of the mystery of the Incarnation. In an article in *Temps modernes*, February 1946, "Foi et bonne foi", Maurice Merleau-Ponty, blaming Christianity for uniting with generous sentiments a conservative and counter-revolutionary conduct, claimed to explain this paradox by the antinomies of theology itself, depending on whether it clings to the religion of the Father or to that of the Son, which is to say, depending on whether it insists on the transcendence or on the incarnation of God. The Reverend Fr. Jean Daniélou has shown very well, in a clearsighted response published by *Dieu vivant*, no. 8, "Transcendance et Incarnation", that there was in this a total misunderstanding of the Christian mystery. "Let us say it quite clearly", he writes, "this comparison of the transcendent aspect of Christianity with reactionary politics and of its incarnate aspect with revolutionary politics signifies precisely nothing. For the Christian, transcendence and incarnation are part of one and the same order of reality which is radically opposed to the political reality, whether reactionary or revolutionary. . . . [Incarnation] is not a degradation of the transcendent into the immanent, it is the assumption of the immanent by the transcendent, of man by God. For God became man only in order to make man God" (pp. 92–93; cf. Daniélou, *Dialogues*, pp. 105–12). Already Auguste Comte had created a similar confusion, seeing in the dogma of the Incarnation a form of passage for the substitution of humanity for the transcendent God (cf. above, p. 197). While it has certainly not been formulated as a thesis among believers, there is some question of its having, here and there, obsessed certain minds a bit.

[121] We have tried to explain the above in a little volume entitled *Paradoxes*

has nothing more to do here on earth, since history, which is nothing if it is not the history of salvation, virtually ended with the Resurrection of Christ. On one side, it is the temptation of a new naturalism, which Christian hope, diverted from its goal, still feeds with its ardor; on the other, it is a forgetfulness of our true condition, a failure to recognize the earthly tasks through which the salvation of creation is to be worked out. This is why it would be good, in closing, to look once again, at least in one of its aspects and in all its original force, at the fundamental distinction that must command our whole attention here.[122]

Saint Augustine, who is at the origin of our progressive philosophies of history, nonetheless still shared ancient conceptions that made him see in the progress of this world the history of a long decline. And the love that he had for Rome, "the true homeland of his spirit",[123] could only accentuate his pessimism when he saw Rome devastated by Alaric and its empire invaded by the Barbarians. He drew from it a twofold lesson at the time, one of detachment and hope: "Do not become attached", he said, "to this old man that the world is! Do not be afraid: your own youth will be renewed like an eagle's."[124] These reflections are always opportune, of course. Whatever might be the progress on which man prides himself or from which he gathers the fruits, it remains and will always remain true that every day, in our hands, "the world is vanishing". But, on the other hand, a more positive view of the human future, such as Saint Augustine could not have had in his century, will make recourse to Christian hope no less necessary, with all the "mortification" it implies. The authentic reign of the "super-

---

(Éd. du Temps présent) [English trans.: *Paradoxes of Faith* (San Francisco: Ignatius Press, 1987)].

[122] For another aspect of the problem, cf. *Recherches de science religieuse*, no. 1 (1949): "Le Mystère du surnaturel".

[123] Gustave Bardy, *L'Église et les derniers Romains* (1948), p. 89.

[124] Saint Augustine, *Sermo* 81, no. 8.

natural" is never established on a depreciation of "nature". On the contrary, "the greater the capacity of the vase, the more it cries out for fullness."[125]

It is the same for Humanity, taken as a whole, as for each individual. Let it develop thus indefinitely in its order, let it cross more and more elevated thresholds: it cannot reach completion without a totally different process—or rather a "passion": a turning around of the whole being, a mysterious passage through death, a revival and a recasting that are nothing other than the evangelical *metanoia.* No external "revolution" will ever dispense with this inner revolution. As it was necessary to consent to be born, one must now consent to die. It is no longer simply a question of self-control: it is self-renunciation. *Whoever would save his life will lose it. . . .* If no one is to escape humanity for a solitary destiny, humanity as a whole must die to itself in each of its members in order to live, transfigured, in God.[126] Such is the first and final word of Christian preaching. Such is the law imposed on humanity in every man—for each is responsible for all, the bearer of his share of the destiny of all. The law, if one accepts the expression, of Christian humanism, which can only be a converted humanism. *Gloria Dei, vivens homo*: the words of Saint Irenaeus express this truth well, but, on the other hand, man has access to Life, in the only total society that can exist, only by saying quite by himself: *Soli Deo gloria.* Whatever, therefore, may be the natural progress gained, even in moral values, whatever might be the

---

[125] Robert Hamel, "Humanisme et christianisme", *Revue pratique d'apologétique,* vol. L (1930), p. 654.

[126] Since, from nature to the supernatural, there are a thousand relations that are both opposition and analogy, one can already find, within the world of nature, an analogy of this opposition in the relation of work activity to the activity of contemplation. So Jean Lacroix writes, p. 61, "Contemplation and work each have their own inclination. . . . For the contemplative, the supreme value is in detachment from the world, for the worker it is in attachment to the world." We are still speaking here of a wholly natural "contemplation", in its object as well as in its principle.

new idea elaborated, something else must intervene in order to confer on all this its definitive value: a transfiguration, incommensurable with any natural transformations. Something very different from a human progress or success, something infinitely more—and something which saves man himself in the midst of human failure. Neither an advance, a discovery, further progress, but a passage beyond all progress—and without which all progress still leaves man his misery. Not merely an objective victory of freedom over the necessities imposed on the human animal; but, in the innermost part of the being, the passage from servitude to rule.[127]

Now this passage is not at all within man's reach. It is not, in fact, a question of any dialectical reversal, even the most incredible of all. Nor is it a question of a new ascension, even the most audacious of all. It is not a question of passing over into a new degree in the same order. The *supernatural* is not a higher, more beautiful or more fruitful nature. It is not, as is sometimes said today through a poor neologism, an overnature. It is the irruption of a wholly different principle. The sudden opening of a kind of fourth dimension, without proportion of any kind to all the progress provided in natural dimensions. A "new creation",[128] the creation of a "new heart".[129] Literally, a "new birth"—whose first benefit for the Christian will be the revival of a new childhood. Nature evolves and advances all through time: through the supernatural, we pass endlessly from time to eternity. The first builds the earthly city: the second introduces us to the kingdom of God.[130] And the latter is not a

---

[127] Cf. Origen, *Fifteenth Homily on Saint Luke*: "Si quis e carcere et vinctorum domo dimittitur, ut ad regnand um vadat, sumat Jesum in manibus suis . . ." (Rauer, p. 103).

[128] Saint Paul, Gal 6:15, 2 Cor 5:17.

[129] Ps 51 (the Miserere).

[130] A distinction not recognized in the last century by Lamennais, when he wrote, for example, in *Le Livre du peuple* (1838), p. 35: "This is your task; it is great. You have to form a universal family; to construct the City of God, to achieve progressively, through uninterrupted work, its work in humanity."

temple made by human hands. It is the "Mountain of Sion, the City of the living God, the heavenly Jerusalem".[131] The bonds are real and close between nature and the supernatural, since it is the first that weaves, so to speak, the body of the second. The Christian does not need, then, to despair of the earth in order to raise his gaze higher; it is not at all in renouncing all better organization of temporal life that he can open himself to divine life. He does not at all have to turn up his nose at research and human inventions. He is not dispensed from carrying on his profession as a man, his whole profession as a man, and this noble profession deserves our enthusiastic self-donation. This is a new reason for living that our ancestors did not have, that of cooperating in the "great metamorphosis" now in process, in view of making the soul of the earth sing.[132] But in doing so, and even in working on himself, man still, so to speak, only prepares the material. No formation of a "new man" will do away with the necessity of the passage to the "New Man",[133] that "New Man" whom Saint Paul described,[134] immortal and incorruptible, which presupposes the whole mystery of the Man-God.[135] Any new stage through which man passes in his history can only open it—or close it, for all natural progress is ambiguous—to the renewal of the Paschal Mystery. . . .

---

[131] Heb 12:22.

[132] Cf. Jacques Sommet, "Genèse et problèmes d'une civilisation du travail", in *Rythmes du monde*, 1947, no. 5, pp. 11–25.

[133] The necessity will appear twofold if one sees in man, as we recalled above, not only nature but sin. For sin is always old, and the victory of Christ is an ever-new miracle. It is at every instant that the *vetustas* and the *novitas* confront each other.

[134] Eph 4:24: "Put on the new man, created in the image of God in true justice and holiness." Cf. 1 Cor 15:53, etc.

[135] It would be necessary to show now how the mystery of man can be fully clarified only by the mystery of Christ. Many a profound suggestion on this subject are to be found in the *Leçons sur le Christ* by Fr. de Montcheuil (Éd. de l'Épi, 1949). We have also recalled the essential Christian teaching in *Catholicisme*, conclusion.

Let man, therefore, confident of divine assistance, take responsibility once again for the work of the six days. Let him prolong it throughout the seventh day. Let him prove to be bold, victorious, inventive. "What man can do, God does not rob him of."[136] But the eighth day, on which alone everything is brought to completion and renewed, is the Day of the Lord: man can only receive it.[137] May he pursue, as long as this world lasts, the activities of Prometheus: let him light a new fire in each century, the material basis for new human strides—for new problems and new anguish. But, at the same time, let him beg for the descent of the only Fire without whose burning nothing can be purified, consumed, saved, eternalized: *Emitte Spiritum tuum et creabuntur, et renovabis faciem terræ—Send forth your Spirit and they will be created, and you will renew the face of the earth.*

---

[136] Msgr. Garrone, "La Solution chrétienne au problème ouvrier", in *Masses ouvrières*, May 1947, p. 10.

[137] Cf. the Epistle of Barnabas, c. 15, n. 9: "I will inaugurate the eighth day, which is to say, a new world." Saint Gregory, *In Ezechielem*, bk. 2, hom. 8, n. 4: "Per octavum etenim gradum illius vitæ mysteria signantur, quam in secretis suis perfecti intelligunt, qui jam cuncta temporalia mente transcendere noverunt, qui præsentem vitam quæ septem diebus curriculo evolvitur plene despiciunt, qui de intima contemplatione pascuntur" (PL 76:1029D).

CHAPTER II

NIETZSCHE AS MYSTIC

In her recollections of Nietzsche, Lou Andreas-Salomé recounts that when he had finished writing *Die fröhliche Wissenschaft* (*The Gay Science*) in 1882, Nietzsche

> thought that he had disembarked onto the shores of an unknown world, a formidable one, a nameless one, about which he knew nothing yet, except that he found himself beyond what can be attacked or destroyed by thought. He believed that he had put an insuperable ocean between himself and all possibility of intellectual refutation. He imagined himself to be treading virgin ground, situated beyond all criticism.[1]

This attitude was not completely new at that time. It was already of a few months' standing. Lately Nietzsche had had the feeling that he was now a different man. He had entered into another universe. In what concerned the most profound depths of his being, he had broken "all links with living men". "Let us leave Mr. Nietzsche back there. . . ."[2] No longer was he the valetudinarian professor, so full of original ideas, whom the companions of his numerous sojourns in the country had come to know. No longer was he a writer, a philosopher, a critic. No longer was he a disciple of the French moralists, nor of any other master for that matter. The romanticism of his first years at Basel and the positivism that followed that period were not merely outstripped and transformed on account of

---

[1] *Nietzsche* (French trans. of *Friedrich Nietzsche in Seinen Werken*), p. 159. Without saying anything of the experiences to which she was doubtless not privy, Lou Salomé notes, beginning in 1882, "the mystical character of his new doctrines" (p. 67).

[2] *Die fröhliche Wissenschaft.* Quoted by Georges Bataille, *Sur Nietzsche, volonté de chance* (Paris: Gallimard, 1945), p. 35.

his having arrived at some kind of intellectual evolution. An individual who had nothing more in common with all this settled inside him and made him "a solitary among solitaries".[3] A gravity hitherto unknown gripped him. He deemed himself the bearer of an overwhelming revelation, charged with a unique mission. "My hour has come", he wrote solemnly to his sister. "In me can be found today the culminating point of Europe's thought and moral effort and many other things besides. Perhaps the time will come when the eagles themselves will fearfully lift their eyes toward me."[4] And to Peter Gast, at about the same time, he wrote this no less astonishing letter:

> The August sun shines brilliantly above our heads. The year is fleeing. Silence and peace descend on the mountains and the forests. On the horizon of my spirit there surface thoughts the like of which I have never yet experienced. . . . I am going to have to live a *few* years yet! Ah! My friend! At times I tell myself that in essence I am leading one of the most dangerous of lives, for I am one of those machines that can *explode*. The intensity of my feelings makes me tremble and laugh at one and the same time. Several times already I have not been able to leave my room for the ridiculous reason that my eyes were inflamed. What was the cause of this? Each time I had overmuch bewailed my sleeplessness in the course of my walks. And these were not tender tears of pitiful emotion, but tears of jubilation. At those times I sang and spoke stupid, foolish things, possessed as I was by a new vision that I am the first of men to know.[5]

---

[3] Cf. a fragment of 1881–1882 (*Volonté de puissance*, French trans. by Bianquis of *Der Wille zur Macht*, vol. 2, p. 365). "O solitude, solitude, my homeland!" will soon be the song of Zarathustra.

[4] He also talked to her of his "great mission". Texts quoted by Ernst Bertram, *Nietzsche, essai de mythologie* (French trans. of *Nietzsche: Versuch einer Mythologie*), p. 873, and Pierre Burgelin, "Actualité de Nietzsche", *Foi et vie* (1938).

[5] From Sils Maria, August 14, 1881. In Nietzsche, *Lettres Choisies*, ed. by Walz, p. 327. In March 1884 he will write the following to Overbeck from Nice: "I do not know why this happens to fall just on my shoulders—but it

What happened then? Notice the words in the last sentence: "a new vision". It is, in effect, very much a vision that we are dealing with here, or something analogous, or something still more as regards its original form. What we have is an ecstasy, an illumination, a thundering intuition. An object was revealed to him that he was "the first of men to know". This thing took place during the first days of the month of August in 1881. Toward the end of July, Nietzsche left Recoaro, a small village in Venetia, where he was sojourning with his dear friend Peter Gast. *Morgenrothe* (*The Dawn of Day*) had just appeared in print. For the third time he went up into the Haute Engadine area, to Sils Maria. He loved this "region of crystalline light and snow, of blue water and dark fir trees, of green and flowery pastures, where grandeur and grace were united".[6] There he resumed his practice of solitary walks. Thus it was one day, as he was coming from a walk along the lake of Silvaplana, with its overhanging woods, that he halted close to the Surlej Rock. It was here that the event happened. There was no companion to witness it. No direct document relates it to us. But we have sure evidence in an agitated page of *Ecce Homo* that the shock of it was sudden and profound. It is a page that is often cited and is important enough for us to place before our eyes again:

> Suddenly, with sureness, with indescribable delicacy, a thing makes itself seen, makes itself heard. It shakes you, it overwhelms you right to your innermost depths. You hear it, you do not look for it any more. You let it fill you without informing yourself about who has bestowed it. A thought blazes forth like a flash of lightning. It imposes itself as a necessity, under a definitive form. I never had to choose it. It is an ecstasy whose formidable tension is resolved at intervals in a torrent of tears, while your walking pace quickens or slows down involuntarily. You are enraptured, taken outside of yourself, and you maintain a clear

is possible that I am *the first* to have an idea that will divide the history of humanity into two parts" (p. 417).

[6] Geneviève Bianquis, *Nietzsche* (Paris: Ed. Rieder, 1933), p. 29.

consciousness of an infinity of delicate thrills and cascades that run through you right to the tips of your toes and fingers. It is a profundity of blessedness such that sorrow and sadness no longer have the effect of a contrast but seem rather a required condition, a shade of meaning called forth in all necessity by this profusion of light. . . . All of this, which is involuntary to the highest degree, is accompanied by a tumultuous feeling of liberty, of independence, of divinity. . . . There you have my experience of the inspiration.[7]

Charles Andler, Daniel Halévy, and Armand Quinot attribute this passage to the ecstasy that followed Rapallo, about which we shall speak later, whereas Miss Geneviève Bianquis cites the ecstasy that is connected to what happened at the Surlej Rock. There is no contradiction here, seeing that Nietzsche manifestly did not claim to determine and date this memory in a unique way but rather to analyze a certain kind of experience that could be reproduced more than one time with variations. All the facets of the analysis do not therefore necessarily apply to each one of the memories that are at the basis of it. Taken as a whole, it seems, however, to be better adapted to Sils Maria than to Rapallo.[8] Nevertheless, Nietzsche holds fast to the psychological aspect of the inspiration. He tells us nothing here that instructs us the very least bit about the contents of his ecstasy. There is nothing more in his letters of the time to Peter Gast or to his sister. During the months that follow he remains silent about the message he has received. "On my horizon there arose thoughts I had not yet had. I do not wish to divulge any of them", he writes to Peter Gast. Similarly he

---

[7] *Ecce Homo* (French trans. by Vialatte), pp. 126–27, or Armand Quinot, Nietzsche, *Les Pages mystiques*, pp. 169–70: or Bianquis, p. 30.

[8] Nietzsche wrote this page in the chapter concerning *Zarathustra*. But this chapter begins with an account of the experience at Sils Maria. For him, "the story of Zarathustra" begins in August of 1881, and since he finished the first book of *Zarathustra* in February 1883, he said that "I have discovered that my pregnancy lasted eighteen months" (*Ainsi parle Zarathoustra* [French trans. by Vialatte of *Also sprach Zarathustra*], pp. 120–21).

will say later that he looked, albeit in vain, for men with souls deep enough for him to be able to communicate to them his thinking without them dying in the process. But it seems, too, that he had first of all to return from his first feelings of wonderment, that he was forced to look for a new interior equilibrium. The revelation that lives in him would need, he says, "tens of centuries to take shape".[9] At the very least he would need some time to himself to assimilate it, to reflect on it, to find formulas for it.

There is, however, another reason yet for his silence. His courage failed him. In *Die fröhliche Wissenschaft*, a simple continuation of *Morgenrothe*, which he completed at Genoa and then at Messina between October 1881 and April 1882, he makes toward the end a glancing, furtive allusion, with an unreal twist to it, as if he dared not do more. The reader would not understand its significance. In August of 1882, which is to say, one year after the event, he will open himself up to Lou Salomé, but not without difficulty nor without mystery. "He confided his thoughts to me, as if they had been a mystery, one unspeakably painful to give voice to. He spoke of it only in obscure words and in a hushed voice, with every indication of the most profound horror." We shall presently understand why this was so. The thought that rose before him "like a star"[10] is not simple. It was an object of terror as well as of jubilation, or rather the one or the other of these two categories, according to the manner in which it is taken. It "blazed forth like a flash of lightning". Was its purpose to illumine or to strike down? He laughed at it and shuddered at it in turn. This terrible and marvelous revelation, this ambivalent thought, is held together in two words: the Eternal Return.

---

[9] To Peter Gast, January 25, 1882 (Charles Andler, *Nietzsche, sa vie et sa pensée* [Paris: Ed. Bossard, 1920–1931], vol. 4, p. 272).

[10] Posthumous fragment, cited by Andler, p. 259, or in *Volonté de puissance* (French trans. by Bianquis [1885] of *Der Wille zur Macht*), vol. 1, p. 295.

The beginning of August 1881, at Sils Maria, 6500 feet above sea-level and much higher than this yet above all things human!

The sun of Knowledge is yet once more at its point of High Noon, and the Eternal Serpent is stretched out ring-wise in its light.[11]

In the autumn of 1882, very much pained by his sentimental adventure with Lou Salomé, Nietzsche had returned to Leipzig. Several of his friends had remarked at the time "that he seemed like a haggard apparition come from an uninhabited region wherein he could not be reached any more".[12] In November he took the road south again. After seeing the Overbecks again at Basel, he arrived at Rapallo, on the Ligurian coast, to spend the winter there. He lived as a solitary with the notebooks in which his doctrine of the Eternal Return was already taking shape in its first outlines. He undertook long walks along the length of the bay at Rapallo, going as far as the promontory at Portofino. Sometimes he sat down to face the sea. It is within this framework that a new and mysterious event took place:

> I was sitting and waiting, without waiting for
> anything,
> Beyond good and evil, tasting
> Light sometimes and sometimes shade,
> Absorbed by this brew,
> Become the sea, noonday, and pure duration, without
> design,
> When suddenly, my friend, what was one became two,
> And Zarathustra passed before me. . . .[13]

---

[11] *Ecce Homo*, p. 120. "Midi et Eternité", fragment of 1881–1882 (Quinot, p. 90).

[12] Andler, vol. 4, p. 348.

[13] Poem addressed to Lou Salomé and published in the second edition of *Die fröhliche Wissenschaft* (1886). Cf. *Le Gai Savoir* (French trans. by Vialatte of *Die fröhliche Wissenschaft*), p. 225. The piece, which bears the title today of "Sils Maria", should, it seems, have been entitled "Portofino" right from the first. We are following Andler here, vol. 4, pp. 330–31.

Contrary to what happened at Sils Maria, we have here a vision. It is a vision that is, without a doubt, precise and sudden: "I could tell you the day and the hour." "Zarathustra", he will go on to say, "has fallen on me, he assaults me." Nevertheless, it is something less absolutely new than what happened at Sils Maria, something less surprising, more prepared for. Also Nietzsche was not shaken right to the depths by contrary impressions. Exulting with joy, he felt no terror. Without a doubt, though, it must be said that it was this vision, it was this radiant image of Zarathustra that positively dispelled all terror and settled him in his joy. It exalted him and reassured him at the same time. Here he is all "atremble with variegated beatitude". Zarathustra is his luminous double, Zarathustra is himself: "The one becomes two." And two make only one. He had already conceived the personage this double would assume, but this by way of a literary fiction. And he, himself, in his hours of depression felt more opposition between the two than fraternity. He asked himself if the preaching of his hero would not entail his own destruction. He did not doubt the idea that he had received, but, at times, he still doubted his hero. This being the case, to the very degree of this doubt of his, the idea, without ceasing to assert itself, became atrocious and intolerable to him. Should he sing of the god who had overwhelmed him or curse with gnashing teeth the demon who was torturing him? . . .[14] Now his last hesitations disappear, as does the return of his anxieties. Without bringing him a new message, Zarathustra came to confirm him in the message already received. From now on he knows with certainty how to interpret for himself the revelation given to him at Sils Maria.

From this source comes that sudden and unexpected fecundity. Ten days end up being sufficient for Nietzsche, starting

---

[14] He brought it to Overbeck's attention in a letter of February 1883, where he told him that this book seemed to him to be his last testament (*Lettres choisies*, p. 373).

from the end of this same month of January, to draft the whole
first book of his prophecy. For it is no longer a matter of critical analyses or observations, as it was in his preceding writings.
And the form is no longer, as it is in *Die Fröhliche Wissenschaft*
still, that of aphorisms.[15] It is a lyrical gushing forth. The inspiration overflows like a river. "It is a poem and a fifth gospel",
he writes to his publisher. "It is a thing for which there is no
name." And to Peter Gast he writes: "This is only a very small
book, but it is the best thing that I have done. I feel my soul is
relieved of a burden. I have never done anything more serious,
nor anything more merry."[16] These pages seem to him to be
"his testament". In April he will write from Genoa to Overbeck: "It seems to me sometimes that I have lived, worked
and suffered only to be able to write this little book of seven
sheets' length, and even that my whole life turns out in this
way to be justified after the fact."[17]

It is tempting to attribute the judgment that he makes on
Zarathustra in *Ecce Homo* to the morbid exaltation that preceded
his downfall.

> This work [he says] is absolutely in a class by itself. . . . A Goethe
> or a Shakespeare would never be able to breathe a single instant
> in this atmosphere of formidable passion and vertiginous heights.
> Dante is merely a believer, and not someone who first and fore-
> most *creates* truth, a spirit who *dominates the world*, a fateful in-
> evitability. The poets of the Veda are priests, unworthy to untie
> the sandlestraps of Zarathustra. And even all this does not give
> an idea of the *azure* distance in which this work lives.[18]

Yes, there is without a doubt in this tone of his an enormous
braggadocio that is a forerunner of the abyss. But in the main

---

[15] Cf. *Le Gai savoir* 341, p. 170.

[16] February 1, 1883 (Andler, vol. 4, p. 333).

[17] From Genoa, April 1883 (*Lettres choisies*, p. 385). Cf. to Karl Hildebrand,
May 24 (p. 201).

[18] *Ecce Homo*, pp. 131–32.

it is quite the same assurance that Nietzsche had evinced from the very first, that assurance which had made him write afterward to another one of his correspondents, Mr. de Seydlitz, that he should betake himself one day on a pilgrimage to Rapallo, "that sacred spot where was born that book of books, *Zarathustra*". He makes us take most seriously the words to his publisher about "a fifth gospel". There is no doubt, moreover, that it must be understood, in the thought of Nietzsche, that this fifth gospel abolishes the preceding ones, the four Christian Gospels. We have confirmation of this in a passage of a letter of April 1883 to Malwida von Meysenbug: "It is a marvelously beautiful story. I have challenged all religions and have made a new Holy Book." From this day on, Nietzsche, an inspired prophet, and more than just a prophet, to be sure, did not pass himself off any more as a mere critic and adversary of Christianity but as a rival and successor to Jesus. He is conscious of being "the decisive and mysterious link that connects two thousands of years one to the other". Already he is aware of himself as the one who will be able to say of himself with obviously literal intent: *Ecce Homo*.

Through this vision at Rapallo, Nietzsche, by convincing himself of the secret depths of his being, had taken definitive possession of his idea of the Eternal Return.

Here a whole series of questions arises that many commentators have not been negligent in assembling and mulling over for a half-century now. How could Nietzsche have believed in the newness of his discovery? How could he have found a source of exaltation in a thought pattern that was really quite oppressive? How, moreover, did he, who was so perspicacious, not discover its incoherences? And how did he not see at least that his ideal of the Overman, incarnated in Zarathustra, stood in contradiction to his faith in the Eternal Return?

Certainly, if any idea could seem hackneyed, it had to be this one. It "could be found everywhere".[19] Nietzsche could not have missed encountering it among those ancient Greeks to whom he had devoted his first enthusiastic admiration: for example, Anaximander, Heraclitus, and also Pythagoras. Lucretius celebrated it in verse, and it was likewise at the heart of stoic cosmology. It was to be found everywhere in India, which the reader of Deussen and Oldenberg must have known well enough. Could he not have read it in Goethe? He had read it in Guyau. It had even found recently a kind of scientific justification in Vogt's new dynamics, which explained the whole universe by indefinitely repeated alternations of dissolution and condensation. Now Nietzsche, who was passing through a phase of scientism at the time, had read the work of Vogt, whose audacity had pleased him.[20] He had copied several passages of it. How then, in view of the sudden enthusiasm of the years 1881–1883, can one avoid following the lead of Henri Bois by speaking of a paramnesiac phenomenon, or the lead of Flournoy by speaking of a cryptomnesiac phenomenon?[21] How could we not say to ourselves with Father Sertillanges: "This brain of fire burns away memories as soon as a new burst of its interior flame comes to surprise it"?[22]

New or not, was such an idea not appropriate for the discouragement of human activity? It not only persuades me that I will have to do again indefinitely all that I am doing, but at the same time it teaches me that already, in the past, I have done it an incalculable number of times. It is thus impossible for me to imagine that I might be able in any way whatsoever to create myself or change myself, to take the least bit of initiative, to

---

[19] Cf. Antonin Sertillanges, *Le Problème du mal* (Paris: Aubier, 1948–1951), vol. 1, p. 346.

[20] Andler, vol. 4, pp. 254–59.

[21] *L'Année philosophique*, 24e année (1913): Henri Bois, "Le Retour éternel de Nietzsche", pp. 145–84.

[22] Sertillanges, vol. 1, p. 346.

effect the least bit of real progress. Neither liberty nor newness is conceivable in the world. I am for an indefinitely repeated future the slave of a past that is itself indefinitely moved back. To all the beings caught up in this infernal cycle, which leaves nothing outside of it, it must be said: "Give up hope." But can it not also be shown without too much trouble, thank God, that such a cycle is completely imaginary? It can be shown by science, whether one accepts or rejects the idea of an infinite number. And how would identical worlds be discernible? And if Nietzsche had such a great opinion of the principle of the conservation of energy, what would he do today with the complementary principle of the degradation of energy? It can also be shown by psychology, for the facts of consciousness can only be the same if they are referred to a same consciousness. Now it is not the same consciousness that reappears from one period to another, since there is no linkage of memory from one to the other. A few "false recognitions", as Nietzsche perhaps proved in fact to be the case, do not furnish a sufficient basis for such a hypothesis to be taken into consideration, and so on.[23]

Did Nietzsche not, moreover, improve on these diverse contradictions by desiring to associate his dream of the Overman to the idea of the Eternal Return? The idea of the Overman, however, was itself not so new. Herder and Goethe, among others, had already conceived of it.[24] Is it not in any case clear that it is necessary to choose between these two things: either a resigned acceptance of a cycle that will always bring back the same unchanged elements, making the same progressions

---

[23] Cf. Benoist-Hanappier, "Le Prophète Nietzsche", *Pages libres*, Sept. 1907; Henri Bois, pp. 148–55. It has been remarked that the feeling of horror evinced by Nietzsche in the wake of his ecstasy invariably accompanies "false recognitions". On the Eternal Return and science: Andler, vol. 4, pp. 62–65; Robert Marchal, "Le Retour éternel", *Archives de philosophie*, vol. 3 (1925).

[24] Cf. D. Tchizenski, "Hegel et Nietzsche", *Revue de la philosophie*, 1929, pp. 330–33.

succeed the same instances of decay, or else a being's effort to grow, to contrive new values, to surpass itself always, and ever to impose its law? Without a doubt it could be replied, with Ernst Horneffer, that the great, strong, happy being has nothing to fear from the law of eternal return, since he can only desire to recover that life which fulfills him. In the measure, therefore, to which he succeeds in raising himself to this ideal, man will necessarily find the perspective of being reborn indefinitely not crushing but rather uplifting. But this is a totally superficial reconciliation, which does not take into account the fact that we cannot change our past, and it presupposes besides a shabby and inexact understanding of Nietzsche's ideal of the Overman. Nietzsche had only contempt for every kind of eudaemonism, and his Overman is not a pleasure-seeker, even in the most noble and refined sense that might be given to this word. "It is a sign of regression", he wrote, "when eudaemonistic values start to come to the fore."[25] Mr. Daniel Halévy also declared in his first *Vie de Frédéric Nietzsche* (Life of Friedrich Nietzsche) that: "The Eternal Return is a bitter truth that suppresses all hope. The Overman is a hope—an illusion. There can be no passing from one to the other. The contradiction between them is complete. If Zarathustra teaches the eternal Return, he will not be able to arouse in souls a passionate belief in overhumanity. And if he teaches the Overman, he will not be able to spread the moral terrorism of the Eternal Return."[26] It was in this very contradiction, according to Mr. Halévy, that could be found the explanation for the gropings and the changes of plan in the rest of the poem. In the final analysis, after a few vain tries at rational justification, the

---

[25] *Volonté*, 551, vol. 1, p. 371. He goes so far as to say: "The superior man is distinguished from the inferior by the intrepidity with which he courts adversity" (ibid.).

[26] Daniel Halévy, *La Vie de Frédéric Nietzsche* (Paris, Calmann-Levy), p. 282. "Friedrich Nietzsche, however, assigns him these two tasks. The disorder and haste of his ideas drive him to this absurdity."

Eternal Return would have been abandoned and would have made its reappearance later only as a simple lyric theme. In fact, there is no question of this in the first *Zarathustra*. The new gospel promulgated in January of 1883 would therefore have superseded at once false Christian hope and the old despairing myth. The second experience would not have confirmed but have discredited the first. The Overman would appear as "a symbol of a real progress that modifies things, a promise of a possible escape beyond chance and fate."[27]

. . . These questions, these criticisms, these analyses show too much *sang-froid*. Did Lou Salomé not inform us that her interlocutor supposed himself to have put "an insuperable ocean between himself and every attempt at intellectual refutation"? Did he not have the feeling that he was "treading virgin ground, ground that was situated beyond all criticism"? Certainly it can be replied that this is a totally subjective feeling, which an objective study does not have to take into account. Nietzsche's convictions do not absolve him of criticism any more than any other mortal. Might they not be a sign to us at least that he has not always been correctly understood? Perhaps there is room for a greater effort to be made so that criticism is not trained on a phantom, even while it believes that it is achieving a comprehension of his ideas. His ideas are not in his case the result of a scientific elaboration. As Andler writes, "in the same way as, with Spinoza, the pantheistic state of his sentiments preexisted his system and his geometric form, thus, with Nietzsche mystical ecstasy preceded his scientific reasoning."[28] He then sought out for it, some of the time, at least, justifications and illustrations in scientific knowledge. But his ideas in themselves, whatever the manner in which they had begun to be insinuated secretly in him before the visions he had at Sils Maria and Rapallo, were of another order. This kind of

---

[27] Ibid., p. 261.
[28] Andler, vol. 6, p. 75.

ennobled scientism, which had seemed for some time to be a necessary definition of Nietzsche's thought, is now quite outmoded. If science does not provide it with any confirmation, Nietzsche will dispense with science, or else he will examine it from another bias.[29] Thus the believer has no trouble in letting go an extrinsic apologetical system, as soon as the latter appears to be ineffective or outdated. His faith does not depend on it. It does not share the same measuring stick. Of what importance, therefore, are the deceptions that science has been able to attribute to Nietzsche? His thought is not at all affected. This is because in its "lofty grandeur" his thought "resembles no other"[30] and is dependent on no other. What then can it properly be said to be?

In a page of his new *Nietzsche*, which corrects to some extent his older study, Mr. Daniel Halévy makes an effort to disentangle his thought. There he finds a metaphysics that is new bound up with a myth that is ancient:

> Everything returns, said the ancients, who were not familiar with the notion of the eternal. Everything returns ceaselessly, writes Nietzsche. Which is to say, eternally. At the same time as there is a Return, there is an Eternal Return. Such is the expression he will always use, and in this expression the accent falls on "Eternal". The use of the Hebrew word, unknown by the Greeks, renews the primitive myth. From age to age, declared the ancients, humanity will see the occurrence of returns. For Nietzsche it is very different: each instant that we live, he says, which is destined to return an infinite number of times, bears the mark of eternity and is itself an Eternal Thing.[31]

---

[29] For "one can no longer imagine a philosophy separated from the natural sciences." And in fact, fragments from 1886–1888 show us Nietzsche continuing to examine the physical sciences in favor of the Eternal Return with as many "hidden theological motives" as those who examine these sciences in favor of creation: *Volonté*, I, II, n. 329 and 331, vol. 13, pp. 298–300.

[30] Quinot, p. 16.

[31] Daniel Halévy, *Nietzsche* (Paris: Grasset, 1944), p. 269.

Provided that it is not pressed too far, this analysis appears to us to be true and just but still insufficient. It is true that Nietzsche has an idea of eternity that did not exist at all in this guise among the ancients. It is also true that in that union that he conceived of becoming and eternity, he put the accent on the latter term:

> Above us shines a multitude of stars,
> Around us rustles Eternity.[32]

It is true as well that this insistence arises from a profound yearning: ". . . For I love thee, O Eternity!"[33] However, these declarations leave the main point uncertain. Namely, how does Nietzsche perceive the relationship between the two elements that appear to him to be united? How does eternity for him prevail over becoming? How can each of the moments that the cosmic wheel of becoming brings back indefinitely be truly, in his eyes, "an eternal thing" itself?

It is here, we believe, that the essential element of Nietzsche's intuition is touched. It is here that the Eternal Return and the Overman are going to show themselves to be bound up together, like "two mysteries meshed with one another".[34]

It is all too clear as well that Nietzsche is not terribly keen on that naïve optimism that humanity has, which could see in the endless return of the ages a means of constantly recommencing anew an animal existence that epitomizes for it all that is good. Nietzsche is not keen on the naïve optimism of a humanity which suffers only one form of anguish, namely, fear lest the cosmic force of renewal waver, and only one concern, that of

---

[32] The "New Columbus", a piece that accompanies the dispatch of *Die fröhliche Wissenschaft* to Lou Salomé, summer 1882 (Quinot, p. 109).

[33] *Les Dithyrambes de Dionysos: Gloire et eternité* (French trans. of *Dionysos-Dithyramben*).

[34] These are the words of Charles Andler, vol. 4, p. 4. But to judge by the commentary that follows them, it does not seem to us that Andler has fully understood the nature of this meshing together. See also p. 36.

assuring by its rites this eternal recommencement. He knows that it is a matter here of an ambiguous reality. It does not escape him that, depending on the way one becomes aware of it, the Eternal Return can appear by turns as the most exalting reality or, on the contrary, as the most crushing reality. In effect, this return is a circle. The person who perceives this can himself be placed in its center or even on its circumference. He can be carried away passively in an immense and desperate rotation, or, on the other hand, he can participate in the dominating force that thus moves the whole cosmos. He can be distended in a scattered state of endless duration, always beginning anew, or, on the other hand, he can find himself gathered together in the moment that gives rise to the whole thing. He can suffer the iron law of universal determinism, but he can, on the other hand, be himself this very law in freedom. In the first case, he is destroyed; in the second, he triumphs.[35] There is no emptiness more horrible nor any plenitude more overflowing. To love fate is merely a *pis aller*, doubtless not practicable, for the person who despairs of escaping it. It is a mediocre submissiveness and not very sincere. But for the person who rises to the point of coinciding with fate, for the person who identifies with it, it truly constitutes the love of supreme liberty. If he

> accepts as a unique and perfect present all that life brings to him . . . , it is because he himself has become the source and the center of life. He has no more need to yield to destiny, for he has raised his own statue right to the heights of destiny. . . . He creates and he conserves in the same breath: in him, as in God, necessity and liberty coincide.[36]

---

[35] It is this which is further expressed by the double apology of the serpent at 1.III of *Zarathoustra*: "This monster slid to the bottom of my throat to choke me. But with a slashing cut of my teeth, I cut off its head and spit it out far from me" ("Le Convalescent", II, p. 202; cf. "De la vision et de l'énigme", II, p. 153).

[36] Gustave Thibon, *Nietzsche ou le déclin de l'esprit*, p. 92.

For such a being the circle of iron becomes a ring of gold. "*Fatum* [fate]", concludes Nietzsche, "is an exalting thought for whoever has come to understand that he is part of it himself."[37] *Amor fati. Ego Fatum* (Love of fate. I am Fate).

Such is precisely the experience of Nietzsche. (We shall see farther on what we should think of its authenticity.) Now this is rightly a mystical experience. "The mystic", Mr. Henri Delacroix has written, "is present at the genesis of things. He places himself at the heart of the source and lets himself be carried by it. Thus he traverses all the forms of being without leaving being."[38] To be present at, to let oneself be carried—it is not enough to use these words in the present case. Nietzsche feels in himself the Force that produces everything and that finds itself intact, unchanged, free and sovereign in each instant of universal becoming. For him, existence is a circle whose center really "is everywhere". Nothing weighs on him, because "at every moment existence commences."[39] It is in this sense we should take the happy expression of Miss Marie-Anne Cochet: "In the month of August 1881, close to the monolith of Surlej, Nietzsche received his baptism of eternity." This author's interpretation, however, is still a little bit too much fixed along the lines of classical intellectualism, at least on this page. According to this interpretation, in effect, "his thought turns around on itself while supposing it is following a straight line, just like horses with their blinkered eyes, who turned the millwheels in days of yore. It will only be free and have mastery of itself when it knows its own

---

[37] *Also sprach Zarathustra*, 1, IV. Cf. *Ecce Homo*, in a less triumphant tone: "The greatness of man is expressed in his *amor fati*. That is my formula; to not ask for change, either of the past or of the future or of eternity. It is not necessary to be content with enduring what is necessary—it is still less necessary to conceal it . . . it is necessary to love it" (p. 67).

[38] *Essai sur le Mysticisme spéculatif en Allemagne au XIVe siècle* (Paris: Alcan, 1900), p. 15.

[39] *Zarathoustra*, 1. III; "Le Convalescent", II, p. 201.

reality."[40] But we have just seen that such a knowledge has a double face. It is, to be sure, an "extreme reconciliation of the world of becoming with the world of Being".[41] Yes, but if one is coming at it from the side of becoming, nothing is more horrible, let us repeat, than Nietzsche's vision of the world, and Nietzsche is the first to experience this and say it. Whereas, if one is coming at it from the side of Being, it constitutes a divine felicity.[42] *Lux mea crux—crux mea lux* (My light is a cross —my cross is a light).

Now Nietzsche's first experience still had something uncertain about it. At the very least, his ecstasy had not sufficed at all to forestall his anxious doubts about his own situation. The role of the vision at Rapallo will be to dispel these doubts. There Nietzsche receives the assurance, which up till then was all too intermittent, that he was very much on the side of Being. He participates actively, freely in *Fatum*. He himself is part of it. His intuition therefore does not relegate him, a paltry individual, to a slavery rendered heavier still by the awareness he would have gained of it. He knows that he is the Overman, he whose lawless will engenders worlds. He is what he has perceived. His thought has not only "taken on flesh" since Sils Maria, it has now received its definitive significance. All ambiguity is lifted. All doubt, all anguish have disappeared. He can henceforth pronounce without hint of a lie the words *amor Fati* (love of Fate) because he can first say without hesitation the words *ego Fatum* (I am Fate). The new Prophet has thus received his investiture. He escapes common humanity. He arises therefore, he is going to pronounce his new gospel,[43]

---

[40] "Nietzsche d'après son interprète français", *Revue philosophique*, vol. 2 (1932), p. 245.

[41] Cf. Halévy, *Nietzsche*, p. 268; Quinot, p. 105.

[42] "A state that the most daring utopian has never dared to dream of!" *Œuvres posthumes*, French trans. by H. J. Bolle, 218 (p. 99).

[43] For he alone, comments Lou Salomé very aptly, p. 269, "possesses the right to proclaim the new law. It is he who has the power to transform it into redemptive felicity."

calling on a new "metanoia" in order to enter into a new kingdom.[44] Like the other kingdom, indeed, more truly than the other one, he is at once its revealer and its object, its messenger and its god. "Noon, the time of the shortest shade. End of the longest error. Culminating point of humanity. *Incipit Zarathustra* (Zarathustra begins)."[45]

Wishing to refute Spinoza's conception of the wise man and his blessedness, Leibniz wrote:

> Spinoza surmises that from the day when man knows that events are the product of necessity, his spirit is considerably strengthened by this knowledge. But there is the following constraint. This knowledge does not make the heart of the sufferer more content. He does not feel the evil that befalls him any the less.

This was certainly not a profound entering into the idea of the philosopher, and one would not have had much difficulty showing that such such a refutation was superficial.[46] In reality, when Spinoza's wise man rises to consider universal Necessity, it is not by means of an ordinary knowledge, which will leave him otherwise in his miserable state. It is rather by a certain kind of intuition thanks to which he is already no longer that "sufferer" whom Leibniz still talks about. The being who obtains third-degree knowledge—if it is not a snare to speak in these terms—is no longer in himself one of the innumerable elements that go to make up *natura naturata* (literally, "natured

---

[44] Cf. *Der Antichrist*: "The kingdom of heaven is a fact of experience, a state of heart."

[45] *Le Crépuscule des idoles* (French trans. by Albert of *Gotzendammerung*), p. 135. One is right to find a double significance in these elliptical lines. On the one hand, in the succession of times, Nietzsche's time marks noonday at its height, for the new prophet, in "killing God" and rejecting the work of Christ, has put an end to human error. On the other hand, the shadeless noonday symbolizes the Overman, who can say the words *Ego Fatum*, placed as he is in the center of the circle of Eternal Return.

[46] *Réfutation inédite de Spinoza par Leibniz*, ed. Foucher de Careil (Paris, 1854), pp. 66–68. Cf. Georges Friedmann, *Leibniz et Spinoza* (Paris: Gallimard, 1946), p. 151.

nature"). He participates in *Natura naturans* (literally, "naturing Nature").

The idea, it is clear, is analogous to that of Nietzsche. There is, nevertheless, a difference between the two, a difference that allows Nietzsche's idea to escape more readily than its counterpart the refutation of Leibniz. We are not making an allusion here to the passionate character of Nietzsche's idea, which contrasts so strongly with Spinoza's impersonal serenity, indeed coldness, as if it sprang from a thought proceeding *more geometrico* (in a geometric fashion). For under the cover of this apparent coldness there was perhaps a smoldering fire, and it could have been said that Spinoza was "intoxicated by God".[47] but in Nietzsche there is no *Natura naturans*. There is no divinity, there are no objective essences, no eternal ideas. There is nothing that resembles a Platonic world. As a result, there is no ontology. As rigorous as the necessity may be that it engenders for those who undergo it, *Fatum* is pure contingency, because it is pure invention, a throw of the dice, a divine fantasy, a dance in the middle of an empty sky. . . . And when Zarathustra discovers that he coincides with such a principle, he discovers rather, to put it plainly, that there is no superior principle to which he needs to be linked. The law of the world is completely, at every moment, sprung from his arbitrariness. He has vanquished completely "the spirit of heaviness". He is eternal in himself, not by participation. Or rather he makes himself eternal. All value proceeds from his will. All his knowledge is creative:

> Supreme star of Being,
> Table of eternal creations. . . .[48]

---

[47] Cf. Andler, vol. 5, p. 75: "As, in Spinoza, the sentimental pantheistic state preexisted his system and its geometric form, so, in Nietzsche, mystical ecstasy precedes his reasoning and engenders it."

[48] *Dithyrambes de Dionysos: Gloire et eternité* (Quinot, p. 264). *Zarathoustra*, I, III, pp. 150–51 and 179–82. Cf. M.-A. Cochet, pp. 246–47: "One does not discover eternity. It is a state that certain men experience in themselves

Nietzsche's idea shares more analogically with Buddhism than with Spinozaism. Nietzsche wanted to establish "a European Buddhism". Without a doubt he exalts life instead of sterilizing it. He seeks the central point from which all of life springs forth, not the central point where all of life is extinguished.[49] He does not celebrate the "destruction of the house", but, on the contrary, he extols its eternal reconstruction.[50] Similarly his conception of the Overman offers no fewer significant resemblances to the conception of the *Buddha*, of the awakened man, who is thereby even more than a man, of him who knows

---

and that they generally project before them as a reality of a transcendent order. The states during which man feels himself to be eternal are precisely superhuman states. Philosophers have most often translated this state by the following words: 'Man is eternal in God.' But Nietzsche says to man that he is only and can only be eternal in himself and that his eternity will be his own creation."

[49] He has, however, admirably celebrated the mystery of the night and of sleep, a metaphor that is dear to the Indian mystic. Cf. the mysterious boat in *Le Gai savoir*, pp. 220–21:

> Suddenly my senses failed
> In an eternal unconsciousness,
> And an abyss opened up, without bottom. . . .
> What was there? blood? drama?
> No! . . . We were dreaming, we were dreaming
> All of us . . . ah! so good! so good!

He also likes to reconcile images of the Sun and the Night (*Gloire et eternité*), and one of his most beautiful poems is "Le Chant de la nuit" in book II of *Zarathoustra*: "I am Light. —ah! why am I not Night? But it is my solitude to be encompassed by Light. —Ah! Why am I not shade, a shade of night? How I would drink at the bosom of Light . . . ! —It is night. The unhappiness of being able to be only Light, and a thirst for shade, and solitude! . . ." (pp. 109–11; Quinot, pp. 133–34). Cf. *Jenseit von Gut und Böse*, where we read in the epilogue:

> He has come, Zarathustra, my friend, the host of
>   hosts!
> The world is now laughing; the black curtain is torn:
> Light is united to darkness!

[50] *Zarathoustra*, I, III; "*Le Convalescent*", II, p. 201.

by a mysterious and total intuition, not the secret of a Being who does not exist, but the secret of universal becoming. "I am not a man, I am not a god. Know that I am a Buddha." Thus could Zarathustra speak. Like Sakyamuni, he is the protagonist of a mysticism without God. And like Sakyamuni, does he not claim, moreover, to be, in his own right, part of a cosmic series of great visionaries?[51] This thought assumes a very Buddhist form: "In each of the successive cycles of human history, there is always an hour when, for an isolated man, then for many men, and then for all men, there arises the all-powerful word, that of the Eternal Return of everything. In such a case noon-hour rings out each time for humanity."[52]

But the analogy goes farther. It is reinforced in that very area where certain people, including Lou Salomé, saw only a contrast. For Nietzsche, says Lou Salomé, "the highest ideal is not called nirvana but *samsara*. The supreme end of life is not to deliver oneself from the cycle of reincarnations but to accept it with joy."[53] This is true. Nietzsche's eternity, the eternity on which Nietzsche puts his accent, is, however, completely in becoming, to such a point that there is nothing other than this becoming. His eternity prevails over becoming. Only it is emptied of all substance, and it has passed completely into the opposite term.[54] It is this that permits Nietzsche to affirm:

---

[51] On Nietzsche and Buddha, one can read Leopold Ziegler, *Der ewige Buddho* (Darmstadt: Reichl, 1922).

[52] Fragment of 1881–1882; *Volonté*, vol. 1, p. 296.

[53] P. 265.

[54] ". . . The ideal of the most impetuous man, the most alive man, the most affirming man on earth, of the man who has not only learned to accommodate himself to what was and what is but who wishes moreover for this state of affairs to continue, such as it was and such as it is, not only for himself but also for the play and the show of life in their entirety, and not only for the show, but still more for him who has need of this show and renders it necessary—because he always has need of himself and renders himself always necessary. . . . How? Would this not be *circulus vitiosus deus* [a vicious, circular god]?" *Par delà le bien et le mal* (French trans. by Albert of *Jenseit von Gut und Böse*, 56), p. 101.

"Even in the domain of the spiritual, we believe solely in becoming." But one should not forget that for Buddhism, too, there is no independent eternity. Buddhist nirvana is not an eternal essence. Buddhist salvation is pure deliverance. It does not consist of passing from the domain of *samsara* into another domain. It ended up being expressed in a doctrine by which Nietzsche would have been enchanted, if he could have known it: the doctrine of *mahayana*, common to the *madhyamika* school and the school of the *Vijnanavadin*, which is the doctrine of "nirvana which is not a stopping".

It is well known that, according to the Great Vehicle, the *bodhisattva*, by virtue of his vow of charity, delays indefinitely his entry into nirvana, even though he has already achieved all the conditions to enter it. But in speaking thus, we are speaking according to appearances. When every "obstruction" has disappeared, "Buddhahood" is achieved. The wise man can still easily enough come and go, think and act, preach and devote himself, be born and die, "as long as the world exists, which is to say, indefinitely."[55] He is no less truly delivered from it. He is not in a separate nirvana. But he is no longer in the prison of *samsara*, since for him, who has seen the underside of things, "nirvana is *samsara*, and *samsara* is nirvana. There is no difference between the two."[56] He has not replaced one illusion by another. He has achieved "that sense of universality where nirvana and *samsara* have only one flavor". His nirvana is a nirvana that is not a stopping, the only true nirvana. Hence Nietzsche's eternity, his *annulus æternitatis* (ring of eternity).[57] It is not at

---

[55] Asanga, *Mahayana Sutralamkara*, chap. 8, v. 22 (trans. Sylvain Lévi, p. 67).

[56] Nagarjuna. And also Asanga, chap. 6, v. 5: "There is in reality no difference between the production and the extinction of personality, between Samsara and Nirvana" (p. 52). Cf. Louis de la Vallée Poussin, *Dogme et philosophie du bouddhisme* (Paris: Beauchesne, 1930), pp. 162–64. The whole reality of nirvana in effect lies in the consciousness that has been achieved of the unreality of *samsara*.

[57] Note at Sils Maria, August 26, 1881. *Œuvres posthumes*, 196, p. 93: cf. 211, pp. 97–98.

all separate from becoming. It is not at all *anything other* than eternal return, that other name for universal *samsara*. Do we not therefore have on both sides a doctrine of eternity in an instant? Not in an instant that opens up a little and disappears so as to allow the appearance of an eternity that is wholly formed, so to speak, outside of itself. Not in some privileged instant where eternity would empty itself, but in an instant taken in itself, wholly charged with an eternal savor.[58]

What a striking analogy, which shows us one more time that the spirit never finds completely new solutions. Nietzsche's "European Buddhism" is none other than the Buddhism of Buddha or of Asanga. The inspiration of the two doctrines is even pretty nearly opposite. What is more, Nietzsche's mysticism has resonances that the mysticism of the great *yogacara* does not know. Never does it throw off that "shudder of joy mingled with tears",[59] which is so specifically Nietzschean. If we wanted another Indian analogy, complementary to the Buddhist analogy, we would find it in the Dance of Siva.[60] The element of pathos would thus be reintroduced—but to the benefit of a more succinct vitalism and with the risk of reestablishing the initial ambiguity. Not at all a perfectly adequate symbol. The personage of Zarathustra himself, such as Nietzsche has constructed him, does not thoroughly express his experience. He does not carry in himself all the "tragedy" that he announces.[61] So Nietzsche will presently return out of his own preference—beginning in 1885—to the symbol of his youth, to Dionysus. "The Great Ambiguous One" will be

---

[58] Cf. the maxim cited by Quinot, p. 256: "To impress on Becoming the character of Being, such is the supreme will to power."

[59] Charles Du Bos, *Journal*, vol. 2, p. 27 (January 14, 1924).

[60] This comparison is made by René Grousset, *Bilan de l'histoire* (Paris: Plon, 1946), pp. 122–23, and by Quinot, p. 24.

[61] We know that the fragment that ends book 4 of the *Die fröhliche Wissenschaft* (and which is taken up again at the beginning of *Zarathustra*), the fragment describing the descent of Zarathustra into the midst of men, is entitled: *Incipit tragedia* (Here begins the tragedy).

presented anew to him on every road he takes. He will dream of giving a synthesis of his thought by setting forth "the philosophy of this god".[62] And the god of ecstasy and orgiastic life will seem to him more apt for defining his frenetic opposition to him whose image will not cease to torment him right to the end. Zarathustra was opposed above all to the Galilean prophet. Dionysus, in his mystic passion, is opposed to the Crucified One at Calvary. . . .[63]

"This thinker does not need anybody to refute him. He undertakes this task himself."[64] In a hundred ways, he himself, in effect, warns us without wanting to of the illusory character of his ecstasy.[65] Poor Nietzsche! The poor great man! So profoundly human, so smitten with purity—victim of so many deceptive phantoms! He aspired to a total Yes. He wanted to persuade himself that he had finally declared it in the simplicity of a rediscovered childhood. "*Amor Fati*! May this henceforth

---

[62] *Dionysos*, fragment from the winter of 1885–1886. Cf. *Le Crépuscule des idoles*. "Ce que je dois aux anciens", 5: "I, the last disciple of the philosopher Dionysus, I, who am master of the eternal return" (p. 235).

[63] Several commentators think that they have observed that toward the end, "Nietzsche makes a strange association of Dionysus with the Crucified One." Cf. Michel Carrouges, *La Mystique du surhomme* (Paris: Gallimard, 1948), p. 31. This is true perhaps only of the very end. Until then, it is not an associative will that he seems to us to perceive in him but rather an opposing design. If, in effect, "a powerful fascination leads him ceaselessly into the sphere of influence of the Crucified One", (Andler, vol. 6, p. 182), nevertheless, "the Crucified One of his invective and the Dionysus of his desires" are identified only "in the chaos and shipwreck of his thought" (Thibon, p. 271). This is the famous note of January 4, 1889, to Koeselitz.

[64] Nietzsche, *le Voyageur et son ombre*, 249 (French trans. by Albert, p. 366).

[65] We are using this word in the singular here, while taking it in a generic sense. Or we may even refer above all to the event of August 1881, for January 1883 only adds a sensible confirmation of it. As Nietzsche will explain it himself, if he gave birth at Rapallo, it was at Sils Maria that he conceived.

be my love. . . . From this day on, I have no further wish than to be an affirmation."[66] "First movement! Holy affirmation! Innocence and forgetfulness!"[67] How far he was from it however! Without entering into an examination along psychiatric lines,[68] it will suffice us by way of overview to pay attention to a few facts that are all too clear. This is not "to put in the foreground the private life of the thinker" with a view to "interpreting on this superficial basis the spiritual depths of a genius". These are the words Mr. Friedrich Wurzbach uses in rightly rejecting such a methodology.[69] But we cannot forget that Nietzsche's claims go much farther than just a thinker's claims. He invites us to a renewed existence whose announcer and exemplar he supposes himself to be. To understand him in his very depths, as he wishes to be understood, we must understand him as he exists. In other words, in his last years Nietzsche the thinker is intimately dependent on Nietzsche the mystic. The value of the former hangs on the authenticity of the latter.

No more is there a question here, be this well understood, of placing his conscious sincerity in doubt. The solitary of Sils Maria truly believed that the emotional shock that disturbed him so deeply was produced by his contact with a marvelous reality and that this contact opened him up to a new world, which offered itself to him like a grace. In this situation what he did, in reality, was only to construct, for better or worse, a mysticism of replacement, to fill the dreadful emptiness that had opened up in him. His true experience, the experience that

---

[66] *Le Gai savoir* 276, p. 137. Cf. *Zarathoustra*, "Des trois métamorphoses": "Yes, for the great game of creation, my brothers, there is need for a sacred Yes", p. 46.

[67] *Zarathoustra*, p. 46.

[68] "Certain alienists", writes Mr. Daniel Halévy, *Nietzsche*, p. 270, "believe that they can detect, in the raptures at Surlej, certain characteristics of euphoric dementia."

[69] Introduction to the translation of Mr. Betz, *Ainsi parlait Zarathoustra*, p. 24.

controls the one we have just analyzed, is of another nature. It is the one he summarized himself in the expression "the death of God". In a few pages of *Die fröhliche Wissenschaft* that are related to it,[70] we find the motherlode of his thought. These pages are the key to all that followed. But it is a completely negative experience—completely opposite to that pure adhesion which he wished afterward to recover at any cost, because man cannot live without it. To escape the despair engendered by the decisive No even while maintaining this No without weakness, he invents the Eternal Return.

"My friends, I must open my heart entirely to you. If the gods exist, how would I endure not being a god?" Let us take care not to give these words a vulgar sense. But we will record this admission nonetheless. God must die, so that man might be set free of his unbearable servitude and be transformed into the Overman. Finally in a resolute consciousness, it is an accomplished fact. "God is dead! Superior men, this God has been your greatest danger. You can only be brought back to life when he lies in the tomb."[71]

Nietzsche is inclined at first to conceive of this man who is set free, restored to life, fully master of an always-higher destiny, without any positive substrate. There is in the depths of him, as Jaspers has noted, "a universal negativity, a limitless dissatisfaction before every aspect of being. And this thrust of dissatisfaction and negation is pursued with such passion, with such a will to sacrifice, that it seems to come from the same depths as the great religions and the beliefs of the prophets."[72] It is this that opposes him as well to all forms of naturalism and positivism. "A Genoese of the intellect",[73] he likes to compare himself to the "blessed Columbus". But "the unknown

---

[70] *Le Gai savoir*, see particularly number 125, "L'Insensé", pp. 104–5.

[71] *Zarathoustra*. "Sur les îles bienheureuses", p. 94; "De l'homme supérior", 2, p. 258.

[72] Karl Jaspers, *Nietzsche*, quoted by Jean Wahl.

[73] Bertram, p. 25.

Indies" toward which he dashes must be his own creation, and always, after it, there will be yet another Indies to discover, to create. . . . "Formidable exuberance of this whole navigational adventure", which started very soon, he tells us, "after 1870".[74] A departure "that is more grandiose and more heroic than all the expeditions to the North Pole or the South Pole"[75] —a departure without end, without a real pole in view. . . . Such is Nietzsche's steadfast ambition, the feature that makes for profound continuity between the two periods that are delimited by the ecstasy of 1881. Only in this summer of 1881, despite all expectation and his first hopeful yearnings, did he "discover a new land".[76] His "unknown Indies" became for him a reality, a shore that he had touched on. It turned out that pure negativity was an impossible dream. The Overman could not build himself in an absolute void. Nietzsche ended up realizing this, and, like a sailor who feverishly stops up a leak in his boat when it is in distress, he fills up this void by which God, who has been banished, threatens anew to invade his old abode. "If we do not wish to fall prey again to the old idea of a Creator",[77] we must put another thing in his place—and this other thing, this will be the Eternal Return. Whether one wishes to or not, this paradox must be upheld, since "he who refuses to believe that the universe is marked by a circular process is constrained to believe in a sovereign, absolute God."[78] Thus the Eternal Return is imperative as the indispensable substitute for a dead god. It alone can seal up the stone of his tomb. . . .

At the very heart of this new experience and in the "great decision" maintained and consolidated, the Nietzschean atti-

---

[74] T. Overbeck, January 1884. To Rohde, from Genoa, March 24, 1881.

[75] Friedrich Wurzbach, introduction to *Zarathoustra*, p. 24.

[76] Letter to his mother and his sister, from Genoa, end of November 1883.

[77] *Volonté*, 332 (1882), vol. 1, p. 296.

[78] Fragment of 1881–1886. *Œuvres posthumes*, n. 209, p. 97. Cf. Andler, p. 258; Sertillanges, p. 346.

tude therefore is indeed less a "positive, affirmative attitude"[79] than an attitude still of opposition and, let us use the word, resentment. In addition, Nietzsche will not stop being haunted, right to his last day, by the figure of Jesus. With respect to Jesus he passes alternately between admiration and denigration, tenderness and sarcasm, which can be explained by a secret jealousy.[80] Even here, it is not the discovery of a new kingdom and the irrepressible affirmation of new values that determine the negations and the criticisms. What comes first is an anxiousness to antagonize in the very act of imitation, through the need to play an analogous and superior role. It is not enough for Nietzsche to make himself the announcer of a new gospel. He aspires to the title of redeemer.[81] He cannot do other than take his own measure with reference to Jesus, and for his part he never stops looking at him surreptitiously out of the corner of his eye, so to speak. All of *Zarathustra* witnesses to this desire to imitate. What is more opposed to what he claims to be? Andler could not help noticing this. "Would he not perhaps", he writes, "have made as good an analysis of the horrors and dangers of rancor if he had not known these by direct experience?"[82] Yes, rancor, and a whole gamut of inclinations of the same kind. Can one imagine the shadow of a similar sentiment at the heart of Jesus' message? In Jesus Christ "all is Yes."[83] Nietzsche, alas, is "the man of resentment".[84] He is such in a

---

[79] *Volonté*, 426 (1884), vol. 2, p. 134.

[80] Cf. *Le Drame de l'humanisme athée*, 3d. ed. (Paris: Editions Spes, 1945), 313–14.

[81] *Zarathoustra*, 1. II; "De la rédemption", p. 137.

[82] Andler, pp. 4, 538.

[83] Saint Paul, 2 Cor 1:19–20. Cf. *De la connaissance de Dieu*, 2d ed., pp. 32–39.

[84] "If I do not know resentment . . . ," he writes in *Ecce Homo*, as if to convince himself (p. 29). It is not impossible, moreover, that among the factors that laid the groundwork of the ecstasy at Sils Maria must be counted Nietzsche's reflection on the case of the apostle Paul. Cf. *Morgenrothe*, 68: ". . . His unbridled will to dominate manifests itself as an anticipation of the

more general way still. He was "the most impotent of men". [85]
Here a few psychological remarks become important. We shall
borrow them from Mr. Henri L. Miéville, who writes:

> It is not to venture too much to place a quite significant emphasis
> in Nietzsche's thought on the subterranean action of "unsettled"
> affective complexes, as the psychoanalysts say. These complexes,
> aggravated by sickness, were complexes of inferiority in the face
> of life. At the time of his relationship with Wagner, his crushing
> friendship with the most tyrannical of geniuses, together with
> the sentimental defeat to which his unavowed and unrequited

joys he will taste in the midst of divine splendors." In this paragraph devoted
to "the Jewish Pascal", to the "first Christian", it seems that Nietzsche described in advance the experience that was soon going to be his own, an experience to which he was already aspiring. Paul is tormented by the Law. "His
unbridled ambition" repulses it. But it possesses "an irresistible charm" that
keeps him from disencumbering himself of it yet. "How he detested it! How
he begrudged it! How keenly he set about hunting around in every possible
quarter to find a proper means of destroying it! . . . But behold how finally
the light of day dawned suddenly on his spirit, thanks to a vision. And it could
not have happened otherwise for this epileptic. He is struck by a liberating
idea. . . . The sick man in his tormented pride feels at the same time that he
is returning to sanity, the moral despair has flown away. . . . The destiny of
the Jews, indeed, the destiny of all mankind seems to him to be linked to this
moment of sudden illumination. He holds the idea of ideas, the key of keys,
the light of lights. Henceforth history revolves around him! . . . (French trans.
by Albert, pp. 74–79). The apostle Paul's nature, writes Miss Marie-Anne Cochet, "irritates and impassions Nietzsche. It is interesting for the purposes of
analysis to see developing in him the desire for a vision like the one that struck
Paul. We should not forget that Nietzsche identifies himself with those whom
he fights as well as with those whom he admires. This is perhaps true in another respect as well, inasmuch as he only fights those whom he admires. He
mimicked orgiastic delirium so as to recover that state. Similarly his concentrated thought on the state of Saint Paul prepares for the vision at Surlej. This
reasoning can also be reversed, and it can be said that the vision at Surlej,
which was already hovering over him, fixed his attention and his feelings on
the vision of Saint Paul. The latter supposition is probably the most accurate
one, since, as a young collegian leaving Pforta, he invoked the 'unknown god'
who would come to him in a thunderbolt. . . ." pp. 242–43.

[85] Nicholas Berdyaev, *Au seuil de la nouvelle époque*, p. 19.

love for Cosima exposed him, could only reinforce his morbid dispositions. We must add to this as well the minimal success of his work as a professor at Basel and later the smarting humiliation that the public's total indifference to his books will cause him. The proof that these complexes existed in his subconscious and that they acted on his thought is furnished by the whole subsequent evolution of the poet of Zarathustra and notably by the pathetic violence—at first contained and then more and more unbridled—of his exacerbated personalism. But insofar as our thought continues to be determined little or a lot by our defensive reflexes, by the desire for compensating satisfactions and by the revolt against old constraints, it is not free. This is true even though our thought may be framed in the most detached and the most audaciously revolutionary language. Its road is mapped out for it beforehand by the influences against which it reacts.[86]

These analyses dovetail with and reinforce the judgment of Miguel de Unamuno:

> Desperate and mad by dint of having to defend himself against himself, he cursed the one he loved the most. Since he was not able to be Christ, he blasphemed against Christ. Puffed up with himself, he wanted to be infinite and dreamed of the eternal return, a shabby counterfeit of immortality, and full of pity for himself, he detested all pity. . . . His doctrine is that of the weak who aspire to be strong, but certainly not of the strong who are truly so in reality![87]

Thus incited and falsified at its very source, what could his experience have been? The intensity with which it was lived is not at all surprising in such a genius. But it is only the intensity of an illusion, splendid clothes thrown on a miserable

---

[86] "L'Aventure nietzschéene et le temps present", *Esprit* (1933–1934), pp. 619–20.

[87] *Le Sentiment tragique de la vie*, (French tr. of *Del sentimiento trágico de la vida en los hombres y en los pueblos* [Paris: Gallimard, 1937]), p. 36.

frame of wretchedness that does not want to acknowledge itself. The Eternal Return—it is Andler again who tells us—
was "the ambrosia from which Nietzsche drew the illusion of
being a god".[88] The unity of this idea, such as he conceived it,
is merely a unity marked by a perceptible merging. It cannot
survive a transitory exaltation, and even in the spirit that will
engender it, one can presently see it being dissociated. For these
are not only "completely opposite points of view" that collide
with one another in this case, such, for example, as "mechanism
and Platonism".[89] These are completely contradictory and irreconcilable conceptions. The whole body of Nietzsche's work
"bears the reflection arising from the barbarous identification
of these antagonistic poles",[90] an identification that is always
compromised.

It is easy enough to propose in words that time is abolished,
that every causal link is ruptured, and so on.[91] It is easy enough
to imagine that "in infinity all straight lines converge" and that
thus "the fate of eternal return renders possible pure contingency."[92] If the one who affirms this to us bore irrefutable signs
at the same time of his superior illumination and his mission,
it would become possible for us to believe it, even though our
experience as poor mortals shows us nothing that approaches it.
That is why just now we gave credit to Nietzsche, before questioning him about himself, in our dismissal of certain overly
simple or overly immediate refutations. But he does not succeed at all in showing us all these contraries united in him-

---

[88] Andler, vol. 4, p. 228.

[89] *Volonté*, 320, vol. 1, p. 295.

[90] Thibon, p. 266.

[91] *Zarathoustra*, "De la redemption". But the prophet must also acknowledge: "That it cannot destroy time and the desire for time, such is the most
solitary affliction of the will. . . . Alas! every prisoner becomes mad! The im-
prisoned will as well frees itself by madness. That time does not go backward,
therein lies the furious anger of the will. 'That which was': this is the name
for the rock that will cannot remove" (p. 127).

[92] Andler summarizing the thought of Nietzsche, vol. 4, p. 317.

self. "To impress on Becoming the character of Being," he explained to us, "behold therein the supreme will to power."[93] Behold therein in any case the statement of the problem that the idea of the Eternal Return wants to address. But has the problem been resolved? This "will to power", was it powerful enough? Has "the marriage of Time and Eternity" according to this formula been consummated?

In *Zarathustra* itself two tendencies are expressed with equal force, which pull the prophet in two opposing directions. A struggle appears to be engaged in here, between a violent passion and an immense nostalgia. On the one hand, Nietzsche utters his war-cry of "Nothing but earth!" "Remain faithful, I adjure you, my brothers, to the earth. Do not thrust your heads into the sand of heavenly things . . . to sin against the earth, that is now the most monstrous crime of all!"[94] He will pride himself on having changed definitively the sense of man: "We no longer trace man's descent from 'the spirit', from 'divinity'. We have placed him among the animals. For us he is the strongest animal, because he is the most crafty. Our spirituality is a consequence of this."[95] The intelligence itself is completely a function of biology: "The most vigorous thinkers are those who are animated by a more abundant and more eager vitality."[96] Perfection "is the extraordinary expansion of one's feeling of power, richness a mighty need to overflow one's banks. . . ."[97] Such declarations have often caused Nietzsche's doctrine to be taken for a crude biologism, an exaltation of strength and animal life, and it is indeed true that for a person to hold to them, one could not but judge the situation so. But the excess nature itself of these declarations causes us to entertain doubts. There is a tone of defiance in them, a willful arrogance, which

---

[93] Quinot, p. 256.

[94] *Zarathoustra*, p. 1.

[95] *L'Antéchrist*, 14 (*Le Crépuscule des idoles*, p. 257).

[96] *Par-delà le bien et le mal*, 23.

[97] "Dionysos philosophos" (fragment of 1887–1888), in *Volonté*, 555, p. 372.

is the sign of a turbulent soul, a fragmented one. —And how, on the other hand, can one not be equally struck by passages with a wholly other tone, passages that carry us into a wholly other climate?

> Deep is sadness,
> Joy deeper than affliction.
> Sadness says: pass on and die!
> But all joy wants eternity,
> Wants deep, deep eternity![98]

Between this "deep eternity" that all joy wants and the height "of sexual instinct, of rapture, of cruelty", into which the Dionysiac trance plunges,[99] "the ring of becoming and return" has not effected a unity. This "nuptial ring" has remained a beautiful symbol—a beautiful, powerless symbol.[100]

Nietzsche does not admit this. But his work cries it out. It contradicts the solution it lays hold of. It shows its gaping faults. "I must persist in my dream under pain of perishing." This is a terrifying admission, for what he called his pearl at that time could have become his salvation, while it is his attachment to an impossible dream that to the contrary will end up leading him to his doom. He who by his demand for sincerity allies himself to the highest of souls has ended up showing a suspicious interest in the idea of the "sacred lie". He who smelled out so subtly and flogged so harshly the unconscious hypocrisies of others, he it is who has become in the final analysis, not a masked man, but the man of the mask, almost, as it were, a theoretician of the self-indulgent, obstinate illusion, an adorer of a fiction that he knows quite well in the depths

---

[98] *Zarathoustra*, "L'Autre chant de la danse", p. 210; "Le Chant d'ivresse", p. 290. See also "Les Sept sceaux", pp. 210–13.

[99] "Dionysos philosophos", in *Volonté*, 555, vol. 2, p. 371.

[100] Cf. *Zarathoustra*. "Les Sept sceaux": "O, how would I not aspire to eternity, to the nuptial ring of rings, to the ring of becoming and return? . . . O, how would I not ardently desire eternity? . . . O, how would I not be eager for eternity? . . .", pp. 210–13.

of his heart to be a fiction.[101] He pretended to create what he could not help suffering.[102] He returned therefore to the illusionism of his first period. Like *Die Geburt der Tragödie* (*The Birth of Tragedy*), *Zarathustra* is "a Wagnerian work".[103] This poem in which he wished to mimic the Gospel is, despite so many beauties, painfully theatrical.[104] One feels that there is a thirst for purity and authenticity in it, but at the same time something inflated and falsely solemn that betrays something counterfeit. And at the very same time as he feels sorry for Pascal as a victim of Christianity, Nietzsche is very close to admitting that he is a victim of his anti-Christian dream—of his lie. Mrs. Lou Andreas-Salomé is not the only one to shudder on reading these revealing words: "Who knows if up till now, in all the important cases, the same phenomenon is not constantly reproduced: the crowd adored a god, and this 'god' in the final analysis was merely a poor victim?"[105]

More than one reflection of his last years on the Eternal Return shows less enthusiasm than disenchanted resignation:

---

[101] Cf. *Die fröhliche Wissenschaft*: "I was abruptly awakened from my dream, but this was so that I might be made aware that I was dreaming, and that I needed to persist in my dream under the pain of perishing." Mr. Friedrich Wurzbach, who comments on this passage in his introduction to *Volonté*, vol. 1, p. 10, has good reason to see therein a "terrifying experience", although the explanation that he gives for it does not seem very certain.

[102] This process was well analyzed by Mrs. Lou Andreas-Salomé, p. 267: "As a backdrop, however, to this whole representation, we find the idea that the universe is merely a fiction created by man and that his divinity, which is to say, his fusion with the fullness of life, depends on a creative act of the human will. . . ." See, among other texts, *Le Gai savoir*, 301: "Illusion du contemplatif", pp. 149–50.

[103] Andler, vol. 6, p. 59. Cf. Charles Du Bos, vol. 2, p. 28: "He wishes to construct anew, he brings back something of that opulent warmth of illusion that was his during his Schopenhauerian and Wagnerian period and against which he himself showed himself to be so pitiless."

[104] On the composition of *Zarathustra*, calqued on that of the Gospels: Andler, vol. 6, p. 3.

[105] *Par-delà le bien et le mal*, 269, p. 319. Cf. Lou Andreas-Salomé, pp. 170–71.

Can you no longer endure it,
Your marvelous destiny?
Love it, you do not have a choice.[106]

Or there is the following reflection, more bitter perhaps, and sadly enigmatic, although still illumined by a remembrance of the radiant moment: "The moment in which I brought to birth the Return is immortal, and it is by my love for this moment that I endure the Return."[107] Or yet again there is this note of June 10, 1887: "The Eternal Return is the most extreme form of nihilism: eternal nothingness (absurdity)." Comparing these words with those that Nietzsche wrote a little while after the ecstasy at Surlej, wherein he said, "That everything should return without ceasing, this is the extreme reconciliation of the world of becoming and being, the summit of meditation", Mr. Daniel Halévy writes:

> In both of these notes what is in question is the Eternal Return. The subject is the same. But what a road has been traveled in the opposite direction, and what a reversal of perspectives! The extreme reconciliation of the world of becoming and the world of being lasted only as long as an ecstatic flash of lightning. In the Eternal Return, considered in the cold light of day, Nietzsche discovers the most extreme form of nihilism, nothingness, the eternal absurdity. This "summit of meditation" that he believed he had touched collapses, and behold Nietzsche surrounded by the ruins of his thought, perched on high, very high, in the vicinity of danger, and without a response to the question: *Wohin?* Where are you going? . . . Of these two notes, the one had opened, the other was closing a cycle of hope.[108]

"Nihilism overcome by himself" can only mean an ephemeral victory, and the arbitrary decision that changes his pessimism into a cry of triumph is powerless to change anything

---

[106] "Maximes et chants de Zarathoustra", 58, in *Ecce Homo*, p. 231.

[107] *Œuvres posthumes*, 228, p. 101.

[108] *Nietzsche*, pp. 475–76.

in the real world. Perhaps this is the reason why, without renouncing the dream he incarnated in the person of Zarathustra, Nietzsche will feel more and more, in a manner contrary to the assurance whose wellsprings were in the vision at Rapallo, that he must distinguish himself forcefully from his counterpart. He is not happy and free as he is. Perhaps this is also why, right to the end, he will harbor the feeling that the revelation he brings is formidable and that he is more a "fate" than an evangelist. . . .[109] And are these not equally significant, these words that he puts in the mouth of his hero: "In truth, I advise you, get far away from me, defend yourself against Zarathustra! Better still, be ashamed of him. Perhaps he has deceived you. . . . You venerate me, but what would happen if your veneration was destroyed one day? Take care not to be crushed by a statue. . . ."[110]

Nietzsche's correspondence forms an insistent commentary

---

[109] Cf. Letter to Brandès, November 20, 1888: "I swear to you that in two years the earth will be writhing in convulsions. I am a fate." Cf. *Ecce Homo*: "Why I am a fate." This is no longer the sense completely of *Ego Fatum*. In one of the rough drafts of the tragedy *Midi et Eternité*, in the third act, Zarathustra had to open up "the redoubtable lodgings of Knowledge". Andler, vol. 6, p. 52.

[110] *Zarathustra*, text quoted by Lou Andreas-Salomé, p. 248. These words take on an even more oppressive meaning if one recalls the conversation Nietzsche had in November of 1882 with Ida Overbeck, as she reported it herself. Ida Overbeck confided to him that she did not find peace in Christianity and that the idea of God did not seem to her to comprise enough real content. Quite moved, Nietzsche replied to her: "You are only saying this in order to come to my own aid. Do not abandon it ever, this idea of God that you have! You possess it unconsciously in yourself, for just as you are, just as I find you, even right to this very minute, a great idea governs your whole life, and this great idea is the idea of God." Then he burst into sobs. His features were distorted. After a moment, his physiognomy assumed a stone-like tranquillity: "As for me, I have renounced this thought. I wish to create anew, I do not have the right to turn back. I will founder and fail in the depths of my passions. They reject me on this side and that. I continually lose my equilibrium, but it is of little importance." Cf. Pierre Dournes, *Nietzsche vivant* (Paris: Bloud & Gay, 1948), p. 96.

on these furtive remarks. We shall not take any argument against him from the suffering that is manifested therein. He would reply in this way to us—and the reply in general would be true to the mark: "Do you not therefore wish to understand that prophetic men are beings who suffer much?"[111] But what is proper to note is that he suffers from his interior division. He is neither unified nor free. Does he truly have that "saved air" that he reproaches so many Christians with not having? He says that he is "profoundly sad". He remains obsessed with "[his] old problems, [those] old problems that are as black as soot."[112] These "cares" weigh him down.[113] "Every year becomes more heavy [for him]."[114] The solitude in which he is sunk is not that of the prophet nor even that of the genius. It is the solitude made for him by a "mistrust" that "changes to a malady", a disposition "that has been developed since [his] tender childhood" and that puts him in a "horrible" state. As early as the beginning of February 1883, even at Rapallo, he wrote to Franz Overbeck something that is scarcely believable —unless in fact it is all too ordinary:

> I will not hide it from you. Things are going very badly. Night overwhelms me more and more. It is as if there had just been a flash of lightning. One moment, I find myself plunged into my element, into my light. And now it is passed. I believe that I am walking ineluctably to my ruin. . . . The barrel of a gun is now a source of relatively pleasant reflections for me. . . .[115]

---

[111] *Le Gai savoir*, 316, p. 156.

[112] A. Overbeck, beginning of 1886. A. Seydlitz, October 26, 1886 (*Lettres choisies*, pp. 229 and 234). Cf. to Overbeck, April 16, 1887, on "the *rack* of problems to which I am bound".

[113] Cf. to Overbeck, October 12, 1886 (ibid., p. 449).

[114] To his sister, May 21, 1887: "The worst periods of sickness, the most unhappy ones, did not seem as painful and as empty of hope as my present existence" (ibid., p. 249). To Overbeck, from Sils Maria, June 30, 1887: "Everything is so destitute of sense!" (ibid., p. 467).

[115] Ibid., pp. 372–73.

And soon afterward, in March: "I am no longer interested in anything. At the very depths of my being, a black and immutable melancholy. . . . The worst is that I no longer understand at all to what purpose I should continue to live, be this only for six months ahead. Everything seems wearisome, painful, *disgusting* to me."[116]

Would it be to abuse confidences to cite similar texts? We well know that we must also take into account his hours of joy. After exaltation Nietzsche, like many others, passed through periods of depression. This is nothing more than a commonplace, as tragic as such a commonplace may also be. It is part of human psychology, all too human, like the anxious need for approval that all those who are weak experience. . . . We shall certainly not reproach him with this, but we shall rather turn our fraternal pity to him. And in returning to his work, in rereading the pages that bear the mark of his higher inspiration, we shall no longer be afraid of blaspheming in discerning their true nature. "The cries of Zarathustra are merely the cries of human confusion, to be compared to such *alleluias* as arose from Easter Saturday's Resurrection."

In reality Nietzsche destroys himself. He has not risen above the despair of "the madman" who looks everywhere with his lantern for the body of the murdered God. What he then proceeded to find in order to escape him only accelerated the crisis. This was already the introduction to it. And in effect, "this thought, which, like the 'Bateau ivre' (drunken boat) of Rimbaud, challenged the high seas without rudder or compass, could not have had any other harbor than rocks and shipwreck."[117] He had a premonition of this a long time in advance. From the summer of 1883 on, having gone back up to Sils Maria, he analyzed with lucidity the "interior conflict" that brought him "nearer and nearer step by step to madness." "I

---

[116] Ibid., p. 381.
[117] G. Thibon, p. 152.

am aware of it", he wrote, "in the most dreadful fashion."[118]
But his *Fatum* came inexorably to possess him. This was completely the opposite of what he still wanted, now and then, to
persuade himself.

Nietzsche "was stoned to death by his own hand". He suffered the mortal fall of the rope dancer "who does not want to
be excelled in his leaping jumps". He suffered a fall that is all
too real, "an all too commonplace physiological shipwreck".[119]
What made this madness a peculiar case was its antecedents,
not its nature. It is useless to look for sublime explanations
here in order to escape the evidence. It is all very well to scoff
at "the bourgeois rationalism" that would be incapable of recognizing in this supposed insanity a freeing from the notion of
time. It is all very well to celebrate the action of the "creative
principle that begets in the cosmos, that shatters its *principium
individuationis*" [principle of individuation] and makes the rational vesture of the spirit burst "like a bubble of soap".[120] It is
all very well to try to believe that the case of Nietzsche "seems
extreme to us only because he represents a mentality of the
future that cannot yet as things stand now in actual fact sustain
itself for a very long time." His thought would seem by this
reckoning incoherent to us because it is developed beyond the
usual norms that we are familiar with and thus clashes with
"an impossibility of transmission" that comes solely from our
sluggishness. . . .[121] These kinds of explanations witness above
all to man's need to believe at any price. It is quite true that the
explosion of something new in the realm of the spirit appears
at first to be drunkenness or madness in the eyes of men. But
the crisis on the streets of Turin and the besotted somnolence
of Weimar do not resemble at all the drunkenness of Pentecost
or the madness of the Cross. . . .

---

[118] Letter to Overbeck, August 1883.
[119] G. Bianquis, p. 59.
[120] Cf. Friedrich Wurzbach, introduction to *Zarathoustra*, p. 24.
[121] Cf. M. A. Cochet, p. 250.

Nietzsche found the innocence that he had looked for so long and hard—but unconsciously. The warning that he addressed to us a while ago now assumes all its tragic contours. This mystic "does not need anybody to refute him. He takes care of this task himself."

INDEX